Refin
— 1
— 2
— 3

MANAGEMENT INFORMATION SYSTEMS

MANAGEMENT INFORMATION SYSTEMS

Larry Long

Prentice-Hall International, Inc.

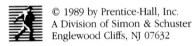 © 1989 by Prentice-Hall, Inc.
A Division of Simon & Schuster
Englewood Cliffs, NJ 07632

Printed in the United States of America

10 9 8 7 6 5 4 3 2

ISBN 0-13-551698-6

Prentice-Hall International (UK) Limited, *London*
Prentice-Hall of Australia Pty. Limited, *Sydney*
Prentice-Hall Canada Inc., *Toronto*
Prentice-Hall Hispanoamericana, S.A., *Mexico*
Prentice-Hall of India Private Limited, *New Delhi*
Prentice-Hall of Japan, Inc., *Tokyo*
Prentice-Hall of Southeast Asia Pte. Ltd., *Singapore*
Editora Prentice-Hall do Brasil, Ltda., *Rio de Janeiro*
Prentice-Hall, *Englewood Cliffs, New Jersey*

OVERVIEW

CONTENTS

PART TWO   The End User Computing Environment

PART THREE   MIS Concepts

PART FIVE   Managing the Information and Computing Resources

A Short Course in Computer Concepts

Hands-on Exercises: Electronic Spreadsheet, Graphics, and Database   526

PREFACE

A management information system, or MIS, is the heart of an organization. Just as the rhythmic beat of the heart pumps blood and life-giving oxygen throughout the body, an MIS is constantly creating and disseminating information, the lifeblood of the organization.

For two decades, top management's perception of the MIS was that of an abstract concept, not a goal. Recently, however, top management is beginning to see the computer-based MIS as a fiscal imperative, clearly a corporate goal. To compete effectively in a world market, executives now realize that they must take full advantage of their information resources. The net result of this turnaround in management thinking is the emergence of information as *the* strategic weapon in the business world. Consequently, the MIS has come to the forefront at all levels of business endeavor.

Fifteen years ago, when I created and taught a course called Management Information Systems, the topic was of little interest to those outside the computer community. Today, the MIS has undergone many changes, and so has the cross-section of people who strive to learn about it. Fifteen years ago, end users were just that—users. Their interaction with the system was passive, for the most part. Today, the role of users has been redefined. Advancing technologies have made it possible (and advantageous) for users to play an active role in all aspects of the development, implementation, operation, and evolution of management information systems. The changing role of the user is a product of emerging information technologies, competitive pressures, and management's awareness that successful companies and individuals are making every effort to exploit the potential of their computing and information resources. While the MIS has added a new dimension to management, it has also burdened managers with greater responsibilities and more to learn.

Professionals in every field are discovering that having MIS knowledge and expertise can open the door to career opportunities. All other factors being equal, those who can contribute to the development of an MIS, and make effective use of an MIS once it is implemented, have a clear advantage over their peers. The material in this book is designed to give managers and potential managers the technical background and management insight needed to fulfill their roles in this age of information.

Audience

Management Information Systems is written in response to the new direction that the American Assembly of Collegiate Schools of Business (AACSB) has set for MIS education in business schools. The text can be used to support first- or second-level courses in either the *business* or *management information systems curriculum*. It is also appropriate for the MIS core course in MBA programs. This flexibility is inherent in the design of the book, which reflects the fact that course objectives and student preparedness vary markedly for MIS courses.

☐ *In support of a first-level course.* The instructor would assign background support modules from "A Short Course in Computer Concepts," as needed, and MIS chapters (1–17), as appropriate, to meet the educational objectives of the course.

☐ *In support of a second-level course or MBA course.* The instructor would assign MIS chapters, as appropriate, to meet the educational objectives of the course. The chapter material is written with the assumption that students have a fundamental understanding of the concepts and terminology associated with computer hardware and software. Of course, the support modules are available to those students who may need a review.

The comprehensive teaching/learning package, with its lab manual, readings book, and videotapes, provides an extra layer of flexibility.

Orientation and Pedagogical Philosophy

Management Information Systems is filled with straight talk. The topic demands it. Contrary to popular belief, the successful creation and implementation of an MIS is more of a sociopolitical challenge than a technical challenge. The consolidation of ideas; the integration of data; the resolution of management conflicts; the setting of objectives; the analysis of costs and benefits; and the inevitable changes in personnel, organization, and procedures are as much a part of the MIS environment as hardware and software. In keeping with the straight-talk orientation, the discussions address what's hot and what's not, what works and what doesn't, what's in and what's out, and what's a marketing ploy and what's real. It is hoped that this straight-talk approach will provide readers with the insight they need to make truly informed MIS-related decisions.

Most of the "MIS books" on the market are actually introductory concepts books with a sprinkling of MIS coverage. This is a *comprehensive* MIS book. All seventeen chapters are devoted to discussing the various facets of the fascinating field of MIS. Fundamental concepts are presented in "A Short Course in Computer Concepts."

Features

- □ *Management Information Systems* covers all emerging trends (for example, end user computing, expert systems, connectivity, MIS planning, CASE tools, prototyping, using MIS to achieve the competitive advantage).

- □ *Management Information Systems* presents the material within the context of the social, economic, ethical, and political pressures of the business community.

- □ *Management Information Systems* includes application case studies (37 in all) at the end of each chapter to help students relate concepts to business practice.

- □ *Management Information Systems* presents clear descriptions of procedures, approaches, techniques, and clear definitions of MIS terms.

- □ *Management Information Systems* includes "A Short Course in Computer Concepts" in six topical modules that offer background material for leveling and review.

- □ *Management Information Systems* has 35 "MIS in Practice" sidebars sprinkled liberally throughout the text to give students insight into the realities of decision making in the MIS arena.

- □ *Management Information Systems* discusses MIS applications and issues in virtually every major industry and in education and government.

- □ *Management Information Systems* is the cornerstone of a comprehensive teaching/learning package.

- □ *Management Information Systems* includes an appendix of hands-on exercises for electronic spreadsheet, graphics, and database software.

- □ *Management Information Systems* has a four-color design that serves to enhance the visual presentation of the material.

- □ *Management Information Systems* contains a handy glossary of over 700 commonly used computer and MIS terms.

- □ *Management Information Systems* reflects a pedagogically sound writing style and philosophy that has proved successful in hundreds of colleges and universities in the United States and throughout the world.

Organization

MIS (Chapters 1–17)

The main body of the text presents the MIS material in seventeen chapters that are divided into five parts.

- □ *Part I—Information: Management's Strategic Advantage*—accomplishes three objectives: MIS is placed in its proper perspective; systems terminology, including decision support systems and expert systems, is explained; and the reader is given some insight into how MIS and computer technology can provide a competitive advantage.

□ *Part II—The End User Computing Environment*—presents the various sources of computer and information services, an overview of the scope and management of end user computing, and a conceptual summary of the hardware and software associated with personal computing.

□ *Part III—MIS Concepts*—presents concepts that must be understood before a person can comprehend the scope and application of management information systems. The major topics include connectivity, data communications, and data management.

□ *Part IV—Systems Planning, Development, and Implementation*—begins with a chapter on MIS planning at both the strategic and operational levels. The middle three chapters discuss the prespecification and prototyping approaches to system development and provide an overview of automated application development tools. Part IV concludes with a chapter consisting of a comprehensive case study that illustrates the information and work flow in a typical manufacturing company.

□ *Part V—Managing the Information and Computing Resources*—presents a variety of management issues, including the allocation of costs to end users, contingency planning, and the acquisition of hardware and software.

The pedagogy of each chapter is carefully designed to keep the reader's interest and to facilitate both learning and teaching.

□ *Chapter opener.* Each chapter opens with a list of *key topics* and a brief *chapter overview*.

□ *Highlighted terms.* In the body of the text, important terms are highlighted in boldface or italic.

□ *Quotations and adages.* Throughout the book, quotations and adages in the margin complement the adjacent material and/or provide food for thought. The sayings reflect both popular and unpopular philosophies.

□ *Photographs.* Almost one hundred color photos are strategically placed throughout the book to enliven the material and to illustrate certain points or concepts. As you will see, each of these carefully selected photos is worth at least a thousand words.

□ *MIS in Practice.* Each chapter contains from one to five "MIS in Practice" sidebars. For the most part, these sidebars have been adapted from my "Turnaround Time" column, which was a regular feature in *Computerworld*, and are presented in the familiar question-and-answer format. The "Q" and "As" are included in the feature to highlight the point that many, perhaps most, computer- and MIS-related decisions are made in that gray area. The titles of the "MIS in Practice" sidebars are listed by chapter in the table of contents.

□ *Chapter endmatter.* Each chapter concludes with *chapter highlights* (bulleted summaries of key points made in the chapter), an alphabetical listing of *important terms*, short-answer *review exercises*, and a comprehensive set of *discussion questions*.

□ *Application Case Studies.* Each chapter is followed by application case studies that emphasize the topics covered in the chapter. The case studies are intended to help students bridge the gap between concept and practice and to provide a backdrop for discussions involving "real-life" applications of MIS concepts. Eight fictitious organizations (Acme Electronics, Circle Oil/Kincaid Service, Compu-Mail, Gabriel Industries, Peterson College, Que Reality, and Zimco Enterprises) are introduced and revisited from different perspectives throughout the book. The titles of the application case studies are listed by chapter in the table of contents.

A Short Course in Computer Concepts

Management Information Systems can be used as a text for a first- or second-level course or at the graduate level. This flexibility is made possible by "A Short Course in Computer Concepts." This "Short Course" is included because the level of computer/information systems knowledge that students bring to an MIS class varies substantially. For those who have studied introductory computer concepts, "A Short Course" provides a good review and update. For those who have had little or no exposure to computers and the information systems environment, the material in "A Short Course" will give them the level of hardware and software knowledge they need to reap the greatest benefits from reading Chapters 1–17.

"A Short Course" consists of six modules, each of which addresses a specific facet of the hardware/software environment. Each module concludes with review exercises and a self-test (with answers). The book is designed so that "A Short Course" can be assigned concurrently with Chapters 1–4.

Hands-on Exercises for Microcomputer Productivity Software

A decade ago, personal computers were somewhat of a novelty. Today, personal computers and personal computing have become as much a part of the business routine as coffee breaks and meetings. The hands-on exercises at the back of the book give students an opportunity to hone their skills in the use and application of integrated electronic spreadsheet packages (spreadsheet, graphics, and database capabilities) and database packages. Many of the students who will take an MIS course will already possess at least intermediate-level hands-on skills in one or more software packages. Those who have not or who need a review can take advantage of the educational versions of commercial software packages and the *Microcomputer Software Lab Manual* that accompany this text.

The Teaching/Learning Package

The comprehensive teaching/learning package that accompanies *Management Information Systems* has set a new standard for MIS texts.

Learning Support Material

MICROCOMPUTER SOFTWARE LAB MANUAL   The *Microcomputer Software Lab Manual* by Nancy Long and Larry Long accommodates the greater emphasis that is being placed on the acquisition of hands-on skills. The lab manual contains hands-on keystroke tutorials for word processing (WordPerfect), electronic spreadsheet (Lotus 1-2-3 and The TWiN), database (dBASE III PLUS), and graphics (Lotus 1-2-3 and The TWiN) software. The tutorials complement the concepts behind these applications software packages covered in Chapter 7, "Personal Computing." Also included in the lab manual are conceptual discussions and keystroke tutorials for MS-DOS.

VIDEO SOFTWARE TUTORIALS   A series of video tutorials for MS-DOS, WordPerfect, Lotus, dBASE III PLUS, and Microsoft Word are made available at no charge to qualified adopters.

SUPPLEMENTARY CASE STUDY TEXT   The *Management Information Systems* learning support package also includes a case study text. *Zimco Enterprises: An MIS Case Study* by Larry Long (Prentice Hall, 1988) centers on the MIS activities and concerns of a fictitious medium-sized manufacturer of consumer products. This readings book expands the presentation of Zimco Enterprises in Chapter 15 of this book into thirteen topical case studies.

Teaching Support Material

INSTRUCTOR'S RESOURCE MANUAL WITH TEST ITEM FILE   For each chapter in this text, the *Instructor's Resource Manual* by Larry Long presents teaching hints, lecture notes, solutions to review exercises and selected discussion questions, and approaches to solutions for the case study assignments. The lecture notes appear in an outline format and include boldface terms, class discussion questions, and references to appropriate transparencies.

COMPUTER-BASED TEST GENERATION   The hard copy of the *Test Item File* is included in the *Instructor's Resource Manual*. A computerized version of the *Test Item File* is available on diskettes for popular microcomputers. Test Generator, Prentice Hall's test generation software, enables instructors to select specific questions or request that the exams be generated randomly. Instructors can also edit test-item-file questions and add questions of their own. When printed, the exam is ready for duplication, and an answer sheet is also produced. Two types of questions (multiple choice and true/false) are provided for each chapter and for each of the modules in "A Short Course in Computer Concepts."

COLOR TRANSPARENCY ACETATES   One hundred and fifty color transparency acetates, which support material in the text and the *Instructor's Resource Manual*, are provided to facilitate classroom explanation. Twenty-five percent of the acetates are taken from the text; the remainder are supplemental.

"AUTHOR HOTLINE"   Professors and college administrators adopting *Management Information Systems* are encouraged to call Larry Long (see details in the *Instructor's Resource Manual*) to discuss specific questions relating to the use of the text and its support package or to discuss more general questions about course organization or curriculum planning.

Acknowledgments

Over a hundred people have made significant contributions to the creation of this text and its teaching/learning package. Several of Prentice Hall's dedicated professionals deserve special recognition: Carol Sobel, Caroline Ruddle, Margaret Rizzi, Dolores Kenny, Jeanne Hoeting, Ellen Greenberg, Lisa Garboski, George Durham, Laura Dulisse, and Gina Chirco Brennan. Editors Dennis Hogan and Gary June supported their visions with commitment and involvement. Production Editor Nancy DeWolfe did the undoable by holding the *MIS* project to an optimistic accelerated schedule, and Linda Conway created true visual harmony. My wife, Nancy, provided pedagogical insight, operational support, and an occasional emotional boost. All did an outstanding job, and I thank them.

The field of MIS is changing too rapidly for any one person to grasp the full extent of its impact on academe and curricula. Fortunately, I had help—lots of it. In that regard, I would like to extend my sincere gratitude to the professors who helped me with the content and overall organization of the book.

M. K. McAlister, University of Alabama at Birmingham

Leslie D. Ball, Babson College

Robert Behling, Bryant College

Dale D. Gust, Central Michigan University

Richard Kerns, East Carolina University

Bruce J. McLaren, Indiana State University

Jerry D. Sawyer, Kennesaw College

John L. Eatman, University of North Carolina at Greensboro

David A. Bryant, Pepperdine University

James T. C. Teng, University of Pittsburgh

Eugene J. Muscat, University of San Francisco

Jamal Munshi, Sonoma State University

William E. Burrows, University of Washington

Larry Long, Ph.D.

MANAGEMENT
INFORMATION
SYSTEMS

CHAPTER 1

Information Processing in Perspective

KEY TOPICS

CHAPTER OVERVIEW

The field of management information systems or MIS encompasses everything that deals directly or indirectly with the computer-assisted flow of information. MIS, the focus of this book, has had a profound impact on the way we live and work and even the way we think. The material in this first chapter helps to put MIS into its proper perspective and sets the stage for the remaining chapters. The first topic to be addressed is the scope of MIS and its impact on society and the corporate culture. The next section responds to the inevitable question—Why study MIS? Information is discussed as a valuable corporate resource and as it relates to data and information systems. This chapter establishes the link between information concepts and the decision-making process, both of which are recurring themes throughout the book. The chapter concludes with a discussion of emerging trends in the MIS field.

COMPUTERS AND INFORMATION PROCESSING

Connectivity, expert systems, CASE, desktop publishing, decision support systems, gigabyte, MIS, WYSIWYG, expansion card, 4GLs, and prototyping—the field of computers and information processing has a language all to its own. Some of the words and phrases are simply new ways to present old concepts. Some evolved out of the need to abbreviate verbal and written communication. Others are hastily concocted, ill-defined, and often redundant buzz words. When you consider that the accumulated total of all knowledge in the area of computers and information processing is doubling every two years, it is no wonder that its language is replete with buzz words, acronyms, and the like. Even with its shortcomings, **computerese**, as it is sometimes called, provides a surprisingly efficient mechanism for communication.

Just a few years ago, paperwork, dated reports, manually completed forms, and telephone tag were the norm in the business world. Today, we are making a transition to an information society. Computer-based information systems enable "knowledge" workers at USAA, an insurance company, to have ready access to the information they need to accomplish their jobs.

USAA

Computers and information processing have become forever intertwined with virtually every facet of the business endeavor. As a result, society in general and the business community in particular have asked all of us who wish to take advantage of this dynamic new field to become comfortable with the concepts and language of computers and information processing. That is what this book is all about.

Prerequisite Knowledge

The material in the chapters portion of this book is written with the assumption that the reader has been exposed to and is familiar with fundamental computer and information processing concepts. If you have not had an opportunity to familiarize yourself with these concepts or you feel that you need a review, you should take the "Short Course in Computer Concepts." The "Short Course," which follows Chapter 17, is presented in seven modules:

Module A—Computer Systems
Module B—Inside the Computer
Module C—I/O and Data Storage Devices
Module D—Software Concepts
Module E—Programming Concepts and Languages
Module F—Design Techniques Overview

Scope of Computers and Information Processing

The fascinating field of computers and information processing encompasses everything that deals directly or indirectly with the computer-assisted flow of information. The scope of the field includes everything from word processing to industrial robots to supercomputers to management information systems. The last term and the title of this book, **management information systems**, or **MIS** (pronounced, em eye es) for short, is commonly used in the business environment as a generic reference to all technologies, procedures, systems, and people associated with computers and information processing. A quick review of the table of contents of this book should give you a feel for the breadth of the MIS field.

The key words throughout this book and in virtually every conversation about the subject are *computers* and *information*. **Computers** are the base technology that enables us to tap the information resource, the value of which will become vividly apparent as you read this chapter. Of course, computers and information are implied in the term "MIS." Besides being a generic reference to the computer and information processing field, the term "MIS" is also used to refer to a particular type of computer-based system. Whether MIS is used as a generic reference to the field or to refer to a type of system is usually apparent from the context in which it is used. MIS as a system is described in detail in Chapter 2, "The MIS and Decision Support Systems."

The new source of power is not money in the hands of the few, but information in the hands of the many.

—— *John Naisbitt*

The Impact of MIS

Computers have been recognized as a valuable business tool for over three decades. During this short history, computers have proven to be incredibly effective processors of data, but only recently, during the decade of the 1980s, have computers won praise for their ability to produce meaningful information. Computers have always produced information, but only a select few people had access to a limited amount of information.

Today, timely information can be made *available* and readily *accessible* to those who need it, whether at the operational or executive levels. To be sure, computers still process data, but their increased potential to produce meaningful information has resulted in MIS taking center stage in many companies. The two major contributors to the emergence of MIS are

☐ *The improved price/performance of computers.* It is now economically feasible to make the power of a computer accessible to more people (see Figure 1–1). In some companies, every employee has a microcomputer for personal computing or a workstation, both of which can be linked to a company's mainframe computer system.

☐ *The availability of user-oriented software.* A wide variety of software packages are available to assist the **end user** in obtaining needed information without the intervention of an MIS professional. The term "end user," or simply **user**, describes anyone who provides input to a computer system and/or uses its output.

This marriage of computers and information that we call MIS is having a dramatic impact on society in general and on corporate culture.

Society in General

Perhaps we are becoming an information society. The way we obtain and use information has forever changed the way we as a society go about the routine of living. A computer monitoring and control system flashes "washer low" when the washer water in our automobiles is low. Our electricity utility invoices contain a bar graph that graphically illustrates monthly power consumption during the past year. We can pay the electricity bill from the comfort of our home through 24-hour home banking. Computer-based traffic control systems expedite intracity travel. In libraries, rows of card catalogs are being replaced by rows of workstations. At the office, one of the first orders of business is to check to see if we have any "electronic" mail. Even newspapers are presenting news in the form of computer-generated statistics and graphs.

On the down side, the emergence of the computer and MIS has raised serious social issues. Personal information is more accessible and, therefore, more vulnerable to abuse. The "take" in an average "electronic" heist is a hundred times that of the more traditional bank robbery. One computer-controlled industrial robot can replace four or more workers.

MIS and associated technologies have the potential for both good and bad. Numerous surveys have attempted to evaluate public opinion on computers and automation. The findings show that the overwhelming majority believe

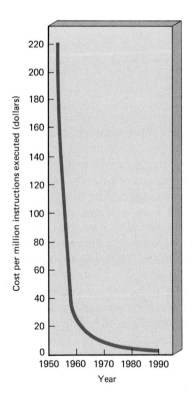

FIGURE 1–1   The Cost of Computers
Advancing computer technology makes it possible for more instructions to be executed at less cost each year.

that computers enhance the quality of life. We take up-to-the-minute weather information and itemized grocery receipts for granted. As a society we have been through the initiation period and are now full members of the information society. Ironically, though, we are only beginning to feel the impact of MIS.

The Corporate Culture

Few would disagree that MIS is having a profound impact on the the way we do business. Over 15 million people interact with a computer system daily in their work, and the number is growing rapidly. Companies are billing and paying one another from computer to computer via *electronic data interchange*, or *EDI*. Financial analysts are consulting *expert systems* before advising clients on investment strategies. Indeed, much of this book is devoted to discussing applications of MIS in the business environment. However, MIS has done much more than change the way we do business; it is also changing the corporate culture.

The company's *corporate culture* is defined by generalizations about human characteristics that can be applied to a particular company—managerial attitudes, work habits, ethics, degree of aggressiveness, communicativeness, and the like. Corporate cultures are molded by the corporation's people, geography, product line, circumstances, and many other factors. One very important factor is the extent to which the company has embraced the use and application of management information systems.

Electronic data interchange (EDI), a technology that permits a computer at one company to interface with one at another company, is causing radical changes in traditional business practices. By establishing a communications link with a supplier's computer system, this inventory manager can determine the status of an order in seconds. Before EDI, the manager would have submitted the request by telephone, then waited hours, even days, for a response from the supplier.

Zenith Data Systems

INFORMATION FLOW   Just as computers and information processing have made the world a global village, they have made companies more intimate. Shared data and the free flow of information have increased workers' and managers' sphere of awareness about their company and their co-workers. Operational managers are now privy to information that top management would like to have had but could not get just a few years ago. Top management receives a continuous flow of information about operations that was previously unavailable. Not only does MIS facilitate the flow of information, it promotes it. For example, the mere existence of *electronic mail*, where messages are transmitted via computer systems, inevitably encourages intracompany communication.

This free flow of information is changing the traditional pyramid structure of organizations. For the most part, the pyramid structure continues to exist, but in successful companies, it has changed markedly. First, it has been flattened; that is, the free flow of information has made it possible to reduce the number of levels of management. Also, informal "dotted-line" relationships have been inserted to formalize interactions between complementary functional areas, such as marketing and engineering, sales and accounting, and so on. One chief executive officer who reduced the layers of management in his company from 13 to 4 called the traditional pyramid organizational structure with preset directions for information flow a "dinosaur." Many other CEOs have also recognized that the technology can be employed to enable a more effective organizational structure.

> Computers can figure out all kinds of problems, except the things in this world that just don't add up.
>
> —— *J. Magary*

DECISION MAKING   Perhaps one of the most visible changes in the corporate culture in almost any progressive company is that *automation has altered the way people think and make decisions*. In the past, making seat-of-the-pants decisions was more the rule than the exception. There was no viable option: needed information was either not available or it could not be obtained within the time frame of the decision. Today, the accessibility and availability of information enables management at all levels to make more informed decisions.

The potential of *MIS has altered management's thinking about how to conduct business*. MIS has expanded management's thinking horizons. For example, the just-in-time approach to the manufacture and distribution of products is dependent on computer technology, timely information, and a change in corporate attitudes. Companies adopting the just-in-time approach manufacture products "just in time" to meet the demand, thereby reducing inventory costs. For just-in-time to work, both management and workers must be willing to adapt quickly to the changing needs of their customers. In converting to just-in-time from a traditional manufacturing environment, people who have been used to a daily routine will be faced with considerably more variety in their jobs.

In the modern MIS environment, *decisions can be made at a lower level*. Information that was previously unavailable or only available to top management can be accessed by the lower levels of management. Forward-thinking executives see this as an opportunity to delegate more authority, thereby freeing up more of their time for corporate planning and other activities that are peculiar to top management. Unfortunately, some executives remain pessimistic and view computers and MIS only as vehicles that erode their power base. The latter will have difficulty competing with the former for promotions during this age of the information society.

ACCOUNTABILITY   Computers and MIS have the capability to monitor performance. Most of the publicity surrounding this controversial capability has centered on measuring performance at the clerical level of activity. For example, a computer system can monitor and report on the number of transactions, and even the number of keystrokes, processed by a data entry clerk each hour. However, an MIS can also be used to monitor the performance of executives, as well. For example, by reviewing hourly production reports, top management can monitor the performance of plant managers on an hourly basis. Computer systems have made people at all levels more accountable for their actions.

MANAGEMENT STYLE   A company's top management probably has the greatest influence on its corporate culture. In company after company, executives who are unwilling to proceed with the implementation of MIS technology are being replaced with those who will. When this happens, the corporate culture moves from plodding and traditional to aggressive and change oriented. For whatever reasons, some unknowing managers and executives see workstations as symbols of clerical activity and, therefore, inappropriate in executive suites.

SUMMARY   Typically, MIS affects, directly or indirectly, virtually every facet of operation within an enterprise. MIS has even changed the physical layout of offices to accommodate local area networks and departmental computing, and of plants to accommodate computer-integrated manufacturing (these topics are discussed in later chapters). By the mid-1990s all white-collar workers and many blue-collar workers will have daily contact with some aspect of computer-based automation. Corporate cultures will continue to change as people adapt to the inevitable emergence of more and more technology in the corporate environment.

WHY STUDY MIS?

Consider the following scenario. A systems analyst is assigned project responsibility for developing a new computer-based accounting system. In keeping with the company's top-down design policy, the analyst schedules a meeting with the controller. The objectives of the meeting are to obtain an overview of corporate objectives relative to accounting systems and to set the tone for the development project.

The analyst has limited knowledge of accounting and has difficulty formulating appropriate questions and evaluating responses. The controller has similar background deficiencies in the MIS area and, consequently, has the same inability to ask intelligent questions and to understand responses.

This all-too-familiar scenario has little potential for an effective interchange of information. Unfortunately, the quality of the resultant computer-based accounting system is directly proportional to the effectiveness of this and subsequent user/analyst interactions.

Although there is always a need for improved technology, the critical resource is intelligent, resourceful people who can relate business needs to technology.

—— *James J. O'Connor*

The moral is clear: user managers and executives should have a working knowledge of MIS concepts and capabilities, and MIS professionals should have an equivalent knowledge of the functional areas they are servicing. Each must acquire this knowledge or suffer the consequences—both corporate and individual. This book provides the background knowledge that a user at any level will need to become an effective interface between the providers of information services and the functional areas. For people pursuing an MIS-related profession, the book provides a foundation of knowledge upon which they can build their careers.

The body of knowledge necessary for users to become active participants in the information revolution is not mystical or illusive—quite the contrary. It consist of relatively straightforward principles, concepts, techniques, and procedures (all of which are discussed in this book). Having acquired a general understanding, all a user needs is a willingness to apply this general understanding to the specifics of a particular MIS environment (for example, a particular word processing package, information system, or decision support system). Realistically, the computerwise user can anticipate a host of peripheral benefits:

- ☐ *More efficient communication.* Had the user in the foregoing scenario been conversant in the field of MIS, he or she and the analyst would not only have been more effective in their communication, but they would have done it in less time.

- ☐ *Higher-quality information systems.* The quality of an information system is directly proportional to the user's ability to articulate his or her needs to the providers of information services (for example, the information services division). Chapter 5, "Providers of Computer and Information Services," discusses where users can go to obtain information services.

- ☐ *An increased mutual responsiveness between users and providers of information services.* Discussions involving MIS applications are one-sided when one of the participants does not understand the other. Informed people can respond intelligently to each other's suggestions and questions.

- ☐ *An improved decision-making process.* Better decisions are a by-product of better information.

- ☐ *Increased productivity.* MIS offers hundreds of ways to increase productivity. The trick is knowing that they exist and how to take advantage of them.

- ☐ *Greater career opportunities.* Anyone who can exploit the potential of the MIS field to the benefit of the organization has a distinct advantage over those who cannot.

Information is central to most of the activities that transpire in the corporate environment. We produce it, evaluate it, or communicate it to others. To harness the information resource, we need to study and feel comfortable with computers and information processing.

COMPUTER LITERACY AMONG MIDDLE MANAGERS

Q. I, along with 30 other middle managers, received a bluntly worded memo from the president of our company that encouraged us to become computer literate as soon as possible. Details were omitted.

Since I am the only middle manager with any semblance of computer knowledge, at least 10 others have asked me for guidance. I consider myself to be computer literate, but the president's memo did not define it, so I am not sure.

At what level of knowledge does one become computer literate?

A. Companies promote it for their employees. Parents demand it for their children. Those who have it believe they have a competitive edge. Those who do not have it seek it out. "It" is computer literacy. Interestingly, in both business and academe, a fundamental question is often left unanswered: "What *is* computer literacy?"

Is it social issues, technical concepts, programming, application skills, and/or hands-on exposure to computers? If so, what is the proper mix?

I define computer literacy in terms of what an individual will have achieved upon attaining computer literacy versus identifying topics of study. You, as a computer-literate person, will:

1. Feel comfortable in the use and operation of a computer system.

2. Be able to make the computer work for you through judicious development or use of software.

3. Be able to interact with the computer—that is, generate input to the computer and interpret output from the computer.

4. Understand how computers are impacting society, now and in the future.

5. Be an intelligent consumer of computer-related products and services.

Note: The foregoing definition of computer literacy prompted a number of responses from Computerworld *readers, one of which follows.*

Q. In your description of computer literacy, "Be an intelligent consumer of computer-related products and services" is the most important.

It is our responsibility in the computer industry to deemphasize computer literacy as a priority goal in our society. I would prefer that my son learn to think, feel, and understand than to find his precocity in the byways of the computer world. Likewise, I seek in a prospective employee one who can think analytically and creatively and can relate to other people in a sensitive manner.

The computer is a fine tool, but can't it be learned as needed to meet the tasks at hand?

A. You imply that computer literacy and learning to "think, feel, and understand" are mutually exclusive activities. Many agree with you. Although I agree that thinking, feeling, and understanding are worthy developmental goals, I contend that computer literacy can be a part of that development and perhaps even hasten progress toward other goals.

When you recommend that the computer be learned as needed, you are suggesting that we be reactive rather than proactive to a need for automation. Those who opt for the reactive approach will probably end up chasing the competition.

---

* The Qs and As appearing in the "MIS in practice" sidebars throughout the book are taken from the Larry Long's "Turnaround Time" column, formerly a regular feature in *Computerworld*, the newsweekly for the computer community. In the column, the author responded to systems analysts, end users at all levels, company presidents, MIS consultants, entrepreneurs, vendors, programmers, government officials, project team leaders, auditors, and others who had a question or a response that related to computers and MIS. The Qs and As are included to give you some insight into the real-life problems, concerns, and situations that confront end users and MIS professionals.

DATA, INFORMATION, AND INFORMATION SYSTEMS

Data Versus Information

Information is the central and recurring theme throughout this book. We have already discussed the information resource and the information society. In this section, the information system is introduced. However, little has been said about information and its origin—data. **Data** (the plural of *datum*) are the raw material from which information is derived. **Information** is what results from the thoughtful analysis, manipulation, and presentation of data in a form that will enhance the decision-making process.

We routinely deal with the concepts of data and information in our everyday experiences. We use data to produce information that will help us make decisions. For example, when we arrive at work in the morning, we collect two pieces of data. We look at the time and recall from our memory or our daily calendars the time of our first meeting. Then we subtract the current time from the starting time of the meeting. This mental computation provides information on how much time we have to prepare for the meeting. Based on this information, we make a decision to hurry up or to relax and work on other projects.

We produce information from data to help us make decisions for thousands of situations each day. In many ways, the contents of this book are just an extension of concepts with which you are already familiar.

Qualities of Information

Just as we describe automobiles in terms of features, color, and size, we describe information in terms of its *accuracy*, *verifiability*, *completeness*, *relevance*, and *timeliness*.

Accuracy and Verifiability of Information

The *accuracy* quality of information refers to the degree to which information is free from error. Information is usually assumed to be accurate unless it is presented otherwise. Sometimes it is not economically feasible to collect information that is 100 percent accurate. For example, a market analyst may poll only a fraction of the potential consumers for a proposed product and extrapolate the results of the information gathered to apply to all potential consumers. In this instance, the market analyst can state that the information gathered from the sample can be applied to all consumers with a certain degree of confidence (for example, 95 percent).

Accuracy and *verifiability* go hand in hand. A decision maker is reluctant to assume that information is accurate unless it is verifiable. For example, executives are usually comfortable with the accuracy of financial information. Financial information can be verified (and usually is by auditors) because records are kept of all transactions that impact the financial position of a company (for example, payments and receipts). Decision makers accept and use unverifiable information, but they do so with caution and skepticism.

Too often managers at all levels are quick to accept computer-generated information as gospel. This can be a mistake. Information is only as good

The trend is to developing information systems that provide on-line access to information. In our fast-paced society, having access to timely information has become a business imperative. This executive knows how to retrieve needed information; those who do not must wait for others to do it for them. For the latter, the quality of the information they receive is diminished because it is less timely.

MicroAge Computer Stores, Inc.

as the data from which it is derived. As the saying goes, "garbage in, garbage out" or **GIGO** (pronounced GUY go).

Completeness of Information

Information can be completely accurate and verifiable, but it may not tell the whole story. The *completeness* quality of information refers to the degree to which it is free from omissions. There is, of course, no relationship between the amount of information supplied to a decision maker and its completeness. Benefit/cost analysis offers a good example of the importance of considering the completeness of information in the decision-making process. If the benefit information is complete and the cost information incomplete, the omission of the rest of the costs may result in an unprofitable project being erroneously approved. Unfortunately, this very situation is a common occurrence in the business world.

Timeliness of Information

The *timeliness* quality of information refers to the time sensitivity of information. Up-to-date information on today's market trends may be of significant value to an executive. The same information will have less value in a month and probably no value in a year. The computer has contributed more toward improving the timeliness quality of information than any of the other information qualities. The power of today's computers has made it possible for managers to have not only the right information, but the right information at the right time. Prior to 1980, managers were conditioned to waiting as much as two weeks for relatively straightforward ad hoc requests for information. Today, similar requests can be handled in minutes.

Relevance of Information

The *relevance* quality of information refers to the appropriateness of the information as input for a particular decision. **Information overload** continues to be a problem for decision makers. Information overload occurs when the volume of available information is so great that the decision maker cannot distinguish relevant information from that which is not. One of the primary causes of information overload is the accumulation of information that is not relevant to a particular decision. For example, the power requirements for mainframe computers are not relevant to decisions involving the acquisition of microcomputers.

Information Systems

Hardware, *software*, *people*, *procedures*, and *data* are combined to create an **information system** (see Figure 1–2). The term information system is a generic reference to a computer-based system that provides the following:

- [] *Data processing* capabilities for a department or perhaps an entire company.
- [] *Information* that people need to make better, more informed decisions.

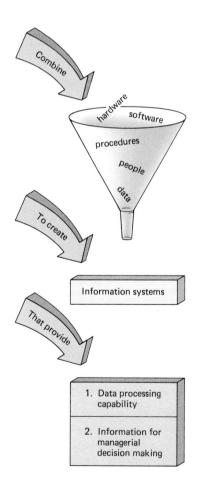

FIGURE 1–2   Information System Ingredients and Capabilities

The data processing capability refers to the system's ability to handle and process data. The more sophisticated information systems provide decision makers with *on-demand reports* and *inquiry capabilities*, as well as *routine periodic reports*.

In Chapter 2, "The MIS and Decision Support Systems," and Chapter 3, "Artificial Intelligence and Expert Systems," information systems in general and other categories of information-producing systems are introduced and discussed.

INFORMATION RESOURCE MANAGEMENT

During the past 50 years, managers have become adept at taking full advantage of the resources of *money*, *materials*, and *people*, but only recently have managers begun to make effective use of the fourth major resource—*information*. In fact, corporate management everywhere is adopting an attitude called **information resource management** (**IRM**). Information resource management is a concept advocating that information is a valuable resource and should be managed accordingly, just like money, materials, and people. Each manager who embraces the concept of IRM is accepting the responsibility to emphasize the management and control of information.

In years past, this executive would fill his attache case with reports, documents, and other work-related papers. Now, he carries his portable personal computer and with it the information resources of his company. From his home (or anywhere there is a telephone) he can establish a communications link with his company and make inquiries to the data base, check on his electronic mail, enter data, or send a memo to the managers in his department.

Amusement parks are adopting the information resource management philosophy. The information gathering process begins when the customer arrives at the gate. This information is used to print tickets, record sales information, and to produce daily, weekly, and monthly activity reports. The desktop computers at the gates are linked to a larger system that handles other administrative duties. Park activity is tracked by day, time, type of weather, and so on to help park management make decisions about staffing levels and other matters affecting overall productivity.

Alpha Microsystems

Objectives of IRM

Information resource management has two objectives: a global objective that applies to a company as a whole and a fundamental objective that applies to the end user of information.

- □ *Global objective of IRM*—to add value to the enterprise through the judicious application of MIS capabilities.
- □ *Fundamental objective of IRM*—to get the right information to the decision maker at the right time in the right form.

Treating Information as a Resource

The IRM concept encourages managers to treat information as a major resource. Managers can adopt the IRM concept by adhering to three guidelines:

1. Use decision support systems and other aids for managerial decision making.

2. Use available information services in support of transaction-based systems.
3. Participate in and encourage the integration of **functionally adjacent systems** (systems that feed each other, have functional overlap, and share all or part of a data base).

The Competitive Advantage

Management in every area of business endeavor is being challenged to become more competitive and, thereby, more profitable. In the past, management has approached this task by focusing its efforts to enhance competitiveness on the resources of people, materials, and money. For example, work-simplification techniques and employee motivation are often used to improve the effectiveness of the people resource. Managers have elevated the movement, storage, and use of the materials resource to an art form. Every medium to large company has at least one and often a team of financial experts to plan the company's investment strategies and the application of its monetary resource. These efforts have proven successful, but they alone are not enough for a company to remain competitive in a world market. In an all-out effort to gain the *competitive advantage*, managers are looking to the information resource. Chapter 4, "Information Systems as a Competitive Strategy," provides many examples of how companies are using information to achieve a competitive advantage.

INFORMATION AND DECISION MAKING

The Decision-Making Environment

The business system model in Figure 1–3 helps to place the decision-making environment in its proper perspective. Most companies have three levels of management: *operational*, *tactical*, and *strategic*.

☐ Strategic-level managers determine long-term strategies and set corporate objectives and policy consistent with these objectives.

☐ Tactical-level managers are charged with the responsibility of implementing the objectives and policies set forth at the strategic level of management. To do this, managers identify specific tasks that need to be accomplished.

☐ Operational-level managers complete specific tasks as directed by tactical-level managers.

Managers at each level have an ongoing need for information. Information is critical in that it is necessary for managers to

☐ Use the resources at their disposal more effectively.

☐ Meet corporate objectives.

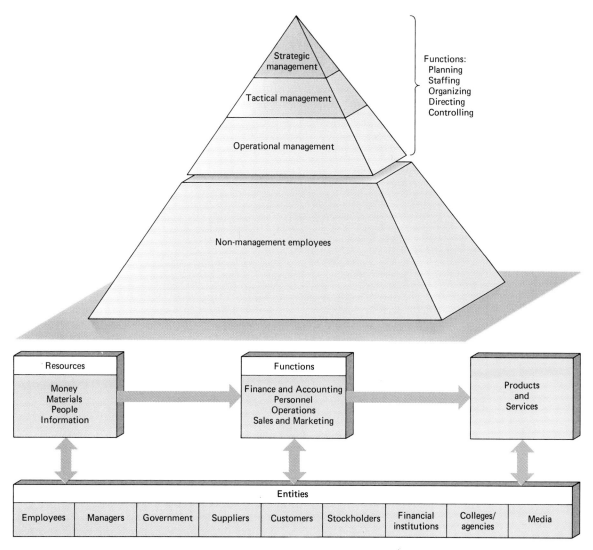

FIGURE 1–3 A Business System Model

☐ Perform the management functions of *planning, staffing, organizing, directing,* and *controlling.*

Figure 1–3 illustrates how the corporate resources of *money, materials* (to include facilities and equipment), *people,* and *information* become "input" to the various functional units, such as operations, sales, and accounting. People use their talent and knowledge, together with these resources, to produce products and services.

The business system acts in concert with several *entities,* such as employees, customers, and suppliers (see Figure 1–3). An entity is the source or destination of information flow, or an entity can be the source or destination of materials or product flow. For example, suppliers are both a source of information and materials. They are also the destination of payments for materials. The customer entity is the destination of products and the source of orders. *Flow diagrams* in Chapter 15, "An MIS Case Study," detail direct interaction between all departments and entities in a business system.

Everybody has problems, and since decisions are made to solve problems, everybody makes decisions. Some are made with a casual nod of the head, others are gut-wrenching experiences for the decision maker. As a rule of thumb, the higher the decision maker is in the organization, the more complex and difficult the decision. Also, the number of people affected by the decision increases with the level of the decision maker. For decisions made at the strategic and tactical levels, each alternative will have avid proponents (and opponents). To a much lesser extent this is also true of operational-level decisions. As a result, the decision maker is constantly smothered with new insight and information. Important corporate decisions are seldom made on a whim. Decision makers are influenced by available information, but they are also influenced by corporate policy, tradition, various pressure groups (for example, vendors), and peers. Decision makers want to make sure that each alternative has been thoroughly evaluated; in so doing, the decision maker is subjected to intense peer pressure and often biased information. Unfortunately, peer pressure can, on occasion, be more influential than reason. However, this is the decision-making environment. Evaluating information at face value is not enough. The decision maker must have the ability to place each piece of information in its proper perspective.

Good Decisions and Bad Decisions

No decision maker can bat 1,000—making the right decision every time. Decision makers who bat 1,000 are not doing their jobs. If a manager waits until the information points conclusively to a particular decision alternative, chances are the manager waited too long to make the decision. Decisions are often sensitive and must be made even if information in support of the decision is limited. For decisions made at the tactical and strategic levels, available information is often inconclusive, and managers must also rely on their *experience, intuition*, and *common sense* to make the right decision. Under conditions of uncertainty, even good managers will make an occasional bad decision.

Types of Decisions

The two basic types of decisions are **programmed decisions** and **nonprogrammed decisions**. Purely programmed decisions address well-defined problems. The decision maker has no judgmental flexibility when making a programmed decision because the actual decision is determined by existing policies or procedures. In fact, many decisions involving such problems can be accomplished by a computer, without human intervention! For example, the decisions required to restock inventory levels for raw materials is often a programmed decision that can be made by an individual or by a computer-based information system. When the inventory level for a particular item drops below the reorder point, perhaps a two month's supply, a decision is made to replenish the inventory by submitting an order to the supplier.

Where all think alike, no one thinks very much.

——— *Walter Lippmann*

Through the mid-1980s, virtually all decisions made by sales clerks were programmed decisions. Now, the greater availability of information made possible through on-line point-of-sale (POS) systems has enabled more of the decisions to be made at the clerical level. This is the case in virtually all types of industry.

Nonprogrammed decisions involve ill-defined and unstructured problems. Such decisions are also called **information-based decisions** because the decision maker needs information to make a rational decision. The information requirement implies the need for managers to apply judgment and intuition in the decision-making process. Corporate policies, procedures, standards, and guidelines provide substantial direction for nonprogrammed decisions made at the operational level, less direction at the tactical level, and little or no direction at the strategic level. The greater the programmability of a decision, the greater the confidence of the decision maker that the most acceptable alternative has been selected. Characteristics of decisions made at the three levels of management are summarized in Figure 1–4.

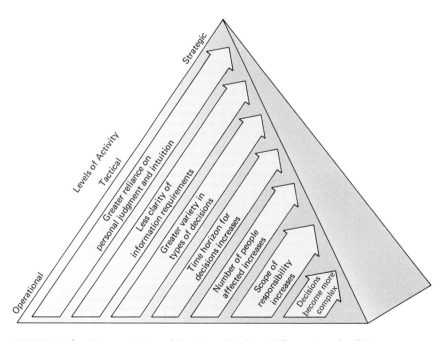

FIGURE 1–4   Characteristics of Decisions Made at Different Levels of Management

A typical strategic-level decision in a consumer goods company involves deciding whether or not to proceed with the introduction of a new product to the marketplace. The information requirements for such a decision are substantial—results of a market test, legal considerations, competitive analysis, manufacturing capacity, and so on.

The Decision-Making Process

Whether a deliberate action or not, people who make information-based decisions go through a decision-making process. The steps in the decision-making process are to

1. Set objectives.
2. Identify constraints.
3. Identify alternatives.
4. Gather appropriate information.
5. Evaluate alternatives.
6. Choose the most acceptable alternative.

The steps in the decision-making process are illustrated in Figure 1–5 and are defined in more detail in the following sections.

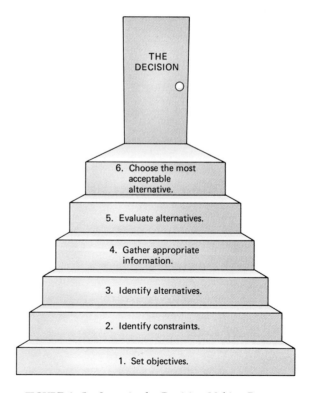

FIGURE 1–5 Steps in the Decision-Making Process

Step 1: Set Objectives

The existence of a problem implies the need for a decision maker to make at least one decision, and typically a series of decisions, to resolve a problem. In this first step, the decision maker sets the objective for the decision. For example, a decision objective might be to decide whether or not to buy a microcomputer. The objective of a follow-up decision might be to determine which microcomputer to purchase.

Step 2: Identify Constraints

Constraints in some way limit the decision maker's choices. Constraints could be defined by legal, economic, or political considerations. Decision constraints are sometimes presented in terms of desired specifications or performance standards. Also, when applicable, corporate policies, procedures, standards, and guidelines serve to limit the scope of the decision maker's options.

Typically, the identification of constraints results in a reduction in the number of possible alternatives. As an example, consider the decision to determine which microcomputer to purchase. The constraints affecting this decision might be identified as follows:

- □ The microcomputer selected must be able to withstand frequent movement within and outside of the office; therefore, it must be either a transportable or lap microcomputer.
- □ The company's microcomputer acquisitions policy states that all new acquisitions must have the capability to run applications software written for the IBM PC.
- □ Corporate guidelines stipulate a minimum system configuration: 640K RAM, 20-megabyte hard disk, one floppy diskette or microdisk drive.
- □ The total purchase price for the micro and all peripheral input/output devices should not exceed $2,000.
- □ The micro selected must be available for delivery within two weeks of the decision date.

Get rid of worthless alternatives, or else someone will commit to them.

———— *Anonymous*

Step 3: Identify Alternatives

The decision-making process involves making a choice between two or more alternatives. In this step the decision maker identifies alternative solutions that meet the constraints outlined in step 2. In most cases, the alternatives are chosen because they provide a solution to the problem, but often one of the alternatives is to do nothing. In the preceding example, 15 micros are identified that meet the "transportable or lap" constraint. Ten of those are IBM PC or compatible and can be configured to meet the minimum configuration specifications. Six of those fall within the budget restrictions, and only three can be delivered on two weeks' notice. Through this process of elimination, the alternatives become Micro A, Micro B, and Micro C. In this example, the "do-nothing" option is not an alternative.

Step 4: Gather Appropriate Information

The information requirements for a given decision vary considerably depending on the complexity and scope of the decision to be made. During this step, the decision maker gathers information that may provide insight as to which alternative to choose. The information could address risks, consequences of choosing a particular alternative, functional specifications, test results, summary of advantages and disadvantages, or virtually any category of information that will influence the decision process. Information requirements are more difficult to define at the strategic levels of management than at the operational level (see Figure 1–4).

The information gathering process is often iterative; that is, one set of information frequently points to other sources of information and so on. The search for relevant information continues until sources are exhausted or available information is sufficient to make a rational decision. Of course, there is always a danger of information overload. An information overload situation can actually add an unnecessary layer of complexity to the already challenging decision-making process.

The MIS environment provides decision makers with the capability to generate quality information. However,

the quality of a decision, or the probability that the right decision is made, is directly related to the quality of information,

which is dependent on the decision maker's ability to gather and assimilate information,

which is dependent on the decision maker's ability to take advantage of the capabilities of MIS.

This fourth step is critical. If the information assembled by the decision maker is incomplete, inaccurate, or out of date, the process becomes more a game of chance than a decision-making process.

Step 5: Evaluate Alternatives

In this step, the decision maker evaluates each alternative. A decision can be rendered based on available information, or a decision maker may wish to employ MIS capabilities to provide more insight into which alternative to choose. For example, at this time the decision maker may wish to employ a computer-based model to predict possible results if a particular alternative is selected. As another example, a manager might prefer that numeric information be presented in another format, perhaps in a bar graph rather than in tabular (rows and columns) form. Throughout this book examples and approaches are presented that show how managers can use MIS capabilities to make more informed and better decisions. The result of step 5 is a ranking of decision alternatives.

Step 6: Choose the Most Acceptable Alternative

In this step, the manager examines the ranking of alternatives and selects the most acceptable alternative, which is often the top-ranked alternative. On occasion, extenuating circumstances cause managers to look past the highest-ranking alternative and select a lower-ranking alternative. Decisions, especially those made collectively by several managers, are often the result of compromise. In these instances, the alternative selected is the *most acceptable* one and not necessarily the *best* one.

When you have to make a choice and don't make it, that is in itself a choice.

——— *William James*

Information is a critical element of the decision-making process, but information does not make decisions, people do. Ultimately, nonprogrammed decisions boil down to the decision maker's experience, intuition, and common sense.

Filtering Information

The four levels of activity within a company are strategic, tactical, operational, and clerical. The top three levels involve management activities and were first introduced and discussed relative to the business system model in Figure 1–3. Computer-based information systems process data at the clerical level and provide information for managerial decision making at the operational, tactical, and strategic levels.

The quality of an information system is judged by its output. A system that generates the same 20-page report for personnel at both the clerical and strategic levels is defeating the purpose of an information system. The information needs at these two levels of activity are substantially different: a secretary has no need, or desire, for such a comprehensive report; the president of the company would never use the report because it would take too long to extract the few pieces of important information.

The key to developing quality information systems is to "filter" information so that people at the various levels of activity receive the information they need to accomplish their job function—no more, no less. **Filtering** information results in the *right information* reaching the *right decision maker* at the *right time* in the *right form*.

Clerical Level

Clerical-level personnel, those involved in repetitive tasks, are concerned primarily with transaction handling. You might say that they process data. For example, in a sales information system, order entry clerks key in customer orders from their workstations. In an airline reservation system, ticket agents confirm and make flight reservations.

Operational Level

Personnel at the operational level have well-defined tasks that might span a day, a week, or as much as three months, but their tasks are essentially short term. Their information requirements are directed at operational feedback. In the sales information system, for example, the manager of the Eastern Regional Sales Department might want an end-of-quarter "Sales Summary" report. The report, illustrated in Figure 1–6, shows dollar volume sales by salesperson for each of the company's four products: Alphas, Betas, Gammas, and Deltas. In the report, the sales records of the top (Cook) and bottom (Ritter) performers are highlighted so that managers can use this range as a basis for comparing the performance of the other salespersons.

Managers at the operational, tactical, and strategic levels often request **exception reports** that highlight critical information. Such requests can be made to the MIS Division, or managers can make inquiries directly to the system using a query language. For example, the eastern regional sales manager used a fourth-generation language (discussed in Chapter 6, "End

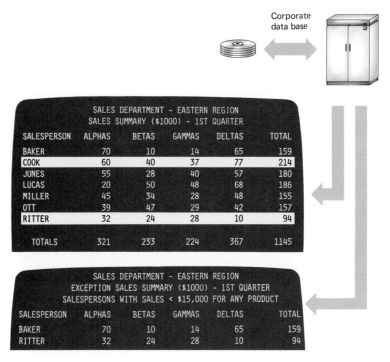

FIGURE 1–6   An Operational-Level Sales Summary and Exception Report
These sales reports are prepared in response to inquiries from an operational-level manager. Contrast the reports in this figure with those in Figures 1–7 and 1–8.

User Computing") to generate the exception report of Figure 1–6. The manager's request was: "Display a list of all eastern region salespersons who had sales of less than $15,000 for any product for this quarter." The report highlights the subpar performances of Baker and Ritter.

The information available for an operational-level decision is often conclusive. That is, the most acceptable alternative can be clearly identified based on information available to the decision maker. At this level, personal judgment and intuition play a reduced role in the decision-making process.

Tactical Level

At the tactical level, managers concentrate on achieving that series of goals required to meet the objectives set at the strategic level. The information requirements are usually periodic, but on occasion, managers require one-time and "what if" reports. Tactical managers are concerned primarily with operations and budgets from year to year. In the sales information system, the national sales manager, who is at the tactical level, might want the "Corporate Sales" report of Figure 1–7. The report presents dollar volume sales by sales region for each of the company's four products. To get a better feeling for the relative sales contribution of each of the four regional offices during the first quarter, the national sales manager requested that the total sales for each region be presented graphically in a circle graph (Figure 1–7).

The information available for a tactical-level decision is seldom conclusive. That is, the most acceptable alternative cannot be identified from informa-

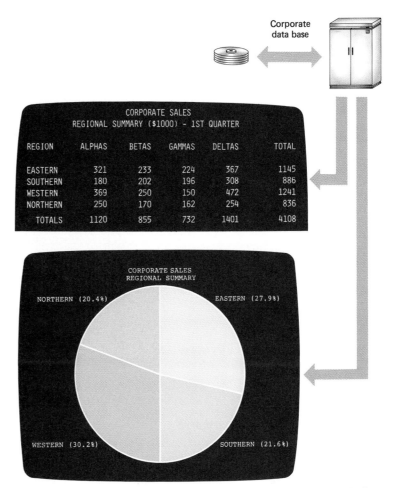

FIGURE 1–7 A Tactical-Level Sales Summary Report Shown in Tabular and Graphic Formats

The sales summary report and circle graph are prepared in response to inquiries from a tactical-level manager. Contrast the reports in this figure with those in Figures 1–6 and 1–8.

tion alone. At this level, most decisions are resolved by applying personal judgment and intuition to available information.

Strategic Level

Managers at the strategic level are objective minded. Their information system requirements are often one-time reports, "what if" reports, and trend analyses. For example, the president of the company might ask for a report that shows the four-year sales trend for each of the company's four products and overall (Figure 1–8). Knowing that it is easier to detect trends in a graphic format than in a tabular format, the president requests that the trends be summarized in a bar graph (Figure 1–8). From the bar graph, the president can easily see that the sales of Alphas and Gammas are experiencing modest growth while the sales of Betas and Deltas are more favorable.

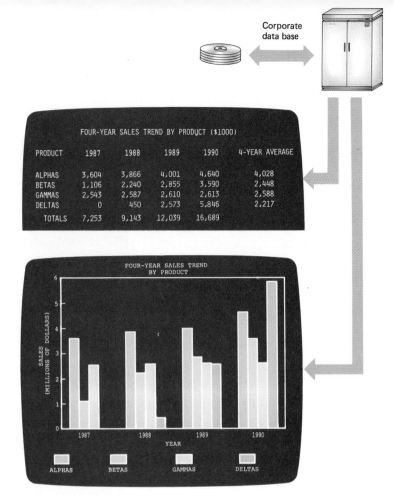

Corporate
data base

FOUR-YEAR SALES TREND BY PRODUCT ($1000)

PRODUCT	1987	1988	1989	1990	4-YEAR AVERAGE
ALPHAS	3,604	3,866	4,001	4,640	4,028
BETAS	1,106	2,240	2,855	3,590	2,448
GAMMAS	2,543	2,587	2,610	2,613	2,588
DELTAS	0	450	2,573	5,846	2,217
TOTALS	7,253	9,143	12,039	16,689	

FOUR-YEAR SALES TREND
BY PRODUCT

FIGURE 1–8   A Strategic-Level Sales-Trend-by-Product Report Shown in Tabular and Graphic Formats
The sales trend report and bar graph are prepared in response to inquiries from a strategic-level manager. Contrast the reports in this figure with those in Figures 1–6 and 1–7.

The information available for a strategic-level decision is almost never conclusive. To be sure, information is critical to strategic-level decision making, but virtually all decision makers at this level rely heavily on personal judgment and intuition.

The information requirements at the various levels of organizational activity are summarized in Figure 1–9.

MIS TRENDS

Even in the ever-changing field of MIS, several trends are emerging.

□ *MIS users are more knowledgeable.* Each year the base of knowledgeable users is increasing dramatically. Recent college graduates are flooding the work force with an appreciation and knowledge of MIS and others are learning about this field at an unprecedented rate.

□ *More computing power is available to the user.* Recent technological innovations have enabled more and more computing power to be made directly accessible to and even controlled by the end user. For example, today's end users can run sophisticated decision support software on their microcomputers that prior to 1980 could only be run in a mainframe computer environment.

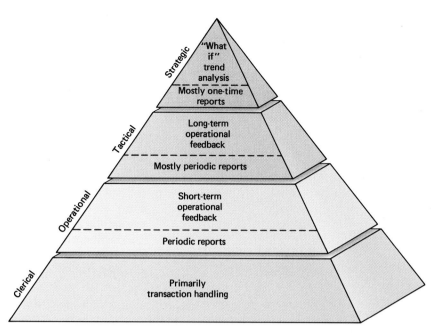

FIGURE 1–9 Information Requirement Profile by Level of Activity

☐ *Resistance to the implementation of emerging MIS technology is subsiding.* For the past four decades, the fear of computers has been so widespread that psychologists have created a name for it—**cyberphobia**. Cyberphobia is the irrational fear of, and aversion to, computers. It is human nature to resist that which we fear and do not understand. Less than 5 percent of the population is comfortable enough with computers to deem themselves "computer literate"; however that percentage is increasing rapidly. Resistance to the implementation of MIS technology decreases as the number of computer-literate people increases.

☐ *Connectivity.* **Connectivity** is a term that has been coined to refer to the concept of linking or connecting computer hardware, computer software, and data bases. The trend in the development of commercially available hardware, software, and data base products is to design the products of the future so that they can be easily interfaced with one another and to provide *bridges* that enable connectivity in existing hardware, software, and data bases. Connectivity is covered in detail in Chapter 8, "Connectivity and Data Communications."

☐ *MIS is becoming one of the primary means of increasing productivity.* A world economy demands that productivity in every area of business endeavor be improved. Top management is asking, "How can computers be employed to improve corporate productivity?" Similar questions are being asked at the individual level. Engineers, accountants, nurses, and countless others are asking, "What can computers do to help me make a greater contribution to my company?"

☐ *Companies are using MIS as a competitive strategy.* Successful companies are using MIS to gain the competitive advantage. Chapter 4, "Information Systems as a Competitive Strategy," addresses this trend in detail and discusses what MIS strategies the various companies are adopting to gain the competitive advantage.

☐ *MIS is becoming integral to the decision-making process.* In the past, and in many companies today, computers have been viewed as administrative tools that are used primarily for transaction processing. The trend is to make better use of the computer's ability of providing information in support of the decision-making process. This trend is discussed at length in Chapter 2, "The MIS and Decision Support Systems."

☐ *The end user is becoming the focus of MIS activity.* In this era of information resource management, users and the providers of information services have become partners in search of better information. There is a direct correlation between the quality of information and the user community's willingness to become actively involved in MIS-related activities.

All trends support the premise that the future of MIS is in the hands of the user. Users are encouraged by top management and MIS professionals to become intimately involved in the development of information systems, from start to finish. In many companies, the functional area manager is appointed to manage the information system development team. The emphasis in the design of virtually all new software is the end user.

For decades the power of computers was entrusted solely to MIS professionals. Today, the power of computers is within the grasp of anyone who wants quality information, increased productivity, or the competitive advantage.

CHAPTER HIGHLIGHTS

■ The terms "management information system" and "MIS" are commonly used in the business environment as a generic reference to all technologies, procedures, systems, and people associated with computers and information processing. Besides being a generic reference, the term "MIS" is also used to refer to a type of computer-based system.

■ The major contributors to the emergence of MIS as a priority concern in the business community are the improved price-performance of computers and the availability of user-oriented software.

■ MIS is having a profound impact on corporate cultures. The free flow of information is changing the traditional pyramid structure of organizations by reducing the levels of management. In almost every progressive company, automation is altering the way people think and make decisions. In an MIS environment, decisions can be made at a lower level in the organization.

Computer systems have made people at all levels more accountable for their actions. As companies move in the direction of MIS, the corporate culture often moves from plodding and traditional to aggressive and change oriented.

■ Information is what results from the thoughtful analysis, manipulation, and presentation of data in a form that will enhance the decision-making process. Information is described in terms of its accuracy, verifiability, completeness, relevance, and timeliness.

■ Information is only as good as the data from which it is derived.

■ Information overload occurs when the volume of available information is so great that the decision maker cannot distinguish relevant information from that which is not.

■ Hardware, software, people, procedures, and data are combined to create an information system. An information system provides companies with data processing capabilities and the company's people with information.

■ Traditionally, managers have been very adept at taking full advantage of the resources of money, materials, and people; but only recently have they begun to make effective use of information, the other resource. Today, executives are embracing the concept of information resource management. The global objective of IRM is to add value to the enterprise through the judicious application of MIS capabilities. The fundamental objective of IRM is to get the right information to the decision maker at the right time in the right form.

■ The higher the decision maker is in the organization, the more complex and difficult the decision. Also, the number of people affected by the decision increases with the level of the decision maker.

■ For decisions made at the tactical and strategic level, available information is often inconclusive, and managers must also rely on their experience, intuition, and common sense to make the right decision.

■ The two basic types of decisions are programmed decisions and nonprogrammed decisions. Purely programmed decisions address well-defined problems. Nonprogrammed decisions, also called information-based decisions, involve ill-defined and unstructured problems.

■ The steps in the decision-making process are

1. Set objectives
2. Identify constraints
3. Identify alternatives
4. Gather appropriate information
5. Evaluate alternatives
6. Choose the most acceptable alternative

■ The quality of a decision is directly related to the quality of the information provided in support of the decision. The quality of the information is dependent on the decision maker's ability to gather and assimilate it. And the decision maker's ability to obtain the information is dependent on his or her ability to take advantage of the capabilities of MIS.

■ Information systems assist in processing data at the clerical level and providing information for managerial decision making at the operational, tactical, and strategic levels.

■ Several trends are emerging in the field of MIS: more knowledgeable users, more computing power for users, less user resistance to the implementation of MIS technology, greater connectivity, increased productivity via MIS, MIS as a competitive strategy, interdependence of the decision-making process and MIS, and the end user orientation of MIS.

IMPORTANT TERMS

bridges (Ch. 8)

competitive advantage (Ch. 4)

computer

computerese

connectivity (Ch. 8)

corporate culture

cyberphobia

data

electronic data interchange (EDI) (Ch. 4)

electronic mail (Ch. 2)

end user

exception reports

expert systems (Ch. 3)

filtering

functionally adjacent systems

GIGO

information

information overload

information resource management (IRM)

information system

information-based decisions

management information systems (MIS)

nonprogrammed decisions

programmed decisions

user

REVIEW EXERCISES

1. MIS is an abbreviation for what term?
2. Describe two ways in which MIS has affected corporate cultures.
3. What are some of the benefits enjoyed by computerwise end users?

4. List and briefly describe the five qualities of information.
5. What is the fundamental objective of IRM?
6. Contrast management functions at the strategic and tactical levels relative to corporate objectives.

---

* Chapter references indicate chapters in which the associated term is discussed in more depth.

7. Does the number of people affected by a decision increase or decrease with the level of the decision maker?

8. What are the two basic types of decisions?

9. List the six steps in the decision-making process.

10. What is meant by the filtering of information?

11. What is the purpose of an exception report?

12. Describe the relationship between data and information.

13. What elements are combined to create an information system?

14. What is IRM, and how does it relate to money, materials, and people?

15. What are the levels of organizational activity, from specific to general?

DISCUSSION QUESTIONS

1. How has the improved price/performance of computers contributed to the emergence of MIS in businesses?

2. The computer has had far-reaching effects on our lives. How has the computer affected your life?

3. What is your concept of computer literacy? In what ways do you think achieving computer literacy will have an impact on your career?

4. Discuss how the complexion of jobs will change as we evolve from an industrial society to an information society. Give examples.

5. Describe how what you did yesterday would change if you did not directly or indirectly use the capabilities of computers.

6. For each of the three levels of management illustrated in the business system model in Figure 1–3, what would be the horizon (time span) for planning decisions? Explain.

7. In general, top executives have always treated money, materials, and people as valuable resources, but only recently have they recognized that information is also a valuable resource. Why do you think they waited so long?

8. It is often said that "time is money." Would you say that "information is money"? Discuss.

9. Give examples of reports that might be requested by an operational-level manager in an insurance company. A tactical-level manager. A strategic-level manager.

10. What is implied in the statement that computers and information processing have made the world a global village?

11. How have computers made people more accountable for their job performance? Would you consider this application good or bad? Justify your response.

12. Why do you think resistance to the implementation of MIS technology is subsiding?

APPLICATION CASE STUDY 1–1
The Decision-Making Process

The Situation

The Edward Gabriel Company, a family-owned business for two generations, began as a small workshop that manufactured hardware for lamps. The business prospered and diversified into other products, such as steel and aluminum tubing for use in the bicycle and automobile industries. Manufacturing and distribution facilities are located in Brooklyn, New York (headquarters), and Newark, New Jersey. Additional distribution facilities are located in Pontiac, Michigan, and Wilmington, Delaware.

The family members decided to go public and relinquish managerial control of the new publicly-held corporation named Gabriel Industries. The Board of Directors asked the Executive Committee, which consists of all the vice presidents, to evaluate and report on the status of all major phases of operations at Gabriel Industries.

The analysis revealed that Gabriel Industries continues to have good profit potential, but a few of the functional areas are not performing well. One of these areas is accounts receivable. The Executive Committee identified several specific problems with the accounts receivable function: invoices and statements are sent to customers as much as two weeks late, late charges are not applied in many cases, and many delinquent customers are not being pursued.

Accounts receivable and other accounting systems are currently run in batch mode on the Accounting Department's minicomputer. The former controller, John Gabriel, was a traditionalist and often resistive to change. One of his mottos was: "If it isn't broken, don't fix it!" John Gabriel had steadfastly refused to integrate his departmental computer-based systems with other corporate systems, all of which are handled by the Computer Services Department.

As a follow-up to the Executive Committee's findings, the board formed a task force to analyze the accounts receivable situation and to recommend a solution. The task force consisted of Mary Pulaski, executive vice president, Jonathan Gilbert, vice president for finance, Martin Bernstein, manager of accounts receivable, and Joan Martinelli, a systems analyst from the Computer Services Department. The task force decided to follow the six steps of the decision-making process described in the chapter material.

The Assignment

1. For each of the steps listed here, perform the indicated task. Note any assumptions that you make. Specify which member(s) of the task force would be the most appropriate person(s) to perform the step.

   a. *Set objectives.* Keep in mind that various members of the task force may be considering different objectives.

   b. *Identify constraints.* List any constraints that may limit the choices available to the task force. These constraints may be defined by corporate policy, personnel limitations, Computer Services Department guidelines, and so on.

   c. *Identify alternatives.* List all possible solutions. These could range from doing nothing to contracting with an outside company to handle the accounts receivable function.

   d. *Gather appropriate information.* List the information the task force needs to make a decision. Describe the source of the needed information and identify who would be responsible for gathering the information.

   e. *Evaluate alternatives.* Suggest a procedure for ranking the alternatives.

   f. *Choose the most acceptable alternative.* How might the task force accomplish this activity? Should each member have an equal voice?

2. The three administrators on the task force might request that their individual information needs be included in the design of an updated accounts receivable system. Speculate on what you think these information requirements might be. For reports and inquiries, specify the title of the report, critical fields and totals, the sequence of the output (for example, in ascending order by customer number or in descending order by amount owed), and the frequency (for periodic reports).

APPLICATION CASE STUDY 1–2
Types of Decisions

The Situation

Compu-Mail is a mail-order retailer of computer hardware, software, and supplies. It stocks approximately 1,700 products at its only location, which is also a walk-in retail outlet. Customers submit orders in two ways. They call in orders using Compu-Mail's 800 number, or they use the forms that appear in Compu-Mail's catalog and in advertisements in computer periodicals.

Order processing is a computer-based batch system in which telephone orders, mail orders, and counter purchases are handled similarly, but with some differences. Orders are processed manually until they have been completely approved and all computations performed, at which point the data are entered into the computer system. For a telephone order, a customer service clerk writes the order details on a sales form and places the sales form in a basket. An order entry clerk periodically collects the completed forms.

The first processing step for a telephone order is to retrieve the unit price and weight of each item ordered from the master catalog and compute the total sales amount. The unit price is multiplied by the quantity ordered, giving the sales amount for that line item. Similarly, the unit weight for that line item is multiplied by the quantity ordered, giving the total weight for that line item. All the line-item sales amounts are then summed, giving the total sales amount for the order. Similarly, all the line-item weights are summed, giving the total weight for the order.

The second step is to check the customer's credit. If the order is a charge, the credit card number and the amount are entered into a dedicated terminal that is on-line to a national credit bureau. The terminal displays one of two responses from the credit bureau—an approval number or a rejection indication. The order entry clerk forwards orders that are rejected to the credit manager. Compu-Mail permits established commercial customers to submit an order with a customer purchase order number. When this occurs, the customer's record must be retrieved from the file. If the customer is not in arrears and the current purchase does not exceed the customer's credit limit, the order is approved. If the order is rejected, it is forwarded to the credit manager, who decides what to do. The credit manager may approve the order, depending on circumstances, or the manager may contact the customer to make alternative payment arrangements.

After the order has been approved, the third processing step involves the determination of the method of shipment and cost. If the customer requests either of the two priority shipping methods, the corresponding surcharge is computed. If priority shipping is not specified, the weight and/or dimensions of the package determine the method (either U.S. mail or a common carrier such as UPS or Federal Express). The cost in either case is determined by the weight and destination zone.

Finally, completed orders are entered into the computer. Periodically, orders are printed by the computer system and are sent to the warehouse for picking and packing. Orders that cannot be completely filled are marked accordingly and are returned to the order entry section for adjustment.

Mail orders are processed similarly to telephone orders, except for a few differences. Critical items on the customer-completed order form are verified for accuracy, specifically the catalog numbers, prices, and the customer's arithmetic. Another difference deals with customers who prepay an order. If the customer has included a personal check as prepayment, the order is held in a pending file until sufficient time has elapsed for the check to clear (from 10 days to 3 weeks, depending on the location of the customer's bank). If the prepayment is the check of a customer company, the clerk consults the customer's record. If the record shows any indication of bad checks, the order is forwarded to the credit manager for disposition.

Counter sales at the retail store are processed like telephone orders except that the sales clerk performs immediately all the steps, unless intervention by the credit manager is required. Personal checks, however, are not accepted for counter sales.

The Assignment

1. Based on the environment described, make a list of decisions that can be programmed.

2. Make a list of decisions that cannot be programmed. For each such decision, specify which employee (customer service clerk, order entry clerk, or credit manager) would make the decision and list the information requirements for the decision.

CHAPTER 2

The MIS and Decision Support Systems

KEY TOPICS

CHAPTER OVERVIEW

At this point in the history of computing and information processing, the two most visible and talked-about information systems are the management information system (MIS) and the decision support system (DSS). The bulk of this chapter is devoted to discussing the scope, function, and purpose of these systems. An overview of general systems theory and important information system concepts helps to set the stage for the MIS and DSS coverage. The remainder of the chapter presents other categories of information systems: data processing (DP) systems, executive support systems (ESS), office information systems, real-time systems, and expert systems. Expert systems are covered in depth in Chapter 3.

SYSTEMS TERMINOLOGY

The MIS and user communities have an amazing affinity for introducing new terminology, acronyms, and buzz words into the computerese vocabulary. This chapter is devoted to demystifying systems terminology. The focus is on those terms and concepts that describe some type of a computer-based information system, especially the management information system and the decision support system. Executives and other end users naturally assume that all professionals in the information services area share a common understanding of these terms. This simply is not true. When conceived, systems terms are left as abstract concepts and are subject to a variety of interpretations and misinterpretations.

Hundreds of MIS terms and concepts have become part of everyday conversations in businesses throughout the world. Many of these terms are a continuing source of confusion to both end users and professionals in the field, especially those terms that describe categories of information systems. There are no commonly accepted definitions for the sometimes abstract "systems" terms. Therefore, the remainder of this chapter is devoted to simplifying and clarifying the following commonly used systems terms:

- □ Information systems
- □ Data processing systems
- □ Management information systems
- □ Decision support systems
- □ Office information systems
- □ Real-time systems
- □ Expert systems

In an attempt to make inherently abstract terms more concrete, the emphasis is on practice as opposed to theory. Each system category is defined in terms of those characteristics typically associated with that type of system as it is found in practice. Each type of system has unique qualities and characteristics, but in practice, there may be some conceptual and functional overlap between the systems. For example, some people describe decision support systems as being subsets of management information systems. The various types of systems are discussed in context with hardware, software, and applications throughout the remainder of the book.

Knowledge is of two kinds. We know a subject ourselves, or we know where we can find information upon it.

———— Samuel Johnson

WHAT IS A SYSTEM?

Perhaps the best place to begin a chapter that is devoted to discussing management information systems, decision support systems, and various other types of computer-based systems is with the concept of a system. Systems exist in all fields of endeavor. There are social systems, fuel-monitoring systems, political systems, biological systems, electrical systems, economic systems, and information systems.

A **system** is any group of *components* (functions, people, activities, events, and so on) that *interface* with and *complement* one another to achieve one or more predefined *goals*. Typically, a system accepts *input*. Various *subsystems* work in concert to produce some kind of *output*. Depending on the system, the input could be aluminum, temperature, data, and so on. Again, depending on the system, the output could be soda cans, cool or warm air, information, and so on.

Systems exist within a defined *boundary*. The conceptual boundary includes

☐ All components of the system.

☐ That which provides input to the system.

☐ That which is influenced by output from the system.

Everything else is external to the system. However, just about every system is a subsystem to another system. For example, the electrical system in your home is a subsystem of a regional power distribution system.

In any system the output from the system is continuously evaluated in a **feedback loop** (see Figure 2–1). The feedback loop is a method of control. If the output from the system begins to deviate from that which is expected, the deviation becomes input to the system via the feedback loop. When the feedback is received, the system makes needed adjustments to ensure that the output is consistent with system goals.

In this book, the word "system" is always used within the context of an information system. It is easy to relate these general systems concepts to information systems. Besides the types of information systems discussed here, we will also discuss systems analysis, the system development process, systems prompt, system design techniques, and more in other chapters.

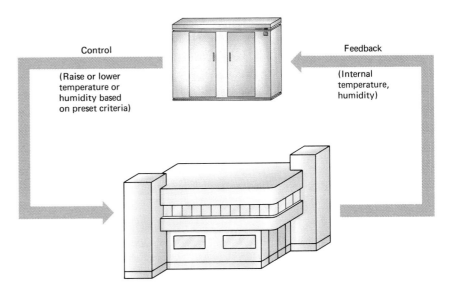

FIGURE 2–1   Process-Control Feedback Loop
Computer-based environmental control systems monitor and control the temperature and humidity in thousands of buildings.

INFORMATION SYSTEM CONCEPTS

The concept of an information system is introduced and briefly described in Chapter 1. The term "information system" is a generic reference to any computer-based system that provides data processing and/or information for decision makers. *All of the systems discussed in this chapter are information systems.* The remainder of this section addresses important concepts that relate to information systems.

Information System Capabilities

Not surprisingly, an information system has the same four capabilities as a computer system: *input*, *processing*, *storage*, and *output* (see Figure 2–2).

Input

The information system input capability can accept

- □ *Source data.* Usually the recording of a transaction or an event.
- □ *An inquiry.* A request for information.
- □ *A response to a prompt.* For example, a "Y" or "N."
- □ *An instruction.* For example, "store file" or "print record."
- □ *A message to another user on the system.*
- □ *A change.* For example, editing a word processing document.

Various devices that enable input to an information system are described in Module C, "I/O and Data Storage Devices," of the "Short Course in Computer Concepts."

Processing

The information system processing capability encompasses

- □ *Sorting.* Arranging data or records in some order (for example, alphabetizing a customer file by last name).

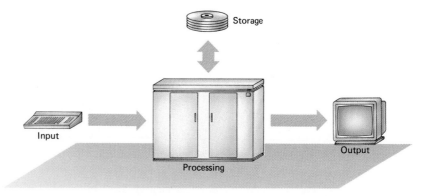

FIGURE 2–2 The Four Fundamental Components of a Computer System
Information systems have the same four capabilities as a computer system.

□ *Accessing, recording, and updating data in storage.* For example, retrieving a customer record from a data base for processing, entering expense data to an accounting system's data base, and changing a customer's address on a marketing data base, respectively.

□ *Summarizing.* The presentation of information in a condensed format, often to reflect totals and subtotals.

□ *Selecting.* The selection of records by criteria (for example, select all employees with 25 or more years of service to the company).

□ *Manipulating.* Performing arithmetic operations (addition, multiplication, and so on) and logic operations (comparing an employee's years of service to 25 to determine if years of service is greater than, equal to, or less than 25).

Storage

The information system storage capability permits information systems to store *data, text, images* (graphs, pictures, and so on), and *other digital information* (voice messages) so that they can be recalled easily for further processing. Various devices that enable the storage capability of an information system are described in Module C, "I/O and Data Storage Devices," of "A Short Course in Computer Concepts."

Output

The information system output capability permits information systems to produce output in a variety of formats:

□ *Hard copy.* For example, printed reports, documents, and messages.

□ *Soft copy.* For example, temporary displays on workstation screens.

□ *Control.* For example, instructions to industrial robots or automated processes.

Various devices that enable output from an information system are described in Module C, "I/O and Data Storage Devices," of "A Short Course in Computer Concepts."

Manual Systems Versus Computer-Based Information Systems

When someone speaks of an information system today, an automated system is implied. The elements of an information system (as described in Chapter 1) are hardware, software, people, procedures, and data. The automated elements (that is, the hardware and software) do not come into play in manual systems. People, procedures, and data are combined to create manual systems. In terms of numbers, the overwhelming majority of systems in industry, government, and education are still manual. This is true of large organizations with hundreds of computers and of two-person companies. Tens of thousands of manual systems have been targeted to be upgraded to computer-based information systems. Ten times that many are awaiting tomorrow's creative users and MIS professionals to identify their potential for computerization.

Both manual systems and computer-based information systems have an established pattern for work and information flow. For example, in a manual payroll system a payroll clerk receives the time sheets from supervisors; the individual employee's records are retrieved from folders stored alphabetically in a file cabinet; the payroll clerk uses a calculator to compute gross and net pay, then manually types the payroll check and stub; and finally, the payroll register, which is a listing of the amount paid and the deductions for each employee, is compiled on a tally sheet with column totals. About the only way to obtain information in a manual payroll system is to thumb through employee folders painstakingly to find and extract the required information.

Today, most payroll systems have been automated. But look in any office in almost any company and you will find rooms full of filing cabinets, tabbed three-ring binders, circular address files, or drawers filled with 3-by-5-inch inventory cards. These manual systems are symbols of opportunities to improve a company's profitability and productivity through the application of MIS technologies.

Function-Based Versus Integrated Information Systems

An information system can be either function based or integrated. A **function-based information system** is designed for the exclusive support of a specific application area, such as inventory management or accounting. Its

Information systems exist in all fields of endeavor, not just business. These astrophysicists rely on an information system to help them in their study of the formation and growth of galaxies.

Courtesy of International Business Machines

data base and procedures are, for the most part, independent of any other system. The data bases of function-based information systems invariably contain data that are maintained in other function-based systems within the same company. For example, much of the data needed for an accounting system would be duplicated in an inventory management system. It is not unusual for companies with a number of autonomous function-based systems to maintain customer data in 5 to 10 different data bases. When a customer moves, the address must be updated in several data bases (accounting, sales, distribution, and so on). This kind of data redundancy is an unnecessary financial burden to a company.

During the past decade, great strides have been made in the integration of function-based systems. The resultant **integrated information systems** share a common data base. The common data base helps to minimize data redundancy and allows departments to coordinate their activities better. Integrated data bases are discussed in detail in Chapter 9, "Data Management," and integrated information systems are discussed in detail in Chapter 15, "An MIS Case Study."

On-Line Versus Off-Line

The four fundamental components of a computer system are input, processing, output, and storage. Each is described in detail in Module A, "Computer Systems," of the "Short Course in Computer Concepts." In a computer system, the input, output, and data storage components receive data from and transmit data to the processor over electrical cables or "lines." These hardware components are said to be **on-line** to the processor. Hardware devices that are not accessible to or under the control of a processor are said to be **off-line**. The concepts of on-line and off-line apply also to data. Data are said to be *on-line* if they can be accessed and manipulated by the processor. All other data are *off-line*.

On-line and off-line are important information system concepts. Consider the payroll example in Figure 2–3. In an *off-line* operation, all supervisors complete the weekly time sheets. The time sheets are then collected and *batched* for input to the computer system. When transactions are grouped together for processing, it is called **batch processing**.

Before the data can be entered and the payroll checks printed, the payroll master file must be placed on-line, if it is not already on-line. To do this, the master file is retrieved manually from a library of interchangeable disks and "loaded" to a storage component called a disk drive. Once loaded, the payroll master file is on-line. The process is analogous to selecting the phonograph record that you wish to play and mounting it on the turntable. Many computer-based files and data bases are stored on permanently installed fixed disks. These files and data bases are on-line at all times that the computer system is operational. The various types of disk storage are discussed in Module C, "I/O and Data Storage Devices," of "A Short Course in Computer Concepts."

An operator at a workstation enters the data contained on the time sheets directly into the computer system in an *on-line* operation. Employee data, such as name, social security number, pay rate, and deductions, are

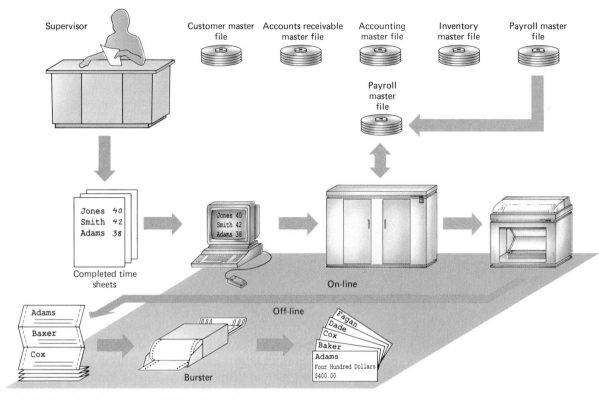

FIGURE 2–3   On-Line and Off-Line Operations
Those processing activities, hardware, and files that are not controlled by, or accessible to, the computer are referred to as off-line.

retrieved from the payroll master file and combined with the number of hours worked to produce the payroll checks. The payroll checks are produced on a printer, which is an output device.

Since the payroll checks are printed on continuous preprinted forms, they must be separated before they can be distributed to the employees. In an *off-line* operation, a machine called a burster separates and stacks the payroll checks.

Data Entry Concepts

Source Data

Most data do not exist in a form that can be "read" by the computer. In the example of Figure 2–3, the supervisor uses a pencil and paper to record manually the hours worked by the staff on the time sheet. Before the payroll checks can be computed and printed, the data on these time sheets must be *transcribed* (converted) into a *machine-readable format* that can be interpreted by a computer. This is done in an *on-line* operation by someone at a workstation. The time sheet is known as the **source document**, and, as you might expect, the data on time sheet are the **source data**.

Not all source data have to be transcribed. For example, the numbers imprinted on the bottom of your bank checks indicate your individual account

Whenever possible, data are collected in machine-readable format. Shown here is the Videx TimeWand, an intelligent bar code reading system. The two-ounce TimeWand enables the off-line collection of up to 16,000 characters of machine-readable time-stamped data. Once data have been collected, the data are uploaded to the host computer for processing.

Videx, Inc.

number and bank. These numbers are already machine readable, so they can be "read" directly by an input device.

Approaches to Data Entry

The term **data entry** is used to describe the process of entering data into an information system. Information systems are designed to provide users with display-screen "prompts" to make on-line data entry easier. The display on the operator's screen, for example, may be the image of the source document (such as a time sheet). A **prompt** is a brief message to the operator that describes what should be entered (for example, "INPUT HOURS WORKED _____").

Data can be entered on a workstation in the following ways:

☐ *Batch processing*, in which transactions are grouped, or batched, and entered consecutively, one after the other.

☐ *Transaction-oriented processing*, in which transactions are recorded and entered as they occur.

To illustrate the difference between batch and transaction-oriented processing, consider an order processing system for a mail-order merchandiser (see Figure 2–4). The system accepts orders by both mail and phone. The orders received by mail are accumulated, or batched, for data entry—usually at night. For phone orders there are no handwritten source documents; persons taking the phone orders interact with the computer via workstations to enter the order data on-line while talking with the customer.

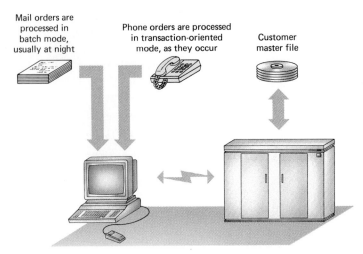

Mail orders are processed in batch mode, usually at night

Phone orders are processed in transaction-oriented mode, as they occur

Customer master file

FIGURE 2–4   Batch and Transaction-Oriented Processing
Mail-order merchandisers accept orders by mail and by phone.

On-Line Data Entry

Most data entered into mainframe computer systems, both batch and transaction oriented, is done on-line. Workstation operators enter data *directly* to the host computer system for processing, as shown in Figure 2–4. The primary advantage of transaction-oriented data entry is that records on the data base are updated immediately, as the transaction occurs. This is quite different from batch data entry, where records are batched periodically. Another advantage of transaction-oriented data entry is that operators can make inquiries to the system. In the example of Figure 2–4, a salesperson can check the availability of an item and tell the customer when to expect delivery.

DATA PROCESSING SYSTEMS

Historical Perspective

The origin of **data processing systems** can be traced back to 1890 and the U.S. Bureau of the Census. The Census Bureau commissioned Herman Hollerith, a statistician, to use his revolutionary punched-card tabulating machine to process the 1890 census. Thus began the emergence of automated data processing. Data processing or **DP**, as the name implies, encompasses using the computer to perform operations on data. For decades, through the mid-1950s, punched-card technology improved with the addition of more punched-card devices and more sophisticated capabilities, but the label "data processing" stuck. During this era everything was data processing: data processing department, data processing professional, and data processing system. **Electronic data processing** or **EDP** was coined to distinguish manual systems from those that are automated (electronic).

Characteristics of Data Processing Systems

The focus of data processing systems is transaction handling and records keeping, usually for a particular functional area. Data are entered and stored in a file format. Stored files are updated during routine processing. Periodic outputs include action documents (invoices) and scheduled reports, primarily for operational-level managers. In essence, data processing systems are inflexible and cannot accommodate data processing or information needs that are not already built into the system. Most enterprises have transcended the scope of DP systems and now provide the flexibility to provide management with information in support of an ever-changing decision-making environment. However, the term "DP" has tremendous momentum and is still used erroneously by some individuals and enterprises as a generic reference to computers and information processing.

In summary, data processing systems exhibit these characteristics:

- □ DP systems focus on transaction handling and records keeping.
- □ DP systems are file oriented.
- □ DP system output is periodic.
- □ DP system processing adheres to a strict production schedule.
- □ DP system information is generated primarily for operational-level management.
- □ DP systems have limited flexibility to accommodate management's ad hoc requests for information.
- □ DP systems are typically function based.

MANAGEMENT INFORMATION SYSTEMS

In the not-too-distant past, most payroll systems were data processing systems that did little more than process time sheets, print payroll checks, and keep running totals of annual wages and deductions. Managers began to demand more and better information about their personnel. As a result, payroll *data processing systems* evolved to human resource *management information systems*. A human resources MIS is capable of predicting the average number of worker sick days, monitoring salary equality between minority groups, making more effective use of available skills, and providing other information that is needed at all three levels of management—operational, tactical, and strategic.

Lack of Common Understanding

If you were to ask any five executives or MIS professionals to define a management information system, the only commonality that you would find in their responses is that there is no agreement on the definition of an

MIS. There is probably less consensus on the meaning of MIS than on any other term or concept in the computerese vocabulary. Considering the widespread use of the term by management and MIS professionals, this is indeed a paradox.

It is economic heresy to think that an executive committee (usually the chief executive officer and vice presidents in a company) would approve the introduction of a new product line without an in-depth understanding of the product, the cost of production, and the market potential. However, this same group of executives routinely approves the development of million dollar management information systems that are ill-defined in purpose, scope, and objectives. This lack of common understanding and, in some cases, the lack of desire to understand, place severe constraints on the system development process and reduces the probability of implementing a high-quality MIS.

Even if each member of an executive committee renders enthusiastic approval for a proposed MIS, each may have different expectations for the system. As a result of this "hit and miss" development strategy, the end product evolves as an ill-defined management information system. This approach to systems development begins with a superficial set of functional specifications and proceeds slowly, often requiring backtracking to make major modifications to completed portions of the system. This backtracking can be avoided if those involved have a common understanding of what is approved in the first place. Ultimately, such systems are implemented, but only after it is apparent that the marginal returns for further modifications do not merit the expenditure of resources. When this happens, seldom is anybody satisfied.

The Management Information System Defined

An MIS has been called a method, a function, an approach, a process, an organization, a system, and a subsystem. The following MIS definitions are offered to give you a feel for what other authors and practitioners perceive a management information system to be:

> The entire set of systems and activities required to manage, process, and use information as a resource in the organization—Ralph H. Sprague, Jr.[1]

> A management information system (MIS) is a business system that provides past, present, and projected information about a company and its environment—David M. Kroenke and Kathleen A. Nolan.[2]

> [An MIS is] a formal method of making available to management the accurate and timely information necessary to facilitate the decision-making process and enable the organization's planning, control, and operational functions to be carried out effectively—James A. F. Stoner.[3]

---

[1] Ralph H. Sprague, Jr., "A Framework for the Development of Decision Support Systems," *MIS Quarterly*, Vol. 4, no. 4, June 1980, pp. 1–26.

[2] David M. Kroenke and Kathleen A. Nolan, *Business Computer Systems*, 3rd ed. (Santa Cruz, Calif.: Mitchell, 1987).

[3] James A. F. Stoner, *Management*, 2nd ed. (Englewood Cliffs, N.J.: Prentice Hall, 1982).

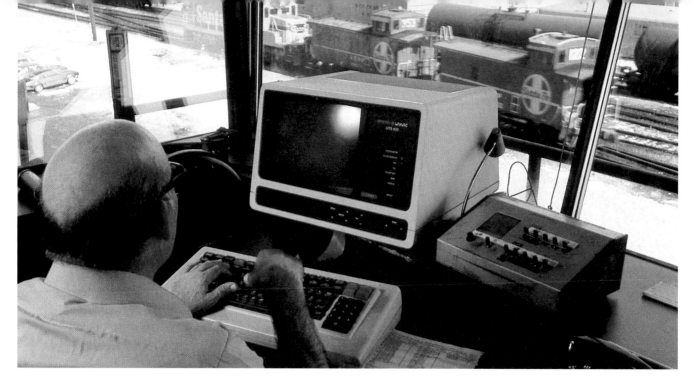

The Santa Fe Railroad's Network Management System at Topeka, Kansas, is an MIS that monitors the location and movement of every train in the system. Each car on each train has a specific destination. Customer service personnel use the system to respond to customer inquiries regarding shipment progress.

Santa Fe Industries

A management information system is a formalized computer information system that can integrate data from various sources to provide the information necessary for management decision making—James O. Hicks, Jr.[4]

MIS is the subsystem [of an organization's information system] relevant to managerial decisions for control and strategic planning—A. Ziya Aktas.[5]

The system that monitors and retrieves data from the environment, captures data from transactions and operations within the firm, filters, organizes, and selects data and presents them as information to managers, and provides the means for managers to generate information as desired is called the management information system (MIS)—Robert G. Murdick.[6]

Many authors are reluctant to commit themselves to a concrete definition, preferring to leave MIS as an abstract concept to be interpreted by the reader relative to his or her own experiences.

---

[4] James O. Hicks, Jr., *Management Information Systems, A User Perspective*, 2nd ed. (St. Paul, Minn.: West, 1987).

[5] A. Ziya Aktas, *Structured Analysis and Design of Information Systems* (Englewood Cliffs, N.J.: Prentice Hall, 1987).

[6] Robert G. Murdick (with John C. Munson), *MIS Concepts and Design*, 2nd ed. (Englewood Cliffs, N.J.: Prentice Hall, 1986).

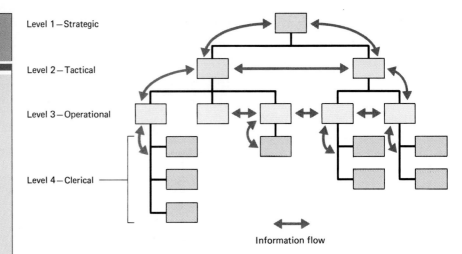

FIGURE 2–5   Information Flow in a Multilevel Organization
An MIS provides the mechanism to enable information flow over all levels and components of a multilevel organization.

Optimally, every user and MIS professional should share a common working definition of management information systems. That being unlikely, the next best thing is for decision makers in a given organization to reach a common understanding of the purpose, scope, and objectives of an MIS. At a minimum, the readers of this text should be on the same wavelength with regard to MIS. To facilitate efficient communication between reader and author, the following working definition of an MIS or management information system is proposed:

> Given a multilevel organization having component groups that perform a variety of functions to accomplish a unified objective, an MIS is an integrated structure of data bases and information flow over all levels and components, whereby the collection, transfer, and presentation of information is optimized to meet the needs of the organization.

The concept of information flow in a multilevel organization (strategic, tactical, and so on) with component parts (finance, accounting, and so on) is graphically illustrated in Figure 2–5. The foregoing definition was formulated to represent the ideal. In reality, an organization can only strive for optimization and total integration. Even if the finished product falls short of the above ideal, user and MIS personnel are shooting at the same target.

Characteristics of Management Information Systems

The following are *desirable* characteristics for an MIS:

☐ An MIS supports the data processing functions of transaction handling and records keeping.

□ An MIS uses an integrated data base and supports a variety of functional areas.

□ An MIS provides operational-, tactical-, and strategic-level managers with easy access to timely but, for the most part, structured information.

□ An MIS is somewhat flexible and can be adapted to meet changing information needs of the organization.

□ An MIS provides an envelope of system security that limits access only to authorized personnel.

The word "desirable" is highlighted in the first sentence of this section because not all of the so-called management information systems possess these characteristics. Some are not well thought out and are cumbersome to use. Some overload managers with information. Many management information systems are vulnerable to tampering from persons inside and outside the company. Others require major system modifications to accommodate small changes in a company's information needs.

The MIS Versus the DP System

The basic distinctions between an MIS an a DP system are summarized as follows:

□ The integrated data base of an MIS enables greater flexibility in meeting the information needs of management than the flat file environment of DP systems (data management concepts are discussed in some detail in Chapter 9, "Data Management").

□ An MIS integrates the information flow between functional areas where DP systems tend to support a single functional area.

□ An MIS caters to the information needs of all levels of management where DP systems focus on operational-level support.

□ The information needs of management are supported on a more timely basis (on-line inquiry capability) with an MIS than with a DP system (usually scheduled reports).

DECISION SUPPORT SYSTEMS

The Decision Support Systems Controversy

What was said in the previous section about the abstract meaning of an MIS can be applied to the **decision support system** or **DSS** as well. Prevailing thought on decision support systems can be divided into two camps. One camp argues that because management information systems support the information needs of all levels of management, why coin another "systems" term. These people treat decision support systems as just another buzz word. The other, larger camp, which is growing in numbers, views the DSS as providing more than just information. These people believe that there is a unique combination of hardware and software called decision support systems that can play an integral role in the decision-making process. There is sufficient evidence to support this premise.

Management information systems are oriented to supporting decisions that involve *structured* problems, such as when to replenish raw materials inventory and how much to order. This type of routine operational-level decision is based on production demands, the cost of holding the inventory, and other variables that depend on the use of the inventory item. The MIS integrates these variables into an inventory model and presents specific order information (for example, order quantity and order date) to the manager in charge of inventory management.

In contrast to the MIS, decision support systems are designed to support decision-making processes involving *semistructured* and *unstructured* problems. A semistructured problem might be the need to improve the delivery performance of suppliers. The problem is partially structured in that information comparing the on-time delivery performance of suppliers during the past two years can be obtained either from hard-copy records or directly from the integrated data base supporting the MIS. The unstructured facets of the problem, such as extenuating circumstances, rush order policy and pricing, and so on, make this problem a candidate for a DSS.

An example of an entirely unstructured problem would be the evaluation and selection of an alternative to the currently used raw material. A decision maker might enlist the aid of a DSS to provide information as to whether it would be advisable to replace a steel component with an equally functional one that is plastic or aluminum. The information requirements for such a decision are diverse and typically beyond the scope of an MIS.

Another distinction that should be made between an MIS and a DSS is that an MIS is designed and created to support a specific application (accounting, inventory control) or set of applications (an integrated MIS). A DSS is a set of decision support tools that can be adapted to any decision environment.

The Decision Support System Defined

Managers spend much of their day obtaining and analyzing information before making a decision. Decision support systems are interactive information systems that rely on an integrated set of user-friendly hardware and software tools to produce and present information that is targeted to support management in the decision-making process. On many occasions, decisions makers can rely on their experience to make a quality decision, or they need look no further than the information that is readily available from the integrated corporate MIS. However, decision makers, especially at the tactical and strategic levels, are often confronted with complex decisions that are beyond their human abilities to synthesize properly the factors involved. These types of decisions are made to order for decision support systems.

Decision support systems help to close the information gap so that managers can improve the quality of their decisions. To do this, DSS hardware and software employs the latest technological innovations (for example, color graphics and database management systems), planning and forecasting models, user-oriented query languages, and even artificial intelligence (discussed in Chapter 3, "Artificial Intelligence and Expert Systems").

THE DECISION SUPPORT SYSTEM CONTROVERSY

Q. One of our vice presidents recently returned from a week-long seminar and asked if we had a decision support system. I asked him if he could be more specific, and he said that he could not. Apparently the seminar leaders told a group of executives that a decision support system would essentially provide them with up-to-the-minute information in any format at any time. We're good, but we're not that good.

I believe that some executive seminars do more harm than good. They give the people in attendance unrealistic impressions of the capabilities of a typical computer center. Do you agree?

A. I agree that the much ballyhooed term "decision support systems" is routinely abused. Many people who write and talk about decision support systems tend to imply that all one has to do to ascend to information heaven is to install a decision support system (DSS). Of course, the implementers know that it's not that simple. It's much easier to put the burden of explanation (and implementation) on an information services division.

DSS is like the term "minicomputer." It means different things to different people. In conversational computerese, communication is much more efficient when people just say what they mean. The typical end user might be better served if people referenced specific decision support tools: fourth-generation (query) languages, electronic spreadsheets, presentation graphics, linear programming models, financial analysis tools, and so on. Reserve the term "decision support system" to be used as a collective reference to all hardware and software decision support tools.

In many cases, the DSS facilitates the decision-making process. For example, a DSS can help a decision maker choose between alternatives. Some DSSs have the capability to rank alternatives automatically based on the decision maker's criteria. Decision support systems also help to remove the tedium of gathering and analyzing data. For example, managers are no longer strapped with such laborious tasks as manually entering and extending numbers (totaling rows and columns of numbers) on spreadsheet paper. Graphics software enables managers to generate illustrative bar graphs and circle graphs in a matter of minutes. And, with the availability of a variety of user-oriented DSSs, managers can get the information they need without having to depend on direct technical assistance from an MIS professional.

In general, an MIS provides periodic, preprogrammed reports, such as a weekly regional sales summary. On the other hand, a DSS is less structured and provides managers with the flexibility to look into the future and ask "what if" questions.

Characteristics of Decision Support Systems

The following are *desirable* characteristics for a DSS:

☐ A DSS aids the decision maker in the decision-making process.

☐ A DSS is designed to address semistructured and unstructured decisions.

- [ ] A DSS supports decision makers at all levels, but it is most effective at the tactical and strategic levels.
- [ ] A DSS makes general-purpose models, simulation capabilities, and other analytical tools available to the decision maker.
- [ ] A DSS is an interactive, user-friendly system that can be used by the decision maker with little or no assistance from an MIS professional.
- [ ] A DSS can be readily adapted to meet the information requirements for any decision environment.
- [ ] A DSS provides the mechanisms to enable a rapid response to a decision maker's request for information.
- [ ] A DSS has the capability to interface with the corporate data base.
- [ ] A DSS is not executed in accordance with a preestablished production schedule.
- [ ] A DSS is flexible enough to accommodate a variety of management styles.
- [ ] A DSS facilitates communication between levels of decision making (for example, graphic presentation of operational-level information for review by top management).

The DSS Tool Box

A decision support system is comprised of a set of decision-support tools that can be adapted to any decision environment (see Figure 2–6). These tools can be categorized as *software tools* and *hardware tools*. The combination of these general-purpose tools helps managers to address decision-making tasks in specific application areas (the evaluation and promotion of personnel, the acquisition of companies, and so on). One of the myths surrounding decision support systems is that a manager need only press a few keys and, like magic, the best decision alternative is conveniently displayed on the manager's workstation. In reality, a good amount of work may be needed to lay the foundation for the decision process. To obtain information in support of a particular decision, a manager, and perhaps an assistant, may need to design a data entry screen for entering data (from external sources or the corporate data base), design and create a simulation model, enter descriptive parameters for a graph, write a program, or perform a variety of other tasks. DSS software tools are designed specifically to help managers accomplish these types of tasks.

DSS Software Tools

Most DSS software tools can be placed in one of the following categories:

- [ ] Applications development
- [ ] Data management
- [ ] Modeling
- [ ] Statistical analysis
- [ ] Planning

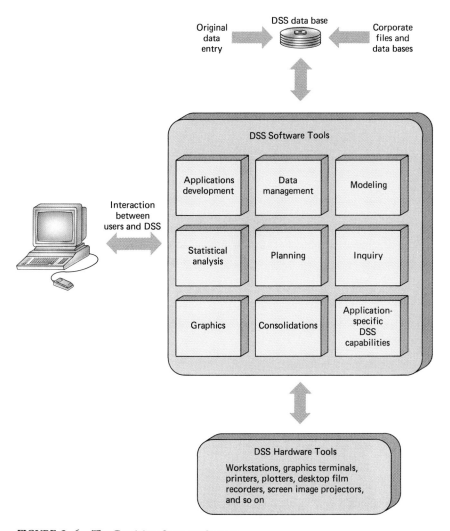

FIGURE 2–6   The Decision Support System
A decision support system is comprised of a set of software and hardware tools that can be adapted to any decision environment.

- ☐ Inquiry
- ☐ Graphics
- ☐ Consolidations
- ☐ Application-specific DSS capabilities

The capabilities of these DSS software tools are explained in the following sections.

APPLICATIONS DEVELOPMENT   Some decision support systems provide managers with the capability to develop computer-based applications in support of the decision-making process. These applications may involve the input of data, the processing and storing of data, and the output of information. Both DSS and MIS applications have input, processing, data storage, and output, but the similarities stop there. DSS applications can be developed by end users for the exclusive support of their decision environment. MIS applications are developed by MIS professionals to service an entire company.

When using DSS applications development capabilities, managers design data entry, output screens, and reports by choosing options from the DSS menus. They can also create a menu-driven interface between the system and the user. For the most part, the design of the DSS data base is transparent to the end user. That is, the user describes what he or she wants in the data base and where to get the data; then the actual design and creation of the data base is handled by the software. Of course, some data entry may be required if the data are not already in machine-readable format. DSS application development tools can provide a "quick and dirty" presentation of the results, or, if more sophistication is desired, managers can use the report-writing capabilities of the software to achieve the most effective communication of results (headings, column labels, summary totals, graphs, and so on). The logic for the application is written in a programming language with English-like instructions. Such programming languages are discussed in detail in Chapter 13, "Prototyping and Application Development Tools."

DSS applications have spawned a new term—**throwaway systems**. Often, DSS applications are developed to support a one-time decision and are then discarded. This is economically feasible because the effort involved in developing a system with a DSS application development tool may be only a fraction of the effort required if the system were developed using traditional procedure-oriented languages such as COBOL and FORTRAN. Although decision support applications are usually developed on an ad hoc basis to help with a particular decision or set of decisions, the resultant application is often applicable to future decisions in its original form or in a slightly modified form.

DATA MANAGEMENT   Each DSS has it own unique approach to data base management, that is, the software mechanisms for storage, maintenance, and retrieval data. This DSS tool is necessary to enable compatibility between a DSS data base and an integrated set of DSS software tools. Decision support systems typically are not ongoing production applications; therefore, a data base is usually created for each application.

Data for a DSS application come from three sources (Figure 2–6):

1. *Existing data in the DSS data base*. These data are available for any DSS application.
2. *Original data entry*. These data are entered, usually via key entry, to the DSS data base.
3. *Computer-based corporate files and data bases*. The DSS data management system provides the capability to extract data from corporate files and data bases. These data are transcribed from a variety of diverse formats to that of the DSS data base.

Once in the DSS data base, the data are available to any of the DSS software tools.

MODELING   Decision support systems enable managers to use mathematical modeling techniques to re-create the functional aspects of a system within

These financial analysts have loaded their data into a decision support system and are using its data management capability to identify decision alternatives.

Cullinet Software, Inc.

the confines of a computer. A plethora of DSS modeling tools are available to enable users to model a wide variety of systems. For example, executives at a manufacturing company might use a DSS tool that permits *linear programming* to create a model that represents the distribution network for the company's products. Executives can use the model to determine the optimal number and location of warehouses, the objective being to minimize the cost of product distribution. To do this, they plug various combinations of warehouse sites into the model and compare the effectiveness of the results. Without the use of a sophisticated model, managers would have to build and use the warehouses before they knew if they had made a good decision. With a DSS model, unacceptable alternatives can be identified before the ground is broken for the first warehouse. The cost of building warehouses out of bits and bytes in a computer-based model is considerably less than building them out of bricks and mortar.

Managers use *network modeling techniques* such as *CPM* (Critical Path Method) and *PERT* (Project Evaluation and Review Technique) to model complex projects. CPM and PERT models enable managers to show the relationships between the various activities involved in the project and to select the approach that optimizes the use of resources while meeting project deadlines.

Simulation is another popular DSS modeling tool. A typical simulation application would involve evaluating the customer traffic at automatic teller machines (ATMs). Suppose, for example, that bank executives want to know how many ATMs would need to be added to the existing network of ATMs to reduce the average peak-period wait time from 3 minutes to less than 1 minute. To make such a decision, managers would simulate the system with different configurations of ATMs. The results of each simulation run would include the average peak-period wait time. Ultimately, the executives would use this information to select the configuration of ATMs that best meets bank objectives.

Some DSS models address a specific decision environment. For example, *inventory models* help managers make decisions involving inventory management. Typically, the optimal decision involves minimizing the costs associated with the acquisition and storage of the inventory item and the penalty cost associated with out-of-stock situations.

STATISTICAL ANALYSIS   The statistical analysis DSS capability manipulates data to provide everything from statistics (such as average, median, and standard deviation) to analytical techniques (such as regression analysis, exponential smoothing, and discriminate analysis) to complex procedures (such as multivariate analysis). Managers use these statistical tools for a broad range of applications. For example, a sales manager might use DSS software to calculate the standard deviation of weekly sales for each salesperson to identify those whose sales vary markedly from their normal weekly sales efforts.

One popular application of DSS statistical tools is *risk analysis*. Risk analysis uses probability and statistics to evaluate the risk involved in making certain projections. For example, a sales manager might ask for a risk analysis of sales projections for amounts between zero and $200 million. The results, illustrated in Figure 2–7, show that the probability of projected sales being at least $100 million is .9, that the probability of projected sales being at

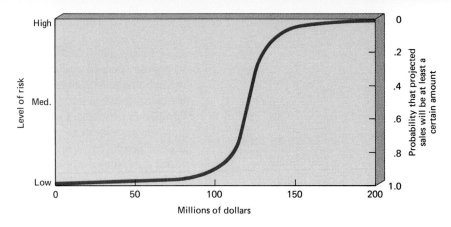

FIGURE 2–7   Risk Analysis
The results of a risk analysis show the probability that projected sales will be at least a certain amount.

least $120 million is .5, and that the probability of projected sales being at least $150 million is .05. These results show that the manager can feel relatively secure with a low-risk estimate of $100 million but that the risk of projecting sales at $150 million is very high. Since budgets are often based on projected sales, there may be too much risk in projecting sales in excess of $100 million.

Another common application of DSS statistical tools is *trend analysis*. Managers employ regression analysis, exponential smoothing, and other statistical techniques to determine trends. Often managers enter historical data, use statistical techniques to fit a curve to the data, and look for trends. For example, a marketing manager might examine monthly sales by region during the past five years for trends. If an identifiable sales trend emerges for a particular sales region, this information is vital input to planning for the coming year's marketing campaigns.

PLANNING   Managers at the tactical and strategic levels are always making decisions that will be implemented at some time in the future, perhaps as much as five years. To help make these decisions, managers rely on the planning capabilities of decision support systems to give them a glimpse into the future. The aids to planning that are commonly supported by DSS software are *forecasting*, *"what if" analysis*, and *goal seeking*.

DSS software tools provide managers with the capability to compile forecasts for everything from work force requirements to revenue projections. For example, managers can use *project management software* to forecast work force requirements for complex projects as well as to plan and schedule the project.

One of the great advantages of decision support systems is the "what if" capability. With the "what if" capability, managers have flexibility to test different decision alternatives. For example, consider the following scenario. The pro rata income statement for next year in Figure 2–8 reflects the best case scenario for Zimco Enterprises. With electronic spreadsheet software, a manager was able to answer the following question.

What if sales increase by 20 percent, cost of goods sold increase by 1 percent, and everything else remains the same for the coming year?

	A	B	C	D
1	==================	=========	=========	=========
2	ZIMCO INCOME STATEMENT ($1000)	Next Year	This Year	Last Year
3				
4	Net sales	$183,600	$153,000	$144,780
5	Cost of sales & op. expenses			
6	Cost of goods sold	116,413	115,260	117,345
7	Depreciation	4,125	4,125	1,500
8	Selling & admin. expenses	19,875	19,875	15,000
9				
10	Operating profit	$43,187	$13,740	$10,935
11	Other income			
12	Dividends and interest	405	405	300
13				
14	TOTAL INCOME	$43,592	$14,145	$11,235
15	Less: interest on bonds	2,025	2,025	2,025
16				
17	Income before tax	41,567	12,120	9,210
18	Provision for income tax	18,777	5,475	4,160
19				
20	NET PROFIT FOR YEAR	$22,790	$6,645	$5,050

	A	B	C	D
21	==================	=========	=========	=========
22				
23				
24	==================	=========	=========	=========
25	Shares outstanding	6,300,000	6,000,000	6,000,000
26	Market price	$21.25	$14.00	$13.00
27	Earnings per share	$3.62	$1.11	$0.84
28				
29	Price-earnings ratio	5.87	12.64	15.45
30	==================	=========	=========	=========
31				
32				
33	==================	=========	=========	=========
34	FORECAST VARIABLES FOR NEXT YEAR'S PRO RATA INCOME STATEMENT			
35				
36	Projected change in sales		20.00%	
37	Projected change in cost of goods sold		1.00%	
38	Projected change in administrative expenses		0.00%	
39	==================	=========	=========	=========
40				

FIGURE 2–8 An Electronic Spreadsheet Template for a Pro Rata Income Statement
The "Next Year" pro rata income statement is extrapolated from the data in the "This Year" income statement and the values of forecast variables. The price-earnings ratio is calculated for each year.

```
A2: 'ZIMCO INCOME STATEMENT ($1000)
                         A                    B            C            D
    ===================================================================================
 1
 2  ZIMCO INCOME STATEMENT ($1000)      Next Year    This year    Last Year
 3  ------------------------------------------------------------------------------------
 4  Net sales                            $157,590     $153,000     $144,780
 5  Cost of sales & op. expenses
 6    Cost of goods sold                  117,565      115,260      117,345
 7    Depreciation                          4,125        4,125        1,500
 8    Selling & admin. expenses            20,670       19,875       15,000
 9                                        ------------------------------------------------
10        Operating profit                $15,230      $13,740      $10,935
11  Other income
12    Dividends and interest                  405          405          300
13                                        ------------------------------------------------
14        TOTAL INCOME                    $15,635      $14,145      $11,235
15  Less: interest on bonds                 2,025        2,025        2,025
16                                        ------------------------------------------------
17  Income before tax                      13,610       12,120        9,210
18  Provisions for income tax               6,148        5,475        4,160
19                                        ------------------------------------------------
20      NET PROFIT FOR YEAR                $7,462       $6,645       $5,050
```

```
A34: 'FORECAST VARIABLES FOR NEXT YEAR'S PRO RATA INCOME STATEMENT
                         A                    B            C            D
    ===================================================================================
21  ===================================================================================
22
23
24  ===================================================================================
25  Shares outstanding                  6,300,000    6,000,000    6,000,000
26  Market price                           $21.25       $14.00       $13.00
27  Earnings per share                      $1.18        $1.11        $0.84
28                                        ------------------------------------------------
29      Price-earnings ratio                17.94        12.64        15.45
30  ===================================================================================
31
32
33  ===================================================================================
34  FORECAST VARIABLES FOR NEXT YEAR'S PRO RATA INCOME STATEMENT
35  ------------------------------------------------------------------------------------
36  Projected change in sales                            3.00%
37  Projected change in cost of goods sold               2.00%
38  Projected change in administrative expenses          4.00%
39  ===================================================================================
40
```

FIGURE 2–9   An Electronic Spreadsheet Template for a Pro Rata Income Statement
*This electronic spreadsheet display is the same as the one in Figure 2–8 except that the forecast
variables in C36, C37, and C38 have been changed from 20%, 1%, and 0% to 3%, 2%, and
4%, respectively.*

To do this, data are entered for the forecast variables (20%, 1%, and 0%) in rows 36 through 38 in the spreadsheet. To examine a worst case scenario, the manager uses the same spreadsheet template (the model for the pro rata income statement) to answer the following question:

What if sales increase by 3 percent, cost of goods sold increase by 2 percent, administrative expenses increase by 4 percent, and everything else remains the same for the coming year?

All the manager needs to do to answer this question is to change the three forecast variables (in cells C36, C37, and C38) from 20%, 1%, and 0% to 3%, 2%, and 4%, respectively. The results of the worst-case scenario are shown in Figure 2–9. The details of the preparation of this electronic spreadsheet example are presented in Chapter 7, "Personal Computing."

The first major step in the planning process is to set one or more objectives, such as "be the number one seller of medicines for colds." The next step in the planning process is the establishment of measurable goals, such as "sell $185 million worth of cold medicine." When using the goal-seeking capability of DSS software, the manager is asking how much certain variables must change to realize the goal. In the example, the manager might be asking:

How many additional salespersons must be added and how much money should be budgeted for the seasonal promotional campaigns in order to realize the sales goal of $185 million?

INQUIRY   DSS software enables managers to make on-line inquiries to the DSS data base using English-like commands. A typical inquiry might be

Display the name, room number, and office telephone extension by department for all employees whose years of service are greater than 25.

Figure 2–10 illustrates the display resulting from the preceding inquiry. The inquiry capabilities are often made possible by fourth-generation languages. Fourth-generation languages are discussed in detail in Chapter 13, "Prototyping and Application Development Tools."

```
          YEARS OF SERVICE GREATER THAN 25

    DEPARTMENT        NAME        ROOM NO.    TEL.

    Accounting      T. Jones     H201A        3133
    Accounting      M. Smith     H210B        3071
    Engineering     Q. Folk      P118         1166
    Purchasing      A. Ross      H412         2215


                                        Total is 5
```

FIGURE 2–10   The Results of a DSS Inquiry
The inquiry: display the name, room number, and office telephone extension by department for all employees whose years of service are greater than 25.

GRAPHICS The use of graphics software has become synonymous with polished presentation. With the graphics DSS software tool, managers can create a variety of **presentation graphics** based on data in the DSS data base. Among the most popular presentation graphics are **bar graphs** (see Figure 2–11), **pie graphs**, and **line graphs**. Other types of graphs are possible. Each of these graphs can be annotated with graph titles, labels for axes, and legends.

Decision makers have found that graphic representations of data have proven to be an effective means of communication. It is easier to recognize problem areas and trends in a graph than it is in a tabular summary of the same data (rows and columns of numeric information).

For many years, the presentation of tabular data was the preferred approach to communicating numeric information. However, this approach was preferred by default: it was simply too expensive and time consuming to produce presentation graphics manually. Prior to the introduction of graphics software, the turnaround time for producing a graph was at least a day, and often a week. Today, managers use graphics DSS software to produce perfectly proportioned, accurate, and visually appealing graphs in a matter of seconds.

In most cases, the data needed to produce a graph already exist in the DSS data base. Managers create graphs by responding to a series of prompts. The first prompt asks the user to select the type of graph to be produced: bar graph, pie graph, line graph, and so on. Once the source of the data has been identified and labels and a title are added, the user can display, print, or plot the graph. The function, concepts, and use of graphics software are discussed in more detail in Chapter 7, "Personal Computing."

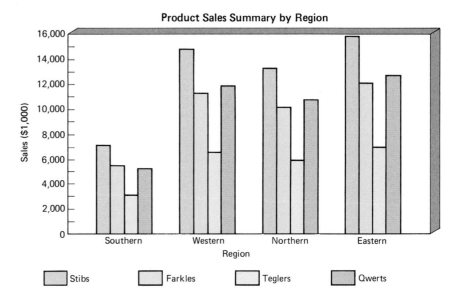

FIGURE 2–11 Clustered-Bar Graph
Regional sales for each of the four products are graphically represented in this clustered-bar graph. Other types of presentation graphics are illustrated in Chapter 7, "Personal Computing."

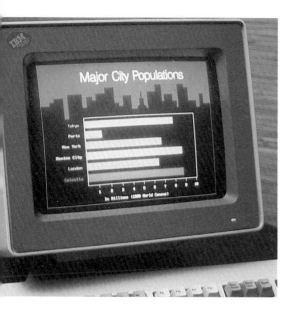

The SAS System, a decision support system, is made up of several components including SAS/Graph, SAS/QC (quality control), SAS/ETS (planning and forecasting), SAS/OR (project management), SAS/STAT (statistical analysis), and more. SAS/Graph enables managers to present data in a variety of charts, maps, plots, and 3-dimensional displays. Also, managers can customize graphs for greater emphasis, for example, adding the skyline as background for a population graph for cities.

SAS Institute Inc., Cary, NC, USA

CONSOLIDATIONS   The ability to consolidate like data from different sources has proven a handy time saver for managers. Consolidation is a routine activity for many managers. One of the most common applications of the consolidation application is that of consolidating financial statements from subsidiary companies into a single corporate financial statement. Another application involves the consolidation of projected line-item budget information into a corporate budget by department. As another example, sales managers use DSS consolidation software to consolidate the sales performance of individual salespersons into regional sales summaries and, later, into a single corporate sales summary.

APPLICATION-SPECIFIC DSS CAPABILITIES   DSS software is being created to support a variety of specific decision environments. For example, one DSS software package is designed especially for people involved in financial analysis. DSS software for financial analysis typically includes such functions as the calculation of rate of return, payback period, present value, future value, annuities, depreciation tables, and loan amortization schedules. Financial decision support systems often give users the capability to prepare a financial statement (profit and loss statement, balance sheet, and sources and uses of funds). Once the financial statement is in the system, managers can examine financial ratios (inventory turnover, current ratio, and so on) and do "what if" and goal-seeking analyses.

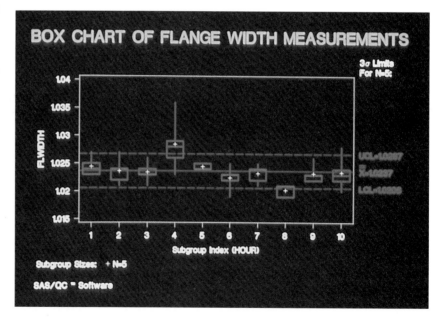

SAS/QC is a component of the SAS System, a decision support system. Plant managers use the SAS/QC component to signal unusual variations in the production process (at hours 4 and 8 in the display).

SAS Institute Inc., Cary, NC, USA

Another popular application-specific DSS package supports managers in the quality control effort. Quality control DSS software enables managers to generate the information they need to monitor variations in production quality during the production process to ensure that quality standards are followed. This type of DSS software is a help to managers because the preparation of quality control tools, such as control charts and acceptance sampling information, is calculation intensive.

DSS Hardware Tools

All the DSS software capabilities described in the previous section are available for mainframe computers and microcomputers. Any input/output device that facilitates interaction with or makes use of the system (workstations, color graphics terminals, printers, plotters, desktop film recorders, screen image projectors, and so on) would be considered a DSS hardware tool. I/O devices are covered in Module C, "I/O and Data Storage Devices," of "A Short Course in Computer Concepts."

Executive Support Systems

User managers and the MIS community are finally getting a handle on the scope and functionality of decision support systems. Now we have the **executive support system**. Like its predecessors, the MIS and the DSS, the term "executive support system" or **ESS** has been introduced with fanfare and anticipation, but without a commonly accepted definition. Proponents of the ESS tout that it is designed specifically to support decision making at the strategic level. Others view it as a subset of decision support systems. Skeptics call it a marketing ploy by software vendors. Like the MIS and DSS, the ESS may eventually gain an identity of its own, but today's commercially available executive support systems look suspiciously like what most managers and MIS professionals have come to know as decision support systems.

We are drowning in information but starved for knowledge.

———— *John Naisbitt*

DSS Summary

Typically, DSS software tools are purchased as an integrated package from a vendor of proprietary software. A sampling of a few of the more comprehensive commercially available tools would include IFPS (Execucom Systems Corporation), EXPRESS (Management Decision Systems, Inc.), SIMPLAN (Simplan Systems, Inc.), and The SAS System (SAS Institute, Inc.). DSS tools provide the framework for creating a variety of applications that aid managers in the decision-making process. Many of the applications can be accomplished by the end user. The more complex applications may require intervention by MIS professionals.

Decision support systems are central to the theme of this book. Many topics that have yet to be introduced fall under the DSS umbrella. Throughout the remaining chapters, various facets (for example, fourth-generation languages) of decision support systems are revisited and discussed in greater depth.

OFFICE INFORMATION SYSTEMS

Office information systems, another category of information systems, is a term generally associated with **office automation**. The term "office automation" refers collectively to those computer-based applications associated with general office work. Office automation applications include *office information systems, word processing, electronic mail, image processing, voice processing*, and *telecommuting*. Office automation and its applications are discussed in detail Chapter 6, "End User Computing." Because "office information systems" is a commonly used "systems" term, it is introduced briefly here in context with other "systems" terms.

Office information systems are small information systems that address traditional office tasks. For example, one office information system allows employees to keep their personal calendars on-line. Another is the on-line office directory that contains basic personnel data. Other office information systems enable employees to organize personal notes, keep diaries, document ideas in a preformatted outline, and keep a tickler file.

REAL-TIME SYSTEMS

For the past four decades engineers have used the term "real time" to refer to systems that operate in a continuous *feedback loop*. In a feedback loop, the process being controlled generates data that become input to the computer system. Since the time lapse between output and input is negligible, the system is said to be happening in real time. During the late 1960s, the computer community decided to use the the real-time concept to describe those management information systems that reflect the current status. To remain continuously up to date, all transactions that impact a system must be recorded as they occur.

The Real-Time MIS

An airline reservation system is a classic example of a **real-time information system** or **real-time MIS** in that it always reflects the current status. An airline reservations agent communicates with a centralized computer via a remote workstation to update the data base the moment a seat on any flight is filled or becomes available. Thereafter, any ticket agent making an inquiry about seat availability would be given the same information. Airline reservation systems are actually management information systems that do much more than keep track of flight reservations. Departure and arrival times are closely monitored so that ground crew activities can be coordinated. The system offers many types of management information needs: the number of passenger-miles flown, profit per passenger on a particular flight, percentage of arrivals on time, average number of empty seats on each flight for each day of the week, and so on.

In practice, most MISs would be considered fully, or at least partially, real time; therefore, when someone refers simply to an MIS, they are usually implying a real-time MIS.

Many computer-controlled machine tools used in manufacturing are real-time control systems that operate in a continuous feedback loop.

Photo courtesy of Hewlett-Packard Company

The Real-Time Control System

The use of the term "real time" may have come full circle. Because most management information systems are real time, the term is being applied more often to computer-based process control systems. In these **real-time control systems**, as the data are received and interpreted by the computer, the computer initiates action to control the ongoing process. For example, real-time control systems monitor and control the environment (temperature, humidity, lighting, security) within skyscrapers (see Figure 2–1). These computer-controlled skyscrapers are often referred to as "smart" buildings. Data collected from real-time control systems are often fed into a management information system for processing. For example, an environmental control system in a smart building records the entry and exit times of individuals who gain access to secured areas via badge readers. These data provide input to an MIS that generates reports for the security office.

EXPERT SYSTEMS: A PREVIEW

The most recent addition to the circle of information systems terminology is the **expert system**. Like the DSS, expert systems are computer-based systems that help managers to resolve a problem or to make better decisions. However, an expert system does this with a decidedly different twist. An expert system is an interactive computer-based system that responds to questions, asks for clarification, makes recommendations, and generally aids in the decision-making process. In effect, working with an expert system is much like working directly with a human expert to solve a problem because the system mirrors the human thought process. It even uses information supplied by a real expert in a particular field (medicine, taxes, geology).

Expert systems are associated with an area of research known as **artificial intelligence**, which is involved with the simulation of human capabilities. Therefore, expert systems are discussed in more detail in Chapter 3, "Artificial Intelligence and Expert Systems."

- Commonly used systems terms are information systems, data processing systems, management information systems, decision support systems, executive support systems, office information systems, real-time systems, and expert systems. All these are information systems.

- A system is any group of components (functions, people, activities, events, and so on) that interface with and complement one another to achieve one or more predefined goals. Typically, a system accepts input and various subsystems work in concert to produce some kind of output.

- An information system has the same four capabilities as a computer system: input, processing, storage, and output. The processing capabilities include sorting; accessing, recording, and updating data in storage; summarizing; selecting; and manipulating.

- An information system can be either function based or integrated. A function-based information system is designed for the exclusive support of a specific application area. Integrated information systems share a common data base.

- In a computer system, the input, output, and data storage components that receive data from and transmit data to the processor are said to be on-line. Hardware devices that are not accessible to or under the control of a processor are said to be off-line.

- When transactions are grouped together for processing, it is called batch processing. In transaction-oriented processing, transactions are recorded and entered as they occur.

- The origin of data processing systems or DP can be traced back to the punched-card tabulating machine that the U.S. Bureau of the Census used to process the 1890 census.

- Data processing systems are file-oriented function-based systems that focus on transaction handling and records keeping and provide periodic output aimed primarily at operational-level management.

- There is probably less consensus on the meaning of management information system or MIS than on any other term or concept in the computerese vocabulary. The author offers the following definition for MIS: given a multilevel organization having component groups that perform a variety of functions to accomplish a unified objective, an MIS is an integrated structure of data bases and information flow over all levels and components, whereby the collection, transfer, and presentation of information is optimized to meet the needs of the organization.

- An MIS supports the traditional data processing functions, plus an MIS relies on an integrated data base to provide managers at all levels with easy access to timely, but structured, information. An MIS is flexible and can provide system security.

- An MIS is oriented to supporting decisions that involve structured problems. In contrast, decision support systems or DSSs are designed to support decision-making processes involving semistructured and unstructured problems.

- Decision support systems are interactive information systems that rely on an integrated set of user-friendly hardware and software tools to produce and present information that is targeted to support management in the decision-making process.

- A DSS supports decision making at all levels by making general-purpose models, simulation capabilities, and other analytical tools available to the decision maker. A DSS can be readily adapted to meet the information requirements for any decision environment.

- A decision support system is comprised of a set of software and hardware tools. The categories of DSS software tools include applications development, data management, modeling, statistical analysis, planning, inquiry, graphics, consolidations, and application-specific DSS capabilities. Any input/output device that facilitates interaction with or makes use of the system would be considered a DSS hardware tool.

- Data for a DSS application come from three sources: existing data in the DSS data base, original data entry, and computer-based corporate files and data bases.

- DSS software is being created to support a variety of specific decision environments, such as financial analysis and quality control.

- The executive support system or ESS is designed specifically to support decision making at the strategic level.

- Office information systems are generally associated with office automation, a term that refers collectively to those computer-based applications associated with general office work. Office information systems are small information systems that address traditional office tasks, such as personal calendars and the office directory.

- There are two types of real-time systems, the real-time information system or real-time MIS and the real-time control system. The former is an information system that always reflects the current status. In the latter, the computer initiates action to control an ongoing process.

- Expert systems, which are associated with an area of research known as artificial intelligence, help managers to resolve a problem or to make better decisions. They are interactive systems that respond to questions, ask for clarification, make recommendations, and generally aid in the decision-making process.

IMPORTANT TERMS

artificial intelligence (Ch. 3)

batch processing

CPM (Critical Path Method)

data entry

data processing (DP) systems

decision support system (DSS)

electronic data processing (EDP)

executive support system (ESS)

expert systems (Ch. 3)

feedback loop

function-based information system

hard copy

integrated information systems (Ch. 15)

linear programming

management information systems (MIS)

office automation (Ch. 6)

office information systems (Ch. 6)

off-line

on-line

PERT (Project Evaluation and Review Technique)

presentation graphics (Ch. 7)

prompt

real-time control system

real-time information system

real-time MIS

simulation

soft copy

sorting

source data

source document

system

throwaway systems

transaction-oriented processing

REVIEW EXERCISES

1. Which of the following information systems can provide support for transaction handling and records keeping: expert systems, management information systems, DP systems, and executive support systems?

2. Name at least six types of information systems.

3. List three output formats for an information system.

4. Name two types of network modeling techniques used in decision support systems.

5. Name three aids to planning that are commonly supported by DSS software.

6. Briefly describe two of the processing capabilities of an information system.

7. In which type of processing are transactions grouped together for processing?

8. What is a throwaway system?

9. List seven items in the DSS software tool box.

10. Which category of information systems is encompassed by the general field of office automation?

11. Distinguish between on-line operation and off-line operation.

12. What advantages does transaction-oriented processing have over batch processing?

13. Which type of information system would come the closest to duplicating the experience of working directly with a human expert to solve a problem?

DISCUSSION QUESTIONS

1. Suppose that you are the president of a company. Give examples of "what if" questions that you would like to submit to the company's accounting and financial information system. One example might be, "What if we made a $5,000,000 capital expenditure; how would that affect the company's tax liability over the next five years?"

2. Several definitions for MIS are presented in this chapter. Describe similarities between any two of these definitions. Describe differences between any two of these definitions.

3. How do you think an executive information system might differ from a decision support system?

4. Give examples of at least three types of systems (not information systems), identifying the components and goals of each system.

5. Discuss the benefits of entering data to an information system at the source in machine-readable format. Give an example application.

6. Contrast DP systems with MIS systems. Contrast MIS systems with DSS systems.

7. Give two examples of semistructured or unstructured problems that would be applicable to decision support systems.

8. Is the phrase "real-time MIS" redundant? Explain.

9. Suppose that the company you work for batches all sales data for data entry each night. You have been asked to present a convincing argument to top management on why funds should be allocated to convert the current system to transaction-oriented data entry. What would you say?

10. Identify the routine periodic outputs generated by a market analysis system in a consumer goods manufacturing company.

APPLICATION CASE STUDY 2–1

The Impact of MIS on the Integration of Business Functions

The Situation

Acme Electronics is a company that assembles components into special-purpose electronic units primarily for aerospace applications. Acme currently has 25 business computer applications (listed below). Applications that are currently computerized are indicated with a (C), and those that are completely manual are indicated with an (M).

- (C) Accounts receivable
- (C) Accounts payable
- (M) Budget planning and control
- (C) Cash receipts
- (C) Customer invoicing
- (M) Cash disbursements
- (M) Cash management
- (M) Check reconciliation
- (M) Customer and product analysis
- (C) Employee payroll
- (M) Fixed assets
- (M) General ledger
- (M) Job costing
- (M) Labor distribution
- (M) Market analysis
- (C) Order entry
- (M) Personnel
- (M) Portfolio management
- (M) Product inventory
- (M) Profit planning and control
- (M) Property accounting
- (M) Purchasing
- (M) Receiving
- (M) Sales analysis
- (M) Work in process

Each of these applications is processed separately, although the outputs from some applications serve as the inputs to others.

A project team has been given the task of designing a truly integrated MIS for ACME. In this early stage, the design team has decided to group existing applications into functionally related areas.

The Assignment

Put yourself in the role of a project team member as you complete the following assignment.

1. Associate the listed applications with one of the four conceptual classifications described in the following.

   a. *Revenue-related applications*: These applications deal with all aspects of bringing money into the company.

   b. *Expenditure-related applications*: These applications deal with all aspects of money leaving the company.

   c. *Conversion-related applications*: These applications deal with all aspects of producing income, that is, converting resources into profit.

   d. *Cash management-related applications*: These applications deal with the overall management of cash flow and profitability.

2. List, in priority sequence, the five existing manual applications that you would automate first. Justify your selections and priorities.

3. List three existing manual applications that you would not recommend for automation during the next two years. Justify your selections.

APPLICATION CASE STUDY 2–2
On-Line Versus Off-Line

The Situation

Gabriel Industries is a diversified manufacturing company with approximately 2,300 employees located in four separate locations. The company has been recently reorganized (see Application Case Study 1-1) and is in the process of examining various functional areas. One of these areas is the personnel/payroll function. This system is currently processed in a batch mode on the Accounting Department's minicomputer at the headquarter's location in Brooklyn, New York. The people in the personnel sections at each of the four locations complete forms for all personnel and payroll activities and send them to the Accounting Department for processing. The actual procedures are described in the following paragraphs.

When a personnel transaction occurs, a personnel change form is completed by a departmental clerk and is sent to the personnel supervisor at the site. The supervisor logs in receipt of the form, checks it for errors, and places it in a folder that serves as a suspense file. The accumulated forms in the suspense file are periodically forwarded to the Accounting Department, generally with the payroll data.

Payroll processing includes the collection of time cards by shop supervisors who review the cards, add any notations (such as an excused absence), and bring the cards to their secretary in the production department. The secretary computes the regular and overtime hours worked for each employee and notes the shift worked. The secretary counts the cards, fills out a transmittal slip, and takes the cards to the personnel clerk. The clerk enters each worker's data on a separate line on a payroll transmittal form. The data on the line include the employee number, the shift, and the number of hours worked. The clerk then sums the hours worked by all employees, counts the number of employees, and sends the transmittal forms to the Accounting Department. The data are then entered into the computer system.

Delays throughout the process continue to cause problems. Time is lost capturing the data, sending the data to the personnel clerk at each site, and sending the accumulated results to the Accounting Department. Frequently, personnel changes are not processed in time to have an impact on the next payroll. Also, sometimes errors are not detected until the completed forms arrive at the Accounting Department, thus delaying the process further. These errors and delays result in the reprocessing of some payroll checks and disgruntled employees.

To alleviate most of the current problems associated with the personnel/payroll system, corporate management has decided to convert the personnel/payroll function to an on-line system. This will be the first on-line system at Gabriel.

The Assignment

Put yourself in the role of the systems analyst as you complete the following assignment.

1. Describe the processing for the on-line system in detail. Use a narrative format and explicitly specify which steps are performed manually and which are performed by the computer.

2. Describe the input validation that you would include for:
   a. Entering personnel/payroll changes.
   b. Entering hours-worked data.

3. List the effects of converting from a batch to an on-line system with respect to:
   a. Changes to hardware.
   b. Changes to software.
   c. Personnel training.
   d. Security and confidentiality.

CHAPTER 3

Artificial Intelligence and Expert Systems

KEY TOPICS

CHAPTER OVERVIEW

Some industry observers are predicting that the information system of the future is the expert system (previewed in Chapter 2). They say that in the not-to-distant future most of us will routinely rely on expert systems to help us make job-related decisions. Expert systems provide us with the insight we need to make higher-quality decisions. Expert systems are within the field of research known as artificial intelligence, or AI. The focus of this chapter is the four categories of AI: knowledge-based and expert systems, natural languages, simulation of human sensory capabilities, and robotics.

ARTIFICIAL INTELLIGENCE

We have access to artificial sweeteners, artificial grass, artificial flowers—why not artificial intelligence? To some extent, we do!

What Is Artificial Intelligence?

Today's computers can simulate many human capabilities, such as reaching, grasping, calculating, speaking, remembering, comparing numbers, and drawing. Researchers are working to expand these capabilities and, therefore, the power of computers by developing hardware and software that can imitate intelligent human behavior. For example, researchers are working on systems that have the ability to reason, to learn or accumulate knowledge, to strive for self-improvement, and to simulate human sensory and mechanical capabilities. This general area of research is known as **artificial intelligence (AI)**, the focus of the material in this chapter.

Artificial intelligence? To some, the mere mention of artificial intelligence creates visions of electromechanical automatons replacing human beings. But, as anyone involved in the area of artificial intelligence will tell you, there is a distinct difference between human beings and machines. Computers will never be capable of simulating the distinctly human qualities of creativity, humor, and emotions! However, computers can drive machines that mimic human movements (pick up objects and place them at a prescribed location) and provide the "brains" for systems that simulate the human thought process within the domain of a particular area of expertise (tax preparation, medical diagnosis, and so on).

Even though significant strides have been made in the area of artificial intelligence, research is still at the embryonic level. Each year AI researchers come up with new discoveries and innovations that serve to redefine artificial intelligence. Some say that AI is such an abstract concept that it defies definition. It seems as if each new revelation in AI research raises more questions than it answers. "It's a moving horizon," says Marvin Minsky, a pioneer in AI research from MIT.

Research in the field of artificial intelligence has been underway since the 1960s, but too often researchers have been frustrated in their attempts to implement their innovations because AI applications demand an enormous amount of computer power. Only recently has the power and cost-effectiveness of computers advanced to the point that AI applications have become economically feasible on a large scale in the real world. Already one area of AI called expert systems has begun to make a major impact on the way people in the business community makes decisions.

Categories of Artificial Intelligence

Research in the field of artificial intelligence can be divided into categories (see Figure 3–1):

- □ Knowledge-based and expert systems
- □ Natural languages

Automation will never be in complete control until the ship of state can be steered by automatic pilot.

—— *Anonymous*

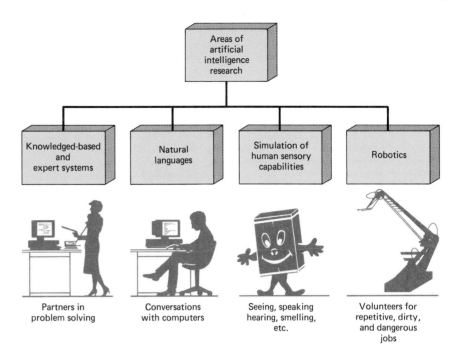

FIGURE 3–1 Categories of Artificial Intelligence

- Simulation of human sensory capabilities
- Robotics

Each category is described briefly now and in more detail later in the chapter.

Knowledge-Based and Expert Systems

A **knowledge-based system** relies on a **knowledge base** that is filled with rules of thumb or **heuristic knowledge** (intuition, judgment, and inferences) about a specific application area, such as computer repair. Humans can use the knowledge-based system and the IF-THEN rules in the knowledge base to help them solve a particular problem. **Expert systems**, introduced initially in Chapter 2 in context with other system concepts, are the most sophisticated implementation of a knowledge-based system. Once the knowledge of one or more human experts has been entered to an expert system's knowledge base, users can tap this knowledge by interacting with the system in much the same way as they would interact with a human expert in that field. Both the user and the computer-based expert system ask and respond to one another's questions until a problem is resolved.

Natural Languages

Natural languages refer to software that enables computer systems to accept, interpret, and execute instructions in the native or "natural" language of the end user, typically English. In theory, the end user is not constrained by the instruction syntax that is inherent in traditional programming languages. In reality, there are limitations. The state of the art of natural languages is still somewhat primitive. Most commercial "natural languages" are designed to provide end users with an interface to the corporate data base or to an expert system.

Simulation of Human Sensory Capabilities

One area of AI research involves computer simulation of human capabilities. This area of AI focuses on equipping computer systems with the capabilities of seeing, hearing, speaking, and feeling (touching). These artificial intelligence capabilities are possible with current technology, to varying degrees.

Robotics

Robotics is the integration of computers and industrial robots. Industrial robots can be "taught" to perform almost any repetitive manipulative task, such as painting a car, screwing on a bolt, moving material, and even complex tasks, such as inspecting a manufactured part for defects.

The Commercialization of Artificial Intelligence

Scientists have been working to build "thinking" machines for decades and, for the most part, paying little attention to the commercial viability of their work. For example, during the formative years of AI, hundreds of researchers were working to develop software that would enable humans to test their chess-playing skills against the skills of a computer. Early chess programs challenged the club player, but today's programs have proven to be formidable opponents for grand masters. Though of questionable commercial value, chess-related research has provided scientists with a greater understanding of the human thought process and how the process can be simulated by computers and software.

In the 1960s and 1970s, the power of multimillion-dollar computers was needed to support even simple commercial AI applications. In the 1980s, computer technology has finally caught up to AI. Now, relatively inexpensive but powerful microcomputers have the power needed to support a wide variety of AI applications. When computer technology made a quantum leap in the early 1980s, dozens of AI companies were born almost overnight. Entrepreneurs and investors were convinced that AI would do for their companies what microcomputers did for Apple Computer, Inc., in 1977.

For several years, artificial intelligence was the darling of the computer and MIS industry. Even though virtually all the companies were experiencing heavy losses, investors remained confident that profits would eventually skyrocket. After two or three years of heavy losses and no profits in sight, most of the companies folded. Reality had set in—people are not willing to buy products that do not contribute to profit. Unfortunately, AI researchers had to learn the hard way that in the business world, it is not profitable to create a solution and then look for a problem. AI companies were being accused of pushing a technology rather than responding to market demands. Since 1987, surviving companies have begun to focus their energies on products that meet the needs of their potential customers.

Executives at AI companies have now recognized that to be commercially viable, AI must be packaged in a manner that will increase productivity or

This 4 megabit (a storage capacity of about 500,000 characters) chip is the state-of-the-art in chip technology. When you consider that the 4 kilobit (about 500 characters) chip was the standard only two decades ago, you realize that scientists are making phenomenal progress in the microminiaturization of electronic circuitry. However, the human brain has 10 trillion circuit elements, about 2.5 million times as many as this state-of-the-art silicon chip. This comparison helps put the field of artificial intelligence into its proper perspective.

aid in the decision-making process. Today, aggressive AI companies are marketing innovative AI products with the potential to have a positive impact on a company's bottom line.

KNOWLEDGE-BASED AND EXPERT SYSTEMS

Today's computers can produce reams of paper, perform billions of calculations, and control the flow of thousands of messages, but at the day's end, computers know no more than they did at the start of the day. One area of artificial intelligence research, called knowledge-based systems, is trying to change this. AI researchers want to give knowledge-based systems two fundamental capabilities:

1. The ability to emulate human reasoning
2. The ability to learn

Many of today's knowledge-based systems are able to emulate human reasoning, but endowing them with other than a rudimentary ability to learn is still a few years away.

Knowledge-Based Systems

A *knowledge-based system* is a computer-based system to which preset IF-THEN rules are applied to solve a particular problem, such as determining a patient's illness. Like management information systems and decision support systems, knowledge-based systems rely on factual knowledge, but knowledge-based systems also rely on *heuristic knowledge*, such as intuition, judgment, and inferences. Both the factual knowledge and the heuristic rules of thumb are acquired from a *domain expert*, an expert in a particular field. The knowledge-based system uses this human-supplied knowledge to model the human thought process within a particular area of expertise. Once completed, a knowledge-based system can approximate the logic of a well-informed human decision maker.

Knowledge is power.

———— *Francis Bacon*

Expert Systems

What Is an Expert System?

In practice, the terms "expert system" and "knowledge-based system" are used interchangeably. Technically speaking, an *expert system* is the highest form of a knowledge-based system. An expert system is an interactive system that responds to questions, asks for clarification, makes recommendations, and generally aids in the decision-making process. The less sophisticated knowledge-based systems are called **assistant systems**. An assistant system helps users to make relatively straightforward decisions. Assistant systems are usually implemented to reduce the possibility that the end user will make an error in judgment rather than to resolve a particular problem.

The technologies needed to develop expert systems, assistant systems, and anything in between are the same. Therefore, in practice, even knowledge-based systems of limited scope and function are referred to as expert systems. Since expert systems are computer-based systems that play an integral role in the decision-making process, some authors and practitioners prefer to place them under the umbrella of decision support systems.

In effect, expert systems simulate the human thought process. To varying degrees, they can reason, draw inferences, and make judgments. Here is how an expert system works. Let's use a medical diagnosis system as an example. Upon examination of a patient, a physician might interact with an expert diagnosis system to get help in diagnosing the patient's illness or, perhaps, to get a "second" opinion. First, the doctor would relate the symptoms to the expert system: male, age 10, temperature of 103°, and swollen glands about the neck. Needing more information, the expert system might ask the doctor to examine the parotid gland for swelling. Receiving an affirmative answer, the system might ask a few more questions and perhaps even ask for lab reports before giving a diagnosis. A final question put to the physician might be whether the patient had been previously afflicted with or immunized for parotitis. If not, the expert system diagnoses the illness as parotitis, otherwise known as the mumps.

In recent years, expert systems have been developed to support decision makers in a broad range of disciplines, including medical diagnosis, oil exploration, financial planning, tax preparation, chemical analysis, surgery, locomotive repair, weather prediction, computer repair, troubleshooting satellites, computer systems configuration, operation of nuclear power plants, newspaper layout, interpreting government regulations, and many others.

Benefits of Expert Systems

The benefits of an expert system are somewhat different from those of other decision support systems and of management information systems.

- *An expert system enables the knowledge of experts to be "canned," so to speak.* The specialized knowledge of real human experts can be captured in the form of an expert system. For example, at Campbell's Soup Company, Aldo Cimino was the only expert troubleshooter for Campbell's giant cookers. He and his 43 years of experience were about to retire, so Campbell's executives decided to "drain his brain" into an expert system. Mr. Cimino may be retired, but Campbell's Soup Company continues to benefit from his years of experience.

- *A single expert system can expand the decision-making capabilities of many people.* In effect, an expert's knowledge can be distributed to and used by anyone associated with a specific decision environment. For example, a number of loan officers in a bank can enlist the aid of an expert system for guidance in approving and rejecting loan applications.

- *An expert system can improve the productivity and performance of decision makers.* By having ready access to an electronic partner with vast expertise in a particular area, decision makers can progress more rapidly to the most acceptable solution.

- *An expert system can provide stability and consistency to a particular area of decision making.* Unlike human beings, an expert system re-

An expert is one who knows more and more about less and less.

—— *Nicholas Butler*

sponds with exactly the same information to each decision situation. When people in similar decision-making situations have access to the advice and guidance of an expert system, the decisions they make tend to be consistent with one another.

□ *An expert system reduces dependencies on critical personnel.* Human beings retire, get sick, take vacations, and only a few of them ever attain the status of expert. Computers do not take coffee breaks. Expert systems can "drain the brain" of the very limited supply of experts so that others can benefit from their expertise, immediately and after they retire.

□ *An expert system is an excellent training tool.* In a manner similar to the way airline companies use flight simulators to train pilots, companies are using expert systems to train decision makers. During training, individuals work through a particular decision with an expert system. After making the decision, they review the documentation of the decision rationale that is generated by the expert system. From this documentation, they learn how decisions are made within the context of a particular environment.

These financial analysts rely on historical and predictive data as well as up-to-the-second stock trading information to advise their clients. They sometimes request a second opinion from an expert system before advising their clients.

What Is "Ask DAN"?

Ask DAN About Your Taxes is a commercially available knowledge–based system that is designed to assist people in the preparation of their annual tax returns. The system contains on-line facsimiles of the official IRS tax forms onto which users enter their data. The system automatically performs all needed calculations based on the data entered. Official IRS tax schedules can be printed directly by the system for submission to the Internal Revenue Service. Of course, *Ask DAN* is updated each year to reflect revisions in the tax laws.

What sets this system apart from some other tax preparation programs are the "Ask DAN" and "Checklist" facilities available to the user. The "Ask DAN" facility is an assistant system that enables users to have a question-and-answer session with DAN, a computerized version of a tax expert. A real live human, named Dan, served as the domain expert (on federal taxes) for the creation of the knowledge base. DAN asks the user questions and, based on the answers provided, asks more detailed questions.

The "Checklist" facility asks questions of the user to determine such things as what income should be declared, what deductions can be taken, and what tax schedules should be submitted. The result includes a checklist of tax items the user should consider and a list of the IRS forms and line numbers to use to report or declare each item.

A Typical "Ask DAN" Session

Let's look at a typical application scenario for *Ask DAN*. James Mitchell, a 22-year-old draftsperson from Pueblo, Colorado, purchased *Ask DAN* to help him prepare his income tax return. James already owns an IBM PC AT. The assistant system runs on IBM PCs and compatibles.

Compile "Checklist"

First, James selects the "Checklist" facility. By asking questions concerning James's income, expenditures, and investments, the system produces a checklist of tax items that James should consider and indicates which forms need to be completed. In James's case, he needs only to file Form 1040.

"Prepare Tax Return"

Now that James knows which form he needs to complete, he selects the "Prepare Tax Return" option from the assistant system's main menu and, interactively, completes Form 1040. James progresses normally until he gets to line 7, "Wages, salaries, tips, etc." Unsure of what figures to enter on this line, James presses the appropriate keys and asks DAN, the intelligent tax consultant!

"Ask DAN"

Any questions addressed to DAN are context sensitive; that is, DAN responds to requests for assistance based on the position of the cursor (for example, line 7 of Form 1040).

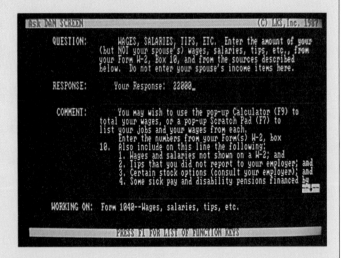

This screen appears when James asks DAN for help on line 7 (wages, salaries, tips, etc.).

Long and Associates

In this case, the screen shown in the adjacent photo appears. After reading DAN's response, James knows he must enter the income amount from his employer-supplied W–2 form. James enters his income ($22,000) at the prompt, and the assistant system returns him to the updated on-line Form 1040.

As James continues filling out the on-line Form 1040, he again becomes puzzled at line 54, "Federal income tax withheld." Again, he calls on DAN for help, and the screen shown in the adjacent photo is displayed. Again, DAN directs James to his W–2 form to obtain the amount for tax withheld. After entering the correct amount ($2,850), James is returned to the on-line Form 1040. Thanks to DAN, James has no further problems in completing Form 1040.

Print Tax Return

Now, James can print the tax information on preprinted IRS-approved forms. James Mitchell's return is relatively straightforward; however, the "Ask DAN" assistant system is equally as helpful to people with complex, multiform returns.

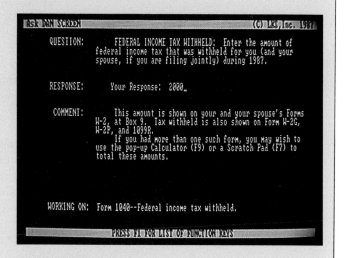

This screen appears when James asks DAN for assistance on line 54 (Federal income tax withheld).

Long and Associates

Selecting an Expert System Application

Not every company has a decision-making environment that is appropriate for expert systems. The situation has to be just right, or the cost of developing an expert system cannot be justified. Typically, the development and implementation of even the most basic expert systems will involve a minimum of one workyear of effort and a substantial monetary outlay for the purchase of software and hardware. Before a decision is made to create an expert system, top management should be made aware of what decision environments are appropriate for the implementation of an expert system.

Those decision environments most conducive to expert systems have the following characteristics:

☐ *A number of people will use the expert system frequently as part of their work routine.* At present, the development costs of an expert system is difficult to justify if only one or two people use it.

☐ *Decisions are complex.* The decision to be made is much more than a simple programmed decision. The decision maker must traverse through complex logic to arrive at a solution, typically a recommended course of action.

☐ *The decision logic can be translated to a hierarchy of rules.* The foundation of an expert system's knowledge base is the heuristic knowledge that is formulated from a hierarchy of rules of thumb.

☐ *Applications typically focus on advice, classification, diagnosis, interpretation, explanation, selection of alternatives, evaluation of situations, or forecasting.* One expert system *advises* financial analysts on the best mix of investments. Others help taxpayers to *interpret* the tax laws and computer repairpersons to *diagnose* the problems of a malfunctioning computer. One type of expert system helps independent insurance agents to *select* the best overall coverage for their business clients.

The number and variety of expert system applications has increased dramatically with the advent of powerful, cost-effective microcomputers. For early versions of expert systems, the minimum hardware configuration was an expensive dedicated superminicomputer. Today, expert systems can run on everything from micros to mainframes.

The Expert System Shell

When someone talks about expert systems, he or she is usually talking about systems that can help decision makers working in a particular *domain of expertise*, such as the configuration of computer systems or commercial lending. As mentioned earlier, these expert systems are the result of substantial development efforts. The software that enables the development of these expert systems has no "intelligence" and is known as the **expert system shell**.

Expert system shells are usually domain-independent proprietary software packages that have no applications "knowledge." An expert system shell contains the generic parts that are needed to create an expert system for a specific application. For example, the expert system shell provides companies with the capabilities needed to construct a knowledge base and the facility by which the user interacts with the knowledge base. The primary components of the expert system shell are the *knowledge acquisition facility*, the *knowledge base*, the *inference engine*, and the *user interface* (see Figure 3–2).

KNOWLEDGE ACQUISITION FACILITY The **knowledge acquisition facility** is that component of the expert system shell that permits the construction of the knowledge base. The knowledge base is created through the cooperative efforts of a **knowledge engineer** and one or more experts in a particular field, called **domain experts** (see Figure 3–2). The knowledge engineer is trained in the use of the expert system shell and in interview techniques. During initial interviews, the domain expert articulates everything he or she knows about how to solve a particular problem to the knowledge engineer. At the end of the initial round of interviews, the information that the expert imparts to the knowledge engineer is often disorganized and incomplete. During the next activity in the acquisition phase of the project, the knowledge engineer observes the expert in the workplace, continually interrogating the expert for more information and confirming that existing rules are complete and accurate. It is not uncommon for the knowledge acquisition phase of an expert system development project to take as long as a year.

The knowledge engineer translates the expert's knowledge into *factual knowledge* and *rules* to create the knowledge base. Some examples might

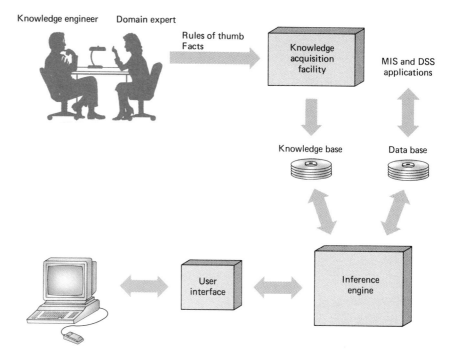

FIGURE 3–2 Components of an Expert System Shell

help you to understand better the difference between factual knowledge and rules. Suppose an expert system was being developed to assist loan officers in a bank. A piece of factual knowledge might be the minimum down payment requirement for home mortgages (for example, a 25 percent down payment). Another example would be the one-time charge associated with processing the loan (for example, one point or 1 percent of the principal amount). Much of the factual knowledge needed to support an expert system is available from the corporation's integrated data base. The crux of the knowledge base is the IF-THEN rules:

- □ The IF portion depicts the *situation.*
- □ The THEN portion depicts the *result* or *goal.*

A rule might be as follows: *IF* the customer's monthly income is less than three times the monthly payment for the mortgage amount, *THEN* examine credit history. Another rule might be: *IF* the customer [with marginal monetary resources] has had a flawless credit history for a period of five years, *THEN* discuss alternative financing with the customer. Ultimately, a completed knowledge base is comprised of the facts that are not directly available from the corporate data base and all applicable rules.

THE KNOWLEDGE BASE   A knowledge base is *not* a data base. The traditional data base environment (fields, records, files) deals with data that have a static relationship between the elements. That is, the employee name and pay rate fields have a fixed relationship with the employee record. The traditional data base environment is discussed in Chapter 9, "Data Management." Appropriate facts and rules are entered to the knowledge base during the acquisition phase. To complete the knowledge base, the knowledge engineer, in cooperation with the domain expert, enters the following into the knowledge base:

☐ The identification of problem(s) to be solved.

☐ Possible solutions to the problem(s).

☐ How to progress from problem to solution (primarily through facts and rules of inference).

The knowledge base interacts with the corporate data base to retrieve the facts (employee name and so on) that are needed to articulate the solution to the user (see Figure 3–2).

Because a knowledge base is heuristic, it provides the expert system with the capability to recommend directions for user inquiry. It also encourages further investigation into areas that may be important to a certain line of questioning, but not apparent to the user. Moreover, a knowledge base grows because it "learns" from user feedback. An expert system learns by "remembering"; that is, it stores appropriate information gleaned from past experiences in its knowledge base. For example, if a user reaches an acceptable solution via an inquiry strategy that is not included in the knowledge base, then the strategy is made a part of the knowledge base to aid future users who have similar problems to solve.

Initially, a knowledge base may be comprised of a few simple rules, but depending on the complexity of the decision environment, it may eventually grow to a thousand or more rules. The first cut at the creation of a knowledge base may contain only a fraction of all the applicable facts and rules. Testing inevitably surfaces oversights and results in facts and rules being added. Additions can be made to the knowledge base without altering the system's overall logic. Once the system becomes operational, the system is continually refined with the addition of more facts and rules or the deletion and revision of existing ones.

INFERENCE ENGINE   The **inference engine** is the nucleus of an operational expert system (see Figure 3–2). It is the vehicle by which the facts and rules in the knowledge base are applied to a problem. The inference engine gives an expert system its ability to reason. It does this by leading the user through a logic path that results in a solution.

The reasoning capabilities of an inference engine are based on one or a combination of the **forward-chaining** and **backward-chaining** inference procedures. In forward chaining, the expert system accepts information from the end user and proceeds to search the knowledge base for an applicable rule. The system continues this interactive approach and uses its built-in logic to reason toward a solution. For example, let's continue with the example of the expert system that was being developed to assist loan officers in a bank. The information entered by the loan officer might be that "the customer's monthly income is less than three times the monthly payment for the mortgage amount." The system would search the knowledge base for rules that apply to this situation. It is possible that several IF-THEN rules would apply. One rule might be: *IF* the customer's monthly income is less than three times the monthly payment for the mortgage amount, *THEN* examine credit history. The end user might respond with "the customer's credit history is flawless." Needing more information to proceed, the expert system might ask for clarification: "How long?" After the loan officer enters "five years," the system might find a link and chain the following rule: *IF* the customer has had a flawless credit history for a period of five years, *THEN* discuss alternative financing with the customer. In forward chaining, the expert system continues to chain applicable IF-THEN rules until a solution is derived or until applicable rules are exhausted. At various points in the chaining process, multiple IF-THEN rules may apply to a particular piece of user information. In these cases, the system may pursue an alternative line of reasoning.

The backward-chaining inference procedure is the reverse of forward chaining. The system accepts a goal or conclusion from the end user and then backtracks through IF-THEN logic to prove the goal or conclusion. The system then searches for an IF-THEN rule for which the THEN clause matches the goal or conclusion. If the IF portion of the situation is consistent with the problem, backward chaining continues with the IF clause becoming the THEN clause for the next search in the knowledge base. For example, in the lending example, a loan officer might have begun the search with the conclusion that he or she should "discuss alternative financing with the customer." The system attempts to verify that this conclusion is correct by following the logic chain backward. The system begins by searching for rules that have the following form: IF [some situation], THEN discuss alternative financing with the customer. It turns out that one of the rules in the knowledge base has that form: *IF* the customer has had a flawless credit history for a period of five years, *THEN* discuss alternative financing with the customer. Backward chaining continues with the IF clause becoming the THEN clause for the next search in the knowledge base until the system finds a rule whose IF segment is not the conclusion of another rule. At this time, the system may begin to ask the user for more information.

THE USER INTERFACE   Heuristic procedures are informal; that is, there are no formal algorithms available to solve the problem. An expert system problem is addressed by one strategy as long as it looks promising. The system always retains the option to switch to another strategy. This heuristic approach requires a flexible **user interface** (see Figure 3–2). This component of an expert system enables the type of interaction between end user and expert system that is needed for heuristic processing. The user interface permits the end user to describe the problem or goal. It permits both the end user and the expert system to structure questions and responses. Along with a response to a particular inquiry, an expert system usually explains and documents the rationale of why a particular course of action was recommended.

The user interface might have several different forms, depending on the expert system's shell. In any case, the interface attempts to insulate end users from the complexities of the system by providing an easy-to-understand method of interacting with the system. A user interface typically employs a variety of techniques and tools to include natural languages, prompts, formatted data entry screens, report generators, and windows.

Locomotive mechanics get troubleshooting help with this computer-based expert system. The mechanic simply keys in responses to questions asked by the "expert" about the malfunction. Through interactive questioning, the expert system eventually identifies the cause of the malfunction and demonstrates repair procedures on the video monitor (screen at left).

General Electric Company

An Example Expert System

Credit card companies are using expert system technology to provide better service to their customers, increase productivity, and save money. A case in point is the American Express Authorizer's Assistant expert system. American Express retains 300 authorizers who provide round-the-clock service to cardholders and customers. For credit card purchases that exceed a preset amount, retailers must contact American Express to obtain authorization before completing the transaction. In cooperation with a human authorizer, the expert system ultimately recommends that a credit charge be approved or denied, or it recommends an alternative line of reasoning and the need for more information. The Authorizer's Assistant expert system was approved for development when the company realized that significant losses were resulting from the bad authorization decisions made by the less experienced authorizers. More experienced authorizers would deny authorization to purchases that would be approved by less experienced authorizers.

To create the Authorizer's Assistant expert system, several human expert authorizers related tried-and-true rules of thumb to a knowledge engineer. From these, a knowledge engineer constructed a knowledge base that contained 520 rules. During the testing phase, the number of rules grew to

Even when the experts all agree, they may well be mistaken.

—— *Bertrand Russell*

850. At the end of the test period, the system demonstrated that it could reduce bad authorization decisions by 76 percent. Authorizer's Assistant is one of American Express's success stories. The system resulted in more consistent decision making, improved authorizer productivity, reduced credit and fraud loses, reduced operating expenses, improved service to customers and cardholders, more accurate decisions, and reduced learning time for authorizers. The system was expensive and time consuming, but the benefits were so overwhelming that American Express recouped its entire investment during the first year of operation!

Expert System Summary

One of the myths surrounding artificial intelligence in general and expert systems in particular is that expert systems will replace human experts. Expert systems augment the capabilities of humans and make them more productive, but they will never replace them. Expert systems and humans complement one another in the decision-making process. The computer-based expert system can handle routine situations with great accuracy, thereby relieving someone from the burden of a detailed manual analysis. Humans can combine the insight of an expert system with their flexible intuitive abilities to resolve complex problems.

In a short period of time, the track record of operational expert systems has been very convincing. Computer-based expert systems have fared well against real expert physicians in the diagnosis of illnesses, against real expert financial analysts in advice to investors, against real computer experts in the configuration of computer systems, against real geologists in the exploration of minerals, and against experts in many other decision environments.

The field of expert systems is literally exploding. Decision makers in every decision environment are developing or contemplating developing an expert system. Attorneys will have mock trials with expert systems to "pre-try" their cases. Doctors will routinely ask a "second opinion." Architects will "discuss" the structural design of a building with an expert system. Military officers will "talk" with the "expert" to plan battlefield strategy. City planners will "ask" an expert system to suggest optimal locations for recreational facilities.

Some computer industry observers believe that expert systems are the wave of the future and that each of us will have "expert" help and guidance in our respective professions. Others say "no way." Time will tell.

NATURAL LANGUAGES

The State of the Art of Natural Languages

The ultimate programming language is the *natural language*. The natural language is actually a program that permits a computer to accept instructions without regard to format or syntax in the native or "natural" language of the end user. To date, there are no pure natural languages. However, natural languages with certain syntax restrictions are available. Researchers are currently working to develop pure natural languages that permit an unrestricted dialogue between us and a computer. Although the creation of such a language is difficult to comprehend, it is probably inevitable. In the interim, the complexities involved in translating one language to another are substantial. For example, a program designed to translate English-to-Russian and Russian-to-English was used to translate "The spirit is willing, but the flesh is weak" into Russian and back to English. The result of the double translation was: "The vodka is good, but the meat is rotten." The result gives us some insight into the complexities involved in the creation of natural language programs. Similar subtleties must be considered when translating English to the language of computers, and vice versa.

Existing natural languages enable more people to take advantage of available information because even casual users can articulate their needs in their native tongue. The premise behind a natural language is that the programmer or user needs little or no training. He or she simply writes, or perhaps verbalizes, specifications without regard for instruction format or syntax. For limited information processing tasks, such as ad hoc inquiries and report generation for a specific application area (human resources, purchasing, and so on), existing natural languages work quite well. Natural languages also provide the *front end* or the user interface to a variety of domain-specific applications, including expert systems. With certain limitations, existing natural languages permit users to express queries in normal, everyday English. For the most part, users can phrase a query any way they want. Examples are presented later in this discussion.

Natural Language Concepts

Here is how a natural language works. Take, for example, the following request:

> Let me see the average salaries by job category in the marketing department.

The natural language software analyzes the sentence in much the same way that we used to diagram sentences during our studies of grammar. This process, known as **parsing**, results in a **parse tree** (see Figure 3–3). The

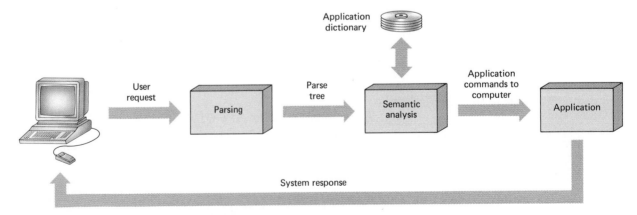

FIGURE 3–3 Interpreting a Natural Language User Request
Following the parsing process, a natural language user request is translated to applications commands through a semantic analysis.

components of the requests are translated to applications commands through a *semantic analysis*. In the semantic analysis, the components are matched, typically beginning with the verb, against key words in the user-created *application dictionary*. The dictionary is essentially a list of command synonyms for English words that might be used in a request for a particular applications environment (marketing, inventory management, medical diagnosis, and so on).

In the example inquiry, the verb "see" would be translated to be the applications command "display." For example, at its most fundamental level, the request is interpreted as "[Let me] see . . . salaries" or, simply, "Display salaries." The "salaries" part of the request indicates that access to the SALARY field, and, therefore, the EMPLOYEE record in the data base, is critical to the response. On closer examination, "average" specifies a function that is to be applied to the SALARY field. The phrase "by job category in the marketing department" identifies the users selection criteria; that is, include in the response only those employees in the marketing department and compute the average salary for each job category. The response to the example inquiry is shown in Figure 3–4.

The user would get the same results if he or she had entered the following request:

What is the average salary in the marketing department for each job classification?

If your query is unclear, the natural language software might ask you questions that will clarify any ambiguities. For example, in the preceding request the system might respond, "I do not understand 'What is?' Do you mean 'Let me see' or 'display'?"

A natural language interprets many common words, but other words peculiar to a specific application or company would need to be added by the user. All common and user-supplied words comprise the **lexicon**, or the dictionary of words that can be interpreted by the natural language. The sophistication of the types of queries that can be accepted are dependent on the comprehensiveness of the lexicon. In the example inquiry, the words "Let," "me," and "see," their meaning, and the context in which they are used would have to be entered into the lexicon before the phrase "Let me see" could be interpreted by the natural language software. Also, in the examples, references to job "category" and "classification" must be defined in the lexicon to mean the same thing.

```
                        MARKETING DEPARTMENT


        Job Category          No. of Employees   Average Salary
        Director                     1              $71,000
        Adminstrative Assistant      4              $26,550
        Product Manager              4              $48,333
        Secretary                    3              $21,480
```

FIGURE 3–4   The Results of a Natural Language Inquiry
The inquiry: Let me see the average salaries by job category in the marketing department.

When using a natural language, all you have to do is ask. To produce this graph, this product manager entered the following request: "Show me a line graph of total sales by region for the past quarter." The graph and an optional tabular summary is generated automatically in response to the request.

Courtesy of International Business Machines

Usually, state-of-the-art natural language software can interpret no more than a one-sentence query at a time. Other typical natural language queries might be

☐ Are there any managers between the ages of 30 and 40 in the northwest region with MBA degrees?

☐ Show me a pie chart that compares voter registrations for Alabama, Georgia, North Carolina, South Carolina, and Florida.

☐ What are the top 10 best selling fiction books in California?

Natural Language Summary

At present, restricted domain-dependent natural languages are commercially available as front ends (user interfaces) for a variety of software packages, including decision support systems, electronic spreadsheets, and expert systems. Eventually, natural languages will provide the front end for all categories of software, from word processing to operating systems.

SIMULATION OF HUMAN SENSORY CAPABILITIES

Knowledge-based systems and natural languages are concerned with the thought process and simulated "intelligence." Therefore, these fields of study fit nicely under the umbrella of artificial intelligence. However, the scope of AI research includes the simulation of all types of human behavior, including those that do not involve "intelligence." This section discusses that category of AI that deals with the simulation of our instinctive human senses (seeing, hearing, and so on). Locomotion (physical movement), which results from an intelligent command, is discussed in the section on robotics.

"Intelligent" machines that can simulate human sensory capabilities have the ability to establish a link with their environments. This link has opened the door to a number of real-world applications. This section presents AI progress in the areas of talking, hearing, and seeing.

Talking: Voice Response Units

If you have ever called directory assistance, you have probably heard something like, "The number is eight-six-one-four-zero-three-eight." If you have not, you have probably been in a car that warned the driver to "fasten your seat belt." These are examples of talking machines and are outputs from voice response units. There are two types of **voice response units**: one uses a *recording* of a human voice and other sounds, and the other uses a *speech synthesizer*.

The first type of voice response unit selects output from user-recorded words, phrases, music, alarms, or anything that you might record on tape, just as a printer would select characters. In "recorded" voice response units, the actual analog recordings of sounds are converted to digital data, then permanently stored in a memory chip. On output, the selected sound is converted back to analog before being routed to a speaker. These chips are mass produced for specific applications, such as output for automatic teller machines, microwave ovens, smoke detectors, elevators, alarm clocks, automobile warning systems, video games, and vending machines, to mention a few.

Speech synthesizers convert raw data to electronically produced speech. To do this, these devices combine sounds resembling the phonemes (basic sound units) that make up speech. A speech synthesizer is capable of producing at least 64 unique sounds. The existing technology produces synthesized speech with only limited vocal inflections and phrasing. Still, the number of applications is growing. In one application, an optical character reader scans books to retrieve the raw data. The speech synthesizer then translates the printed matter into spoken words for blind persons. In another application, the use of speech synthesizers is opening a new world to speech-impaired children who were once placed in institutions because they could not communicate verbally. As the quality of the output improves, speech synthesizers will enjoy a broader base of applications. Speech synthesizers are relatively inexpensive and are becoming increasingly popular with many personal computer owners.

> The real problem isn't whether machines think but whether men do.
>
> —— B. F. Skinner

Hearing: Speech Recognition

Computers are great talkers, but they are not very good listeners. It is not uncommon for a **speech recognition system** to misinterpret the slamming of a door for a spoken word. Nevertheless, speech recognition systems can be used to enter limited kinds and quantities of information. Despite its limitations, speech recognition has a number of applications. Salespersons in the field can enter an order simply by calling the computer and stating the customer number, item number, and quantity. Quality control personnel, who must use their hands, call out defects as they are detected. Baggage handlers at airports simply state the three-letter destination identifier ("L-A-X" for Los Angeles International), and luggage is routed to the appropriate conveyer system. Physicians in the operating room can request certain information on a patient while operating. A computer-based audio response unit or a speech synthesizer makes the conversation two way.

Here is how it works. When you speak into a microphone, each sound is broken down and examined in several frequencies. The sounds in each frequency are **digitized** and are matched against similarly formed *templates* in the computer's electronic dictionary. The digitized template is a form that can be stored and interpreted by computers (1s and 0s). In speech recognition, the creation of the data base is called *training*. Most speech recognition systems are *speaker dependent*; that is, they respond to the speech of a particular individual. Therefore, a data base of words must be created for each person using the system. When creating the data base, persons using the system must repeat as many as 20 times each word that is to be interpreted by the system—thus the "training." This is necessary because we seldom say words in the same way every time. There will probably be a different inflection or nasal quality even if we say the word twice in succession.

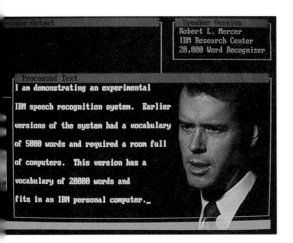

An experimental version of a speech recognition system being demonstrated here can interpret 20,000 spoken words. With this type of microcomputer-based capability, executives will be able to dictate most of their correspondence directly into a word processing system, occasionally inserting words that are not part of the system's vocabulary.

Courtesy of International Business Machines

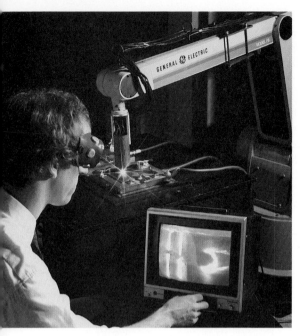

This robot has "eyes." The TV monitor in the foreground shows what is seen by the robot. This welding robot uses its vision system to steer itself along irregularly-shaped joints as it makes the weld.

General Electric Company

State-of-the-art *speaker-independent* systems have a limited vocabulary, perhaps "yes," "no," and the 10 numeric digits. Although the vocabulary is limited, speaker-independent systems do not require training and can be used by anyone. However, they do require a very large data base to accommodate anyone's voice pattern.

Voice inflections, grammatical exceptions, and words that have several meanings have combined to make speech interpretation difficult, but not impossible. For example, "I'm OK!" differs from "I'm OK?" For human beings, distinguishing these subtle differences is second nature. However, these subtleties have vastly complicated the plight of AI researchers. Even so, researchers are developing speaker-independent data bases of several thousand words that enable the transcription of complete spoken sentences with a high degree of accuracy. It is only a matter of time before programmers can enter their programs in spoken English rather than through time-consuming keystrokes and managers can dictate their correspondence directly to the computer. Today, we must see and touch our workstations to interact with a computer, but in a few years, we will be talking with computers as we move about our offices and homes.

Seeing: Vision Systems

The simulation of human sensory capabilities is extremely complex, especially vision. For example, a computer does not actually see and interpret an image the way a human being does. To give computers eyesight, a camera provides the input needed to create the data base. A vision system, complete with camera, digitizes the images of all objects to be interpreted. The digitized form of each image is then stored in the data base. When the system is placed in operation, a camera enters the image to a digitizer. The digitized image to be interpreted is then compared to the prerecorded digitized images in the computer's data base. The computer interprets the image by matching the structure of the input image with those in the data base. This process is illustrated by the digital vision inspection system in Figure 3–5.

As you can imagine, **vision input systems** are best suited to very specialized tasks where only a few images will be encountered. These tasks are usually simple, monotonous ones, such as inspection. For example, in Figure 3–5 a digital vision inspection system on an assembly line rejects those parts that do not meet certain quality control specifications. The vision system performs rudimentary gauging inspections and then signals the computer to take appropriate action (see Figure 3–5).

Human Sensory Capabilities Summary

AI research is continually enhancing the abilities of computers to simulate human sensory capabilities. Research is ongoing in the areas of speech, speech recognition, vision and in other areas of human sensory perception as well, such as touch and smell. In the not-too-distant future, we will be able to have meaningful verbal conversations with computers. These computers will be able to talk, listen, and even smell the roses!

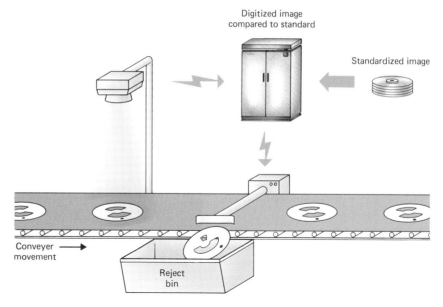

FIGURE 3–5   Digital Vision Inspection System
In this digital vision inspection systems, parts are examined by a digital vision system for defects. If the digitized image of the part does not match a standard digital image, the defective part is placed in a reject bin.

ROBOTICS

Rudimentary Robotics

To date the area of artificial intelligence experiencing the greatest commercial success is robotics. *Robotics* is the integration of computers and **industrial robots**. By 1990, the "steel-collar" work force throughout the world will be made up of over 250,000 industrial robots. Contrary to what some might believe, these robots are quite different in appearance and function from those portrayed in science fiction movies. The most common industrial robot is a single mechanical arm that is controlled by a computer. The arm, called a manipulator, has a *shoulder, forearm*, and *wrist* and is capable of performing the motions of a human arm. The manipulator is fitted with a *hand* that is designed to accomplish a specific task, such as painting, welding, picking and placing, and so on.

An industrial robot is best at repetitive tasks, tasks that require precision movements, moving heavy loads, and working in hazardous areas. These types of tasks exist in virtually every kind of industry, from hospitals to cannery row. The automotive industry is the largest user of robots (painting, welding) and the electronics industry (circuit testing, connecting chips to circuit boards) is second. Even surgeons are using robots to assist in brain surgery. They can be set up to manipulate the surgical drill and biopsy needle with great accuracy, thereby making brain surgery faster, more accurate, and safer.

Q. The work that I did in automating certain plant operations resulted in the elimination of five jobs. Ultimately 25 jobs will be eliminated. After that, we have no definite plans for further automation.

   We don't anticipate any people being laid off. Nevertheless, rumors are flying that most of our 250 workers will be replaced by robots. This simply is not true, but nothing I say seems to convince them otherwise. Do you have any suggestions?

A. Our society is transitioning to an information society. The question is not whether we automate, but when and how much we automate. This is a time when management and labor must be open and frank with one another. I would suggest that you invite a labor representative to serve on the team that will evaluate any future proposals to automate plant operations. This gesture implies that labor will be fully informed of and involved in any future automation, from concept to implementation.

   This may not be what plant personnel want to hear, but it may provide some small comfort. Tell them that during the next decade more jobs will be lost because of a lack of automation than an implementation of automation.

Teaching Robots to Do Their Job

A computer program is written to control the robot just as a program is written to print payroll checks. The program includes such commands as when to reach, in which direction to reach, how far to reach, when to grasp, and so on. Once programmed, robots do not need much attention. One plant manufactures vacuum cleaners 24 hours a day, seven days a week, in total darkness!

Outfitting Robots with Intelligence and Human Sensory Capabilities

Most robots are programmed to reach to a particular location, find a particular item, and then place it somewhere else. This simple application of robotics is called "pick and place." Instead of a grasping mechanism, other robots are equipped with a variety of industrial tools, such as drills, paint guns, welding torches, and so on. Of course, it will be a very long time before our companions and workmates are robots. However, industrial robots are being equipped with rudimentary sensory capabilities, such as vision, that enable them to simulate human behavior better. A robot with the added dimension of vision can be given some intelligence. Robots without intelligence simply repeat preprogrammed motions. Even though the state of the art of vision systems is low, a robot can be "taught" to distinguish between dissimilar objects under controlled conditions. With the addition of this sensory subsystem, the robot has the capability to make crude but important decisions. For example, a robot equipped with a vision subsystem can distinguish between two boxes coming down the conveyor. The robot can be programmed to place a box of particular dimensions on an adjacent conveyer and to let all other boxes pass.

   If vision system technology continues to improve, more and more robots will have "navigational" capabilities. Most robots are stationary, and those that are not can detect the presence only of an object in their path, or they are programmed to operate within a well-defined work area where the position of all obstacles is known. Within the decade of the 1990s, robots will be able to move about the work area just as people do.

The Reality of Robots

Few people, even robotics experts, anticipated the explosion of interest of the industrial community in robots. Most attribute this interest to the economy and to management's attempt to remain competitive by reducing cost wherever possible. During the next decade we can anticipate that many less desirable jobs will be relegated to robots. This concerns and affects a great many people.

   Robots will eliminate between 1 and 2 million blue-collar jobs during the 1980s. However, a new stratum of employees is emerging in the field

The precise, untiring movement of computer-controlled industrial robots helps assure quality in the assembly of everything from electrical components to automobiles. Here, a robot applies spot welds.

TRW Inc.

of manufacturing. These people design, build, sell, install, program, repair, and troubleshoot robots. Also, robots have enabled some companies to survive, thereby saving jobs. By 1995, the net result of the implementation of robotics is predicted to be a plus in the number of jobs. In the meantime, unions are challenging the wisdom of replacing their workers with robots. On the other hand, management reminds workers that robots can do the same repetitive task for one-sixth of the cost. Unions cite social responsibility. Management cites competitive strategy.

Opponents of robots may slow the pace at which workers in repetitive and hazardous tasks are replaced, but we can only conclude that robots will eventually replace human labor wherever their doing so is cost effective. We have only to review recent history to confirm this conclusion. Today's earth movers do the work of 100 nineteenth-century laborers with shovels. In the nineteenth century, people were convinced that mechanization would eliminate needed jobs and have a negative effect on the quality of life. Today, instead, we enjoy higher employment and a higher quality of life.

A realization of the inevitable has spawned new partnerships between management, labor, and the government. For example, a research venture is underway to develop robotics devices to replace sewing machines in the garment industry. The research is sponsored by a textile workers' union, private enterprise, and the U.S. Department of Commerce. They recognize that U.S. enterprises have traditionally flourished through technological innovation and that it is difficult for U.S. workers to compete with foreign suppliers of labor-intensive consumer goods. Perhaps all garment jobs will be lost if nothing is done. Or perhaps many jobs will be saved if high technology can be introduced into the traditionally labor-intensive garment industry.

CHAPTER HIGHLIGHTS

■ In the area of research known as artificial intelligence (AI), researchers are working on systems that have the ability to reason, to learn or accumulate knowledge, to strive for self-improvement, and to simulate human sensory and mechanical capabilities.

■ Only recently have the power and cost-effectiveness of computers advanced to the point that AI applications have become economically feasible on a large scale in the real world.

■ Research in the field of artificial intelligence can be divided into four categories: knowledge-based and expert systems, natural languages, simulation of human sensory capabilities, and robotics.

■ The knowledge-based system uses human-supplied knowledge to model the human thought process within a particular area (domain) of expertise.

■ The two fundamental capabilities of knowledge-based systems

are their ability to emulate human reasoning and their ability to learn.

■ The factual knowledge and the heuristic rules of thumb acquired from a domain expert are the primary input to an expert system's knowledge base.

■ An expert system is the highest form of a knowledge-based system, but in practice, the two systems terms are used interchangeably.

■ An expert system is an interactive system that responds to questions, asks for clarification, makes recommendations, and generally aids in the decision-making process. The less sophisticated knowledge-based systems are called assistant systems. Assistant systems help users to make relatively straightforward decisions.

■ The following are several of the more prominent benefits of expert systems: they enable the knowledge of experts to be "canned," they can expand the decision-making capabilities of many people, they can improve the productivity and performance of decision makers, and they can provide stability and consistency to a particular area of decision making.

■ The expert system shell is a domain-independent proprietary software package that enables the development of expert systems. The primary components of the expert system shell are the knowledge acquisition facility, the knowledge base, the inference engine, and the user interface.

■ The knowledge acquisition facility of the expert system shell permits the construction of the knowledge base. The knowledge base is created through the cooperative efforts of a knowledge engineer and one or more domain experts.

■ The knowledge base of an expert system contains facts, rules of inference, the identification of problem(s) to be solved, possible solutions to the problem(s), and how to progress from problem to solution.

■ An expert system's inference engine is the vehicle by which the facts and rules in the knowledge base are applied to a problem. The reasoning capabilities of an inference engine are based on one or a combination of the forward-chaining and backward-chaining inference procedures.

■ The user interface component of an expert system enables the type of interaction between end user and expert system that is needed for heuristic processing.

■ Natural languages are programs that permit a computer to accept instructions without regard to format or syntax in the native language of the end user. To date, there are no pure natural languages. Natural languages provide the user interface with a variety of domain-specific applications.

■ The natural language software parses a user inquiry into a parse tree that is translated to applications commands through a semantic analysis.

■ Artificial intelligence research is ongoing in the areas of speech, speech recognition, vision, touch, and smell. There are two types of voice response units: one uses a recording of a human voice and other sounds, and the other uses a speech synthesizer. Speech recognition systems can be used to enter limited kinds and quantities of information. Vision input systems are best suited to very specialized tasks where only a few images will be encountered.

■ Robotics is the integration of computers and industrial robots. Most industrial robots have a single mechanical arm called a manipulator. The manipulator is fitted with a hand that is designed to accomplish a specific task, such as painting, welding, picking and placing, and so on.

■ Industrial robots are being equipped with rudimentary sensory capabilities, such as vision, that enable them to better simulate human behavior. A robot with the added dimension of vision can be given some intelligence.

IMPORTANT TERMS

application dictionary	expert system	knowledge base	robotics
artificial intelligence (AI)	forward chaining	knowledge-based system	semantic analysis
assistant system	heuristic knowledge	knowledge engineer	speech recognition system
backward chaining	industrial robots	lexicon	speech synthesizer
digitized	inference engine	natural languages	user interface
domain experts	knowledge acquisition facility	parse tree	vision input systems
expert system shell		parsing	voice response units

REVIEW EXERCISES

1. What do expert systems and assistant systems have in common? What is the primary difference between the two?

2. Domain experts would typically be associated with what area of AI research?

3. List three benefits of experts systems.

4. What are the primary components of an expert system shell?

5. What is the function of an expert system's inference engine?

6. In the field of robotics, to what does "navigation" refer?

7. Briefly describe the types of tasks that are appropriate for industrial robots.

8. What is the basic difference between an expert system's knowledge base and a data base?

9. What is the lexicon of a natural language?

10. Name five human sensory capabilities that, to some extent, can be simulated with computer technology.

11. What are the devices called that convert raw data to electronically produced speech?

12. Which component of the expert system shell permits the construction of the knowledge base?

13. Which component of the expert system shell permits both the end user and the expert system to structure questions and responses?

14. What are the two fundamental capabilities of knowledge-based systems?

15. What are the four categories of artificial intelligence research?

16. Give two examples of what would be considered heuristic knowledge.

17. Only recently have AI applications become economically feasible on a large scale. Why?

18. Name two types of systems whose logic employs the use of IF-THEN rules.

19. Other than facts and rules, what else does a knowledge engineer enter into an expert system's knowledge base?

DISCUSSION QUESTIONS

1. The American Express Authorizer's Assistant, discussed in this chapter, paid for itself in one year. Explain briefly how you think the system was able to
   a. Provide more consistent decision making.
   b. Improve authorizer productivity.
   c. Reduce credit and fraud loses.
   d. Reduce operating expenses.
   e. Improve service to customers and cardholders.
   f. Enable more accurate decisions.
   g. Reduce learning time for authorizers.

2. Expert systems have been created that assist human financial analysts in providing advice to investors. Give examples of three pieces of factual knowledge and three rules that might be a part of the knowledge base that supports such an expert system.

3. Describe a specific decision environment (not mentioned in the text) that would be appropriate for the implementation of an expert system.

4. Describe a specific decision environment (not mentioned in the text) that would be appropriate for the implementation of an assistant system.

5. The following rule is part of an expert system's knowledge base:

   > If presentation graphics is an anticipated application, then consider a color monitor.

   The expert system is designed to help people configure microcomputer systems to meet the needs of the intended end users. The system uses both the forward- and backward-chaining procedures. Give examples of rules to which the decision logic would chain forward from the foregoing rule and backward from the foregoing rule.

6. In reference to artificial intelligence, Marvin Minsky of MIT said, "It's a moving horizon." What do you think he meant?

7. For the past two decades AI researchers have been accused of creating solutions that do not address real-world problems. Now they are more interested in the commercial viability of their work. What transpired in recent years to cause this radical shift in emphasis?

8. Explain in general terms what a natural language would do with the following command: List all fixed inventory items in the purchasing department that were purchased prior to 1985. Give an example of what a response to the request might look like. Fixed inventory items would include items such as desks, chairs, lamps, and so on.

9. Research in artificial intelligence is accelerating much faster than anyone would have imagined in 1980. Perhaps this increase in research can be attributed to AI's potential for increasing productivity in the plant and improving decision making. Is this the case, or will it mean fewer paychecks? Discuss.

10. Management, labor, and government are cooperating to develop robots that will surely eliminate some jobs. Why are they doing this?

11. Compare today's vision input systems with those portrayed in such films as *2001* and *2010*. Do you believe that we will have a comparable vision technology by the year 2001?

12. Describe an MIS application (not mentioned in the text) that might make use of speaker-independent speech recognition systems.

APPLICATION CASE STUDY 3–1
Expert Systems

The Situation

Que Realty, a real estate company with 16 offices and a sales staff of 96 full-time and 37 part-time real estate agents, has a high turnover rate among agents. The turnover rate is high for two reasons. First, many new agents get discouraged and leave before they establish themselves and make their first big sale. Second, many successful agents are lured away by other real estate companies. Que Realty is like most other realty companies in that at any given time, about half the sales staff is inexperienced.

Over 80 percent of Que Realty's sales volume is in residential real estate. At Que, each agent's objective is to show potential home buyers only those properties that a prospective buyer is likely to find appealing. The inexperienced agents have problems matching clients to the available homes. These mismatches invariably result in wasted time and unhappy clients. Some clients have been so upset that they have complained to Joan Magee, the owner of Que Realty, and have refused to do further business with the company. Ms. Magee hired a consultant on a contract basis to alleviate the situation.

After reviewing the situation, the consultant decided to develop an expert system to help both inexperienced and veteran agents do a better job of matching buyers with available properties. The purpose of the system is to create a profile of a house that meets the buyer's needs. Ms. Magee arranged for the consultant to interview David Meissner, Que's most successful agent. Mr. Meissner has been selling real estate for 35 years and has been with Que for 17 years. He was the sales leader at Que for 13 years. He accomplished this feat while showing fewer homes than his colleagues at Que. Dave Meissner summarized his approach by saying, "I work smarter, not harder!" He is retiring in a few months and is proud to have been selected to share his expertise. Que, of course, is paying him to participate in the project.

During the interview, Dave Meissner said that he asks his clients a series of questions relating to their needs and desires. Based on the client's responses, he rates each factor's importance. He then considers these factors when searching the list of available homes to determine which ones to show the client. To help in the design of the expert system, the consultant and Dave agree on the following scale for client responses to questions: critical, important, advantageous, and immaterial.

Dave always asks his clients for the following data:

1. Number of adults and their relationship (spouse, parent, and so on)

2. Number of children and their ages

3. Workplace location(s)

4. Style of house preferred

5. Amount of land desired

6. Type of setting (such as a development, rural, inner city)

7. Need for access to public transportation

8. Special needs (for example, office in home, handicapped access)

9. Special interests (for example, photo darkroom, boarding horses)

10. Financial details (down payment available, income, and so on)

11. Timing details (earliest and latest occupancy dates, dependence on sale of current house, and so on).

The Assignment

Put yourself in the role of the consultant as you complete the following assignment.

1. Prepare rules for the questions Dave says he always asks by using the format shown here. Write at least one rule for each of the questions, making any necessary assumptions (for example, style of house must be selected from a specified list consisting of ranch, bilevel, two-story colonial, and so on).

IF   : <condition>
THEN   : <action or result>
REASON : <the rationale>

Example 1

IF   : <There is an adult who is not a spouse>
THEN   : <Ask about privacy needs>
REASON : <Client may desire separate entrance or detached living quarters for parents, in-laws, and so on)

Example 2

IF   : <Quality of schools is critical>
THEN   : <SCHOOLDISTRICT = Parkland OR Southern>
REASON : <Only houses in these two outstanding school districts will be considered.>

(*Note*: SCHOOLDISTRICT is capitalized here because it represents a variable in the AI system, and OR is capitalized because it represents an operator.)

2. Assume that the expert system will be implemented and run interactively on a microcomputer. Design screens for two of the rules you developed in the first question. One of the screens should present the agent with a menu of possible client responses from which to choose, and the other should accept free-form, unstructured responses entered in plain English.

3. Describe how you would test the accuracy of Que's expert system. That is, does the expert system generate a profile that accurately reflects the needs of the client?

4. Describe how you would determine the effectiveness of the system. That is, how well does the system do what it is intended to do? Assume that it is accurate, as defined in the previous question.

5. Develop a plan for training Que's agents to use the expert system. Include the topics to be covered, the length of the training session(s), where training would be conducted, who would conduct the training, and class sizes.

APPLICATION CASE STUDY 3–2
Natural Languages

The Situation

Que Realty has developed an expert system that helps real estate agents to identify the type of residence a prospective buyer would be most likely to purchase (see Application Case Study 3-1). This system has helped agents to use their time and the time of their clients in the most effective manner. And, much to owner Joan Magee's excitement, sales have increased dramatically.

Currently, information about each residence for sale is contained on an 8½-by-11-inch preprinted form. This form is completed by the listing agent. Data on the form include such items as house location; schools children would attend; number, type, and measurements of rooms; current taxes; and estimated utilities costs. Most listings also include a photo of the property. The forms are stored in three-ring binders and are grouped geographically by township, section of the city, and so on. New listings are inserted into the binders as soon as they are completed and photocopied, an activity that is not always done promptly or correctly. Each of Que's 16 sales offices maintains at least one up-to-date listings binder. Finding the listings that correspond to the profile recommended by the expert system can be a time-consuming process because each listing in the desired section of the binder must be individually scanned by the agent. Furthermore, misfiled listings are unlikely to be identified. Although Joan Magee is very pleased with the results obtained by implementing the expert system, she has asked a consultant to develop a better solution for the storage and retrieval of real estate listings.

The computer-based design suggested by the consultant has two major components:

1. A data base with random access capability that contains the listing data

2. A natural language interface to be used with the listings data base

The photographs will be coded and stored in sequence in a photo album. Eventually, Que will incorporate the scanning, digitizing, and storing of the photo images on disk. When this is completed, agents and clients will be able to view or print the photo images together with the text of the listing.

The Assignment

Put yourself in the role of the consultant as you complete the following assignment.

1. A parsing algorithm is a necessary component of the software for a natural language interface. The algorithm decomposes a sentence (S) into a tree structure that consists of noun phrases (NP), verbs (V), determiners (D), and nouns (N). The parse tree for the sentence "The girl saw a horse" is shown on the next page.

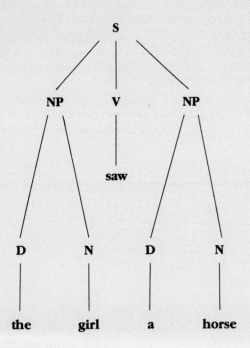

Draw a parse tree for each of the following sentences:

   a. John Alpert sold listing #14738.

   b. I want to see all the houses in Center City.

2. Give three alternatives to articulate the command in question 1b.

3. A second component of a natural language interface is the lexicon of words that it can understand. Standard lexicons are available, but they must be augmented for specific applications, such as Que's listing system.

   a. List five verbs that you would add to Que's lexicon.

   b. List five nouns that you would add to Que's lexicon.

4. Consider the following realistic inquiry:
I want to see all four-bedroom houses in a good school district, with easy access to Interstate 78, on a large lot, and costing no more than $185,000.

   a. Which portions of the inquiry are likely to be interpreted without difficulty by the system?

   b. Which portions of the inquiry are not likely to be understood by the system?

   c. List three alternatives to specifying the amount "$185,000."

   d. List three alternatives of specifying the restriction "no more than."

CHAPTER 4

Information Systems as a Competitive Strategy

KEY TOPICS

CHAPTER OVERVIEW

In recent years, top management has begun to view computers and MIS in a different light. For decades these resources were simply thought of as support functions. Now they are viewed as strategic weapons that, if used creatively, can provide a company with a clear competitive advantage. This chapter presents ways in which a broad cross section of innovative and progressive companies has leveraged computer and information technologies to realize an advantage over their competitors.

GAINING THE COMPETITIVE ADVANTAGE WITH INFORMATION SYSTEMS

A highly competitive world market is pressuring corporate executives into a desperate search for solutions. Those with a genuine desire to survive and flourish are doing everything they can to improve profitability. Companies are adopting no smoking policies to lower the cost of insurance premiums. Unions are accepting wage concessions. Executives are flying coach rather than first class. At least one layer of management has been eliminated in most companies during the last decade. These are examples of a few of the thousands of approaches being taken by executives to improve profitability. Ironically, only recently has corporate America begun to realize that computers and information systems can improve profitability and provide the all-important *competitive advantage*.

The days are gone when good management and hard work would invariably result in success and profits. Now that these corporate qualities have become prerequisites for survival, managers are seeking strategies that can give their companies the competitive advantage, especially those strategies that involve computer and information technology. John S. Scott, president and CEO of Richardson-Vicks, Inc., said, "We recognize that we should exploit the technology to achieve competitive advantage. . . . We further recognize that this is a moving target. Success in technological advantage may last only a limited period of time. We plan to press on with other opportunities to maintain a competitive advantage." Richardson-Vicks is a consumer goods company specializing in medicine for colds. In this highly competitive era, the judicious use of computers and information systems can make the difference between profitability and failure in just about every kind of industry.

New and innovative uses of computers and information systems are being implemented every day. Even so, the business community is still in the early stages of automation. Each company has a seemingly endless number of opportunities to use computer and information technologies to achieve a competitive edge.

Management Attitudes

Information Systems as a Strategic Weapon

The attitudes of top management toward business automation have changed dramatically during the 1980s. Coming into the 1980s, more often than not top management viewed computers and data processing as a support capability that would forever be relegated to routine data processing tasks, such as churning out invoices and payroll checks. In many companies, management had exhausted all other avenues for improving profitability before turning to MIS for solutions. On the other hand, the management of aggressive companies recognized early on that MIS is much more than an expense—it is a strategic weapon that can be very effective in the business battlefield.

Traditional Attitudes

Unfortunately, a good many executives do not have a grasp of the potential of MIS and, therefore, believe that competitive advantages being enjoyed by their competitors will be short lived. Top management at one airline company took great pride in the fact that it did not have an on-line reservations

The information system is fast becoming the ultimate strategic weapon in the business world. For example, an automobile manufacturer lowered the cost of producing automobiles while retaining maximum flexibility in what is made. To do this, a computer-based information system was installed to control the assembly line and enable the communication and implementation of last-minute order changes.

Courtesy of International Business Machines Corporation

system. That company has ceased to exist. The stark reality of the business world is that MIS solutions will continue to provide companies with opportunities to create competitive advantages and to negate the competitive advantage of a competitor. Companies whose executives maintain the data processing attitude will lose ground and eventually revert to survival mode. Historically, tradition-minded managers tend to introduce (or accept) change only when they had to. Now they have to.

Cost, Risk, and Change

The obvious question becomes, "If MIS is so clearly the solution to establishing a competitive advantage, why isn't everybody doing it?" There are three primary reasons.

> We need a generation of business people who neither fears the computer nor stands in awe of it, people who have the imagination and creativity to harness the computer's potential and use it to rethink and improve the management strategies of the future.
>
> ————— *Peter Scanlon*

1. *MIS solutions are often expensive and time consuming.* The implementation of information systems to achieve a competitive advantage is a

TAKING THE GIANT LEAP

Q. Six months ago I hired a new director of information systems. He took over a difficult situation and has been doing very well. The MIS steering committee has approved all of his recommendations to date, but all of us were taken by surprise when he proposed doubling his budget during the next three years, from $3 million to $6 million. He stated that this increase is needed to bring us up to parity with our peer companies.

We are seriously considering approving most, if not all, of the proposed increase. But before doing so, we would like to know if other companies are making similar commitments in an attempt to "catch up."

A. In truth, relatively few companies have adopted the giant-leap strategy in an attempt to become state-of-the-art users of computer technology, but more should. If you are way behind now, you can't catch up "gradually."

Half of all MIS departments are grossly underfunded. If MIS funding were doubled in these departments, the net result would be a positive contribution to the organization's bottom line. These companies, of which yours may be one, are not taking full advantage of the potential of computers.

Of course, good MIS management is a necessary prerequisite. If your new manager has a well-conceived long-range plan and you remain confident in his abilities, go for it.

perfect example of a situation in which you have to spend money to make money. Studies have shown that relative to revenues, the companies with the best performance records spend twice as much on computers and information systems as do the companies with the worst performance records.

2. *There is usually an element of risk in the implementation of information systems.* Traditionalist managers would opt to maintain the status quo rather than subject themselves to the risk of failure, even at the expense of losing market share. Of course, if achieving the competitive advantage were inexpensive and easy, everybody's advantage would be nobody's advantage.

3. *The implementation of information systems inevitably means change.* People inherently resist change.

The economic environment and fierce competition have focused attention on the computer and information resources. Those enterprises that challenge their managers and executives to tap the potential of these resources are gaining the competitive advantage. These successes are putting pressure on status quo managers to change their attitudes.

Information Is Power

Just as top management is well known for keeping a tight grip on the purse strings, it is also reluctant to share information. After all, managers often equate information with power. Most MIS solutions result in more information being available to more people, including subordinates and even customers. To achieve the MIS-based competitive advantage, managers must be willing to adopt an attitude that if information can be beneficial to someone else, it should be shared.

The Bottom-Line Attitude

The "you're only as good as your last quarter" attitude runs against the grain of information systems solutions. When resources are allocated based on maximizing profits for the next reporting quarter (three-month period), long-term projects are continually postponed until the next quarter. Fortunately, the pressure of a world market is beginning to force management to rethink the wisdom of maintaining an attitude that focuses on the quarterly bottom line. The strategic use of MIS demands commitments to strategies that have lead times of up to five years. A management group that thinks ahead and plans for the long term may get a five-year jump on a competitor that does not.

Reactive Versus Proactive Thinking

Some managers have traditionally reacted to the actions of competitors. Essentially, they are counterpunchers. For example, they might respond to an advertising blitz by a competitor with one of their own. In this instance, they can react within days. However, to respond to a competitor's MIS-based competitive advantage may take years! To remain competitive in today's intense market environment, management must adopt a proactive attitude. A company can only react so many times before it is out of business. As you read through this chapter, you will see that some of the MIS-based competitive advantages achieved by proactive companies can actually cripple the competition.

Being proactive does not imply that corporate management must blaze new trails through hidden forests. It does, however, imply that the company should position itself to be among the leaders in technological innovation. To do this, top management and MIS professionals must stay abreast of leading-edge technology. A few companies are convinced that being first is worth the extra expense associated with being on the "bleeding edge." Others are content with letting the competitor make the mistakes that inevitably accompany the implementation of leading-edge technology. In the meantime, they position themselves to move in with similar or superior technology within a few months after their competitor gains the advantage. The "bleeding-edge" philosophy not only presses the limits of the technology, it often presses the limits of customer patience when the inevitable implementation problems begin to have an impact on the customer.

Strategic Planning

Companies are gaining the competitive advantage by making MIS an integral part of the corporate strategic planning process. For decades, research and development, finance, and marketing have been the dominate areas of consideration in corporate strategic planning. Other functions were viewed as support functions, including production and data processing. Today, distinct competitive advantages are being realized by innovations in factory automation and in MIS, therefore, forward-thinking executives are making technology their strategic weapon.

This chapter contains a number of examples of how companies are employing computers and information systems to gain a competitive advantage. Long before any of these competitive advantages became apparent to customers and competitors, corporate executives evaluated the cost and risk of the project and integrated this information into their strategic plans. Strategic plans typically contain general objectives (for example, increase market share) and sometimes specific measurable goals (for example, capture a 20 percent share of the market). The details of implementing these objectives are left up to MIS professionals and functional area personnel.

LEVERAGING INFORMATION SYSTEMS

If corporations had instincts, their first instinct would be to survive. To survive, a company must make a profit. Once profitability is established, the corporate instinct is to do whatever is needed within the bounds of business ethics to continue to improve profitability. Improved profitability can be achieved in many ways. There are literally hundreds of traditional approaches to realizing higher profits: expanding the product line, work force reduction, adjusting pricing, and so on. More and more often, aggressive

A man with a new idea is a Crank, until the idea succeeds.

—— Mark Twain

companies are leveraging information systems to achieve a competitive advantage that ultimately leads to increased profitability (see Figure 4–1).

There is one major difference between improving profitability through traditional approaches (for example, adjusting pricing) and those that involve computer and information systems technologies. The traditional approaches typically involve changes within the context of "business as usual." In contrast, MIS solutions that result in decisive competitive advantages tend to alter the fundamental functionality of a company and, sometimes, the entire industry. Examples of where such changes are taking place are discussed later in this chapter.

Profitability is enhanced by

□ *Increasing sales.* MIS technology can be leveraged to increase sales in a number of ways. It can be used to increase market share, to conduct informative market research, to create new business, to encourage customer loyalty, and to do research and development that results in enhancing and expanding the product line.

□ *Increasing productivity and reducing cost.* Increased productivity and cost reduction go hand in hand. Anything that can be done to reduce costs while retaining or improving operational capabilities has a positive impact on profitability. Having exhausted virtually all the traditional approaches to cost reduction, executives are looking to MIS for more opportunities.

□ *Improving customer service.* All things being equal, customers tend to take their business to the companies that can provide the best service. Management information systems are helping to make great strides in the area of customer service.

□ *Managing resources more effectively.* Every company has the following resources: money, facilities (including materials and equipment),

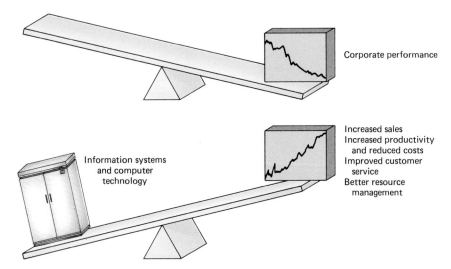

FIGURE 4–1   Leveraging Information Systems and Computer Technology
Information systems and computer technology can be leveraged to achieve a competitive advantage.

Because this real estate company subscribes to an on-line multi-list service, it is enjoying a distinct competitive advantage. Real estate agents relying on traditional manual approaches are unable to offer the level of service made possible by the computer-based system.

Courtesy of International Business Machines

people, and information. However, not every company is making effective use of these resources. Management information systems are the strategic weapons that executives are using to take full advantage of their resources.

Examples of competitive advantages for enhancing profitability are discussed within the context of the foregoing categories. Of course, they are not mutually exclusive (see Figure 4–2). For example, a particular competitive strategy may result in both increased productivity and improved customer service.

FIGURE 4–2   Ways to Leverage MIS to Enhance Profitability
As depicted in the figure, competitive strategies involving MIS are not necessarily mutually exclusive.

LEVERAGING INFORMATION SYSTEMS TO INCREASE SALES

Competitive strategies for increasing sales by leveraging computer and information systems technologies are illustrated in Figure 4–3 and discussed in the following sections.

Increasing Market Share

Even junkyards have gone high tech. Traditionally, dealers in recycled auto parts have been local businesses that catered to customers in the immediate vicinity of the yard. If they did not have what the customer needed, they would call a competitor at the other end of town or in a nearby city. If none of them had the part, the customer would be out of luck.

Today, over 600 "local" auto salvage dealers have banded together in a computer network to create a national market for their products. If a customer asks any of the 600 participating dealers for a water pump for a 1970 Monte Carlo and the dealer does not have one, the salesperson keys in a request that is routed simultaneously to the other 599 dealers. Typically, within minutes the salesperson receives at least one positive response and a price. If more than one dealer responds, the salesperson can select the best deal.

The net effect of this system is to increase each of the participating salvage dealer's share of the recycled auto parts market. Without the system, a dealer is limited to selling what he or she has in stock or to what he or she can find by making a few telephone calls. With the system, the networked salvage dealer has three distinct advantages:

1. The dealer can almost always meet the customer's needs.
2. In effect, there is a national market for everything in the dealer's inventory.
3. The dealer has a distinct competitive advantage over non-networked dealers in the local area because customers will eventually migrate to the dealer with the best record of performance.

Success in the junk business is never having to say "I'm sorry, but we don't have it and can't get it."

Market Research

The most prominent system in the retail sales industry is the *point-of-sale* (*POS*) system. However, not all POS systems are the same. In the most basic systems, the cash-registerlike POS workstation simply records the transaction of the sale and perhaps associates the sale with a particular department. Also, not all POS workstations are linked directly to a centralized computer. In these situations, data are collected off-line and periodically dumped to a centralized mainframe computer system.

The more sophisticated POS systems provide companies with a clear competitive advantage. The POS systems of retailers that use information systems as a strategic weapon are on-line to a centralized computer system. This direct link gives salespersons greater capability to serve the customer and gives market researchers the information they need to develop strategies to maximize sales. These POS systems permit on-line inquiries by salespersons, such as customer credit limit checks, and the inventory status of the

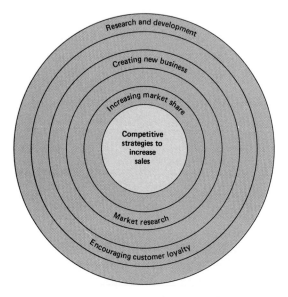

FIGURE 4–3 MIS Strategies for Increasing Sales

item sold is updated immediately. This immediate feedback is valuable input
to market research and analysis. For example, a department store chain
relies on its on-line POS system to identify fast-selling items so that these
items can be reordered before the stock is depleted. This system also
identifies slow-moving items so that management can reduce the price accordingly. Retailers with limited POS capabilities are at a distinct disadvantage.
Companies with the more sophisticated POS capabilities will be able to
restock fast-selling items before their competitors realize that they are out
of stock.

Creating New Business

One way to gain a competitive advantage is to be there first with information
about a product and at timely intervals thereafter. The key to the successful
implementation of this strategy is knowing when to arrive with the information
and when to return with more information. Several manufacturers that specialize in baby products have employed this strategy and used management
information systems to establish a competitive advantage. Management at
these companies knows that each birth expands the market for their products
and represents a new business opportunity. One manufacturer of baby products gives an ample supply of sampler kits to hospitals so that these kits
can be distributed to expectant mothers during the hospital's prenatal orientation sessions. The kits include samples of products and informative literature,
but perhaps the most important component of the package is a return card.
The mother-to-be completes a card that includes critical marketing information, such as name, address, and expected date of birth. The information
on the card is all the company needs to be there first and at timely intervals
thereafter.

The circumstances are perfect for the effective use of a marketing-
oriented MIS. The baby products company enters this information into an
MIS that automatically triggers the delivery of prenatal promotional literature
(coupons) and samples (shampoo) just prior to the expected delivery date.
Thereafter, the company sends the consumer a monthly newsletter that focuses
on the needs and expectations of mother and baby during the coming month.
The newborn newsletter arrives just before the expected date of delivery.
The second newsletter arrives a month later and then every month for the
first year. The company provides a valuable service to potential consumers
of its products while keeping its name and products in the forefront of the
consumer's mind.

A baby's needs are well defined during the first year. The system ensures
that the mother receives samples and coupons just prior to the baby's need
for small, medium, or large diapers. Of course, the same is true of baby
food, toys, and other products.

After the first year, the company can use the system to anticipate the
baby's needs on a quarterly basis. Competing companies must use the more
costly shotgun approach to reach the consumer. The rifle approach, made
possible by a sophisticated MIS, provides the company with a definite competitive advantage.

Encouraging Customer Loyalty

A manufacturer of machine tool parts developed a system to provide better
service to distributors of its products. One of the side benefits of the system

*The more sophisticated point-of-sale (POS) systems do
much more than record sales and generate receipts.
Because this department store chain's POS system is
integrated with the inventory control system, buyers
can obtain up-to-the-minute information that enables
them to react quickly to the buying trends of their
customers.*

Courtesy of International Business Machines

**CORPORATE ATTITUDES
TOWARD THE INFORMATION RESOURCE**

Q. Five years ago I purchased a personal computer for my home and quickly became interested in how I could apply it to my work. Seven years later I routinely use personal computers in my work as a product manager.

I am one of eight product managers in the marketing department, but I am the only one who actively uses computers. During the last few months, there has been a continuous parade of managers, including top management, stopping by to talk with me about how I am applying computer technology to my work.

On numerous occasions my manager has stated that he is proud of my work with computers and that he is very satisfied with my overall job performance. Ironically, he does not encourage the other marketing managers to use available personal computers as a tool in their work.

I have never worked anywhere else, but it is hard for me to believe that our competition's managers would adopt such a laissez-faire attitude toward computers and information. Is this the case?

A. People say that this is the "computer revolution" and that we are entering the "age of information." This is true, but we are doing it more slowly than flashy television advertisements would have us believe.

Information resource management via computers is an attitude that must be nurtured—it doesn't just happen. It is hard to say whether your company is typical, but I would estimate that fewer than 15 percent of the companies in the United States have adopted the attitude that information is valuable and should be treated as a resource. In these companies, managers take every opportunity to encourage their subordinates to use the tools of automation.

is that it can be employed to encourage customer loyalty or, in other words, "lock the customer in." The manufacturer created a computer-based system that would permit distributors to place orders and make inquiries regarding pricing, availability of parts, and delivery dates directly to the manufacturer's computer system. To encourage distributors to use the system, the manufacturer gave each of its distributors a workstation with a direct link to the computer system. Distributors like this capability because they are essentially in direct contact with the supplier when talking with one of their customers. With the system, distributors can give their customers a delivery date within minutes. The same information may take a week or more to obtain from another supplier.

The distributors not only enjoy the convenience of the services available through the system, but they have become comfortable with its use. The net effect of the system is increased sales for the manufacturer and very loyal distributors of its products. Eventually, other competing suppliers will follow suit with similar technological capabilities, but they may be too little, too late.

Research and Development

Clearly, improving a product and product differentiation are proven approaches to increasing sales. Both usually begin with the research and development department. Companies that have been traditionally low tech or mechanical are integrating the functionality of information technology into their products to improve the product or to differentiate the product from that of the competitor. Time and time again, the first company in a given marketplace to do this successfully realizes gains in market share. This has already happened with microwave ovens, automobiles, dishwashers, and myriad other products. The race to "one up" the competition with innovative uses of information technology is never ending. For example, each manufacturer of automobiles is trying to provide the driver and passengers with more information (the value of the information notwithstanding). The following information is available on certain production models: inside and outside temperature, miles per gallon (instant and accumulated), shift indicators, washer water level, and much more. Automobile manufacturers are hoping that they can achieve a competitive advantage with the introduction of even more information, such as a continuous readout of the pressure in all four tires. One automobile manufacturer is developing a computer-based navigation system that uses satellites to obtain a fix on the location of the car. The car's location is noted on a video display of a road map. Prototypes of the system are now being tested—and they work!

LEVERAGING INFORMATION SYSTEMS TO INCREASE PRODUCTIVITY AND REDUCE COSTS

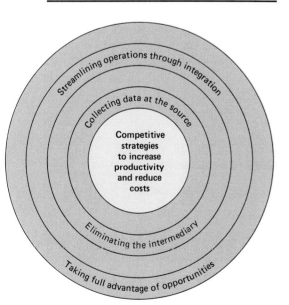

FIGURE 4–4 MIS Strategies for Increasing Productivity and Reducing Costs

Competitive strategies for increasing productivity and reducing costs by leveraging computer and information systems technologies are illustrated in Figure 4–4 and discussed in the following sections.

Collecting Data at the Source

In recent years, health care has become a competitive industry. Overcapacity and the emergence of for-profit hospitals have forced hospital administrators to pursue the competitive advantage aggressively. The best way to do this is to offer better service at a better price. This means improving the quality of health care and increasing productivity. To do this, hospital administrators are turning to information systems for a solution. Mr. R. W. Fleming, chairman of the Department of Administration at the Mayo Clinic, echos this observation. He said, "the medical care field faces some very real needs for increased efficiency and productivity. Computer technology offers a means to deal with those needs. Data transfer, improved clerical efficiency, and improved utilization of physicians' time are all areas in which computer technology may provide substantial benefits."

If a hospital can use management information systems to improve productivity to the point that they can offer services that are priced less than the competition, they will enjoy a competitive advantage. A cost reduction program involving information systems would normally encompass several facets of hospital operation. A study at one hospital revealed that nurses devoted over 40 percent of their time to recording what they do. For example, nurses must log every prescription that they deliver and every time they respond to a patient call. At that hospital a computer-based data collection system was developed and installed that enables data to be captured in machine-readable format (for example, bar codes) from bedside terminals at the point of care. The system not only reduces the time that nurses spend recording data about their activities from 40 percent to 5 percent, but the system also frees up time that can be devoted to direct patient care. In this case, the implementation of an MIS resulted in both cost reduction and improved services.

Throughout this hospital, data are captured as close to the source as possible to help curb the rising cost of health services. In this medical laboratory, data generated by the analytical equipment are fed directly into the computer system that analyzes the data and reports the results. Other related data (patient number) are entered via keyboard.

Courtesy of International Business Machines

Eliminating the Intermediary

One of the best ways to reduce the cost of a product or service is to eliminate the intermediary, usually the person or people who sell the products or services to the consumers. Companies that sell directly to the consumer can offer products or services at a substantially reduced cost. For example, USAA Insurance Company has been able to keep premiums low by handling all transactions (sales and service) over the telephone, thereby eliminating field agents and the cost of commissions. This break with insurance tradition is made possible by judicious applications of information systems. The information that USAA service representatives need to interact effectively with policyholders and potential policyholders is at their fingertips at all times. Agents for competing companies typically do not have access to this kind of information and more often than not must contact the insurance company directly for quotes, approvals, and procedures to follow for various circumstances.

Computer and information technology has enabled USAA, an insurance company, to eliminate the intermediary. Since it does not have a field sales force, it is able to offer insurance to its customers at competitive rates.

USAA

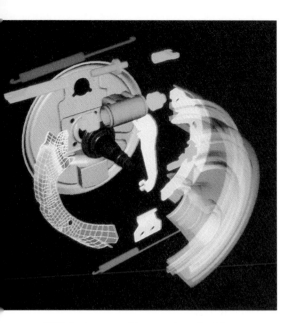

With the prospect of increased productivity, manufacturing companies have been rushing to install more and more applications of computer-aided design (CAD). The photo illustrates how CAD enables engineers to see, test, and modify a design from any viewpoint. The components of this automobile brake assembly are highlighted in different colors.

Courtesy of International Business Machines

You might expect that the impersonal nature the telephone-oriented service offered by USAA would be a concern to policyholders, but this is not the case. *Consumer Reports* consistently ranks USAA at or near the top of all insurance companies in customer satisfaction. USAA's chairman Robert F. McDermott said:

> Today, in the decade of the 1980s, a company's success and survival is directly related to how well it is able to compete in the marketplace on technological grounds. It is imperative that we take full advantage of the opportunities that new and emerging information processing technology will offer us over the next few years. Systems and communications technologies are strategic weapons, not "cost centers."

Streamlining Operations Through Integration

Computer and information technologies are the vehicles by which manufacturing companies are streamlining operations. The integration of computers and manufacturing is called **computer-integrated manufacturing (CIM).** In computer-integrated manufacturing, the computer is used at every stage of the manufacturing process, from the time a part is conceived until it is shipped. The various computer systems are linked together via data communications and feed data to one another. An engineer uses a **computer-aided design (CAD)** system to design the part. The design specifications are produced and stored on a magnetic disk. The specifications, now in an electronic data base, become input to another computer system that generates programs to control the robots and machine tools that handle and make the part. These computer-driven tools are even linked to the company's MIS computers to provide data for order processing, inventory management, shop floor scheduling, and general accounting. Some CIM systems go one step farther and provide a link between the manufacturer and the customer.

Several companies in each industry are working feverishly toward the implementation of total CIM. Few, if any, have achieved total CIM, but many have achieved at least a degree of CIM. CIM is the classic situation that calls for tremendous changes in management attitudes. To create the efficiency in design required of a CIM environment, management in all phases of the company must cooperate. The degree to which CIM can be implemented depends on the level of management cooperation that can be achieved and the company's level of technological sophistication. Each increment of implementation of CIM means substantial improvements in productivity and reduced costs. Companies have been able to reduce inventory levels, reduce the elapsed time between design and production, improve quality control, and eliminate much of the manual data entry that takes place in a typical manufacturing environment. These savings give CIM companies the competitive advantage.

Taking Full Advantage of Opportunities

Perhaps the most price-sensitive market of all is the grocery business. A company can lure customers from a competitor by lowering prices by a few pennies on selected items. Supermarket managers are continually seeking ways to lower prices and reap the competitive advantage. Thousands of supermarkets have installed automated checkout systems to take advantage of the existence of the machine-readable Universal Product Code (UPC)

Supermarket checkout systems are an established cost-saving technology, nevertheless most supermarkets continue to use the traditional manual approach. The automated systems use laser scanners to read the bar code that identifies each item. Price and product descriptions are retrieved from a data base and recorded on the sales slip.

Courtesy of International Business Machines Corporation

that is imprinted on each item. The automated checkout systems not only speed the checkout process, but they save money that can be passed on to customers in the form of lower prices. Supermarkets experience gains in checker productivity from 20 percent to 50 percent. Besides the gains in checker productivity, the system electronically tallies purchases, speeds cash flow, updates the inventory, and alerts store personnel to bad checks. Even though thousands of automated checkout systems have been installed, five times as many supermarkets do not have them. These supermarkets are at a disadvantage because their operating costs are higher, their checkout process is slower, and management is unable to monitor inventory levels on a timely basis.

Within a few years, all supermarkets will have automated checkout systems—and what then? Some supermarkets are not waiting. They are seeking new competitive strategies involving information systems. Several supermarkets have installed workstations in the stores so that customers can make inquiries about the location of an item. Other stores give each customer a personalized shopping list and coupons based on the customer's shopping history. These strategies focus on improving customer service. The next section presents other strategies that are designed to emphasize customer service.

LEVERAGING INFORMATION SYSTEMS TO IMPROVE CUSTOMER SERVICE

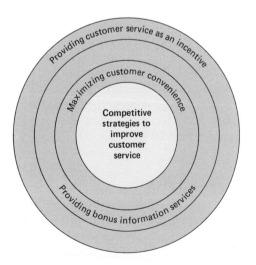

FIGURE 4–5 MIS Strategies for Improving Customer Service

Competitive strategies for improving customer service by leveraging computer and information systems technologies are illustrated in Figure 4–5 and discussed in the following sections.

Maximizing Customer Convenience

Financial institutions, especially banks, have been among the most progressive users of MIS. Deregulation of the banking industry has sent bank executives scurrying for strategic advantages. In addition to using MIS for data processing and the generation of information, banks are also using it to gain the competitive advantage in the area of customer service, specifically customer convenience. The race to provide customers with the most convenient banking began in the 1977 in New York City with the implementation of the first user-friendly **automatic teller machines (ATMs)**. Citibank reaped the benefits of being first. Of course, during the past decade, other banks implemented their own ATMs, but not before Citibank almost tripled its market share. During the 1980s this scenario has been replayed in every multibank city in the country; that is, the first bank to offer the convenience of ATMs increased its market share. Of course, ATMs provide more than a customer convenience. An ATM transaction costs the bank less than half that of a transaction made with a human bank teller!

Today, most banks have 24-hour ATMs, thereby negating any competitive advantage that one bank might have over another. However, in an attempt to regain the advantage, some banks are cooperating to provide an extra measure of customer convenience. Recognizing that our society is becoming increasingly mobile, cooperating banks are linking their computers so that customers can complete banking transactions at the ATMs of participating banks in various locations throughout the country. This competitive advantage

The banking industry would prefer that its customers use ATMs for banking transactions rather than tellers. This bank gives customers who come in the bank the option of selecting a teller or an ATM. The average ATM transaction takes less time, but most importantly, it costs less than half that of a teller transaction. The more that customers use ATMS, the more that banks can reduce the cost of their services.

Courtesy of International Business Machines Corporation

may be short lived because eventually all banks will be part of an ATM network.

The saga of making banking more convenient is being carried one step farther. If 50 ATMs are good, then 100 must be better. To regain the competitive advantage, banks are making more ATMs available to customers in grocery stores, gambling casinos, or anywhere the customer might need some extra cash. At present, the more prolific banks have the competitive advantage, but not for long.

The next level of banking convenience is enabling the customer to do his or her banking at home. Some banks are hoping to gain the competitive advantage by offering *home banking* systems. Subscribers to a home banking service use their personal computers as workstations to pay bills, to transfer funds, and to make inquiries about the status of their accounts. Some systems also provide subscribers with other services, such as "electronic" shopping, electronic mail, and up-to-the-minute stock market quotations.

Information technology has become such a strategic weapon in the banking industry that second-tier banks are merging to be able to justify expensive technological solutions to competitive situations. Unfortunately, the technological revolution in banking may be the swan song for small nonaffiliated banks.

Providing Bonus Information Services

The Thrift chain of pharmacies is using information systems as a strategic weapon. The weapon is a potential life-saving information service that Thrift provides free of charge. Each store has a workstation that is connected to a central computer in Pittsburgh, Pennsylvania. When a customer asks a pharmacist to fill one or more prescriptions, the pharmacist enters the name of the drug or drugs prescribed and the patient's name (see Figure 4–6). If the customer does not have a record on file, the customer is asked to fill out a customer profile that includes such information as address, drugs that cause allergic reactions, and other pertinent information. The system accesses the patient's record and checks other drugs that the patient is presently taking. The possible drug interactions of the prescribed drug(s) and

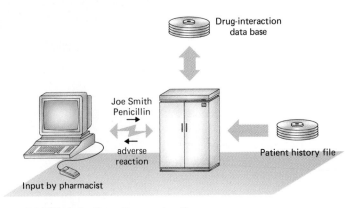

FIGURE 4–6 Drug-Interaction System
Drugs currently being administered to Joe Smith are matched against penicillin and the drug-interaction data base to check for a possible adverse reaction.

the drugs currently being taken are checked against the drug-interaction data base and potentially hazardous interactions are identified. This system minimizes the possibility of an adverse drug interaction and a potentially fatal accident. If the system flags an interaction that could be severe, the customer is warned and the physician(s) involved is notified. The system also warns customers if a prescription contains a drug that may cause an allergic reaction.

A drug-interaction system helps physicians and pharmacists prepare and administer the proper drug to a patient. Literally thousands of drugs can be prescribed by an attending physician, and a mistake in selecting drug pairs could cause an adverse chemical reaction that might be serious, even fatal. Thrift has demonstrated that service in the form of information can be a strategic weapon against the competition.

Providing Customer Services as an Incentive

In the preceding example, a drugstore chain achieved a competitive advantage by offering its customers valuable information services. Let's take one step back in the economic chain and view the drug distributors as the entrepreneurs and the druggists as the customers. Several players in the highly competitive drug distribution business are providing druggists with a variety of information services as incentives to do business with them. The fundamental technology being exploited by aggressive drug distributors is **electronic data interchange** or **EDI**.

ELECTRONIC DATA INTERCHANGE EDI is using computers and data communications to transmit data electronically between companies. For example, invoices, orders, and many other intercompany transactions, including the dissemination of information, can be transmitted from the computer of one company to the computer of another. For example, Figure 4–7 contrasts the traditional interaction between a customer and supplier company with interactions via EDI. EDI is a strategic advantage that some companies have over their competitors. It reduces paper processing costs and delays, it reduces errors and corrections costs, it minimizes receivables and inventory disputes, and it improves relations between trading partners.

No EDI, no business.

——— *Edward E. Lucente*

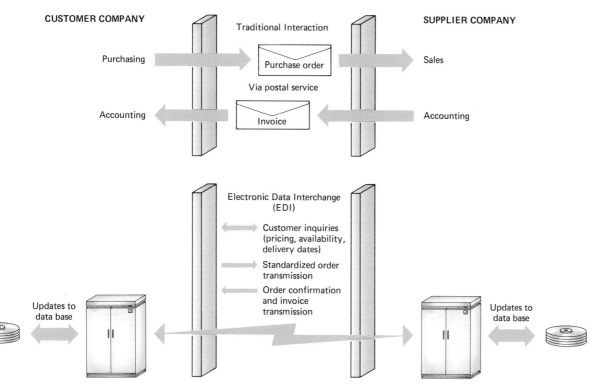

FIGURE 4–7 Interactions Between Customer and Supplier
*In the figure, the traditional interaction between a customer company and a supplier company
is contrasted with similar interactions via electronic data interchange.*

Just a few years ago, the lack of an industry standard for electronic data interchange was a formidable hurdle that was slowing the growth of EDI. Recognizing that EDI was going nowhere without a standard, industry leaders cooperated with the American National Standards Institute (ANSI) to develop a cross-industry, cross-functional standard that would enable trading partners to talk to one another via data communications. The standard, called **X.12**, describes communications protocols (see Chapter 8, "Connectivity and Data Communications") and provides standards for 20 (eventually to be 60) transaction sets, such as purchase orders and invoices. The standard has been the impetus behind the explosion of EDI during the past few years.

Executives are no longer debating whether or not to implement EDI; they are more concerned about the speed at which it can be implemented in their companies. They have essentially two choices. They can elect to create the hardware- and software-based EDI system in-house, or they can use a third-party provider of EDI services. By far the most expeditious way to take advantage of EDI is to go with a third-party provider. A third party provider is an intermediary who helps to facilitate EDI between trading partners who have incompatible hardware and software. Although in-house development of EDI capabilities may take longer, the resultant system does not involve the expense of an intermediary.

EDI IN THE WHOLESALE DRUG DISTRIBUTION INDUSTRY   EDI has altered the basic constructs of the wholesale drug distribution industry and it is likely to do the same with other industries as well. In the drug industry, it is a win-win situation. *Strategic alliances* involving EDI ultimately benefit all parties involved.

Traditionally, druggists at over 50,000 drugstores devote many hours each week to taking inventory and creating handwritten lists of the items they need to restock the inventory. Druggists who have computer systems usually enter order data into their own local system. The system prints the purchase orders, often in triplicate, and the orders are sent by mail to one or more wholesale distributors. It is not unusual for a single order to contain hundreds, even thousands, of items. When the wholesaler receives the hard-copy order, key entry operators enter the orders to their computer system. The trend today is for the drug wholesalers to provide EDI capabilities to their customers as an incentive to do business with them. Those who provide this capability are realizing a competitive advantage and substantial increases in market share. Those who do not provide EDI capabilities are struggling or going out of business.

Druggists use distributor-supplied hand-held bar code scanners to expedite the order entry process. The only data keyed in by the druggist is the quantity. Order data are loaded from the portable data entry device directly to the druggist's computer system, and an electronic order is transmitted from the retailer to the distributor via data communications. This approach eliminates the need for hard-copy orders and redundant key data entry.

Besides expediting the order entry process, the wholesaler provides the druggist with other information-based incentives as well. For example, druggists have only to ask for sales reports by department and product. Also, the products are even shipped with price labels that have the customer-designated profit margin included. In an ongoing effort to provide the best customer incentives and gain the competitive advantage, drug wholesalers are continuing to up the ante. One distributor provides computer-generated suggestions for the most effective visual presentation of products. Another processes insurance forms and provides records needed for the preparation of income tax returns.

This druggist has a direct link to the distributor's central computer system via EDI. Using his workstation, he can request up-to-the-minute pricing information and enter orders. Such systems benefit both the customer and the supplier.

Photo courtesy of Hewlett-Packard Company

Let's take one more step back in the economic chain (from the drug distributor) to the manufacturer of the drugs. Of course, drug manufacturers would prefer to sell directly to the druggists, thereby eliminating the intermediary or the wholesale distributor. To do this, however, they must be either very aggressive in pricing or provide information services commensurate with those offered by the distributors. Today, with their computer-based competitive advantage, drug wholesalers distribute more than two-thirds of all pharmaceuticals, considerably more than a decade ago.

LEVERAGING INFORMATION SYSTEMS FOR BETTER RESOURCE MANAGEMENT

Competitive strategies for improving the effectiveness of resource management by leveraging computer and information systems technologies are illustrated in Figure 4–8 and discussed in the following sections.

The Money Resource

The three fundamental maxims of money management are

1. Collect money owed as soon as possible.
2. Pay invoices as close to the due date as possible.
3. Invest money on hand.

The premise behind this trilogy of maxims is to optimize the company's cash flow; that is, keep the pot of money available for investment as large as possible at any give point in time. The net effect of doing so is increased income and possibly a competitive advantage. Of course, the solution to optimizing cash flows lies in the judicious use of information systems.

COLLECT MONEY OWED AS SOON AS POSSIBLE   Smart retailers are integrating their point-of-sale systems with **electronic funds transfer** (**EFT**) systems so that what is now a *credit* transaction will be a *cash transfer* transaction. That is, when a customer purchases an item, the amount of the sale is debited, via EFT, from the customer's checking account in a bank and credited to the account of the retail store in that same bank. The transaction takes place in real time. No further funds transfer is needed. By using EFT to make the payment, the cost of postage, credit hassles, paper processing, bad checks, and the float (the cost of not being able to use the amount of the purchase for up to two months) are eliminated. All things considered, the retailer's cost for an EFT payment transaction is about 20 percent of one that involves some form of paper processing. Also, from a customer's perspective, the convenience of the EFT transaction more than offsets the loss of the benefits derived from the float.

PAY INVOICES AS CLOSE TO THE DUE DATE AS POSSIBLE   Just as EFT can provide an advantage for the creditor, it can also provide an advantage for the debtor. In the past, companies have waited until the due date before making payment for invoices. Although the strategy still holds, the advent of intercompany networking through EDI and EFT have prompted vendors to negotiate not

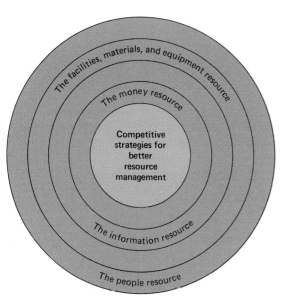

FIGURE 4–8   MIS Strategies for Better Resource Management

There is no substitute for talent. Industry and all the virtues are of no avail.

—— *Aldous L. Huxley*

only the price, but the exact date on which payment will be made. In this way, both debtor and creditor reap the benefits of the paperless transaction. The company that is not using EDI and its capability to pay bills on the due date as leverage for price negotiations is losing the competitive advantage to those who can.

INVEST MONEY ON HAND   The more uncertain a company's financial personnel are about a company's cash flow, the more money they tend to keep on hand (liquid funds). A real-time cash management system can increase a company's revenue by providing executives with timely information concerning the exact amount of money owed, the amount of money that is due and when it will be received, and how much money is on hand. With this information, a company's investment strategist can use decision support systems in combination with direct computer links to brokers and banks to maximize the amount of money available for investments.

The Information Resource

Some consumer goods companies (toothpaste, cookies, shampoo, and so on) focus all their marketing efforts on the front end of a sales effort—that is, on on-site sales calls and promotional campaigns aimed at retailers and on advertising campaigns aimed at consumers. After completing the front-end effort, consumer goods companies wait a few months, gather sales data, and evaluate the effectiveness of their advertising dollar. In consumer goods industries, sales are directly proportional to the amount of money spent on advertising. Of course, there is a point at which additional expenditures have an adverse effect on the bottom line. Advertising expenses can be as much as 25 percent of revenues, so knowing exactly how much to spend and where to spend it can give a company a tremendous advantage. Recognizing the enormous outlay required for advertising, some consumer goods companies seek the competitive advantage by having the best market information. These companies are equally interested in the front end, the middle, and the back end of a sales effort because they know that follow-up and information systems can double the effectiveness of monies spent on sales campaigns.

Aggressive consumer goods companies have mechanisms in place that enable them to track the effectiveness of their marketing campaigns in different regions of the country on a daily basis. Sophisticated models tap demographic data, historical sales data, and current sales data to provide marketing managers with information that will help them make decisions about how to fine tune the campaign to maximize advertising effectiveness. For example, output from the model might indicate that newspaper advertisements are more effective in New England than television commercials. The model might indicate that the reverse is true of the Southeast. Also, the models often highlight untapped potential in the marketplace.

Such systems enable companies to record and track the buying habits of regions, states, cities, and for some products, even individuals. These systems also monitor how responsive regions, states, and so on are to marketing campaigns. The use of marketing models has enabled several consumer goods companies to reduce advertising expenditures by as much as 20 percent while improving the overall effectiveness of advertising campaigns.

A product manager for a soft-drink company relies on an information system to monitor the success of marketing campaigns. The system enables the company to make the most effective use of its advertising dollars.

More often than not, the better informed marketing staff gets the business. In the past, a company would accept a certain number of bad decisions as the price of doing business because the competition was making an equal number of bad decisions. Today, the company that is not trying to eliminate or at least minimize bad decisions is in danger of losing market share and the competitive advantage. To gain the advantage, companies must manage information carefully and make the most effective use of all forms of decision support systems.

The Facilities, Materials, and Equipment Resources

Too often, companies take their facilities, material (inventory), and equipment resources for granted. Hospitals and airlines have found that attention to these resources can yield the competitive advantage.

PROVIDING BETTER SERVICE WHILE INCREASING REVENUE   Many hospitals are operating in the red. To get back in the black, hospitals are implementing procedures to control costs better. For the first time, they are implementing systems that optimize the use of their facilities' resource while maximizing revenue. Several hospitals have implemented a physician's accounting system to give them the competitive advantage. The system provides hospital administrators with information about how each physician is using hospital facilities. For example, such systems identify physicians who tend to admit patients who could just as well be treated as outpatients. These patients typically generate less revenue for the hospital and take up a bed that could best be used by a seriously ill patient. Hospital administrators council these physicians and remind them that an inordinate number of their patients were admitted unnecessarily. Increased revenue and the competitive advantage are side benefits of a physician's accounting system. The real benefit is being able to accommodate a greater number of patients who have a medical need to be admitted to the hospital.

MAKING THE MOST OF HARDWARE AND SOFTWARE   Arguably the most extensive management information systems are the airline reservation systems that airline and travel agents use to make and revise passenger reservations. Agents update a centralized data base the moment a seat on any flight is filled or becomes available. Of course, airline reservations systems, which were first mentioned in Chapter 2, "The MIS and Decision Support Systems," provide a plethora of information for management.

In the mid-1970s, executives at American Airlines and United Airlines thought that they could parlay their expertise in on-line information systems into a strategy that would eventually yield a significant competitive advantage. Each airline needed to develop an information system that would permit airline and travel agents to make reservations for scheduled flights with their respective airlines. Upon further study, both airlines concluded that their proposed systems could just as well be designed to permit agents to make reservations for other airlines as well. American Airlines completed its Sabre System first in 1976. Today, the Sabre System involves more than 100,000 workstations and printers and can process 1,450 transactions per second. The Apollo System of United Airlines was installed five months later. Today American and United not only make money on passenger fares, but they also use their computer and information systems to contribute to profits. Each time a travel agent uses the Sabre or the Apollo system to make a reservation for a competing airline, the travel agent is charged a certain amount. Moreover, agencies that subscribe to an airline reservation service tend to give substantially more business to airlines associated with that service.

The Sabre and Apollo systems are examples of the strategic use of MIS, and they are are also a good example of competitive strategies run amok. Other airlines had no choice but to cooperate with American and United. Consumers and competing airlines accused American and United of using their reservations systems for consumer deception and unfair competition. Having complete control over the systems, naturally American and United listed their flights first. This and other biases built into early versions of the systems prompted Congress to become critical of their unfair advantage. Shortly thereafter, most biases were eliminated, but American and United still retain the competitive advantage by continuing to charge agents for making reservations with competing airlines.

By being first, the Sabre and Apollo systems helped American Airlines and United Airlines to garner the lion's share of the market, 36 percent and 26 percent, respectively. However, three other airlines have similar systems. Texas Air (Eastern, Continental, and other airlines) has System One with 15 percent of the market, TWA and Northwest have PARS Service Partnership with 13 percent of the market, and Delta Airlines has Datas II with 10 percent of the market. Because these airlines are reacting to a competitor's innovative competitive strategy, they face an uphill battle. However, the newcomers know that agencies will opt for the service that provides the best features and price/performance. To be the best, each service is trying to

With the competitive advantages afforded by airline reservations systems diminishing, airlines are adopting other technology-based strategies. For example, several airlines have installed computer-based luggage handling systems. When you travel by air and check your luggage through to your destination, a three-character destination tag (e.g., LAX is Los Angeles, OKC is Oklahoma City) is attached to each piece of luggage. At some airports, this coded data element (destination) is read by an optical scanner and your luggage is automatically routed, via conveyor, to the appropriate pickup station.

squeeze every ounce of sophistication it can out of available computer and information technologies.

The People Resource

The most valuable resource that any company has is its people. Time and time again, education has proven to be one of the most cost-effective investments that a company can make. There are many sources of education: on-the-job (OJT) training, college courses, seminars, professional conferences, and independent study, to mention a few. Some companies feel that the judicious use of **computer-based training** (**CBT**) has enabled them to be more effective in their use of people resources, the net result of which has been a competitive advantage. CBT, which has added a new dimension to education, has many benefits:

□ A CBT system can give "individual" attention to a student.

□ CBT is interactive and is quick to respond to a student's input.

□ CBT is capable of multidimensional communication (sound, print, graphics, and color).

□ CBT can demonstrate and present material, provide opportunities for drill and practice, test for understanding of the material, evaluate the test results, and provide follow-up instruction based on test results.

□ CBT systems can interact with students to enhance the learning process. Through interactive computer graphics, a CBT system can demonstrate certain concepts more effectively than can books, manuals, or even teachers.

□ CBT is self-paced so that the student controls the speed of learning.

□ CBT can be used for drill and practice as well as training.

Educational software packages have been developed that reinforce and complement virtually every business-related topic, from word processing to project management. Other approaches to employee education are more expensive and are not as versatile. Companies using CBT are saving money and getting the most out of their people. This, they feel, gives them a slight competitive edge.

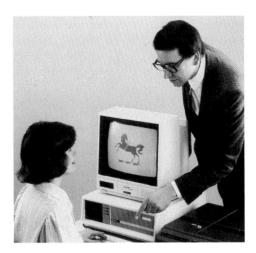

Lloyd Bank, a financial institution in Britain, employs an interactive videodisc system to train its employees in teller and customer service techniques. Lloyds notes the systems has reduced training time by as much as 30 percent for its 48,000 employees in some 1,500 branches. Each program begins with a display of the bank's logo.

Philips and DuPont Optical Company

Ours is the age which is proud of machines that think, and suspicious of men who try to.

———— *H. Mumford Jones*

CHASING A SPEEDING BULLET

The Sabre System gave American Airlines a clear competitive advantage. The advantage lasted five months, until United Airlines introduced the Apollo System to the marketplace. Today, TWA, Delta, and Eastern have similar systems. Using information systems as a competitive strategy has proven successful for American and United, but it is inevitable that the competing companies will implement a technological innovation that will eventually negate any advantage. The race to win the competitive advantage with information systems is ongoing, but it is like chasing a speeding bullet. If one company gets a jump on the competition, you can bet that the competition is aggressively pursuing MIS strategies that will improve their position in the marketplace.

Relatively seldom does a company introduce a system like Sabre or Apollo that changes the basic constructs of an industry. In practice, most of the competitive strategies involve a combination of innovative and tried-and-proven MIS-related solutions, the accumulation of which may give companies a competitive advantage.

CHAPTER HIGHLIGHTS

■ Corporate America is beginning to use computers and information systems to improve profitability and achieve a competitive advantage.

■ Because MIS solutions are often expensive and risky and cause change, not all companies are striving to implement MIS-based competitive advantages.

■ Managers often equate information with power. Consequently, a few managers are reluctant to share critical information, even with those who have a need to know. This attitude runs counter to the concept of a good MIS.

■ Computer and information systems technologies are now strategic weapons. Companies are gaining the competitive advantage by making MIS an integral part of the corporate strategic planning process.

■ Within a company, profitability is enhanced by increasing sales, increasing productivity and reducing cost, improving customer service, and managing resources more effectively. Companies are applying MIS solutions in each of these areas.

■ Dealers in recycled auto parts have leveraged MIS technology to increase their market share. To do this, over 600 "local" auto salvage dealers have banded together in a computer network to create a national market for their products.

■ Retailers with the more sophisticated point-of-sale systems have a clear competitive advantage in the area of market research. With all POS terminals having a direct link to the centralized data base, market researchers have access to the up-to-the-minute information they need to develop strategies that can maximize sales.

■ Management information systems can be used to create new business. One way to create new business and gain a competitive advantage is to be there first with information about a product and at timely intervals thereafter. Several manufacturers that specialize in baby products have created information systems that employ this strategy.

■ One manufacturer of machine tool parts achieved a competitive advantage by effectively locking its customers into its system. It did this by giving wholesale distributors direct access to an MIS with so many convenient features that the distributors would not consider shifting their business to a competing manufacturer.

■ Companies are using computer technology to improve their products and to differentiate their products from those of competitors, both proven approaches to increasing sales.

■ At one hospital a computer-based data collection system was developed and installed that enables data to be captured in machine-readable format from bedside terminals. By collecting data at the point of care, the hospital has achieved a competitive advantage by reducing cost while offering improved services.

■ The USAA Insurance Company has employed computers and information systems to eliminate field agents and the cost of commissions, while retaining a very high level of customer satisfaction. By eliminating the intermediary, the company can offer insurance at a reduced cost and thereby enjoy a competitive advantage.

■ Companies employing the concepts of computer-integrated manufacturing or CIM have been able to reduce inventory levels, reduce the elapsed time between design and production, improve quality control, and eliminate much of the manual data entry that takes place in a typical manufacturing environment. By using CIM to streamline product development and production, these companies have achieved a competitive advantage.

■ Supermarkets are using automated checkout systems to speed the checkout process and offer products at a lower price. These systems enable supermarkets to take full advantage of the automation opportunities afforded by the availability of the UPC that is imprinted on all packaged grocery items.

■ Since the introduction of the first automatic teller machine (ATM), banks have been seeking the technology-based competitive advantage by offering customers more and more convenience in banking. First, banks began to create regional and national networks of ATMs. Then, banks began to make ATMs even more accessible to their customers. Recently, some banks are providing home banking services for customers with personal computers.

■ The Thrift chain of pharmacies is enjoying a competitive advantage because it provides a potential life-saving information service to its customers. Because of their drug-interaction system, Thrift customers can be reasonably assured that they will not be given drugs that will have an adverse interaction.

■ Electronic data interchange or EDI is using computers and data communications to transmit data electronically between companies. For example, invoices, orders, and many other intercompany transactions, including the dissemination of information, can be transmitted from the computer of one company to the computer of another. The American National Standards Institute developed the X12 communications protocol standard that would enable trading partners to talk to one another via data communications. The existence of the standard has resulted in the rapid growth of EDI during the past few years.

■ The strategic alliances established between the wholesale drug distribution industry and drug retailers via EDI has altered the basic constructs of the industry. The trend today is for the drug wholesalers to provide EDI capabilities to their customers as an incentive to do business with them. Those who provide this capability are realizing a competitive advantage and substantial increases in market share.

■ Smart retailers are integrating their point-of-sale systems with electronic funds transfer systems so that what is now a credit transaction will be a cash transfer transaction. By using EFT to make the payment, the cost of postage, credit hassles, paper processing, bad checks, and the float are eliminated. This MIS strategy makes a positive contribution to profitability.

■ A real-time cash management system can increase a company's revenue by providing executives with timely information concerning the exact amount of money owed, the amount of money that is due and when it will be received, and how much money is on hand.

■ Some companies achieve the competitive advantage by making better use of the information resource. Aggressive consumer goods companies have mechanisms in place that enable them to track the effectiveness of their marketing campaigns in different regions of the country on a daily basis. Sophisticated models provide marketing managers with information that will help them make decisions about how to fine tune the campaign to maximize advertising effectiveness.

■ Hospitals are implementing systems that optimize the use of their facilities' resource while maximizing revenue. Several hospitals have implemented a physician's accounting system. The system provides hospital administrators with information that enables them to make more effective use of patient rooms.

■ The Sabre System of American Airlines and the Apollo System of United Airlines are vivid examples of how a company can create a significant competitive advantage through judicious use of its hardware and software resources. Although other airlines offer similar systems to travel agents, American and United still enjoy the advantage that they created over a decade ago.

■ Computer-based training has enabled some companies to be more effective in their use of people resources, the net result of which has been a competitive advantage.

■ Using information systems as a competitive strategy has proven successful for many companies, but it is inevitable that the competing companies will implement a technological innovation that will eventually negate any advantage. This aggressiveness makes the race to win the competitive advantage with information systems an ongoing endeavor.

IMPORTANT TERMS

automatic teller machines (ATMs)

computer-aided design (CAD)

computer-based training (CBT)

computer-integrated manufacturing (CIM)

electronic data interchange (EDI)

electronic funds transfer (EFT)

home banking

point of sale (POS)

strategic alliances

X.12

REVIEW EXERCISES

1. If MIS solutions are so clearly the reasons that many companies are enjoying a competitive advantage, why haven't all companies made MIS a top priority?

2. List four ways that information systems can be leveraged to increase productivity and reduce cost.

3. What is meant when someone says that a company is on the bleeding edge of technology?

4. In what year did Citibank in New York City implement the first user-friendly automatic teller machines?

5. Why does an executive attitude that emphasizes the importance of the quarterly bottom line run against the grain of information systems solutions?

6. List five ways that information systems can be leveraged to increase sales.

7. What is the major difference between improving profitability through traditional approaches and through those that involve computer and information systems technologies?

8. Briefly describe one of the ways that information systems can be leveraged for better resource management.

9. What is the name of the ANSI standard for EDI data communications?

10. Name five airline reservations systems. Which two have over 60 percent of the market for reservations systems?

11. List three ways that information systems can be leveraged to improve customer service.

12. What is the function of a third-party provider of EDI services?

13. List three advantages of computer-based training.

14. Briefly describe the CIM concept.

15. What machine-readable code provides the basis for automated checkout systems in supermarkets?

16. What term is used to describe the linking of computers of different companies?

DISCUSSION QUESTIONS

1. Describe MIS strategies that companies in the construction industry could employ to achieve a competitive advantage.

2. Describe MIS strategies that any specific federal agency or body (FBI, CIA, the Senate, IRS, White House, and so on) could employ to reduce the burden on the taxpayer and/or provide better service.

3. Describe MIS strategies that companies in the frozen foods industry could employ to achieve a competitive advantage.

4. Banks are offering their customers money and prizes just to try automatic teller machines, yet only a handful of banks have more than 30 percent of their customer base using ATMs. Why are bankers so anxious for their customers to use ATMs and why are so many people avoiding them?

5. Describe MIS strategies that companies in the software industry could employ to achieve a competitive advantage.

6. Describe MIS strategies that universities could employ to achieve a competitive advantage in their efforts to attract the better students.

7. A company retained a computer consultant to determine if it should computerize certain aspects of corporate operation. The consultant's response was, "You can't afford not to." What is the implication of the consultant's assessment?

8. Why do you suppose truckers are resisting the implementation of satellite monitoring systems when they know that such a system will reduce costs and provide management with better control information?

9. Describe MIS strategies that companies in the electricity utilities industry could employ to achieve a competitive advantage.

10. Describe a routine periodic report that is generated each day by a point-of-sale system in a department store chain. Each week. Each month. Each year.

11. Department stores use hand-held wand scanners to interpret the bar codes imprinted on the price tags of the merchandise. Why don't they use slot scanners as supermarkets do?

12. What type of customer/supplier relationship would reap the greatest benefits from EDI?

13. "Automate, migrate, or evaporate." Discuss this statement from the points of view of manufacturing management and of labor.

14. Why do so many executives equate information with power?

15. The insurance company featured in the chapter has no field insurance agents, yet it is ranked consistently at or near the the top of all insurance companies in customer satisfaction. How can this be?

16. During the 1950s, 1960s, and even the 1970s, research and development, finance, and marketing dominated thinking in the area of corporate strategic planning. Only recently has top management begun to integrate MIS in the corporate strategic planning process. Why did they wait for so long?

17. Describe MIS strategies that companies in the motion picture industry could employ to achieve a competitive advantage.

18. In a cooperative effort, 600 dealers in recycled auto parts have implemented a computer network that has given the participants in the network a distinct advantage over their local competitors. What other industry could benefit from a similar network?

19. Discuss the potential relationship between EDI and EFT. Between POS and EFT.

20. Realistically speaking, can a company "lock a customer in" to its product line by offering them a variety of customer-oriented information services, such as on-line inquiry, periodic reports, EDI, and so on? Justify your response.

21. Describe MIS strategies that companies in the book publishing industry could employ to achieve a competitive advantage.

22. The hospital data collection system that was discussed in the chapter reduced the time that nurses spend recording data about their activities from 40 percent to 5 percent. Assuming that the number of nurses on staff remained the same after system implementation, how do you think the cost of the system was justified?

APPLICATION CASE STUDY CASE 4–1
Gaining the Competitive Advantage

The Situation

Kincaid's Service Station, an independent affiliate of Circle Oil Company, sells gasoline at self-service and full-service pumps and performs a wide range of automobile repairs and services. Other products sold include tires, batteries, and oil, to mention a few. As an affiliate, all products that are sold directly to customers must be purchased from Circle. However, parts that are installed while performing repairs can be purchased from any supplier. Bruce Kincaid, the owner, accepts cash, personal checks (only from customers he knows), and several popular credit cards as payment for products and services. Customers may also use the Circle credit card.

Until recently, Circle credit card purchases were processed in the following manner.

1. The customer presents the credit card to the attendant, who places a sales slip and the card into an imprinting machine. The amount to be charged is entered on the machine by adjusting the sales levers. The attendant moves a bar across the sales slip, thus imprinting the customer's name, the customer's account number, and the amount on the slip. At the same time, the machine also imprints the name and number of the service station on the sales slip. Details regarding the transaction (for example, the type of gasoline and the number of gallons sold) are written on the sales slip. If the amount to be charged exceeds Circle's limit for a single transaction, the attendant must telephone Circle's operations center to receive approval for the charge. The customer signs the sales slip and the attendant compares the signature on the slip to the signature on the card. If they correspond, a copy of the sales slip is given to the customer.

2. Periodically, usually once a week, Bruce Kincaid sends the accumulation of sales slips to Circle's operations center. At the center, the OCR (optical character recognition) documents are scanned, and the data are entered to the system. For each sales slip, a customer's account is updated to reflect the date and amount of the transaction. The Kincaid account is updated to reflect the date and amount of each transaction.

3. The operations center:

   a. Sends a monthly statement to customers who have an outstanding balance.

   b. Sends a monthly statement to Kincaid's along with a check for the total of all Circle credit purchases (less a nominal service charge) during the preceding month.

This procedure is currently being used by most of the major oil companies.

Recently, Circle required its retail dealers to convert to an on-line system. This new system operates in the following manner.

1. The customer presents the credit card to an attendant, who places the card into a terminal. The terminal reads the magnetic stripe on the back of the card. If the sale was fuel, the attendant keys in the pump number and the sale amount is retrieved from the automated metering system. If the sale was for anything except fuel, the attendant keys in only the amount of the purchase. There are no item numbers, and no sales analysis is performed. The customer's account number and the amount of the purchase are transmitted directly to a computer system in Circle's operations center. The terminal displays one of two responses:

   a. *Transaction approved*: A sales slip containing the details of the transaction is generated at the terminal. The customer signs the sales slip and is given a copy. The attendant files the station's copy of the sales slip. The on-line transaction debits the customer's account and credits the Kincaid account.

   b. *Transaction not approved*: The attendant follows standard procedures, depending on the reason for the rejection.

2. The operations center:

   a. Sends a monthly statement to customers who have an outstanding balance.

   b. Sends a monthly statement to Kincaid's along with a check for the total of all Circle credit purchases (less a nominal service charge) during the preceding month.

The Assignment

1. Describe shortcomings of the old Circle credit card system.

2. Describe the competitive advantages enjoyed by Kincaid's Service Station as a result of the implementation of the new on-line system in each of these strategic areas: increased sales, increased productivity and reduced costs, improved customer service, and better resource management. Do the same for Circle Oil Company.

3. Based on your response to question 2, why might other service stations want to become affiliates of Circle?

4. Contrast the former and current systems from the perspective of the retail customer. List the advantages and disadvantages of the new system for the retail credit card customer.

5. List the problems with the old system (see question 1) that are not corrected by the new system. Suggest solutions to correct these problems.

6. Assume that the time of day when a transaction is sent to the operations center can be captured and made a part of the transaction record. Suggest ways in which this additional information can be of competitive value to Kincaid's Service Station. To Circle Oil Company.

7. What information could you offer a trucking company as an incentive to purchase fuel only from Circle affiliate stations?

APPLICATION CASE STUDY 4–2
Leveraging Information Systems

The Situation

Que Realty is a progressive real estate operation. The company has already implemented an expert system to match clients with houses (see Application Case Study 3-1) and an on-line listing system with a natural language interface (see Application Case Study 3-2). These two systems have considerably enhanced individual and organizational productivity and income. Joan Magee, Que's owner, is so impressed with the results of these two systems that she has again hired a consultant, this time with an open-ended assignment: "Analyze our operations and find ways to make us more productive!"

The consultant begins by interviewing Joan Magee, other administrators, the senior agent David Meissner, and a representative sample of agents. Their common complaint is that they want to do things *now* and they want to be able to do them *faster*. Commonly mentioned tasks include:

☐ Calculating monthly payments for mortgages and taxes.

☐ Entering a new listing into the data base.

☐ Preparing sales agreements.

☐ Preparing closing papers.

☐ Making inquiries into the listing data base when not in the office.

☐ Getting copies of sales agreements or other documents from another Que office.

Although not all the tasks described by the staff can be revolutionized by the application of high technology, some of them can be, and most can be performed more efficiently or in a more timely manner.

The Assignment

Put yourself in the role of the consultant as you complete the following assignment.

1. Make a list of commercially available state-of-the-art technology, both hardware and software, that you feel might be applicable to the situation. Use "A Short Course in Computer Concepts" following Chapter 17 as a starting point. In your list of hardware, include lap computers and facsimile equipment.

2. Apply the knowledge from the list developed in question 1 to the specific tasks. For each task:

   a. Describe the task.

   b. Give a brief brief description of an improved method of accomplishing the task.

   c. Describe the effect on productivity or other aspects of competitiveness mentioned in the chapter.

3. Which three tasks would you work on first? Why?

CHAPTER 5

Providers of Computer and Information Services

KEY TOPICS

CHAPTER OVERVIEW

Just about everyone, from chief executive to line worker, is a potential user of computer- and information-related services. Interestingly, the user does not always know where to go to obtain these services, be it the creation of a decision support system or help with the operation of a microcomputer. Almost all the information services provided to end users come from sources discussed in this chapter. These providers of information services are introduced in the first section and are discussed in some detail later in the chapter, especially as they relate to the information services division and the information center. This chapter also contains an overview of job categories for MIS professionals.

PROVIDERS OF COMPUTER AND INFORMATION SERVICES: AN OVERVIEW

Where does an end user go for computer- and information-related services? At some time or another, end users will need help with implementing an on-line accounting system, creating an electronic spreadsheet template, designing a data base to do market research, using a public electronic mail service, configuring a microcomputer system for desktop publishing, printing an ad hoc report, using and applying word processing, obtaining up-to-the-minute quotes on bonds and securities, simulating materials movement in a proposed plant, generating presentation graphics, or providing an endless number of other information services. Throughout the remainder of the book, computer- and information-related services are referenced collectively simply as **information services.**

Two decades ago, virtually all end user requests for information services were directed to the data processing department. More often than not, the request would become part of the *backlog* of an ever-growing list of user requests for service. That has changed. The end user can choose from a variety of providers of information services, both from internal sources (within the company) and external sources (not affiliated with the company).

For purpose of explanation, internal providers of information services are divided into five categories and external providers into four categories. These providers are introduced in this section and are discussed in detail later in the chapter.

Internal providers of information services are

☐ *The centralized information services division.* The **information services division** evolved from the data processing department. The information services division (or department) is the data and information "nerve center" of an organization. Most organizations—hospitals, insurance companies, universities, movie studios, cities, and so on—have an information services division. The *data* are supplied by the various user groups. In return, the information services division provides the hardware, software, and operational support needed to produce *information.* The basic responsibility of an information services division is to be responsive to the organization's information processing needs.

☐ *Departmental computing.* A relatively new buzz word, **departmental computing**, has not yet evolved to the point that people have a universally understood concept of what it is. Essentially, departmental computing is any type of computing done at the departmental level. The feature of departmental computing that distinguishes it from the support of an information services division is that the managers of the department being serviced assume full responsibility for the use and operation of all departmental computing resources.

☐ *The information center.* An **information center** is a "hands-on" facility in which computing resources, including training, are made available to end users.

☐ *User liaisons.* **User liaisons** serve as the technical interface between various providers of information services and the individual user or user group. Besides offering advice and guidance, a user liaison can direct a user to the appropriate provider of information services.

□ *End user computing.* A computerwise end user can use available hardware and software to provide information services for himself or herself. This option has become very popular and is a major emphasis of this book. Part II, which includes this chapter, Chapter 6, "End User Computing," and Chapter 7, "Personal Computing," focuses on the end user computing environment.

External providers of information services are

□ *Commercial information services, consulting services, and data bases.* The computer revolution is creating a tremendous demand for computer-related services. In response to this demand, a number of service organizations have emerged. These include *service bureaus, facilities management companies, turnkey companies, consulting firms, computer repair stores,* and *data base services,* to mention a few.

□ *Information networks.* As the percentage of businesses and homes with microcomputers increases, so does the potential for **information networks**. Information networks provide specific services to an end user through a communications link to a micro. This two-way system provides the end user with information (for example, airline flight schedules) and permits the end user to enter data (for example, reservations for airline flights). Representative services provided by information networks are described in the detailed discussion of this topic.

THE CENTRALIZED INFORMATION SERVICES DIVISION

Man, unlike any other thing organic or inorganic in the universe, grows beyond his work, walks up the stairs of his concepts, emerges ahead of his accomplishments.

——— *John Steinbeck*

Most companies employ MIS professionals who work within the organization constructs of a centralized computer center. The combination of hardware and software and the people who run the computers and develop the software is often referred to as the *information services division* or the *information services department.* The division or department, depending on the company's organizational structure, may be called *data processing,* or *DP; information systems,* or *IS; management information systems,* or *MIS; computer information services,* or *CIS;* or anything the company so desires. Words commonly used in such titles are "information," "services," "systems," "processing," "management," and "computer." For continuity, the term "information services division" will be used throughout the remainder of this book.

The information services division handles the organization's information needs in the same way that the finance department handles the organization's money needs. The division provides data processing and information-related services to virtually every business area. For example, programmers and systems analysts might work with plant managers and engineers to develop a computer-based production and inventory control system.

During the 1960s and 1970s, growth in the use of computer and information technologies was so rapid that information services divisions simply reacted to the needs of the corporation and the individual departments. During the 1980s, information services divisions have emphasized planning and are playing a bigger role within the corporate structure. Many have established charters that help to define the role of the information services division. The following charter is representative:

The hub of any information services division is the central computing facility that houses the mainframe computer systems.

Courtesy of Unisys Corporation

The information services division is charged with the support of those information processing requirements that are consistent with corporate objectives. Information services division responsibilities complementary to this charge are

1. Engaging in development, the ongoing operation, and maintenance of production information systems.
2. Acting as an advisor to users throughout the corporation on computer-related matters.
3. Serving as a catalyst for improving operations through system enhancements or new systems development.
4. Coordinating data and systems integration throughout the corporation.
5. Establishing standards, policies, and procedures relating to computers and information processing.
6. Evaluating and selecting hardware and software.
7. Conducting end user education programs.

With the charter in place, there is seldom any question about who does what. Of course, charters vary from coː ɔany to company. Roles and responsibilities for users and the information services divisions are discussed in more detail later in this section.

The information services division has some unusual characteristics that set it apart from other organizational entities (marketing, production, and so on).

1. The information services division is at the beck and call of any person or department within an enterprise.

2. The information services division is shrouded with a technical, almost mystical, veil, which is more perceived than real.

3. The information services division engages in ongoing interaction with virtually all corporate departments.

4. Most functional areas (accounting, personnel, and so on) within the organization are dependent on support from information services to carry out their daily activities.

Only recently has top management accepted the reality of the interdependency between the information services division and the user groups. Executives now know that decisions involving marketing, accounting, or any other functional area must be made within the context of available MIS resources.

Evolution and Growth Patterns

Most of the traditional entities within a company have been in existence since the beginning of the Industrial Revolution. However, the information services division is a relative newcomer. Most divisions were created and grew within the framework of an operating company. Like people, some matured faster than others. The overall growth in the information services function is the sum total of the growth in

☐ The number of data processing and information systems.

☐ The sophistication of information systems.

☐ Management techniques.

☐ Attitudes toward information services.

Representative growth patterns are illustrated in Figure 5–1.

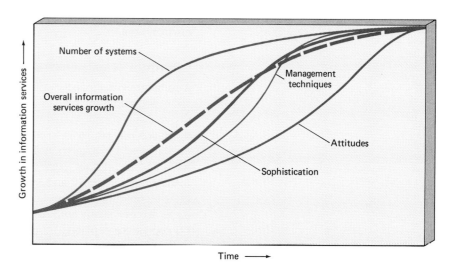

FIGURE 5–1 Growth Patterns for the Information Services Function
The overall growth in the information services function is the sum total of the growth in several major areas.

Growth in the Number of Data Processing and Information Systems

When an information services division is created, data processing and information systems with a readily identifiable potential for contribution to profit are given the highest priority. Typically, such applications as payroll, accounts receivable, and general ledger are among the first to be automated. As traditional systems become operational, managers in departments that do not use the computer begin to see potential applications that can benefit them or their departments. The second wave of information systems usually includes such systems as inventory control, order entry and processing, and market analysis. Once the basic systems become operational and users gain confidence in automation, the information services division is deluged with requests for services, called **service requests**. Today, the average backlog of service requests submitted to information services divisions is over three years. That is, a routine user request for service that is submitted today may not be addressed for years!

Growth in the Sophistication of Information Systems

Information services divisions grew as fast as the technology would permit during their formative years. Most began with batch-oriented systems that had their own autonomous files. These systems were modified to meet changing information needs until the accumulation of revisions made the systems so inefficient that they could no longer keep pace with the needs of users. These systems were redesigned to incorporate the latest technology. Eventually, the systems in mature companies reflected the state of the art of the technology; that is, on-line systems with an integrated data base.

Today, very sophisticated hardware, software, and personnel are within the economic reach of those relatively few companies that have not yet entered the world of computers. These companies, if they have the patience and perseverance to do it right the first time, can actually make a quantum leap in sophistication and go directly to an on-line, integrated data base environment.

Growth in Management Techniques

A company's first manager of information services is usually more concerned about programming than good management. Initially, the manager responds to the hastily conceived demands of users and corporate executives. Typically, there are no standards, controls, or planning. Inevitably, the MIS staff size increases and management has more flexibility to implement management tools and techniques, such as system development methodologies, project management systems, and systems planning procedures. The first management techniques to be implemented are usually manual. As growth continues, these are eventually automated; that is, manual systems development methodologies are replaced by computer-assisted software engineering (CASE) tools. System development methodologies and CASE tools are discussed in depth in Chapter 11, "Systems Development and Management," and Chapter 13, "Prototyping and Application Development Tools," respectively.

Growth in the Attitudes Toward Information Services

Organizational attitudes are usually the critical factor in determining rates of growth in the number of systems, in sophistication, and in management techniques. In start-up information services divisions, communication between user and MIS specialist is inefficient and sometimes nonexistent. There is resentment that information services divisions are impinging on the unwritten proprietary rights of the functional areas. A lack of knowledge creates a distrust among the user community. Only after computer-based systems have proven to be assets to the company does the overall attitude change from distrust to reluctant acceptance. During this period every manager is demanding that his or her project be given top priority, creating a crises-oriented environment. Also, during this somewhat difficult period, users develop an attitude of respect for the potential of information services. This respect becomes acceptance. This acceptance opens the door for a coordinated plan for the growth of information services.

Roles and Responsibilities

The quality of an information system and the potential profitability of a corporation are very much dependent on a clear definition of end user and information services division roles and responsibilities. If there is any confusion about who should do what and when, management should insist that these roles and responsibilities be articulated in the form of procedures and policy.

Representative roles and responsibilities for end users and the information services division are summarized in Figure 5–2 and discussed in the following sections.

Roles and Responsibilities	
Users	**Information Services Division**
■ Serving on the information services policy committee	■ Development, ongoing operation, and maintenance of production information systems
■ Being receptive to change	■ Acting as an advisor to users throughout the corporation on computer-related matters
■ Submitting systems service requests	■ Serving as a catalyst for improving operations through system enhancements or new systems development
■ Signing off on information services projects	
■ Providing and participating in training	
■ Entering data	■ Coordinating data and systems integration throughout the corporation
■ Funding information services	■ Establishing standards, policy, and procedures relating to computers and information processing
■ Periodically evaluating information systems	■ Evaluating and selecting hardware and software
	■ Conducting end user education programs

FIGURE 5–2 Roles and Responsibilities: User and Information Services Division

End Users

The roles and responsibilities of end users are listed and discussed in the following sections.

SERVING ON THE INFORMATION SERVICES POLICY COMMITTEE   Most medium and large companies have a high-level information services steering committee. The committee, which is usually made up of user executives, approves major requests for information services, sets priorities, resolves interdepartmental differences, and establishes corporatewide information services policy. This important high-level committee is discussed in more detail later in this chapter.

BEING RECEPTIVE TO CHANGE   Computerization, by its very nature, means change. People, by nature, resist change. It is not uncommon for an entire functional area department to resist the implementation of an information system, even when departmental personnel are assured and believe that the end product will make their jobs more productive and personally gratifying. It is the responsibility of user managers to create the proper environment for acceptance of the inevitable changes that accompany the implementation of a computer-based information system.

SUBMITTING SYSTEMS SERVICE REQUESTS   The responsibility of compiling and submitting a request for services from the information services division resides with the end user.

SIGNING OFF ON INFORMATION SERVICES PROJECTS   Even if he or she is not a member of the system development project team, the user manager should stay abreast of project activities that affect areas within his or her scope of responsibility. After all, the resultant product will have a major impact on the functional area's procedures, operation, and success. At each major project milestone, the user manager is asked to "sign off" on what has been accomplished to date. The signature indicates satisfaction and concurrence not only with the basic system design, but also with the detailed specifications. User managers and appropriate staff members should meet with project team personnel to make sure that they understand and concur with every aspect of the proposed system.

PROVIDING AND PARTICIPATING IN TRAINING   User managers and user personnel are responsible for providing functional area training for information services personnel (for example, inventory models, AICPA accounting principles, marketing strategies, and so on). The user may require some computer/information systems-related training. The administration of this training is the responsibility of the information services division. The user's responsibility is participation.

ENTERING DATA   Traditionally, user personnel are responsible for providing input to the system. In on-line systems, this usually entails the transcription of source data to machine-readable format.

FUNDING INFORMATION SERVICES   Depending on corporate policy, the user department may be responsible for funding all, some, or none of the services rendered by the information services division. Those corporations that have adopted a *chargeback system* typically bill users for internal consulting, analyst and programming services, hardware utilization, on-line storage utilization, and materials. Chargeback systems are discussed in Chapter 16, "Managing Information Services."

PERIODICALLY EVALUATING INFORMATION SYSTEMS An information system is "owned" by (the property of) the user departments, not the information services division. It is therefore the user manager's responsibility periodically to initiate formal reviews of the department's information systems.

Information Services Division

The roles and responsibilities of the information services division are listed and discussed in the following sections.

STAYING ABREAST OF THE TECHNOLOGY With the state of the art of technology changing almost daily, no corporation can afford to neglect opportunities for cost-effective increases in computing capabilities. To take advantage of available technology, information services personnel must make a concerted effort to stay abreast of the technology. Any technological innovations that have the potential to increase productivity, improve effectiveness, or create a competitive advantage should be brought to the attention of user management.

SERVING AS A CATALYST Information services personnel should be catalysts in the identification of opportunities for new MIS applications. Any MIS opportunities that have the potential to improve data processing or decision making should be presented to management.

PROVIDING A SOURCE FOR ADVICE Information services personnel are a source of advice and consultation for the user community. The information services division should provide a mechanism by which users can request advice on any facet of computers and MIS.

ASSISTING USERS IN THE SYSTEM DEVELOPMENT PROCESS The system development process is a 50:50 proposition whereby functional area expertise is combined with technical expertise and the result is a computer-based information system. Prior to 1980, the prevailing attitude of both user and information services personnel was that system development was the responsibility of information services. Today, the information system is owned by the user and is therefore the responsibility of the appropriate user manager. The information services division is responsible for assisting users with their information systems projects.

PROVIDING OPERATIONAL CAPABILITY FOR INFORMATION SYSTEMS The information services division is responsible for the hardware-based portion of the production information system. This encompasses all machine room activities, system control, and the distribution of the output. This, of course, does not apply

The trouble with our age is all signposts and no destination.

—— *L. Kronenberger*

to departmental computing environments, where departments manage their own computer centers.

Information services division personnel are responsible for the physical and logical maintenance of the data base. However, any changes to the data base are prompted by user input; therefore, the accuracy of the data base is the responsibility of the user.

MAINTAINING INFORMATION SYSTEM DOCUMENTATION   For any given information system, the documentation package includes system and programming documentation, "run instructions" for computer operators, data base documentation, and the user manual. Any enhancements to a system must be reflected in the aforementioned documents. These documents are distributed and maintained by information services personnel.

PROVIDING AN ENVIRONMENT FOR CORPORATE INTEGRATION   The common denominator in a corporation is not money—it is data. Data comprise the vehicle by which to integrate functionally adjacent corporate entities. Every corporation, educational institution, and government agency is wrought with redundancies in data and procedures. It is the responsibility of the information services division to provide the technological capacity (hardware and technical expertise) to minimize or eliminate these redundancies through system integration.

PROVIDING USER EDUCATION PROGRAMS   Education of the user in the area of computers and information processing is widely recognized as a significant contributor to an organization's success. Typically, the information services division is charged with this responsibility.

DEVELOPING AND MAINTAINING STANDARDS AND PROCEDURES   The information services division is responsible for the development and maintenance of standards and procedures relating to computers and information processing. Any given computer center will have hundreds of standards and procedures, ranging from programming conventions, to standard procedures for systems development, to standardized microcomputer networks.

ASSISTING IN THE MIS STRATEGIC PLANNING PROCESS   The strategic MIS planning function is the responsibility of the high-level MIS steering committee, if one exists. However, information services personnel serve as functionaries to develop the plan for approval by the steering committee. MIS strategic planning is discussed in detail in Chapter 10, "MIS Planning."

INTERACTING WITH VENDORS   As a matter of corporate policy, both hardware and software vendors should be directed, at least initially, to a central location. Since information services managers routinely interact with a variety of vendors, information services is the logical point for the initial vendor interaction. This approach minimizes the possibility of an inexperienced user being sold a "bill of goods" by an unscrupulous vendor. (Overall, the integrity of vendors is high.) Another reason for this approach is to achieve standardization of hardware and software within the corporation.

ACQUIRING HARDWARE   Any acquisition of computing hardware should be centralized. It is only logical that the information services division be assigned this responsibility. Again, the primary reason for the centralization of this activity is to maintain hardware and, possibly, software compatibility, and to take advantage of volume discounts.

Organization and Personnel

There is no standard or traditional organizational location for the information services division. Since information services must be organizationally located to render service to all areas of the company, organizational alternatives will invariably reflect emotions, biases, prejudices of top executives, and the politics and traditions of the corporation. The two most common approaches are

1. The largest user of information services has responsibility and provides support to other organizational entities.
2. Information services is centralized under a high-level neutral office, usually that of the president.

The advantages of the first alternative are skewed to the largest user. The second embodies the advantages of centralization and neutrality.

When information services is located under the chief financial officer (CFO), as illustrated in Figure 5–3, the information services division usually provides superior support to the parent department. However, this structure causes conflict in corporate information services priorities, promotes a low level of support to smaller users, and makes MIS strategic planning almost impossible.

Limited resources are available for the development and maintenance

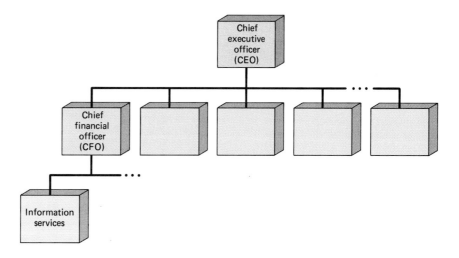

FIGURE 5–3   Information Services Subordinate to the Largest User

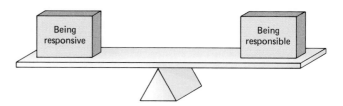

FIGURE 5–4   The Information Services Balancing Act
The information services division must maintain a balance between being responsive to user information needs and being responsible.

of information systems. Therefore, information services must maintain a balance between *being responsive* to user information needs and *being responsible* (see Figure 5–4). For example, an information services manager cannot divert previously committed resources from one project in an attempt to be responsive to another user. Unless extreme circumstances dictate this action, information services management cannot disregard its responsibility to keep approved projects on schedule. This is an almost daily conflict that information services and user managers must resolve. With an organizational structure that provides organizational neutrality for the information services division (see Figure 5–5), projects can be prioritized with the corporate good in mind. Also, neutrality encourages the integration of information services and the preparation of realistic MIS strategic plans.

Organization of an Information Services Division

In some information services divisions, one person is the chief cook and bottle washer. Other divisions have several thousands of people. Both small and large "shops" (a slang term for information services divisions) must accomplish the same functions of systems analysis, programming, technical support, data communications, operations, and so on. Differences in the way they are staffed and organized are due primarily to the degree of specialization.

Figure 5–6 illustrates how an information services division in a medium-to large-sized corporation might be organized. This chart illustrates a representative organizational structure that could vary considerably, depending

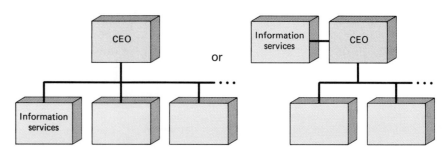

FIGURE 5–5   Information Services Positioned for Organizational Neutrality
In the figure, the centralized information services division is shown as subordinate to a high-level neutral office in both a line capacity (left) and a staff capacity (right).

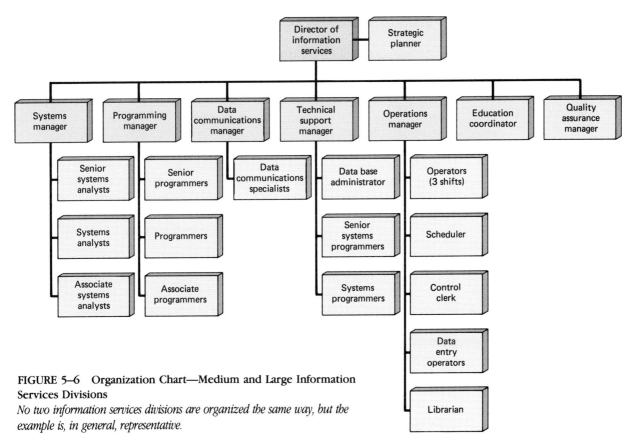

FIGURE 5–6 Organization Chart—Medium and Large Information Services Divisions
No two information services divisions are organized the same way, but the example is, in general, representative.

on circumstances. The various components and specialist positions shown in Figure 5–6 are discussed in the next section.

A typical organizational structure for a small company is illustrated in Figure 5–7. Some specialty areas are not noted in the chart. Personnel in small companies double up on duties. For example, a programmer might also be the data base administrator.

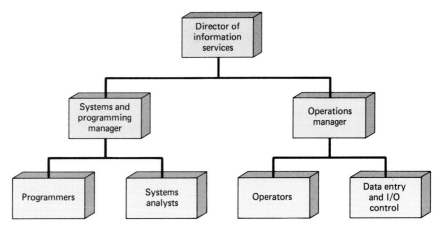

FIGURE 5–7 Organization Chart—Small Information Services Divisions
This example organization is representative of a small information services division.

Q. Our yearly MIS budget is 2 percent of sales and comprises a substantial portion of administrative costs. Since so much has been written about the importance of organizational neutrality, I have initiated an evaluation of organizational alternatives.

I feel that our present level within the organization limits our capability to be responsive. Three years ago, I reported to the comptroller. I am still the director of MIS, but now, believe it or not, I report to an assistant comptroller.

Would you endorse a suggestion that I report to the president?

A. The only definitive statement that I can make about your particular circumstance is that no head of a corporate information services (MIS) function should ever report to an assistant comptroller.

The director of a well-organized and properly chartered centralized information services organization should be at a high level, perhaps a vice president. The optimum level is based on scope of services, the manner and degree to which information services affect events and activities in other functional areas, and to a lesser extent, the capabilities and potential of the MIS personnel. Budget share is seldom a good indicator of corporate significance.

Information Services Functional Components and Specialists

The purpose of this section is to acquaint you with the functional components and professionals associated with the MIS function. There is no "best" way to staff for the effective delivery of information services. However, each of the following components and job specialties is either implicitly or explicitly included in every company that employs MIS.

INFORMATION SERVICES MANAGEMENT   Information services managers perform the traditional management functions: planning, organizing, staffing, directing, and controlling. The **chief information officer** (**CIO**), often a vice president, has responsibility for all information services activity in the company. At least half the CIO's time is spent interacting with user managers and executives. In this capacity, the CIO coordinates the integration of data and information systems and serves as the catalyst for new systems development. The remainder of the CIO's time is devoted to managing the information services division. The CIO or information executive must be somewhat futuristic, predicting what information technologies will become reality so that the company can position itself to use MIS as a strategic weapon.

The term "CIO" is an outgrowth of the more common "CEO" (chief executive officer) and "CFO" (chief financial officer). CFO and CEO are familiar business titles, but CIO is relatively new. The CIO is responsible for integrating computers and MIS into the business function, for ongoing MIS operations, and for the planning and implementation of the corporation's MIS strategies. The CIO is (or should be) part of the inner circle of the corporate management team because he or she deals daily with major issues and concerns that cut across functional and organizational boundaries.

SYSTEMS ANALYSIS   The systems analysis group is composed of **systems analysts**. The systems analysts, or simply "analysts," analyze, design, and implement information systems. The analysts work closely with people in the user areas to design information systems that meet their data processing and information needs. These "problem solvers" are assigned a variety of tasks, which might include feasibility studies, system reviews, security assessments, long-range planning, and hardware/software selection.

The role of these "problem solvers" is expanding with the technology. For example, with recent innovations in programming languages (see Chapter 13, "Prototyping and Application Development Tools"), users and analysts can work together at a workstation to design *and* implement certain information systems—without programmer involvement!

PROGRAMMING   The programming component includes **applications programmers**, or simply programmers, who translate analyst-prepared system and input/output specifications into programs. Programmers design the logic, then code, debug, test, and document the programs. Programmers write programs for a certain application, such as market analysis or inventory management.

Sometimes called "implementers" or "miracle workers," programmers are charged with turning system specifications into an information system. To do this, they must exhibit logical thinking and overlook nothing. A good programmer is *perceptive*, *patient*, *persistent*, *picky*, and *productive*—the "five P's" of programming.

Some companies distinguish between *development* and *maintenance* programmers. Development programmers create *new* systems. Maintenance programmers enhance existing systems by *modifying* existing programs to meet changing information processing needs. At a typical company, about 50 percent of the applications programming tasks are related to maintenance and 50 percent to new development.

A person holding a **programmer/analyst** position performs the functions of both a programmer and a systems analyst. The more senior people in the programming group are often programmer/analysts.

DATA COMMUNICATIONS   The **data communications specialists** design and maintain computer networks that link computers and workstations for data communications. This involves selecting and installing appropriate hardware, such as modems, data PBXs, and front-end processors, as well as selecting the transmission media (all discussed in Chapter 8, "Connectivity and Data Communications"). Data communications specialists also develop and implement the software that controls the flow of data between computing devices.

TECHNICAL SUPPORT   The technical support group designs, develops, maintains, and implements *systems software*. Systems software is fundamental to the general operation of the computer; that is, it does not address a specific business or scientific problem.

The technical support group is usually made up of systems programmers and the data base administrator. **Systems programmers** develop and maintain systems software. The **data base administrator** (**DBA**) position evolved with the need to integrate information systems. The data base administrator designs, creates, and maintains the integrated data base. The DBA coordinates discussions between user groups to determine the content and format of the data base so that data redundancy is kept to a minimum. The integrity and security of the data base are also responsibilities of the data base administrator.

OPERATIONS   People in the operations group perform a variety of jobs, each of which is described in the following paragraphs.

The **computer operators** perform those hardware-based activities that are needed to keep production information systems operational. An operator works in the machine room, initiating software routines and mounting the appropriate magnetic tapes, disks, and preprinted forms. The operator is in constant communication with the computer while monitoring the progress of a number of simultaneous production runs, initiating one-time jobs, and troubleshooting. If the computer system fails, the operator initiates restart procedures to "bring the system up."

The **scheduler** strives to utilize the valuable hardware resources at optimum efficiency. Along with production systems, the scheduler allocates and schedules computer time for program development and testing, system acceptance testing, data and file conversion, ad hoc jobs, preventive maintenance, general maintenance, and system down time for hardware upgrades.

The **control clerk** accounts for all input to and output from the computer center. Control clerks follow standard procedures to validate the accuracy of the output before it is distributed to the user department.

Data entry operators, sometimes called the key operators, use key entry devices to transcribe data into machine-readable format. At most companies, only a small data entry group is attached to information services because the majority of the data entry operators are "distributed" to the user areas.

The **librarian** selects the appropriate interchangeable magnetic tapes and disks and delivers them to the operator. The operator mounts the tapes and disks on the storage devices for processing and then returns them to the librarian for storage. The librarian maintains a status log on each tape and disk. Medium- and large-sized companies may have hundreds, even thousands, of tapes and disks. The librarian is also charged with maintaining a reference library filled with computer books, periodicals, and manuals, as well as internal system and program documentation (that is, logic diagrams, program listings).

EDUCATION   The **education coordinator** coordinates all computer-related educational activities. Anyone who works with computers or selects a computer-related career automatically adopts a life of continuing education. Computer technology is changing rapidly, so learning is an ongoing process. The education coordinator schedules users and computer specialists for technical update seminars, video training programs, computer-assisted instruction, and others, as needed. The coordinator sometimes conducts the training sessions.

ADMINISTRATION   Administration is the support function that handles the paperwork and administrative details associated with the operation of an information services division.

PLANNING   Although planning is a management function, the complexities of MIS planning demand that at least one **MIS planner** be dedicated to the planning function in medium and large companies. MIS planning is covered in detail in Chapter 10, "MIS Planning."

QUALITY ASSURANCE   The quality assurance group encourages the do-it-right-the-first-time approach to system development. **Quality assurance specialists** are assigned the task of monitoring the quality of every aspect of the design and operation of information systems, including system efficiency and documentation. They also ensure that MIS specialists and users adhere to standards and procedures.

INFORMATION SERVICES AUDITING   The purpose of the audit group is to audit both the information services division and information systems. Typically, the **information services auditor** is part of the internal audit group. Information services auditing is discussed in more detail in Chapter 14, "System Implementation."

The High-Level MIS Steering Committee

The much ballyhooed high-level **MIS steering committee** is the vehicle that executives have adopted to enable them to decide their own MIS destinies.

The open society, the unrestricted access to knowledge, the unplanned and uninhibited association of men for its furtherance—these are what make a vast, complex, ever growing, ever changing, ever more specialized and expert technological world, nevertheless a world of human community.

——— *J. Robert Oppenheimer*

MIS managers are welcoming the direction and support provided by these user-based committees. The names and charges given to this committee vary widely from one company to the next. Common names include "Computer Advisory Committee," "Executive DP Steering Committee," "MIS Advisory Council," "Information Services Priorities Committee," and "Information Systems Policy Committee." For the high-level steering committee to be operationally effective, its members should be at the policymaking level, preferably at the vice-presidential level. An effective high-level steering committee is an essential ingredient to the success of any corporate information services function.

During the past decade the MIS steering committee has been a popular addition to many corporations' organizational structures. Unfortunately, many of these committees were founded because it was the "in" thing to do and they were not given a definitive charge; consequently, many have been ineffective. The charge of the MIS steering committee should be well defined. For example, the following charge has proven successful in a number of organizations:

☐ *Support the use of information services for an effective and efficient corporate operation.* The MIS steering committee should be visible in its encouragement of information services.

☐ *Periodically present a report and recommendations on information services to the chief executive officer and the board of directors.*

☐ *Approve and reject requests for major information services.* For example, a medium-sized corporation might designate major projects as those requiring more than one workyear of effort or a $50,000 expenditure.

☐ *Set priorities among approved information systems development projects.* A typical committee would have a queue of approved projects for which priorities are continually evaluated and updated, depending on corporate needs.

☐ *Monitor the progress of major information services projects and the performance of ongoing production systems.* On occasion, the committee will have to evaluate the merits of allocating additional resources to projects that are expected to run substantially over budget. The committee might also make go/no-go decisions when it becomes apparent that the finished project will fall short of expectations.

☐ *Arbitrate differences between user departments and/or divisions arising from information services operations and/or proposed operations.* For many years, the director of data processing was placed in a position of having to choose between two or more functional area alternatives. Major procedural conflicts should be resolved by the MIS steering committee and those departments most affected by the decision, not by information services management.

☐ *Set policy that relates to information services and affects all departments.*

The foregoing are suggested responsibility areas and do vary depending on the type of industry and committee emphasis.

Organization Summary

Figure 5–8 graphically summarizes the relationship among MIS specialty positions, the high-level MIS steering committee, users, and the development and operation of an information system. A *user* request for a computer-related service, called a service request, is compiled and submitted to the information services division. Because resources are limited, not all requests are filled. The merits of minor service requests are evaluated by the *director of information services*, and major requests are routed to the *MIS steering committee*. The director or the committee approves those requests that appear to offer the greatest benefits to the organization. Major requests are incorporated into the MIS planning process by the *MIS planner* and assigned a priority by the MIS steering committee.

A project team is formed to develop and implement the information system. The project team is typically made up of *programmers, systems ana-*

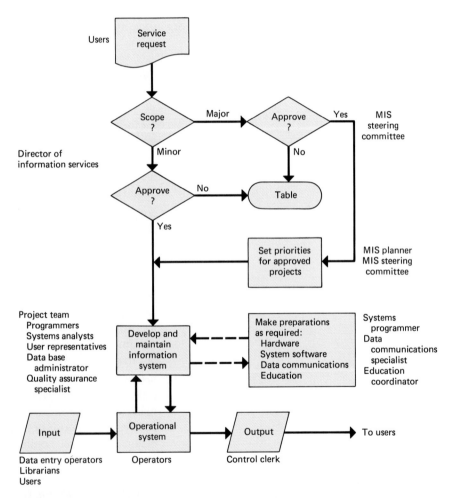

FIGURE 5–8 Position Functions and Information Systems
This chart summarizes the relationship among the various information services positions, the MIS steering committee, and user personnel in the development and operation of an information system.

lysts, *user representatives*, the *data base administrator*, and a *quality control specialist*, or some combination of these specialists. *Systems programmers* and *data communications specialists* make changes to the hardware configuration, data communications network, and systems software, as required. The *education coordinator* schedules needed training sessions for both computer specialists and users. Once the system is implemented and becomes operational, operations people handle the routine input, processing, and output activities. *Data entry operators* transcribe the raw data to machine-readable format. The *librarian* readies magnetic storage media for processing. *Operators* initiate and monitor computer runs and distribute the output to *control clerks*, who then check the output for accuracy before delivering it to the *user*.

DEPARTMENTAL COMPUTING

Departmental computing has become a generic reference to any type of computing done at the departmental level. The trend to departmental computing is causing hardware, software, and processing to be moved closer to the people who use them. Departmental computing is defined differently by different people or vendors, depending on their objectives. Information services specialists have been referring to this concept as **distributed processing** for over a decade. Microcomputer vendors define departmental computing in terms of micros and micro networks. Some users define it in terms of an autonomous information service function within the organizational structure of a functional area department. A few vendors are using the term in an attempt to define another market for their products.

The concept of departmental computing has emerged because users are becoming sophisticated enough (or desperate enough) to assume responsibility for their own computer(s) and information systems. Departmental computing could be as basic as using a micro-based electronic spreadsheet to do "what if" analysis or, at the other end of the spectrum, a superminicomputer with departmental workstations supporting an on-line MIS. In the more sophisticated implementations of departmental computing, functional area managers are finding themselves managing their own miniature information services divisions, often including programmers, analysts, operators, and other MIS professionals.

The Emergence of Departmental Computing

Through the mid-1970s, the prevailing thought was to take advantage of the economies of scale and strive for total integration of corporate information services by centralizing the entire information services function. These centralized facilities grew rapidly until they became so complex that their ability to be responsive to users was severely diminished. This lack of responsiveness was a major factor in reversing the trend to total centralization. Another factor was the rapid decrease in the cost of hardware, especially for small computers. The introduction of microcomputers into the business community in the early 1980s added fuel to the fire for decentralization.

The movement toward decentralization began in the mid-1970s, not as departmental computing (circa 1987), but as **distributed data processing** or, later, simply distributed processing. Distributed processing is not only a technological concept, but it is also an organizational concept. The concept is built around a philosophy that, if implemented correctly, will render benefits to both centralized and decentralized information services.

In distributed processing, computer systems are arranged in a network, with each computer being connected to one or more of the other computers. A distributed processing network is usually designed around geographical and/or functional considerations, with most networks reflecting a combination of both. For example, in Figure 5–9 minicomputers are placed in a company's regional warehouses in Chicago, Atlanta, and Los Angeles to support local information processing needs (geographic distribution) and in the several functional area departments, such as accounting and personnel, at its corporate headquarters in Dallas (functional distribution) to support their local information processing needs. Since all minis are part of the network that includes the central mainframe computer, the corporate data base and information systems can be integrated.

The trend toward departmental computing, or distributing processing closer to the people who use it, is visibly encouraged by the type of hardware

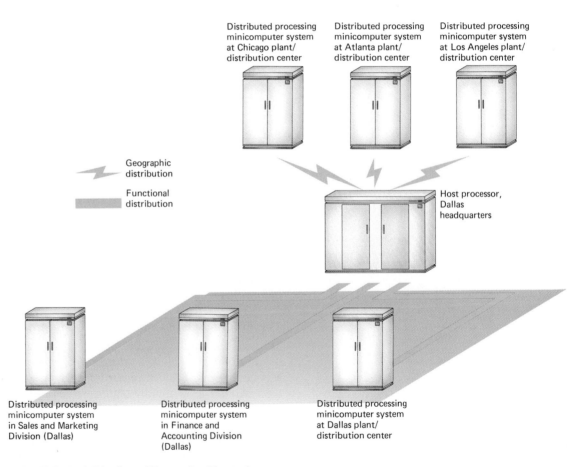

FIGURE 5–9   A Distributed Processing Network
The distributed processing network demonstrates both geographic and functional distribution of processing.

CENTRALIZED DECENTRALIZATION

Q. We are a small company of slightly fewer than 1,000 employees. Currently, our centralized MIS division services our four locations, all of which are in the same state. Against all of my arguments to the contrary, our steering committee voted to decentralize and has asked me to draw up a plan to accomplish the move. I feel that such a move is premature and will hinder our efforts to be responsive. Is there anything I can say or do to reverse their hasty decision?

A. There is no such thing as pure decentralization of information services. You can distribute people, hardware, software, data, and procedures, but somebody has to mind the store, whether you choose geographic or functional decentralization. Is your committee suggesting that each site maintain separate data bases? Who will set standards, ensure compatibility, and establish policy?

I've long been a proponent of moving processing capability closer to those who use it, but not at the expense of integration and coordination. Approach the steering committee with a plan for what I call "centralized decentralization." That is, outline a plan that distributes computing resources according to the committee's wishes, but accompany it with an organizational structure with central authority for coordinating the information services function.

and software being developed and offered by vendors. Initially, departmental computing, as it is now called, was limited to networked or stand-alone minicomputers placed in user departments or locations. With the coming of age of microcomputers as business tools, the scope of departmental computing is much broader. The dominant characteristic of the software designed for departmental computing is its **user-friendliness**. That is, a person with relatively little experience can interact successfully with the system. The dominant characteristic of the hardware designed for departmental computing is its **open architecture**. That is, users have the flexibility to configure the system with a variety of peripheral devices.

End user computing, the foundation of departmental computing, is discussed in detail in Chapter 6, "End User Computing."

Controlling Departmental Computing

With so many hardware and software options from which to choose, user managers need the advice and guidance of a centralized information services function to maintain corporate compatibility, consistency, and integration of information processing. The centralized group is usually charged with

- □ Evaluating and selecting hardware.
- □ Establishing standards, procedures, and documentation policy.
- □ Doing short- and long-range planning for overall corporate information processing.
- □ Maintaining an integrated corporate data base.
- □ Staying current on available information technology.
- □ Supporting information services and user education programs.

The trend is definitely to decentralization through departmental computing, but realistically, the MIS environment is so complex, and the need for overall integration so great, that there will always be a need for strong centralized control.

One of the objectives noted in this company's MIS strategic plan is to provide greater user accessibility to the computer and information services through departmental computing. Currently, five departments, including the marketing department shown in the photo, have installed a minicomputer for local processing. The departmental minis are part of a companywide network that includes the corporate mainframe.

Courtesy of International Business Machines

THE INFORMATION CENTER

A good many companies still have managers who submit handwritten drafts for typing, secretaries who frequently refer to dictionaries, clerks who use hand calculators throughout the day, administrative personnel who assemble reports with glue and paper cutters, executives who would like to (but cannot) do "what if" analysis, or researchers who use pencils and graph paper to plot their results. These companies are prime candidates for one or more information centers. *Information centers* can provide personnel with the opportunity to learn to use computers and to be more productive with their time.

An information center is a "hands-on" facility in which computing resources and training are made available to end users. Users come to an information center because they know that they can find the computing resources and technical support that they need to help them with their personal short-term business information and computing needs. Companies with information centers report a seemingly insatiable demand for these facilities.

Today, users, from clerks to top management, routinely go to an information center to get the information they need, usually in less time than it would take to explain their need to an MIS specialist from the information services division. Information centers are strategically located to provide ease of access for users. For example, information centers might be located at a company's headquarters office and at each of its four plants. The availability of information centers has reduced the number of one-time user service requests received by the information services division by as much as 80 percent. With users literally taking matters into their own hands, programmers and analysts in the information services division have more time to devote to ongoing development projects.

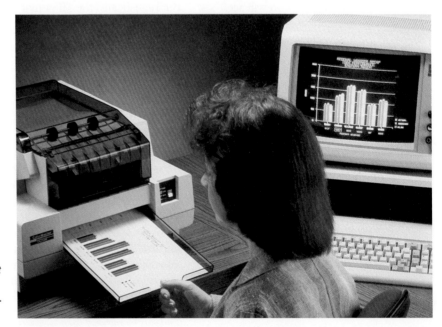

In an information center, end users use graphics software to prepare professional-looking visuals for presentations. They then use a plotter to draw the image directly on paper or a blank acetate. Some information centers have desktop film recorders that can reproduce screen images on 35mm film.

CalComp

Information Center Resources

The typical information center makes a plethora of hardware and software resources available to end users. The hardware or computing resources in an information center might include

- *Workstations* that enable users to interact directly with the business's central computer system and the integrated corporate data base.
- *Microcomputers* for "personal" or stand-alone computing.
- *Printers* (near letter quality, letter quality, and near typeset quality) for hard copy or printed output.
- *Plotters* for the preparation of presentation graphics.
- *Desktop publishing* equipment.
- *Desktop film recorders* that reproduce a high-resolution graphic image on 35-millimeter film.
- *Screen-image projectors* that project computer-generated graphic images to a large screen for viewing by a group of people.

The information center would also make a variety of software packages available for use. Software that would be considered standard in an information center includes

- *Word processing.* Word processing software permits users to enter, store, manipulate, and print text.
- *On-line thesaurus.* An on-line thesaurus is used in conjunction with word processing software and is always ready with possible synonyms for a user-selected word.
- *Electronic dictionary and spelling checker.* A spelling checker checks the spelling of every word in a word processing document against an electronic dictionary.
- *Mail merge.* Mail merge software provides the facility to merge the text generated by word processing with data from a data base (for example, merge a name and address data base with a form letter).
- *Desktop publishing.* Desktop publishing software provides the capability to produce near-typeset-quality copy for newsletters, advertising pieces, and so on from the confines of a desktop.
- *Electronic spreadsheet.* Electronic spreadsheet software permits users to work with the rows and columns of a matrix (or spreadsheet) of data.
- *Data management.* Data management or *database software* permits users to create and maintain a data base and to extract information from the data base.
- *Presentation graphics.* Presentation graphics software permits users to create charts and line drawings that graphically portray the data in an electronic spreadsheet or data base.
- *Idea processor.* Idea processor software helps users to organize and document their thoughts and ideas.

□ *Communications.* Communications software permits users to send and receive transmissions of data to/from remote computers, and to process and store the data as well.

□ *Decision support system.* The cross section of DSS software selected for use in an information center would depend on user needs (simulation, statistical analysis, "what if," financial analysis, and so on).

□ *Expert system shell.* The expert system shell enables users to create their own expert systems.

□ *Electronic bulletin board.* Most information centers sponsor an electronic bulletin board, which is the electronic counterpart of a wall-mounted bulletin board. End users use the electronic bulletin board to exchange ideas and information via a centralized data base.

□ *Fourth-generation query languages.* This category of user-oriented programming languages has English-like commands and is used primarily for inquiry and reporting.

All these hardware devices and software tools are discussed in detail in other chapters or in "A Short Course in Computer Concepts" following Chapter 17.

Information Center Personnel

Perhaps the most important component of an information center is the people who assist users. These people, called **information center specialists**, conduct training sessions, answer questions, create systems that complement the information center function, and generally *help users to help themselves*. Because user computing needs span the gamut of computers and information processing, the information center specialist must be a generalist who is comfortable with micros, a wide variety of micro applications, and user-oriented mainframe software.

Information Center Services

The theory behind the concept of an information center is that the users have a place to go, not necessarily to request information services, but to help themselves meet their own information needs. Besides providing access to user-oriented hardware and software, information centers provide three basic services: training, consulting, and software development.

TRAINING The first step toward becoming a successful user of computing and information resources is learning how to use these resources. Recognizing this, information center specialists provide ongoing training on the use and application of available hardware and software resources. The training is provided in at least three formats: small-group seminars, individual instruction, or computer-based training (CBT). Typically, seminars on software, such as word processing or query languages, are scheduled at least once per quarter. Seminars on more specialized software, such as expert system shells or desktop publishing, are scheduled as the need arises. Information center seminars could be from 4 to 40 hours in duration. Information center specialists provide individualized instruction as time permits. Much of the

Information center specialists assist users in the use and application of hardware and software until they can become self-sufficient. Here, a facilities planner is learning FOCUS, a fourth generation language and database system, so that she can do "what if" analysis.

Information Builders, Inc.

software used by information centers is accompanied by some form of CBT, often an interactive tutorial illustrating the features and operation of the software.

CONSULTING   The information center is the place where users go to get answers to their computer-related questions. The user might need help merging a spreadsheet graph into a word processing document, or debugging a query language program, or finding a cable to link a laser printer with a micro.

SOFTWARE DEVELOPMENT   Initially, information centers were charged with helping users to help themselves. However, in recent years, information centers have been pressured to justify their existence. To do so, information center specialists have been charging user departments for certain services. The service that proved most profitable has been developing small micro-based systems for users. For example, users are routinely asking information center specialists to develop dBASE III PLUS systems. dBASE III PLUS is a proprietary database package for micros. Of course, charging users for information services is nothing new. Most information services divisions have been charging user departments for all services during the past decade.

The Future of Information Centers

Over two-thirds of all existing information centers were created during the years 1982 through 1984. It is no coincidence that this time period parallels the introductory years of IBM's enormously successful IBM PC. Although information centers have been extremely successful, some say that the future of information centers is tenuous. These people feel that information centers will go as quickly as they came. They say that users are much more technologically sophisticated than in the early 1980s and that users no longer need help. They say that the growth of departmental computing has dampened the user's need to go outside of the office for computing capabilities.

Certainly, the growth in the number of information centers has slowed, but that is to be expected because most medium- to large-sized companies already have at least one. Still, there remains a tremendous need for information centers. Only 5 percent of the work force would be considered computer literate. The average backlog of approved projects in information services divisions is in excess of three years. In other words, the user community still needs information centers, now and for the foreseeable future.

USER LIAISONS

The intensity of computer and information processing activity is very high in companies that seek to achieve the competitive advantage. In this environment, someone who is organizationally attached to a particular functional area must be given the responsibility for taking full advantage of the potential of computer-based information systems. More often than not, this person is the *user liaison*. The user liaison is given a variety of titles, such as "internal consultant," "functional specialist," and "account executive." The user liaison

THE FACILITIES MANAGEMENT OPTION

Q. For the past five years I have had responsibility for the MIS department (about 20 people). I'll be the first to admit that I have neglected it in favor of my primary responsibilities in accounting and finance.

Being in the public sector, we cannot keep up with MIS salaries and, as a result, have lost most of our best people. With our current MIS staff, our MIS department is faltering.

Momentum is building to get out of the MIS business and bring in a facilities management group. Such a group has proposed that they take over the entire MIS operation. They said that they can move into our present facility and use their software to do everything we are doing now, and do it for less than we are currently spending. Is this possible?

A. Do *what* for less? It may be possible for the facilities management company to reduce MIS costs and maintain the status quo over the short term, but is that what you want? You are apparently not satisfied with things the way they are.

Implied in the company's proposal is that services over and above the existing level of service will be billed. Don't overlook this important cost consideration.

External operation of the computer center has proved a smart decision for many organizations, but not for all. You never "get out of the MIS business." Top management has an ongoing responsibility to relate information needs and priorities to the MIS department. Whether run by an outside company or internally, it is top management's responsibility to provide strategic direction.

I detect from your letter that you expect to be absolved of further MIS responsibilities once the facilities management company takes over. However, it doesn't work that way. If you continue to be aloof from MIS, then don't expect any quantum leaps in the quality of the MIS services.

is a "live-in" computer specialist who coordinates all computer-related activities within a particular functional area. The user liaison is intimately familiar with the functional area (for example, marketing and accounting) as well as the technical end of computers and information processing. A company with four major functional areas would probably have at least four user liaisons. The user liaison is often the impetus behind movements to upgrade existing systems or develop new systems.

Computers are synonymous with change, and any type of change is usually met with some resistance. We can attribute much of this resistance to a lack of knowledge about computers and, perhaps, to a fear of the unknown. It is human nature to fear that which we don't understand, be it an extraterrestrial being or computers. Fear of the computer is so widespread that psychologists have created a name for it: **cyberphobia**. Cyberphobia is the irrational fear of, and aversion to, computers. Within the business community, there are many cyberphobics and people with limited computer skills. These people do not have the inclination, knowledge, or time to interface effectively with an MIS specialist, so they articulate what they want in general terms to the user liaison. The user liaison then does whatever is necessary to fulfill the user's request. This may involve anything from working with the MIS professionals from the information services division to actually doing the programming for a department-based information system.

COMMERCIAL INFORMATION SERVICES, CONSULTING SERVICES, AND DATA BASES

Commercial Information Services

The computer revolution is creating a tremendous demand for computer-related services. In response to this demand, a number of service organizations have emerged. These include *service bureaus, facilities management companies, turnkey companies, consulting firms,* and *computer repair stores,* to mention a few.

SERVICE BUREAUS   **Service bureaus** provide almost any kind of information processing service. These services include, but are not limited to, developing and implementing information systems, providing computer time (timesharing), and transcribing source data. A service bureau is essentially a public computer center. Service bureau employees who work under contract to develop information systems for a client company are referred to as "contract programmers" and "contract systems analysts."

FACILITIES MANAGEMENT COMPANIES   **Facilities management companies** offer an alternative to firms that would like to have an internal information services division but do not want the responsibility of managing it. Employees of facilities management companies physically move into a client company's computer center and take over all facets of the center's operation. Facilities management companies are often engaged for turnaround situations, where the client company wants its information services function to make a quantum leap in sophistication and capability that cannot be accomplished with existing staff.

TURNKEY COMPANIES AND SYSTEM INTEGRATORS   A **turnkey company** contracts with a client to install a complete system, both hardware and software. One of the major selling points of a turnkey company is that the hardware and/or software are installed with minimum involvement by personnel from the purchasing company. Rather than purchase the hardware and software separately and install an information system, a company may contract with a turnkey company to handle everything. Such companies are also called **system integrators** because they integrate various hardware and software products to provide a solution to a problem, such as desktop publishing (for example, integrating PageMaker software, the Mac SE personal computer, and the Laserwriter laser printer).

Consulting Services

The peaks and valleys of MIS requirements and the lack of internal expertise in specialty areas have made the use of outside consultants and contract programmers and analysts an economic necessity. Consulting firms provide advice relating to the use of computers and the information resource. Consultants usually have specialized expertise that is otherwise not available to clients. Contract programmers, analysts, and other MIS specialists are retained primarily for work force augmentation, and not because they have unique skills. For example, they may be hired to develop a high-priority information system for which internal resources are not available.

The jobs of consultants are not limited to implementation of hardware and software. One of their challenges is to design computer work areas that will be aesthetically pleasing while providing comfort and efficiency.

TRW Inc.

Data Base Services

A variety of applications-specific data bases are available commercially. Market researchers can obtain data bases that summarize sales by demographics for a particular type of product (shampoo or cough medicine). Druggists can purchase a data base that contains drug pairs that when taken together may result in an adverse reaction. Politicians can purchase data bases that contain voter preferences. Entrepreneurs can purchase data bases that contain the names and addresses of the most likely buyers of their products.

INFORMATION NETWORKS

Microcomputers are normally used as stand-alone computer systems, but they can also double as remote workstations. This dual-function capability provides users with the flexibility to work with the micro as a stand-alone system or to link with a larger computer and take advantage of its increased capacity. With a micro, users have a world of information at their fingertips. The microcomputer can be used in conjunction with the telephone system to transmit data to and receive data from an information network.

A growing trend among end users is to subscribe to the services of an *information network*. These information networks have one or several large computer systems that offer a variety of information services, from hotel reservations to daily horoscopes. Besides a micro, all that is needed to take advantage of these information networks is a **modem** (the interface between the telephone line and a micro), a telephone line, and a few dollars. The user would normally pay a one-time fee. For the fee, users get an account number that will permit them to establish a link with the network. Billing is based on usage of the services provided by the information network.

The following list summarizes the types of entertainment, information, and services available through information networks:

☐ *Home banking*. Check account balances, transfer money, and pay bills in the comfort of the office or home.

☐ *News, weather, and sports*. Get the latest releases directly from the wire services.

☐ *Games*. Access to hundreds of single and multiplayer games. Users can even play games with friends in other states!

☐ *Financial information*. Get up-to-the-minute quotes on stocks, securities, bonds, options, and commodities.

☐ *Bulletin boards*. Offer, by way of special-interest electronic bulletin boards, users a forum for the exchange of ideas and information. The largest information network, CompuServe, now has over 200,000 subscribers. Its closest rival is The Source. CompuServe has over 100 bulletin boards to choose from on topics ranging from graphics showing the FBI's most wanted fugitives, to gardening, to astrology, to IBM personal computers. There are thousands of privately sponsored **bulletin board systems** (**BBSs**). One in Denver is devoted to parapsychology. Some senators sponsor BBSs to communicate with their constituents. Others are devoted to religion.

As a subscriber to an information network, this scientist can use key words to scan the text of the most recent medical journals to see if anything has been written that might have some impact on the direction of his research. For example, he can ask the system to identify all articles published in the New England Journal of Medicine *during the past year that reference epinephrine; then he can request the the full text of applicable articles.*

Zenith Data Systems

- □ *Electronic mail.* Send and receive mail to and from other network users. Each network subscriber is assigned an ID and an electronic mailbox. To retrieve mail, a subscriber must enter a secret password.

- □ *Shop at home.* Select what you want from a list of thousands of items offered at discount prices. Payment is made via electronic funds transfer (EFT) and orders are delivered to your doorstep.

- □ *Reference.* Look up items of interest in an electronic encyclopedia. Scan through various government publications. Recall articles on a particular subject.

- □ *Education.* Choose from a variety of educational packages, from learning arithmetic to preparing for the Scholastic Aptitude Test (SAT). A user can even determine his or her IQ!

- □ *Real estate.* Check out available real estate by scanning the listings for the city to which the user may be moving.

- □ *Travel.* Plan your own vacation or business trip by checking airline schedules and make your own reservations. You can even charter a yacht in the Caribbean or rent a lodge in the Rockies.

■ The combination of hardware and software and the people who run the computers and develop the software is often referred to as the information services division.

■ The basic responsibility of an information services division is to be responsive to the organization's information processing needs.

■ Most functional areas within an organization are dependent on support from the information services division to carry out their routine activities.

■ The overall growth in the information services function is the sum total of the growth in the number of data processing and information systems, the sophistication of information systems, management techniques, and attitudes toward information services.

■ Today, the average backlog of service requests submitted to information services divisions is over three years.

■ Among other things, the end user is responsible for serving on the information services policy committee, being receptive to change, signing off on information services projects, funding of information services, and periodically evaluating existing information systems.

■ Among other things, the information services division is responsible for staying abreast of the technology, assisting users in the system development process, providing operational capability for information systems, and assisting in the MIS strategic planning process.

■ The system development process is a 50:50 proposition whereby functional area expertise is combined with technical expertise, resulting in a computer-based information system.

■ The two most common approaches to locating information services within the corporate organization structure are to position information services under the largest user or to centralize information services under a high-level neutral office. The latter is the preferred approach.

■ A director of information services must maintain a balance between being responsive to user information needs and being responsible.

■ Both small and large information services divisions must accomplish the same functions. Differences in the way they are staffed and organized are due primarily to the degree of specialization.

■ The chief information officer (CIO) is responsible for integrating computers and MIS into the business function, for ongoing MIS operations, and for planning and implementing the corporation's MIS strategies.

■ Systems analysts do the analysis, design, and implementation of information systems. Applications programmers translate analyst-prepared system and input/output specifications into programs.

■ The technical support group designs, develops, maintains, and implements systems software. Systems software is fundamental to the general operation of the computer; that is, it does not address a specific business or scientific problem.

■ Within an information services division's operations group, computer operators perform hardware-based activities, the scheduler optimizes hardware efficiency, control clerks account for all input to and output from the computer center, data entry operators transcribe data into machine-readable format, and the librarian delivers appropriate tapes and disks to operators.

■ Quality assurance specialists monitor the quality of every aspect of the design and operation of information systems, including system efficiency and documentation.

■ The MIS steering committee supports the use of information services, reports on information services to the CEO, approves and rejects requests for major information services, set priorities, monitors the progress of major information services projects and systems, arbitrates MIS-prompted differences among user groups, and sets MIS policy.

■ Through the mid-1970s, centralized information services divisions grew rapidly until they became so complex that their ability to be responsive to users was severely diminished. This lack of responsiveness was a major contributor to the growth of distributed processing and, later, departmental computing.

■ Departmental computing is any type of computing done at the departmental level.

■ The trend in MIS is to decentralization through departmental computing, but there will always be a need for strong centralized control.

■ An information center is a "hands-on" facility in which computing resources, including training, are made available to end users.

■ The availability of information centers has reduced the number of one-time user service requests received by the information services division by as much as 80 percent.

■ The hardware or computing resources in an information center might include workstations, microcomputers, printers, plotters, desktop publishing equipment, desktop film recorders, and screen-image projectors. Software that would be considered standard in an information center would include word processing, on-line thesaurus, electronic dictionary and spelling checker, mail merge, desktop publishing, electronic spreadsheet, data management, presentation graphics, idea processor, communications, decision support system, expert system shell, electronic bulletin board, and fourth-generation query languages.

■ Information center specialists conduct training sessions, answer questions, create systems that complement the information center function, and generally help users to help themselves.

■ User liaisons serve as the technical interface among various providers of information services and the individual user or user group.

■ A number of organizations provide computer-related services, for example, service bureaus, facilities management companies, turnkey companies, consulting firms, data base services, and computer repair stores, to mention a few.

■ A growing trend among end users is to subscribe to the services of an information network. These information networks have large computer systems that offer a variety of information services.

IMPORTANT TERMS

applications programmer
bulletin board system (BBS)
chief information officer (CIO)
computer operator
control clerk
cyberphobia
data base administrator (DBA)
data base service
data communications specialist
data entry operator
database software (Ch. 7)
departmental computing

desktop publishing (Ch. 7)
distributed data processing
education coordinator
electronic dictionary (Ch. 7)
electronic spreadsheet (Ch. 7)
facilities management company
fourth-generation query language (Ch. 4)
idea processor
information center
information center specialist
information network

information services auditor
information services division
librarian
mail merge (Ch. 7)
MIS planner
MIS steering committee
modem
on-line thesaurus (Ch. 7)
open architecture
programmer/analyst
quality assurance specialist
scheduler

service bureau
service request
system integrator
systems analyst
systems programmer
user-friendliness
user liaison
turnkey company
word processing (Ch. 7)
workstation

REVIEW EXERCISES

1. Contrast development programmers with maintenance programmers.

2. What role does the high-level MIS steering committee play in MIS strategic planning?

3. What is the function of the chief information officer?

4. Who is responsible for the physical and logical maintenance of a company's data base? Who is responsible for the accuracy of the data base?

5. Name four positions in the operations group of an information services division.

6. Expand the following acronyms: DBA, BBS, CIO, and CFO.

7. Who "owns" an information system?

8. List four end-user responsibilities in relation to the MIS function.

9. Certain unique characteristics of an information services division set it apart from other functional divisions. Briefly describe these characteristics.

10. Who, in the operations groups, accounts for all input to and output from the computer center?

11. The information systems in mature companies typically reflect the state of the art of the technology. These systems have what two characteristics in common?

12. When an information services division is created, which type of data processing and information systems are given the highest priority? Give an example.

13. List a minimum of six services provided by a commercial information network.

14. What type of hardware would be appropriate for an information center?

15. What is the function of a user liaison?

16. Name six computer specialist positions commonly represented in a company's information services division.

17. What is the product of a turnkey company?

18. List three representative responsibilities of a high-level MIS steering committee.

19. Distributed processing networks are usually designed around what two considerations?

20. What is the dominant characteristic of the software designed for departmental computing? The hardware?

21. What are the three basic services provided by a typical information center?

22. What type of company contracts with a client to install a complete system, both hardware and software?

23. The fear of computers is now an official phobia. What is the name of this phobia?

24. List five software packages that you might expect to find in a typical information center.

DISCUSSION QUESTIONS

1. Revise the organizational chart of Figure 5–6 such that only four people report to the director of information services.

2. What rationale would you use for appointing the director of information services, a vice president, to the MIS steering committee? What rationale would you use for omitting the director from the committee?

3. A company of 1,000 people is in the process of establishing a high-level MIS steering committee. Management has decided that the committee's charge will be similar to the one presented in this chapter and that all five vice presidents (Finance, Sales, Administration, Operations, and MIS) should serve on the committee. However, management is still debating the issues of who should chair the committee and how often it should meet. Make recommendations and justify your rationale.

4. Many, perhaps most, of the information services divisions do not have the luxury of full-time quality control specialists. In their absence, who do you think handles the quality control function?

5. It is not unusual for the top information executive to be excluded from a corporation's inner circle of executives, even though the CIO's scope of responsibility exceeds that of some of the members of the elite group. Why is this the case?

6. Describe the growth pattern in attitudes toward information services from the start-up of the function to its maturity.

7. Discuss the similarities between a company's information services function and its finance function.

8. Until about 1980, most hardware and software vendors interacted directly with MIS professionals. Now, vendors are attempting to sell their products directly to the end users. Some companies have adopted a policy that requires vendors to be cleared through a central authority before they are permitted to contact an end user. What prompted these companies to implement such a policy?

9. Ultimately, who is responsible for the success or failure of an information system—user management or information services management? Justify your response.

10. Name four external providers of information services.

11. Give an example of how a CIO can be responsive to a user request and not be responsible.

12. Rather than using the resources of an information center and making their own ad hoc inquiries, some user managers still rely on MIS personnel. What arguments would would you make to convince these managers that information centers can benefit them, their companies, and their information services divisions?

13. In many companies, the CIO reports to the president in a staff capacity and the other vice presidents report to the president in a line capacity. Discuss the advantages of such an organization.

14. One of the stated responsibilities of an information services division is "serving as a catalyst for the development of new information systems." How might the vice presidents of an operations division interpret this charge?

15. Discuss the advantages and disadvantages of having user liaisons organizationally attached to all major functional areas in a company.

16. A representative charter for an information services division is presented in the chapter material. Which two charter items do you think are the most controversial? Why?

17. A systems analysis manager suggested to the director of MIS that both programmers and systems analysts should report to a single manager. Discuss the pros and cons of the suggestion.

18. Discuss the desirable characteristics of a good systems analyst.

19. Some companies will have only one level of programmer or systems analyst, where other companies will have two, three, and even four levels. Discuss the advantages of having several levels for a particular position (for example, Programmer I, Programmer II, and so on).

20. One company uses an electronic bulletin board system to announce internal position openings. Identify other management uses of the BBS that involve the enterprisewide distribution of information.

APPLICATION CASE STUDY 5–1
Providers of Information Services

The Situation

Peterson College is a private, liberal arts college with a day enrollment of 825 students. The school also has an evening enrollment of 1,350 students, which is a full-time equivalent (FTE) of 750 students. That is, 1,350 part-time students take as many courses in a year as do 750 full-time students. Full-time staff consists of 54 day faculty and 89 salaried or hourly administrative and maintenance personnel. In addition, there is a pool of approximately 200 evening instructors that provide the equivalent of 50 FTE faculty.

Peterson College enrolled its first class 28 years ago on a newly constructed campus in a pleasant suburban setting. The school has been successful in attracting day and evening students. It consistently fills its freshman class and is experiencing a steady rise in evening enrollments. The positive enrollment status, combined with sound fiscal management, has resulted in a slight positive cash flow each year since the first 5 years of operation. The school will pay off its original 30-year indebtedness 2 years from now. The long-term master plan calls for the construction of a library; the renovation of the main classroom building, the dormitories, and the student center; and a reevaluation of the school's operating procedures.

The college's Planning Committee has formed an Administrative Computing Task Force that consists of the treasurer, the registrar, and two local computer center executives. The Task Force's charge is to develop a strategic plan for administrative computing at Peterson College. The Planning Committee has decided that the current academic computing center is to remain totally separate from any future administrative computing facilities, primarily for security reasons. The Task Force hired a consultant to investigate current procedures and to make initial recommendations regarding the appropriateness of automating the administrative units of the college. The consultant interviewed the heads of the major administrative units on campus (see the accompanying organization chart) for the purpose of obtaining information on the primary tasks performed and the extent of any current automation. The discussions are summarized here.

- *Continuing Education*. This office performs functions related to the recruiting, admission, and counseling of part-time students. In addition, the office markets and runs a variety of noncredit short courses and seminars. All operations are performed manually except for extensive use of word processing on two microcomputers.
- *Registrar's Office*. This office performs functions related to registration for classes and processing grades. The registrar's staff produces a variety of reports manually, such as the

Dean's List (a list of students who have achieved a grade point of at least 3.25 out of a possible 4.0). The Dean's List is prepared by class in descending sequence by grade point within each class. A service bureau produces student class schedules, class lists, student grade reports, and "student grade labels" that are manually attached to a student's existing transcript.

- *Library*. The library performs functions related to the acquisition and circulation of books and audiovisual materials. All operations are performed manually, with the exception of interlibrary loans. The library has an on-line terminal connected to the On-line Computer Library Center (OCLC) system. Inquiries and requests for interlibrary loans are made on a terminal via this system. Practically all college, public, and industry libraries are subscribers to the OCLC system.
- *Controller's Office*. This office performs bookkeeping and accounting functions related to student tuition (for example, grants) as well as traditional accounting functions, such as accounts payable, payroll, and general ledger. These functions, with the exception of payroll, are performed manually or by using an "ancient" magnetic ledger card accounting machine. The payroll is sent to a service bureau for processing.
- *Bookstore*. The bookstore performs functions related to retail sales to students, faculty, and college offices. Students pay for items when they are purchased. College employees can charge sales to an account number, but they must pay cash for personal items. These charges are processed through the Business Office. Textbook requests, orders, and inventory are processed using database management software on a microcomputer. All other items are processed manually.
- *Admissions Office*. This office performs functions related to attracting students, processing applications from students, accepting students, and processing the deposits from accepted students. The staff maintains a record for each accepted student on a microcomputer. They use database management and word processing software for these applications. As part of its marketing effort, the Admissions Office annually purchases a commercially prepared magnetic tape that contains approximately 40,000 prospective students' names and addresses. The academic computer center prints labels from the tape, and the college's Word Processing Center prints an individualized letter that is sent to students inquiring about the college.
- *Development Office*. This office performs functions related to the solicitation of individual and organizational donations to the college. The staff maintains a data base of approxi-

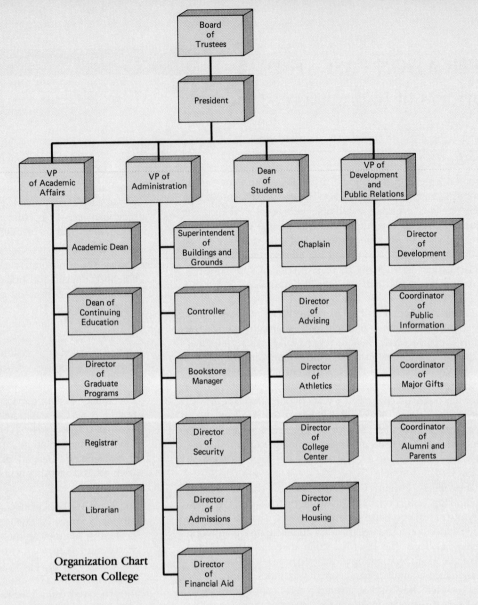

**Organization Chart
Peterson College**

mately 4,000 donors on one of the office's two microcomputers. The staff also makes extensive use of word processing software on both microcomputers.

The Assignment

1. For each of the groups the consultant interviewed, do the following:

   a. List the most appropriate provider(s) of computer and information services (if any is necessary) to enable this administrative unit to operate more efficiently and effectively and also to integrate its operations with other college units. Use the categories provided in the chapter: the centralized information services division; departmental computing; the information center; user liaisons;

commercial information services, consulting services, and data bases; and information networks.

   b. Describe the rationale for your selection.

2. Draw an organization chart for a centralized administrative computing department, even if you think one should not be established. Include the name of the office and the titles of all personnel in the office. [Hint: The total number of personnel in this department is likely to be less than 10 in an organization the size of Peterson College.]

3. Many organizations have a high-level MIS steering committee to help guide the activities of the information services function. List the personnel who you think should be members of Peterson College's MIS steering committee (see the college's organization chart).

APPLICATION CASE STUDY 5–2
The Information Center

The Situation

Gabriel Industries is a medium-sized manufacturing company (see Application Case Study 1–1, "The Decision-Making Process"). The Executive Committee evaluated the major operational areas in the company and recommended that several of these areas be analyzed in more detail. The Executive Committee created a task force to prepare a report listing areas whose operations could be improved by the application of information technology.

The task force compiled a long list of applications that would benefit by being automated. The head of the task force presented this list at a meeting of the Executive Committee. John Robson, manager of the Computer Services Department, was present at the meeting and was asked to react to the task force's report. He had several reactions: (1) he agreed that the items on the list were valid; (2) he said that there were many other applications that could benefit from automation; and (3) he adamantly stated that the current resources of the Computer Services Department were inadequate to implement the task force's recommendations, not to mention any other applications, within any reasonable time frame.

John Robson's comments caused a stir among the Executive Committee members because they were interested in improving operations at Gabriel as rapidly as possible. The initial dismay of the committee's members rapidly changed into a quest for a solution, and they asked John Robson for recommendations regarding the large backlog of potential computer applications. He had several suggestions:

1. Hire additional systems analysts and programmers to work on the larger, integrated applications.

2. Encourage users themselves to implement smaller, locally functional applications on microcomputers.

3. Establish an information center to help users with their own applications.

The Executive Committee liked Robson's suggestions and asked him to make a more detailed presentation one month from now.

The organization chart for the Computer Services Department is shown here. The systems and programming manager also serves as the data base administrator for the department.

The Assignment

John Robson has asked you to perform the planning for the implementation of an information center for Gabriel Industries.

1. Write a charter for the information center. Use the charter for the information services division shown in this chapter as a guide.

2. Give a staffing plan for the information center. For each job classification, give
   a. The job title.
   b. The job description (duties/responsibilities).
   c. The number of people in this category.
   d. Potential sources for acquiring these people (transfer from within the Computer Services Department, transfer from other departments, new hire, and so on).

3. Modify the organization chart for the Computer Services Department to include the personnel in the information center.

4. Describe how information center personnel can keep abreast of the continual changes in the field of MIS.

5. Describe the facilities (office space, hardware, software, and so on) required by the information center.

6. List the criteria for selecting the software that is to be made available to users.

7. Describe your strategy for justifying the expenses that will be incurred in establishing and operating the information center.

8. Briefly describe seminars and short courses that should be offered on a one-time and ongoing basis.

9. In what ways do you think top management can help to motivate users to develop their own applications?

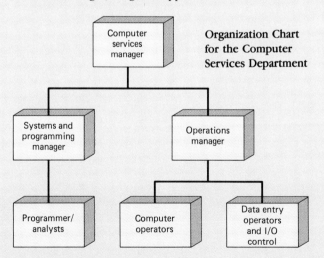

Organization Chart for the Computer Services Department

CHAPTER 6

End User Computing

CHAPTER OVERVIEW

End user computing is the catch phrase of the modern MIS era. The entire business community has embraced the concept of end user computing, but both user and MIS management have expressed concern that it must be coordinated, or it could get out of hand. This chapter is devoted to discussing the topic of end user computing—its scope, its resources, and its management.

THE TREND TO END USER COMPUTING

End User Computing

Most computer-based information systems are the result of cooperative efforts between the information services division and one or more user departments. In these partnership efforts, MIS professionals typically handle the technical aspects of development, and end users provide input on functional specifications. In some information system projects, end users handle both the technical and functional aspects of the project. The latter is known as **end user computing**. In support of end user computing, the information services division provides any needed technical advice and operational support on the company's mainframe.

A continuing string of user-oriented hardware and software products has made end user computing an increasingly enticing option in most businesses. End user computing is exactly what the phrase implies: users, with specialties in areas other than MIS, using their expertise to make the computer work for them. End user computing is not necessarily independent of corporate MIS activities because many of the mainframe-based tools, such as certain decision support systems, are supported by the information services division. However, once users are trained in the use and application of the software, what they do with it is entirely up to the individual users.

The Growth of End User Computing

End user computing is not just growing, its exploding! Once users become familiar with computers and have implemented those applications that justified the purchase of the hardware, they begin to branch out and find even more applications. Moreover, end user computing is contagious. Nonusers quickly see the opportunities that are created by end user computing and jump on the bandwagon.

For three decades, users opted for a somewhat passive role in the growth of MIS. However, today, users are becoming active participants in the information society. This activism can be attributed to the availability of MIS capabilities and a more sophisticated user community. In truth, a few users would like to continue in a passive role, but the cat is out of the bag, so to speak. Too many users have already demonstrated the value of end user computing. It is now apparent to those few who would prefer to be spoon-fed by information services that end user computing is the wave of the future.

Although the trend to end user computing is overwhelming, reluctant managers continue to ask, "Is end user computing necessary?" They want to know why the information services division does not continue to handle all the company's information processing needs. In short, there is no alternative. User information demands are increasing beyond the information services division's ability to meet these demands. The priorities of an individual manager are often in conflict with corporate priorities. For example, a manager may desperately need a small system to service ad hoc information needs, but long-term projects dealing with general corporate needs tend to dominate the agenda of information services divisions.

We have modified our environment so radically that we must now modify ourselves to exist in this new environment.

—— *Norbert Wiener*

End user computing is a relatively new term, but the trend was actually started in the mid-1970s with distributed processing. Distributed processing, discussed in Chapter 5, "Providers of Computer and Information Services," makes processing capabilities more accessible to the people who use these capabilities. In the early 1980s, the trend to end user computing was further fueled by the introduction of business-oriented microcomputers and a wide range of user-oriented software products, both for the micro and mainframe environments. Now that computing capabilities, user-oriented software, technical training, and technical assistance are readily available to the end user community, end user computing has become one of the driving forces behind the growth of MIS.

CATEGORIES OF END USER COMPUTING

Like so many automation-oriented buzz words, "end user computing" evolved without being formally defined. Consequently, the scope of what people refer to as end user computing has several interpretations. Technically speaking, any non-MIS professional using a computer falls in the category of end user computing. However, most people (including the author) do not include corporatewide information systems, such as the order entry, payroll, accounting, and inventory control systems, within the realm of end user computing.

End user computing spans all four levels of corporate activity: clerical, operational, tactical, and strategic. However, most of the end user computing activity is concentrated at the operational and tactical levels. Clerical-level personnel are involved with routine tasks that are supported by corporatewide information systems. Many top executives are unable or unwilling to set aside needed training time, even though end user computing has proven to be of great value to management at the strategic levels.

Conceptually, end user computing can be viewed at three levels: the individual, the department, and the corporation. Each has information processing needs.

- *At the individual level*, a single person identifies the need and uses his or her expertise and available technology to meet this need. At this level, the applications have a direct impact on an individual's job function and an indirect impact on the department and the company (productivity and effectiveness).

- *At the department level*, end user computing is a cooperative effort. The department manager provides direction by selecting hardware and suggesting applications. Department employees might work together to implement a local area network that provides support for a variety of applications, such as office automation or the sharing of local data bases.

- *At the corporate level*, end user computing is changing every facet of corporate endeavor from product development, to sales, to administration, to corporate strategy. To accommodate the evolution of end user computing, top management is establishing policy and procedures to control its growth.

Small businesses, such as this retail sporting goods store, do not have a corporate hierarchy and a centralized mainframe computer system. But their need for computer-based systems is no less intense. This type of situation is analogous to a department in a larger organization where end user computing is usually a cooperative effort.

Courtesy of International Business Machines Corporation

End user computing helps users plan; make decisions; write reports; communicate with their colleagues; store, recall, and process information; and learn. These benefits can be realized in the four categories of end user computing (see Figure 6–1):

☐ Decision support

☐ Personal productivity improvement

☐ User-developed information systems

☐ Office automation

All of these categories of end user computing are available in both micro and mini/mainframe environments. Decision support and information processing were first supported primarily on minis and mainframes and eventually migrated to the micro environment. Personal productivity improvement began in the micro environment with word processing and electronic spreadsheet applications and eventually migrated to the mini/mainframe environment. Office automation had its origins in the mid-1970s with dedicated word processing systems and has since expanded in scope and to all sizes of general-purpose computers. These four categories are discussed in detail in the following sections.

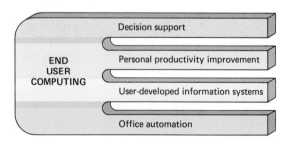

FIGURE 6–1 Categories of End User Computing

Decision Support

Decision support systems are interactive, computer-based information systems that rely on an integrated set of user-friendly hardware and software tools to produce and present information that is targeted to support management in the decision-making process. The characteristics, concepts, scope, and types of decision support systems (DSSs) are discussed in detail in Chapter 2. A DSS is comprised of a set of decision support tools that can be adapted to any decision environment (see Figure 6–2). These tools, which are discussed in detail in Chapter 2, are the following:

☐ *Applications development.* Some decision support systems provide end users with the capability to develop computer-based systems in support of the decision-making process. These applications typically involve the input of data, the processing and storing of data, and the output of information. Although these user-developed systems are usually developed on an ad hoc basis to provide information for a particular

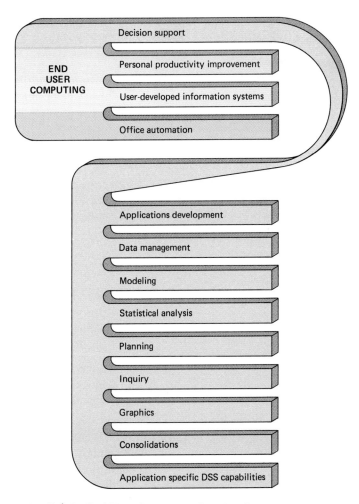

FIGURE 6–2   End User Computing: Decision Support

In the construction business, the accuracy of cost estimates may mean the difference between making or losing money. This engineer relies on a decision support system that uses historical data and updated cost data to produce reliable estimates of project costs.

Courtesy of International Business Machines Corporation

decision, the resultant system is often applicable to future decisions in its original or a slightly modified form.

☐ *Data management.* Each DSS software package has its own unique approach to data base management; that is, the software mechanisms for the storage, maintenance, and retrieval of data. This DSS tool is necessary to enable compatibility between a DSS data base and an integrated set of DSS software tools.

☐ *Modeling.* Decision support systems enable managers to use mathematical modeling techniques to re-create the functional aspects of a system within the confines of a computer. Models are appropriate when decisions involve a number of factors. For example, models are often used when uncertainty and risk are introduced, when several decision makers are involved, and when multiple outcomes are anticipated. In these cases, each decision needs to be evaluated on its own merit.

☐ *Statistical analysis.* The statistical analysis DSS capability includes everything from statistics such as average, median, and standard deviation; to analytical techniques such as regression analysis, exponential smoothing, and discriminate analysis; to complex procedures such as multivariate analysis. Risk analysis and trend analysis are common applications of DSS statistical tools.

☐ *Planning.* End user managers are often faced with making decisions that will be implemented at some time in the future. To help them get a glimpse into the future, managers rely on DSS software that permits forecasting, "what if" analysis, and goal seeking.

☐ *Inquiry.* DSS software enables managers to make on-line inquiries to the DSS data base using English-like commands. End users who query corporate data bases are able to communicate with computers in much the same language that they would use to communicate with their colleagues.

☐ *Graphics.* With the graphics DSS software tool, managers can create a variety of presentation graphics based on data in the DSS data base, including bar graphs, pie graphs, and line graphs.

☐ *Consolidations.* DSS software tools are available that enable the consolidation of like data from different sources (for example, the consolidation of financial statements from subsidiary companies into a single corporate financial statement).

☐ *Application-specific DSS capabilities.* DSS software is being routinely introduced to the marketplace that supports a particular decision environment, such as financial analysis and quality control.

To make a given decision, different users will seek different information in different forms. For example, one might choose modeling while another might prefer "what if" analysis. One manager might prefer to evaluate the results in a tabular format and another manager might prefer to evaluate the same results in a graphic format.

Personal Productivity Improvement

Many of the tasks accomplished at the clerical and operational levels of activity can be time consuming and tedious. To a lesser extent this is also true for managers at the tactical and strategic levels. For example, each month sales managers (operational level) used to spend hours, even days, documenting and summarizing sales figures on desktop-sized spreadsheet paper. They would use pen, ink, and straightedges to present the data in graphic form. The graphs would then be forwarded to appropriate management personnel with individual cover letters, all prepared manually on a typewriter. This process could easily take a week. Now, with the introduction of personal productivity improvement tools, such as electronic spreadsheets, presentation graphics, and word processing software, end users can do similar monthly reporting and other such activities in a fraction of the time that it took to do them manually.

Perhaps the most popular category of end user computing is using microcomputers in conjunction with *productivity software*. Microcomputer-based productivity software is a series of commercially available programs that can help end users save time and obtain the information they need to make more informed decisions (see Figure 6–3). These productivity tools, considered to be the foundation of personal computing in the business world, are listed on the following page.

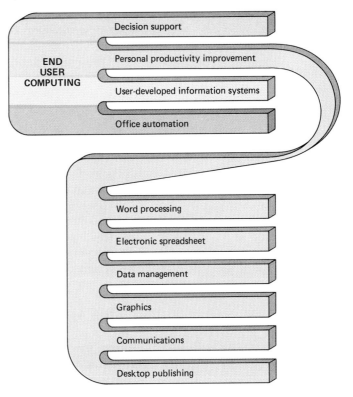

FIGURE 6–3   End User Computing: Personal Productivity Improvement

Of the personal productivity tools, desktop publishing is getting the lion's share of the attention. Not only can users bypass the expense of professional typesetting and page layout, they can drastically reduce the time needed to prepare a camera-ready document. In the photo, an ad designer is creating an ad piece. To do this he is using a microcomputer, with a keyboard and mouse for input, and a laser printer in conjunction with PageMaker, a desktop publishing software package.

Aldus Corporation

Give a user a program and you satisfy him for a day. Teach a user to program and you satisfy him for life.

——— *James Martin and E. A. Hersbey III*

- ☐ Word processing
- ☐ Electronic spreadsheet
- ☐ Data management
- ☐ Graphics
- ☐ Communications
- ☐ Desktop publishing

Each of these tools is mentioned briefly in Chapter 5, "Providers of Computer and Information Services," in the discussion of standard software resources in information centers. The function, concepts, and use of these and other productivity tools are described in detail in Chapter 7, "Personal Computing."

User-Developed Information Systems

The information demands in a typical business are endless. To give you an idea of management's demand for information, the average information services division carries a three-and-a-half-year backlog of service requests. We have heard that "time is money"; it is also true that "information is money." Users cannot wait three years for the information they need. Most can't wait a week. End user computing has shown managers that they do not have to wait, so many users are taking matters into their own hands. With the help of user-friendly software tools, such as query languages, database management systems, electronic spreadsheets, and decision support systems, end users are developing their own information systems.

The combination of departmental computing, powerful micros, and user-friendly software has resulted in a rapid expansion in the base of computerwise users. These users have the tools and knowledge to meet many of their own information processing needs. In fact, a greater percentage of an organization's ever-growing information processing needs are being met with little or no involvement on the part of the professional programmers associated with an information services department. This trend is illustrated in Figure 6–4. Notice that each year a growing percentage of a company's information processing needs is being met by the user community.

User-developed information systems are limited in scope and sophistication, and they are usually *function based*; that is, they are designed to support an individual's or a department's information needs. In contrast, information systems developed by the information services division are *integrated* and are designed to support several departments or the company as a whole.

Office Automation

During the last 10 years, much has been said and written about **office automation**. The term refers collectively to those computer-based applications associated with general office work. With the increasing technical sophistication of the user community, office automation or **OA** has begun to fall within the scope of end user computing. User departments that take full advantage of office automation have experienced productivity increases of

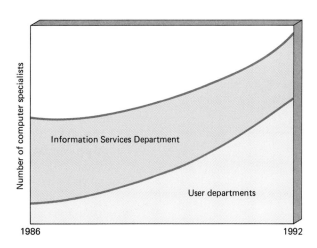

FIGURE 6–4 Computer Specialist Positions in Transition
The trend to end user computing has increased the number of computer specialists in the user areas.

50 to 100 percent. Surprisingly, less than 15 percent of all companies can claim extensive use of office automation applications. Therefore, OA is an application with tremendous growth potential. Office automation applications include word processing (also considered a productivity tool), electronic mail, image processing, voice processing, and office information systems (see Figure 6–5). Each of these applications is discussed in the paragraphs that follow.

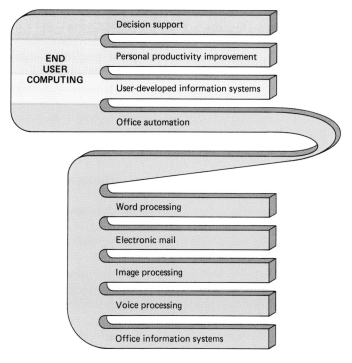

FIGURE 6–5 End User Computing: Office Automation

WORD PROCESSING   Word processing, the cornerstone of office automation, revolves around written communication and is found wherever there is an office with a computer. Word processing, which is discussed in detail in Chapter 7, is available on virtually every micro, mini, and mainframe computer.

ELECTRONIC MAIL   Computer networks enable us to route messages to each other. A message can be a note, letter, report, or chart or even the manuscript of a book. Each person in a company can be assigned an "electronic mailbox" in which messages are received and stored on secondary storage, such as magnetic disk. To "open" and "read" **electronic mail**, or **E-mail**, the user simply goes to the nearest workstation and recalls the message from storage.

A national sales manager can inform regional sales managers of a price reduction via electronic mail and avoid the time-consuming ritual of "telephone tag." The message would originate on a workstation at the national headquarters. It would then be routed to the electronic mailboxes of the regional managers. Each manager "opens the mail" by displaying the message on his or her workstation.

IMAGE PROCESSING   Image processing involves the creation, storage, and distribution of pictorial information. There are two levels of image processing sophistication.

At the first level, **facsimile** equipment, which has been around since the 1960s, transfers images of hard-copy documents via telephone lines to another office. The process is similar to making a copy on a copying machine, except that the original is inserted in a facsimile, or "fax," machine at one office and a hard copy is produced on another fax machine in another office. A marketing manager who needs quick approval on a new ad piece might elect to send facsimile copies of the ad piece to the regional sales managers.

Recent technological innovations have expanded the scope of image processing. An **image processor** uses a camera to scan and digitize the image; then the digitized image is stored on a disk. The image can be handwritten notes, photographs, drawings, or anything that can be digitized. In digitized form, the image can be retrieved, displayed, altered, merged with text, stored, and sent via data communications to one or several remote locations.

VOICE PROCESSING   Voice processing includes **voice message switching** and **teleconferencing**. The workstation for voice message switching (a store-and-forward "voice mailbox" system) is a touchtone telephone. Voice message switching accomplishes the same function as electronic mail, except the hard copy is not available. When you send a message, your voice is digitized and stored on a magnetic disk for later retrieval. The message is routed to the destination(s) you designate (using the telephone's keyboard); then it is heard upon request by the intended receiver(s). A voice store-and-forward system permits you to send one or many messages with just one phone call.

Teleconferencing enables people in different locations to see and talk to each other and to share charts and other meeting materials visually. The voice and video of teleconferencing are supported by the telephone network. The idea behind teleconferencing is that people who are geographically scattered can meet without the need for time-consuming and expensive travel.

The use of teleconferencing has fallen short of initial expectations because people have found that electronic interaction is not a substitute for direct human interaction. The controlled teleconferencing environment does not transmit subtle nonverbal communication, which is so important to human understanding.

OFFICE INFORMATION SYSTEMS Several small information systems address traditional office tasks. For example, one system allows people to keep their personal *calendars* on-line. As workers schedule activities, they block out times in their electronic calendars. There are definite advantages to having a central data base of personal calendars. Let's say that a public relations manager wants to schedule a meeting to review the impact of some unexpected favorable publicity. To do this, the manager enters the names of the participants and the expected duration of the meeting. The *conference scheduling* system searches the calendars of affected people and suggests possible meeting times. The manager then selects a meeting time, and the participants are notified by electronic mail. Of course, their calendars are automatically updated to reflect the meeting time.

Another common office application is the company *directory*. The directory contains basic personnel data: name, title, department, location, and phone number. To "look up" someone's telephone number, all you have to do is enter the person's name on your workstation, and the associated data are displayed. The beauty of the directory data base is that it is always up to date, unlike hard-copy directories which never seem to have the current titles or phone numbers.

Other systems permit users to organize *personal notes*, keep *diaries*, document ideas in a *preformatted outline*, and keep a *tickler file*. When users log on in the morning, the tickler file automatically reminds them of "things to do" for that day.

RESOURCES AVAILABLE FOR END USER COMPUTING

The wave of the future is coming and there is no fighting it.

——— *Anne Morrow Lindbergh*

The variety of computing resources available to end users is growing every day. These resources are discussed in four categories: hardware, software, education, and technical support.

Hardware

Today's microcomputers and minicomputers have the power of the mainframe computers of a few years ago. A single minicomputer or a multiuser micro can service many users and accommodate a broad spectrum of applications. The most visible symbol of end user computing is the hardware: workstations, microcomputers, minicomputers, printers, and so on. Top management is in agreement that computing resources should be made accessible to end users. The benefits are overwhelming. Even so, there is a trade-off between accessibility and proliferation. There is a fine line between providing users with the necessary resources and having more user-based hardware than can be adequately controlled.

Software

End user computing software resources can be grouped into five basic classifications:

- □ User-oriented fourth-generation languages
- □ Microcomputer productivity software
- □ Natural languages
- □ Decision support systems
- □ Expert systems

Each is discussed in the paragraphs that follow.

User-Oriented Fourth-Generation Languages

The trend in software development is to using high-level, user-friendly, *fourth-generation languages* (**4GL**s). Such languages enable managers to create their own applications systems. The principles and use of fourth-generation languages are discussed in Chapter 13, "Prototyping and Application Development Tools." There are two types of 4GLs. The first is designed primarily for MIS professionals and for the development of production information system. These products are usually, though not always, associated with a vendor's database management system software. Production-oriented 4GLs include ADR's Ideal, Software AG's Natural 2, and Cincom's Mantis. The other type of 4GL is designed to be used primarily by end users. Users write programs to query (extract information from) a database and for creating function-based information systems. User-oriented 4GLs include Mathematica Products Group's RAMIS II and Information Builders' FOCUS.

Over the years, most companies have accumulated large amounts of computer-based data. Prior to fourth-generation languages (mid-1970s), these data were not directly accessible to users. Users had to describe their information needs to a professional programmer, who would then write a program in a procedure-oriented language, like COBOL, to produce the desired results. Fulfilling a typical user request would take at least a couple of days and as much as two weeks. By then, the desired information may no longer be needed. With fourth-generation languages, these same ad hoc requests, or queries, can be completed in minutes by the user, without involving computer professionals!

With four to eight hours of training and practice, a user can learn to write programs, make inquiries, and get reports in user-oriented 4GLs. Once they become familiar with user-oriented 4GLs, users often find that it is easier and quicker to sit down at the nearest workstation and write a program than it is to relate inquiry or report specifications to a professional programmer. With 4GLs, managers can attend to their own seemingly endless ad hoc requests for information and even write their own production information systems. If the data base is already in place, about 75 percent of a typical

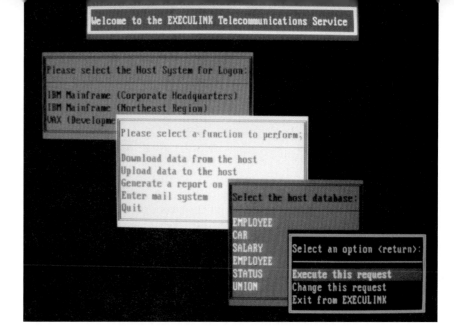

All user-oriented software products are being designed with the end user in mind. This user-friendly PC FOCUS display illustrates how easily a user can use communications software to download data from a host computer to a microcomputer. The first window gives the user a choice of three host computer systems. Once the link is established, a second window is superimposed on the first and gives the user a menu of possible functions. The third window is displayed in response to the user selecting the "download" option and contains a list of available data bases. When the user selects a data base to download, the final window asks the user to confirm the request.

Information Builders, Inc.

user's information needs can be met with 4GLs. 4GLs benefit everyone concerned—users get the information that they need quickly, and, because programmers have fewer ad hoc programming assignments, they can focus their efforts on the ever-increasing backlog of information systems projects. Of course, professional programmers use 4GLs to increase their productivity as well. Programmers claim productivity improvements over third-generation procedure-oriented languages (COBOL, FORTRAN, BASIC, and so on) of 200 to 1,000 percent.

The problem with 4GLs is that they are less efficient than third-generation languages. That is, 4GLs require more computer capacity to perform a particular operation. Proponents of 4GLs claim that the added cost of the hardware is more than offset by the time saved in creating the programs with 4GLs. Critics claim that 4GL capabilities are limited (when compared to third-generation languages) and that users end up fitting their problems to the capabilities of the software.

Microcomputer Productivity Software

Microcomputer productivity software, which includes word processing, electronic spreadsheet, data management, and other software, is discussed earlier in this chapter.

Natural Languages

Natural language software accepts instructions without regard to format or syntax in the native or natural language of the end user. At this time, there are no pure natural languages. However, natural languages with certain syntax restrictions are available. These natural languages permit end users to express their information needs in plain English. Concepts of and examples of natural languages are presented in Chapter 3, "Artificial Intelligence and Expert Systems."

Decision Support Systems

There is a plethora of decision support system software that is designed especially for the end user computing environment. DSS software, which includes "what if" analysis, electronic spreadsheet, simulation, and other decision support software, is summarized in an earlier section of this chapter and is discussed in detail in Chapter 2, "The MIS and Decision Support Systems."

Expert Systems

An expert system is an interactive computer-based system that responds to questions, asks for clarification, makes recommendations, and generally aids in the decision-making process. Expert systems help end users to solve problems by playing the role of expert during an interactive session with a user. Users can create their own expert systems, or they can purchase one of the limited number of commercially available expert systems (for example, medical diagnoses, computer repair, tax preparation). Concepts of and examples of expert systems are presented in Chapter 3, "Artificial Intelligence and Expert Systems."

Education

Education is the foundation ingredient in end user computing. There is no shortcut to becoming an active participant in the end user computing movement. Each person must educate himself or herself in the use and application of the hardware and one or more of the software tools that comprise end user computing. With approximately 95 percent of the work force calling themselves computer illiterates, making the educational resource available to those who want and need it is a massive undertaking. Most companies make at least one of the following sources of computer-related education available to employees: periodic in-house seminars, self-paced videotape courses, one-on-one advisors (in information centers), tuition reimbursement (for college courses), and a library of computer books and educational materials. Of course, many still learn in a less formal setting via OJT (on-the-job training).

Technical Support

Any company that embraces the concept of end user computing must accept the responsibility of educating its employees and providing them with technical support. On occasion, users, and even MIS specialists, need help. When they do, they need to know that there is a place to go or a person to call who can provide them with assistance. Informally, technical support is available from colleagues with more experience and knowledge. Formally, technical support is available through the information center, user liaisons, and, for particularly difficult problems, specialists in the information services division.

Making the Most of End User Computing Resources

The availability of resources does not guarantee that they will be used or used judiciously with purpose. Reluctant users must be motivated to take advantage of the resources and the activities of enthusiastic users must, on occasion, be curtailed.

Users are encouraged to participate in end user computing as long as what they do complements corporate objectives. When applications of end user computing do not support corporate objectives, the net result is a negative impact on the corporation. For example, the accounting division might create a series of information systems that supports only their needs, while ignoring the importance of integration and the impact of their design on other divisions. In general, autonomous systems breed expensive data and work flow redundancy and should be avoided.

For the most part, the applications of end user computing are selected by the individual users or by the user departments. Users should be encouraged to select those information processing applications that yield the greatest benefits to the company. There is an endless number of "nice to have" applications that provide marginal benefits to the user and to the company. Users should be encouraged to defer the implementation of marginal applications indefinitely and to focus their energies on high-return applications.

MANAGEMENT OF END USER COMPUTING

End user computing has changed the way top management views information services. Companies have been reorganized (information centers, user liaisons) to accommodate end user computing. Many position descriptions have been updated to make certain computer skills prerequisite knowledge for job applicants. As a result of the continuing emphasis on end user computing, the number of installed computer applications in companies has increased geometrically. Forecasters are predicting that by 1990, 50 to 80 percent of the all computing capabilities will be dedicated to the support of end user computing. Managing the explosion of end user computing may be the single greatest challenge facing the business community.

With the advent of end user computing, users have greater flexibility to do what they wish with their computing environment. Just a few years ago, user managers were dependent on the information services division for the approval, development, and support of all computer applications. Almost overnight, end users have graduated from being dependent users to being creators and implementers. Now users must deal with all aspects of information systems development, implementation, and operation. In the past, the information services division handled all operational duties, such as running the mainframe computer, and all administrative functions, such as controls, backup, and security. In their new role, users will eventually assume responsibility for all facets of end user computing, but during the transition phase, someone needs to coordinate its growth. By default, much of the management of end user computing has fallen on the shoulders of the information services division.

During the early stages of end user computing (early 1980s), user and MIS management had their hands full just coping with its rapid growth. Although growth continues to be brisk, the rate of growth has slowed to the point that end user computing can be managed. Corporate management is beginning to address some basic questions: Who pays for what? Who is responsible for what? Is purchasing centralized? What policies are needed? Should hardware/software standards be established? These are literally burning questions in many companies.

The Role of Information Centers and the Information Services Division

The two primary information services support groups, information centers and the information services division, are playing critical roles in the emergence of end user computing. Information centers evolved from a need to provide quick solutions to immediate information processing problems. Information centers, discussed in detail in Chapter 5, "Providers of Computer and Information Services," continue to provide educational support, technical advice, and accessibility to user-oriented hardware and software. More and more, however, information center personnel are doing development work as well. Because information centers are not a policymaking body, managers of these centers are not in a position to control what users do with their computer knowledge and skills.

For the most part, directors of information services divisions are embracing and fostering end user computing. On the positive side, users are taking on development projects that would otherwise be relegated to information services. This reduces the MIS backlog and enables the division to be more responsive to corporatewide information processing needs. On the negative side, end user computing is placing the burden of control on the information services division. To make matters worse, this control is often informal; that is, MIS management is powerless to enforce its directives on control, security, and so on. Unless policies regarding the management of end user computing are established at the top levels of the corporation, the information services division's role can be no more than that of a catalyst and advisor.

Coordination and Control of End User Computing

End user computing is a topic of great concern for MIS managers and user managers with information systems experience. They know that their companies are courting disaster if the growth of end user computing is left unchecked. The controls in place in information services divisions have evolved to a high level of sophistication over the past 30 years (see Chapter 14, "System Implementation"). End user computing is in the embryonic stage of development, and so are its controls. More often than not, the individual user is responsible for ensuring that the system he or she created is secure from unauthorized access, the system is properly documented and backed up, and the necessary system controls are in place. In the mainframe environment, these controls are taken for granted. Information services divisions have strict program control procedures. For example, if a programmer modifies a program, he or she has to follow the program change procedure. Just a few years ago, only 5 to 10 people in a company of 500 people would be writing programs. That same company may have 100 or more people writing programs, another hundred may be involved in some form of end user computing, and the remainder may have access to at least parts of the data base. User-developed systems that deal with sensitive data are open invitations to computer criminals.

A centralized authority, perhaps an arm of the information services division, should be empowered to coordinate and control end user computing. This authority's scope of responsibility would typically include enforcing policies and procedures that deal with the following areas:

☐ *The integration of data bases and information systems.* The centralized authority can serve as a clearinghouse to ensure that data bases and information systems are not duplicated and that users with similar information needs can cooperate to meet these needs.

□ *Auditing and controls.* Direct control is not always necessary, but when the system and/or its associated data base deal with sensitive information (salaries, corporate profit/loss, pricing information, client information), the centralized authority may need to help users in the design phase to ensure that the system includes the proper controls and can be audited properly. User-generated systems that provide input to the corporate data base must include the same rigorous controls as mainframe-based systems (data verification, documentation, program change controls).

□ *Limiting access.* Sensitive systems must use passwords and personal identification numbers to limit access to persons with a need to know.

□ *Backup.* Every system, especially those that are volatile (frequent changes to data base), must adhere to proper backup procedures.

□ *Hardware acquisition.* To maintain compatibility, most companies have adopted a policy that spells out which computers and peripheral devices can be purchased in support of end user computing.

□ *Software acquisition.* To maintain compatibility, most companies have adopted a policy that spells out which software can be purchased in support of end user computing.

Issues in End User Computing

Within a given company, many issues have surfaced and been resolved during the evolution of end user computing, but the three that get the lion's share of management's attention are software piracy, the proliferation of microcomputer hardware, and viruses.

Software Piracy

The unlawful duplication of proprietary software, called *software piracy*, is making companies vulnerable to legal action by the affected vendors. To protect themselves, most companies that support end user computing have established a strongly worded policy that discourages employees from the unlawful duplication of proprietary software. Nevertheless, the problem continues to exist. Often, software pirates duplicate proprietary software for use on their home microcomputers. Vendors are hoping that the threat of a suit will encourage companies to honor their copyrights and to police the distribution of proprietary software better. Top management is hoping that a policy and the threat of dismissal will be a deterrent. Unfortunately, both vendors and top management are disappointed with the results of their actions and software piracy continues to be a serious issue. The software piracy issue is addressed again in Chapter 16, "Managing the Information and Computing Resources."

The PC Proliferation Problem

It is not unusual for a company to have hundreds, even thousands, of workstations, most of which are microcomputers. All micros can serve as standalone systems or as workstations. During the early 1980s when the business community began to recognize the personal computer as a valuable business tool, user managers purchased PCs by the truckload with little regard for compatibility considerations. By the mid-1980s, the "PC proliferation problem," as it had become known, had become acute and needed attention. It was not at all uncommon for an information services division to be providing informal technical support for dozens of different microcomputers and micro software packages.

Initially, users viewed the purchase price of the micros as the majority of the expense associated with buying and using a micro. Some found out later that the successful implementation of a micro may result in costs of several times the purchase price. One of the problems was that the price alone of a micro was well within the discretionary purchasing limits of user managers. Managers were buying micros without any forethought as to what they wanted to do with them or what the ultimate costs would be.

Many companies confronted the "PC proliferation problem" by establishing a microcomputer review committee. The typical committee had the following fundamental charges:

1. Establish guidelines for the acquisition of microcomputer hardware, specifying which micros and associated peripheral devices would be supported by the information services division and the information center.

2. Establish guidelines for the acquisition of microcomputer software, specifying which microcomputer productivity software tools (e.g., electronic spreadsheet, word processing, database, graphics, and communications) would be supported by the information services division and the information center.

3. Review and approve/disapprove all user requests to purchase microcomputer hardware or software.

4. Set up and monitor a volume microcomputer purchase program that enables departments and employees to purchase micro hardware and software at substantial discounts.

5. Educate users in the purchase and acquisition of microcomputer hardware and software.

Viruses

One important issue facing end user computing is the growing threat of viruses. A **virus** is a program that literally "infects" other programs and data bases. Virus programs are written with malicious intent and are loaded to the computer system of an unsuspecting victim, often an end user. Viruses have been found at all levels of computing, but the end user computing environment is particularly susceptible to virus infiltration because of the lack of system controls in this environment.

The virus is so named because it can spread from one system to another like a biological virus. There are many types of viruses. Some act quickly by erasing user programs and data bases. Others grow like a cancer, destroying small parts of a data base each day. Some viruses act like a time bomb. Such viruses lay dormant for days or months, but eventually are activated and wreak havoc on any software on the system. Some viruses attack the hardware and have been known to throw the mechanical components of a computer system, such as disk access arms, into costly spasms. Viruses can spread from one computer network to another. Also, they spread from one system to another via common diskettes.

Since first appearing in the mid-1980s, viruses have erased bank records, damaged hospital records, destroyed the programs in thousands of microcomputers, and even infected part of the systems at NORAD (strategic defense) and NASA. Disgruntled employees have inserted viruses in disks that were distributed to customers. The motives of those who would infect a system with a virus run from electronic vandalism to revenge to terrorism. There is no monetary reward, only the "satisfaction" of knowing that their efforts have been very costly to individuals, companies, governments, and so on.

Viruses are a serious problem. They have the potential to impact an individual's career and even destroy companies. For example, a company that loses its accounts receivables records could be a candidate for bankruptcy. Antiviral programs exist, but these programs can be circumvented by a persistent (and malicious) programmer. The best way to cope with viruses is to recognize that they exist and to take precautionary measures. For example, one company requires micro users to turn off their micros and reload their personal copy of the operating system before each use. In the mainframe environment, systems programmers must continually search for suspicious-looking programs and be particularly wary of downloading programs from computer systems outside of the company.

BECOMING A POWER USER

The term **power user** was coined to describe a computerwise end user who takes full advantage of the capabilities of end user computing. The casual user employs only a fraction of the capabilities of end user hardware and software. The power user presses the limits of the hardware and software. To become a power user

□ *Learn the use and application of end user computing resources.* The first step to becoming a power user is to achieve computer literacy, and then learn the use and application of a workstation and/or a microcomputer and at least one of the end user software tools.

□ *Practice skills.* Develop skills through practice. For example, use test data to create a spreadsheet, a data base, or graph.

You can bet that John Frank, the president of Zenith Data Systems, is a power user. While en route to Chicago's O'Hare Airport, he is using his battery-powered portable personal computer to put the finishing touches on a product launch presentation.

Zenith Data Systems

176

Perhaps the most valuable result of all education is the ability to make yourself do the thing you have to do, when it ought to be done, whether you like it or not. This is the first lesson to be learned.

—— *Thomas Huxley*

☐ *Apply your knowledge and resources to your working environment.* For example, create a "sales summary" spreadsheet that can be used for "what if" analysis.

☐ *Experiment with and apply the advanced features of end user computing resources.* Spend time experimenting with the advanced features of the hardware and software tools of end user computing. For example, use the file merge capability of a word processing package to consolidate the text in several files and reformat the text into a multicolumn newsletter format. Once you have become familiar with an advanced feature, use it in a work-related application.

☐ *Update skills continually.* The accumulated total of computer capabilities doubles every two years, and so it is with the field of end user computing. To remain current, power users subscribe to trade periodicals, such as *Personal Computing* and *Computerworld*. When they see a product or an application that interests them, they request more information, or perhaps they order the product. Power users frequently exchange information via special-interest electronic bulletin boards (Lotus 1-2-3, IBM PS/2, FOCUS, and so on).

Of course, the power user is continually searching for new applications for his or her knowledge and the resources of end user computing.

CHAPTER HIGHLIGHTS

■ End user computing involves users, who have specialties in areas other than MIS, using their expertise to make the computer work for them. In end user computing, users handle both the technical and functional aspects of information system-related projects.

■ The trend to end user computing was started in the mid-1970s with distributed processing and, in the early 1980s, was further fueled by the introduction of business-oriented microcomputers and a wide range of user-oriented software products.

■ End user computing spans all four levels of corporate activity, but is concentrated at the operational and tactical levels. It helps users plan; make decisions; write reports; communicate with their colleagues; store, recall, and process information; and learn.

■ The four categories of end user computing are decision support, personal productivity improvement, user-developed information systems, and office automation.

■ Decision support systems are interactive, computer-based information systems that rely on an integrated set of user-friendly hardware and software tools to produce and present information that is targeted to support management in the decision-making process. The categories of DSS software tools include applications development, data management, modeling, statistical analysis, planning, inquiry, graphics, consolidations, and application-specific DSS capabilities.

■ Probably the most popular area of end user computing involves using microcomputers in conjunction with productivity software. The most visible of these software productivity tools include word processing, electronic spreadsheet, data management, graphics, communications, and desktop publishing.

■ With the help of user-friendly software tools, end users are developing their own information systems. In fact, a greater percentage of an organization's ever-growing information processing needs are being met with little or no involvement from MIS professionals.

■ Office automation refers collectively to those computer-based applications associated with general office work. They include word processing, electronic mail, image processing, voice processing, and office information systems.

■ Computer networks enable us to route messages to each other via electronic mail or E-mail.

■ Image processing involves the creation, storage, and distribution of pictorial information. The base technologies for the two levels of image processing sophistication are facsimile equipment and image processors.

■ Several small information systems address traditional office tasks, for example personal calendars, conference scheduling systems, directories, personal notes, diaries, preformatted outlines, and tickler files.

- The resources available to end user computing include hardware, software, education, and technical support.

- Hardware resources available for use in end user computing encompass any combination of input/output, storage, and processor hardware that can be adequately controlled by the end user.

- The software resources for end user computing can be grouped into five basic categories: user-oriented fourth-generation languages, microcomputer productivity software, natural languages, decision support systems, and expert systems.

- The trend in software development is to using high-level, user-friendly, fourth-generation languages. Such languages enable managers to create their own applications systems.

- Natural languages permit end users to express their information needs in plain English. Natural language software accepts user-entered instructions without regard to format or syntax in the native or natural language of the end user.

- Expert systems help end users solve problems by playing the role of a human expert during an interactive session with a user.

- Any company that embraces the concept of end user computing must accept the responsibility of educating its employees and providing them with technical support. Technical support is usually available through the information center, user liaisons, and specialists in the information services division.

- Forecasters are predicting that by 1990, 50 to 80 percent of all computing capabilities will be dedicated to the support of end user computing. Managing the explosion of end user computing may be the single greatest challenge facing the business community.

- The two primary information services support groups, information centers and the information services division, are playing critical roles in the emergence of end user computing. Information centers provide educational support, technical advice, accessibility to user-oriented hardware and software. And center personnel do development work as well. Typically, the information services division coordinates and manages end user computing.

- A centralized authority empowered to coordinate and control end user computing would typically enforce policies and procedures that deal with the following areas: the integration of data bases and information systems, auditing and controls, limiting access, backup, hardware acquisition, and software acquisition.

- The three issues involving end user computing that are receiving the most attention by management are software piracy, the proliferation of microcomputer hardware, and viruses.

- The unlawful duplication of someone else's copyright program is referred to as software piracy.

- During the early 1980s, user managers purchased personal computers with little regard for compatibility considerations. This action gave rise to what is now known as the "PC proliferation problem."

- Viruses are programs that are written with malicious intent and then loaded to the computer system of an unsuspecting victim, often an end user. The virus is so named because it can spread from one system to another like a biological virus.

- The power user is a computerwise end user who takes full advantage of the capabilities of end user computing.

IMPORTANT TERMS

backup (Ch. 9)	fourth-generation languages (4GLs) (Ch. 14)	power user	virus
electronic mail (E-mail)	image processor	software piracy (Ch. 16)	voice message switching
end user computing	office automation (OA)	teleconferencing	
facsimile			

REVIEW EXERCISES

1. What started the trend to end user computing?

2. Risk analysis would fit into which category of end user computing? Goal seeking would fit into which category of end user computing?

3. List the areas of responsibility of the centralized authority in charge of coordinating end user computing.

4. Briefly describe the role that information centers play in end user computing.

5. List those computer applications that fall under the umbrella of office automation.

6. Which of the office automation applications has the potential to lighten the load of the U.S. Postal Service?

7. Give examples of three types of office information systems.

8. What name has been given to the unlawful duplication of someone else's program?

9. What is the difference between a casual end user and a power user?

10. Contrast the two types of fourth-generation languages.

11. Word processing is included in which two of the four categories of end user computing?

12. During the next few years, which organizational entity is being charged with the management of end user computing?

13. Name five commercially available fourth-generation languages.

14. What is a program called that has an adverse affect on other programs and data bases?

15. What type of system responds to user questions, asks for clarification, makes recommendations, and generally aids in the decision-making process?

16. What is the "PC proliferation problem"?

17. Name and briefly describe the six microcomputer tools that are collectively referred to as productivity software.

18. What advantages does an image processor have over facsimile equipment?

19. Most the the end user computing activity takes place at which two levels of activity?

DISCUSSION QUESTIONS

1. Some user managers believe that end user computing is a flash-in-the-pan trend that will soon go the way of the pet rock. These managers are content to let the information services division handle all their information processing needs. What would you say to these managers to convince them that end user computing may well be the wave of the future?

2. Discuss the motives of someone who would employ a virus to infect the data base of a bank. Of a university. Of a foreign government.

3. How has end user computing affected the priorities of MIS projects?

4. Describe decision circumstances that would invite the use of mathematical modeling techniques. Give an example.

5. The average backlog of service requests to an information services division is in excess of three years. In what way has this backlog contributed to the growth of end user computing?

6. Discuss the advantages and disadvantages of fourth-generation languages.

7. Contrast information systems developed by the information services division with those developed exclusively by end users.

8. Millions of clerical-level end users spend much of their working day interacting with a computer system. For the most part, these people are trained to enter data and make simple inquiries to a specific MIS (for example, an airline reservations system). Would these people be considered part of the 5 percent of the work force that is computer literate? Explain.

9. Describe the types of applications that are best suited to end user computing. Give an example.

10. Discuss some of the problems that management may need to resolve during the early stages of a company's growth into end user computing.

11. Discuss the importance of controls in end user computing.

12. Suppose that a company has a policy that prohibits software piracy. Several employees of the company admit to software piracy. The affected software vendor files suit against the company (not the employees) for damages. Discuss the case from the perspective of the plaintiff. Discuss the case from the perspective of the defendant.

13. Which office automation applications have the potential to reduce the amount of time that white-collar workers spend on the telephone? Explain.

14. What advantages does voice message switching have over electronic mail? What advantages does electronic mail have over voice message switching? Why do you suppose that some companies have opted to implement both?

15. The ACME Corporation is in the top 10 percent of all manufacturing companies in the number of micros per white-collar worker. Does this reflect frivolous spending or a conscious effort to promote end user computing and make effective use of available technology? Explain.

16. Should a company specify what microcomputer hardware and software users can buy, or should users be permitted the flexibility to choose whatever they want? Justify your position.

17. Many companies encourage their micro users to be "computer literate" by providing an in-house education program. Should users study computers on company time or on their own time? Explain.

APPLICATION CASE STUDY 6–1
Office Automation

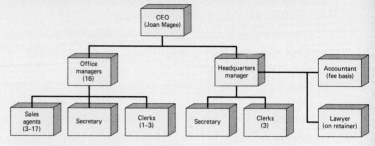

Organization Chart for Que Realty

The Situation

Que Realty is a successful independent real estate sales company. Que has 96 full-time and 37 part-time real estate agents who work out of 16 offices. Joan Magee, Que's owner, is an avid proponent of using information technology as a competitive strategy. Under her leadership, information systems have been implemented for matching clients with houses (see Application Case Study 3–1, "Expert Systems") and for storing and retrieving listings from an on-line data base (see Application Case Study 3–2, "Natural Languages").

Ms. Magee hired a consultant two months ago to investigate the feasibility of automating tasks that the agents stated they would like to see operate faster and more efficiently (see Application Case Study 4–2, "Leveraging Information Systems"). After analyzing the tasks mentioned by the agents, as well as other aspects of Que's operations, the consultant came to the conclusion that the application of office automation would resolve many of the agents' complaints.

Joan Magee prepared an organization chart that depicts Que Realty's structure. She thought that with this chart (shown here) and an understanding of Que's operations (see previous case studies mentioned), the consultant should be able to design an integrated office automation system.

Joan Magee is Que's owner and chief executive officer (CEO). She is responsible for making major policy decisions and managing the overall operation of the company. Ms. Magee is located in Que's headquarters office, together with the headquarters manager, a secretary, and 3 clerks. The headquarters staff handles all the company's bookkeeping and legal functions. Que utilizes the services of an accountant on a fee basis. The accountant audits the books, prepares the financial statements (balance sheet, income statement, and profit and loss statement), and provides advice on financial matters. Que has a lawyer who works on a retainer basis. The lawyer assists with complex sales and represents Que in any litigation that may arise. The accountant and lawyer are not employees of Que Realty. Each of the 16 sales offices has a manager, a secretary, 1 or more clerks, and a number of real estate agents. The smallest office currently has 3 agents and the largest has 17 agents. The number of clerks in the sales offices varies from 1 to 3, depending on the number of agents in an office and the volume of sales.

The Assignment

Put yourself in the role of the consultant and design an office automation system for Que Realty that responds to the tasks the agents listed as needing to be improved and to the tasks that you feel would enhance operations at Que. The common complaint by the agents is that whatever their specific task is, they want to do it *now*, and they want to do it *faster*. The tasks most frequently mentioned are

☐ Calculating monthly payments for mortgages and taxes.

☐ Entering a new listing into the data base.

☐ Preparing sales agreements.

☐ Preparing closing papers.

☐ Making inquiries into the listing data base when not in the office.

☐ Getting copies of sales agreements or other documents from another office.

1. Add any other tasks that you, as a consultant, think could benefit from the application of office automation technology. For example, although not mentioned, agents might benefit from being able to retrieve and listen to their phone message while away from the office.

2. For each task identified by the agents and you, identify which office automation application(s) would be appropriate to address the task.

3. Specify the hardware necessary to implement the office automation applications that you specified in the previous question. The "Short Course in Computer Concepts" following Chapter 17 provides an overview of computer hardware.

4. Describe the resistance you might encounter from any Que personnel when you implement the office automation system. In your description, include the job title(s) (secretary, for example), the elements of the office automation system that might be resisted, and possible reasons for the resistance. What precautionary steps would you take to preempt or overcome any anticipated resistance?

5. Give a plan to train Que's staff to use the office automation system. Specify which personnel would be trained on which applications.

APPLICATION CASE STUDY 6–2
Management of End User Computing

The Situation

Gabriel Industries is a medium-sized manufacturing company that has recently organized an information center (see Application Case Study 5–2, "The Information Center"). The information center staff periodically conducts seminars to introduce users to microcomputer hardware and software. Users have responded enthusiastically to the seminars, and several departments have purchased microcomputers and implemented information systems. However, some problems have surfaced.

John Robson, the manager of the Computer Services Department, has discovered that some users have purchased hardware and software without obtaining prior approval from the information center staff. Two microcomputers and several major software items that were purchased were not on the "approved list," meaning that the information center is not prepared or obliged to support these systems. When confronted about her deviation from the approved list, Barbara Goldman, manager of advertising and public relations, stated "We can handle it, don't worry about it!" She was incensed at the implication that personnel in her department were not competent enough, and also resented interference with what she felt was an internal departmental operation. She told John Robson that "It's my money and I'll spend it as I see fit!" Gabriel's policy permits department managers to make purchases without higher approval of items costing less than $2,000. Barbara Goldman used this policy to purchase her microcomputer system piece by piece. She compiled separate purchase orders for the processor unit, color monitor, and laser printer.

Another potential problem that John Robson discovered quite informally is that several users are no longer making backups of data on a regularly scheduled basis. So far, this has not caused any serious problems, that is, nobody has had a hard disk crash or erased a major file or data base, although some small files have had to be re-created.

Paul Klahr, manager of the Personnel Department, uses an information system that stores data on each employee's employment history with Gabriel. Data include items such as job and salary history, training and education undertaken, medical and insurance data, and so on. The system runs on the department's microcomputer and was written in dBASE IV by Susan Waterman, an employee in the department. Ms. Waterman, who learned dBASE IV by attending a seminar given by the information center staff, became very interested in programming and became proficient in the use of the language. She decided to make a career change

from personnel to programming and left Gabriel to accept a position that offered a significantly higher salary. Paul Klahr wants to add several enhancements to this information system. Also, two bugs have surfaced in the system, although neither affects the primary functioning of the system, but both need to be corrected. The problem is that nobody in the Personnel Department knows dBASE IV, although several people use the information system. Paul Klahr has asked John Robson to help, but John Robson insists that the Computer Services Department has a serious backlog of mainframe-oriented work and cannot spare staff to help the Personnel Department with micro-based locally produced systems.

The Assignment

You are a programmer/analyst in the Computer Services Department. John Robson has given you the task of addressing the problems that have developed with end user computing at Gabriel Industries. Specifically, you are to make recommendations regarding each of the following situations that were described in the case study:

1. *Nonapproved purchases*: A nonapproved purchase occurs when a user purchases hardware or software that is not on the "approved list" and has not been specifically approved by the information center staff. Give recommendations regarding

   a. What to do about nonapproved purchases already made.

   b. How to prevent future nonapproved purchases.

2. *Failure to perform backups*: Give recommendations regarding

   a. The responsibilities of the information center when a user has a problem resulting from the lack of adherence to proper backup procedures.

   b. How to motivate users to make backups, especially since there are no "horror stories" to date.

3. *Managing user programmers*: Give recommendations regarding

   a. Training a backup person.

   b. Creating and maintaining adequate documentation for user-written systems.

   c. Retaining user programmers.

CHAPTER 7

Personal Computing

CHAPTER OVERVIEW

To say that personal computing has made an enormous impact on how we do business is an understatement. Microcomputer-based personal computing has altered the thinking of all workers and managers who strive to make a greater contribution to their employers. This chapter focuses on the primary tools of personal computing, the microcomputer and the six most popular software productivity tools (word processing, desktop publishing, electronic spreadsheet, presentation graphics, database software, and communications software). The chapter begins with an overview of personal computing, including a historical perspective. The overview is followed by a discussion of pertinent micro concepts. The software productivity tools are discussed in sufficient depth to enable you to understand their purpose and to give you a feel for their functionality and how they could be applied to real-world problems.

PERSONAL COMPUTING

Lo! Men have become the tools of their tools.

—— *Henry Thoreau*

The office without a microcomputer is more the exception than the rule. Microcomputers sit easily on a desktop and can be operated by one person. The growth of this kind of computing, called **personal computing**, has surpassed even the boldest forecasts of the mid-1970s. Inexpensive microcomputers have made automation economically feasible for virtually any business environment. As a result, microcomputer software is available to support thousands of common and not-so-common business applications. There is, of course, an established need for applications such as payroll, accounting, sales analysis, project management, and inventory control. There are also hundreds of industry-specific software packages for thoroughbred breeding, medical laboratories, professional football, veterinarians, art dealers, and just about any other industry type. Also, personal computers provide managers with access to a variety of decision support systems (simulation, modeling, forecasting, "what if" analysis), many of which were available only on mainframe computers a few years ago. Most of the new commercially available expert systems are being created for personal computers (tax reporting, medical diagnosis, and so on).

Thousands of commercially available software packages run on microcomputers, including *word processing*, *desktop publishing*, *electronic spreadsheet*, *presentation graphics*, *database*, and *communications* software. In contrast to software that is designed for a specific application, these and other software packages are general-purpose software and provide the framework for a great number of business and personal applications.

These software packages are often characterized as *productivity tools* because they help to relieve the tedium of many time-consuming manual tasks. Thanks to word processing software, retyping is a thing of the past. Desktop publishing software makes it possible to produce near-typeset-quality copy for restaurant menus, newsletters, brochures, and a thousand other items without the assistance of a commercial printer. Electronic spreadsheets permit us to perform certain arithmetic and logic operations without writing programs. Say goodbye to grid paper, plastic templates, and the manual plotting of data: graphics software prepares bar, circle, and line graphs without us drawing a single line. With database software, we can format and create a data base in minutes. Communications software enables micro users to establish a communications link with other micros or with larger computers. The functions, concepts, and uses of these micro software tools are discussed in this chapter.

HISTORICAL PERSPECTIVE ON PERSONAL COMPUTING

Personal Computer Milestones

The history of personal computers or microcomputers is of special significance to us because their entire history has occurred within our lifetime. In terms of the way people live and work, John V. Atanasoff's invention of the electronic digital computer (1942) can be considered one of the most significant events in history. But not until 1975 and the introduction of the *Altair 8800* personal computer, a product of the microminiaturization of electronic circuitry, was computing made available to individuals and very small companies. This event has forever changed how we as society perceive computers. The Altair 8800, which sold for $650 ($395 as a kit), was marketed by a small electronics company called Micro Instrumentation and Telemetry Systems (MITS). After *Popular Electronics* featured the Altair 8800 on its cover, MITS received thousands of orders. People wanted their own personal computer. By 1977, 30 other companies were manufacturing and selling personal computers.

Perhaps the most prominent entrepreneurial venture during the early years of PCs was the *Apple II* computer. It all began in 1976 when two young computer enthusiasts, Steven Jobs and Steve Wozniak (then 21 and 26 years of age, respectively) collaborated to create and build their Apple II computer. Seven years after they opened a makeshift production line in Jobs' garage, Apple Computer, Inc., earned a spot on the *Fortune* 500, a list of the 500 largest corporations in the United States.

In 1981 International Business Machines (IBM), the giant of the computer industry, tossed its hat into the PC ring with the announcement of the *IBM PC*. In the first year, 35,000 were sold. In 1982, 800,000 were sold, and the IBM PC was well on its way to becoming the "standard" for the micro industry. When software vendors began to orient their products to the IBM PC, many microcomputer manufacturers created and sold *clones* of the IBM PC. These clones, called *IBM PC compatibles*, run most or all of the software designed for the IBM PC.

Some industry analysts argue that IBM's dominance in the micro industry has helped to stabilize the growth of an industry in its infancy. Others argue that the overwhelming influence of the IBM PC tends to stifle the efforts of those entrepreneurs who want to push the limits of modern technology. In any case, whatever IBM does in the personal computer arena has immediate and far-reaching effects on personal computing. The successor to the IBM PC, the *IBM Personal System/2* (introduced in 1987), will almost certainly become a milestone in PC history.

This architect is interacting with a member of the IBM Personal System/2 series, IBM's successor to the popular IBM PC series. The PS/2 Models 30 and 50 are designed to rest on a desktop. The component that houses the processing and disk storage capabilities for PS/2 Models 60 and 80 (shown here) is designed to rest on the floor.

Courtesy of International Business Machines Corporation

Several other personal computers have established their place in PC history. Introduced in 1982, the *Commodore-64* was significant because it signaled the buying public that powerful micros could be manufactured and sold at a reasonable cost—$599. In the same year, Compaq Computer Corporation bundled the equivalent of an IBM PC in a transportable case and named it the *Compaq Portable*. Thus began the era of the portable computer. In 1984, Apple Computer introduced the *Macintosh* with a very "friendly" graphic user interface—proof positive that computers can be easy and fun to use.

PC Software Milestones

During the early years, you had to be a programmer if you wanted to use a micro to address a particular application. During this period, the personal computer industry was waiting for the software industry to catch up. Today, it is the other way around. The software industry continues to grow at a fever pitch.

During the late 1970s, *CP/M* (Control Program for Microcomputers) was the dominant *operating system*. A micro's operating system provides the interface between the hardware and the applications software. When IBM chose *MS-DOS* from Microsoft Corporation, it, like the IBM PC, eventually became the standard for the industry. The IBM version of MS-DOS is called *PC-DOS*.

Several software packages are assured prominent places in PC history. With the introduction of *VisiCalc*, the first electronic spreadsheet program, in 1979, micros became a viable business tool. Before that micros were used primarily in the educational environment and by the hobbyist. VisiCalc blazed the trail for *Lotus 1-2-3*, another electronic spreadsheet program. The success of Lotus Development Corporation's 1-2-3 is now legend. Ashton-Tate's *dBASE II*, a database software package introduced in 1979, made it possible for micro users to create their own information systems, without the aid of a professional programmer. In 1979, MicroPro International Corporation introduced *WordStar*, a word processing package that to this day enjoys an almost cultlike following.

This quick stroll through the short history of personal computers highlights only a few of the many significant innovations and events that have occurred since the announcement of the Altair 8800.

THE MICROCOMPUTER

A microcomputer or PC is just a small computer. Perhaps the best definition of a micro is *any computer that you can pick up and carry*. But don't be misled by the *micro* prefix. You can pick up and carry some very powerful computers! Personal computers come in three different physical sizes: *pocket PCs*, *lap PCs*, and *desktop PCs*. The pocket and lap PCs are light (a few ounces to 8 pounds) and compact and can operate without an external power source, so they earn the "portable" label as well. There are also a number of "transportable" desktop PCs on the market, but they are more

This realtor uses her NEC lap PC to take notes during appraisals, evaluate mortgage options, and record client criteria. The portable PC has two 3½-inch microdisk drives, 640K bytes of random access memory, and 512K bytes of read-only memory.

cumbersome to move. They fold up to about the size of a small suitcase, weigh about 20 pounds, and usually require an external power source. Desktop PCs are not designed for frequent movement and are therefore not considered portable. The power of a PC is not necessarily in proportion to its size. A few lap PCs can run circles around some desktop PCs.

Like any computer, a microcomputer is an electronic device capable of interpreting and executing programmed commands for *input*, *output*, *computation*, and *logic operations*. PCs may be technically complex, but they are conceptually simple. The **processor** is the "intelligence" of a **microcomputer system**. The system has only four fundamental components—*input*, *processing*, *output*, and *storage*. Note that a microcomputer system (not a micro) is made up of the four components. The actual microcomputer is the processing component and is combined with the other three to form a *microcomputer system* (see Figure 7–1). Microcomputer concepts are discussed in more detail in Module A, "Computer Systems," in "A Short Course in Computer Concepts." Input devices (keyboard, mouse), output devices (printers, plotters), and storage devices (disks, tapes) are discussed in Module C, "I/O and Data Storage Devices."

In only a decade, PC technology has advanced from PCs that did not offer enough to be useful business tools to PCs that offer word processing, electronic spreadsheet, and database capabilities to PCs that can do almost anything a mainframe computer can do. Some vendors refer to their top-of-the-line micros as *microframes*, to associate them with the capabilities of mainframe computer systems.

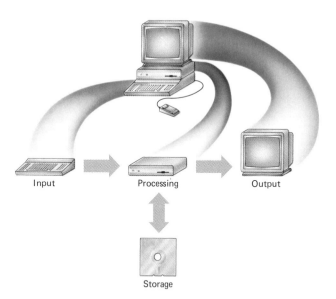

Input   Processing   Output

Storage

FIGURE 7–1   The Four Fundamental Components of a Microcomputer System
In a microcomputer system, the storage and processing components are often contained in the same physical unit. In the illustration, the diskette storage medium is inserted into the unit that contains the processor.

WORD PROCESSING

Function

Word processing is using the computer to enter, store, manipulate, and print text in letters, reports, books, and so on. Once you have used word processing, you will probably wonder (like a million others before you) how in the world you ever survived without it!

Concepts

Creating a Document

To begin preparation of a document, all you have to do is begin keying in the text. But before you do, it is always a good idea to *format* the document. When you format a document, you are describing the size of the print page and how you want the document to look when it is printed. As with the typewriter, you must set the left and right margins, the tab settings, line spacing (for example, lines/inch), and character spacing (for example, characters/inch). You must also specify the size of the output document, then set margins for the top and bottom of the text.

Text is entered in **replace mode** or **insert mode**. When in replace mode, the character that you enter *overstrikes* the character at the cursor position. For example, suppose that you typed the word "the" but you wanted to type "and". To make the correction in replace mode, you would position the cursor at the "t" and type a-n-d, thereby replacing the "the" with "and". When in insert mode, you can enter *additional* text. For example, to correct the misspelled "outpt", place the cursor on the second "t" and add a "u". In insert mode, the computer manipulates the text such that it *wraps around*, sending words that are pushed past the right margin into the next line, and so on, to the end of the paragraph.

Word processing permits *full-screen editing*. That is, you can insert or replace text at any position in the document. You can browse through a multiscreen document by *scrolling* a line at a time or a "page" (a screen) at a time, that is, viewing parts of a word processing document that extend past the bottom or top of the screen.

Common Word Processing Features

Features common to most word processing software packages are mentioned and discussed briefly in this section. The *block* operations are among the handiest of word processing features. They are the block *move*, the block *copy*, and the block *delete* commands. These commands are the electronic equivalent of a "cut and paste" job. The move feature permits you to select a block of text (for example, a word, a sentence, a paragraph) and move it to another portion of the document (see Figure 7–2). At the end of the move procedure, the entire block of text that was selected or "marked" is moved to the designated location (see Figure 7–3). The copy command works in a similar manner except that the text block selected is copied to the location that you designate. To delete a block of text, the block is marked, and the delete block option is selected.

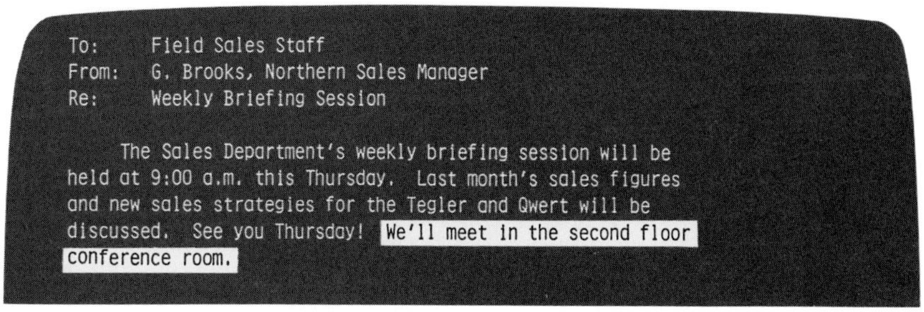

```
To:      Field Sales Staff
From:    G. Brooks, Northern Sales Manager
Re:      Weekly Briefing Session

        The Sales Department's weekly briefing session will be
held at 9:00 a.m. this Thursday.  Last month's sales figures
and new sales strategies for the Tegler and Qwert will be
discussed.  See you Thursday! We'll meet in the second floor
conference room.
```

FIGURE 7–2   Word Processing: Marking Text for a Block Operation
The last sentence of the memo is marked to be moved.

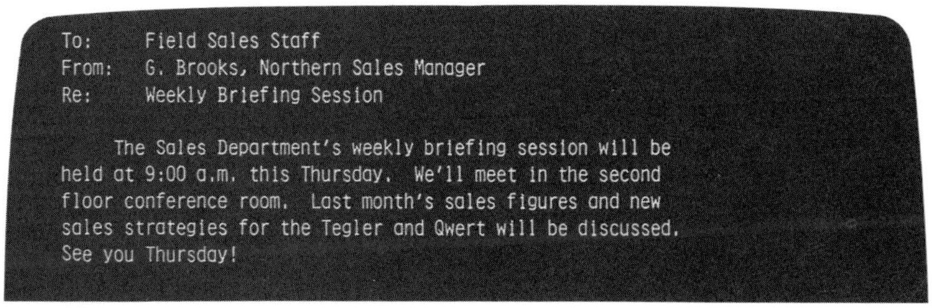

```
To:      Field Sales Staff
From:    G. Brooks, Northern Sales Manager
Re:      Weekly Briefing Session

        The Sales Department's weekly briefing session will be
held at 9:00 a.m. this Thursday.  We'll meet in the second
floor conference room.  Last month's sales figures and new
sales strategies for the Tegler and Qwert will be discussed.
See you Thursday!
```

FIGURE 7–3   Word Processing: Move Text
This memo is the result of the marked block in Figure 7–2 being moved to a position following the first sentence.

The *search* or *find* feature permits you to search through the entire document and identify all occurrences of a particular character string. For example, if you wanted to search for all occurrences of "Thursday" in the memo of Figure 7–3, you would simply initiate the search command and type in the desired *search string*, "Thursday" in this example. The cursor is immediately positioned at the first occurrence of the character string "Thursday" so you can easily edit the text to reflect the new meeting day. From there, you can "find" other occurrences of "Thursday" by pressing the appropriate key. As an alternative approach to making the Thursday-to-Friday change, you could use the *search and replace* feature. This feature permits selective replacement of occurrences of "Thursday" in the memo with "Friday".

Several other valuable word processing features enhance the appearance and readability of a document. These features are illustrated in Figure 7–4.

To print a document, all you have to do is ready the printer (turn it on and align the paper) and select the print option on the main menu. Some word processing systems present you with a few final options. For example, you can choose to print the document single or double spaced, or you can print specific pages or the whole document.

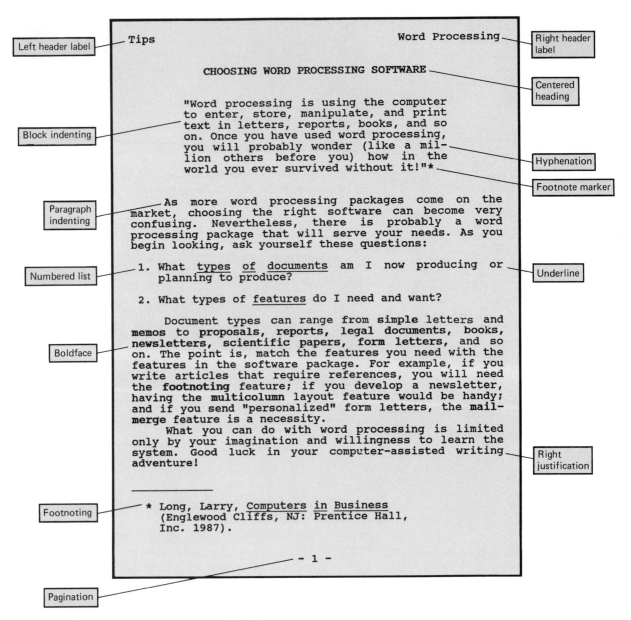

FIGURE 7–4   Word Processing: Features Overview
Many of the more common capabilities of word processing software are illustrated in this example printout of a text file.

Advanced Word Processing Features

The features discussed in this section are available with the more sophisticated word processing packages. For example, a simple command creates a *table of contents* with page references for the first-level headings. An alphabetical *index of key words* can be created that lists the page numbers for each occurrence of designated words. One of the most tedious typing chores, *footnoting*, is done automatically (see Figure 7–4). Another feature permits a *multicolumn* output (for example, one or more columns of text on a single page). These features would be ideal for writers.

Add-on Capabilities

A number of software programs are designed to enhance the functionality of word processing programs. These add-on capabilities are usually in the form of stand-alone programs. That is, they are programs that either come with a word processing package or are purchased separately.

Have you ever been writing and been unable to put your finger on the right word? Some word processing packages have an **on-line thesaurus**! Suppose that you have just written: "The Grand Canyon certainly is beautiful." But "beautiful" is not quite the right word. Your electronic thesaurus is always ready with suggestions: "pretty," "elegant," "exquisite," "angelic," "pulchritudinous," "ravishing," and so on.

If spelling is a problem, then word processing is the answer. Once you have entered the text and formatted the document the way you want it, you can call on the **spelling checker** capability. The spelling checker checks every word in the text against an **electronic dictionary** (usually from 75,000 to 150,000 words) and alerts you if a word is not in the dictionary.

The **grammar checker** highlights grammatical concerns and deviations from conventions. For example, it highlights split infinitives, phrases with redundant words ("very highest"), misuse of caps ("JOhn" or "MarY"), sexist phrases, double words ("and and"), and sentences that are written in the passive voice (versus the active voice).

Use

You can create just about any kind of text-based document with word processing: letters, reports, books, articles, forms, memos, tables, and so on. The features of some word processing packages go beyond the generation of text documents. For example, some word processing systems provide the capability to merge parts of the data base with the text of the document. An example of this *mail merge* application is illustrated in Figure 7–5. In the example, Zimco Enterprises announced the enhanced version of its Qwert. Each regional sales manager sent a "personal" letter to every Zimco customer in his or her respective region. There were thousands of customers in each region. Using word processing, a secretary could enter the letter once, store it on the disk, then simply merge the customer name-and-address file (also stored on the disk) with the letter. The letters could then printed with the proper addresses and salutations. Figure 7–5 illustrates how the Qwert announcement letter could be merged with the customer name-and-address file to produce a "personalized" letter.

The mail merge example is a good illustration of the use of **boilerplate**. Boilerplate is existing text that can in some way be customized to be applicable to a variety of word processing applications. One of the beauties of word processing is that you can accumulate text on disk storage that will eventually help you to meet other word processing needs. You can even buy boilerplate.

The legal profession offers some of the best examples of the use of

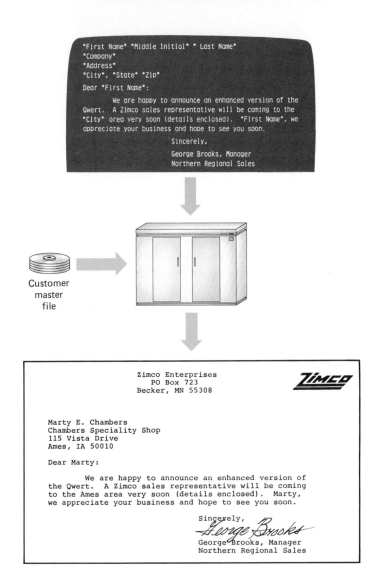

FIGURE 7–5 Merging Data with Word Processing
*The names and addresses from a customer master file are retrieved from secondary storage and are merged with the text of a letter. In the actual letter, the appropriate data items are inserted for *First Name*, *Company*, *Address*, *City*, and so on. In this way, a "personalized" letter can be sent to each customer.*

boilerplate. Simple wills, uncontested divorces, individual bankruptcies, real estate transfers, and other straightforward legal documents may be as much as 95 percent boilerplate. Even more complex legal documents may be as much as 80 percent boilerplate. Once the appropriate boilerplate has been merged into a document, the lawyer edits the document to add transition sentences and the variables, such as the names of the litigants. Besides the obvious improvement in productivity, lawyers can be relatively confident that their documents are accurate and complete when they use boilerplate. Lawyers, of course, do not have a monopoly on boilerplate. The use of boilerplate is common in all areas of business, education, government, and personal endeavor.

Word processing is the perfect example of how automation can be used to increase productivity and foster creativity. It minimizes the effort that you must devote to the routine aspects of writing, so that you can focus your attention on the creative aspects of writing. Most word processing users will agree that their writing style has improved measurably. The finished product is less verbose, better organized, devoid of spelling errors, and of course, more visually appealing.

DESKTOP PUBLISHING

The ultimate extension of word processing is **desktop publishing**. In fact, some are calling desktop publishing software the next generation of word processing software. Desktop publishing refers to the capability of producing *near-typeset-quality copy* from the confines of a "desktop." The concept of desktop publishing is changing the way companies, government agencies, and individuals approach the printing of newsletters, brochures, user manuals, pamphlets, restaurant menus, periodicals, greeting cards, and thousands of other printed items.

Traditionally, drafts of documents to be printed are delivered to commercial printers to be typeset. Desktop publishing has made it possible to eliminate this expensive typesetting process for those printed documents that required only near typeset quality. In practice, near typeset-quality copy is acceptable for most printed documents. Relatively few documents need to be prepared using the expensive commercial phototypesetting process. The output of the desktop publishing process is the *camera-ready copy*. Duplicates of the camera-ready copy are reproduced by a variety of means, from copy machines to commercial processing.

The primary components required for desktop publishing are *desktop publishing software*, a *microcomputer*, and a *laser printer*. The more sophisticated desktop publishing environments include *image processors* (see Chapter 6, "End User Computing") that can be used to digitize images, such as photographs. Image processors, also called scanners, re-create a black-and-white version of text or an image (photograph) in an electronic format that can be manipulated and reproduced under computer control. Desktop publishing software is essentially sophisticated word processing software (all of the capabilities described in the previous section of this chapter) plus *page-composition software*. The page composition software enables users to design and make up pages.

The page make-up process involves the integration of graphics, photos, text, and other elements into a visually appealing *page layout*. Besides the positioning of the elements, the user must also select the desired mix of type sizes and fonts. One problem with desktop publishing is that it has put the capability to produce camera-ready documents in the hands of the masses, many of whom do not have the artistic skills needed to produce an aesthetically pleasing and functionally readable copy. Recognizing this, many companies are adopting standards and policies that apply to all copy that contains the company logo and is released to the public.

Combine words, graphics, imagination, creativity, software, and hardware and what do you have? You have the makings for desktop publishing, one of the hottest applications of computer technology. People in virtually every business endeavor are designing, creating, and producing more and more of their printed materials in-house. Before desktop publishing, businesses submitted drafts of their ads, memos, manuals, brochures, and so on to professional typesetters as a matter of routine. Desktop publishing has eliminated this costly and time-consuming process for many printed items.

PageMaker, a product of Aldus Corporation, is one of today's popular desktop publishing software packages. With PageMaker, you can produce finished professional-looking documents in four steps.

1. *Prepare text and graphics.* Use your word processing software to create and edit the text of your document. For needed illustrations and graphics you can use electronic clip art (prepackaged electronic images), computer-created graphics (pie graph), or scanned images (photos).

2. *Develop a format.* By using PageMaker's master page feature, you can define margins, set number of columns and column widths, and add design elements and more to design the format for each page of the document.

3. *Place graphics in text.* With PageMaker's "Place" command, you can adjust the position of the text and resize your graphics to fit your needs. The display is WYSIWYG, that is, "what you see is what you get" when the document is printed. If what you see is not what you want, then you

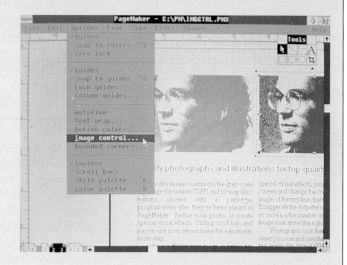

This display illustrates a representative screen that a user might encounter during a PageMaker session. Notice the contrast between the two images. The dot pattern in the images can be modified to achieve special visual effects. A pull-down menu is superimposed over the WYSIWYG display.

Aldus Corporation

can use the mouse to reposition text and graphics to the desired locations.

4. *Print the document.* Once the WYSIWYG display is as you would like it to appear, use a laser printer to produce the finished camera-ready copy.

ELECTRONIC SPREADSHEET

Function

The name "electronic spreadsheet" describes the software's fundamental application. The spreadsheet has been a common business tool for centuries. Before computers, the ledger (a spreadsheet) was the accountant's primary tool for keeping the books. Professors' grade books are set up in spreadsheet format.

Electronic spreadsheets are simply an electronic alternative to accomplishing thousands of traditionally manual tasks. No longer are we confined to using pencils, erasers, and calculators for applications that deal with rows and columns of data. Think of anything that has rows and columns of data, and you have identified an application for spreadsheet software. For example, how about income (profit and loss) statements, personnel profiles, demographic data, and budget summaries—to mention a few? Because electronic spreadsheets so closely resemble many of our manual tasks, they are enjoying widespread acceptance.

All commercially available electronic spreadsheet packages provide the facility to manipulate rows and columns of data. However, the *user interface*, or the manner in which you enter data and commands, differs from one package to the next.

Concepts

The example used to illustrate and demonstrate electronic spreadsheet concepts is the Zimco Enterprises' pro rata income statement shown in Figure 7–6. The vice president of finance and accounting at Zimco uses an electronic spreadsheet **template** of Zimco's income statements (Figure 7–6) for the past two years to do financial planning. The template, which is simply a spreadsheet model, contains a column that allows him to produce a pro rata income statement for next year. In Figure 7–6, the income statements are shown on the first screen. The second screen contains the calculations for the price-earnings ratio and the display of the variables used to produce the pro rata income statement for next year. In the example of Figure 7–6, the vice president projected sales, cost of goods sold, and administrative expenses to be 20%, 1%, and 0%, respectively.

Viewing Data in a Spreadsheet

Scrolling through a spreadsheet is much like looking through a magnifying glass as you move it around a page of a newspaper. You scroll left-right (horizontal scrolling) and/or up-down (vertical scrolling) to view various portions of a large spreadsheet (see Figure 7–7). For example, since only 20 lines of the spreadsheet template in Figure 7–6 can be displayed at once, the vice president must "page up" or "page down" to see the complete spreadsheet.

Organization

Electronic spreadsheets are organized in a *tabular structure* with **rows** and **columns**. The intersection of a particular row and column designates a **cell**. As you can see in Figure 7–6, the rows are *numbered* and the columns are *lettered*. Single letters identify the first 26 columns, and double letters are used thereafter (A, B, . . . , Z, AA, AB, . . . , AZ, BA, BB, . . . , BZ).

Data are entered and stored in a cell, at the intersection of a column and a row. During operations, data are referenced by their **cell address**. A cell address identifies the location of a cell in the spreadsheet by its column and row, with the column designator first. For example, in the income statement example of Figure 7–6, C2 is the address of the column heading "This Year," and C4 is the address of the net sales amount for this year ($153,000).

	A	B	C	D
1	=================			
2	ZIMCO INCOME STATEMENT ($1000)	Next Year	This Year	Last Year
3	-------			
4	Net sales	$183,600	$153,000	$144,780
5	Cost of sales & op. expenses			
6	Cost of goods sold	116,413	115,260	117,345
7	Depreciation	4,125	4,125	1,500
8	Selling & admin. expenses	19,875	19,875	15,000
9		-------	-------	-------
10	Operating profit	$43,187	$13,740	$10,935
11	Other income			
12	Dividends and interest	405	405	300
13				
14	TOTAL INCOME	$43,592	$14,145	$11,235
15	Less: interest on bonds	2,025	2,025	2,025
16		-------	-------	-------
17	Income before tax	41,567	12,120	9,210
18	Provision for income tax	18,777	5,475	4,160
19		-------	-------	-------
20	NET PROFIT FOR YEAR	$22,790	$6,645	$5,050

	A	B	C	D
21	=================			
22				
23				
24	=================			
25	Shares outstanding	6,300,000	6,000,000	6,000,000
26	Market price	$21.25	$14.00	$13.00
27	Earnings per share	$3.62	$1.11	$0.84
28		-------	-------	-------
29	Price-earnings ratio	5.87	12.64	15.45
30	=================			
31				
32				
33	=================			
34	FORECAST VARIABLES FOR NEXT YEAR'S PRO RATA INCOME STATEMENT			
35	-------			
36	Projected change in sales		20.00%	
37	Projected change in cost of goods sold		1.00%	
38	Projected change in administrative expenses		0.00%	
39	=================			
40				

FIGURE 7–6   Electronic Spreadsheet: A Pro Rata Income Statement Template
This electronic spreadsheet template (both screens) is the basis for the explanation and demonstration of spreadsheet concepts. The "Next Year" pro rata income statement is extrapolated from the data in the "This Year" income statement and the values of forecast variables. The price-earnings ratio is calculated for each year.

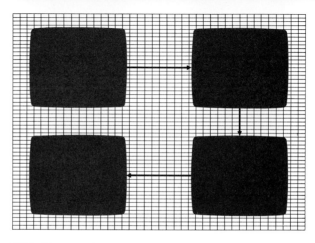

FIGURE 7–7 Electronic Spreadsheet: Scrolling
Scroll vertically and horizontally to view those portions of an electronic spreadsheet or word processing document that do not fit on a single screen.

In the spreadsheet work area (the rows and columns), a movable highlighted area "points" to the *current cell*. This highlighted area, which is appropriately called the **pointer**, can be moved around the spreadsheet with the cursor control keys to any cell address. To add or edit an entry at a particular cell, the pointer must be located at the desired cell. The content or resultant value (for example, from a formula) of each cell is shown in the spreadsheet work area. The current cell, however, is displayed in reverse video (for example, black on white or, for color monitors, black on a color).

Cell Entries

To make an entry in the spreadsheet, simply move the pointer with the cursor control keys to the appropriate cell and key in the data. To *edit* or replace an existing entry, you also move the pointer to the appropriate cell. The new or revised entry appears first in the edit line beside the cell address (see Figure 7–6); then it is moved to the appropriate cell when you press the enter key.

Text and Formula Entries

An entry to a cell is classified as a *text entry* (also called a *label entry*), a *numeric entry*, or a *formula entry*. Strictly speaking, numeric entries fall under the "formula" heading in some spreadsheet programs. In Figure 7–6, the values in C4 and D4 are numeric. A text entry, or a label, is a word, phrase, or any string of alphanumeric text (spaces included) that occupies a particular cell. In the example of Figure 7–6, "This Year" in cell C2 is a text entry, as is "Net Sales" in A4 and "FORECAST VARIABLES FOR NEXT YEAR'S PRO RATA INCOME STATEMENT" in A34.

Cells C10 and C14 in Figure 7–6 contain formulas, but it is the numeric results (for example, $13,740 and $14,145) that are displayed in the spreadsheet. The formula value of C10 (see Figure 7–8) computes the operating profit (for example, net sales less the cost of sales and operating expenses or +C4 − C6 − C7 − C8). With the pointer positioned at C10, the formula appears in the cell contents line in the user interface panel and the actual numeric value appears in the spreadsheet work area. When the pointer is positioned at C4, the actual numeric value (153000) is displayed as the cell contents in the user interface and an optional *edited* version (with $ and comma) is displayed in cell C4 (see Figure 7–8).

Spreadsheet formulas use standard notation for **arithmetic operators**: + (add), − (subtract), * (multiply), / (divide), ^ (raising to a power, or exponentiation). The formula contained in C10 (top of Figure 7–8) computes the operating profit for "This Year." Compare this formula:

$$+C4 - C6 - C7 - C8$$

with the formula in cell D10 (here):

$$+D4 - D6 - D7 - D8$$

The formulas are similar, but the first formula references those amounts in column C and the second formula references those amounts in column D.

Formulas are the essence of spreadsheet operations. A formula causes the spreadsheet software to perform numeric and/or string calculations and/or logic operations that result in a numeric value (for example, 13740) or an alphanumeric character string (for example, "ABOVE 25% LIMIT"). A formula may include one or all of the following: *arithmetic operations*, *functions* (average, square root, present value of annuities), *logic operations* (greater than, less than, and so on), and *string operations* (for example, joining or concatenating character strings).

When you design the spreadsheet, keep in mind where you want to place the formulas and what you want them to accomplish. Since formulas are based on relative position, you will need a knowledge of the layout and organization of the data in the spreadsheet. When you define a formula, you must first determine what you wish to achieve (for example, calculate net profit). Then you select a cell location for the formula (for example, C20) and create the formula by connecting cell addresses with operators,

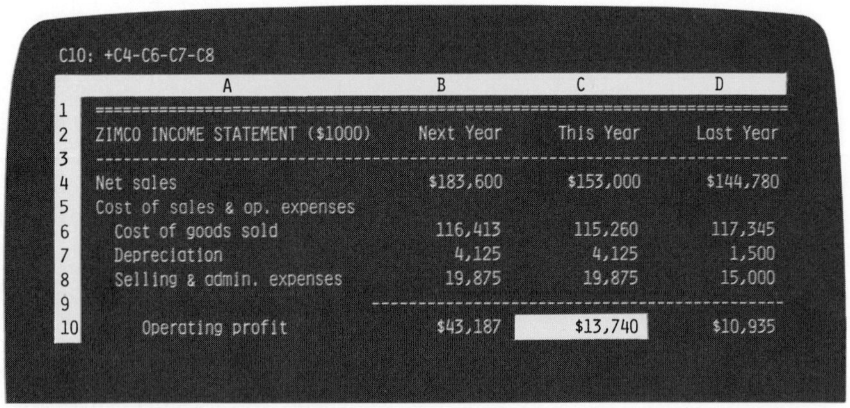

```
C10: +C4-C6-C7-C8
```

	A	B	C	D
1	===			=
2	ZIMCO INCOME STATEMENT ($1000)	Next Year	This Year	Last Year
3	- - - - - - - - - - - - - - - - - - - -			
4	Net sales	$183,600	$153,000	$144,780
5	Cost of sales & op. expenses			
6	Cost of goods sold	116,413	115,260	117,345
7	Depreciation	4,125	4,125	1,500
8	Selling & admin. expenses	19,875	19,875	15,000
9		- - - - - -	- - - - - -	- - - - - -
10	Operating profit	$43,187	$13,740	$10,935

FIGURE 7–8   Electronic Spreadsheet: Formulas
The actual content of C10 is the formula in the user interface panel in the upper left-hand part of the screen. The result of the formula appears in the spreadsheet at C10.

as appropriate. In many instances, you will copy the formula to other locations (for example, C20 was copied to D20 in Figure 7–6).

Spreadsheet applications begin with a blank screen and an idea. The spreadsheet that you create is a product of skill and imagination. What you get out of a spreadsheet is very dependent on how effectively you use formulas.

Formatting Data for Readability

The appearance of data in a spreadsheet can be modified to enhance readability. For example, the value .2 was entered as the projected change in sales in C36 (Figure 7–6), but it appears in the spreadsheet display as a percentage (that is, 20.00%). This is because the **range** C36..C38 (C36, C37, and C38) was *formatted* so that the values are automatically displayed as percentages rather than as fractions. A range of cells is defined by the end points of adjacent cells in a column (example range is A17..A20), a row (example range is B2..D2), or a rectangular block (example range is B6..D8 or B8..D6) The methods of formatting data vary considerably among spreadsheet software packages.

Currency amounts can be formatted so that commas and a dollar sign are inserted. For example, in Figure 7–6 the value for net sales for "This Year" is entered as 153000 in C4, which is formatted for currency. Notice that it is displayed as $153,000.

Numeric data can be defined so that they are displayed with a fixed number of places to the right of the decimal point. In Figure 7–6, the format of the net sales data in the range B4..D4 is currency with the number of decimal places fixed at zero. The format of the market price data in the range B26..D26 is currency with the number of decimal positions fixed at two. Numbers with more decimal digits than specified in the format are rounded when displayed.

Use

Spreadsheet Templates

The electronic spreadsheet of Figure 7–6 is a template, or a model, of past years' income statements and a pro rata income statement. It can be used over and over for different purposes by different financial analysts with different sets of data. Next year, the data now in the "This Year" column, will be moved to the "Last Year" column and a new set of data will be entered for "This Year".

With electronic spreadsheets, a template is easily modified to fit a variety of situations. Another analyst may wish to modify the template slightly to handle quarterly income statements (only the column headings would be changed).

Spreadsheet Summary

The possibilities of what users can do with electronic spreadsheet software and micros are endless. For example, the vice president of finance can add the Zimco balance sheets for the last two years to the spreadsheet of Figure 7–6 to create a variety of helpful "what if" scenarios.

When used as a data management tool, electronic spreadsheet software organizes data elements, records, and files into columns, rows, and tables, respectively. For instance, in a name and address file, each row in the spreadsheet would contain the data items for each individual record (for example, Jeffrey Bates, 1401 Oak St., Framingham, MA 01710). All the records are combined in a table of rows (records) and columns (data elements) to make a file. Many of the capabilities of specialized data management or database software (discussed in the database software section) are also capabilities of electronic spreadsheet software. These include sorting records, extracting records that meet certain conditions (for example, STATE="MA"), and report generation.

The special section at the end of the book, entitled "Hands-on Exercises: Electronic Spreadsheet, Graphics, and Database," contains exercises for electronic spreadsheet software.

PRESENTATION GRAPHICS

Function

With presentation graphics software, you can create a variety of graphics from data in an electronic spreadsheet or a data base. Among the most popular presentation graphics are **bar graphs**, **pie graphs**, and **line graphs** (as seen in Figures 7–10, 7–12, and 7–13, respectively). Other types of graphs are possible. Each of these graphs can be annotated with graph *titles*, *labels*, and *legends*.

Some graphics software lets you create and store original drawings. To do this, however, your personal computer must be equipped with a mouse, joystick, digitizing board, or some type of device that permits the input of curved and angular lines. To make drawing easier to do, such software even offers a data base filled with a variety of frequently used symbols, such as rectangles, circles, cats (yes, even cats), and so on. Some companies draw and store the image of their company logo so that it can be inserted on memos, reports, and graphs.

Graphic representations of data have proven to be a very effective means of communication. It is easier to recognize problem areas and trends in a graph than it is in a tabular summary of the same data. For many years, the presentation of tabular data was the preferred approach to communicating tabular information. This was because it was simply too expensive and time consuming to produce presentation graphics manually. Today, you can use graphics software to produce perfectly proportioned, accurate, and visually appealing graphs in a matter of seconds. Prior to the introduction of graphics software, the turnaround time was at least a day, and often a week.

Concepts

Usually, the data needed to produce a graph already exist in a spreadsheet or data base. The graphics software leads you through a series of prompts, the first of which asks you what type of graph is to be produced: bar graph, pie graph, line graph, and so on. You then select the data that are to be plotted. You can also enter names for the labels. Once you have identified the source of the data and entered the labels, and perhaps added a title, you can display, print, or plot the graph. Any changes made to data in a spreadsheet or data base are reflected in the graphs as well.

Use

Zimco Enterprise's vice president of sales and marketing is an avid user of spreadsheet and graphics software. The spreadsheet of Figure 7–9 is an annual summary of the sales for each of Zimco's four products by sales region. This spreadsheet is used in the following sections to demonstrate the compilation of bar, pie, and line graphs.

Bar Graphs

To prepare the bar graph of Figure 7–10, the vice president first had to specify appropriate ranges; that is, the values in the "Totals" row (range B10..E10 of Figure 7–9) are to be plotted, and the region names (range B3..E3 of Figure 7–9) are to be inserted as labels along the horizontal or x axis. The vice president also added a title for the graph (Sales Summary by Region), titles for the x axis (Region), and the vertical or y axis [(Sales ($1,000)].

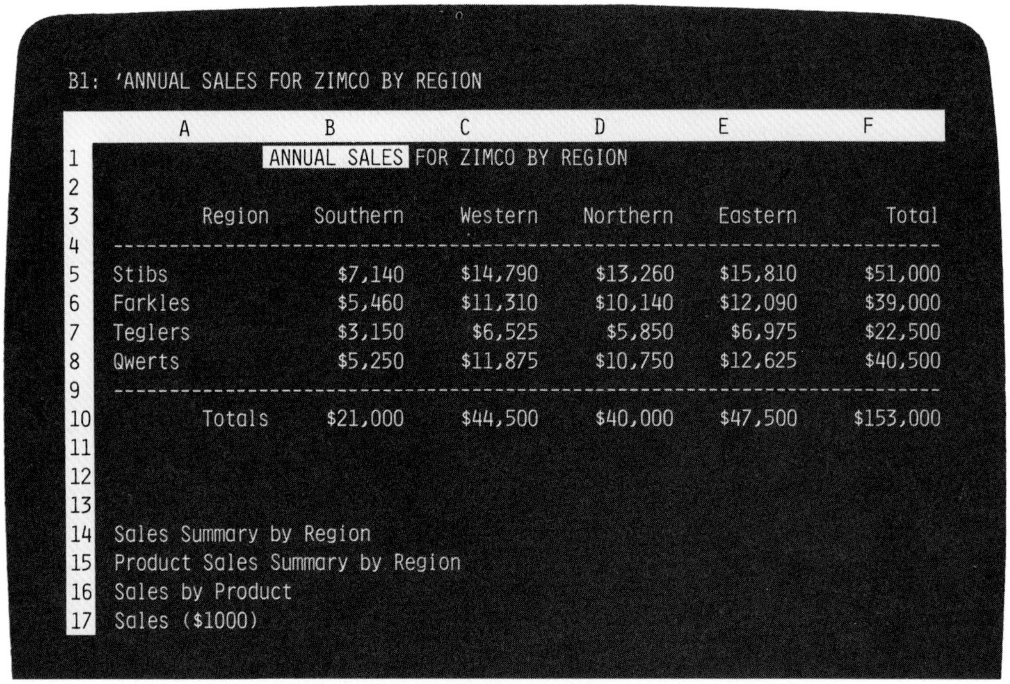

```
B1: 'ANNUAL SALES FOR ZIMCO BY REGION

         A          B          C          D          E          F
 1              ANNUAL SALES FOR ZIMCO BY REGION
 2
 3          Region    Southern    Western    Northern    Eastern      Total
 4      -----------------------------------------------------------------
 5   Stibs            $7,140     $14,790    $13,260    $15,810     $51,000
 6   Farkles          $5,460     $11,310    $10,140    $12,090     $39,000
 7   Teglers          $3,150      $6,525     $5,850     $6,975     $22,500
 8   Qwerts           $5,250     $11,875    $10,750    $12,625     $40,500
 9      -----------------------------------------------------------------
10          Totals   $21,000     $44,500    $40,000    $47,500    $153,000
11
12
13
14   Sales Summary by Region
15   Product Sales Summary by Region
16   Sales by Product
17   Sales ($1000)
```

FIGURE 7–9 Electronic Spreadsheet: Sales Data for Graphs
The bar, pie, and line graphs of Figures 7–10 through 7–13 are derived from these sales figures.

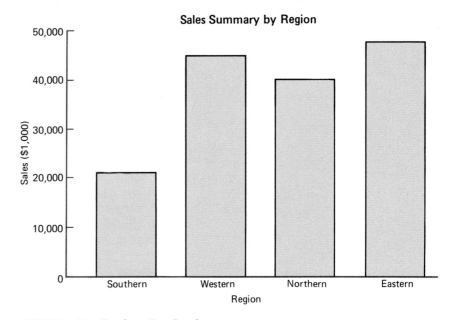

FIGURE 7–10   Graphics: Bar Graph
The "Total" sales for each region in Figure 7–9 are graphically represented in this bar graph.

The sales figures for each region in Figure 7–9 (range B5..E8) can be plotted in a *stacked-bar graph*. The resultant graph, shown in Figure 7–11, permits the vice president to understand better the regional distribution of sales. The *clustered-bar graph* in is an alternative presentation to the stacked-bar graph in Figure 7–11. These graphs visually highlight the relative contribution that each product made to the total sales for each region.

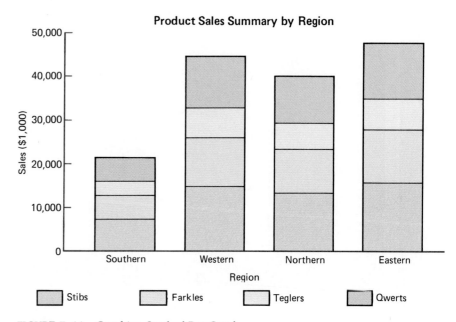

FIGURE 7–11   Graphics: Stacked-Bar Graph
Regional sales for each of the four products in Figure 7–9 are graphically represented in this stacked-bar graph.

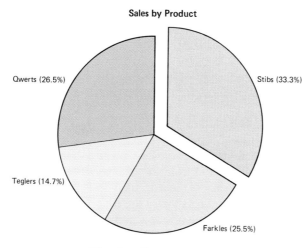

Sales by Product

Qwerts (26.5%)

Stibs (33.3%)

Teglers (14.7%)

Farkles (25.5%)

FIGURE 7–12   Graphics: Pie Graph
*Total sales by product (i.e., the "Totals"
row, B10..E10) in Figure 7–9 are
graphically represented in this pie graph.
The "Stibs" piece of the pie is exploded for
emphasis.*

Pie Graphs

Pie graphs are the most basic of presentation graphics. A pie graph graphically
illustrates each "piece" of data in its proper relationship to the whole "pie."
To illustrate how a pie graph is constructed and used, refer again to the
"Annual Sales" spreadsheet in Figure 7–9. The vice president of sales and
marketing produced the sales-by-product pie graph in Figure 7–12 by specifying that the values in the "Total" column be the "pieces" of the pie. To
emphasize the product with the greatest contribution to total sales, she decided to *explode* (or separate) the Stibs piece of the pie.

Line Graphs

A line graph connects similar points on a graph with one or several lines.
The Zimco vice president used the same data in the spreadsheet of Figure
7–9 to generate the line graph of Figure 7–13. The line graph makes it
easy for her to compare sales among regions for a particular product.

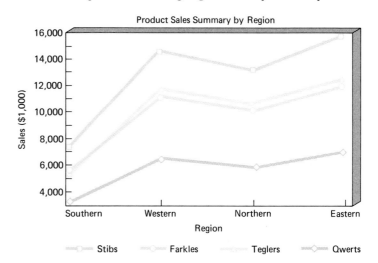

FIGURE 7–13   Graphics: Line Graph
*This line graph shows a plot of the data of Figure 7–9. A line connects the
sales for each product by region.*

The special section at the end of the book, entitled "Hands-on Exercises: Electronic Spreadsheet, Graphics, and Database," contains exercises for graphics software.

DATABASE SOFTWARE

Function

With database software, you can create and maintain a data base and extract information from the data base. To use database software, you first identify the format of the data, then design a display format that will permit interactive entry and revision of the data base. Once the data base is created, its *records* (related data about a particular event or thing) can be deleted or revised and other records can be added to the data base. "Database," as one word, is an alternative terminology for data management software. "Data base," as two words, refers to the highest level of the hierarchy of data organization. The six levels of the hierarchy are *bit*, *character*, *data element* or *field* (name, zip code, part number), *record* (employee record, customer record), *file* (employee file, customer file), and *data base*. The first level is transparent to the end user. The other levels of the hierarchy are important considerations in the use of database software.

All database software packages have these fundamental capabilities:

1. Create and maintain (for example, add, delete, and revise records) a data base.
2. Extract and list all records or only those records that meet certain conditions.
3. Make an inquiry (for example, the average value of a particular field in a series of records).
4. Sort records in ascending or descending sequence by primary, secondary, and tertiary fields.
5. Generate formatted reports with subtotals and totals.

The more sophisticated packages include a variety of other features, such as spreadsheet-type computations, graphics, and programming.

Concepts

Many similarities exist between commercially available word processing packages and between commercially available electronic spreadsheet packages. With word processing, you see and manipulate lines of text. With electronic spreadsheets, you see and manipulate data in numbered rows and lettered columns. This is not the case with database packages. All commercial software packages permit the creation and manipulation of data bases, but what you see on the screen may be vastly different for the various packages. However, the concepts embodied in these database packages are very similar. The conceptual coverage that follows is generic and can be applied to all database packages; however, the examples are oriented to *dBASE III PLUS*, a product of Ashton-Tate.

The organization of the data in a microcomputer data base is similar to the traditional hierarchy of data organization. Related **fields**, such as course identification number, course title, and course type, are grouped to form **records** (for example, the course record in the COURSE data base in Figure 7–14). A collection of related records make up a data **file** or a **data base**. In data management software terminology, "file" and "data base" are often used interchangeably. The hierarchy of data organization is discussed further in Chapter 9, "Data Management."

The best way to illustrate and demonstrate the concepts of database software is by example. Zimco's education coordinator uses a micro-based database software package to help him with his record-keeping tasks. To do this, he created a COURSE data base (see Figure 7–14) which contains a record for each course that Zimco offers to its employees and for several courses at State University, for which Zimco provides tuition reimbursement. Each record in the COURSE data base contains the following fields:

- Identification number (supplied by Zimco for in-house courses, by vendors, and by State University)
- Title of course
- Type of course (in-house, multimedia, college or vendor seminar)
- Source of course (Zimco staff or supplier of course)
- Duration (number of hours required to complete course)

Creating a Data Base

To create a data base, the first thing you do is to set up a *screen format* that will enable you to enter the data for a record. The data entry screen

Record#	ID	TITLE	TYPE	SOURCE	DURATION
1	100	MIS Orientation	in-house	Staff	24
2	201	Micro Overview	in-house	Staff	8
3	2535	Intro to Info. Proc.	media	Takdel Inc	40
4	310	Programming Stds.	in-house	Staff	6
5	3223	BASIC Programming	media	Takdel Inc	40
6	7771	Data Base Systems	media	Takdel Inc	30
7	CIS11	Business COBOL	college	St. Univ.	45
8	EX15	Local Area Networks	vendor	HAL Inc	30
9	MGT10	Mgt.Info.Systems	college	St. Univ.	45
10	VC10	Elec. Spreadsheet	media	VidCourse	20
11	VC44	4th Generation Lang.	media	VidCourse	30
12	VC88	Word Processing	media	VidCourse	18

COURSE data base

FIGURE 7–14 Database: COURSE Data Base
The COURSE data base contains a record for each course that Zimco offers to its employees.

format is analogous to a hard-copy form that contains labels and blank lines (for example, medical questionnaire, employment application). Data are entered and edited (deleted or revised) with database software one record at a time, as they are on hard-copy forms.

THE STRUCTURE OF THE DATA BASE   To set up a data entry screen format, you must first specify the *structure* of the data base by identifying the characteristics of each field in the data base. This is done interactively, with the system prompting you to enter the field name, field type, and so on (see Figure 7–15). For example, the ID field in Figure 7–15 is a five-character field. The *field name* is ID, the *field length* is five characters, and the *field type* is character. A character field type can be a single word or any alphanumeric (that is, numbers, letters, and special characters) phrase up to several hundred characters in length. For numeric field types, you must specify the maximum number of digits (field length) and the number of decimal positions that you wish to have displayed. Since the course durations are all defined in whole hours, the number of decimal positions for the DURATION field is set at zero (see Figure 7–15).

ENTERING AND EDITING A DATA BASE   The screen format for entering, editing, and adding records to the COURSE data base is shown in Figure 7–16. This screen is generated automatically from the specifications outlined in the structure of the COURSE data base (see Figure 7–15). To create the COURSE data base, the education coordinator issued a command that called up the data entry screen of Figure 7–16; then he entered the data for first record; then the second record, and so on. On most data management systems, the records are automatically assigned a number as they are entered. The reverse video portion of the screen in Figure 7–16 comprises the data for the five fields in record "1". Records can, of course, be added to the data base and edited.

Setting Conditions for Record Selection

Database software also permits you to retrieve, view, and print records based on preset conditions. You set conditions for the selection of records by

Field no.	Field name	Field type	Field length	Decimal positions
1	ID	Character	5	
2	TITLE	Character	20	
3	TYPE	Character	8	
4	SOURCE	Character	10	
5	DURATION	Numeric	4	0

FIGURE 7–15   Database: Structure of the COURSE Data Base

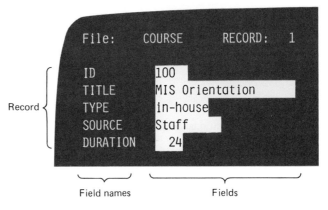

```
File:      COURSE        RECORD:    1

   ID          100
   TITLE       MIS Orientation
   TYPE        in-house
   SOURCE      Staff
   DURATION     24
```

Record {

‿‿‿‿‿   ‿‿‿‿‿‿‿‿‿‿‿
Field names   Fields

FIGURE 7–16   Database: Data Entry Screen Format
*Illustrated is the screen format for entering, editing, and adding records
to the COURSE data base. This screen is automatically generated from
the specifications outlined in structure of the COURSE data base (see
Figure 7–14).*

composing a *relational expression* that reflects the desired conditions. The
relational expression normally compares one or more field names to numbers
or character strings using the *relational operators* [= (equal to), > (greater
than), < (less than), and combinations of these operators]. Several expressions
can be combined in a single condition with *logical operators* (AND, OR,
and NOT).

The education coordinator wanted a listing of all in-house seminars,
so he issued commands to *locate (search* for), then *list* the records of all
courses that are of TYPE "in-house" in the COURSE data base (see Figure
7–14). To retrieve these records, he set the condition to

TYPE='in-house'

Depending on the database package, the *search string* is enclosed in single
or double quotation marks (for example, "in-house"). We'll use single quotation marks. To produce the output of Figure 7–17, the education coordinator
keyed in the command

LIST FOR TYPE='in-house'

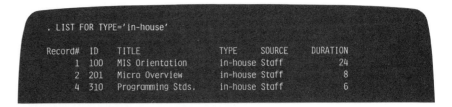

```
. LIST FOR TYPE='in-house'

Record#  ID    TITLE              TYPE      SOURCE   DURATION
     1   100   MIS Orientation    in-house  Staff        24
     2   201   Micro Overview     in-house  Staff         8
     4   310   Programming Stds.  in-house  Staff         6
```

FIGURE 7–17   Database: Conditional Search and List
*For the command, LIST FOR TYPE='in-house', only the records from the COURSE data base
(Figure 7–14) are displayed for which TYPE='in-house'.*

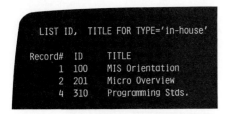

```
. LIST ID, TITLE FOR TYPE='in-house'

Record#  ID      TITLE
      1  100     MIS Orientation
      2  201     Micro Overview
      4  310     Programming Stds.
```

FIGURE 7–18 Database: Conditional Search and List, Specified Fields Only
For the command, LIST ID, TITLE FOR TYPE='in-house', only the ID and TITLE fields are displayed for the records from the COURSE data base (Figure 7–14) for which TYPE='in-house'.

Of course, one of the options is to route the output to a display screen or to a printer. If the education coordinator wanted only the ID and TITLE for those records that meet the condition TYPE='in-house', he would enter a command like this

LIST ID, TITLE FOR TYPE='in-house'

Figure 7–18 shows the output.

Data Base Inquiries

Database software permits inquiries that involve parts or all of one or more records. To extract and then list (also display, print, or edit) selected records from a data base, you must first establish the condition or conditions. The following relational expressions establish conditions that will select or extract records (noted to the right of the expression) from the COURSE data base of Figure 7–14.

TYPE='in-house' .AND. DURATION < =10	records 2 and 4 (see Figure 7–19)
SOURCE='VidCourse' .OR. SOURCE='Takdel Inc'	records 3, 5, 6, 10, 11, 12
DURATION > 15 .AND. DURATION < 25	records 1, 10, 12
ID='CIS11'	record 7

The process of selecting records by setting conditions is sometimes called *filtering*; that is, those records or fields that you don't want are "filtered out" of the display. The concept of filtering is introduced in Chapter 1, "Information Processing in Perspective."

Sorting Records

Data can also be sorted for display in a variety of formats. For example, the COURSE data base in Figure 7–14 has been sorted and is displayed in ascending order by course identification number (ID). To obtain this sequencing of the data base records, the education coordinator selected ID as the *key field* and requested an ascending sort of the COURSE data base. Numbers are considered "less than" alphabetic characters; therefore, the numeric IDs are listed before those that begin with a letter.

```
. LIST FOR TYPE='in-house' .AND. DURATION<=10
Record# ID      TITLE            TYPE      SOURCE    DURATION
      2 201     Micro Overview   in-house  Staff            8
      4 310     Programming Stds. in-house Staff            6
```

FIGURE 7–19 Database: Conditional Expression with AND Operator
For the command, TYPE='in-house' .AND. DURATION<=10, only the records from the COURSE data base (Figure 7–14) are displayed for which TYPE='in-house' and DURATION >= (less than or equal to) 10.

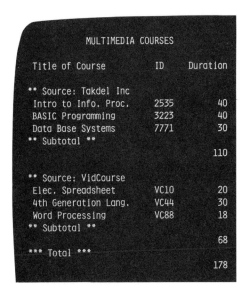

```
            MULTIMEDIA COURSES

 Title of Course       ID     Duration

 ** Source: Takdel Inc
 Intro to Info. Proc.  2535       40
 BASIC Programming     3223       40
 Data Base Systems     7771       30
 ** Subtotal **
                                 110


 ** Source: VidCourse
 Elec. Spreadsheet     VC10       20
 4th Generation Lang.  VC44       30
 Word Processing       VC88       18
 ** Subtotal **
                                  68

 *** Total ***
                                 178
```

FIGURE 7–20 Database: Formatted Reports
This formatted report was compiled by merging a predefined report format with the COURSE data base after it has been sorted by ID within SOURCE.

Customized Reports

Database software provides the capability to create customized or formatted reports. This capability allows you to design the *layout* of the report. This means that you have some flexibility in spacing and can include titles, subtitles, column headings, separation lines, and other elements that make a report more readable. You describe the layout of the *customized* report interactively, then store it for later recall. The result of the description, called a *report form*, is recalled from disk storage and merged with a data base to create the customized report. Managers often use this capability to generate periodic reports (for example, weekly training status report).

Once a month Zimco's education coordinator generates four reports that summarize the offerings for each type of course; that is, one report summarizes Zimco's course offerings for TYPE='in-house', another for TYPE='media' (multimedia), and so on. One of these formatted reports is shown in Figure 7–20. This summary report of "MULTIMEDIA COURSES" was compiled by merging a predefined report format with the COURSE data base that was sorted by ID within SOURCE, that is, with the SOURCE field as the primary key and the ID field as the secondary key.

Use

Database software earns the "productivity tool" label by providing users with the capability to organize data into an electronic data base that can be easily maintained and queried (permit user inquiries). The examples illustrated and discussed in the "concepts" section merely scratch the surface of the potential of database software. With relative ease, you can generate some rather sophisticated reports that involve subtotals, calculations, and programming. You can even change the structure of a data base (for example, add another field).

The special section at the end of the book, entitled "Hands-on Exercises: Electronic Spreadsheet, Graphics, and Database," contains exercises for database software.

COMMUNICATIONS SOFTWARE

Practice does not make perfect; perfect practice makes perfect.

——— *Vince Lombardi*

Function

Communications software makes the microcomputer more than a small stand-alone computer. With communications software, a micro can transmit and receive data to/from a remote computer. Communications software automatically "dials up" a remote computer (another micro or a mainframe) and then "logs on" (establishes a link with a remote computer). Once on-line, you can communicate and share data with a remote computer.

After logging on, communications software allows you to **download** files; that is, you can request and receive data or program files that are transmitted from a remote computer. Once the files have been downloaded to your micro, you can select any of the microcomputer productivity tools to work with the files. Once processing is complete, you can use the communications software to **upload** the file to a remote computer. Uploading is the opposite of downloading.

Concepts

You use communications software to link your microcomputer via telephone lines to another computer system anywhere in the world. However, to do this, your micro must be equipped with a *modem*. The modem links your micro with the telephone line that connects the two computers. On most microcomputers, the modem is an optional plug-in circuit board. You can purchase it with your micro, or you can add it later as the need arises. A modem can also be purchased as a separate unit and connected to the micro with an electrical cable.

In essence, communications software enables your micro to emulate any one of a number of popular terminals, like those that are commonly serviced by mainframe computers. To do this you need to specify certain data communications parameters, such as the type of terminal you plan to emulate, whether or not parity bits are to be added, the number of stop bits used, the rate of data transmission (300 to 9,600 baud), and so on. One baud is approximately equal to one bit per second. Data communications concepts are discussed in Chapter 8, "Connectivity and Data Communications."

The communications software can be set up to dial up and log on automatically to frequently accessed computer systems. It will even redial if a busy signal is detected. A micro with a modem and communications software can be on the receiving end as well. That is, it can automatically answer "calls" from other computers.

One very handy feature of communications software is that it enables you to record all input/output during an interactive session to a disk file. At a later time, you can recall the session from disk storage and browse through it at a more leisurely rate. The information gathered during an interactive session can be integrated into a word processing document, such as a letter or report.

Use

Many *information services*, such as flight and hotel information, stock quotes, and even restaurant menus, are available to microcomputer owners with communications capabilities. A few information services are gratis, but most require a fee. The fee normally consists of a set monthly charge plus an amount based on usage. A few of the more popular commercial information services are CompuServe, The Source, Dow Jones, Western Union, and News-Net.

Just about every city with a population of 25,000 or more has at least one *computer bulletin board*, often sponsored by a local computer club. Members "post" messages, announcements, for-sale notices, and so on to the computer bulletin board by transmitting them to a central computer, usually another micro. To scan the bulletin board, members again use communications software to link up to the central computer. This software component also opens the door to sending and receiving *electronic mail*, either through a local bulletin board or an information network or via a public electronic mail service.

INFORMATION CENTER PERSONNEL

Q. The two people in our newly established information center and 20 programmers report to me. I am comfortable with managing programmers, but have not fared well with the two people in the information center.

Our information center has five micros, and eventually it will have several terminals. Having no experience in this area, I did not know whom to hire, so I recruited one person from corporate training and the other from my programming staff.

I thought that would be the perfect combination, but I have had nothing but complaints. The programmer tries to impress people with his knowledge, and the trainer simply cannot answer questions about the hardware or software.

What type of background is best for persons working in information centers?

A. It seems as if there are a dozen concepts for information centers. I see an information center as a place that has the tools to help users to help themselves. These tools include hardware, software, technical support, and education.

To date, no credentials package has emerged for information center personnel. In such an environment, you must have people with a solid technical base who can use and explain the use of available tools. They can come from either MIS or the user community.

After technical competence, you can look for certain desirable personality traits. People working directly with users must genuinely want them to learn so that they can eventually work independently. They must have patience and recognize that a user is not going to learn in one hour what took him or her years to learn.

A common failing in information centers is that support personnel would rather just do the work than show users how to do it themselves. In the long run, this is counterproductive.

In the coming years, we'll probably see a shift to smaller briefcases. With communications software and an ever-growing number of home computers, people won't need to lug their paperwork between home and office every day. For a great many white-collar workers, at all levels, much of their work is on computers. Continuing their work at home is simply a matter of establishing a link between their home and office computers.

The combination of microcomputers and communications software has fueled the growth of *cottage industries*. The world has been made a little more compact with the computer revolution. Stockbrokers, financial planners, writers, programmers, and people from a wide variety of professions may not need to "go to the office." They can live wherever they choose. Micros make it possible for these people to access needed information, communicate with their clients, and even deliver products of their work (for example, programs, stories, or recommendations).

INTEGRATED MICROCOMPUTER SOFTWARE

Function

Seldom do we produce a graph (graphics) without adding some explanatory text (word processing). Producing a hard copy of a memo (word processing) may be unnecessary if we can send it via electronic mail (communications). If you think about it, all the micro productivity tools can be integrated to increase the capabilities of the individual software packages.

Integrated microcomputer software, or simply **integrated software**, is the integration of two or more of the major productivity tools (i.e., word processing, electronic spreadsheet, database, graphics, and communications software). These integrated packages permit us to work as we always have—on several projects at a time—but with the assistance of a computer.

Concepts

Integrated software lets you work the way you think, and think the way you work. Several projects are at the tips of your fingers, and you can switch easily among them with relative ease. When you do this, you are switching from one *window* (for example, spreadsheet) to another window (for example, word processing). You can even "look through" several windows on a single display screen; however, you can only manipulate text or data in one window at a time. This is called the *current window*. Windows can overlap one another on the display screen.

Use

A manager might use all micro productivity tools to handle a variety of administrative duties. In one window, a manager might use electronic spreadsheet software to track product sales by region. At the end of each week, the manager might summarize and plot sales data in a bar graph in another window. In still another window, the manager might write a memo recommending the top field sales representatives for special recognition. Another window might contain personal "things-to-do" notes in an outline format. The manager can distribute the memo via electronic mail by uploading it to the company's mainframe (via communications software). This example illustrates how the capabilities of the individual software packages complement the capabilities of the others.

PERSONAL COMPUTING SUMMARY

Several hundred micro productivity software packages are available commercially. Over 30 integrated micro software packages are available. Commercially available software packages vary greatly in capabilities and price. Before buying, have an idea of how you plan to use the software; then investigate thoroughly to make sure it has the features you want.

Personal computing is evolving to group computing on a personal level via networking. Micros can be linked together in a *network* and some of the more powerful microcomputers have the capabilities to support several users. Network versions of micro software (electronic spreadsheet, word processing) prevent file overwrite and permit the sharing of peripherals. A network version of a software package costs about 30 percent more plus an additional amount for each workstation over one. The network approach to personal computing makes economic sense and provides end users with more opportunities to share resources (hardware, software, data).

If a man has a talent and cannot use it, he has failed. If he has a talent and uses only half of it, he has partly failed. If he has a talent and learns somehow to use the whole of it, he has gloriously succeeded, and won a satisfaction and a triumph few men ever know.

—————— *Thomas Wolfe*

To be sure, personal computing offers tremendous opportunities for end users to improve their productivity and the quality of their decisions; however, personal computing needs to be placed in its proper perspective. Numerous television commercials and magazine ads oversimplify the work that goes into providing management information. For example, a representative commercial portrays a smiling high-level manager pressing a few keys to the strains of a Strauss waltz and up pops a graph that prompts the "I've got it" look. Except for the Strauss waltz, the commercial is true to life, but it only shows the conclusion of the effort. To be able to produce the graph, the end user had to be trained on the use and application of the hardware and software, and the data had to be entered and meticulously massaged into the proper format for graphing. However, even when you take into account the training and the data preparation activities that go into producing graphs, the productivity gains made possible by this and other micro software packages are nothing short of phenomenal.

CHAPTER HIGHLIGHTS

■ Personal computing is individuals using microcomputers to meet their information and processing needs.

■ Thousands of commercially available software packages run on microcomputers, including the popular productivity tools (word processing, desktop publishing, electronic spreadsheet, presentation graphics, database, and communications software).

■ The Micro Instrumentation and Telemetry Systems company introduced the first commercially available microcomputer, the Altair 8800, to the public in 1975. Other milestones in PC hardware history include the Apple II, the IBM PC, the IBM Personal System/2, the Commodore-64, the Compaq Portable, and the Macintosh.

■ With the introduction of VisiCalc, the first electronic spreadsheet program, in 1979, micros became a viable business tool. Other milestones in PC software history include CP/M, MS-DOS, Lotus 1-2-3, dBASE II, and WordStar.

■ Personal computers come in three different physical sizes: pocket PCs, lap PCs, and desktop PCs.

■ A microcomputer is an electronic device capable of interpreting and executing programmed commands for input, output, computation, and logic operations. A microcomputer system has four fundamental components—input, processing, output, and storage.

■ Word processing is using the computer to enter, store, manipulate, and print text in letters, reports, books, and so on. To begin preparation of a document, format the document and begin keying in the text. Text is entered in replace mode or insert mode.

■ The block move, copy, and delete commands are among the handiest of word processing the features. Other common features include the search, search and replace, and the wide variety of print options.

■ Word processing advanced features include the generation of a table of contents, the generation of an index of key words, automatic footnoting, and multicolumn output.

■ Word processing add-on capabilities include the on-line thesaurus, spelling checker (with an electronic dictionary), and grammar checker.

■ The mail merge example is a good example of the use of boilerplate. Boilerplate is existing text that can in some way be customized to be applicable to a variety of word processing applications.

■ Desktop publishing refers to the capability of producing near typeset-quality copy from the confines of a "desktop." The primary components required for desktop publishing are desktop publishing software, a microcomputer, and a laser printer. Some include an image processor, as well.

■ All commercially available electronic spreadsheet packages provide the facility to manipulate rows and columns of data. However, the user interface differs from one package to the next.

■ Electronic spreadsheets are organized in a tabular structure with rows and columns. The rows are numbered and the columns are lettered. The intersection of a particular row and column designates a cell. During operations, data are referenced by their cell address (for example, B3 or C14).

■ An entry to an electronic spreadsheet cell is classified as a text, numeric, or a formula entry. Spreadsheet formulas use standard notation for arithmetic operators ($+ - * / \wedge$). A formula may include one or all of the following: arithmetic operations, functions, logic operations, and string operations.

■ A range of cells in an electronic spreadsheet is defined by the end points of adjacent cells in a column, a row, or a rectangular block.

■ Many of the capabilities of specialized data management software are also capabilities of electronic spreadsheet software. These include sorting records, extracting records that meet certain conditions, and report generation.

■ With presentation graphics software, you can create a variety of graphics from data in an electronic spreadsheet or a data base. Among the most popular presentation graphics are bar graphs (including the stacked-bar and clustered-bar graphs), pie graphs, and line graphs. Each of these graphs can be annotated with graph titles, labels, and legends.

■ Database software permits users to create and maintain a data base and extract information from the data base. Once the data base is created, its records can be deleted or revised and other records can be added to the data base.

■ The six levels of the hierarchy of data organization are bit, character, data element or field, record, file, and data base. The first level is transparent to the end user. The other levels of the hierarchy are important considerations in the use of database software.

■ In database software, the user-defined structure of a data base identifies the characteristics of each field in the data base. The screen format for entering, editing, and adding records to a data base is generated automatically from the specifications outlined in the structure of the data base.

■ Database software permits users to retrieve, view, and print records based on preset conditions. To do this, users set conditions for the selection of records by composing a relational expression that reflects the desired conditions. Several expressions can be combined in a single condition with logical operators (AND, OR, and NOT). The process of selecting records by setting conditions is sometimes called filtering.

■ With communications software, a micro can transmit and receive data to/from a remote computer. Communications software provides the capability to "dial up" a remote computer automatically and then "log on." Once on-line, the user can communicate and share data with a remote computer via the downloading and uploading of files. To use communications software, micros must be equipped with a modem.

■ Integrated microcomputer software is the integration of two or more of the major software productivity tools. Integrated software permits users to work on several projects at a time by switching from one window to the next.

■ Personal computing is evolving to group computing on a personal level via networking. Micros can be linked together in a network and some of the more powerful microcomputers have the capabilities to support several users.

IMPORTANT TERMS

Apple II
arithmetic operators
bar graphs
boilerplate
cell
cell address
clones
clustered-bar graph
communications software
Compaq Portable
cottage industries
current cell
current window
dBASE II
dBASE III PLUS
database software

desktop PCs
desktop publishing
download/upload
electronic dictionary
electronic spreadsheet
fields
file/data base
filtering
full-screen editing
grammar checker
IBM PC
IBM PC compatibles
IBM Personal System/2
insert mode
integrated microcomputer software
lap PCs

line graphs
logical operators
Lotus 1-2-3
MS-DOS
Macintosh
mail merge
microcomputer system
microframes
near-typeset-quality copy
on-line thesaurus
PC-DOS
page-composition software
personal computing
pie graphs
pocket PCs
pointer

presentation graphics software
processor
range
records
relational expression
replace mode
rows/columns (spreadsheet)
scrolling
search string
spelling checker
stacked-bar graph
template
window
word processing
WordStar

1. What are the four fundamental components of a microcomputer system?

2. Name a microcomputer input device other than the keyboard.

3. In terms of physical size, how are PCs categorized?

4. Text is entered in a word processing program in either of what two modes? What mode would you select to change "the table" to "the long table"? What mode would you select to change "pick the choose" to "pick and choose"?

5. What causes text to wrap around in word processing?

6. Give a word processing example of when you might issue a global search and replace command.

7. Describe the layout of an electronic spreadsheet.

8. Give an example of an electronic spreadsheet cell address. Which portion of the address depicts the row and which portion depicts the column?

9. Give an example of each of the four types of electronic spreadsheet ranges.

10. Give examples of the three types of entries that can be made in an electronic spreadsheet.

11. What types of operators are used to compare numeric and string values in an electronic spreadsheet?

12. Write the electronic spreadsheet formula that would compute the average of the range A1..D1.

13. In an electronic spreadsheet, when would you need to scroll horizontally? Vertically?

14. What is a spreadsheet template?

15. What is the relationship between a field, a record, and the structure of a data base?

16. Name and give an example for each level of the hierarchy of data organization.

17. Give examples and descriptions of at least three other fields that might be added to the record for the COURSE data base of Figure 7–14.

18. Name three types of graphs commonly used for presentation graphics.

19. What is the source of the data needed to produce graphs?

20. Name and graphically illustrate (by hand) two variations on the bar graph.

21. What types of input devices enable you to produce original line drawings when using micro productivity software?

22. What is meant when a portion of a pie graph is exploded?

23. Briefly describe the concept of integrated microcomputer software.

24. What is the software capability that enables viewing of electronic spreadsheet data and a bar graph at the same time?

1. Discuss the emerging role of personal computers in electronic funds transfer.

2. How might a microcomputer help in the day-to-day administration of an appliance store (20 employees)?

3. Customer service representatives at Zimco Enterprises spend almost 70 percent of their day interacting directly with customers. Approximately one hour each day is spent preparing courtesy follow-up letters, primarily to enhance goodwill between Zimco and its customers. Do you think the "personalized" letters are a worthwhile effort? Why or why not?

4. The five PCs in the purchasing department of a large consumer goods manufacturer are used primarily for word processing and data base applications. What would be the benefits and burdens associated with connecting the PCs in a local area network?

5. Most word processing packages have a default document size. Discuss other defaults that you might expect a word processing package to have.

6. Discuss the difference between the pointer and the cursor in an electronic spreadsheet.

7. What is the purpose of setting conditions for a data base?

8. In data base terminology, what is meant by the term "filtering"?

9. Describe two types of inquiries to a data base that involve calculations.

10. Under what circumstances is a graphic representation of data more effective than a tabular presentation of the same data?

11. Is it possible to present the same information in a stacked bar and a line graph? How about stacked bar and pie graphs?

12. Why would you download data? Upload data?

13. One popular information service is home banking. Describe an interactive session with at least one transaction to both a checking and savings account. Begin from the time you turn on your microcomputer.

APPLICATION CASE STUDY 7–1
Personal Computing

The Situation

Que Realty is a real estate sales company with 16 offices and 96 full-time and 37 part-time real estate agents. The support staff at each office consist of a manager, a secretary, and one or more clerks. A manager, a secretary, and 3 clerks are located at Que's headquarters as well. In addition, Que uses the services of an outside lawyer and accountant. Que's organizational structure is illustrated in Application Case Study 6–1. Que's operations are described in Application Case Study 3–1, Application Case Study 3–2, and Application Case Study 4–2.

Joan Magee, Que's owner, recently attended a workshop on personal computing. The workshop included classroom instruction and hands-on experience with word processing, spreadsheet, and database software. Ms. Magee was impressed with the capabilities and ease of use of both the microcomputers and the software. She was convinced that her employees could improve their productivity using these and other microcomputer tools.

The Assignment

Joan Magee has hired you as a consultant to help her employees select and use software and hardware effectively.

1. Describe the training that you would recommend to provide Que's employees with the knowledge needed to accomplish the following functions. For each function, specify the course title, intended audience, mode of training (classroom, hands-on lab, and so on), length of course, and facilities required.
   a. Familiarity with microcomputer hardware.
   b. Familiarity with microcomputer software principles. This includes an introduction to an operating system (such as DOS or UNIX) and a general understanding of the capabilities and limitations of word processing, spreadsheet, database, desktop publishing, graphics, communications, and integrated software packages.
   c. Selecting software and hardware.
   d. Working knowledge of one electronic spreadsheet package.
   e. Working knowledge of one database package.
   f. Working knowledge of one desktop publishing package.
   g. Working knowledge of one graphics package.
2. Why should Que have standard, companywide packages for applications such as word processing, electronic spreadsheet, database, and communications? In your response, discuss centralization versus decentralization of the various applications. For example, should all documents created with word processing be accessible to all users?

3. If you were developing the specification for a word processing package for companywide use, what would you include for each of the following?
   a. Advanced features.   b. Add-on capabilities.
4. Describe circumstances under which someone at Que should be permitted to use a word processing package other than the company standard.
5. For Que's desktop publishing software,
   a. Which personnel in the company would be primary users of desktop publishing?
   b. List the documents that are likely to be created using desktop publishing software.
   c. List the hardware that is necessary to implement desktop publishing at Que.
6. For Que's companywide electronic spreadsheet software:
   a. List the personnel in the company who would be the most likely users of spreadsheet software and briefly describe the applications for each person on your list.
   b. Manually illustrate templates for two different spreadsheet applications in the foregoing list. Use the example in Figure 7–6 as a guide for possible formats. Be careful to restrict your templates to the display area of a standard monitors (24 lines by 80 columns).
7. For Que's presentation graphics software,
   a. List the personnel in the company who would be the most likely users of graphics software and briefly describe the applications for each person on your list.
   b. Sketch an example of a bar graph, a pie graph, and a line graph for one of the spreadsheet examples described in the previous question.
8. For Que's companywide database software,
   a. List the personnel in the company who would be the most likely users of database software and briefly describe the applications for each person on your list.
   b. For two different applications in your list, give the name of the data base, list the fields in each record in the data base, and give the dBASE command to produce a selective listing from the data base.
9. List the personnel in the company who would be the most likely users of communications software and briefly describe the applications for each person on your list. Be sure to include applications that interact with entities external to Que, such as lending institutions.
10. What hardware would you recommend to support personal computing at Que, and where it should be located?

CHAPTER **8**
Connectivity and Data Communications

KEY TOPICS

CHAPTER OVERVIEW

In the 1960s, computers numbered in the tens of thousands. Today, computers are numbered in the tens of millions. In short, information is everywhere. Making this information more accessible to a greater number of people is the challenge of the next decade. To do this, the business and MIS communities are seeking ways to interface or connect a diverse set of hardware, software, and data bases. Connectivity, as it is called, is necessary to facilitate electronic data interchange, end user computing, and free flow of information within an enterprise. The chapter material focuses on connectivity concepts and the base technology of connectivity—data communications.

DATA COMMUNICATIONS

Computers and MIS have been the driving force behind our transition from an industrial to an information society. In an industrial society, tasks at the clerical and operational levels are typically repetitive, decisions are programmed, and the information requirements are minimal. On those rare occasions when a clerk would need supplemental information, he or she would simply contact the person who was most likely to have access to this information. All too often the needed information was not available from any source.

The clerks of yesterday are today's **knowledge workers**. Their scope of responsibility has expanded, and they have a much greater need for easy and ready access to information. In today's competitive environment, relying solely on verbal communication for information transfer can be inefficient, untimely, and very expensive. Of course, knowledge workers continue to interact with co-workers, but they need a more efficient way of retrieving information—enter MIS. To achieve an efficient and effective interface between knowledge workers, links need to be established between their workstations and data bases. Just as telephones provide a link for voice communication, a similar link is needed for data and information communication.

Data communications is, very simply, the collection and distribution of "electronic" data from and to remote facilities. Data are transmitted from computers to workstations and other computers over land, in the air, and under the sea. Telephone lines, satellites, and coaxial cable are a few of the many ways that data are transmitted. The technical aspects of data communications are discussed later in this chapter.

Through the mid-1960s, a company's computing hardware was located in a single room called the machine room. The only people who had direct access to the computer were the people in the machine room. Since that time, microcomputers, workstations, and data communications have made it possible to move hardware and information systems "closer to the source" and to the people who use them. Before long, workstations will be as much a part of our work environment as desks and telephones are now.

Several other terms describe the general area of data communications. **Telecommunications** encompasses not only data communications, but any type of remote communication, such as the transmission of a television signal. **Teleprocessing**, or **TP**, is the combination of *tele*communications and data *processing* and is often used interchangeably with the term "data communications." The integration of computer systems, workstations, and communication links is referred to as a **computer network**.

THE ERA OF COOPERATIVE COMPUTING

Intracompany Networking

This is the era of **cooperative computing**. Information is the password to success in today's business environment. To obtain meaningful, accurate, and timely information, businesses have decided that they must cooperate internally and externally to take full advantage of available information. To promote internal cooperation, they are moving in the direction of *intracompany networking* (see Figure 8–1). For example, information maintained in the personnel department is made readily accessible to people throughout

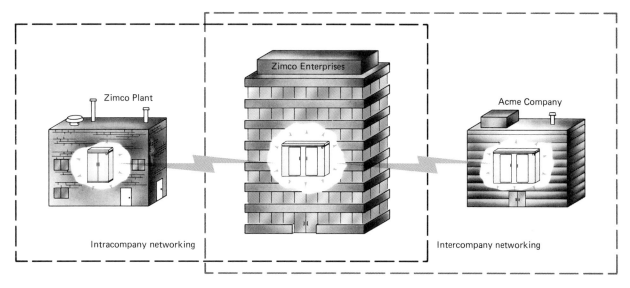

FIGURE 8–1   Intracompany and Intercompany Networking

the company on a *need-to-know* basis. The same is true of information maintained by purchasing, engineering, or any other department. At the individual level, managers or knowledge workers are creating microcomputer-based systems and data bases to help them in the performance of their jobs. Often these personalized systems and data bases have the potential to benefit other people in the company. When this happens, these systems are made a part of the company's network to permit the sharing of these information resources.

Intercompany Networking

Companies have recognized that they must cooperate with one another to compete effectively in a world market. They are doing this via *intercompany networking* (see Figure 8–1) or, more specifically, electronic data interchange (EDI). For example, at General Foods 25 percent of all shipments are a result of computer-to-computer order processing. That is, customers submit their orders to General Foods via EDI. By 1990, 50 percent of all shipments of General Foods products will be as a result of EDI.

This office is one of 15 regional customer support centers. Each workstation is linked to a local minicomputer, which is connected via a high-speed communications line to the company's headquarters office in Atlanta, Georgia. The regional minis are also used for local processing.

Courtesy of International Business Machines Corporation

In the 1990s, EDI will be more the rule than the exception. Executives in progressive companies are well aware that the competitive edge belongs to those companies that take advantage of EDI. Chapter 4, "Information Systems as a Competitive Strategy," contains discussions of EDI concepts and strategies.

External Computing Support

The phenomenal growth of micros in the home is causing companies to expand their MIS capabilities to permit linkages with home and portable PCs. This form of cooperative computing increases system efficiency while lowering costs. For example, in over 100 banks, services have been extended to home micro owners in the form of *home banking* systems. Subscribers to a home banking service use their personal computers as workstations linked to the bank's mainframe computer system to pay bills, transfer funds, and inquire about account status.

The Internal Revenue Service (IRS) now permits tax returns to be filed from the taxpayer's home PC. This service saves the taxpayer and the IRS both time and money. For the taxpayer, the on-line system performs all the necessary table searches and computations, and it even cross-checks the accuracy and consistency of the input data. For the IRS, no further data entry or personal assistance is required. Also, brokerage firms permit customers to access up-to-the-minute stock market quotations and to issue buy/sell orders directly from their personal computers. Several supermarkets are experimenting with "electronic" shopping. In the 1990s, virtually every type of industry will provide the facility for external links to their mainframe computer systems.

WHAT IS CONNECTIVITY?

The scope of computer and information system technology is doubling every two years. Accompanying this rapid growth is an equal increase in the number of catch phrases, buzz words, and new terms. If MIS specialists were asked to vote on which of these phrases, words, or terms would represent the driving force of computers and MIS in the 1990s, they would probably say **connectivity**. Let's explore this concept further.

Connectivity—Theory and Practice

Connectivity refers to the degree to which hardware devices can be functionally linked to one another. Some people expand the scope of connectivity to include other aspects of MIS, such as software and data bases. Connectivity has become such an important consideration that virtually all future decisions involving hardware, software, and data base management must be evaluated with respect to connectivity. Corporate management has made connectivity a high-priority strategy. Management realizes that connectivity is the key to unlocking the full potential of the information resource.

To get the most out of the information resource, it must be shared. To do this, the company must strive toward full connectivity.

□ Connectivity means that a marketing manager can use a microcomputer to access information in a data base on the finance department's mini-computer.

□ Connectivity means that a network of microcomputers can route output to the same laser printer.

□ Connectivity means that a manufacturing company's mainframe computer can communicate with the mainframe computers of suppliers.

In these examples there must be an electronic connection between these hardware devices—thus the derivation of the term connectivity.

In practice, people interpret the meaning of connectivity within the context of their own perspectives. A personal computer enthusiast sees it as the capability to transfer files between personal computers. MIS professionals, in particular, data communications specialists, see it as the passing of data between hardware devices of any kind. Vendors of user-oriented query languages see it as the degree of connection between software products that use query languages. In its broadest sense, connectivity is more than the physical connection of hardware devices; it is the functional connection of an organization's MIS and information resources.

Connectivity—The Technological Challenge

Technologically, it is relatively easy to make an electronic connection between two computer systems, but realizing any meaningful transfer of information from the connection is another matter. Most computer systems and data base software packages were not designed to permit the efficient sharing of resources with different types of computers systems and data bases. *Incompatible* computer systems differ, often dramatically, in architecture (basic design) and the manner in which they store data. In essence, they do not speak the same language. This incompatibility is best explained by an analogy. You can pick up a telephone and dial anywhere in the world, even China. However, if you do not speak Chinese or the person on the other end does not speak English, information transfer is impossible without the assistance of a translator.

The technological challenge confronting connectivity in an incompatible environment is formidable. To achieve connectivity, a hardware and/or software interface must be designed and implemented that enables the efficient modification of the output of one system such that it can be intercepted and interpreted by another system. Efficiency is the key word. Connectivity is possible in almost every situation, but in some situations, either the *system overhead* or the *response times* are prohibitively high. That is, the expense of the extra processing required to modify the output and the excessive time delay between user input and system response may make connectivity infeasible.

Connectivity—A Hardware Vendor's Perspective

Vendors of hardware and software products have made little effort to provide the facility for connectivity outside of their line of products. To permit connec-

MIS *in practice*

THE WORKER-TO-WORKSTATION RATIO

Q. I am the software development manager for a manufacturing company with about 1000 employees.

Six hundred people work in the plant and 400 work in the office or field sales. We are moving rapidly toward on-line interactive systems and currently support about 200 terminals. This figure includes 20 portable terminals used by our field sales staff.

Have any statistics been compiled that reflect the average ratio of terminals to employees for the various types of industries? We would like to know where we stand with respect to our peer companies.

A. I will qualify my remarks by noting that the number of installed workstations is not nearly as important as the quality and availability of software and data. I am not aware of any such ratios. Most companies of your size and larger do not know where their workstations are located, much less how many.

In MIS, the average ratio of workstations to programmers/analysts is approaching one to one. Based solely on my observations, I would surmise that your ratio of one to five reflects a greater use of workstations than most manufacturing companies. A one-to-five ratio may be low for insurance, banking, and other companies whose employees are primarily white collar.

The same logic that supports the one programmer/one workstation theory will soon be applicable to office workers as well.

If you weigh the cost of not having a workstation available when an employee needs it against the cost of the device, the scales are tipped heavily in favor of all office workers having their own workstation.

I would expect those companies that are aggressively developing on-line systems to approach a one-to-one ratio for office workers within a few more years. By then, the typical workstation will be a micro that can be networked or used as a stand-alone system.

tivity, vendors need to cooperate and set standards. Until recently, vendors and business were not very concerned about data communications compatibility. Traditionally, centralized information services divisions have had complete control, and they were careful to ensure compatibility within their scope of processing and service. In a controlled environment, they were able to minimize the connectivity problems associated with the proliferation of vendors in a single computing environment. Now the situation has changed. The widespread use of micros and the emergence of departmental computing has diluted centralized control. Micros, minis, and a wide variety of applications software have been purchased and installed by users. Now users want to connect their incompatible hardware and software to the company's mainframe resources and the resources of other users. This connectivity challenge is shared by small mom-and-pop organizations and by billion-dollar multinationals.

To accommodate user requests for greater connectivity and to make the most effective use of all computing and information resources, today's information services divisions must position themselves to handle linkages for a wide variety of hardware, software, and data bases. Moreover, the push to implement electronic funds transfer (EFT) and electronic data interchange applications intensifies concerns about connectivity. Connectivity concerns have actually changed the buying habits of companies. Executives are much more deliberate in their decision making. They do not want to buy into a technology that may be obsolete in a few years because of changing connectivity standards. This need for internal and external connectivity has prompted top management personnel in companies throughout the world to demand that vendors focus their efforts on providing better connectivity.

Although vendors are still reluctant to cooperate with one another, the individual vendors are beginning to stress the importance of connectivity. For example, IBM, DEC, and others are committed to providing the facility to link all hardware devices and software products within their respective product lines.

Connectivity—A User's Perspective

To the user, the ideal implementation of connectivity would be to make all corporate computer and information resources accessible from his or her workstation environment. This ideal is referred to as **total connectivity**. Realistically, industry analysts are predicting that total connectivity is still a decade or more away. Nevertheless, users are expecting, even demanding, that the information services divisions at least strive for total connectivity.

Total connectivity, or the networking of all hardware, software, and data bases, is a goal of many companies. Total connectivity will permit user access to:

- ☐ Mainframe computers.
- ☐ Local area networks (LANs).
- ☐ Personal computer network file servers.
- ☐ Outside information services.
- ☐ Departmental computers.
- ☐ Other companies' computers via EDI.
- ☐ All other hardware/software environments in the company.

In total connectivity, a message can be sent from any user to any other point in the network, be it a workstation, a micro, a printer, or a mainframe.

One of the fundamental assumptions of connectivity is that the the linking of hardware, software, and data bases be *transparent* to the user. That is, the user would simply request the information he or she needs without being concerned about the technical complexities of connectivity.

Connectivity—A Technological Perspective

To the MIS specialists charged with establishing the link between the various elements of a system, the implementation of connectivity can be incredibly complex. To achieve almost any level of connectivity (connectivity is implemented in degrees), these technical specialists must juggle communication protocols (rules), official and de facto standards, different approaches to data base design, different computer system architectures, and user information requirements. Each of these considerations poses formidable technological hurdles. To overcome these hurdles while shielding users from the complexity of connectivity is a herculean task. Nevertheless, almost every information services division has made a commitment to strive for a higher level of connectivity.

These communications specialists are designing a computer network in West Germany that will use the OSI (Open Systems Interconnection) communications standard.

Courtesy of International Business Machines Corporation

Connectivity Summary

Technologically, total connectivity is possible; however, it is not likely in the near future. If vendors were to cooperate and set standards for connectivity, it would still take years for vendors to redesign their product lines to accommodate the standards. Also, companies have enormous investments in their existing hardware and software environments. It is not likely that a company would scrap its current environment and replace it with a compatible environment, even if such an environment were available on the open market. One industry analyst described the prospects for improved connectivity as a "muddy mess." There are too many "catch-22s" at work for both vendors and consumers. For example, if vendors change their product lines to accommodate connectivity better, they run the risk of being shunned by existing customers for leaving them with obsolete equipment and software.

For the time being, companies are using jury-rigged solutions to implement connectivity. For example, to permit communication between a network of microcomputers in the marketing department and a departmental minicomputer in the plant may require substantial interim processing. In the ideal implementation of connectivity, the connection is direct with no interim processing needed. Approaches to linking incompatible environments are discussed later in this chapter.

Even a "muddy mess" has some clear water. The greatest strides have been in the area of intercompany networking. The ANSI **X.12** communications protocol has been adopted for the exchange of invoices, orders, corporate electronic payments (via participating banks), and other electronic data interchange transactions. International standards-making bodies are developing standards, such as the *Open Systems Interconnection* (*OSI*) and *Integrated Services Digital Network* (*ISDN*). Others are gaining de facto standard status, such as IBM's *Systems Network Architecture* (*SNA*).

DATA COMMUNICATIONS HARDWARE

Data communications hardware is used to transmit data in a computer network between workstations and computers, and between computers. This hardware includes modems, down-line processors, front-end processors, and data PBXs. The integration of these devices (except the data PBX) with workstations and computer systems is illustrated in Figure 8–2 and discussed in the paragraphs that follow.

The Modem

Telephone lines were designed for voice communication, not data communication. The **modem** (*mo*dulator/*dem*odulator) converts computer-to-workstation electrical *digital* signals to *analog* signals so that the data can be transmitted over telephone lines (see Figure 8–3). The digital electrical signals are "modulated" to make sounds similar to those you hear on a touch-tone telephone. Upon reaching their destination, the analog signals are "demodulated" by another modem to computer-compatible electrical signals

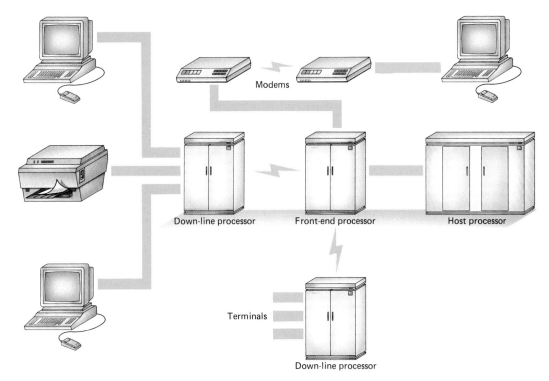

FIGURE 8–2   Hardware Components in Data Communications
Devices that handle the movement of data in a computer network are the modem, down-line processor, front-end processor, and host processor.

for processing. The process is done in reverse for workstation-to-computer communication.

On most workstations, the modem is an optional device that is contained on a circuit board and simply plugged into an empty slot in the workstation. To make the connection with a telephone line, you simply plug the telephone line into the modem, just as you would if connecting a telephone. Modems have varying degrees of "intelligence." For instance, some modems can automatically dial up the computer (*auto-dial*), then establish a link (*log on*), and even answer incoming calls from other computers (*auto-answer*).

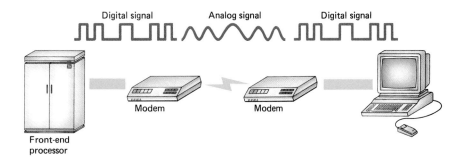

FIGURE 8–3   The Modulation/Demodulation Process
Electrical digital signals are modulated to analog signals for transmission over telephone lines and then demodulated for processing at the destination.

For transmission media other than telephone lines, the modulation/demodulation process is not required. A modem is always required when you "dial up" the computer on a telephone line. If you need a telephone hookup (for a voice conversation) on the same line and do not want to hassle with disconnecting the phone with each use, you can purchase a modem with an **acoustical coupler**. To make the connection, you mount the telephone handset directly on the acoustical coupler. Some workstations have not only a built-in modem but a built-in telephone as well.

The Down-Line Processor

The **down-line processor**, also called a **cluster controller**, is remote from the *host processor*. It collects data from a number of low-speed devices, such as workstations and serial printers. The down-line processor then transmits "concentrated" data over a single communications channel (see Figure 8–4).

The down-line processor, also called a **concentrator** or **multiplexor**, is an economic necessity when several low-speed workstations are located at one remote site. One high-speed line connecting the down-line processor to the host is considerably less expensive than several low-speed lines connecting each workstation to the host. An airport airline reservations counter might have four workstations. Each workstation is connected to a down-line processor, which in turn is connected to a central host computer. An airport might have one or several down-line processors, depending on volume of passenger traffic.

A microcomputer can be made to emulate the function of a down-

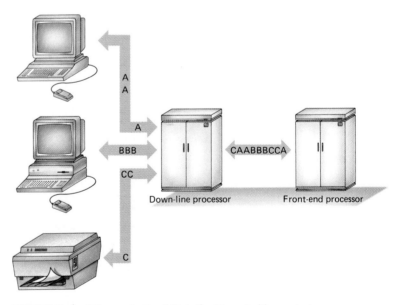

FIGURE 8–4 "Concentrating" Data for Remote Transmission
The down-line processor "concentrates" the data from several low-speed devices for transmission over a single high-speed line. Data received from a front-end processor are interpreted by the down-line processor and routed to the appropriate device.

line processor. This occurs when a network of micros is linked to a mainframe computer.

The Front-End Processor

The workstation or computer sending a **message** is the *source*. The work-station or computer receiving the message is the *destination*. The **front-end processor** establishes the link between the source and destination in a process called **handshaking**.

If you think of messages as mail to be delivered to various points in a computer network, the front-end processor is the post office. Each computer system and workstation is assigned an **address**. The front-end processor uses these addresses to route messages to their destination(s). The content of a message could be anything from a program instruction to an "electronic" memo. Figure 8–5 illustrates how a memo would be sent from the president of a company to two vice presidents and the plant manager. It is not uncommon

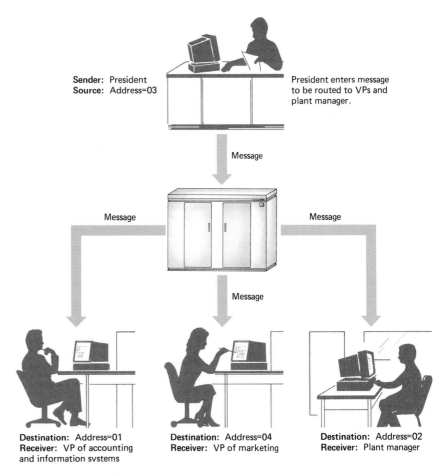

Sender: President
Source: Address=03

President enters message to be routed to VPs and plant manager.

Message

Message

Message

Message

Destination: Address=01
Receiver: VP of accounting and information systems

Destination: Address=04
Receiver: VP of marketing

Destination: Address=02
Receiver: Plant manager

FIGURE 8–5   Message Routing
In the illustration, the president sends a message to two vice presidents and the plant manager.

for a front-end processor to control communications between a dozen down-line processors and 100 or more workstations.

The front-end processor relieves the host processor of communications-related tasks, such as message routing, parity checking, code translation, editing, and cryptography (the encryption/decryption of data). This processor "specialization" permits the host to operate more efficiently and to devote more of its resources to processing applications programs.

The Data PBX

The old-time telephone PBX (private branch exchange) switchboard has given its name to a new generation of devices for **data PBX** switching. The data PBX is actually a computer that electronically connects computers and workstations much as telephone operators manually connected people on the old PBX switchboards.

As discussed in previous chapters, there is definitely a trend to making information systems more responsive to end users by "distributing" processing capabilities closer to the people who use them. Because of this trend, a single organization is likely to have at least one mainframe computer, several minis, and many micros and workstations. The data PBX, serving as the hub of data activity, permits these computers and workstations to talk to one another. Figure 8–6 illustrates how several computer systems can be linked via a data PBX.

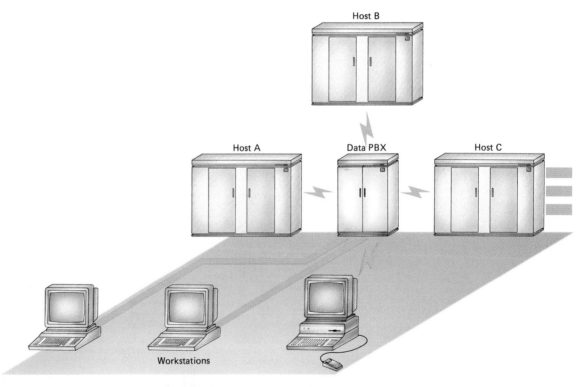

FIGURE 8–6 Computers and Workstations Linked to a Data PBX
Any two of the host computers or workstations can be linked together for data transmission by the data PBX.

THE DATA COMMUNICATIONS CHANNEL

Transmission Media

A **communications channel** is the facility by which data are transmitted between locations in a computer network. Data are transmitted as combinations of bits (0's and 1's). A *channel's capacity* is rated by the number of bits that can be transmitted per second. A regular telephone line can transmit up to 9600 **bits per second** (**bps**), or 9.6K bps (thousands of bits per second). Under normal circumstances, a 9.6K-bps line would fill the screen of a video monitor in 1 or 2 seconds.

In practice, the word **baud** is often used interchangeably with bits per second. In reality they are quite different. Baud is a measure of the maximum number of electronic signals that can be transmitted via a communications channel. It is true that a 300-bps modem operates at 300 baud, but both 1200-bps and 2400-bps modems operate at 600 baud. A technical differentiation between baud and bits per second is beyond the scope of this book. Suffice it to say that when someone says "baud," and he or she is talking about computer-based data communications, that person probably means bits per second. The erroneous use of baud is so common that some communications software packages ask you to specify baud rather than bits per second.

Data rates of 1500K bps are available through common carriers, such as American Telephone & Telegraph (AT&T). The channel, also called a **line** or a **data link**, may be comprised of one or a combination of the transmission media discussed next.

Telephone Lines

The same transmission facilities that we use for telephone conversations can also be used to transmit data. This capability is provided by communications companies throughout the country and the world.

Optical Fiber

Very thin transparent fibers have been developed that will eventually replace the copper wire traditionally used in the telephone system. These hairlike **optical fibers** carry data faster and are lighter and less expensive than their copper-wire counterpart.

The differences in the data transmission rates of copper wire and optical fiber are tremendous. In the time it takes to transmit a single page of Webster's *Unabridged Dictionary* over copper wire (about 6 seconds), the entire dictionary could be transmitted over a single optical fiber.

Another of the many advantages of optical fiber is its contribution to data security. It is much more difficult for a computer criminal to intercept a signal sent over optical fiber (via a beam of light) than it is over copper wire (an electrical signal).

Coaxial Cable

Coaxial cable contains electrical wire and is constructed to permit high-speed data transmission with a minimum of signal distortion. Coaxial cable is laid along the ocean floor for intercontinental voice and data transmission. It is also used to connect workstations and computers in a "local" area (from a few feet to a few miles).

This antenna atop a skyscraper transmits and receives data communications signals to and from a satellite. Incoming signals from the satellite are routed to their ultimate destination via conventional earth-based communications channels, such as coaxial cable, microwave, and the telephone system. Signals to be transmitted arrive from same types of channels.

Courtesy of International Business Machines Corporation

Microwave

Communications channels do not have to be wires or fibers. Data can also be transmitted via microwave radio signals. Transmission of these signals is *line-of-sight*; that is, the radio signal travels in a direct line from one repeater station to the next until it reaches its destination. Because of the curvature of the earth, microwave repeater stations are placed on the tops of mountains and towers, usually about 30 miles apart.

Satellites have made it possible to overcome the line-of-sight problem. Satellites are routinely launched into orbit for the sole purpose of relaying data communications signals to and from earth stations. A satellite, which is essentially a repeater station, is launched and set in a **geosynchronous orbit** 22,300 miles above the earth. A geosynchronous orbit permits the communications satellite to maintain a fixed position relative to the surface of the earth. Each satellite can receive and retransmit signals to slightly less than half of the earth's surface; therefore, three satellites are required to cover the earth effectively (see Figure 8–7). The big advantage of satellites is that data can be transmitted from one location to any number of other locations anywhere on (or near) our planet.

Data Transmission in Practice

A communications channel from computer A in Seattle, Washington, to computer B in Orlando, Florida (see Figure 8–8), would usually consist of several different transmission media. The connection between computer A and a

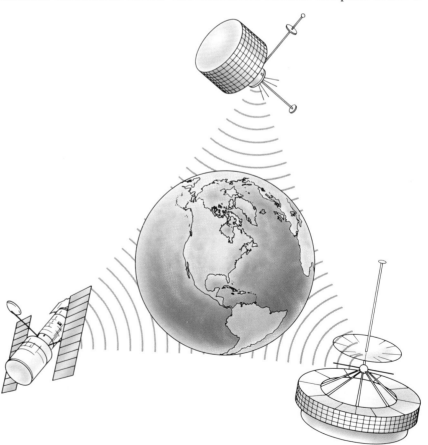

FIGURE 8–7   Satellite Data Transmission
Three satellites in geosynchronous orbit provide worldwide data transmission service.

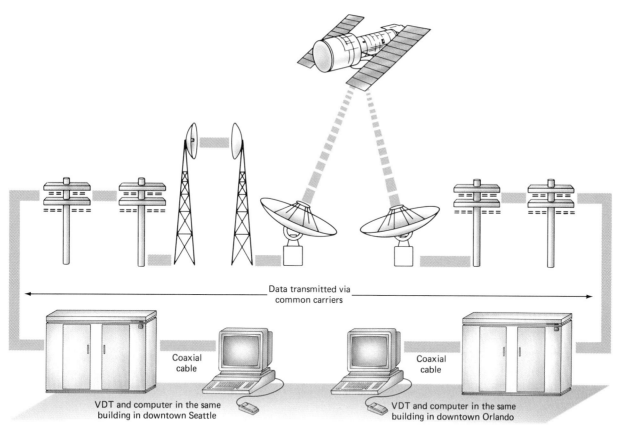

FIGURE 8–8 Data Transmission Path
It's more the rule than the exception that data are carried over several transmission media between source and destination.

workstation in the same building is probably coaxial cable. The Seattle company might use a communications company, such as AT&T, to transmit the data. The company would then transmit the data through a combination of transmission facilities that might include copper wire, optical fiber, and microwave radio signals.

DATA TRANSMISSION SERVICES

Common Carriers

It is impractical, not to mention illegal, for companies to string their own coaxial cables between two locations, such as Philadelphia and New York City. It is also impractical for them to set their own satellites in orbit. Therefore, companies turn to **common carriers**, such as AT&T and Western Union, to provide channels for data communications. Data communications common carriers, which are regulated by the Federal Communications Commission (FCC), offer two basic types of service: private lines and switched lines.

A **private line** (or **leased line**) provides a dedicated data communications channel between any two points in a computer network. The charge for a private line is based on channel capacity (bps) and distance (air miles).

A **switched line** (or **dial-up line**) is available strictly on a time-and-distance charge, similar to a long-distance telephone call. You make a connection by "dialing up" the computer; then a modem sends and receives data.

As a rule of thumb, a private line is the least expensive alternative if you expect to use the channel more than three hours per day and you do not need the flexibility to connect with several different computers.

Specialized Common Carriers

A **specialized common carrier**, such as a **value-added network (VAN)**, may or may not use the transmission facilities of a common carrier, but in each case, it "adds value" to the transmission service. The value added over and above the standard services of the common carriers may include electronic mail, data encryption/decryption, and code conversion for communication between incompatible computers.

COMPUTER NETWORKS

Network Topologies

Each time you use the telephone, you use the world's largest computer network—the telephone system. A telephone is an end point, or a **node**, that is connected to a network of computers that route your voice signals to another telephone, or node. The node in a computer network can be a workstation or another computer. Computer networks are configured to meet the specific requirements of an organization. The basic computer **network topologies**—star, ring, and bus—are illustrated in Figure 8–9. A network topology is a description of the possible physical connections within a network. The topology is the configuration of the hardware and indicates which pairs of nodes are able to communicate.

The **star topology** involves a centralized host computer that is connected to a number of smaller computer systems. The smaller computer systems communicate with one another through the host and usually share the host computer's data base. Both the central computer and the distributed computer systems are connected to workstations (micros or video display terminals). Any workstation can communicate with any other workstation in the network. Banks usually have a large home-office computer system with a star network of minicomputer systems in the branch banks.

The **ring topology** involves computer systems that are approximately the same size, and no one computer system is the focal point of the network. When one system routes a message to another system, the message is passed around the ring until it reaches its destination address.

The **bus topology** permits the connection of workstations, peripheral devices, and microcomputers along a central cable called a **transmission medium**. Devices can be easily added to or deleted from the network. Bus topologies are most appropriate when the devices linked are close to one another (see the discussion of local area networks that follows).

A pure form of any of these three topologies is seldom found in practice. Most computer networks are *hybrids*—combinations of these topologies.

Networks offer what bureaucracies can never deliver—the horizontal link.

—— *John Naisbitt*

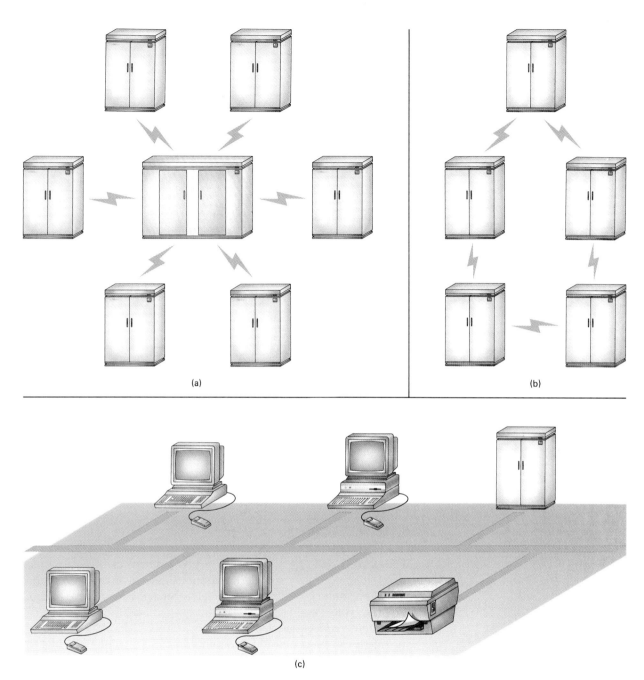

FIGURE 8–9   Network Topologies
(a) Star; (b) ring; (c) bus.

Three-Tier and Two-Tier Networks

The various types of networks are sometimes classified as **three-tier** or **two-tier networks**, referring to the number of layers of computers in the network. A three-tier network has three layers of computers. At the top is the host mainframe that is linked to multiple minicomputers. Each mini is linked to multiple micros. The three-tier concept was the norm until the capabilities of micros began to approach that of the multiuser minis of the mid-1980s. The increased power of the microcomputer made three-tier networks redundant at the bottom two levels, thus prompting the concept of the two-tier network. A two-tier network has only two layers of computers, usually a mainframe computer that links directly to multiple minicomputers and/or microcomputers. The tier concept is most often associated with the star topology or a hybrid that is based on the star topology.

The Micro/Mainframe Link

Micros, initially designed for use by a single individual, have even greater potential when they can be linked with mainframe computers. To give micros this dual-function capability, vendors develop the necessary hardware and software to enable **micro/mainframe links**. There are three types of micro/mainframe links:

1. The microcomputer serves as a dumb terminal (that is, I/O only with no processing) that is linked to the mainframe.
2. Microcomputer users request that data be downloaded from the mainframe to their micros for processing.
3. Both microcomputer and mainframe work together to process data and produce information.

Micro/mainframe links of the first two types are well within the state of the art, but achieving the third is more involved. The tremendous differences in the way computers and software are designed make complete micro/mainframe integration of activities difficult and, for some combinations of micros and mainframes, impossible.

Local Area Networks

A **local area network** (**LAN**), or **local net**, is a system of hardware, software, and communications channels that connects devices on the same premises, such as in a suite of offices. A local net permits the movement of data (including text, voice, and graphic images) between mainframe computers, personal computers, workstations, I/O devices, and even data PBXs. For example, your micro can be connected to another micro, to mainframes, and to shared resources, such as printers and disk storage. The distance separating devices in the local net may be a few feet to a few miles.

The unique feature of a local net is that a common carrier is not necessary to transmit data between computers, workstations, and shared resources. Because of the proximity of devices in local nets, a company can install its own communications channels (such as coaxial cable or optical fiber).

Like computers, cars, and just about everything else, local nets can be built at various levels of sophistication. At the most basic level they permit the interconnection of PCs in a department so that users can send messages to one another and share files and printers. The more sophisticated local

A local area network links microcomputers so that students and instructors can share hardware and software resources.

Courtesy of International Business Machines Corporation

nets permit the interconnection of mainframes, micros, and the gamut of peripheral devices throughout a large, but geographically constrained area, such as a cluster of buildings.

In the near future, you will be able to plug a workstation into a communications channel just as you would plug a telephone line into a telephone jack. This type of data communications capability is being installed in the new "smart" office buildings and even in some hotel rooms.

Local nets are often integrated with "long-haul" networks. For example, a bank will have home-office teller workstations linked to the central computer via a local net. But for long-haul data communication, the bank's branch offices must rely on common carriers.

LINE CONTROL

Polling and Contention

When a workstation or a microcomputer is connected to a computer over a single communications channel, this is a **point-to-point connection**. When more than one workstation or micro is connected to a single communications channel, the channel is called a **multidrop line**. Workstations on a multidrop line must share the data communications channel. Since all workstations cannot use the same channel at once, line-control procedures are needed. The most common line-control procedures are **polling** and **contention**.

In polling, the front-end processor "polls" each workstation in rotation to determine whether a message is ready to be sent (see Figure 8–10). If a particular workstation has a message to be sent and the line is available, the front-end processor accepts the message and polls the next workstation.

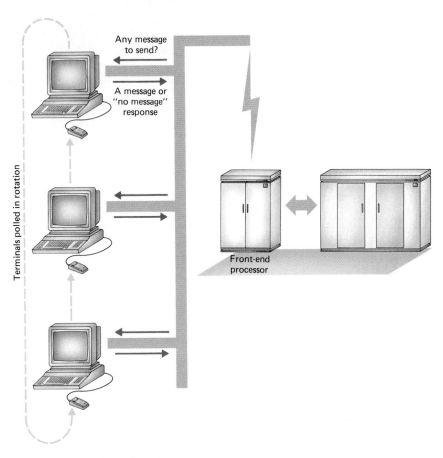

Terminals polled in rotation

Any message to send?

A message or "no message" response

Front-end processor

FIGURE 8–10   The Polling Process
Each terminal is polled in rotation to determine if a message is ready to be sent.

Programmers can adjust the polling procedure so that some workstations are polled more often than others. For example, tellers in a bank are continuously interacting with the system. A loan officer, however, may average only two inquiries in an hour. In this case, the teller workstations might be polled four times for each poll of a loan officer's workstation.

In contention, a workstation with a message to be sent automatically requests service from the host processor. A request might result in a "line busy" signal, in which case the workstation waits a fraction of a second and tries again, and again, until the line is free. Upon assuming control of the line, the workstation sends the message and then relinquishes control of the line to another workstation.

Communications Protocols

Communications protocols are rules established to govern the way that data are transmitted in a computer network. The two general classifications of protocols, **asynchronous** and **synchronous**, are illustrated in Figure 8–11.

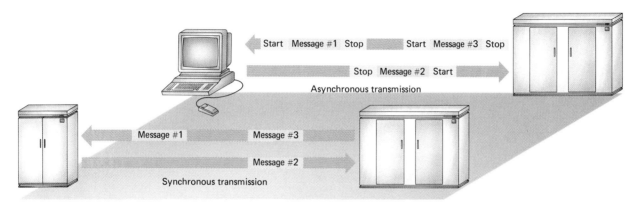

FIGURE 8–11   Asynchronous and Synchronous Transmission of Data
Asynchronous data transmission takes place at irregular intervals, where synchronous data transmission requires timed synchronization.

In asynchronous data transmission, data are transferred at irregular intervals on an as-needed basis. *Start/stop bits* are appended to the beginning and end of each message. The start/stop bits signal the receiving workstation/computer at the beginning and end of the message. A message could be a single character or a string of characters, depending on the communications protocol. Asynchronous transmission, sometimes called start/stop transmission, is best suited for data communication involving low-speed I/O devices, such as workstations and serial printers.

In synchronous transmission, the source and destination operate in timed synchronization to enable high-speed data transmission. Start/stop bits are not required in synchronous transmission. Data transmission between computers and between down-line processors and front-end processors normally is synchronous.

APPROACHES TO CONNECTIVITY

Now that you have a feel for the technologies associated with data communications and have an appreciation for the technological challenges of connectivity, it is time to discuss approaches to achieving degrees of connectivity. Perhaps the most effective way to achieve connectivity within the confines of an organization is to stay with one vendor. Even then, purchases must be limited to those hardware devices that are compatible. This approach is feasible for very small companies and start-up companies. For larger companies, this straightforward solution is not an option. These companies already have many different vendors represented, and the expense of a total conversion is prohibitive.

Companies with established operating environments use gateway and bridge technologies to achieve connectivity. **Gateways** help to alleviate the problems associated with linking incompatible micros, minis, and mainframes. A gateway is a combination of hardware and software that permits networks

> Bureaucracy defends the status quo long past the time when the quo has lost its status.
>
> ——— *Laurence Johnston Peter*

using different communications protocols to "talk" to one another. The use of a gateway normally implies a requirement for a protocol conversion.

Most commercially available gateways connect microcomputer-based LANs to mainframes. In the micro/mainframe link, discussed earlier in this chapter, the micro is linked to a down-line processor that in turn is connected to a front-end processor, which is linked to the mainframe. A LAN-to-mainframe gateway makes it possible for one of the micros in a LAN to emulate the function of a down-line processor. Although efficiency may suffer slightly, the company can actually save money because down-line processors are considerably more expensive than microcomputers.

Some companies have numerous small departmental local area networks. Instead of integrating these microcomputer-based LANs into a large network, they use **bridges** to enable these LANs to continue operation in their present format with the added advantage of being able to "talk" to each other. Bridges, which are protocol-independent hardware devices, permit communication between devices on separate local area networks. Bridges provide a relatively straightforward solution to enable LANs to communicate with one another.

For the foreseeable future, many connectivity questions can be answered with planning, restrictive policies, gateways, and bridges. However, with total connectivity being the goal of most progressive companies, the computer and MIS community will continue to focus its sights on overcoming the barriers to total connectivity.

CHAPTER HIGHLIGHTS

■ To obtain meaningful, accurate, and timely information, businesses have decided that they must cooperate internally and externally to take full advantage of available information. To promote internal cooperation, they are promoting intracompany networking. To compete in a world market, they are encouraging intercompany networking, or electronic data interchange.

■ Connectivity refers to the degree to which hardware devices can be functionally linked to one another. Some people expand the scope of connectivity to include other aspects of MIS, such as software and data bases. Connectivity is viewed differently depending on the perspective of the observer (user, vendor, MIS specialist).

■ The ANSI X.12 communications protocol has been adopted for the exchange of invoices, orders, corporate electronic payments, and other electronic data interchange transactions.

■ Technologically, it is relatively easy to make an electronic connection between two computer systems, but realizing any meaningful transfer of information from the connection is another matter.

■ Modern businesses use data communications to transmit data and information at high speeds from one location to the next.

Data communications, or teleprocessing, makes an information system more accessible to the people who use it. The integration of computer systems via data communications is referred to as a computer network.

■ The data communications hardware used to facilitate the transmission of data from one remote location to another includes modems, down-line processors or cluster controllers (or concentrators or multiplexors), front-end processors, and data PBXs. Modems modulate and demodulate signals so that data can be transmitted over telephone lines. The last three are special-function processors; they not only convert the signal to a format compatible with the transmission facility but they also relieve the host processor of a number of processing tasks associated with data communications.

■ A communications channel (line, or data link) is the facility by which data are transmitted between locations in a computer network. A channel may be composed of one or more of the following transmission media: telephone line, optical fiber, coaxial cable, and microwave radio signal. A channel's capacity is rated by the number of bits that can be transmitted per second.

- Common carriers provide communications channels to the public, and lines can be arranged to suit the application. A private, or leased, line provides a dedicated communications channel. A switched, or dial-up, line is available on a time-and-distance charge basis.

- Computer systems are linked together to form a computer network. The basic topologies for configuring computer systems within a computer network are star, ring, and bus. In practice, most networks are actually hybrids of these topologies.

- The connection of microcomputers to a mainframe computer is called a micro/mainframe link.

- A communications channel servicing a single workstation is a point-to-point connection. A communications channel servicing more than one workstation is a multidrop line. The most common line-control procedures are polling and contention.

- Data communications protocols are rules for transmitting data. The asynchronous protocol begins and ends each message with start/stop bits and is used primarily for low-speed data transmission. The synchronous protocol permits the source and destination to communicate in timed synchronization, for high-speed data transmission.

- Companies with established operating environments use gateway and bridge technologies to achieve connectivity. Gateways help to alleviate the problems associated with incompatible hardware. A gateway permits networks using different communications protocols to "talk" to one another. Bridges enable LANs to continue operation in their present format with the added advantage of being able to "talk" to other LANs.

IMPORTANT TERMS

acoustical coupler
address
asynchronous
auto-answer
auto-dial
baud
bits per second (bps)
bridges
bus topology
channel capacity
cluster controller
coaxial cable
common carrier
communications channel
communications protocol
computer network
concentrator
connectivity

contention
cooperative computing
data communications
data PBX
data link
dial-up line
digital/analog
down-line processor
front-end processor
gateways
geosynchronous orbit
handshaking
host processor
intracompany networking
intercompany networking
Integrated Services Digital
  Network (ISDN)
knowledge worker

leased line
line
local area network (LAN)
local net
log on
private line
message
micro/mainframe link
modem
multidrop line
multiplexor
network topology
node
Open Systems
  Interconnection (OSI)
optical fiber
point-to-point connection
polling

ring topology
source/destination
specialized common carrier
star topology
switched line
synchronous
Systems Network Architecture
  (SNA)
telecommunications
teleprocessing (TP)
three-tier network
total connectivity
transmission medium
transparent
two-tier network
value-added network (VAN)
X.12

REVIEW EXERCISES

1. Would EDI be more closely associated with intercompany networking or intracompany networking?

2. What technologies do companies with established operating environments use to achieve connectivity?

3. What is meant by "geosynchronous orbit," and how does it relate to data transmission via satellite?

4. What is the unit of measure for the capacity of a data communications channel?

5. Expand the following acronyms: SNA, TP, bps, VAN, and LAN.

6. What is the purpose of a multiplexor?

7. What is the relationship between teleprocessing and a computer network?

8. At what channel capacity is the bits per second equal to the baud?

9. What computerese term refers to the degree to which hardware devices can be functionally linked to one another?

10. What device converts digital signals to analog signals for transmission over telephone lines? Why is it necessary?

11. Why is it not advisable to spread microwave relay stations 200 miles apart?

12. What is the ideal implementation of connectivity called?

13. Briefly describe the function of a data PBX.

14. What is the purpose of the ANSI X.12 communications protocol?

15. Describe circumstances for which a leased line would be preferred over a dial-up line.

16. Consider this situation: A remote line printer is capable of printing 800 lines per minute (70 characters per line average). Line capacity options are 2.4K, 4.8K, or 9.6K bps. Data are transmitted according to the ASCII encoding system (seven bits per character). What capacity would you recommend for a communications channel to permit the printer to operate at capacity?

DISCUSSION QUESTIONS

1. For the most part, *Fortune* 500 companies are relying primarily on gateways and bridges to achieve connectivity. What is the alternative?

2. What is the relationship between EDI, EFT, and connectivity?

3. Discuss connectivity from the perspective of any non-IBM hardware vendor. From the perspective of IBM.

4. Corporate management in every type of industry is making connectivity a high-priority strategy. Why?

5. Describe how information can be made readily accessible, but only on a need-to-know basis?

6. Argue for or against the author's premise that this is the era of cooperative computing.

7. List and discuss those characteristics that would typify a knowledge worker.

8. Corporate management is evaluating a proposal to allow employees to telecommute one day each week, that is, to work at home with a direct link to the company via a workstation. Argue for or against this proposal.

9. How is a specialized common carrier, such as a value-added network, able to improve on the services offered by a common carrier and offer these services at a reduced cost?

10. Suppose that you are a systems analyst for a municipal government. You have been asked to justify the conversion from a batch to an on-line incident-reporting system to the city council. What points would you make?

11. The five PCs in the purchasing department of a large consumer goods manufacturer are used primarily for word processing and data base applications. What would be the benefits and burdens associated with connecting the PCs in a local area network?

APPLICATION CASE STUDY 8–1

An Interstate Network

The Situation

Gabriel Industries is a diversified manufacturing company with 2,300 employees. Manufacturing and distribution facilities are located in Brooklyn, New York, and Newark, New Jersey. Additional distribution facilities are located in Pontiac, Michigan, and Wilmington, Delaware. The corporate offices are located at the Brooklyn site. The company's organizational structure is shown here.

Currently, all computing facilities are in Brooklyn. These consist of a mainframe operated by the Computer Services Department; a minicomputer operated by the Accounting Department; and microcomputers in the Advertising and Public Relations, Personnel, and Engineering departments. All companywide applications are run in batch mode on the mainframe, although an on-line payroll system is under development (see Application Case Study 2–2, "On-Line Versus Off-Line"). The microcomputers are used solely for departmental applications that do not overlap with the applications of other departments.

John Robson, the manager of the Computer Services Department, is convinced that to remain competitive, Gabriel Industries needs state-of-the-art management information systems. This means linking all the corporation's facilities, departments, and personnel

together with an integrated, on-line information systems. In addition, John Robson wants to take advantage of EDI.

Additional background information about Gabriel Industries and the status of computerization in the company is contained in Application Case Study 1–1, "The Decision-Making Process"; Application Case Study 5–2, "The Information Center"; and Application Case Study 6–2, "Management of End-User Computing."

John Robson would like a communications network that has the following capabilities:

☐ All companywide or interdepartmental information systems are to be on-line systems that use the mainframe, with the exception of some accounting systems that are to be on-line systems using the Accounting Department's minicomputer.

☐ Each distribution facility will maintain its inventory on its own microcomputer, and each location will be able to make inquiries into the inventory databases.

☐ Each salesperson will have a laptop microcomputer with communications capabilities and will be able to connect to the mainframe from a customer location to check inven-

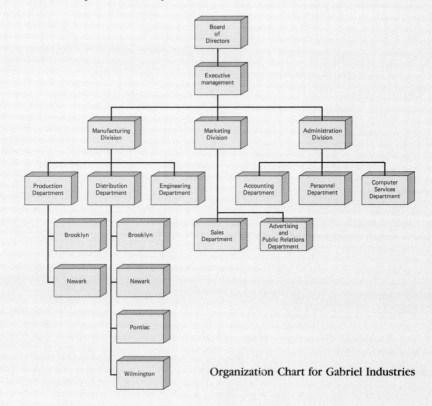

Organization Chart for Gabriel Industries

tory, get quotes, place orders, and check on the status of existing orders.

☐ Customers will be able to place orders with Gabriel via EDI.

☐ Gabriel will be able to place orders via EDI with suppliers who support EDI.

☐ Gabriel will transmit payroll W-2 forms to the IRS via EDI at the end of each calendar year.

☐ All executives and department managers will have an individual workstation for making inquiries and performing other functions.

The Assignment

1. Design a network for Gabriel Industries. For your design,

   a. Draw the network configuration and identify each node. Specify the location of the node, the type of node (workstation, minicomputer, and so on) and the department or the title of the individual to whom a remote hardware is assigned.

   b. Specify the data communications hardware at each node in the network.

   c. Which transmission services are used in the network?

   d. Provide specifications for the various data communications channels.

e. Specify the line control procedures (polling versus contention). Justify your recommendations.

2. What impact will the implementation of your network design have on the Computer Services Department regarding

   a. *Personnel*: Would any additional personnel be required? If yes, for each type of position, specify job title and responsibilities. If no, who would perform the additional work necessary to implement and maintain the network?

   b. *Organization*: Modify the Computer Services Department's organization chart (see Application Study 5-2, "The Information Center") to include any additional personnel, if needed.

   c. *Facilities*: What additional facilities (space, utilities, and so on) would be required?

   d. *Training*: What additional training would have to be provided to each of the following and who would provide the training: computer services personnel? End users?

   e. *Expenses*: List the expenses that would be incurred with the implementation of the network for one-time expenses (nonrecurring expenses); for recurring expenses (ongoing expenses). For each item in this list, specify whether the expense is fixed (*F*) or variable (*V*) in nature. A fixed expense does not change with volume while a variable expense will increase as volume increases. In a network, volume refers to the number of messages (transactions or inquiries) that the network processes.

APPLICATION CASE STUDY 8–2
A Local Area Network

The Situation

Peterson College, a four-year private liberal arts college, has recently developed a plan for administrative computing (see Application Case Study 5–1, "Providers of Information Services"). The school's long-term master plan includes the construction of a library building and renovation of the main classroom building and the dormitories. The college recently opened a satellite campus in rented quarters located 17 miles northeast of the main campus and is exploring the feasibility of another satellite location 15 miles south. The college has an undergraduate major and minor in computer science and has just received approval for an M.S. in management information systems. The first classes in this graduate program will be held this fall semester. The college's Planning Committee has asked Monica Roberts, the director of academic computing, to develop a plan for academic computing, taking into

consideration the recent expansion of the college and the factors in the college's long-term master plan.

Current public academic computing facilities at the main campus consist of an eight-year-old minicomputer with 16 terminals and a microcomputer laboratory containing 10 IBM PCs, 12 IBM-PC-compatibles, 7 Apple IIe computers, 7 dot-matrix printers, 1 daisy-wheel printer, 1 laser printer, and 1 plotter. Each of the dot-matrix printers and the daisy-wheel printer are shared by 3 or 4 microcomputers that use "share switches." These operate as follows. Up to 4 microcomputers are wired into the share switch, which is wired to a printer. When a person at a microcomputer is ready to use the printer, he or she sets the dial on the share-switch box to the letter corresponding to his or her microcomputer. If the printer is busy, the person must wait until it is free. The laser printer is attached to the microcomputer that is used by the consultant on duty. The plotter is attached to one of the micros, which is also attached to one of the shared printers. The Psychology Department has a laboratory containing 6 IBM-PC compatible microcomputers, 2 dot-matrix printers, and 1 terminal that is hardwired to the minicomputer. In addition, the Chemistry Department has 2 Apple IIe's and 1 dot-matrix printer and the Biology Department has 1 Apple IIe. All these facilities are in the main classroom building. The satellite location has a laboratory containing 4 IBM-PC compatibles, 3 Apple IIe's, and 2 dot-matrix printers.

The staff in the Academic Computing Center consists of the director, Monica Roberts, 2 chief operators (students) who alternate working in the evenings when the center is busiest, and approximately 15 student consultants who work during the day and on weekends. The Chief Operators are responsible for performing backups and such duties as software maintenance on the minicomputer's operating system, writing useful utility programs, and so on. An Academic Computing Advisory Committee provides Ms. Roberts with guidance on matters regarding policy and planning. The membership consists of the associate academic dean, the dean of continuing education, Ms. Roberts, the chair of the Computer Science Department, and 4 faculty members from different disciplines.

The first part of Monica Roberts's plan for academic computing at Peterson College included the following desired capabilities and facilities:

☐ Replace the minicomputer with a newer model. This purchase would involve a considerable initial expense, but would provide a significant reduction in maintenance costs.

☐ Give all microcomputers in the main laboratory access to a dot-matrix printer, the daisy-wheel printer, the laser printer, and the plotter.

☐ Permit all micros the capability of downloading files from the minicomputer and uploading files to it.

☐ Have a cluster of 3 or 4 microcomputers and a printer in each of the three dormitories and in the Learning Center, which is located in the main classroom building.

☐ Provide each faculty member with a microcomputer in his or her office.

☐ Provide access to the library's proposed on-line catalog from any workstation (micro or terminal, on or off campus).

☐ Provide access to computing facilities at other cooperating colleges from any workstation. This capability would necessitate some restrictions, since other colleges plan to charge back the use of their facilities to Peterson College.

☐ Provide access to Peterson College's computing facilities for students and faculty at other selected institutions.

☐ Provide access to the minicomputer from the current and proposed satellite campuses.

☐ Provide access to the minicomputer from off-campus workstations, that is, for individuals who have a workstation at

home or at their place of employment. This is essential for the masters students and desirable for faculty and undergraduate students.

The Assignment

1. Design a communications network for Peterson College that has the capabilities outlined by Monica Roberts. For your design,

   a. Draw the network configuration and identify each node. Specify the location of the node, the type of node (workstation, minicomputer, and so on), and the department or the title of the individual to whom a remote hardware is assigned.

   b. Specify the data communications hardware at each node in the network.

   c. Which transmission services are used in the network?

   d. Provide specifications for the various data communications channels.

   e. Specify the line control procedures (polling versus contention). Justify your recommendations.

2. What impact will the implementation of your network design have on the Academic Computer Center regarding

   a. *Personnel*: Would any additional personnel be required? If yes, for each type of position, specify job title and responsibilities. If no, who would perform the additional work necessary to implement and maintain the network?

   b. *Facilities*: What additional facilities (space, utilities, and so on) would be required?

   c. *Training*: What additional training would have to be provided to each of the following and who would provide the training: academic computer center personnel? end users (students and faculty)?

3. Describe the role of the Academic Computing Advisory Committee in the design and implementation of the network.

4. The director of the library would like overdue notices and similar documents to be printed on the library's proposed minicomputer. To do this, the library's minicomputer needs access to the databases on the mainframe in the college's proposed administrative computer center. These databases would contain information such as student grades and faculty salaries.

   a. Since the proposed network will enable public access to the library system's on-line card catalog, does this pose a security problem? Explain.

   b. In this situation, what precautions can be taken to minimize or eliminate potential security risks.

   c. Should the library rather than the administrative computer center print the overdue notices and other similar outputs? Explain.

APPLICATION CASE STUDY 8–3
A Network-Based Commercial Service Operation

The Situation

Que Realty has developed an expert system that matches clients with houses (see Application Case Study 3–1, "Expert Systems") and an on-line listing system with a natural language interface (see Application Case Study 3–2, "Natural Languages"). Joan Magee, Que's owner, is impressed with the results of the two systems. The implementation of these systems is directly responsible for the increases in the productivity of Que's real estate agents. Ms. Magee is highly knowledgeable in the real estate area and feels that other realtors would be willing to pay for the benefits that could be derived from the use of Que's systems. To this end, she has formed another company, Que Software. Que Software is currently modifying these systems for general use and will eventually market them to the industry as a turnkey package with the name Que-List. Long-term plans for Que Software include the development of other real estate-related turnkey systems.

Que-List will be marketed to regional realtor associations that want an on-line multiple listing system. Such systems permit any member realtor access to information on any real estate listing in the region. Realtors like the multiple listing approach because they have a greater variety of properties to sell. A realtor association would purchase the hardware and software as a turnkey system from Que Software and then operate the system for its members. The acquisition and ongoing operation of the system are financed by member fees. Once a realtor association adopts a multiple listing system (MLS), be it manual or computer based, all the realtors in the region participate. Joan Magee believes that Que-List's natural language interface and client-matching expert system will make the package highly competitive with other proprietary software packages aimed at this market.

Que-List will have the following functions:

□ *Entering a listing*. When an agent obtains a new listing from a seller, the agent completes a form. The data on the form are entered into the system by the listing agent or a clerk.

□ *Printing the listing book*. All the current listings are printed once a week, four listings to a page. The listings include factual data and a picture of the property. The printout is duplicated and distributed to all members. The members discard the previous listing book. The listings are grouped by school district and are in sequence by increasing price within each school district.

□ *Entering a sale*. When an agent sells a property, the property is transferred from the listings data base to the "comparable file." This file contains all the properties sold within the last 18 months. The record in the comparable file contains the basic listing data as well as the sale price and terms. The comparable file is printed in the same sequence as the listing book and is distributed quarterly. The printout is used by agents to compare a current or prospective listing with similar properties that have been sold recently.

□ *Making inquiries*. An agent can obtain a list of properties that meet specified criteria, have been listed since the last listing book was printed, and have been sold since the last printing of the comparable file.

The Que-List system can be accessed from any workstation equipped with dial-up communication capabilities.

The Assignment

The following questions apply to the development of the Que-List system.

1. Specify the data communications hardware that will be needed at the realtor association's data center. Justify your recommendations.

2. Specify the data communications hardware at various user nodes and justify your recommendations for

   a. A real estate office with multiple workstations.

   b. A real estate office with a single workstation.

   c. A laptop workstation.

3. List the alternatives for data transmission services. Discuss the economics of the various alternatives, including speed versus cost trade-offs as well as other considerations.

4. Are hard copy printouts of the listing book and comparable file necessary? That is, can't an agent merely browse as needed at a workstation and then print out only those listings of particular interest? Discuss.

CHAPTER 9

Data Management

KEY TOPICS

CHAPTER OVERVIEW

This chapter is devoted to presenting traditional and emerging approaches to data organization and management, with an emphasis on the database management system (DBMS) and related concepts. After an overview discussions on the sources of data and data management, the chapter is divided into three parts. The first part addresses the hierarchy of data organization. The hierarchy is prerequisite knowledge to understanding the concepts embodied in traditional and data base approaches to data storage. The second part presents examples of sequential and random processing that use traditional file organization. The last part provides an overview of the data base environment and the three most popular types of DBMSs: the hierarchical DBMS, the network or CODASYL DBMS, and the relational DBMS.

DATA SOURCES AND DATA MANAGEMENT

Sources of Data

This chapter is about organizing and managing data, but where do data come from? And how are data compiled?

Obtaining the data necessary to extract information and generate output is always one of the more challenging tasks in information processing. Data have many sources. They can be compiled as a result of a telephone call (telephone orders); received in the form of letters and turnaround documents (for example, utility bills with returnable stubs); and collected on remote workstations, perhaps as part of a point-of-sale transaction. Some data are generated outside the company (when a customer submits an order specifying type and quantity of products). Most data, however, are generated internally (expenses, inventory activity, hours worked, and so on).

Data can come from strange places. For example, metal sensors in the streets relay data to a central computer that controls traffic. Long-distance telephone calls generate destination and duration data for billing purposes. The digitizing of an image, perhaps an X-ray, creates data. Even hardware errors provide a source of data.

The data that we need are not always readily available. Existing data are usually not in the proper format, or they are not complete or up to date. Once consistent and reliable sources of data have been identified for a particular application, procedures must be established to obtain these data. To do this, users and MIS professionals work together to establish a scheme for collecting and organizing the data and a method by which to manage the data. The material in this chapter will provide some insight into how this is done.

Data Management

Data management encompasses the storage, retrieval, and manipulation of data. This chapter includes discussions of the concepts and methods involved in computer-based data management. Traditional methods of data organization are presented first, then database management systems.

Your present or future employer will probably use both the traditional and the data base approaches to data management. Many existing information systems were designed using traditional approaches to data management, but the trend now is to use the data base approach to develop new information systems.

Collecting data is much like collecting garbage. You must know in advance what you're going to do with the stuff before you collect it.

—— *Mark Twain*

THE HIERARCHY OF DATA ORGANIZATION

This section is devoted to discussing the *hierarchy of data organization*. The hierarchy is introduced briefly in the database software section of Chapter 7, "Personal Computing." Each information system has a hierarchy of data organization, and each succeeding level in the hierarchy is the result of combining the elements of the preceding level (see Figure 9–1). Data are logically combined in this fashion until a data base is achieved. The six levels of the hierarchy are *bit, character, data element* or *field, record, file*, and *data base*. The first level, bits, is handled automatically, without action

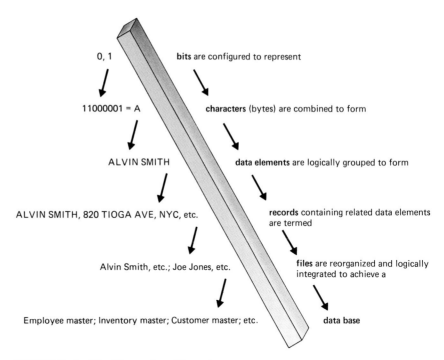

0, 1

bits are configured to represent

11000001 = A

characters (bytes) are combined to form

ALVIN SMITH

data elements are logically grouped to form

ALVIN SMITH, 820 TIOGA AVE, NYC, etc.

records containing related data elements are termed

Alvin Smith, etc.; Joe Jones, etc.

files are reorganized and logically integrated to achieve a

Employee master; Inventory master; Customer master; etc.

data base

FIGURE 9–1   The Hierarchy of Data Organization

on the part of either the programmer or the end user. The other five levels are important design considerations for any information processing activity. The following paragraphs explain each level of the hierarchy and how each relates to the succeeding level.

Bits

The computer's seemingly endless potential is, in fact, based on only two electrical states—*on* and *off*. The physical characteristics of the computer make it possible to combine these two electronic states to represent letters and numbers. An "on" or "off" electronic state is represented by a **bit**. "Bit" is short for *b*inary dig*it*. In the **binary numbering system** (base 2) and in written text, the on-bit is a 1 and the off-bit is a 0.

Bits may be fine for computers, but human beings are more comfortable with letters and decimal numbers (the base-10 numerals 0 through 9). Therefore, the letters and decimal numbers that we input to a computer system must be translated to 1's and 0's for processing and storage. The computer translates the bits back to letters and decimal numbers on output. This translation is performed so that we can recognize and understand the output, and it is made possible by **encoding systems**, such as **EBCDIC** and **ASCII**. In the eight-bit EBCDIC encoding system, 11000010 represents the letter B, and 11110011 represents a decimal number 3. In the seven-bit ASCII encoding system, a B and a 3 are represented by 1000010 and 0110011, respectively. Bits, encoding systems, and other concepts relating to the internal operation of computers are discussed in more detail in Module B, "Inside the Computer," of "A Short Course in Computer Concepts" following Chapter 17.

The data base on this sales representative's portable PC contains pertinent client information, such as name, address, and product preferences. The data base also contains data that enable on-the-spot price quotations. To make inquiries involving product availability and delivery dates, the representative establishes a communications link with the company's centralized mainframe computer system and its data base. He can then use his portable PC as a remote workstation.

Photo courtesy of Hewlett-Packard Company

Characters

A **character** is represented by a group of bits that are configured according to an encoding system, such as ASCII or EBCDIC. In terms of data storage, a character is usually the same as a **byte**. A byte is the combination of bits that represent a character (11000010 is an EBCDIC B). Whereas the bit is the basic unit of primary and secondary storage, the character is the basic unit for human perception. When we enter a program instruction on a workstation, each character is automatically encoded to a bit configuration. The bit configurations are decoded on output so that we can read and understand the output.

Data Elements or Fields

The **data element** or **field** is the lowest-level *logical* unit in the data hierarchy. For example, a single character (such as, "A") has little meaning out of context. But when characters are combined, they form a logical unit, such as a name (for example, "Alicia" or "Alvin"). A data element is best described by example: social security number, first name, street address, marital status—all are data elements.

An address is not necessarily one element, but four data elements—street address, city, state, and zip code. If we treated the entire address as one data element, it would be cumbersome to print, since the street address is normally placed on a line separate from city, state, and ZIP code. Also, since name-and-address files are often sorted by ZIP code, it is a good idea to store the ZIP code as a separate data element.

When it is stored on secondary storage, a data element is allocated a certain number of character positions. The number of positions allocated is the *field length*. The field length of a telephone area code is 3. The field length of a telephone number is 7.

Whereas the data element or field is the general, or generic, reference, the specific "value" of a data element is called the **data item**. For example, a social security number is a data element, but "445487279" and "440214158" are data items. A street address is a data element, but "1701 El Camino" and "134 East Himes Street" are data items.

Data Elements	Data Items
Employee/social security number	445447279
Last name	SMITH
First name	ALVIN
Middle initial	E
Department (coded)	ACT
Sex (coded)	M
Marital status (coded)	S
Salary (per week)	800.00

FIGURE 9–2 A Portion of an Employee Record
The data elements listed are commonly found in employee records. Example data items appear next to each data element.

Records

A **record** is a description of an event (for example, a sale, a hotel reservation) or a thing (for example, a person or a part). Related data elements describing an event or a thing are logically grouped to form a record. For example, Figure 9–2 contains a partial list of data elements for a typical employee record. It also shows the data items for an *occurrence* of a particular employee record: "Department," "Sex," and "Marital status" are *coded* for ease of data entry and to save storage space.

In general, the record is the lowest-level logical unit that can be accessed from a file. For example, if the personnel manager needs to know just the marital status of Alvin E. Smith, his entire record will be retrieved from secondary storage and transmitted to primary storage for processing.

Files

A **file** is a collection of related records. The employee master file contains a record for each employee. An inventory file contains a record for each inventory item. The accounts receivable file contains a record for each customer. The term "file" is also used to refer to a named area on a secondary storage device that contains a *program* or *textual material* (such as a letter).

Data Bases

The **data base** is the data resource for all computer-based information systems. In essence, a data base is a collection of files that are is some way logically related to one another. In a data base, the data are integrated and related so that data redundancy is minimized. In a situation where an employee moves and records are kept in a traditional file environment, the address must be changed in all files that maintain address data. In a data base, employee address data are stored only once and are made available to all departments. Therefore, only one update is needed.

Database management system software, which is discussed later in this chapter, has enabled many organizations to move from traditional file organization to data base organization, thereby enjoying the benefits of a higher level of data management sophistication.

TRADITIONAL APPROACHES TO DATA MANIPULATION AND RETRIEVAL

In traditional file processing, files are sorted, merged, and processed by a **key data element**. For example, in a payroll file the key might be "employee name," and in an inventory file the key might be "part number."

When you write programs based on the traditional approaches, data are manipulated and retrieved from secondary storage either *sequentially* or *randomly*. Typically, magnetic tape is used for **sequential access** only. Magnetic disks have **random-access** or **direct-access** capabilities as well as sequential-access capabilities. You are quite familiar with these concepts, but you may not realize it. Magnetic tape is operationally similar to the one in home and car tape decks. The magnetic disk can be compared to the phonograph record. When playing music on a cassette tape, you have to wind the tape forward to search for the song you want. With a phonograph record, all you would have to do is move the needle "directly" to the track containing the desired song. This simple analogy demonstrates the two fundamental methods of storing and accessing data—sequential and random. The function and operation of data storage devices, such as magnetic tape and disk, are covered in support Module C, "I/O and Data Storage Devices," of "A Short Course in Computer Concepts." Sequential and random processing are presented in detail in the sections that follow.

Sequential Processing

Sequential files, used for **sequential processing**, contain records that are ordered according to a key data element. The key, also called a **control field**, in an employee record might be social security number or employee name. If the key is social security number, the employee records are ordered and processed numerically by social security number. If the key is employee name, the records are ordered and processed alphabetically by last name. A sequential file is processed from start to finish. The entire file must be processed, even if only one record is to be updated.

The principal storage medium for sequential files is magnetic tape. Direct-access storage devices (DASD), such as magnetic disks, can be used also for sequential processing.

Principles of Sequential Processing

Sequential processing procedures for updating an inventory file are illustrated in Figures 9–3, 9–4, and 9–5. Figure 9–3 lists the contents of an inventory **master file**, which is the permanent source of inventory data, and a **transaction file**, which reflects the daily inventory activity.

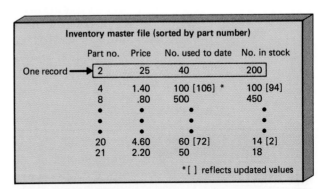

FIGURE 9–3 Inventory Master and Transaction Files
Both files are sorted by part number. The numbers in brackets [ ] reflect the inventory master file after the update. Figures 9–5 and 9–6 graphically illustrate the update process.

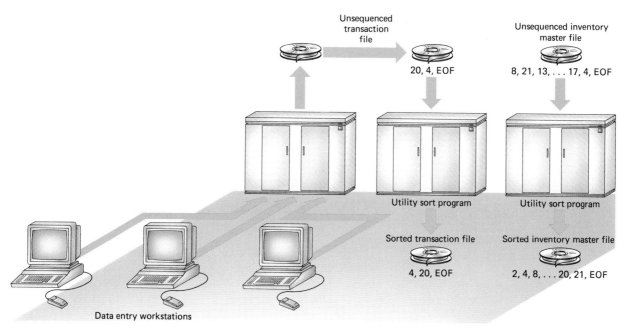

Unsequenced
transaction
file

20, 4, EOF

Unsequenced inventory
master file

8, 21, 13, . . . 17, 4, EOF

Utility sort program

Utility sort program

Sorted transaction file

4, 20, EOF

Sorted inventory master file

2, 4, 8, . . . 20, 21, EOF

Data entry workstations

FIGURE 9–4   Sorting
Unsequenced inventory master and transaction files are sorted prior to sequential processing.
Normally, the master file would be sorted as a result of prior processing.

Prior to processing, the records on both files are sorted and arranged in ascending sequence by part number (the key). A utility sort program takes a file of unsequenced records and creates a new file with the records sorted according to the values of the key. The sort process is illustrated in Figure 9–4.

Figure 9–5 shows both the inventory master and transaction files as input and the *new inventory master file* as output. Since the technology does not permit records to be "rewritten" on the master file, a new master file tape is created to reflect the updates to the master file. *A new master file is always created in sequential processing for master file updates.* The processing steps are illustrated in Figure 9–5 and explained as follows:

☐ *Prior to processing.* If the two input tapes are *not sorted* by part number, they must be sorted as shown in Figure 9–4. The sorted tapes are then mounted on the tape drives. A blank tape, mounted on a third tape drive, will ultimately contain the updated master file. The arrows under the part numbers in Figure 9–5 indicate which records are positioned before the read/write heads on the respective tape drives. These records are the *next* to be read. Each file has an **end-of-file marker (EOF)** that signals the end of the file.

☐ *Step 1.* The first record (4) on the transaction file (T) is read and loaded to primary storage. Then the first record (2) on the master file (M) is loaded to primary storage. A comparison is made of the two keys. Because there is not a match (4 ≠ 2), the first record on the master file is written to the new master file tape without being changed.

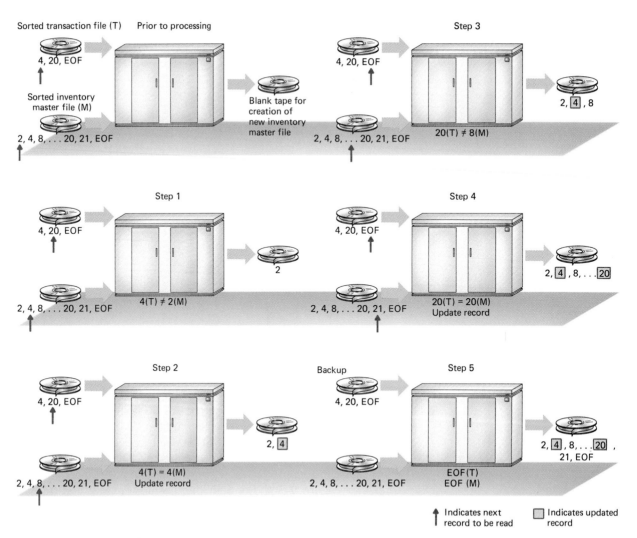

FIGURE 9–5 Sequential Processing

An inventory master file is updated using sequential processing and magnetic tapes. Processing steps are discussed in the text. Notice in step 5 that the backup is a by-product of sequential processing.

□ *Step 2.* The next record (4) on the master file is read and loaded to primary storage. After a positive comparison (4 = 4), the record of part number 4 is updated (see Figure 9–3) to reflect the use of six items and then written to the new master file. In Figure 9–3 note that the "number in stock" data item is reduced from 100 to 94 and the "number used to date" is increased from 100 to 106. Updated records in Figure 9–5 are enclosed in boxes.

□ *Step 3.* The next record from the transaction file (20) and the next record from the master file (8) are read and loaded to primary storage. A comparison is made. Since the comparison is negative (20 ≠ 8), the record for part 8 is written to the new master file without being changed.

☐ *Step 4*. Records from the master file are individually read and loaded, and the part number is compared to that of the transaction record (20). With each negative comparison (for example, 20 ≠ 17), the record from the old master file is written, without change, to the new master file. The read-and-compare process continues until a match is made (20 = 20). Record 20 is then updated and written to the new master file.

☐ *Step 5*. A read is issued to the transaction file and an end-of-file marker is found. All records on the master file following the record for part number 20 are written to the new master file, and the end-of-file marker is recorded on the new master file. All tapes are then automatically rewound and removed from the tape drives for off-line storage and processing at a later time.

Backup

The transaction file and old master file are retained as **backup files** to the new master file. Fortunately, backup is a by-product of sequential processing. After the new master file is created, the old master file and the transaction file comprise the backup. If the new master is destroyed, the transaction file can simply be run against the old master file to re-create the new master file.

Backup files are handled and maintained by *generation*, with the up-to-date master file being the current generation. This tape cycling procedure is called the **grandfather-father-son method** of file backup. The "son" file is the up-to-date master file. The "father" generation of backup is noted in step 5 of Figure 9–5. Most computer centers maintain a "grandfather" file (from the last update run) as a backup to the most recent backup.

Random or Direct-Access Processing

A **direct-access file**, or a **random file**, is a collection of records that can be processed randomly (in any order). This is called **random processing**. Only the value of the record's key field is needed in order for a record to be retrieved or updated. More often than not, magnetic disks are the primary storage medium for random processing.

You can access records on a direct-access file by more than one key. For example, a salesperson inquiring about the availability of a particular product could inquire by *product number* and, if the product number is not known, by *product name*. The file, however, must be created with the intent of having multiple keys.

Principles of Random Processing

In Figure 9–6, the inventory master file of Figure 9–3 is updated from an on-line workstation to illustrate the principles of random processing. The following activities take place during the update:

☐ *Step 1*. The first transaction (for part number 20) is entered into primary storage from an on-line workstation. The computer issues a read for the record of part number 20 on the inventory master file. The record

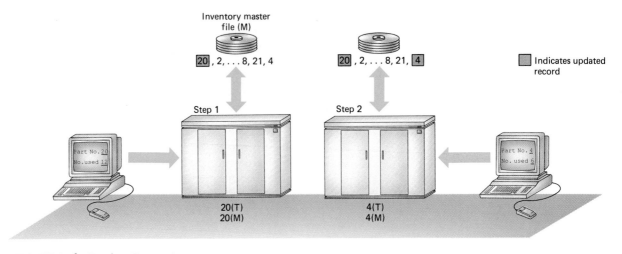

Inventory master file (M)

20 , 2, . . . 8, 21, 4   20 , 2, . . . 8, 21, 4   ☐ Indicates updated record

Step 1   Step 2

Part No. 20
No.used 12   Part No. 4
No.used 6

20(T)   4(T)
20(M)   4(M)

FIGURE 9–6   Random Processing
An inventory master file is updated using random processing and magnetic disks. Processing steps are discussed in the text.

is retrieved and transmitted to primary storage for processing. The record is updated and written back to the *same* location on the master file. The updated record is simply written over the old record.

☐ *Step 2.* A second transaction (for part number 4) is entered into primary storage. The computer issues a read for the record of part number 4 on the inventory master file. The record is retrieved and transmitted to primary storage for processing. The record is then updated.

Since only two updates are to be made to the inventory master file, processing is complete. However, unlike sequential processing, where the backup is built in, random processing requires a special run to provide backup to the inventory master file. In the backup activity illustrated in Figure 9–7, the master file is "dumped" from disk to tape at frequent intervals, usually daily. If the inventory master file is destroyed, it can be re-created by dumping the backup file (on tape) to disk (the reverse of Figure 9–7).

As you can see, random processing is more straightforward than is sequential processing, and it has those advantages associated with on-line, interactive processing. Figure 9–8 summarizes the differences between sequential and random processing.

Backup

Inventory master file   Inventory master file

FIGURE 9–7   Backup Procedure for Random Processing
Unlike sequential processing, a separate run is required to create the backup for random processing.

	Sequential Processing	Random Processing
Primary storage medium		
Preprocessing	Files must be sorted	None required
File updating	Requires complete processing of file and creation of new master file	Only active records are processed, then rewritten to the same storage area
Data currency	Batch (at best, data are a day old)	On-line (up-to-the-minute)
Backup	Built-in (old master file and transaction file)	Requires special provisions

FIGURE 9–8 Differences Between Sequential and Random Processing

Random-Access Methods

The procedures and mechanics of the way a particular record is accessed directly are, for the most part, transparent to users, and even to programmers. However, some familiarity will help you understand the capabilities and limitations of direct-access methods. The **indexed sequential-access method**, or **ISAM** (pronounced *EYE-sam*), is a popular method that permits both sequential and random processing.

When accessing a record from magnetic disk, the disk access arm, and therefore the read/write head, must be positioned over the track containing the desired record. In ISAM, the access of any given record is, in effect, a series of sequential searches through several levels of indices. These indices minimize the search time for locating the record to be processed. Figure 9–9 illustrates how indices are used to locate a particular record using ISAM.

When an ISAM file is created, several data records are grouped together, or *blocked*, and an **index file** is created. The index file is also blocked, but in a hierarchical manner. The number of levels of index blocks varies with the size of the file. Each index block contains "index records." Extra index records are included in each block to leave space for records to be added in the future.

Each index record contains a value of a key and a **pointer** (see Figure 9–9). The pointer indicates whether to go to the next level of index blocks or directly to a data block. The pointer is a *physical address* depicting the disk location (that is, the disk pack, disk face surface and/or sector, track, and record number) of the first index record in an index block or the first data record in a data block. To simplify the example in Figure 9–9, the actual disk addresses are omitted and are replaced with the numbers of the index blocks (2 and 3) and data blocks (1, 2, 3, and 4).

The key value in each index record is the *highest-value key* contained in the next level index block or the data block. For example, the first record in index block 1 (the second and highest level of index blocks) contains a pointer to index block 2 (in the first level of index blocks); therefore, the

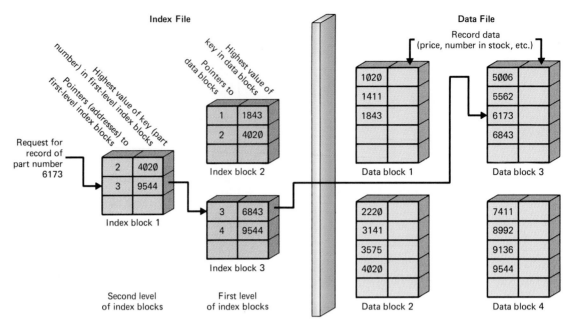

FIGURE 9–9   Retrieving an ISAM Record
The figure illustrates how the record for part number 6173 would be located and retrieved using the indexed sequential-access method. Processing steps are discussed in the text.

highest key value (4020) in index block 2 is included in the first record of index block 1. The second record in index block 1 contains a pointer to index block 3 and the highest key value (9544) in index block 3.

As you step through the following example, you should get a basic understanding of how an ISAM file works. Suppose you would like to retrieve the record for part number 6173 in Figure 9–9.

□ *Begin the search with index block 1.* The search begins with the first record of index block 1, the highest-level index block. Each index block is searched sequentially, beginning with the first index record to determine which block to search at the next level. Since 6173 is greater than the highest key value in index block 2 (4020), the search proceeds to the next index record in index block 1. Since 6173 is less than 9544, the search is directed to index block 3 (in the first level of index blocks).

□ *Continue the search at the next level of index blocks.* The search always begins with the highest-level index block (second level in the example) and progresses through each successive level in the index file and eventually to the data file. Since the search is directed to index block 3, the records of index block 3 are searched sequentially until the search is directed to the next index level or, in the example, a data block. Since 6173 is less than 6843, there is no need to search any more records in index block 3. In the example, the search is directed to data block 3.

□ *Search the data block for the desired record.* Data block 3 is searched sequentially until the record for part number 6173 is located. The third record of data block 3 contains the record for part number 6173.

□ *Read the desired record.* The record is read and transmitted to main memory for processing.

It should be emphasized again that the search and retrieval process is transparent to the programmer. The programmer has only to issue a "read" for part number 6173. The computer and ISAM software do the rest.

THE DATA BASE ENVIRONMENT

To a large extent, a user's understanding of a database depends on what he or she sees of it. To an even larger extent, a user's acceptance and use of a database (concept or tool) depends on his or her understanding of it.

—— *Anonymous*

Data Integration

The traditional sequential and random files discussed earlier in this chapter are typically designed to meet the specific information and data processing requirements of a particular functional-area department, such as accounting, sales, or purchasing. Different, but in many ways similar, files are created to support these functions. Many of the data elements on each of these files are common. For example, each of these functional areas has a need to maintain customer data, such as customer name, customer address, and the contact person at the customer location. When the name of the contact person changes in a traditional file environment, each file must be updated separately.

Through the early 1980s, most installed information systems were implemented in a crisis environment and with a single functional objective in mind. The integration of information systems was not a priority. As result, many companies are saddled with massive system, procedural, and data redundancies. These redundancies promote inefficiencies and result in unnecessary expenses. Today, companies are using **database management system (DBMS)** software as a tool to integrate data management and information flow within an organization.

Costly data redundancy can be minimized by designing an *integrated data base* to serve the organization as a whole, not just one specific department. The integrated data base is made possible by database management system software. Notice that "database" is one word when it refers to the software that manages the data base. "Data base" is two words when it refers to the highest level of the hierarchy of data organization (see Figure 9–1).

Benefits of a Data Base Environment

There are many reasons why a company would begin with or convert to a data base environment.

Greater Access to Information

Most organizations have accumulated a wealth of data, but translating these data to meaningful information has, at times, proven difficult, especially in a traditional file environment. The structure of an integrated data base provides enormous flexibility in the types of reports that can be generated and the types of on-line inquiries that can be made.

Better Control

A database management system allows data to be centralized for improved data security. Also, by centralizing data, advanced *data structures* can be used to control data redundancy. "Data structures" refer to the manner in which the data elements and records are related to each other.

More Efficient Software Development

The programming task is simplified with a database management system because data are more readily available. Also, in a data base, data are *independent* of the applications programs. That is, data elements can be added, changed, and deleted from the data base, and this does not affect existing programs. Adding a data element to a record of a traditional file may require the modification and testing of dozens, and sometimes hundreds, of programs.

Approaches to Data Base Management

The processing constraints of traditional files are overcome by database management systems software. To do this, database management systems rely on sophisticated data structures. The data structures vary considerably among commercially available DBMS software packages. However, there are three fundamental approaches to the design of DBMS software:

- ☐ The **hierarchical DBMS**
- ☐ The **network DBMS** or **CODASYL DBMS** (The *C*onference for *Da*ta *Sy*stems *L*anguages or CODASYL is an industry-funded organization in which volunteers from different organizations cooperate to develop and recommend standards for database management systems, programming languages, and other computer-related activities.)
- ☐ The **relational DBMS**

The examples presented in the following sections should help you to understand better the principles and advantages of the three types of database management systems.

Hierarchical DBMS

BACKGROUND   Although network and relational DBMS technologies are considered superior to hierarchical DBMS technology, the hierarchical approach remains the most commonly used. This is more a result of momentum than choice. In 1968, IBM announced its *Information Management Systems* (*IMS*), a hierarchical DBMS product. At the time, it was the only game in town and became enormously popular. IMS was designed to be run on the hardware of the day. A large mainframe in 1968 had approximately the same speed and capacity as a top-of-the-line desktop micro of today. With limited hardware capabilities, IMS designers opted for the simplicity of the hierarchical design. Although IMS has been upgraded many times, it is still

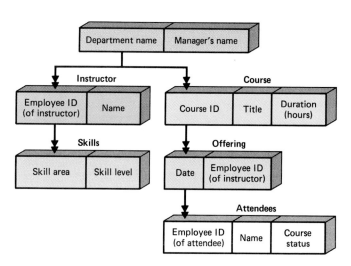

FIGURE 9–10   A Structure for a Hierarchical Data Base
The data base records for instructor, [instructor] skills, course, [course] offering, and [course] attendees are linked to the root in a hierarchical manner to form the structure of a hierarchical data base.

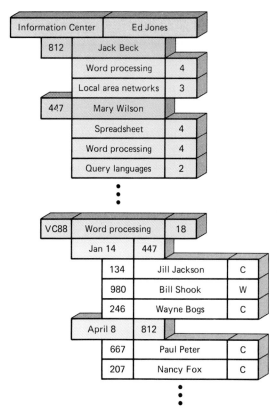

FIGURE 9–11   A Partial Occurrence of the Hierarchical Data Base Structure of Figure 9–10
Mary Wilson (employee ID of 447) taught the January 14 offering of the word processing course.

a hierarchical system and does not have the scope of features of the more sophisticated network and relational DBMSs. It does, however, have two decades of momentum and IMS users are reluctant to scrap their sizable investments and start over with a network or relational DBMS. Nevertheless, virtually all new development in the area of database management systems uses network and/or relational technologies.

A HIERARCHICAL DBMS EXAMPLE   Hierarchical DBMSs are based on the tree data structure, actually an uprooted tree turned upside down. Hierarchies are easy to understand and conceptualize. A company's organizational chart is a good example of the tree data structure. At the top of the chart is the president, with the vice presidents in the second level and subordinate to the president. Those people reporting to the vice presidents occupy the third level.

Hierarchical structures are equally appropriate for data management. Consider the employee data base in Figure 9–10. In the example, an information center in a large company has several full-time in-house instructors, each of whom gives courses on a variety of subjects. The data base includes the skill areas and associated skill levels for each instructor. For example, an instructor might have skills in word processing and local area networks at skill levels 4 and 3, respectively. A particular course (word processing) may be given several times a year, possibly by different instructors. Each offering of a course is attended by at least one employee who either completes (C) the course or withdraws (W), thereby prompting a "C" or "W" to be entered to the course status field (see Figures 9–10 and 9-11).

Figure 9–11 shows a partial occurrence of the information center's hierarchical data base structure. The hierarchical structure of the data base and the occurrence are analogous to the data element and the data item (for example, employee name, Jack Beck). One is the definition—the category or abstract—and the other is the actual value or contents.

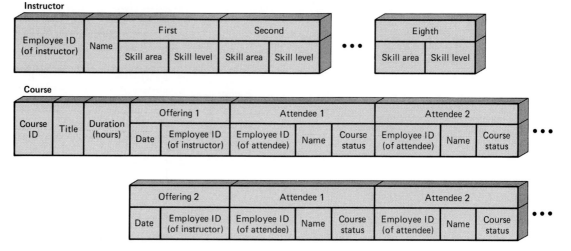

FIGURE 9–12   Record Layouts
*These record layouts for a course file and an instructor file are traditional file alternatives to
the hierarchical data base structure of Figure 9–10.*

In hierarchical DBMSs, a group of fields is called a **segment** and can
be likened to the record in a traditional file. The segment or **data base
record** is similar to the record of a traditional file in that it is a collection
of related data elements and is read from, or written to, the data base as a
unit. The relationship between a segment at a higher level and a segment
connected by a line to a lower level is that of a *parent* and *child* or *children*.
In Figure 9–10, the instructor segment is the "parent" of the skills segment.
The possibility of "children" (for example, instructors with multiple skills)
is denoted by a double arrow on the connector line. In a hierarchical data
base, no segment has more than one parent. The *root*, or highest level,
does not have a parent.

The information center tree illustrated in Figure 9–10 could be linked
with other trees, perhaps the employee tree, to create informative reports.
For example, the employee ID data items in the attendees' segments could
be used to "point" to more detailed information about a particular attendee
(department affiliation, extension number, and so on).

If this application were designed using traditional approaches to data
management, there would probably be two files, the course file and the
instructor file. The record layout for these two files might appear as shown
in Figure 9–12.

Network or CODASYL DBMS

The network approach to data management carries the hierarchical approach
to the next level of sophistication by permitting children to have more than
one parent.

A NETWORK DBMS EXAMPLE   Consider the following situation. A library currently
maintains a file that contains the following data elements on each record:

- Title
- Author(s)

Title	ISBN number	Publication year	Publisher	Publisher's address	Author 1	Author 2	Author 3	Author 4

FIGURE 9–13 Record Layout
This record layout is for a traditional book inventory file in a library.

□ Publisher

□ Publisher's address

□ Classification

□ Publication year

The head librarian wants more flexibility in obtaining decision-making information. Many of the librarian's requests would be impractical with the existing traditional file (see Figure 9–13). A data base administrator recommended restructuring the file for a network database management system. The data base administrator is an MIS specialist who designs and maintains the data base.

Not surprisingly, the analysts found certain data redundancies in the existing file. Since each book or title has a separate record, the *name* of an author who has written several books is repeated for each book written. A given publisher may have hundreds, even thousands, of books in the library—but in the present file, the *publisher* and *publisher's address* are repeated for each title. To eliminate these data redundancies, the data base administrator suggested the records or segments shown in Figure 9–14.

Next, the data base administrator established the relationships between the records. There is a *one-to-many* relationship between the publisher and title records. That is, one publisher may publish any number of titles. The publisher-title relationship is represented in Figure 9–14 by a connecting line between the two records. A double arrow toward the title record represents the possibility of more than one title per publisher. The publisher-title combination is called a **set**. Other sets defined by the data base administrator are title-author and author-title. Figure 9–14 is a graphic representation of the logical structure of the data base, called a **schema** (pronounced *SKEE-muh*).

In the data base schema of Figure 9–14, a particular author's name appears only once. The author's name is then linked to the title records of those books that he or she has authored. The publisher record is linked to all the titles that it publishes. When accessing a record in a program, you

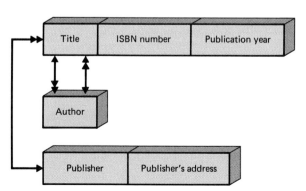

FIGURE 9–14 A Network or CODASYL Data Base Schema
The record layout of the traditional book inventory file in Figure 9–13 is reorganized into data base records and integrated into a data base schema to minimize data redundancy. Relationships are established among the data base records so that authors, titles, and publishers can be linked as appropriate.

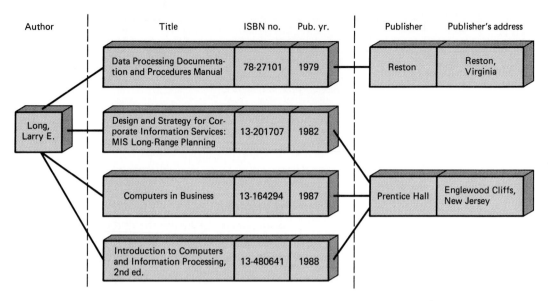

| Author | Title | ISBN no. | Pub. yr. | Publisher | Publisher's address |

FIGURE 9–15 An Occurrence of the Network Data Base Structure of Figure 9–14
Notice that publishers can be linked to authors via the title record, and vice versa.

simply request the record of a particular title, author, or publisher. Once you have the author's record, you can use the links between records to retrieve the titles of the books written by that author. Similarly, if you request the record of a particular publisher, you can obtain a list of all titles published by that publisher.

Figure 9–14 is a representation of the schema and Figure 9–15 shows an occurrence of the data base structure.

QUERIES TO THE DATA BASE   This data base design eliminates, or at least minimizes, data redundancy and permits the head librarian to make a wide range of inquiries. For example:

☐ What titles were written by Mark Twain?

☐ List those titles published in 1986 by Prentice Hall (alphabetically by title).

Responses to these and other similar inquiries are relatively easy to obtain with a database management system. Similar inquiries to the library's existing traditional file (Figure 9–13) would require not only the complete processing of the file, but perhaps several data preparation computer runs for sorting and merging.

If the head librarian decides after a year to add, for example, Library of Congress numbers to the title record, the data base administrator can make the revision without affecting existing programs.

Relational DBMS

RELATIONAL VERSUS NETWORK DBMSS   The relational approach to database management systems has been gaining momentum through the 1980s. In contrast to the network DBMS, data are accessed by *content* rather than by *address*. That is, the relational approach uses the computer to search the data base

It is better to know some of the questions than all of the answers.

——— *James Thurber*

for the desired data rather than accessing data through a series of indices and physical addresses, as with both the hierarchical and network DBMSs. In relational DBMSs, the data structures, or relationships between data, are defined in *logical*, rather than *physical*, terms. That is, the relational data base has no predetermined relationship between the data, such as the one-to-many sets in the network schemas (see Figure 9–14). In this way, data can be accessed at the *data element* level. In network structures, the entire data base record must be retrieved to examine a single data element.

Until recently, relational DBMSs have been to slow to be effective in the real world, especially in transaction-oriented environments. Even with the increased speed of computers and innovations in relational technology, network data base management systems outperform relational DBMSs for transaction processing. However, for applications where the transaction volume is low and the need for flexible decision support systems (query and "what if") is high, relational DBMSs outperform network DBMSs. Because relational structures provide greater flexibility in accessing information, relational DBMSs provide companies with greater opportunities to increase productivity.

A RELATIONAL DBMS EXAMPLE   Let's stay with library applications for our relational DBMS example, but let's shift emphasis from book inventory to book circulation. The objective of a circulation system is to keep track of who borrows which books, then monitor the timely return of the books. In the traditional file environment, the record layout might appear as shown in Figure 9–16. In the record shown, a library patron can borrow from one to four books. Precious storage space is wasted for patrons who borrow infrequently, and the four-book limit may force prolific readers to make more trips to the library.

The data base administrator recommended the relational DBMS organization shown in Figure 9–17. The data base contains two *tables*, each con-

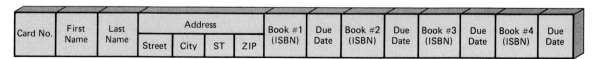

Card No.	First Name	Last Name	Address				Book #1 (ISBN)	Due Date	Book #2 (ISBN)	Due Date	Book #3 (ISBN)	Due Date	Book #4 (ISBN)	Due Date
			Street	City	ST	ZIP								

FIGURE 9–16   Record Layout
This record layout is for a traditional book circulation file in a library.

Patron Data

Card No.	First Name	Last Name	Address			
			Street	City	ST	ZIP
1243	Jason	Jones	18 W. Oak	Ponca City	OK	74601
1618	Kay	Smith	108 10th St.	Newkirk	OK	74647
2380	Heather	Hall	2215 Pine Dr.	Ponca City	OK	74604
2644	Brett	Brown	1700 Sunset	Ponca City	OK	74604
3012	Melody	Beck	145 N. Brook	Ark. City	KS	67005
3376	Butch	Danner	RD#7	Tonkawa	OK	74653
3859	Abe	Michaels	333 Paul Ave.	Kaw City	OK	74641

Books-on-Loan Data

Card No.	Book No. (ISBN)	Due Date
1618	89303-530	4/7
1243	12-201702	4/20
3859	13-48049	4/9
2644	18-23614	4/14
2644	71606-214	4/14
2644	22-68111	4/3
1618	27-21675	4/12

FIGURE 9–17   A Relational Data Base Organization
The record layout of the traditional book circulation file record of Figure 9–16 is reorganized and integrated into a relational data base with a "Patron Data" table and a "Books-on-Loan Data" table.

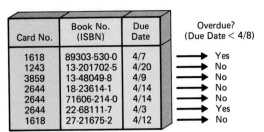

Card No.	Book No. (ISBN)	Due Date	Overdue? (Due Date < 4/8)
1618	89303-530-0	4/7	→ Yes
1243	13-201702-5	4/20	→ No
3859	13-48049-8	4/9	→ No
2644	18-23614-1	4/14	→ No
2644	71606-214-0	4/14	→ No
2644	22-68111-7	4/3	→ Yes
1618	27-21675-2	4/12	→ No

Overdue Books (4/8)			
Card No.	Name	Due Date	ISBN Number
1618	Kay Smith	4/7	89303-530-0
2644	Brett Brown	4/3	22-68111-7

FIGURE 9–18 Queries to a Relational Data Base

The figure graphically illustrates the resolution and output of an April 8 query to the data base: "List all books overdue."

taining rows and columns of data. A row or **tuple** in a table is roughly equivalent to an occurrence of a data base record in a hierarchical or network data base. The column headings, called **attributes**, are analogous to fields (data elements) of the hierarchical and network data bases.

The first table contains patron data, and the second table contains data relating to books out on loan. Each new patron is assigned a number and issued a library card with a number that can be read with an optical wand scanner. The patron's card number, name, and address are added to the data base. When the patron borrows a book, the librarian at the circulation desk uses a wand scanner to enter the card number and the book's ISBN number. These data and the due date, which are entered on a keyboard, become a row in the "on loan" table. Notice that by using a relational DBMS, there is no limit to the number of borrowed books that the system can handle for a particular patron.

QUERIES TO THE DATA BASE Suppose the circulation librarian wanted a report of overdue books as of April 8 (4/8). The query would be: "List all books overdue" (query date is 4/8). The search criterion of "due date < (before) 4/8" is applied to the "due date" column in the "on loan" table (see Figure 9–18). The search surfaces two overdue books; then the system uses the card numbers to cross-reference delinquent patrons in the "patron" table to obtain their names and addresses. The report at the bottom of Figure 9–18 is produced in response to the librarian's query. Data on each book, including publisher, author, and ISBN number, might be maintained in another table in the relational data base.

Commercial Database Management Systems

There are well over 200 commercially available DBMS software packages. Each year some prove to be unprofitable products and are removed from the market, but the gap is soon filled with innovative new products. Some microcomputer DBMSs sell for under $50, and some mainframe versions sell for over $250,000. Industry giant IBM dominates the minicomputer and mainframe DBMS market with the two-decade-old IMS, a hierarchical DBMS, and the recently introduced *DB2*, a relational DBMS. With IMS and DB2, IBM has 50 percent of the DBMS market. DB2, announced in 1985, is far from the market leader, but all indicators say that it will be the market leader in the early 1990s, if not sooner. Cullinet Software, Inc., is a distant, but solid, second with *IDMS, IDMS/R*, and *IDMS/SQL*. Other major players include Applied Data Research, Inc.'s *Datacom*, Software AG of North America, Inc.'s *ADABAS*, Cincom Systems, Inc.'s *Total* and *Supra*, Oracle Corporation's *Oracle*, On-Line Software International's *RAMIS*, and Relational Technology Inc.'s *Ingress*.

The runaway market leader among microcomputer DBMS products has been the dBASE series (*dBASE II, III, III PLUS*, and *IV*). These Ashton-Tate products hold over one-third of the market. Other commercially successful products include Borland International's *Paradox* and *Reflex*, Microrim, Inc.'s *R:base System V*, Micro Data Base Systems, Inc.'s *Knowledgeman*, and Condor Computer Corporation's *Condor 3*.

Q. We are in the process of evaluating database management systems and expect to begin the conversion process within the year. As an IBM user, we have a variety of options and generally understand the trade-offs. I would appreciate having any insights you might have regarding recent breakthroughs or current research that might affect our decision.

A. Existing commercially available database management systems are passive and respond only when queried. Current research on "alerter" systems promises to enhance the functional capabilities of information systems by enabling the user to assume a dynamic attitude toward the data base. Briefly stated, an alerter system monitors a data base and takes predefined actions when it detects the occurrence of a dynamically specified condition. Alerter systems will add a new dimension to current commercially available data bases and, therefore, to the computer-assisted decision-making process.

I would anticipate that alerters will soon be a commercial reality. Initial alerters will be dependent on a specific DBMS; therefore, you might ask potential vendors about their plans for incorporating alerter capabilities.

It is not always possible to pigeonhole a commercial DBMS as hierarchical, network, or relational. In practice, there are as many approaches to developing database management system software as there are DBMS products. To achieve the flexibility of relational technology and the transaction processing capabilities of network technology, a vendor might create a DBMS software package that embodies the best of both technologies. Cullinet's IDMS/R is a good example of such a package. In fact, some commercial DBMSs are hybrids of all DBMS technologies, and some even make use of traditional file organization.

The application development tools that accompany commercial DBMS packages help to differentiate the various packages. A DBMS package can be purchased with none or all of the following development tools: fourth-generation query language, application or code generator, data dictionary, report generator, screen generator, prototyping tool, and others. These tools are discussed in Chapter 13, "Prototyping and Application Development Tools."

Standards for Database Management Systems

For the most part, the 200 plus DBMS products on the market differ markedly in approach and the manner in which they store and retrieve data. Moreover, vendors have created their own proprietary data base query languages for data definition, retrieval, manipulation, and control. Typically, to respond to the query "List all books overdue" in the relational DBMS example, a query language program would have to be written (or generated automatically). The existence of a plethora of query languages has made it difficult, though not impossible, for data in one data base to be combined logically with that of another. However, this hurdle will be less of a concern in the coming years.

IBM's **SQL (Structured Query Language)**, pronounced "sequel," has been the de facto standard data access query language for relational data bases for several years. Recently, SQL was made the official standard by both ANSI (American National Standards Institute) and ISO (International Standards Organization). This means that in the future, vendors of relational DBMS software will design their packages such that they can interpret SQL commands. It also means that SQL can be used to permit the sharing of data between dissimilar software packages and DBMSs. This should spur the growth of both intercompany and intracompany networking.

Most industry observers, even skeptics, are predicting that IBM's DB2 will be the de facto industry standard and may someday garner as much as two-thirds of the DBMS market. In fact, DB2 is already a market itself; that is, software vendors are developing productivity tools that are designed specifically for the DB2 environment.

With SQL and DB2 becoming industry standards, human skills (programming, data base administration) and software will have greater portability. That is, both humans and software can move easily from one computing environment to the next. When moved, humans will need little or no training and the software will need little or no modification. The overwhelming majority of people who have SQL programming skills and/or DB2 design skills are MIS specialists.

DBMS Summary

The days of the centralized data base may be numbered. Emerging DBMS standards may enable MIS specialists to overcome the hurdle of data base connectivity. The ideal data storage scheme would optimize the use of available resources. Such a scheme would store data in the most convenient places within a computer network, depending on data entry requirements, storage capacity availability, processing load requirements, and so on. To implement this ideal data storage scheme, MIS specialists must use a **distributed DBMS**. A distributed DBMS permits the interfacing of data bases located in various places throughout a computer network (departmental minicomputers, micro-based local nets, the corporate mainframe, and so on). The distributed DBMS functions as if it was centralized. The fact that it is distributed is transparent to the end user. That is, a user requesting an ad hoc report would make the request and not be concerned about the source of the data or how the data are retrieved. Unfortunately, the software for distributed DBMSs is still on the drawing board. However, talk of functionally distributed DBMSs will intensify as we move into the 1990s.

For the purpose of comparison, we should revisit the *knowledge base* (see Chapter 3, "Artificial Intelligence and Expert Systems"). A knowledge base contains rules and strategies as opposed to the data base, which contains

The emergence of high-density optical laser disk technology has made it economically feasible to store images as well as textual data in a data base. In this application, optical laser technology is used to store maps of British Telecom underground telephone lines and equipment. All maps are stored in the form of still pictures at different scales and can be retrieved with a microcomputer-based data management system.

Philips and DuPont Optical Company

data that have a static relationship between the elements. Expert systems rely primarily on knowledge bases, but they must also interact with the corporate data base to retrieve facts (part number and quantity on hand). The facts from the data base are needed to present the expert system's solution and its rationale for the solution to the user.

We all keep data, both at our place of business and at home. DBMS software and the availability of computing hardware make it easier for us to extract meaningful information from these data. In time, working with data bases will be as familiar to us as reaching in a desk drawer file for a manila folder.

CHAPTER HIGHLIGHTS

■ Data come from many sources. The source and method of data entry are important considerations in information processing. Some data are generated outside the organization, but most are generated as a result of internal operations.

■ Most organizations use both the traditional and data base approaches to data management. The trend is to the data base approach.

■ The six levels of the hierarchy of data organization are bit, character (or byte), data element (field), record, file, and data base. The first level is transparent to the programmer and end user, but the other five are integral to the design of any information processing activity. A string of bits is combined to form a character. Characters are combined to represent the values of data elements. Related data elements are combined to form records. Records with the same data elements combine to form a file. The data base is the company's data resource for all information systems.

■ Encoding systems, such as EBCDIC and ASCII, enable computers to store characters of data as a configuration of binary bits. For example, in EBCDIC, 11000001 represents the letter A, and 11110001 represents a decimal number 1.

■ In traditional file processing, files are sorted, merged, and processed by a key data element. Data are retrieved and manipulated either sequentially or randomly.

■ Sequential files, used for sequential processing, contain records that are ordered according to a key data element, also called a control field. A sequential file is processed from start to finish, and a particular record cannot be updated without processing the entire file.

■ In sequential processing, the records on both the transaction and the master file must be sorted prior to processing. A new master file is created for each computer run in which records are added or changed.

■ The direct-access or random file permits random processing

of records. The primary storage medium for direct-access files is magnetic disk.

■ The indexed sequential-access method is one of several access methods that permit a programmer random access to any record on the file. In ISAM, the access of any given record is, in effect, a series of sequential searches through several levels of an index file. This search results in the disk address of the data block that contains the record in question.

■ In random processing, the unsorted transaction file is run against a random master file. Only the records needed to complete the transaction are retrieved from secondary storage.

■ A traditional file is usually designed to meet the specific requirements of a particular functional-area department. This approach to file design results in the same data being stored and maintained in several separate files. Data redundancy is costly and can be minimized by designing an integrated data base to serve the organization as a whole and not any specific department. The integrated data base is made possible by database management system software.

■ The benefits of a data base environment have encouraged many organizations to convert information systems that use traditional file organization to systems that use an integrated data base. Database management systems permit greater access to information, enable greater control of data, minimize data redundancy, and provide programmers more flexibility in the design and maintenance of information systems.

■ Database management systems rely on sophisticated data structures to overcome the processing constraints of traditional files. Three common types of DBMSs are the hierarchical DBMS, the network or CODASYL DBMS, and the relational DBMS.

■ Because of the tremendous momentum of IBM's IMS DBMS, the hierarchical approach to data base management remains the most commonly used.

■ Hierarchical DBMSs are based on the tree data structure. In hierarchical DBMSs, the segment or data base record is similar to the record of a traditional file in that it is a collection of related data elements and is read from, or written to, the data base as a unit. The relationship between segments is that of a parent and child or children. In a hierarchical data base, no segment has more than one parent. The root, or highest level, does not have a parent.

■ In network DBMSs, data links are established between data base records. One-to-one and one-to-many relationships between data base records are combined to form sets. The data base schema is a graphic representation of the logical structure of these sets.

■ In relational DBMSs, data are accessed by content rather than by address. There is no predetermined relationship between the data; therefore, the data can be accessed at the data element level. The data are organized in tables in which each row or tuple is roughly equivalent to an occurrence of a segment in a hierarchical or network DBMS.

■ There are well over 200 commercially available DBMS software packages. IBM dominates the minicomputer and mainframe DBMS market with the two-decade-old IMS and the recently introduced DB2. Other popular DBMSs include IDMS, IDMS/R, IDMS/SQL, Datacom, ADABAS, Total, Supra, Oracle, RAMIS, and Ingress. The market leaders among microcomputer DBMS products are dBASE III PLUS and its successor dBASE IV. Other popular micro DBMSs are Paradox, Reflex, R:base System V, Knowledgeman, and Condor 3.

■ To achieve the flexibility of relational technology and the transaction processing capabilities of network technology, some software vendors are creating DBMS software packages that embody the best of both technologies.

■ IBM's SQL was recently made the official standard data access query language for relational data bases by both ANSI and ISO.

■ Industry observers are predicting that IBM's DB2 will soon emerge as the de facto industry standard DBMS.

■ The ideal data storage scheme, which will eventually be made possible by distributed DBMSs, would optimize the use of available resources. A distributed DBMS will permit the interfacing of data bases located in various places throughout a computer network such that the location of the data is transparent to the user.

■ A knowledge base contains rules and strategies as opposed to the data base, which contains data that have a static relationship between the elements.

IMPORTANT TERMS

ADABAS

ASCII

attributes

backup files

binary numbering system

bit

byte

character

child

Condor 3

control field

DB2

dBASE II, III, III PLUS, and IV

data base

data base record

data element

data item

data structures

database management system (DBMS)

Datacom

direct access

direct-access file

distributed DBMS

EBCDIC

encoding systems

end-of-file marker (EOF)

field

field length

file

grandfather-father-son method

hierarchical DBMS

hierarchy of data organization

IDMS

IDMS/R

IDMS/SQL

Information Management Systems (IMS)

index file

indexed sequential-access method (ISAM)

Ingress

key data element

knowledge base (Ch. 3)

Knowledgeman

master file

network or CODASYL DBMS

Oracle

Paradox

parent

pointer

RAMIS

R:base System V

random access

random file

random processing

record

relational DBMS

root

SQL (Structured Query Language)

schema

segment

sequential access

sequential files

sequential processing

set

Supra

Total

transaction file

tuple

1. Which approach to data base management is based on the tree data structure?

2. Name four commercially available DBMSs for mainframes and minicomputers. For microcomputers.

3. Give two examples of encoding systems.

4. What are the six levels of the hierarchy of data organization?

5. What is the official ANSI and ISO standard for data access query languages for relational data bases?

6. What is the lowest-level logical unit in the hierarchy of data organization?

7. What is the logical structure of a CODASYL data base called?

8. Which level in a hierarchical data base does not have a parent?

9. Name two possible key data elements for a personnel file. Name two for an inventory file.

10. In the grandfather-father-son method of file backup, which of the three files is the most current?

11. What is the purpose of an end-of-file marker?

12. Under what circumstances is a new master file created in sequential processing?

13. What is the EBCDIC bit configuration for the letter C? For the number 2? [Hint: Extrapolate the bit configurations from the examples in the chapter material and the "Chapter Highlights."]

14. What is meant when someone says that data are program independent?

15. Describe the search procedure to locate and retrieve the record for part number 3575 in the ISAM file of Figure 9–9.

16. Use the technique of Figure 9–5 to illustrate graphically the sequential processing steps required to update the inventory master file of Figure 9–3. The transaction file contains activity for part numbers 8 and 21. Assume that the transaction file is unsequenced.

17. Use the technique of Figure 9–6 to illustrate graphically the random processing steps required to update the inventory master file of Figure 9–3. The transaction file contains activity for part numbers 8 and 21. Provide for backup.

18. The attribute of a relational DBMS is analogous to which level of the hierarchy of data organization?

1. Even though network and relational DBMS technologies are considered superior to hierarchical DBMS technology, the use of the latter remains strong because of the momentum of IBM's IMS. Why are IMS users reluctant to convert their data bases to a more technologically advanced DBMS?

2. Identify the data elements that would provide the links between these four categories of data in an integrated data base: manufacturing/inventory, customer/sales, personnel, and general accounting. For example, the customer account number data element is common to all data categories except personnel.

3. Prior to the implementation of an integrated data base in 1981, a midwestern company maintained 113 separate computer-based files. Most of these files supported autonomous, departmental information systems and had numerous instances of redundant data. Discuss the impact that redundant data have on the integrity and accuracy of data.

4. Contrast the advantages and disadvantages of sequential and random processing. Do you feel there will be a place for sequential processing in 1995? If so, where?

5. SQL and DB2 are well on their way to becoming industry standards. How will this have an impact on the software industry, in general, and consumers of computer hardware and software?

6. Identify some of the major hurdles that must be overcome before the distributed DBMS can become a reality.

7. Assume that the registrar, housing office, and placement service at your college all have computer-based information systems that rely on traditional file organization. Identify possible redundant data elements.

8. Identify the sources of data that eventually become input to an accounting information system.

9. The author contends that a fundamental knowledge of the capabilities and limitations of ISAM is important, even though ISAM storage and search procedures are transparent to the programmer. Do you agree or disagree? Why?

10. What do you feel is the most significant advantage to using a database management system? Why?

APPLICATION CASE STUDY 9–1
Data Management for Order Processing

The Situation

Compu-Mail sells computer hardware, software, and supplies to retail customers. Most sales are made by mail or telephone, although there also is a walk-in store. Order processing is currently a computer-based batch system; however a preliminary analysis was conducted to determine which of the decisions in the system could be automated (see Application Case Study 1–2, "Types of Decisions"). The analysis led to the conclusion that order processing should be upgraded to an on-line system. The new on-line system is expected to have the following capabilities:

- □ *Order processing.* All orders are entered directly into the system via terminals. Telephone orders are entered by customer service clerks, mail orders are entered by order entry clerks, and counter sales are entered by sales clerks. The customer's name is entered, and the system retrieves the corresponding name and address. If the customer is new, a record is created. For each item ordered, the clerk enters the item number and quantity ordered and determines whether a sufficient quantity is on hand. If "yes," a line item entry, including price and weight, is generated. If "no," the item is shown as back-ordered. Once all orders have been entered, the system sums all the sales amounts for the order. The clerk enters the method of payment, and the system checks the customer's credit, interrogating the national credit bureau for credit card charges or Compu-Mail's data base when payment is by purchase order or check. Rejected orders are printed and sent to the credit manager for further action. The clerk then enters the method of shipment, and the system determines the shipping cost and the total dollar amount for the order. The order is printed in the warehouse for picking and packing.

- □ *Purchasing.* The system prints a list of all the items that need to be replenished. A purchasing agent selects a vendor for an item, enters the vendor number, item number, order quantity, and date needed. The system sorts all the ordered items by vendor number and generates the orders. It is desirable to be able to monitor replenishment orders so that action can be taken if an order is late in arriving.

- □ *Receiving.* When a replenishment order is received from a vendor, the system increases the amount on hand, decreases the amount on order, and checks to see if there are any back orders for this item. If there are, an order is printed in the warehouse for picking and packing.

The Assignment

For the three functions described in the situation,

1. Prepare a data organization design using traditional files. For each file, specify
   a. The file name.
   b. The processing mode (sequential or random).
   c. The record layout.
   d. The key data element(s).
2. Prepare a data organization design using a hierarchical DBMS. Graphically illustrate the structure, including
   a. A name for each segment.
   b. The fields in each segment.
   c. The key data element(s) for each segment.
   d. The connections between segments (show the arrows entering all segments except the root).
3. Prepare a data organization design using a network DBMS. Graphically illustrate the schema, including
   a. A name for each record.
   b. The fields in each record.
   c. The key data element(s) for each record.
   d. The sets connecting records (name each set and show the arrows entering all records).
4. Prepare a data organization design using a relational DBMS. For each tuple, specify
   a. The tuple name.
   b. The attributes in each tuple.
   c. The key data element(s) for each tuple.
5. Which data management organization (traditional files, hierarchical, network, or relational) would you recommend? Justify your selection.

APPLICATION CASE STUDY 9–2
Data Management for Student Housing

The Situation

Peterson College is a small, private liberal arts school with a day enrollment of 825 students (see Application Case Study 5–1, "Providers of Information Services"). Approximately 70 percent of these students live on campus in four dormitories, in one remodeled house, and in rooms rented from a hospital within easy walking distance. A room may house 1, 2, or 3 students. Students are not permitted to bring household appliances into their rooms, but they can rent a minirefrigerator from the school for a monthly fee. A deposit, returnable at the end of the semester, is also required. The school does not require a general damage deposit, but it does assess room damages against the residents of the room and distributes general damages among all students on a floor. Regina Dacey, the director of housing, feels that she could provide better service for resident students if she had ready access to timely, accurate information regarding the status of rooms, furnishings, and students. Specifically, she wants a database that can respond to the following types of requests:

1. Given a student's name, what is the dormitory and room number, and who are the roommates?

2. Given a dormitory and room number, who are the residents?

3. Given a dormitory and room number, what are the contents of the room as inventoried at the beginning of the current semester?

4. Given a refrigerator number, to whom is it rented, and where?

5. Given a dormitory and floor, who are the students who live on that floor?

6. Given a dormitory and floor, who is resident advisor (R.A.) in charge?

7. Given a student's name, what is the student's disciplinary history?

The Assignment

For Regina Dacey's requests as described,

1. Prepare a data organization design using traditional files. For each file, specify

a. The file name.

b. The processing mode (sequential or random)

c. The record layout.

d. The key data element(s).

2. Prepare a data organization design using a hierarchical DBMS. Graphically illustrate the structure, including

a. A name for each segment.

b. The fields in each segment.

c. The key data element(s) for each segment.

d. The connections between segments. Show the arrows entering all segments except the root.

3. Prepare a data organization design using a network DBMS. Graphically illustrate the schema, including

a. A name for each record.

b. The fields in each record.

c. The key data element(s) for each record.

d. The sets connecting records (name each set and show the arrows entering all records).

4. Prepare a data organization design using a relational DBMS. For each tuple, specify

a. The tuple name.

b. The attributes in each tuple.

c. The key data element(s) for each tuple.

5. Peterson College is in the process of developing a plan for coordinating and integrating administrative computing. However, implementation of the plan is some time away and Ms. Dacey would like her system in place as soon as possible. She has no computer background, nor do any of her staff. Discuss ways in which Ms. Dacey could get her database implemented.

6. Which data management organization (traditional files, hierarchical, network, or relational) would you recommend? Justify your selection.

APPLICATION CASE STUDY 9–3
Data Management for Real Estate Operations

The Situation

Que Software is a newly formed company that develops and markets turnkey packages for the real estate industry. The company's first product, Que-List, is a multiple listing system (MLS) designed to be supported by regional realtor associations (see Application Case Study 8–3, "A Network-Based Commercial Service Operation"). In addition to the standard features of other MLSs, Que-List contains a client-matching expert system (see Application Case Study 3–1, "Expert Systems") and a natural language interface (see Application Case Study 3–2, "Natural Languages"). Que Software has decided to upgrade Que-List by including the capability to respond to the following management requests:

□ Given an agent's name, display the listings the agent obtained that are currently on the market and those that were sold during the last 18 months, flagging the ones sold by the agent with an asterisk.

□ Given an agent's name, display the properties sold during the last 18 months, flagging the ones listed by the agent with an asterisk.

□ Given a particular office, display the manager's name and the sales history for all office listings during the past 18 months.

The Assignment

Que-List has the following basic functions:

□ Entering a listing
□ Printing the listing book
□ Entering a sale
□ Making inquiries

These functions are described in detail in Application Case Study 8–3, "A Network-Based Commercial Service Operation." For the basic Que-List functions plus the management capabilities described in the situation,

1. Prepare a data organization design using traditional files. For each file, specify
   a. The file name.
   b. The processing mode (sequential or random)
   c. The record layout.
   d. The key data element(s).

2. Prepare a data organization design using a hierarchical DBMS. Graphically illustrate the structure, including
   a. A name for each segment.
   b. The fields in each segment.
   c. The key data element(s) for each segment.
   d. The connections between segments (show the arrows entering all segments except the root).

3. Prepare a data organization design using a network DBMS. Graphically illustrate the schema, including
   a. A name for each record.
   b. The fields in each record.
   c. The key data element(s) for each record.
   d. The sets connecting records (name each set and show the arrows entering all records).

4. Prepare a data organization design using a relational DBMS. For each tuple, specify
   a. The tuple name.
   b. The attributes in each tuple.
   c. The key data element(s) for each tuple.

5. Which data management organization (traditional files, hierarchical, network, or relational) would you recommend? Justify your selection.

CHAPTER 10
MIS Planning

KEY TOPICS

CHAPTER OVERVIEW

With virtually every area of business endeavor jumping on the MIS bandwagon, MIS planning and coordination have become key issues among managers. Each wants to maximize the return of every dollar invested in computer and information technologies. To do this, they are turning to MIS planning, the central theme of this chapter. The first part of the chapter provides an overview to MIS planning and its relationship to corporate planning. The remainder of the chapter discusses the two stages of MIS planning: MIS strategic planning and MIS operational planning.

RELATIONSHIP BETWEEN CORPORATE AND MIS PLANNING

It is a paradox that in our time of drastic rapid change, when the future is in our midst devouring the present before our eyes, we have never been less certain about what is ahead of us.

——— *Eric Hoffer*

Now that executives in progressive companies are beginning to focus their energies on information resource management (IRM), *MIS planning* has become a high-priority activity. Until the mid-1980s, most MIS-related planning emphasized hardware, with little attention being given to information systems and other areas of MIS. MIS planning has evolved as a critical activity in recent years because:

☐ Companies have found that MIS can be used to achieve a competitive advantage.

☐ Companies can use MIS to increase productivity.

☐ Corporate executives have become more acutely aware of the strategic importance of integrating their data bases and information dissemination.

As with any technically oriented activity, the learning process is slow, and several years may elapse before a given company can compile an effective MIS plan.

Traditionally, planners who create **corporate strategic plans** have oriented the strategies in their plans to their company's product or service. Only recently have these planners begun to consider the plan's effect on the MIS function. Whether corporate strategic plans, also called *long-range plans*, include a new product line, new warehouses, increases in personnel, or a new compensation structure, virtually everything in the plan has a substantial and direct effect on information services. In essence, MIS was not even in the management loop prior to the mid-1980s, primarily because of its status as a support function. Now that executives are looking to MIS for the competitive advantage, it is of strategic significance. Therefore, corporate planners are paying close attention to planning in the computer and MIS areas.

MIS planning is subordinate to and in support of corporate strategic planning. The most effective corporate planners invite frequent input from MIS planners. On the flip side, the corporate plans must be drafted in a manner that provides direction and guidance to MIS planners. For example, if the corporate strategic plan calls for a doubling of the number of distribution facilities for the firm's products, the MIS plan must incorporate plans to accommodate the additional distribution facilities.

The information services divisions in most enterprises have become the nucleus of corporate operation. This is because the common denominator in any company is the data and information gathered and disseminated throughout the various functional areas. Because of their new-found importance and critical position within the company, MIS managers must make a concerted effort in the area of MIS planning. This chapter is devoted to the two primary areas of MIS planning, **MIS strategic planning** and **MIS operational planning**. Other areas of MIS planning, *contingency planning* and *capacity planing*, are covered in Chapter 16, "Managing Information Services," and Chapter 17, "Acquiring Hardware and Software," respectively.

STRATEGIC VERSUS OPERATIONAL MIS PLANNING

Q. I was moved from development work into MIS planning about 18 months ago. Since that time I have completed two MIS plans. One was operational and the other was in response to top management's request for a strategic plan for MIS.

Both have been well received in the MIS department, but top management thinks our MIS strategic plan is still too operational. I have been asked by the director of MIS to revise the last plan to emphasize strategic planning. Do you have any suggestions about how to proceed?

A. Many MIS "strategic" plans are no more than management summaries of more detailed operational plans that concentrate on new systems development, major enhancements, and hardware upgrades. Top management's response to your strategic plan indicates to me that you may have fallen into this same trap.

You may be better off starting from scratch than trying to revise the existing MIS strategic plan. At this point, top management is not going to be satisfied with a condensed operational plan. An operational plan is subordinate to a strategic plan. They want a plan that articulates those MIS strategies that are consistent with, and complementary to, corporate objectives.

If you have not already done so, review the corporate strategic plan to see if it identifies any directions for MIS (often it does not). Invite input from corporate planners. Follow any corporate planning guidelines to the extent possible.

Keep in mind that top management wants a strategic plan that focuses on what has to be done to achieve specific results. Through a series of discussions with top management and MIS managers, derive a consensus of what the function of MIS is to be. Then set a series of strategic objectives. In the plan, accompany each strategic objective with a brief explanation of how that objective is to be met. In all probability, the operational plan will need to be revised so that it is consistent with your new strategic plan.

Finally, keep the strategic plan to 20 pages or less.

MIS PLANNING OVERVIEW

The Consequences of Not Planning

Planning is one of the five management functions, but often, planning is given a lower priority than are the more immediate management functions of staffing, organizing, directing, and controlling. Typically, MIS and user managers deal with the routine crises of day-to-day activities before they turn to long-range planning, and, sometimes, there is no time left for planning. Although the importance of planning has become a time-honored business maxim, planning is often deferred until executives realize that not planning will have an adverse impact on the bottom line. For those companies involved in competitive struggles, planning can no longer be deferred. Now that progressive companies are actively pursuing the competitive advantage via automation, the bottom line has come into play and MIS planning has become a priority activity.

Almost every corporation can relate to the situation where the lack of MIS planning has resulted in the information services division and/or the corporation being placed in a predicament that could have been avoided with planning. In the past, MIS managers could operate by the seat of their pants and handle each situation as it arose. This management style is no longer a viable option. Too much is at stake. For example:

☐ A large department store chain implemented a new point-of-sale (POS) system but, because of management's lack of planning, it did not schedule time to train managers and salespersons on the use of the new system. During the month following the implementation of the POS system, salespersons spent as much as an hour logging a single sales transaction. The result was an enormous loss of sales and untold goodwill.

☐ A company ordered new hardware only to find that the available machine room space could not accommodate it. Because of lack of planning, the new hardware remained in the hallway, and implementation of two major systems was delayed for six months while the facilities were expanded.

☐ A company's rapidly expanding information services division continued to grow in numbers of employees, but available office space remained constant. At the saturation point, space was allocated in another building 20 miles away. The split in personnel and subsequent inefficiencies experienced through lack of project coordination cost the company millions of dollars.

All these corporate oversights could have been avoided with prior long-range planning.

If you were to identify the common threads among today's successful enterprises, one of the threads would surely be a commitment to a comprehensive MIS planning effort. Management personnel who neglect the MIS planning function may be doomed to a short-term, crisis-oriented environment.

The Benefits of Information Services Planning

Although executives understand the importance of MIS planning, some must be convinced that diverting limited resources away from operational support to the planning effort is good business practice. The benefits of MIS planning are convincing. These are the primary benefits of MIS planning:

☐ *MIS planning promotes better communication between top management, user management, and MIS professionals.* The process of planning encourages cooperation and communication among all affected persons. Continuous feedback from all levels of personnel and all functional areas is a prerequisite to successful MIS planning.

☐ *MIS planning results in a more effective use of corporate resources.* MIS planning encourages the development of integrated information systems so that the company can enjoy the efficiencies associated with such systems. The planning process causes proposals for system development projects that do not contribute to corporate goals to be rejected. In effect, the implementation of an MIS plan causes resources to be allocated in a manner that best addresses business needs. Also, MIS planning enables the judicious scheduling of all resources, including personnel and hardware.

Because user information needs are the driving force behind MIS planning, the planning process necessitates frequent interactions between MIS planners and managers at all levels of the company.

Photo courtesy of Hewlett-Packard Company

☐ *MIS planning provides a vehicle for accountability.* MIS planning can be used as a benchmark for measuring the performance of individuals and departments. This makes individuals and organizational entities more accountable for their actions.

☐ *MIS planning encourages self-evaluation.* The MIS planning process forces MIS and user managers to take a hard look at at all facets of information processing within their respective realms of responsibility. The results of this introspection are ideas and a better understanding for all.

☐ *MIS planning enables managers to cope with long system development lead times.* The lead times associated with the development and implementation of an information system can be substantial. A single system development project can span up to four years. The evaluation, selection, and installation of support hardware can take a year of more. The same is true of user training. The existence of an MIS plan is helpful to both MIS and user mangers. For example, user managers can use the information in the plan to prepare properly for those periods that place heavy demands on their staffs (such as during system conversion).

The Impact of MIS Planning

The MIS planning process has a direct and lasting impact on all levels of management, on competitors, and on customers.

IMPACT ON EXECUTIVE MANAGEMENT   Until recently, executives have been surprisingly unaware of the value of information and, therefore, have been reluctant to involve themselves in MIS-related activities. If an executive does not realize the value of information, then he or she must be convinced, usually by the chief information officer. Once executives recognize the strategic significance of MIS, they must take it upon themselves to learn about the capabilities of computers and information processing and how these capabilities can be applied to their businesses. In effect, they must become computer and MIS literate. Once they comprehend the scope and potential of MIS, executives will begin to allocate a substantial amount of their time to MIS-related activities.

IMPACT ON FUNCTIONAL AREA MANAGERS   The impact of MIS planning is most acute on functional area managers. The planning process encourages these managers to think "integration." Many plant managers, accounting managers, personnel managers, and others have been content to treat their functional areas as autonomous operating entities. In an integrated MIS environment, many MIS-related decisions must be made in concert with several functional area managers. For example, user managers are often asked to come to an agreement on the format of shared data (such as the coding scheme for the part number data element). Because information services affects virtually every area of corporate operation, the MIS planning effort causes user managers to formalize their thinking. For decades user managers have had the flexibility to work at their own pace, but this is not possible in the age of information. In an environment of integrated information flow, management coordination is paramount.

Like executives, user managers have an implied responsibility to become computer and MIS literate. Some companies have actually adopted a policy that all management personnel must achieve a certain level of computer and MIS literacy.

IMPACT ON COMPETITORS   The strategic significance of computer and MIS technologies will be one of the most talked about subjects in corporate boardrooms during the next decade. Every well-informed executive is aware that aggressive competitors are planning ways to gain the competitive advantage. When implemented, a well-conceived MIS plan could spell disaster for competitors, especially those that do not have an MIS plan. At a minimum, these competitors are risking the loss of market share.

IMPACT ON CUSTOMERS   With electronic data interchange growing in acceptance (see Chapter 4, "Information Systems as a Competitive Strategy"), a customer's information system may become an integral part of a company's integrated information system. Intercompany networking requires that companies cooperate with their customers in their respective planning efforts.

The Two-Stage MIS Planning Process

MIS planning is usually accomplished in two stages:

☐ *Stage 1. MIS strategic planning*. Strategic-level planning focuses on the identification and description of long-term strategies for MIS. These strategies are documented in an **MIS strategic plan**.

☐ *Stage 2. MIS operational planning*. Operational-level planning focuses on the identification, description, and scheduling of tasks that need to be accomplished to implement the strategies set forth in the MIS strategic plan. The result of this second stage of planning is the **MIS operational plan**.

In progressive companies, both stages of planning are repeated each year. The remainder of the chapter is devoted to MIS strategic planning and MIS operational planning.

MIS STRATEGIC PLANNING

The Scope of MIS Strategic Planning

A company will typically have several operational information systems and other information systems in various stages of planning and development. For example, a manufacturing company might be conceptualizing a system to permit electronic data interchange between customer computer systems, developing an on-line skills inventory system for the personnel department, running any number of operational information systems from inventory management to accounting, and determining whether or not to scrap their out-

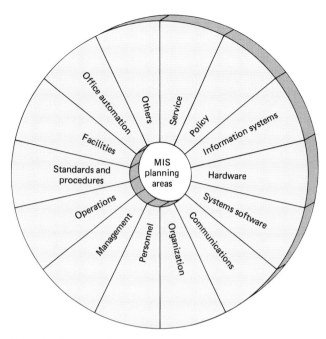

FIGURE 10–1   MIS Planning Areas

Strategic planning is worthless—unless there is first a strategic vision.

——— *John Naisbitt*

dated order processing system. All information systems, whether proposed or currently operational, are within the scope of the MIS planning process.

MIS planning involves more than just information systems. It encompasses all facets of the information services environment that directly or indirectly have an impact on the application of computer and information technology. For example, an MIS plan might include planning in each of the following areas (see Figure 10–1): service, policy, information systems, hardware, systems software, communications, organization, personnel, management, operations, standards and procedures, facilities, office automation, and others as required (such as artificial intelligence). Of course, information systems continue to be the driving force behind MIS strategic planning. This is because everything else, including hardware, facilities, and personnel, is considered support. Any MIS environment revolves around the applications supported by its information systems.

The results of the MIS strategic plan identify general strategies for meeting the company's MIS objectives. For example, a company's MIS objective might be to make EDI capabilities available to customers. A supporting strategy might be to develop an information system that accepts customer orders via EDI. The completed MIS strategic plan would include strategies in support of all MIS objectives. Examples of MIS objectives are presented later in this section.

Management's Role in MIS Planning

Most companies are striving to achieve the ideal in information resource management while pursuing the competitive advantage with computer and information technology. Pursuing IRM and the competitive advantage demand the long-term vision that can be realized only through a coordinated effort by executives and user managers. The MIS strategic plan is the documentation of and the commitment to these visions. Management's role in the planning process is twofold.

☐ *Feedback and cooperation.* Management is responsible for relating their individual and collective visions to planners and for cooperating with planners and other managers throughout the planning process. Operational-level managers may devote as much as four weeks a year to the MIS planning process. Top executives may dedicate as much as two weeks a year.

☐ *Commitment.* Management is responsible for making a commitment to the MIS plan. By approving an MIS plan, managers are saying that when the time comes, they will commit the resources necessary to implement the plan.

Some companies are not in a position to create an effective MIS plan. Unfortunately, the crisis-oriented approach to management practiced by some companies precludes managers from participating in the MIS planning process. These companies simply react to user information needs and to competitors. Also, they tend to keep cumbersome information systems operational long after they become a burden to operational effectiveness. This type of environment is simply not conducive to MIS planning.

Organizing for Planning

The manner in which the planning function is staffed depends on the size of the company. The following are rules of thumb for staffing the MIS planning function:

☐ *For small companies with fewer than 25 MIS professionals.* The director of information services is the functionary and carries out the activities of the planning process.

☐ *For medium-sized companies with between 25 and 175 MIS professionals.* These companies can easily justify a full-time MIS planner.

☐ *For large companies with more than 175 MIS professionals.* These companies can justify a small planning group of two of more full-time planners.

The key persons or groups in the MIS strategic planning process are:

☐ The director of information services (the chief information officer or CIO).

☐ Managers of the various operational areas within the information services division (programming, systems analysis, technical support, and so on; see Chapter 5, "Providers of Computer and Information Services").

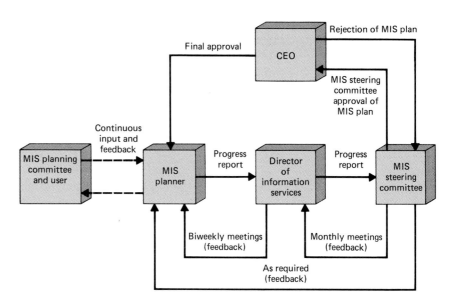

FIGURE 10–2   An Example Approval Process for an MIS Strategic Plan
Shown here is the interaction between principals during the MIS strategic planning process.

- ☐ Functional area managers (accounting, purchasing, marketing, and so on).
- ☐ Corporate executives (CEO, president, and vice presidents).
- ☐ The high-level MIS steering committee (described in Chapter 5).
- ☐ The MIS planning committee (a standing committee of MIS and user managers formed to provide continuous input to the MIS planning process).

MIS strategic planning is an iterative process that requires a formal, ongoing feedback mechanism and well-defined authority for both intermediate and final approval. Although MIS and corporate organizational structures have well-defined lines of authority, approval authority for MIS planning is often vague. To avoid approval delays, a formal approval process should be defined by the high-level MIS steering committee before planning commences. One approach to formalizing the approval process is shown in Figure 10–2. This figure illustrates the ongoing interaction between principals in the MIS strategic planning process.

Planning Tools

Two popular planning tools frequently used in MIS planning are *critical success factors* and IBM's *Business Systems Planning*.

Critical Success Factors

The **critical success factors (CSF)** method is a procedure that helps planners to define an organization's information processing requirements. The CSF method, which was developed at MIT's Sloan School of Management, provides a procedure that managers can follow to identify those areas of business activity that are "critical" to the successful operation of the functions within a particular manager's scope of responsibility. In theory, you would think that managers would do this type of self-examination as a matter of routine. In practice, most managers seldom give this topic the kind of serious consideration that it deserves—thus the CSF method.

The CSF method provides a rigorous procedure that, if followed, enables managers to identify the most important factors in their jobs and in the operation of their functional areas. Once identified, these manager-defined CSFs become valuable input into the MIS planning process. Planners use CSFs to give them added insight into the identification MIS objectives and, in MIS operational planning, the prioritization of projects. For example, if both the vice president of sales and the vice president of accounting identify electronic data interchange as their number one critical success factor, then the implementation of EDI would surely be given a very high priority in the MIS plan.

Of course, CSFs change over time as circumstances change, and they must be periodically revised. Eventually, updated CSFs provide programmers and systems analysts with insight into the design of information systems.

Business Systems Planning

Business Systems Planning or **BSP** is a structured process that many companies use to establish a foundation for the MIS planning process. The premise behind BSP, a creation of the IBM Corporation, is that data are a corporate resource that must be carefully evaluated with respect to organizational needs. The fundamental characteristics of IBM's BSP are presented here.

- It is a team business study.
- The emphasis of the study is on business processes.
- The approach to analysis is structured and top-down (see Figure 10–3).
- Implementation is bottom-up (see Figure 10–3).

In theory, the BSP methodology is an intense 14-week effort that demands considerable time commitments on the part of upper and middle management. In reality, companies seldom complete the BSP study within months of the suggested time frame. The results of a comprehensive BSP study would include:

1. Descriptions of business objectives.
2. Descriptions of processes and subprocesses within the company.
3. Identification of who is responsible for these processes.
4. What data are associated with which processes, departments, and systems.
5. Problems being confronted by management.
6. Graphic depiction of an information systems network showing the relationships between systems and subsystems.
7. Prioritized list of future development projects.

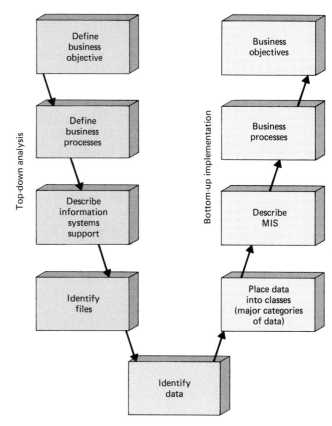

FIGURE 10–3   Business Systems Planning
*In Business Systems Planning, the approach to analysis is structured
and top-down, and implementation is bottom-up.*

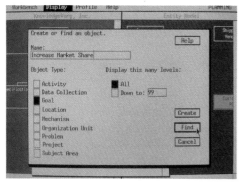

*Several automated tools are available to assist MIS
planners during the planning process. The Planning
Workstation from KnowledgeWare, Inc., gathers,
models, and analyzes knowledge about an
organization, such as business goals, business
functions or activities, data entities, problems, and
organizational units and locations. The software also
depicts the interrelationships of these objects. The tool
can then suggest subject area data bases and
candidate development projects so that the planning
in the systems development area is consistent with
strategic business goals and objectives. The Planning
Workstation uses a variety of planning tools to capture
and analyze planning information.*

KnowledgeWare, Inc., Atlanta, GA, USA

As with any methodology, BSP has its strengths and weaknesses. The
following are strengths of BSP:

☐ BSP is a structured approach that gets management involved in and
attuned to the importance of integrating data within a company.

☐ BSP encourages communication between MIS professionals, end users,
and management.

☐ BSP provides documentation of the existence, use, and need for data
within a company.

The following are weaknesses of BSP:

☐ BSP results in an enormous amount of documentation, with some
saying it is too much to be assimilated effectively.

☐ Companies have difficulty translating a mountain of technical data into
a working systems plan.

In practice, the majority of BSP efforts get bogged down in data definitions
and descriptions before any kind of MIS plan is completed. Even so, the
BSP methodology is often praised for its ability to promote meaningful communication between MIS, user management, and top executives.

Steps in MIS Strategic Planning

Just as programmers and systems analysts follow a system development methodology during the development of information systems, MIS planners follow a methodology to compile an MIS plan. Methodologies describe step-by-step procedures that are to be followed to accomplish a particular objective (an MIS plan or an information system). Planning methodologies are typically more informal than system development methodologies, which are discussed in Chapter 11, "Systems Development and Management." MIS planners follow the steps in the methodology and use whatever tools they have at their disposal to complete activities described in the methodology. Of course, planning methodologies vary from company to company; however, the following fundamental steps are common to most MIS strategic planning methodologies.

- ☐ *Step 1*: Resolve basic planning issues.
- ☐ *Step 2*: Gather pertinent information.
- ☐ *Step 3*: Conduct a situation assessment.
- ☐ *Step 4*: Identify planning constraints.
- ☐ *Step 5*: Set objectives.
- ☐ *Step 6*: Compile MIS strategic plan.

These steps are illustrated in Figure 10–4 and are explained in the following discussion.

Step 1: Resolve Basic Planning Issues

Prior to the beginning of the MIS planning process, certain planning issues should be resolved, considered, or at least identified as having some effect on the planning process. For example, what is the planning horizon? There is no typical planning horizon, but the average is between three and five years. Another common issue to be resolved is the determination of who has primary responsibility for the compilation of the MIS strategic plan and the MIS operational plan. The idea behind this step is to ensure that everyone involved is on the same wavelength prior to commencing the planning process.

Step 2: Gather Pertinent Information

Those charged with the responsibility of MIS planning have five primary sources from which to gather information: individuals in key positions, committees (high-level steering committee), written documents (external auditor's report, organizational charts), vendors, and literature (periodicals, books). Planners tap these sources of information initially and then frequently during the planning process.

Step 3: Conduct a Situation Assessment

In most companies, the MIS strategic plan is updated annually to reflect current information and changing circumstances. The first real planning activity each year is the *situation assessment*. A situation assessment is conducted to evaluate the current status of the MIS function, not only within the informa-

FIGURE 10–4 Steps in MIS Strategic Planning
These six fundamental steps are common to most MIS strategic planning methodologies.

> The most reliable way to anticipate the future is by understanding the present.
>
> ——— *John Naisbitt*

tion services division but, as MIS is implemented, in all areas of the company. The purpose of this activity is to provide the planning team with a definition, or "benchmark," of where the information services division and the functional areas stand with respect to their use of computer and information technologies. Essentially, the situation assessment highlights the company's strengths and weaknesses in the MIS areas. The end product of the situation assessment is a status report.

The three primary benefits of a situation assessment are:

☐ It provides a candid assessment of where the company stands with respect to the computer/information services technology as compared to other similar companies and the state of the art of the technology.

☐ It highlights areas for improvement within the information services division and throughout the company.

☐ It provides a foundation for the initiation of the annual MIS strategic planning effort.

Some of the areas typically investigated during a situation assessment (see Figure 10–5) are adherence to the previous MIS plan, quality and effectiveness of information systems, hardware capacity, systems software, organization and staffing, personnel expertise, morale, operations and controls, standards and procedures, physical facilities, immediate and long-term priorities, security, and MIS-user relations.

During the situation assessment, all ongoing information systems and major development projects are reviewed and evaluated with respect to their effectiveness and contribution to corporate goals. Planners determine if the operational aspects of the systems are consistent with corporate strategies and if the systems are meeting the information and data processing needs of the organization. They evaluate the systems relative to the state of the art of computer and information technology and relative to systems of competitors. The results of the system-by-system evaluation are documented and made a part of the situation assessment. The entire situation assessment provides a major input into the MIS strategic planning process. Figure 10–6 contains an excerpt from a situation assessment for a medium-sized consumer goods company. The excerpt provides an assessment of the areas of "operations and controls" and "quality and effectiveness of information systems." Notice in Figure 10–6 that the situation assessment identifies areas of concern but does not recommend solutions. This comes later in the MIS planning process.

Some companies are not mature enough in their use of MIS to recognize the importance of a situation assessment and MIS planning. These companies have adopted the popular philosophy, "If it works, don't fix it." On the surface this sounds like a workable philosophy, but when applied to the MIS environment, it can be expensive and possibly spell disaster. For example, the following is a typical scenario in such a company. A distributor of automotive parts has a seven-year-old batch-oriented order processing system. The system is error free, and it is understood by virtually everyone in the company. However, the ongoing operation of the system involves several hundred hours per month of costly manual data entry. Moreover, the system provides only a limited amount of information for management decision making,

The Situation Assessment

Areas of Investigation:

- Adherence to previous MIS plan
- Quality and effectiveness of information systems
- Hardware capacity
- Systems software
- Organization and staffing
- Personnel expertise
- Morale
- Operations and controls
- Standards and procedures
- Physical facilities
- Immediate and long-term priorities
- Security
- MIS-user relations

FIGURE 10–5 The Situation Assessment: Areas of Investigation
Listed are some of the areas that are typically investigated during a situation assessment.

Operations and Controls

Down time, response time, turnaround time, and the adequacy of system controls (system quality notwithstanding) are the primary operational issues of concern. System down time for on-line systems is adequate with operational readiness above 99 percent. This is consistent with the industry average.

Response time problems continue to plague all on-line systems with the recent implementation of several on-line systems. It is not uncommon to experience increased response times with implementation of new systems. Therefore, until the problem has been specifically identified, users must be tolerant. Response times should improve as the new system reaches a steady state of operation. If this does not happen, then the hardware capacity may need further evaluation.

The one- to two-week turnaround time for reports generated from certain critical systems (e.g., sales) is unacceptable. Current hardware and software do not have the capacity or capability to produce timely reports, especially during promotional campaigns.

Existing input/output and data controls continue to meet current operational needs.

Quality and Effectiveness of Information Systems

The Information Services Division has taken a quantum leap in the sophistication of information systems during the last 18 months. The leap is attributed to the addition of the IMS-based on-line *accounts receivable* and *accounts payable* systems, the IMS-based batch *general ledger* systems, and the *human resource development* system (batch, non-IMS). Even so, these systems are data processing/reporting systems that do not permit managers to take full advantage of the availability of information. These and other existing systems do not provide the timely information for managerial decision making that is so critical to the consumer goods marketplace. However, several of the recently purchased packages can be upgraded to provide this capability.

Frequent system changes and minor requests for services are sometimes not put into proper perspective by the user groups. Information services resources expended on accommodating these changes and services are often inordinately high, especially when the worth of the end product to the company is considered. This practice is continued because of an unrealistic chargeback system and the lack of priorities.

As far as new systems development is concerned, the *payroll* system is at the end of its life cycle (implemented in 1978) and is due for a complete overhaul. Accumulation of patches and revisions to the order processing system makes the system difficult to maintain. It is also in cycle for a major overhaul. The *sales and marketing* system never got off the ground in the area of marketing. That is, enhancements in the areas of consumer spending and adding competitive data on the data base are still in the planning stages.

The Information Services Division is currently coordinating the implementation of common systems in the subsidiaries that use IBM's AS/400 system. To date, three subsidiaries have implemented a common *order processing* system.

The company is 5 to 10 years behind in the application of state-of-the-art management information systems. Emphasis has been on basic data processing/reporting systems. There are literally hundreds of systems with the potential for automation throughout the enterprise. Moreover, data bases exist or can be developed that can provide meaningful and timely information for managerial decision making. These cost-effective opportunities have been overlooked by users and the Information Services Division. This can, in part, be attributed to the crisis-oriented environment within the Information Services Division during the past three years. Also, users have been reluctant to take the initiative for automating certain functions and for requesting critical information.

The quality of existing information systems is best characterized by a user manager. He said, "The existing systems are neither an asset nor a hindrance."

Some users have found time-sharing services more responsive and have opted to go outside the company. These users, primarily in marketing, are currently spending over $250,000 annually for these services.

FIGURE 10–6 The Situation Assessment: Topical Area Discussions
Shown here is an excerpt from a situation assessment for a medium-sized consumer goods company. The excerpt focuses on the areas of "operations and controls" and "quality and effectiveness of information systems."

most of which is at least a week old. Since there is no situation assessment to expose this and other inefficient systems, management is content not to explore the potential of an enhanced system. By staying with this archaic system, the company not only lost money but it lost its competitive advantage to a company that replaced its batch order processing system with an EDI system.

Step 4: Identify Planning Constraints

The identification of the planning constraints is actually a by-product of the situation assessment. While conducting the situation assessment, planners note anything that would be expected to limit the scope or direction of the MIS planning effort. For example, a corporate freeze on hiring over the next year would be a constraint, as would a finite and saturated office space. Some constraints might involve corporate policy. For example, one company has a policy that discourages departmental computing.

Step 5: Set Objectives

Perhaps the most important step in the MIS planning process is the setting of objectives for information services over the planning horizon. These objectives should be subordinate to and in support of the objectives set forth in the corporate strategic plan. Typically, the high-level MIS steering committee and top management will offer guidance in setting objectives. To set objectives, planners must be aware of the scope and quality of service desired, policy requirements, organization deficiencies, and so on. At this point in the planning process, it is still premature to address information system requirements.

Rather than compile objectives in a random list, MIS planners will often group objectives within each of several major planning areas. Examples of possible strategic objectives for a small manufacturing company are listed here for each of the planning areas listed in Figure 10–1.

SERVICE

☐ To support the information requirements of all levels of business activity in a timely, responsive, and cost-effective manner.

☐ To provide support for all areas of end user computing.

POLICY

☐ To establish policy for computer and information resources that provides guidelines for common situations and a framework by which the information services division, corporate management, and user management can cope with exceptional situations.

INFORMATION SYSTEMS

☐ To integrate existing and proposed information systems into a corporatewide management information system with an integrated data base.

☐ To encourage the expeditious development of information systems that will help to provide a competitive advantage.

☐ To provide on-line inquiry capability in appropriate proposed and existing systems.

☐ To emphasize user friendliness and distributed processing in systems design.

☐ To make judicious use of proprietary software packages.

□ To conduct periodic system reviews.

□ To take full advantage of decision support and expert system technologies.

HARDWARE

□ To continue to upgrade and expand existing hardware to accommodate the growing data processing and information needs of the corporation.

□ To provide greater user accessibility to the computer and information services through departmental computing and microcomputer-based local area networks.

□ To integrate state-of-the-art hardware technology into the design of existing and proposed systems.

SYSTEMS SOFTWARE

□ To provide systems software support for distributed processing.

□ To support user-oriented query languages.

COMMUNICATIONS

□ To emphasize data communications in the design of future information systems.

□ To implement more effective approaches to verbal and written communication.

ORGANIZATION

□ To structure the organization within the information services division and the information center to meet operational commitments and be responsive to the company's information services needs.

PERSONNEL

□ To recruit and retain outstanding individuals with management potential.

□ To improve the quality of existing MIS professionals through career development.

□ To provide career alternatives for personnel who are not inclined to management.

□ To maintain a high level of morale.

MANAGEMENT

□ To recognize the importance of good management.

□ To improve management's ability to manage through the effective use of proven management approaches and techniques.

□ To improve management's ability to manage through the effective use of available technological tools.

□ To promote the concept of information resource management at all levels of the organization.

☐ To provide sufficient operational capability to achieve acceptable response times and turnaround times during peak periods.

STANDARDS AND PROCEDURES

☐ To develop and implement the standards and standardized procedures necessary to create the proper framework for information systems development and maintenance and for effective interaction with users.

FACILITIES

☐ To provide ergonomically sound working space for all personnel who work with computing equipment.

☐ To work with corporate facility planners to ensure consideration of future communications, hardware, and security requirements.

☐ To establish and maintain information centers at all plant sites.

OFFICE AUTOMATION

☐ To coordinate the integration of office automation equipment and applications into the company's computer network and into future information systems designs.

☐ To encourage office automation in support of increased productivity for office personnel.

Step 6: Compile MIS Strategic Plan

The MIS strategic plan is a brief document that represents the collective thinking of planners and top corporate management. Once written and approved, this document provides direction for the compilation of the MIS operational plan.

The MIS strategic plan is, as the name implies, a strategic-level document. At a minimum, the MIS strategic plan contains the general MIS objectives set in Step 5. Also included in the plan are the detailed goals that support the MIS objectives. Goals, as opposed to objectives, are more specific and are stated in terms of results. Take one of the foregoing *MIS objectives* as an example.

> To provide sufficient operational capability to achieve acceptable response times and turnaround times during peak periods.

The following is an example of one of the *goals* that might support this MIS objective.

> To keep response times under one second and turnaround times to less than one hour during peak periods.

Another *MIS objective* might be:

> To provide greater user accessibility to the computer and information services through departmental computing and microcomputer-based local area networks.

A supporting *goal* might be:

> To improve the ratio of white-collar workers to workstations to 3 to 1 within 18 months.

The MIS strategic plan can also include specific strategies to achieve these goals. For example, consider the following *goal*.

> To keep response times under one second and turnaround times of less than one hour during peak periods.

Planners might adopt any or all of the following *strategies* to achieve this goal.

> Upgrading the processor of the host mainframe computer.

> Adopting a chargeback policy that encourages users to schedule batch processing jobs during off-peak hours.

> Off-loading as much communications-related processing tasks as possible from the host processor.

As another example, the *goal* might be:

> To improve the ratio of white-collar workers to workstations to 3 to 1 within 18 months.

The supporting *strategy* might be:

> Install a volume purchase program that permits substantial hardware discounts to departments and individuals.

Depending on the audience and the level of detail desired in the MIS strategic plan, the strategies are sometimes included as part of the MIS operational plan.

MIS OPERATIONAL PLANNING

The Scope of MIS Operational Planning

The second stage of the MIS planning process involves the compilation of the MIS operational plan. Once the MIS objectives, goals, and strategies have been determined and presented in the MIS strategic plan and the plan is approved, management and planners can begin work on the operational-level plan. In this second stage of planning, managers examine the strategies and identify specific projects or tasks that need to be accomplished to implement the objectives set forth in the MIS strategic plan. Depending on the size of the company, managers may identify from five to several hundred MIS-related projects that need to be completed. Once identified, the information systems projects must be prioritized based on corporate need and availability of resources.

The MIS strategic plan is essentially a well-conceived wish list. An important part of MIS operational planning is determining the order in which the strategies in this "wish list" are to be implemented. As is often the case, corporate managers would prefer that all systems be implemented during the first year. This, of course, is seldom an option, so each company must plan within the context of available resources. Given priority guidelines, MIS management and planners schedule the projects (start date and completion date). This implementation schedule and an implied (and sometimes specific) allocation of resources comprise the crux of an MIS operational plan.

Steps in MIS Operational Planning

The MIS strategic plan provides strategic direction for the creation of the operational-level MIS plan. Strategic-level objectives can be formulated using the six-step planning process described in the previous section. Going through the BSP methodology and identifying the critical success factors can also provide insight into the formulation of strategic objectives. Ultimately, however, these objectives must be translated into an optimum mix of implementable projects. Then, these projects must be prioritized and scheduled for implementation. This is the essence of an MIS operational plan.

MIS operational planning is a five-step process.

- □ *Step 1*: Identify projects.
- □ *Step 2*: Select optimum mix of projects.
- □ *Step 3*: Establish priorities.
- □ *Step 4*: Allocate resources and schedule projects.
- □ *Step 5*: Compile the MIS operational plan.

The fundamental steps in the MIS operational planning process are illustrated in Figure 10–7 and explained in the following discussion.

Step 1: Identify Projects

Computer and MIS resources are scheduled and allocated by activities. Therefore, the specific activities necessary to carry out the objectives set forth in the MIS strategic plan must be identified. Management and planners identify two types of activities: *project-oriented* (one-time) and *ongoing* activities. Examples of project-oriented activities are:

- □ The development of a prototype system for a proposed financial and accounting information system.
- □ An MIS security audit.
- □ An enhancement to the customer service subsystem of the marketing information system.
- □ The presentation of three in-house seminars on "The Effective Use of Business Graphics."
- □ A mainframe upgrade.

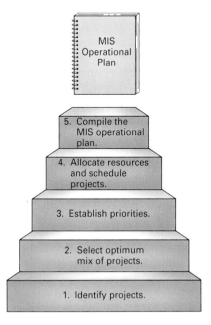

FIGURE 10–7 Steps in MIS Operational Planning

Examples of ongoing activities are:

- Operational support, control, and maintenance of the personnel resource information system.
- MIS planning.
- Compilation and distribution of *Compu-Talk*, a monthly information services division newsletter.

A small company (less than 300 employees) would probably have a list of 25 to 100 projects and ongoing activities. A large company could have hundreds. Given that resources are limited, not all activities can be accomplished. Some must be deferred indefinitely. Therefore, management and planners must determine the mix of activities that would best fit the needs of the company.

Step 2: Select Optimum Mix of Activities

Prior to selecting the optimum mix of activities, existing and proposed projects are given some type of rating relative to risk. The risk refers to the validity of the personnel, money, and time estimates associated with a project, and to the probability of completing a project. To select and propose all high-risk projects would jeopardize the success of the information services division and, perhaps, the company. On the other hand, across-the-board selection of low-risk projects would probably eliminate certain needed projects from consideration, especially those that might provide a competitive advantage. The best approach is to select an optimum mixture of high- and low-risk projects. To do this, each project should be evaluated relative to its complexity, level of technology required, and scope or size (see Figure 10–8).

Those projects that are highly structured provide the project coordinator with a clear view of what needs to be done. These projects will have low to medium risk, depending upon the sophistication of the technology involved and/or size of the project. Similarly, the projects that do not have a clear beginning and end will have a medium to high risk. An example of a low-risk project would be the introduction of a series of in-house user-oriented seminars on the use of electronic spreadsheets. An example of a high-risk project would be the implementation of an on-line expert system to support loan officer decision making in a large bank.

Figure 10–9 illustrates graphically the proper mixture of high- and low-risk MIS projects. The "proper" area would vary about the center depending upon the venturesome nature of the corporation (willingness to accept risk).

Planners use something like the evaluation matrix in Figure 10–10 to assess project risk. To use the matrix, planners identify the projects to be evaluated and list them at the top of each column. Next, they establish criteria for risk evaluation and list the criteria with the relative risk importance (portion of 100 percent) on the rows. Note that complexity, level of technology, and scope/size are only suggested criteria. Several informed persons would then rate the projects by each criterion relative to project risk. For example,

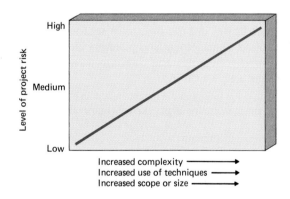

FIGURE 10-8 Criteria for Assessing the Risk Associated with a Project

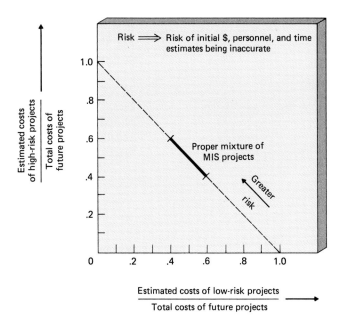

FIGURE 10-9   MIS Project Mix
Within each company, there is an optimum mixture of high- and low-risk MIS projects. The best mixture of projects for any given company would vary about the "proper" area on the chart depending on the level of risk the company is willing to accept.

Project No. Criteria	No. 1 Upgrade of batch personnel system to online	No. 2 Feasibility study for AS/400 system	No. 3 Annual security analysis	No. 4 Machine room construction	No. 5 MIS reorganization
Complexity 40	30	35	15	10	15
Use of technology 30	30	20	10	25	5
Scope/size 30	10	10	10	25	10
Total risk	70	65	35	60	30

FIGURE 10–10   Project Risk Evaluation Matrix
This evaluation matrix can be used as a tool to assess the level of project risk. In the figure, five projects are evaluated relative to three weighted criteria.

if Project 1 were extremely unstructured and complex, an evaluator might rate the project risk as 38 of 40 (highest risk). If Project 1 were within the corporate technological expertise and were limited in scope and size, the evaluator might give the project a 10 of 30 rating for technology and a 15 of 30 rating for scope. The total risk of Project 1 for one evaluator might be 38 + 10 + 15 = 63, an overall medium level of risk. Every evaluator would go through the same exercise for each project, and the individual results would be combined to form a consensus risk evaluation. Figure 10–10 shows a final summary.

Choosing the right mix of projects can have long-term significance. For example, if a company selects primarily high-risk projects, the possibility exists that most of the projects could overrun their budget by a large amount and be well behind schedule. On the other hand, if the mix is primarily low-risk projects, competitive companies may end up with the competitive advantage. A company's mix of existing and proposed information systems at any given time is referred to as the **applications portfolio**.

Step 3: Establish Priorities

Identifying projects to be developed is the easy part of MIS operational planning. The tough part is setting project priorities. Unless extenuating circumstances prevail, existing projects and ongoing activities would be given the highest priorities. Each company must set its own criteria for the establishment of priorities. However, the following are representative criteria:

- ☐ *A federal regulation or an internal mandate*. For example, the Internal Revenue Service might change the payroll withholding guidelines.
- ☐ *Potential to make a positive contribution to the company's cash flow*.
- ☐ *Potential to provide a competitive advantage*.
- ☐ *Interdependence of projects*. For example, a proposed on-line personnel reporting system may supply the data base for a proposed upgrade to the payroll system.

By evaluating the mix of proposed projects against preset corporate criteria, the planner prepares a prioritized list of projects.

Step 4: Allocate Resources and Schedule Projects

The fourth step in the preparation of the MIS operational plan is to allocate resources and schedule the projects. The scheduling process requires that the planner make estimates of costs and personnel requirements for each activity proposed.

The scheduling of MIS activities is essentially a trade-off between maintaining the priorities set in the previous step and minimizing the fluctuation in personnel requirements (that is, work load leveling). Obviously, all projects cannot be started immediately, so they are staggered based on priorities to permit the optimum effectiveness of available resources. At any given time, a company may have dozens and even hundreds of approved activities that are ready to be scheduled. The high-priority projects are scheduled, and as

I will go anywhere provided it is forward.

———— *David Livingstone*

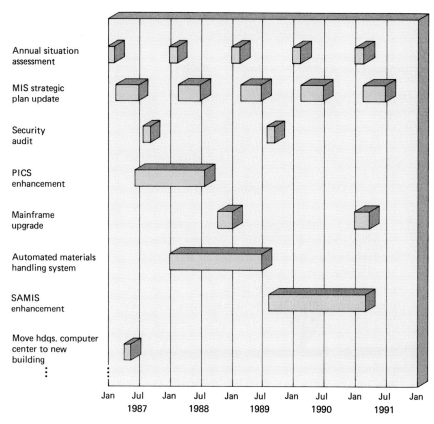

FIGURE 10–11   MIS Project Schedule Chart (Partial)
The MIS project schedule chart graphically illustrates the scheduled start and end dates for all approved projects.

resources become available, the next round of projects is scheduled. A portion of a company's project schedule chart is shown in Figure 10–11. The complete chart would graphically illustrate the scheduled start and end dates for all approved projects.

Step 5: Compile the MIS Operational Plan

At a minimum, a completed MIS operational plan should contain:

☐ An overview description of each proposed MIS activity.

☐ A prioritized list of all approved MIS activities.

☐ A schedule illustrating the start and projected completion dates for all priority projects (usually those beginning within the coming year).

Typically, the strategic and operational MIS planning processes are repeated each year. After the first MIS plans are completed, the planning process becomes a maintenance activity. That is, last year's MIS strategic and operational plans are updated to reflect current situations.

MAKING ESTIMATES AND SETTING PRIORITIES

Q. One of your columns mentions using the "Delphi" and "nominal group techniques" for making time, manpower, and cost estimates and for setting priorities on MIS projects. I am not familiar with these techniques and would appreciate any information you could provide.

A. I received a sufficient number of inquiries about these techniques to merit dedicating a column to their explanation. The versions presented are modified to accommodate better the realities of the MIS environment. The amazingly simple Delphi and nominal group techniques (NGT) provide a rigorous framework by which a group of persons (committee, panel, project team, and so on) can arrive at consensus opinions and/ or estimates. These techniques are effective when each person in the group has knowledge of the problem or task and the ability to provide the group with the rationale for his or her opinion.

Of the two, the Delphi technique is more appropriate for making time, manpower, and cost estimates. The following steps describe Delphi's iterative approach:

1. *Have a leader present the task and appropriate background information.*
2. *Require each person to submit a written estimate.*
3. *Plot estimates.* Each estimate is plotted on a linear scale for all to see.
4. *Calculate and mark the upper and lower quartiles and the median on the same scale.*
5. *Explain rationale for extremes..* Those estimators whose estimates fall in the lower and upper quartiles are asked to explain their rationale for their low or high estimates.
6. *Discuss.* The leader coordinates an open discussion.
7. *Repeat steps 2 through 6.* The dispersion of the estimates should be reduced with each iteration. The process continues until the returns for increasing the accuracy of the estimate do not merit another iteration.
8. *Take the estimate to be the median or the mean (as appropriate).* The dispersion of the estimates is an indication of the risk involved.

Although the nominal group technique can be used for making estimates, it is more helpful in enumeration and identification of important considerations, and for setting priorities. As an example, NGT could be used for setting priorities for a queue of approved MIS projects. NGT's iterative approach is as follows:

1. *The leader presents the task and appropriate background information.*
2. *Silent generation.* Each member of the group compiles a list of pertinent considerations, items, projects, and so on. In some cases the list to be considered will be given (i.e., queue of approved MIS projects).
3. *Leader lists items for all to see.* The leader obtains one point, without discussion, from each participant in rotation until all items are exhausted.
4. *Clarification process.* If individual items are unclear to the other participants, appropriate persons are asked for explanations.
5. *Voting and ranking.* Depending upon the number of items, an odd number somewhat less than the total of the list would be selected. For example, seven might be selected for a list of 15 items. Each participant selects what he or she believes to be the top seven (in our case) items, then assigns a ranking to each item by starting with the extremes and working to the middle (i.e., 1, 7, 2, 6, and so on). For ease of tabulation, each person notes the ranking for each item on a separate card.
6. *Totaling the scores.* The rankings for each item are summed and listed for all to see (most significant first).
7. *Discussion.* The leader coordinates an open discussion.
8. *Repeat steps 5 through 7.* The process continues until it is apparent that further iterations will not significantly improve the results.

Reflect back on the last occasion that you were called upon to participate in a group charged with making estimates or setting priorities. In all probability, yours, like so many others, was not a pleasant experience, and the result was less than 100 percent acceptable. These techniques are designed to improve the plight of those in similar circumstances.

■ MIS planning has evolved as a critical activity in recent years because now MIS can be used to achieve a competitive advantage, MIS can boost productivity, and executives have a greater awareness of the strategic importance of MIS.

■ MIS planning is subordinate to and in support of corporate strategic planning.

■ Planning is one of the five management functions; however, planning is often deferred until executives realize that not planning will have an adverse impact on profit.

■ The following are the primary benefits of MIS planning.

   □ It promotes better communication between top management, user management, and MIS professionals.

   □ It results in a more effective use of corporate resources.

   □ It provides a vehicle for accountability.

   □ It encourages self-evaluation.

   □ It enables managers to cope with long system development lead times.

■ The MIS planning process has a direct and lasting impact on all levels of management, on competitors, and on customers.

■ MIS planning is usually accomplished in two stages. During the first stage, MIS strategic planning, the focus is on the identification and description of long-term strategies for MIS. During the second stage, MIS operational planning, the focus is on the identification, description, and scheduling of tasks that need to be accomplished to implement the strategies set forth in the MIS strategic plan. In progressive companies, both stages of planning are repeated each year.

■ The results of MIS planning are presented in an MIS strategic plan and an MIS operational plan.

■ MIS planning encompasses all facets of the information services environment that directly or indirectly impact the application of computer and information technology (for example, service, policy, information systems, hardware, systems software, communications, organization, personnel, management, operations, standards and procedures, facilities, office automation, and others as required).

■ The results of the MIS strategic plan identify general strategies for meeting the company's MIS objectives.

■ Management's role in the planning process is twofold. First, management is responsible for relating its individual and collective visions to planners and for cooperating with planners and other managers throughout the planning process. And, second, management is responsible for making a commitment to the MIS plan.

■ The manner in which the planning function is staffed depends on the size of the company. As a rule of thumb, in companies with under 25 MIS professionals, the director of information services does the MIS planning. Companies with between 25 and 175 MIS professionals usually have a full-time MIS planner. Companies with over 175 MIS professionals usually have a small planning group.

■ The key persons or groups in the strategic planning process are the director of information services, MIS managers, functional area managers, corporate executives, the MIS steering committee, and the MIS planning committee.

■ Two popular planning tools frequently used in MIS planning are critical success factors and IBM's Business Systems Planning.

■ The critical success factors method is a rigorous procedure that, if followed, enables managers to identify the most important factors in their jobs and in the operation of their functional areas.

■ Business Systems Planning or BSP is a structured process that many companies use to establish a foundation for the MIS planning process. The premise behind BSP is that data are a corporate resource that must be carefully evaluated with respect to organizational needs.

■ The results of a comprehensive BSP study would include descriptions of business objectives; descriptions of processes and subprocesses; responsibilities; data cross-references to processes, departments, and systems; problems confronting management; an information systems network; and a prioritized list of projects.

■ The following fundamental steps are common to most MIS strategic planning methodologies:

   □ Resolve basic planning issues.

   □ Gather pertinent information.

   □ Conduct a situation assessment.

   □ Identify planning constraints.

   □ Set objectives.

   □ Compile MIS strategic plan.

■ During the MIS planning process, a situation assessment is conducted to evaluate the current status of the MIS function throughout the company. The purpose of this activity is to provide the planning team with a definition of where the information services division and the functional areas stand with respect to their use of computer and information technologies.

■ The identification of the planning constraints is a by-product of the situation assessment. While conducting the situation assessment, planners note anything that would be expected to limit the scope or direction of the MIS planning effort.

■ Perhaps the most important step in the MIS planning process is the setting of objectives for information services over the planning horizon. These objectives should be subordinate to and in support of the objectives set forth in the corporate strategic plan. MIS planners will often group objectives within each of several major planning areas.

■ The MIS strategic plan contains general MIS objectives and the detailed goals that support these objectives. Goals, as opposed to objectives, are more specific and are stated in terms of results. The MIS strategic plan also can include specific strategies to achieve these goals.

■ During MIS operational planning, the second stage of planning, managers identify specific projects or tasks that need to be accomplished to implement the objectives set forth in the MIS strategic plan.

■ MIS operational planning is a five-step process:

☐ Identify projects.

☐ Select optimum mix of projects.

☐ Establish priorities.

☐ Allocate resources and schedule projects.

☐ Compile the MIS operational plan.

■ During MIS operational planning, computer and MIS resources are scheduled and allocated by project-oriented (one-time) activities and ongoing activities.

■ Prior to selecting the optimum mix of activities during MIS operational planning, each existing and proposed project is given some type of rating relative to risk. The risk refers to the validity of the personnel, money, and time estimates associated with a project and to the probability of completing a project.

■ A company's mix of existing and proposed information systems at any given time is referred to as the applications portfolio.

■ During MIS operational planning, the planner prepares a prioritized list of projects by evaluating the mix of proposed projects against preset corporate criteria.

■ During the final stages of the preparation of the MIS operational plan, the planner allocates resources and schedules the projects. The scheduling process requires that the planner make estimates of costs and personnel requirements for each activity proposed.

■ At a minimum, a completed MIS operational plan should contain an overview description of each proposed MIS activity, a prioritized list of all approved MIS activities, and a schedule illustrating the start and projected completion dates for all priority projects.

IMPORTANT TERMS

applications portfolio
Business Systems Planning (BSP)
capacity planning
contingency planning
corporate long-range plan

corporate strategic plan
critical success factor (CSF)
MIS planning
MIS operational plan
MIS operational planning

MIS strategic plan
MIS strategic planning
ongoing activities
project-oriented activities
situation assessment

REVIEW EXERCISES

1. MIS planning is subordinate to what type of planning?

2. In which stage of the MIS planning process are the MIS objectives established?

3. What is the focus of MIS strategic planning?

4. Distinguish between objectives and goals.

5. Describe the scope of MIS strategic planning.

6. List six areas, other than information systems, that might be included in an MIS strategic plan.

7. List two benefits of MIS planning.

8. The identification of the planning constraints is a by-product of which step in the MIS strategic planning process?

9. What is the focus of MIS operational planning?

10. Name two areas of MIS planning other than MIS strategic planning and MIS operational planning.

11. Name two popular planning tools that are frequently used in MIS planning.

12. Expand the following acronyms: CSF and BSP.

13. List the key persons or groups involved in the MIS strategic planning process.

14. As a rule of thumb, who would be responsible for MIS planning in a company with fewer than 25 MIS professionals?

15. List the six steps that are common to most MIS strategic planning methodologies.

16. List five of the areas typically investigated during a situation assessment.

17. Name three sources of information that might be helpful to an MIS planner.

18. What is the purpose of the situation assessment?

19. What are the strengths of Business Systems Planning?

20. What two types of activities are identified by managers and planners during the MIS operational planning process?

21. List the five steps in the MIS operational planning process.

22. Briefly describe the contents of a completed MIS operational plan.

DISCUSSION QUESTIONS

1. Prior to the beginning of the MIS planning process, certain planning issues should be resolved. Give two original examples of such issues.

2. Why is it so important that an MIS planning methodology include a formal approval process?

3. Give three original examples each of project-oriented activities and ongoing activities.

4. Explain why the crisis-oriented approach to management practiced by some companies is not conducive to MIS planning.

5. Discuss how MIS planning might have an impact on the customers of an electric utility company.

6. What dangers does an information services division face when management includes an inordinately high number of high-risk projects in the applications portfolio? What are the dangers to the company?

7. Companies seldom complete a BSP study within the suggested time frame. Why?

8. In the chapter material, the author likened the MIS strategic plan to "a well-conceived wish list." Discuss the similarities.

9. Typically, a situation assessment identifies areas of concern but it does not recommend solutions. Why?

10. Explain how MIS planning encourages self-evaluation.

11. Pick any three of the example MIS objectives presented in the chapter material and give at least one example of a supporting goal for each of the three MIS objectives. Suggest strategies for achieving these goals.

12. In the typical corporation, both the MIS strategic plan and the corporate strategic plan deal with all facets of corporate operation. Why not combine them into a single plan?

13. In an attempt to convince a CEO that MIS planning is a worthy activity, a CIO said, "Consider the potential cost of not planning." Discuss these costs.

14. The scope of the MIS strategic plan includes the events and activities that are affected by or under the control of the information services division. Describe areas within a sales and marketing division that would be within the scope of the MIS strategic plan. What areas in this division would not be considered within the scope of the MIS strategic plan?

15. Discuss the relationship between the MIS strategic plan and the MIS operational plan.

16. One of the charges of an MIS steering committee is to set priorities among major information systems projects that have been approved for development. In companies that do not have an MIS steering committee, the director of information services usually sets the MIS priorities. Discuss the advantages of having an MIS steering committee set the priorities.

17. Discuss the criteria that an MIS steering committee might use to set priorities for major information systems development projects.

18. It is not uncommon for MIS managers to be very outspoken against conducting an annual situation assessment. Why?

APPLICATION CASE STUDY 10–1
MIS Strategic Planning

The Situation

Peterson College recently conducted a study of its operating procedures in conjunction with the preparation of its long-term master plan. The College's Planning Committee formed an Administrative Computing Task Force to develop a plan for administrative computing at the school. The Task Force hired a consultant to conduct a preliminary investigation of the major functional units of the College (see Application Case Study 5–1, "Providers of Information Services"). The Task Force concluded that administrative computing at Peterson College should be integrated and centrally controlled. The Board of Trustees created the position of director of administrative computing that reports to the treasurer. Sharon Regotti was hired to fill the position. One of the reasons she was selected is that she had participated in the establishment of a new computer center. Ms. Regotti decided that her first major task should be to develop an MIS strategic plan.

The Assignment

Begin the preparation of an MIS strategic plan for administrative computing at Peterson College by responding to the following questions:

1. Resolve the following basic planning issues:
   a. What should be the planning horizon?
   b. Who should have primary responsibility for the completion of the MIS strategic plan? The MIS operational plan?
   c. Who has participatory responsibility in the completion of the MIS strategic plan? The MIS operational plan?

2. List individuals and committees at the college who would be helpful sources of information during the MIS planning process (use the organization chart in Application Case Study 5–1, "Providers of Information Services"). Briefly describe their contributions to the MIS planning process.

3. Write a situation assessment, in summary form, depicting the current state of administrative computing at Peterson College.

4. List any anticipated constraints to MIS planning.

5. For each of the following MIS objectives, give one goal that would support the objective and list specific strategies to achieve the goal:
   a. To integrate existing and proposed information systems into a collegewide management information system with an integrated data base.
   b. To work with college facility planners to ensure consideration of future communications, hardware, and security requirements. [Note: Facility planners will be working with the architects on the remodeling of several campus buildings and on plans for the new library.]
   c. To provide on-line inquiry capability in appropriate existing and proposed information systems.

CHAPTER 11

Systems Development and Management

KEY TOPICS

CHAPTER OVERVIEW

One of the purposes of MIS planning, discussed in Chapter 10, is to identify the information systems to be developed or enhanced. The next step, the development and implementation of these systems, is addressed in this and the next three chapters (12, 13, and 14). The material in this chapter helps to put systems development into its proper perspective. The chapter begins with an overview of the system life cycle and continues with topics that are considered important background knowledge for discussions of the actual development process in subsequent chapters. These topics include feasibility analysis, making the decision to make or buy software, legal considerations, and project management. The chapter also introduces two fundamental approaches to systems development—prespecification and prototyping. Both are discussed in detail in Chapters 12 and 13, respectively. The last section presents a variety of proven axioms that, if followed, will result in the development of higher quality information systems.

THE SYSTEM LIFE CYCLE

An information system is analogous to the human life form. It is born, grows, matures, and eventually dies. The **system life cycle** has four stages, as shown in Figure 11–1.

Birth Stage

In the *birth stage* of the system life cycle, someone has an idea as to how the computer can assist in providing better and more timely information.

Development Stage

The idea becomes a reality during the *development stage* of the system life cycle. During the development stage, systems analysts, programmers, and users work together to analyze a company's information processing needs and design an information system. The design specifications are then translated into programs, and the system is implemented.

Production Stage

Upon implementation, the information system enters the *production stage* and becomes operational, serving the information needs of the company. The production stage is the longest of the four stages and will normally last from 4 to 7 years. During the production stage, information systems are continuously modified, or "maintained," to keep up with the changing needs of the company.

Death Stage

The accumulation of system modifications to a dynamic information system eventually takes its toll on system efficiency. The *death stage* arrives when an information system becomes so cumbersome to maintain that it is no longer economically or operationally effective. At this time, the system is discarded and the system life cycle is repeated.

The average life of an information system is about 7 years. Many would argue that with the advances in computer and MIS technologies coming at an unprecedented rate, 7 years is too long. When you consider that three generations of programmers will work to develop and maintain an information system during the production stage of the life cycle, 7 years is a long time. The average programmer turnover rate is about 2.2 years; that is, on the average, programmers stay in one position for about 2.2 years.

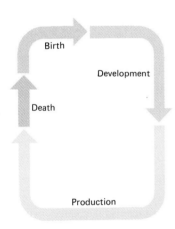

FIGURE 11–1 The System Life Cycle

ASSESSING SYSTEM FEASIBILITY

Before committing corporate resources to the development and implementation of an information system, especially an expensive one, management must assess the feasibility of the system. However, before this can be done, management must define the scope of the system. The scope of the proposed system can be defined casually in the form of a narrative description, or, at the other end of the spectrum, it can be defined by a working model of the system called a *prototype system*. (Prototype systems are discussed later in this chapter.) Of course, assessing the feasibility of a proposed system is easier if the scope of the project is well defined. A prototype of the proposed system provides the best information for making feasibility decisions, but building one is not always possible or desirable. Creating a prototype system is considerably more expensive than is the preparation of a simple narrative description.

At a minimum, the proposed system should be described in sufficient detail to enable managers to make an informed decision. A definition of the proposed system should include a nontechnical description of the fundamental operation of the system and of any interactions between existing and proposed systems. Based on whatever information is available (narrative description, prototype system, and so on), management must answer these four questions to assess system feasibility adequately.

1. Is the proposed information system technologically feasible?
2. Is the proposed information system economically feasible?
3. Is the proposed information system consistent with corporate objectives?
4. Is the proposed information system consistent with existing and other proposed information systems?

Technological Feasibility

Technological feasibility is not an issue when all a company's MIS professionals are skilled in state-of-the-art computer and information technologies, when the company has or is planning to install the latest innovations in hardware and software technologies, and when all systems and data bases are compatible with one another. In practice, this utopian situation does not exist. Management can create meticulous plans for the implementation of sophisticated state-of-the-art information systems, but, in the end, management must ask, "Do we have the technological capabilities to create this system?" Often the answer is no. When management is not sure, then the project, if approved, becomes a high-risk project. High-risk projects are addressed within the context of MIS planning in Chapter 10, "MIS Planning."

To put technological risk into perspective, consider this analogy: Would you be willing to lease office space in a 50-story skyscraper that was built by a firm that had never built anything higher than a 2-story home?

Economic Feasibility

Whether in business or government, managers do not decide to implement a computer-based solution just because it sounds like a good idea or it might be fun. An information system, robotics, computer-assisted instruction, or any other use of the computer is like any other investment opportunity—it must be economically justified. In the final analysis, uses of the computer are normally deemed economically feasible if, and only if, *the benefits are greater than the costs.*

Benefits

The benefits of a proposed information system are either *tangible* or *intangible*. The tangible benefits result in monetary savings or earnings. For example, a plant production scheduling system saves a company money by providing information that helps its managers use resources more efficiently than they might without one.

Intangible benefits are difficult to quantify, but they are a major consideration when justifying expenditures on MIS and computer solutions. For example, the prestige and convenience associated with a bank's automatic teller machines may lure customers from other banks. As another example, a sales analysis system may help salespersons to identify sales prospects better, but the system does not make the sale. The system does, however, improve business effectiveness. Intangible benefits, such as the availability of critical and timely information, cannot be readily translated into earnings or savings, but they are real benefits, so they must be noted and considered when making decisions on economic feasibility.

Costs

The two types of costs associated with computers and information systems are *one-time* costs and *recurring* costs. The one-time costs include all expenses associated with the development and implementation of a particular use of computer technology. The biggest share of the one-time costs are usually personnel, hardware, and software.

In evaluations, recurring costs are sometimes overlooked. These are costs that are incurred after implementation. The one-time cost of purchasing a product or developing a system may be only a fraction of the recurring costs, especially for an information system. Depending on the system being evaluated, recurring costs could include the programmers' time for systems maintenance, ongoing training, data entry, computer time and data storage, paper and other consumable materials, hardware upgrades, and charges for data communications services.

Benefit/Cost Analysis

Managers weigh benefits against costs by using what is called **benefit/cost analysis**. Simply stated, if the tangible benefits outweigh the cost, the system is normally approved.

Managers are often faced with evaluating the economic feasibility of proposals where the estimated costs are greater than the estimated savings or earnings. In these cases, managers must subjectively weigh the anticipated loss against the intangible benefits. If the intangible benefits appear to be greater than the loss, the system is usually given the go-ahead. For example, during the late 1970s, most banks were evaluating the feasibility of installing automatic teller machines or ATMs. At that time, the benefit/cost ratio was uniformly less than one, yet most banks opted to approve the installation of ATMs. They did so because any anticipated losses were more than offset by intangible benefits, such as increased prestige and improved customer convenience.

IN-HOUSE VERSUS PROPRIETARY SOFTWARE

There are two basic approaches to satisfying a company's information processing needs. The first is to use company employees and/or outside consultants to create an information system that is customized to meet user specifications. The other alternative is to purchase and install a **proprietary software package**. Proprietary software is developed by a software vendor with the intent of selling the end product to a number of potential buyers. With these two options, managers are faced with a classic "make-versus-buy" decision. Some systems should be made in-house and others should be purchased. Each approach has its advantages and disadvantages. The best *application portfolios* have an optimal mix of the two.

In-House Development of Information Systems

Most organizations have the capability to develop information systems using in-house personnel. However, personnel resources are always limited and must be used judiciously. Very few companies can afford the luxury of developing all software in-house; therefore, the projects assigned to in-house MIS professionals must be selected carefully. Typically, systems are selected for in-house development for one of two reasons.

> The nice thing about teamwork is that you always have others on your side.
>
> ——— *Margaret Carty*

- □ A proprietary software package is not available for the application.
- □ A proprietary software package is available for the application, but the company's information processing requirements are so unique that the cost of modifying the package to meet these needs is prohibitive.

There are many ways to design an information system as their are systems analysts and end users. Invariably, each person involved has his or her ideas about how to proceed with the design of an information system. The information systems development process is discussed in detail in Chapters 12, 13, and 14.

Using Proprietary Software

Categories of Proprietary Software

Most proprietary software packages fit into one of these six categories.

- □ Applications software (for example, inventory control, accounts payable)
- □ Systems software (for example, operating systems, programming languages)
- □ Personal productivity software (for example, electronic spreadsheet, word processing)
- □ Data management software (for example, DBMS)
- □ Hardware-related software (for example, performance measurement)
- □ Software engineering tools (for example, computer-assisted software engineering or CASE)

This accountant is interacting with a type of proprietary software package called a financial information system. This system is distributed by Cullinet Software, Inc. The accounts payable subsystem, shown here, enables the accounts payable staff to respond quickly and effectively to management and vendor inquiries.

Cullinet Software, Inc.

The categories of primary interest to user managers are applications software and productivity software. The user manager is usually the ultimate authority for acceptance or rejection for these two categories of proprietary software. The applications software category is emphasized in the remainder of this section. Productivity software packages are discussed in Chapter 6, "End User Computing," and Chapter 7, "Personal Computing."

When a company purchases a proprietary applications software package, it will usually receive the programs (on magnetic tape, diskettes, or microdisks) and associated documentation. Depending on the scope and complexity of the software, on-site education, on-site consultation, and the use of a hotline may be bundled with the price of the software. There are literally thousands of proprietary software packages on the market, from billing systems for veterinarians to general ledger accounting systems for billion-dollar multinational companies. If there is a market for a software product, chances are that some entrepreneur has developed a package to meet the need.

The Make-Versus-Buy Decision

Some companies spend months, even years, developing in-house systems that could have been purchased in the form of a proprietary software package and implemented immediately. Other companies purchase proprietary software packages and spend months, even years, modifying these packages to meet their information needs. In both circumstances, management probably made the wrong make-versus-buy decision. As a rule of thumb, the efforts of programmers, systems analysts, and users should be channeled to the development of systems whose characteristics are unique to that particular company. Those applications that are relatively straightforward are prime candidates for proprietary software packages.

The company that does not take advantage of the potential of proprietary software is not utilizing corporate information services' resources effectively. On the other hand, there are detrimental ramifications for those companies that use packaged systems across the board. These companies forfeit the opportunity to develop valuable in-house expertise. Programmers and analysts who have limited expertise in new system development sometimes have difficulty responding to ad hoc requests and to developing specialized information systems.

User Acceptance of Proprietary Software

When systems are developed by in-house personnel, many traditional procedures (for example, method of accounting, inventory reorder procedures) remain intact. In contrast, the procedures followed by available proprietary software packages are almost always substantially different from those currently in place. When a company purchases a proprietary software package, it is usually faced with two options—change the traditional procedures or modify the proprietary software package. Procedural changes are always hard to accept. Of the proprietary software packages installed during the past decade, over half were modified by the licensee and a third were modified by the vendor for the licensee. Less than 20 percent were installed without modification, and these were usually installed in very small companies.

During the past decade, many companies learned a valuable lesson the hard way! They found out that the expenses associated with the modification of proprietary software may exceed the cost of a commensurate system that is developed in-house. The wise functional area manager will make every effort to implement a packaged system with few or no changes to the software. Of course, some modifications may be critical, but, as a general rule, it is much easier and less expensive to change internal procedures to fit the package than it is to change the software to fit existing procedures. For example, if a packaged billing system uses a six-digit numeric customer number and the company traditionally has used a four-digit alphanumeric customer number, the more prudent approach would normally be to adopt a six-digit account number.

The Not-Invented-Here Syndrome

People in general have delicate egos, and so it is with users and MIS professionals. The ego of a user manager who has developed procedures that have been successful for 20 years is somewhat damaged when he or she finds it necessary to modify these procedures to accommodate a proprietary software package. MIS specialists sometimes consider it a slap in the face when management decides to discard an existing in-house developed information system and purchase a software package, thus denying them the opportunity to use their creativity to develop a new and better system. The result is the *not-invented-here syndrome*; that is, people do not want a new system unless they create it.

It is human nature for programmers and analysts (and sometimes users) to believe that they can develop a better information system than some software vendor on the other side of the country. Even when user and MIS professionals agree that the rational decision is to implement a packaged system, the not-invented-here syndrome is still a factor. In-house people are relegated to modifying and implementing someone else's creation. For some, this is a hard pill to swallow. It is simply more fun and more professionally rewarding to create than to modify. Because of this, MIS specialists, in particular, may be less than enthusiastic about proprietary software packages.

Proprietary Software Pitfalls

Potential buyers of proprietary software packages may benefit by heeding the following warnings:

- ☐ *Recognize that a proprietary software package is not a panacea.* Some managers have unrealistic expectations of a packaged system and as a result are often disappointed with the result. Just because an MRP (manufacturing resource planning) system is operational and people are satisfied with it at ABC, Inc., does not mean that the package will yield the same results at XYZ, Inc.

- ☐ *Don't be first.* It is unfortunate, but many software vendors routinely field test their software at the expense of their clients.

- ☐ *Don't sign the contract before the package is on the market.* A software product may be "90 percent complete" according to the vendor, but "90 percent complete" products often take months, even years, to finish.

- ☐ *Don't assume that the package will require only minor modifications.* The technical ramifications of what may appear to be minor functional modifications can be, and often are, extensive.

□ *Don't proceed without complete or almost complete user acceptance.* Invariably, the implementation of packaged software requires some compromises on the part of all users involved. The user who has not approved the system prior to signing the contract will be reluctant to make the necessary compromises.

□ *Recognize that the purchase price may be as little as 25 percent of the fully installed cost of a packaged system.* Too often, required software modifications are deemed minor and not considered in the economic analysis. In almost every case, software modifications are a major cost of system implementation.

□ *The conversion and implementation phases demand a similar amount of effort, whether the software is purchased or developed in-house.* The implementation of an information system is a formidable task—period.

APPROACHES TO SYSTEMS DEVELOPMENT

There are two fundamental approaches to the development of in-house information systems:

1. The systems development methodology or prespecification approach
2. The prototyping approach

These approaches are included in this chapter to introduce you to the alternatives and are covered in detail in Chapter 12, "Systems Analysis and Programming," and Chapter 13, "Prototyping and Application Development Tools." Chapter 14, "System Implementation," is applicable to both approaches.

Systems Development Methodologies

Because systems development is a team effort, most companies have adopted a standardized **systems development methodology** that provides the framework for cooperation. This step-by-step approach to systems development is essentially the same, be it for an airline reservation system or an inventory management system. As members of a project team progress through the procedures outlined in a systems development methodology, the results of one step provide the input for the next step and/or other subsequent steps. These methodologies, like software, can be purchased commercially or developed in-house.

A company's methodology is usually presented in a manual and depicts the following:

1. Descriptions of the activities to be performed
2. The relationship and sequence of these activities
3. The key evaluation and decision **milestones**—significant points in the development process (for example, programming is completed)

By adhering to a systems development methodology, management can take full advantage of the benefits of the *standardization cycle.* The standardization

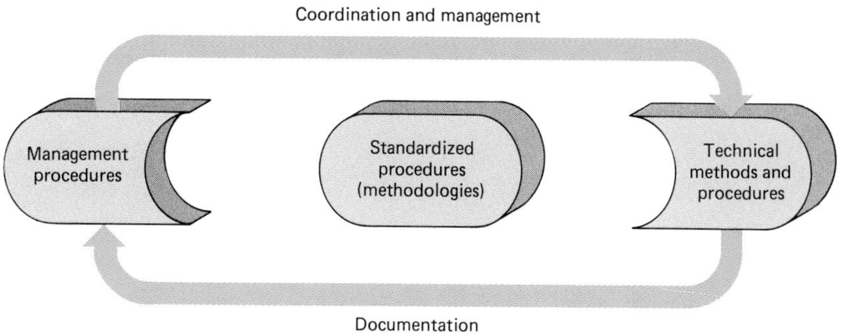

FIGURE 11–2　The Standardization Cycle

cycle in Figure 11–2 illustrates the relationship among standardized procedures (systems development methodologies), technical methods, management, and documentation. Given a methodology that includes technical methods (programming) with accompanying procedures, documentation provides management with the capability to review whether the project is meeting objectives and/or an acceptable level of quality. Through documentation, management also has the capability to monitor project progress. This documentation provides the framework by which management can coordinate and control what takes place within the structure of the standard procedures; thus the cycle is complete.

The methodological approach to systems development is a tool that MIS and user managers can use to coordinate the efforts of a variety of people engaged in a complex process. One of the major premises of a systems development methodology is that users articulate their information processing needs to the project team during the early stages of the project and then make a commitment to stick to these systems specifications through system implementation. These specifications include everything from the functionality of the system to the format of the system's output screens and reports. Because of this premise, this approach to systems development is also called the **prespecification** approach.

Advantages and Disadvantages of Methodologies

A systems development methodology provides a framework by which those involved can coordinate their activities. It also encourages project team members to produce up-to-date and complete documentation (for example, data base design, program logic diagrams, and so on) so that everyone on the project team understands what has been done and what is being done.

Because a methodology identifies and sequences development activities, the project can be planned, monitored, and controlled. Project teams that do not use a methodology of some kind tend to rush through a development project, bypassing important steps along the way. As a result, they often overlook important design considerations, and documentation is neglected. Their rush to finish the system inevitably reduces the overall quality of the end product. A poor-quality information system may result in lower development costs, but it requires considerably more maintenance after implementation. In the long run, a poorly designed system will usually cost more than will a high-quality information system.

It is considered poor judgment to attempt to traverse a chasm in two leaps.

—— *Anonymous*

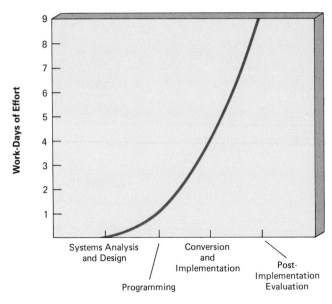

Phases of System Development

FIGURE 11–3   The Cost of an Error
This chart depicts the relative personnel time required to correct a logic error when first detected in the different phases of systems development.

Too few people on a project can't solve the problems—too many create more problems than they solve.

———— *Anonymous*

Figure 11–3 highlights the economics of doing it right the first time. An oversight left undetected becomes more and more difficult to correct as the project progresses from one phase to the next. A logic error that would take about an hour to correct in the systems analysis and design phase of a systems development methodology would take nine workdays to correct after the system is implemented!

All the foregoing advantages assume that users know what processing capabilities and information they want. This is not always the case. In fact, it is more the exception than the rule. Users typically have a good idea what they want, but have difficulty defining exact system specifications until they get a better feel for the operation of the proposed system. Nevertheless, users are asked to decide on and commit to detailed specifications during the early stages of the project. Inevitably, as users gain familiarity with the emerging design of a proposed system, they see opportunities to improve the usefulness of the information and to increase processing efficiencies. However, by this time programming is underway toward achieving the original design specifications. Making changes after the specs are *frozen* (approved and not to be changed) means adding cost to the project and jeopardizing the project schedule. However, as any MIS manager can tell you, if enough heat is applied (pressure from top management), *frozen specifications* can be melted. The prespecification approach to system development leaves little room for flexibility in design. This is its major disadvantage.

A Five-Phase Systems Development Methodology

Systems development methodologies vary in scope, complexity, sophistication, and approach. In practice, systems development methodologies may

Software packages are available that enable project team members to design systems interactively at their workstations. Automated design tools, such as Teamwork/SA from Cadre Technologies, have helped programmers and systems analysts to make significant strides in productivity improvement. With Teamwork/SA, systems analysts can depict the work and information flow in a system that uses any of a variety of structured design techniques.

Cadre Technologies Inc.

be divided into 3, 5, or even 10 phases, but the chronology of the activities remains essentially the same. The best methodologies are those that continually involve the user. After all, systems development is a 50:50 proposition—users are responsible for the functional specifications and MIS specialists are responsible for the implementation of those specs. A five-phase systems development methodology is discussed in this chapter to give you an overview of what is involved in developing and implementing an information system. The phases are:

☐ *Phase I—Feasibility Study.* During phase I, the objective is to determine whether a proposed information systems project is economically and procedurally feasible.

☐ *Phase II—Systems Analysis and Design.* During phase II, systems analysts and users work together to compile detailed system specifications. These specifications are then submitted to programmers for coding in phase III.

☐ *Phase III—Programming.* During phase III, the software needed to support the system is developed.

☐ *Phase IV—Conversion and Implementation.* During phase IV, data files are created, and the new system is implemented and put into operation.

☐ *Phase V—Postimplementation Evaluation.* Phase V begins the *production stage* of the life cycle (see Figure 11–1). During this stage, the system is evaluated periodically to ensure that it continues to meet the information processing needs of the company.

Traditional approaches to phases I, II, and III are covered in detail in Chapter 12, "Systems Analysis and Programming." Automated approaches to accomplishing the tasks in the first three phases are discussed in Chapter 13, "Prototyping and Application Development Tools." Phases IV and V are covered in Chapter 14, "System Implementation." These five phases are equally applicable to systems development in small, one-person businesses and in large companies with several layers of management.

The Responsibility Matrix

A systems development methodology makes it easy to identify *who* does *what*, and *when*. To help you understand better the structure of a systems development methodology, a five-phase methodology is illustrated graphically in Figure 11–4 in the form of a **responsibility matrix**.

The major activities for each of the five phases are listed along the left-hand side of the responsibility matrix. Although some of the activities are accomplished at the same time, they are generally presented in the order in which they are begun.

The individuals and groups directly involved in the development of an information system are listed across the top of the matrix. Each is described as follows:

- □ *Project team*. The project team normally consists of systems analysts, programmers, perhaps the data base administrator, and at least one user who will eventually use the system. Systems analysts design the system and develop the system specifications. The programmers use these specs as guidelines to write the programs. The data base administrator assists the team in designing and creating the data base.
- □ *Information services management*. This group includes the director and other managers in the information services division.
- □ *User management*. This group encompasses all user managers (for example, director of personnel, vice president of marketing) who affect or are affected by the proposed development project.

The entries in the matrix reflect the extent and type of involvement for each of the foregoing individuals and groups.

A Denotes *approval* authority.

C Denotes that the individual/group may be called in for *consultation*.

R Denotes who has primary *responsibility* for a particular activity.

P Denotes that although the individual or group does not have primary responsibility, it has *participating responsibility*.

Phases of Systems Development	Project team	MIS management	User management
Phase I Feasibility study			
I-1. Service request		C	R
I-2. Project team appointment		R	P
I-3. Feasibility evaluation	R	A	A
Phase II Systems analysis and design			
II-1. Existing system review	R		C
II-2. System objectives	R	C	C
II-3. Design constraints	R	C	C
II-4. Requirements definition	R		P
II-5. General system design	R		C/A
II-6. Data base design	R		
II-7. Detail system design	R		C/A
Phase III Programming			
III-1. System specifications review	R		
III-2. Program identification and description	R		
III-3. Program coding, testing, and documentation	R		
Phase IV Conversion and Implementation			
IV-1. System test	R		P
IV-2. System conversion	R		P
Phase V Postimplementation Evaluation			
V-1. Postimplementation evaluation	R		C
V-2. System maintenance		R	P

Key: A = Approval   R = Primary responsibility
         C = Consultation   P = Participating responsibility

FIGURE 11–4   Systems Development Responsibility Matrix
The project team has direct responsibility for most systems development activities, but MIS and user managers have participating responsibilities and are called upon for consultation and approval.

Companies using systems development methodologies or the prespecification approach usually have a responsibility matrix or something similar to it. The more detailed methodologies may have literally hundreds of activities. The manual for a company's systems development methodology normally contains detailed descriptions for the numbered activities in the responsibility matrix and standardized forms to aid project team members in the development process. Figure 11–5 contains an example of a standardized form, called the "Cost Report," that is used during Phase I—Feasibility Study to summarize the costs of the feasibility study; the estimated costs of design, development, and implementation; and the monthly recurring costs associated with an operational information system.

Form:	COST REPORT		No. F120	Date	
System Title:				ID	

Budget Center _____

Cost Item	Phase I	Phase II–IV		Phase V — Estimated Monthly Recurring Costs			
	Actual Cost	Estimated Cost	Actual Cost	Year 1	Year 2	Year 3	Year 4
Labor							
Mat/Eq User							
Computer Center							
Travel Per diem							
Transportation							
Miscellaneous							
Budget Center							
Total Cost							
Savings–F110							
Net Cost							

FIGURE 11–5 Standardized Form

This is one of many standardized forms that might accompany a systems development methodology. The "Cost Report" form is used to summarize estimates of one-time and recurring costs associated with a particular project. The costs are presented by phase for each budget center. The circled numbers are cross-references to detailed explanations in the methodology manual on how to complete a particular item in the form.

Prototyping

Prior to the early 1980s, virtually all in-house systems development was done in accordance with some methodology, or it was done very informally with no guidelines for programmers and analysts. The informal approach was inefficient and difficult to manage. In recent years, the technology has finally begun to have a positive impact on the systems development process. Sophisticated hardware and software are now available that enable the project team to work with users to develop a **prototype system**, a model of a full-scale system. This approach is called **prototyping**. The objectives of prototyping are threefold.

□ To analyze the current situation.

□ To identify information needs.

□ To develop a scaled-down model of the proposed system.

In effect, a prototype system permits users a "sneak" preview of the completed system. A typical prototype system:

□ Handles the main transaction-oriented procedures.

□ Produces critical reports.

□ Permits rudimentary inquiries.

Once users gain hands-on experience with the prototype system, they are in a better position to comment on the proposed design and to fine-tune their information processing needs.

Prior to the early 1980s, a prototype system would probably have cost almost as much as a completed full-scale information system. But, today, project team members can use fourth-generation languages and application generators to create a subset of the proposed system that, to the user at a workstation, appears and acts very much like the finished product. Chapter 13, "Prototyping and Application Development Tools," describes the prototyping process and the tools and technologies that make prototyping possible.

Systems Development in Practice

Over the years, MIS managers have become accustomed to the structure and success of systems development methodologies, and they are reluctant to give them up. Nevertheless, the trend is to taking advantage of the latest technology and to prototyping. In practice, tradition and trend are merging. Relatively few companies rely solely on prototyping for system development. Those that have adopted the prototyping philosophy have created hybrid approaches that combine the best of the two approaches so that they can realize the advantages of the structure of a systems development methodology and the flexibility of prototyping.

LEGAL CONSIDERATIONS IN SOFTWARE DEVELOPMENT

Companies try to develop systems and use the computer within the boundaries of any applicable law. Unfortunately, the laws are not always clear, because many legal questions involving computers and information processing are being debated for the first time. To no one's surprise, computer law is the fastest-growing type of law practice.

Laws governing computer and information processing are few, and those that do exist are subject to a variety of interpretations. A few federal laws are in force, and most of the states have adopted laws, but these are only the skeleton of what is needed to direct an orderly and controlled growth of automation. Only now are lawmakers beginning to recognize the impact of computers, and legislation is slow in coming. Critics say that the bottleneck is our lawmakers' reluctance to become computer literate.

Negligence

The two main causes of illegal information processing activity are negligence and fraud. Negligence causes someone external to the organization to be unnecessarily inconvenienced and is usually a result of poor input/output control. For example, a woman who was essentially communicating with a computer was continually sent dunning notices and visited by collection agencies for not making payments on an automobile. This was after she had completed payment in full. Although the company's records and procedures were in error, the company forcibly repossessed the automobile without thoroughly checking its procedures and the legal implications. The woman had to sue the company for the return of her bought-and-paid-for automobile. The court ordered the automobile returned and the company to pay her a substantial sum as a penalty.

This is a clear case of a misinterpretation of a computer maxim—*GIGO* (garbage in, garbage out). GIGO does *not* stand for "garbage in, gospel out." Some people take the accuracy of computer output for granted. The company blamed the incident on a mistake by the computer. The court stated that people enter data and interpret output and that the people affected should be treated differently from punched cards. *Trust in the infallibility of a computer does not constitute a defense in a court of law.* This incident points out the importance of careful system design and exhaustive testing.

Fraud

The other area of illegal information processing activity is a premeditated or conscious effort to defraud the system. For example, a couple of programmers at one bank created an unauthorized savings account into which they placed thousands of "extra" pennies each day. They did this by modifying programs to round down on all interest calculations and put the "extra" penny in one of the programmer's savings accounts rather than in the customer's savings account. Eventually those pennies became a considerable sum of money. This is an example of fraud. Any illegal entry into a computer system for the purpose of personal gain is considered fraud. Over 50 percent of all computer frauds are internal; that is, they are committed by employees of the organization that is being defrauded. About 30 percent of those defrauding employees are MIS specialists who work in an information services division.

The Privacy of Personal Information

More media and legislative attention has been attracted to the issue of an individual's privacy than to negligence or fraud. The individual must be afforded certain rights regarding the privacy of data or of information relating to him or her. However, these rights have yet to be uniformly defined by our lawmakers. In the absence of definitive legislative guidelines, the following principles are offered for consideration.

1. People should be made aware that data are being collected about them and aware of how these data are to be used.

2. A person should be permitted to inspect his or her personal data and information.

3. A person should be permitted to supplement or clarify personal data and information.

4. Data and information found erroneous or irrelevant must be removed.

5. Disclosure of personal information should be limited to those with a need to know.

6. A log should be maintained of all persons inspecting any individual's personal information.

7. Adequate safeguards must be in place to ensure the security of personal data and information (for example, locked doors, passwords).

MANAGEMENT OF SYSTEMS DEVELOPMENT PROJECTS

Quality and Commitment

Most systems development projects are accomplished by interdisciplinary project teams under the direction of a project leader. The objective of the project leader is to install a quality system within budget on or prior to a preset deadline. This is not an easy task. One problem is that, for any given project, members of the team are usually drawn from three or more organizational entities, such as programming, systems analysis, and the affected user groups. This creates a situation where each member may have two supervisors—his or her regular supervisor and the project leader. The key to success in this *matrix management* environment is for each supervisor to respect all personnel commitments to projects not under his or her control. For example, the sales manager cannot commit the assistant sales manager for 30 percent of his or her time to a major development project and then revoke that commitment once the project is underway. On the surface, this appears to be a minor problem, but this often happens and, when it does, it invariably has disastrous effects on team progress.

The Project Leader

The project leader has traditionally been selected from the ranks of systems analysts; however, some organizations are appointing users as project leaders. Some managers are convinced that the project leader should be intimately familiar with the technology and procedures involved in developing the proposed system. This requirement narrows the field to MIS professionals. Other managers are equally convinced that the most important quality of a project leader is that he or she be intimately familiar with the functional area being addressed by the proposed system. This requirement usually implies that a user should be appointed as the project leader. Each approach has had its successes and failures. During the early 1980s, the trend was to make users project leaders. Information services divisions were having difficulty obtaining full user cooperation, so they made users the project leaders and therefore the *owners* of the proposed system. By doing this, the user becomes responsible for the quality and on-time completion of the project.

SYSTEMS DEVELOPMENT AND QUALITY ASSURANCE

Q. I have recently been hired by the information systems department of a well-known company. The company management has decided to create a quality assurance group with the emphasis on protecting the firm's on-line production systems from undue downtime, either from program or other software errors. My managers do not seem to be able to give us a clear-cut direction on how to do this and have asked the newly formed quality assurance organization to present its views on how to perform this function. We have come up with numerous proposals but keep running into walls. Any advice you have will be welcome.

A. Studies have shown that it takes approximately 50 times the effort to rectify errors found after implementation than for those found during the design phase. The message is loud and clear! The quality assurance group should be an integral part of the development effort from the time the project is approved, not just after implementation.

The quality assurance function, though well established in some organizations, is nonexistent in most. Properly charged, the QA group can have a positive effect on the quality of design, documentation, and ultimately, the efficiency and effectiveness of the system. Quality assurance encourages the do-it-right-the-first-time approach. A good many computer centers are tiring of having to do systems over and have opted to establish a QA group and integrate it into the systems development process.

Project Management Variables

There are four variables in project management (see Figure 11–6):

- Quality
- Scope
- Resources (people and money)
- Time (schedule)

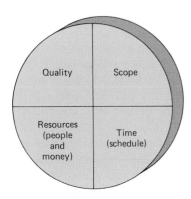

FIGURE 11–6 The Four Variables in Project Management

Changing any one of these variables affects one or more of the other variables.

One major problem facing information services managers is that once the quality and scope of the proposed system are agreed upon, the resources are committed, and the schedule is completed, a high-level manager changes something. For example, he or she might change the scope, availability of resources, or the deadline (time). Changing any one of these variables affects one or more of the other variables. For example, suppose that halfway through a project, a user decides to add another layer of sophistication to the proposed information system. That is fine, but to do so, something has to give in one or more of the other variables. If the scope of the project is increased without a commensurate increase in resources, the quality of the end product will suffer. A project cannot retain a desired level of quality if cutbacks are made in personnel commitments without a commensurate decrease in the scope of the project. Once these relationships are understood by all concerned, project management becomes a doable task. A primary reason that MIS managers have promoted project sponsorship by the user is to eliminate or minimize frequent changes or, at a minimum, to encourage users to recognize the impact of their requests on the project.

AXIOMS FOR SYSTEMS DEVELOPMENT

The following axioms, if taken to heart by both MIS and user personnel, will result in better information systems and an overall smoother corporate operation.

□ *Don't defer automation indefinitely.* There is a point at which it becomes economically advisable for a transaction-based manual system to be automated (see Figure 11–7). In manual systems, the typical solution to problems associated with increased volume is to hire more people. With this solution, the cost of processing the five-hundredth transaction is the same as the cost of processing the first. Although the initial outlay for automating a system is substantial in terms of time and dollars, the cost per transaction processed decreases as volume increases. Figure 11–7 is based solely on transaction processing and does not reflect the intangible or informational benefits derived from a computer-based system.

□ *Divide and conquer.* Address systems development by dividing the system into modules that are small enough to be intellectually manageable. Lack of communication is one of the most serious deterrents to quality information systems. Once systems are modularized, interactions can be effectively concentrated on a single segment of the system. The result is an efficient transfer of information between user and MIS personnel.

□ *Don't begin detailed specifications prematurely.* The project team should not advance from one level of generalization to the next until the current level is understood and agreed upon by all concerned. Depending on the complexity of an information system, there may be as many as eight levels of generalization. The project team should resist the temptation to address "bits and bytes" during the early stages of systems

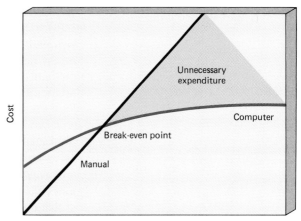

FIGURE 11–7 The Break-Even Point
Every manual system has a break-even point. When the number of transactions processed exceeds this point, it is economically advantageous to convert to a computer-based information system.

development. Unfortunately, in the prespecification approach, it is not uncommon for members of the project team to begin programming long before the general systems design is complete. Skipping levels of generalization will invariably result in unnecessary reworking.

☐ *Include performance criteria in the system design.* The quality and/or performance of an information system should be measurable. The criteria for success should be identified prior to development, and the capability to evaluate the system relative to these criteria should be built into the system design. This allows user managers to determine if the system is meeting objectives and to pinpoint operational deficiencies. For example, one criterion might be a requirement to enable the processing of 500 user inquiries per hour during peak processing periods while keeping response times under 1.5 seconds.

☐ *Emphasize consistency of quality throughout the systems development process.* Quality should be continuous and consistent throughout the systems development process. For example, one of the activities in the responsibility matrix of Figure 11–4 cannot be slighted in favor of another. The only way this can be achieved is through good project management. The resultant system is no better than the quality of the output of the lowest-quality activity. In the example of Figure 11–4, neglecting of the system acceptance test in favor of an intense effort during parallel operation violates the consistency of effort rule. In these cases, quality always suffers.

☐ *Adopt a systems development methodology.* The benefits of following the guidelines of a systems development methodology far exceed the burdens. The merits of a methodology are discussed earlier in this chapter.

☐ *Develop a prototype of the proposed system.* The prototyping process enables users to familiarize themselves better with the proposed system and to provide more meaningful direction to the design team. The benefits of creating a prototype system have been discussed earlier in this chapter.

☐ *Document during development.* Documentation can be used to structure the development process. Some project teams neglect documentation until after implementation. Project teams adopting this strategy find themselves covering the same territory more than once. For example, a user manager is interviewed by the project team and no notes are taken. Studies have shown that without written documentation, only a small percentage of what transpires at a meeting can be recreated after several weeks' elapsed time.

☐ *Abort obviously ineffective projects.* As the say goes, "Don't throw good money after bad." Projects should be terminated once it becomes apparent that the output of a particular project will not live up to the user's expectation or is no longer consistent with corporate objectives. Sometimes momentum, blind commitment, or wishful thinking cause poorly conceived and/or poorly designed systems to be completed and installed. Information systems with unhappy users have little chance of any long-term success.

If there's one pitch you keep swinging at and keep missing, stop swinging at it.

——— *Yogi Berra*

- The four stages of a computer-based information system comprise the system life cycle. They are birth, development, production, and death.

- A feasibility study is usually conducted before management commits corporate resources to the development and implementation of an information system. The scope of the feasibility study encompasses technological feasibility, economic feasibility, a comparison of system and corporate objectives, and an investigation of the proposed system's compatibility with existing and other proposed information systems.

- In the final analysis, uses of the computer are normally deemed economically feasible if, and only if, the benefits are greater than the costs. The benefits of a proposed information system are either tangible or intangible.

- Managers use benefit/cost analysis to weigh the benefits of a proposed system against the associated costs. The two types of costs associated with computers and information systems are one-time costs and recurring costs.

- There are two basic approaches to satisfying a company's information processing needs. The first is to use company employees and/or outside consultants to create an information system that is customized to meet user specifications. The alternative is to purchase and install a proprietary software package.

- Most proprietary software packages fit into one of these six categories: applications software, systems software, personal productivity software, data management software, hardware-related software, and software engineering tools.

- When a company purchases a proprietary software package, it is usually faced with two options—change the traditional procedures or modify the proprietary software package.

- The not-invented-here syndrome sometimes has an impact on user and MIS acceptance of a proprietary software package.

- Buyers of proprietary software packages should be aware of possible pitfalls. Some rules to follow to avoid these pitfalls include: don't sign the contract before the package is on the market, don't assume that the package will require only minor modifications, and don't proceed without complete or almost complete user acceptance.

- The two fundamental approaches to the development of in-house information systems are the systems development methodology or prespecification approach and the prototyping approach.

- The process of developing a computer-based information system is essentially the same, regardless of the information system being developed. Some companies follow a systems development methodology that provides the framework for cooperation between the various people involved in a development project.

- A systems development methodology is usually presented in a manual and depicts the activities to be performed, the relationship and sequence of these activities, and the key milestones.

- One of the major premises of a systems development methodology is that users articulate their information processing needs to the project team during the early stages of the project and then make a commitment to stick to these systems specifications through system implementation.

- An oversight in system design that is left undetected becomes more and more difficult to correct as the project progresses from one phase to the next.

- In the long run, a poorly designed system will usually cost more than will a high-quality information system.

- Systems development methodologies vary in scope, complexity, sophistication, and approach. The activities in the methodology can be presented in a responsibility matrix. The matrix shows when and to what extent individuals and groups are involved in each activity of the systems development process.

- A representative project team charged with developing an information system will normally consist of systems analysts, programmers, perhaps the data base administrator, and at least one user.

- Sophisticated hardware and software are now available that enable the project team to work with users to develop a model of a full-scale system called a prototype system. This approach to the development of in-house information systems is called prototyping.

- The objectives of prototyping are to analyze the current situation, identify information needs, and develop a scaled-down model of the proposed system.

- A typical prototype system handles the main transaction-oriented procedures, produces critical reports, and permits rudimentary inquiries.

- A prototype system, which is created primarily with fourth-generation languages and application generators, enables users to test out the fundamental operation of a proposed system prior to full implementation.

- Some companies have adopted a hybrid approach to systems development that enables them to combine the structure of the prespecification approach with the flexibility of prototyping.

- The two main causes of illegal information processing activity are negligence and fraud. Negligence causes someone external to the organization to be unnecessarily inconvenienced and is usually a result of poor input/output control. Fraud is a premeditated or conscious effort to defraud the system.

- The privacy of personal information is an important issue in the ongoing operation of information systems. The individual must be afforded certain rights regarding the privacy of information relating to him or her.

■ The objective of an MIS project leader is to install a quality system within budget on or prior to a preset deadline.

■ In some companies, users are appointed as project leaders for MIS projects. As such, they "own" the system and are responsible for the quality and on-time completion of the project.

■ The four variables in project management are quality, scope, resources, and time. Changing any one of these variables affects one or more of the other variables.

■ If followed, these and other axioms can result in better information systems and an overall smoother corporate operation: don't defer automation indefinitely; rather, divide and conquer, emphasize consistency of quality throughout the systems development process, develop a prototype of the proposed system, and document during development.

IMPORTANT TERMS

benefit/cost analysis

frozen specifications

GIGO (garbage in, garbage out)

intangible benefit

matrix management

milestones

prespecification

proprietary software package

prototype system

prototyping

responsibility matrix

system life cycle

systems development methodology

tangible benefit

REVIEW EXERCISES

1. In which stage of the information system life cycle are systems "conceived"? "Maintained"?

2. What are the two main causes of illegal information processing activity?

3. What is normally included in a manual for a systems development methodology?

4. Name the project management variables.

5. What are the two basic approaches to satisfying a company's information processing needs?

6. What four questions must be resolved to assess the feasibility of a proposed information system adequately?

7. Associate each of the following types of software with a particular category of proprietary software: DBMS, marketing information system, and presentation graphics.

8. Name the two types of costs associated with computers and information systems.

9. What is the not-invented-here syndrome?

10. When are uses of the computer normally deemed to be economically feasible?

11. Why does the operating expense per transaction for a computer-based information system decrease as the volume increases?

12. What type of system is a model of a full-scale information system?

DISCUSSION QUESTIONS

1. Much needed legislation in the computer and MIS areas is slow in coming. Critics say that the bottleneck is our lawmakers' reluctance to become computer literate. Suggest other reasons.

2. Under what circumstances should management consider "melting" frozen specifications?

3. A company is investigating the feasibility of enhancing the existing human resources information system to include a skills inventory subsystem. The subsystem will enable managers to search for employees who have particular skills. Give two examples of intangible benefits that might result from such a subsystem. Give two examples of tangible benefits.

4. Some companies prefer to incorporate all benefits into the benefit/cost analyses, including intangible benefits. They claim that by presenting intangible benefits in terms of dollars and

cents, they can take the subjectivity out of the evaluation. Is this the case? Explain.

5. If all managers in positions of authority are in agreement that a proposed MIS is needed and will be a value to the company, is there any reason to conduct a feasibility study? Explain.

6. Discuss the advantages and disadvantages of appointing a senior systems analyst to be the project leader on a multimillion-dollar MIS project. Do the same for the appointment of a user to the project leader position.

7. What is to be gained by incorporating the ability to measure system performance into the design of an information system?

8. Discuss the advantages and disadvantages of the prespecification approach to systems development.

9. In general, is it better to change internal procedures to fit a particular proprietary software package or modify the software to fit existing procedures? Discuss.

10. One of the recommendations in the chapter regarding the purchase of proprietary software is "don't be first." Why?

11. In the chapter, seven principles for dealing with the privacy of personal information are presented. Discuss the merits of each of these principles. Can you suggest other applicable principles?

12. A company recruits people to become programmer/analysts. All project team members do both programming and systems analysis. In what ways would this affect the systems development methodology presented in the responsibility matrix of Figure 11–4? Discuss the effects this arrangement would have on career development.

13. Would it be possible for a company with 600 employees to maintain a skeleton information services division of about five MIS professionals and use commercially available packaged software for all their computer application needs? Explain.

14. Corporate management is routinely confronted with a "make-versus-buy" decision regarding software. Discuss the advantages and disadvantages of each alternative.

15. Discuss the rationale for the "divide-and-conquer" approach to system design.

16. Figure 11–3 illustrates how it is increasingly time-consuming to correct a logic error in a system design as the project progresses. Explain why this is the case.

17. Large companies are less apt to choose proprietary software solutions than are small and medium-sized companies. Why?

APPLICATION CASE STUDY 11–1
Economic Feasibility

The Situation

John Robson, the manager of the Computer Services Department at Gabriel Industries, was asked to evaluate six projects from the standpoint of technological risk and business priority (see Application Case Study 10–2, "MIS Operational Planning"). The projects, which are referenced or described in Applications Case Study 10–2, are

1. Developing and implementing a new accounts receivable system.
2. Upgrading the batch personnel/payroll system to on-line.
3. Implementing an information center.
4. Designing and implementing a corporate communications network.
5. Upgrading the material requirements planning (MRP) system to include just-in-time inventory planning.
6. Upgrading the batch order processing system so that Gabriel's customers can place orders using EDI.

Prior to making his final recommendations regarding the order of implementation for the proposed projects, John Robson plans to investigate the economic feasibility of the projects.

The Assignment

1. In preparation for the economic feasibility analyses of the projects, John Robson has asked you to do the following for *each* of the six projects:

a. *List potential tangible benefits.* That is, without attempting to estimate the actual dollar amounts, identify benefits that may result in quantifiable monetary savings or earnings. For example, the "just-in-time" ordering of materials will reduce the inventory holding cost.

b. *List potential intangible benefits.* That is, identify benefits that are difficult to quantify but may make a contribution to the organization's objectives. For example, upgrading of the personnel/payroll system will reduce payroll errors, resulting in fewer complaints from employees. This, in turn, is likely to improve employee morale.

c. *List probable one-time cost items.* That is, without attempting to estimate the actual dollar amounts, identify costs that occur only once. For example, when implementing the data communications network, a one-time cost will be incurred for the installation of the data channels.

d. *List probable recurring cost items.* That is, without attempting to estimate the actual dollar amounts, identify costs that occur repeatedly. For example, any project that requires the purchase of additional hardware will incur ongoing maintenance charges. For each item in this list, specify whether the expense is fixed (*F*) or variable (*V*) in nature. A fixed expense does not change with the volume of information processing activity, while a variable expense increases as volume increases.

2. If the project requires specific application programs, do you recommend that Gabriel develop the software in-house or acquire proprietary software? Justify your choice.

APPLICATION CASE STUDY 11–2

Legal Considerations in Software Development

The Situation

Que Software has developed an on-line multiple listing system for realtors (see Application Case Study 8–3, "A Network-Based Commercial Service Operation," and Application Case Study 9–3, "Data Management for Real Estate Operations"). The system, called Que List, will be marketed to regional realtor associations as a turnkey package. Typically, realtor associations have a board of governors who have overall responsibility for the operation of the association. A small staff carries on the day-to-day operations. When a board of governors selects the Que-List system, Que Software installs the hardware and software, provides documentation, and trains the association's staff. Also, unlimited use of a telephone "hot line" for one month is included in the purchase price of Que-List. Thereafter, the hot-line service is available on a per call charge, or unlimited usage can be continued for an annual fee. Updates to the Que-List system (if any) are provided at no cost for one year; thereafter, they must be purchased from Que Software.

Real estate agents or their clerks enter the listings (properties for sale) into the system from their workstations in the real estate offices or from their portable personal computers. Agents and clerks record any changes to the status of the property (reduction in sale price, sold) in a similar manner.

The realtor association is responsible for the ongoing operation of the system, for the maintenance of the hardware, for the installation of software upgrades as provided by Que Software, and for the adherence to proper backup procedures.

The Assignment

For a Que-List system to function properly, people at several layers of responsibility must meet their obligations. These layers are

□ *Que Software*: develops and installs the system (both as an organizational entity and individual employees).

□ *The realtor association*: operates the system for its members (both as an organizational entity and individual employees).

□ *Real estate agents and their clerks*: data entry.

□ *Property sellers and buyers*: relate correct information to agents.

Your assignment is to analyze the legal considerations pertaining to the Que-List system.

1. Que Software has certain obligations to realtor associations who purchase the Que-List system. Complete the following sentences:

   a. "Que Software warrants that the Que-List system will...."

   b. "Que Software is not responsible for any ... and is not liable for any resultant damages."

2. Discuss the potential for negligence, fraud, and invasion of privacy by personnel in a real estate office. Consider the viewpoints of clients and of other realtors.

3. Discuss the realtor association's responsibilities and liabilities regarding

   a. Modification of the Que-List software.

   b. Performing backups of the software and the database.

   c. Providing on-line access to the Que-List system.

4. Discuss the responsibilities and liabilities regarding the proper functioning of the Que-List system for

   a. Personnel employed by Que Software (systems analysts, programmers, salespersons, and so on).

   b. Personnel employed by a realtor association (programmers, computer operators, and so on).

CHAPTER 12

Systems Analysis and Programming

KEY TOPICS

CHAPTER OVERVIEW

This chapter contains an explanation of the activities that a project team completes during the systems analysis, systems design, and programming stages of the prespecification approach to systems development. MIS professionals have completed these or similar activities during systems development for the past three decades. Even with the recent onslaught of technological advances in software development techniques, these traditional activities have tremendous momentum and continue to be very popular among MIS professionals. New technologies for enhancing the effectiveness of the traditional approach to software development, including prototyping, are discussed in Chapter 13, "Prototyping and Application Development Tools."

THE SYSTEMS DEVELOPMENT PROCESS

You can freeze the users' specs, but they won't stop expecting.

—— *Anonymous*

A Cooperative Effort

The systems development process is a cooperative effort between users and MIS professionals. MIS professionals are familiar with the technology and how it can be applied to meet a business's information processing needs. On the other hand, users have in-depth familiarity with their respective functional areas and the information processing needs of the organization. The skills and knowledge of these two groups complement one another and can be combined to create any type of information system during the systems development process. The process is applicable to any of the information systems discussed in Chapter 2, "The MIS and Decision Support Systems," or Chapter 3, "Artificial Intelligence and Expert Systems." However, the end product of the traditional systems development process is usually a management information system.

The Prespecification Approach to Systems Development

In Chapter 11, "Systems Development and Management," each of the two fundamental approaches to the in-house development of information systems is briefly described: *systems development methodology* (or *prespecification*) and *prototyping*. This chapter contains follow-up discussions of the activities that take place during the systems analysis, systems design, and programming stages of a typical systems development methodology. The prototyping approach is covered in Chapter 13, "Prototyping and Applications Development Tools." The prespecification approach is based on the premise that exact information processing needs can be identified and systems specifications can be determined during the early phases of a development project. In theory, once set, the specifications are frozen (cannot be revised) until implementation is complete. In practice, specs are sometimes revised during the development process. The advantages and disadvantages of this approach are discussed in Chapter 11.

The Service Request

Increased productivity and information are critical to economists, plant supervisors, engineers, nurses, advertising executives, and managers in every profession. These people are continually searching for applications for information processing that results in increased productivity and better, more timely information. There are two ways to initiate the systems development process. The first is to incorporate the idea for a system into the MIS plan. The MIS plan, a product of user and MIS cooperation, identifies, describes, and prioritizes system development projects (see Chapter 10, "MIS Planning"). The other way to initiate the systems development process is via the **service request**. The user takes the initiative and submits a service request to the individual or committee with the authority to approve or reject the request. Minor ad hoc requests for information services are evaluated within the context of existing approved projects. Major requests are usually integrated into the MIS planning process.

The service request, which is normally compiled by the user, gets the ball rolling. When user departments do not have the technological expertise or resources to meet certain information needs (for example, departmental computing), they submit a service request to the information services division. The request is typically for one of the following:

☐ A new information system
☐ An enhancement of an existing system (this includes one-time requests to meet specific information requirements)

Because the extent of the requests usually exceeds the capabilities of available personnel and computing resources, each request must be evaluated relative to its contribution to the corporate need and its consistency with the MIS strategic and operational plans. A completed service request would include the following information:

☐ The objectives for the proposed system
☐ The fundamental operation of the proposed system
☐ The scope of the proposed system
☐ The problems associated with the present system
☐ The justification for the proposed system
☐ The long-range objectives for the proposed system

An example of a completed service request for a college residence operations system is shown in Figure 12–1.

Assessing the feasibility of a proposed system is discussed in Chapter 11. Based on the results of the feasibility study, a decision is made either to *table* the project or to *approve* it. Approval triggers one of two activities: the purchase and implementation of a proprietary software package or the initiation of an in-house development project. This chapter emphasizes the latter.

Setting the Stage for Systems Development

A project team is appointed by managers of the information services division and the affected user departments. One member of the team is appointed project leader. As explained in Chapter 11, the project leader can be either a user or an MIS specialist.

Every information systems project has a deadline. The project team leader is assigned a certain number of programmers, systems analysts, users, and other personnel with specialized expertise, depending on the scope and orientation of the project. Based on the deadline and the resources available, the project leader establishes an implementation schedule. A typical project schedule shows a projected start date and a completion date for each phase in the systems development methodology (see Figure 12–2).

You may be able to con some people into committing to an unreasonable deadline, but you can't bully them into meeting it.

—— *Anonymous*

OBJECTIVES FOR PROPOSED SYSTEM

Primary Objectives:
1. To automate the room assignment procedure
2. To automate the inventory record keeping task

Supporting Objectives:
1. To provide the staff of Residence Operations with an instrument to use in making more efficient and effective decisions
2. To integrate existing procedures

FUNDAMENTAL OPERATION OF PROPOSED SYSTEM

The basic work flow of the present system will be followed. Areas to be computerized include:

1. Freshman roommate and room assignment procedure
2. Inventory control
3. Student billing to include damage billing
4. File updates (to be on-line)
5. Report generation including:
   On-campus population by building and room number
   Off-campus population
   Home address labels
   Statistical reports of residence halls population
   Room assignment notification

SCOPE OF PROPOSED SYSTEM

Other Organizational Interfaces:
1. Bursar and Registrar — to supply student information
2. Campus Maintenance — for general repairs and upkeep on residence halls
3. Dining Service — to inform of the number of students on the various meal plans
4. Admissions Office — to handle housing assignments

Volumes
The proposed system must be able to process approximately 2,100 students in the residence halls. The general student files will include approximately 4,000 students.

PRESENT SYSTEM PROBLEMS

There are a number of problems with the present system:

1. Excessive paper work
2. Time-consuming procedures for assigning rooms and roommates
3. No cross-reference between room inventory and occupancy (i.e., lack of inventory control)
4. No way to systematically isolate recurring maintenance problems

JUSTIFICATION

The proposed system should eliminate those problems noted above, as well as provide information for better decisions. Service to the student will be improved through more responsive procedures.

LONG-RANGE OBJECTIVES

The proposed system will ultimately be incorporated into the proposed student information system, scheduled for implementation in three years.

FIGURE 12–1   A Service Request
This service request was completed for a college residence operations system.

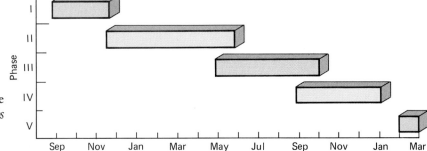

FIGURE 12–2   Bar Graph of a Project Schedule
Systems development project teams often use bar graphs to schedule activities and track progress toward implementation.

SYSTEMS ANALYSIS

The following results are realized during the systems analysis stage of the systems development process:

- ☐ Existing system review
- ☐ System objectives
- ☐ Design constraints
- ☐ Requirements definition

Each of these results defines an activity that is to be accomplished.

Existing System Review

Before designing a new or enhanced MIS, the members of the project team must have a good grasp of the existing work and information flow, be it manual or computer-based. If the existing system is computer-based, it is usually accompanied by some type of documentation. If the existing system is manual, the project team may need to compile a basic documentation package that includes a list and examples of all reports and documents, system data elements and files, and a graphic illustration of the current work and information flow.

The work and information flow of the present system is documented by reducing the system to its basic component parts: *input*, *processing*, and *output*. A variety of design techniques can be used to depict graphically the logical relationships between these parts. Perhaps the most popular, although not necessarily the best for all situations, is **flowcharting**. Other more "structured" techniques include **data flow diagrams** and **hierarchical plus input-processing-output** (**HIPO**). Data flow diagrams are introduced later in the systems design portion of this chapter. Flowcharting, HIPO, and other design techniques are discussed in in Module F, "Design Techniques Overview," of "A Short Course in Computer Concepts."

System Objectives

Once the existing system is documented, the project team can begin to identify the obvious and not-so-obvious problem areas, including procedural bottlenecks, inefficiencies in information flow and storage, duplication of effort, deficiencies in information dissemination, worker discontent, problems with customer interaction, inaccuracy of operational data, and so on. Once these are identified, project team members can concentrate their energies on the identification of opportunities for the coordination of effort, the integration of functionally adjacent systems, and the use of information.

By this time, the project team should know what can be achieved with the judicious application of information. However, this knowledge needs to be formalized as system objectives. The project team arrives at general system objectives by engaging in interactive discussions with all end user managers who will ultimately be affected by the proposed system. In the end, everyone should be satisfied that the system objectives are consistent with business needs and complementary to the MIS strategic plan. And everyone concerned should have a clear picture of the direction in which the project is heading.

Design Constraints

The proposed system will be developed subject to specific constraints. The purpose of this activity is to detail, at the onset of the systems development process, any hardware, costs, schedule, procedural, software, data base, and operating constraints that may limit the definition and design of the proposed system. If constraints are not defined early in the project, the scope and/or direction of the project may need to be revised once the project is underway. Such revisions are unnecessary and costly. Constraints typically fall into these categories:

□ *Hardware constraints*. If the system is not designed within the limits of available hardware, provision must be made to upgrade the present hardware.

□ *Cost constraints*. Cost constraints include any limits on developmental, operational, or maintenance costs.

□ *Schedule constraints*. Schedule constraints would take into consideration such things as availability of hardware or software and corporate cycles (for example, billing cycle and year-end closing).

□ *Procedural constraints*. Describe any limitations on the sequence in which existing functions are performed or on the degree of standardization imposed by corporate policy.

□ *Software constraints*. Identify any software to which the proposed system must interface (for example, an operating system or a fourth-generation language) and any limitations on the use of proprietary software (for example, a single-site license agreement).

□ *Data base*. Describe any constraints on the use of particular data bases and on modifications to these data bases.

□ *Operating constraints*. These constraints usually relate to system reliability, accuracy, response time, turnaround time, capacity, frequency of processing, and so on.

These and any other constraints that may in some way limit the design of the proposed system are identified before the system's information processing requirements are defined.

Requirements Definition

Functional Specifications

An information system provides data processing capabilities and information for decision making. In this activity the project team completes a needs analysis that results in a definition of the data processing and information requirements for the proposed system. To accomplish this task, the project team begins by gathering information.

- They interview users.
- They ask users to respond to written questionnaires.
- They examine the documentation of the existing system.
- They study the decisions made within the context of the proposed system.

Probably the best way to determine system requirements is the user interview. The people who are currently using the system and will be using the proposed system are the best source of information. User feedback during interviews is the basis for the project team's **functional specifications** for system input, processing, and output requirements (information needs). The functional specifications describe the logic of the system from the perspective of the user (input/output, work and information flow).

At this point, the emphasis turns toward *output requirements*. In the systems development process, the team begins with the desired output and works backward to determine input and processing requirements. Outputs are typically printed reports, workstation displays, or some kind of transaction (for example, purchase order, payroll check). At this time, outputs are described functionally. The actual layout and detailed content of a display screen or report is specified during the system design phase.

The User Sign-Off

In the prespecification approach to systems development, the user is asked to "sign off" at certain stages of the process. The **user sign-off** is the signature of an authorized user that in effect says:

- The user has examined the work to date in detail.
- All work and specifications completed to date are consistent with user objectives.
- The user is committed to the specifications as defined by the project team.

The prespecification approach to systems development requires the user to sign off on the design specifications at various stages of the process. This programmer/ analyst is demonstrating the proposed layouts of the input/output screens for an inventory management subsystem to the plant manager. The plant manager is encouraged to make recommendations to improve the layouts and other aspects of the system design until he signs off, after which time, the specs are frozen.

> The trouble with doing something right the first time is that nobody appreciates how difficult it was.
>
> —— *Walt West*

The reason for periodic user sign-offs is twofold: First, to ensure that the user is involved and is made aware of project progress, and second, to enable the project team to make steady progress toward project completion.

Prior to the formal user sign-off, project teams often had difficulty making continuous forward progress. During this period, users might informally concur with current project specifications, and then, a month later, they would ask for something substantially different. During the 1960s and much of the 1970s, this three-steps-forward-two-steps-backward approach to systems development was more the norm than the exception. The user sign-off was made a part of the systems development process to eliminate, or at least minimize, costly backtracking.

The key to successful implementation of an MIS is to do it right the first time. To do this, system designers must be deliberate in their analysis of the system and involve all people who will be affected by the system. A conscientious project team that keeps users informed of progress and invites their feedback each step of the way will invariably end up with a quality management information system. The user sign-off is a handy tool that can be used to facilitate this interaction.

SYSTEMS DESIGN

The following results are realized during the systems design stage of the systems development process:

- □ General system design
- □ Data base design
- □ Detailed system design

Each of these results defines an activity that is to be accomplished.

General System Design

System Design—The Creative Process

The design of an MIS is more a challenge to the human intellect than it is a procedural challenge. Just as an author begins with a blank page and an idea, the members of the project team begin with empty RAM (random-access memory) and the information requirements definitions. From here, they must create what can sometimes be a very complex information system. The number of ways that a particular information system can be designed is limited only by the imagination of the members of the project team.

A well-designed computer-based system inevitably requires that major changes be made in procedures, in the form of the input, in the type of output, and in the way the system interacts with users and other computer systems. This point cannot be overemphasized—think "Change!" when designing an information system. By definition, members of MIS project teams are agents of change.

One popular, but less than creative, approach to design is to "computerize" the existing system. That is, design an upgraded system that simply mirrors the logic and procedures of the existing system. This is not a very effective approach to system design. It is considered poor technique, not to mention a demonstration of lack of creativity, to design an MIS within the confines of human capabilities and limitations (if the existing system is manual) or obsolete technology (if the existing system is automated). When state-of-the-art MIS capabilities are ignored in the design of a system, the system's shortcomings become painfully apparent soon after implementation.

Completing the General System Design

The project team analyzes the existing system and assesses information processing requirements and then develops a **general system design** of the proposed system. The general system design, and later the detailed design, involves continuous communication between members of the project team and all levels of users (clerical through strategic), as appropriate. After evaluating several alternative approaches, the project team translates the system specifications into a general system design.

At a minimum, the documentation of the general design of the proposed system includes the following:

- ☐ A graphic illustration that depicts the fundamental operation of the proposed system (for example, data flow diagrams).
- ☐ A written explanation of the graphic illustration.
- ☐ General descriptions of the outputs to be produced by the system, including display screens and hard-copy reports and documents. (The actual layout—for example, spacing on the page or screen—is not completed until the detail system design.)

Beware analysis paralysis.

———— *Anonymous*

Chapter 15, "An MIS Case Study," contains numerous examples of data flow diagrams that depict the work and information flow in an MIS.

Data Base Design

The data base is the common denominator in any system. It contains the raw material (data) necessary to produce the output (information). In manufacturing, for example, you decide what you are going to make, then you order the raw material. In the process of developing an information system, you decide what your output requirements are; then you determine which data are needed to produce the output. In a sense, the output requirements can be thought of as input to data base design.

With the trend to integrated on-line systems and DBMS technology, at least part, and perhaps all, of the data base may already exist. Creation of the data base may not be necessary; however, it is likely that data elements will need to be added to the data base.

The first step in data base design is to compile a **data dictionary**. A data dictionary, illustrated in Figure 12–3, is simply a listing of all data elements in the data base. An existing data base will already have a data dictionary. The data elements, together with certain descriptive information, are listed along the left-hand side of the data dictionary "matrix." The data dictionary

No.	Name	Description	Format	Coded	Responsibility	Best sellers' list (R)	Over due report (R)	On-loan report (R)	Patron data base (D)	Book data base (D)	Checkout display (S)	Acq. data entry (S)	Data base update (S)
1	TITLE	Complete title of book	X(150)	No	Acquisitions	X	X	X		X	X	X	X
2	ISBN	ISBN number	9(13)	No	Acquisitions				X	X	X	X	X
3	PUBYR	Year of publication	9(2)	No	Acquisitions	X				X		X	X
4	AUTHOR	Name of an author	X(25)	No	Acquisitions	X				X		X	X
5	PUBL	Name of publisher	X(25)	No	Acquisitions					X		X	X
6	DUE	Due date of book	9(6)	No	Circulation		X			X	X		
7	CARDNO	Patron card number	9(4)	Yes	Circulation					X	X		
8	FNAME	First name of patron	X(10)	No	Circulation			X		X	X		

Report (R)   Data base (D)   Display screen (S)

FIGURE 12–3   Data Dictionary

Companies maintain an up-to-date data dictionary with descriptive information for all data elements. The use or occurrence of these data elements is cross-referenced to appropriate files, reports, and source documents. The entry in the "Format" column describes the data element's length and whether it is numeric (9) or alphanumeric (X).

provides the bases for the creation or modification of a data base. Data base management systems and structures (hierarchical, network, and relational) are discussed and illustrated in Chapter 9, "Data Management."

The matrix portion of Figure 12–3 is completed *after* the data base organization has been determined and *after* the reports and input screens are designed. The data elements are then cross-referenced to reflect their occurrence in data base records, reports, and input screens.

Detailed System Design

The **detailed system design**, which is the detailed input/output, processing, and control requirements, is the result of analysis of feedback from users on the general system design. The general system design depicts the relationship between major processing activities and has enough detail for users to determine whether or not that is what they want. The detailed design includes *all* processing activities and the input/output associated with them.

The detailed design is the cornerstone activity of the systems development process. It is here that the relationships between the various components of the system are defined. The system specifications are integrated with the project team's imagination and skill to create an information system. The detailed system design is the culmination of all previous work. Moreover, it is the *blueprint* for all project team activities that follow.

A number of techniques aid programmers and analysts in the design process. Each of these techniques permits the design of the system to be

Until recently, automated design tools were very expensive and limited to the mainframe environment. Only large companies could justify the cost of these proprietary software packages. Today, sophisticated software for automated system design is reasonably priced and available for the microcomputer environment. Excelerator/RTS™ from Index Technology Corporation, a totally integrated PC-based package, offers all the capabilities needed to design and document even the most complex of systems.

Index Technology Corporation

graphically illustrated. One of these techniques, data flow diagrams, is briefly discussed here. Flowcharting, HIPO, and other design techniques are discussed in in Module F, "Design Techniques Overview," of "A Short Course in Computer Concepts." Other automated aids to systems development are presented in Chapter 13, "Prototyping and Application Development Tools."

Structured System Design

It is much easier to address a complex design problem in small, manageable modules than as one big task. This is done using the principles of **structured system design**. The structured approach to system design encourages the top-down design technique. That is, the project team divides the system into independent modules for ease of understanding and design. The HIPO **structure chart** in Figure 12–4 illustrates how a payroll system can be conceptualized as a hierarchy of modules. In the hierarchy, the system is decomposed into modules at finer levels of detail until a particular module can best be portrayed in terms of procedural logic. Eventually, the logic for each of the lowest-level modules is represented in detailed in step-by-step diagrams that illustrate the interactions between input, processing, output, and storage activities for a particular module.

Data Flow Diagrams

Data flow diagrams, or **DFD**s, enable analysts to design and document systems using the structured approach to systems development. Only four symbols are needed for data flow diagrams: entity, process, flow line, and data store. The symbols are summarized in Figure 12–5, and their use is illustrated in Figure 12–6.

□ *Entity symbol.* The entity symbol, a square with a darkened border, is the source or destination of data or information flow. An entity can be a person, a group of persons (for example, customers or employees), a department, or even a place (for example, warehouse). The interac-

FIGURE 12–4 HIPO Structure Chart
This structure chart breaks a payroll system down into a hierarchy of modules.

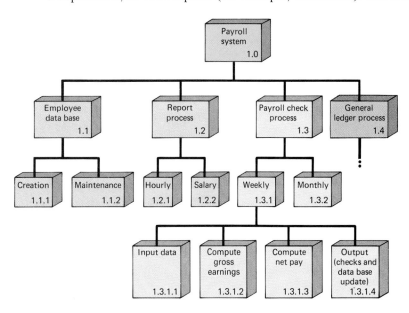

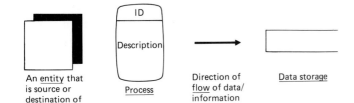

An entity that
is source or
destination of
data/information

ID

Description

Process

Direction of
flow of data/
information

Data storage

FIGURE 12–5   Data Flow Diagram Symbols

tions between the various entities in a typical business system are illustrated Figure 1–3 in Chapter 1, "Information Processing in Perspective."

☐ *Process symbol*. Each process symbol, a rectangle with rounded corners, contains a description of a function to be performed. Process symbols also can be depicted as circles. Typical processes include "enter data," "calculate," "store," "create," "produce," and "verify." Process symbol identification numbers are assigned in levels (for example, processes 1.1 and 1.2 are subordinate to process 1).

☐ *Flow line*. The flow lines indicate the flow and direction of data or information.

☐ *Data store*. These data storage symbols, open-ended rectangles, identify storage locations for data. A storage location could be a file drawer, a shelf, a data base on magnetic disk, and so on.

In the example of Figure 12–6, a data flow diagram documents that portion of a personnel system that produces payroll checks. Processes 1 and 2 deal with the employee data base, but in process 3 the actual payroll checks are produced. In the bottom portion of Figure 12–6, process 3 is *exploded* to show greater detail. Notice that the second-level processes within the explosion of process 3 are numbered 3.1, 3.2, 3.3, and 3.4. Process 3.1 could be exploded to a third level of processes to show even greater detail (for example, 3.1.1, 3.1.2, and so on).

There is no one best analytical or design technique. If you elect to take a course on systems analysis and design, you will gain a deeper understanding of data flow diagrams and the other techniques discussed in "A Short Course in Computer Concepts." Most companies encourage their MIS professionals and users to use the combination of techniques that best fits the circumstances for a particular system or program.

The principles of data flow diagrams, flowcharting, HIPO, or any of a dozen other design techniques are not difficult to learn. However, applying these techniques to the design of information systems requires practice, practice, and more practice. You can learn how to do word processing, but that does not mean that you are going to write the great American novel. These techniques are just tools. It's your skill and imagination that make an information system a reality.

The Presentation of Information

Within the context of an information system, information can be presented in many ways. During the systems design process, members of the project team work in close cooperation with the users to describe each output

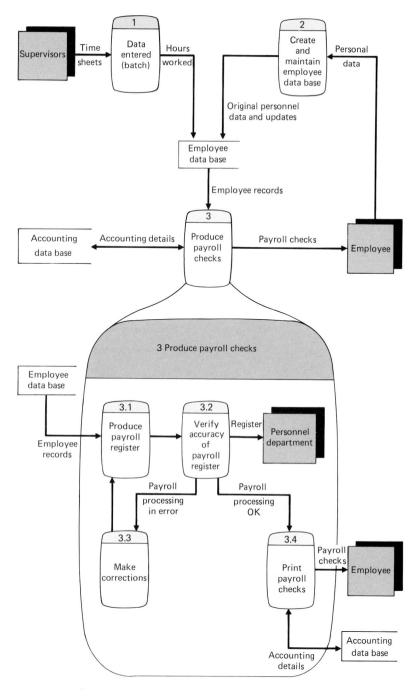

FIGURE 12–6 Data Flow Diagram

In the example data flow diagram of a payroll system, process 3 is exploded to show greater detail.

that will be generated from the proposed system. An output could be a hard-copy report, a display of information, or a transaction document (an invoice). Transaction documents are typically periodic (monthly invoices). Reports, or generally the presentation of information in either hard-copy or soft-copy format, can be either *periodic* or *ad hoc*.

Most reports fit into one of the following classifications based on content.

☐ *Comprehensive reports.* The comprehensive report presents all pertinent information about a particular subject. For example, a comprehensive report might contain the past and current salaries for each employee in the information services division.

Information Services Division Salaries

Name	Last Year	This Year	% Change
Abel	$30,000	$33,000	+10%
Acker	22,000	23,320	+ 6
Bitner	35,000	37,800	+ 8
Danner	45,000	48,150	+ 7
Furr	34,500	37,950	+10
Grotz	41,200	43,260	+ 5
Kapp	28,400	29,820	+ 5
Ronca	55,000	60,500	+10

☐ *Summary reports.* The summary report presents a summary of information about a particular subject. For example, a report might contain the total and an average of the past and current salaries for the employees in the information services division.

Information Services Division Salary Summary

	Last Year	This Year	% Change
Total	$291,100	$313,800	+7.8%
Average	36,388	39,225	+7.8
No. employees	8		

☐ *Exception reports.* Exception reports highlight critical information. For example, a manager might wish to have an exception report that lists only those employees in the information services division who received salary increases of 10 percent or more.

Information Services Division Salaries

Name	Last Year	This Year	% Change
Abel	$30,000	$33,000	+10%
Furr	34,500	37,950	+10
Ronca	55,000	60,500	+10

Both periodic and ad hoc reports also can be classified with respect to time. Not surprisingly, time-based classifications deal with the past, the present, and the future.

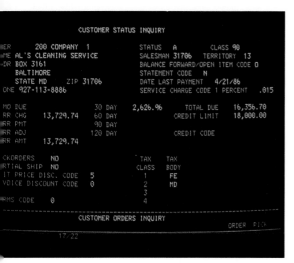

During detailed system design, the project team creates the detailed specifications for all input to and output from the system. Typically, analysts and users experiment with several alternatives before selecting the one that displays the information in the most effective manner. Project team members worked closely with affected users, primarily customer service personnel and salespersons, to create the layout for the "Customer Status Inquiry" in the photo.

Courtesy of International Business Machines Corporation

□ *Historical reports.* Historical reports are generated from data that were gathered in the past and do not reflect the current status. Reports based solely on historical data are rare in practice. Most historical reports involve comparisons between current and historical data, such as those in the preceding examples.

□ *Status reports.* Status reports reflect the current status. For example, the following report presents the salary ranges for the three levels of personnel in the information services division.

**Information Services Division
Salary Ranges**

Level	Salary Range
Professional	$37,800–60,500
Technical	33,000–37,950
Administrative	23,320–29,820

□ *Predictive reports.* Predictive reports are often the output of models that are based on current and historical data. An example of a predictive report might be a forecast of next year's budget requirements for the information services division.

Information Services Division Budget Worksheet

Category	Predicted Budget Requirements
Salaries	$ 338,000
Hardware	350,000
Software	150,000
Materials	44,000
Travel	40,000
Education	25,000
Miscellaneous	68,000
Total	$1,015,000

Both periodic and ad hoc reports can be classified with respect to content and time. The various types of reports are summarized graphically in Figure 12–7.

Of course, not all reports contain numbers and text. Some of the most effective ways of presenting information involve the use of graphics. The presentation of information in the form of graphics is discussed in Chapter 7, "Personal Computing."

The User Interface

Once the input and output requirements have been defined, the project team designs the **user interface**. The user interface is the mechanism by which the end user interacts with the system. It is through the user interface that the end user issues commands, such as requesting a display of a report

FIGURE 12–7   Summary of Types of Reports
Periodic and ad hoc reports can be classified with respect to content and time.

or making a routine inquiry to the data base. User interfaces are usually designed as a hierarchy of **menus**. The user issues commands and initiates operations by selecting activities to be performed from this hierarchy of menus. These hierarchies are sometimes called **menu trees**. When the users select an item from the **main menu**, they are often presented with another menu of activities, and so on. Depending on the items selected, the user may progress through as few as one and as many as eight levels of menus before processing is initiated for the desired activity.

A menu can appear as a **bar menu**, a **pull-down menu**, or a **pop-up menu**. The menu options in a bar menu are displayed across the screen. The result of a menu selection from a bar menu at the top of the screen is often a pull-down menu. The subordinate menu is "pulled down" from the selected menu option and displayed as a vertical list of menu options. The entire menu is shown in a **window** directly under the selected menu option and over whatever is currently on the screen. A window is a rectangular display that is temporarily superimposed over whatever is currently on the screen. Like the pull-down menu, the pop-up menu is superimposed over the current screen in a window. A pop-up menu can be called up in a variety of ways, including function keys or as the result of a selection from a higher-level pop-up menu.

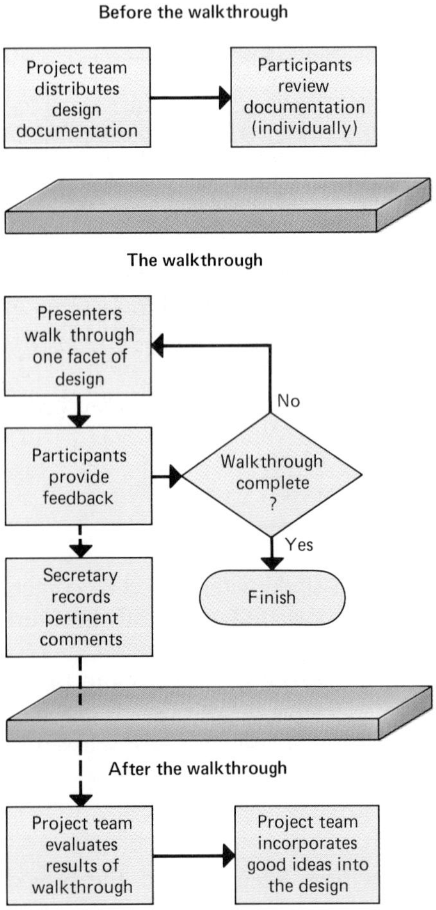

Structured Walkthrough

We are human beings, and we make mistakes. We overlook things and do not always select the best way to design a program or a system. To do the best job possible, project team members often ask other interested and knowledgeable persons to review and evaluate what they have done. They invite input and feedback within the context of a peer-review procedure called a **structured walkthrough**. A structured walkthrough is effective in minimizing the possibility of something being overlooked or done incorrectly.

The people involved in a structured walkthrough include the following:

□ *Members of the project team*. One or all of the project team members act as presenters and explain that portion of the system that they authored.

□ *Coordinator*. The coordinator is in charge of the walkthrough and coordinates the interaction between presenters and participants.

□ *Participants*. The participants are selected on the basis of their knowledge of and interest in the topic being presented. They should have no direct involvement with the project.

□ *Secretary*. The secretary keeps a written record of significant points made during the structured walkthrough.

□ *Neutral manager* (optional). A neutral manager is often invited to attend the first walkthrough. The mere presence of a manager encourages everyone involved with the walkthrough to attend to the matter at hand. (Presenters sometimes take critical comments personally and the ensuing debate can actually result in a breakdown of communication.)

FIGURE 12–8 The Structured Walkthrough

The procedures of a structured walkthrough are illustrated in Figure 12–8. The material to be reviewed (usually the documentation of the system design) is distributed several days in advance to appropriate persons. This lead time gives the participants and others an opportunity to examine the material at their convenience so that they will be prepared to make a meaningful contribution at the walkthrough. During the actual walkthrough, the presenter(s) explains the design and the accompanying documentation. This is done by "walking through" the system, step by step, perhaps with the aid of one of the design tools (for example, data flow diagrams). Participants make suggestions and the merits of these suggestion are discussed interactively by all in attendance. Pertinent comments are recorded by the secretary. After the walkthrough, the project team evaluates all recommendations and incorporates the good ideas into the system design.

Structured walkthroughs are valuable for obtaining meaningful feedback during the systems development process. Several structured walkthroughs are scheduled for most information system projects. When project team members know that their work is going to be scrutinized by their colleagues, the quality of the end product is enhanced.

Systems Analysis and Design: Mainframes Versus Microcomputers

Applications designed for micros are usually oriented to supporting an individual or a department. Applications designed for mainframe computers are usually oriented to supporting an enterprise. Although the scope and orientation of the application are different, the approaches used for the development of information system are essentially the same for both types of computers.

PROGRAMMING

Programming languages have continually improved during the past four decades. Early or first-generation programming languages required the programmer to write many complex instructions to accomplish simple tasks. Each new generation of programming languages reduced the number of instructions required to perform tasks and made the instructions easier to comprehend and code. The first three generations of languages are discussed and illustrated in Module E, "Programming Concepts and Languages," in "A Short Course in Computer Concepts." Significant improvements have been made in programming technology during the past decade. The more recent user-oriented fourth-generation programming languages are introduced in Chapter 6, "End User Computing." The principles and use of these languages are discussed in Chapter 13, "Prototyping and Application Development Tools."

The following results are realized during the programming phase of the systems development process:

☐ System specifications review
☐ Program identification and description
☐ Program coding, testing, and documentation

PROGRAMMING PRODUCTIVITY

Q. As the newly appointed supervisor of Corporate Systems Development, I am very interested in increasing the productivity of my staff and would like to obtain information on techniques for improving programming productivity.

I would appreciate any information you might have.

A. The I-want-it-yesterday syndrome surrounding the MIS activity has delayed attempts of many to increase productivity in general and in programming specifically. But attention to a few basic concepts, tools, and techniques can render enormous increases in programmer productivity.

- □ *Mode of program development*—benefits of interactive program development are overwhelming.

- □ *Choice of programming language*—match to application requirements; use state-of-the-art compilers; use fourth-generation languages and application generators where appropriate.

- □ *Automated program development tools*—analysis, design, coding, test data generation, and documentation can be expedited by using automated tools.

- □ *DBMS*—to make programs independent of data structure.

- □ *Systems development methodology*—integrated procedures for structured analysis, design, and documentation.

- □ *Library of reusable code*—modules that are indexed and cataloged for easy reference.

- □ *Chief programmer teams*—with flexibility to relocate line programmers to priority projects.

- □ *Structured walkthroughs*—peer reviews to ensure the accuracy and quality of the end product.

- □ *Scheduling*—to level work load and keep individual assignments at or above 100 percent.

- □ *De-emphasis on extremely efficient code*—today, a savings of 2 milliseconds/transaction does not merit the expenditure of 2 workmonths of effort.

- □ *Recruiting practices*—all programmers are not created equal; 10 percent more salary may yield 100 percent more production.

- □ *Retention*—one person retained may result in a work-year of effort saved in the recruiting and training of a replacement.

Although this list is not exhaustive, it should provide a starting point for self-examination.

Each of these results defines an activity that is to be accomplished. With detailed specifications in hand, programmers are now ready to write the programs needed to make the proposed system operational.

System Specifications Review

During the programming phase, programming becomes the dominant activity, and the programmers really go to work. The system specifications completed during system analysis and design are all that is needed for programmers to write, or "code," the programs to implement the information system. Before getting started, programmers must review the system specifications created during system analysis and design. These include:

- □ Printer output layouts of reports and transactions.
- □ Workstation input/output screen layouts.

- □ Data dictionary.
- □ Files and data base design.
- □ Controls and validation procedures.
- □ Data entry specifications.
- □ General system design.
- □ Detailed system design.

Once programmers have reviewed and understand these specs, the programming task is begun. A superior programming effort will go for naught if the system specifications are incomplete and poorly written. As the saying goes, "Garbage in, garbage out."

Program Identification and Description

An information system needs an array of programs to create and update the data base, print reports, permit on-line inquiry, and so on. Depending on the scope of the system and how many programs can be generated using application development tools, as few as three or four or as many as several hundred programs may need to be written before the system can be implemented. At this point, all programs needed to make the system operational are identified and described. A typical program description would include:

- □ Type of programming language (COBOL, BASIC, FOCUS, Ideal, and so on).
- □ A narrative of the program, describing the tasks to be performed.
- □ Frequency of processing (for example, daily, weekly, on-line).
- □ Input to the program (data and their source).
- □ Output produced by the program.
- □ Limitations and restrictions (for example, sequence of input data, response-time maximums, and so on).
- □ Detailed specifications (for example, specific computations and logical manipulations, any tables).

Program Coding, Testing, and Documentation

Armed with system specifications and program descriptions, programmers can begin the actual coding of programs. The development of a program is actually a project within a project. Just as there are certain steps that the project team takes to develop an information system, there are certain steps a programmer takes to write a program (see Figure 12–9).

Everything should be made as simple as possible, but not simpler.

———— *Albert Einstein*

Step 1. Describe the problem.

Step 2. Analyze the problem.

Step 3. Design the general logic of the program.

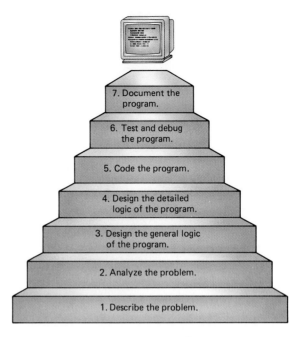

FIGURE 12–9   Steps in Writing a Program

Step 4. Design the detailed logic of the program.

Step 5. Code the program.

Step 6. Test and debug the program.

Step 7. Document the program.

These steps are described in more detail in the following sections.

Step 1. Describe the Problem

The "problem" is described in the program descriptions. For example, a problem might be to write a program that accepts numeric quiz scores and assigns a letter grade. Another problem might be to write a program that identifies and prints the names of customers whose accounts are delinquent.

Step 2. Analyze the Problem

In this step the programmer breaks the problem into its basic components for analysis. "Divide and conquer" is one of the key strategies for both systems analysts and programmers. Although different programs have different components, a good place to start with most programs is to analyze the *output, input, processing,* and *file-interaction* components. The programmer would then identify important considerations in the design of the program logic. At the end of the problem analysis stage, the programmer should have a complete understanding of what needs to be done and a good idea of how to do it.

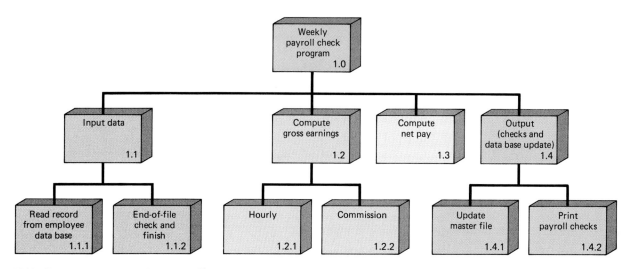

FIGURE 12–10 Program Structure Chart
*The logic of a payroll program to print weekly payroll checks can be broken into modules
for ease of understanding, coding, and maintenance.*

Step 3. Design the General Logic of the Program

Next, the programmer has to put the pieces together in the form of a logical
program design. Any of the systems design tools mentioned earlier in the
chapter are applicable to program design as well. As in the information system,
the program is also designed in a hierarchical manner, or from the general
to the specific. For example, Figure 12–10 illustrates a structure chart for a
program to print weekly payroll checks (hourly and commission employees
are processed weekly). The structure chart permits a programming problem
to be broken down into a hierarchy of tasks. A task can be broken down
into subtasks, as long as a finer level of detail is desired. The most effective
programs are designed so they can be written in **modules**, or independent
tasks. It is much easier to address a complex programming problem in
small, more manageable modules than as one big task. This is done using
the principles of **structured programming**.

In structured programming, the logic of the program is addressed
hierarchically in logical modules (see Figure 12–10). In the end, the logic
of each module is translated into a sequence of program instructions. The
modules interact with one another by passing data back and forth. By dividing
the program into modules, the structured approach to programming reduces
the complexity of the programming task. Some programs are so complex
that if taken as a single task, they would be almost impossible to conceptualize,
design, and code.

In the general design of a particular program, the programmer creates
a logic diagram for the overall program and for each module. These diagrams
depict the major processing activities and the relationships between these
activities. By first completing a general flow diagram, the programmer makes
it easier to investigate alternative design approaches. The example program
flowchart of Figure 12–11 illustrates the general design of task 1.3, "Compute
net pay," from the structure chart of Figure 12–10. Once the programmer

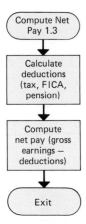

FIGURE 12–11   General Flowchart

The logic of module 1.3, "Compute Net Pay," of Figure 12–10 is depicted in a general flowchart.

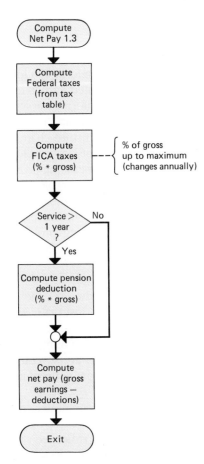

FIGURE 12–12   Detailed Flowchart

The logic of the general flowchart in Figure 12–11 is depicted in a detailed flowchart.

is confident that he or she has identified the best approach, a more detailed flow diagram can be completed.

Step 4. Design the Detailed Logic of the Program

The detailed design contains more detail in the graphic representation of the program logic. This level of detail includes all processing activities and their relationships, calculations, data manipulations, logic operations, and all input/output.

The flowchart in Figure 12–12 is a more detailed representation of the logic presented in the general flowchart in Figure 12–11. In programming, the level of detail portrayed in the graphic representation of the logic is a matter of personal preference. The flowcharts in Figures 12–11 and 12–12 illustrate the difference between general and detailed logic diagrams. Other programmers might prefer to have more or less detail.

Step 5. Code the Program

Whether a programmer "writes" or "codes" a program is a matter of personal preference. In this context, the terms are the same. In step 5, the graphic and narrative design of program development steps 1 to 4 is translated into machine-readable instructions, or programs. If the logic is sound and the design documentation (for example, flowcharts, data flow diagram, and so on) is thorough, the coding process is relatively straightforward.

The best way to write a program is to work directly from the design documentation and compose the program interactively at a workstation or PC. Programs are much easier to write when broken down into several small and more manageable modules. Programmers have shown time and time again that it takes less time to code ten 50-line modules than it does to code a single 500-line program.

When a programmer writes a program, the following documentation should be on hand:

☐ The data dictionary (with standardized names for variables, for example, NET, HOURS)

☐ The coding scheme for coded data elements

☐ The file layouts and data base schemas

☐ Printer and video display layouts

☐ Data entry specifications

☐ The program design documentation (for example, HIPO charts, flowcharts, program descriptions, and so on)

Every programming task does not require original code. Many organizations maintain libraries of frequently used program modules, called **reusable code**. For example, several programmers might use the same reusable code as the basis for one of their input modules.

Step 6. Test and Debug the Program

Once the program has been entered into the system, it is likely that the programmer will encounter at least one of those cantankerous **bugs**. A

THE CHIEF PROGRAMMER TEAM

Q. I have heard the chief programmer team concept mentioned several times during recent conferences and would appreciate knowing more about it.

A. The chief programmer team is formed to accommodate the hierarchical modular development of programs. Top-down design is paralleled in the team organization.

The basic team consists of a chief programmer, assistant chief programmer, librarian, and up to four programmers. The *chief programmer* identifies the modules (of no more than three workweeks each) in a hierarchical manner, writes the job control and "driver" program(s), and assigns and supervises the development of subordinate modules. The *assistant* or *backup chief programmer* maintains an overall knowledge of the project and does production programming. The *librarian's* functions may include maintaining the documentation library, assisting in program testing, and monitoring test file status. *Programmers* should have a range of skill levels so that easy and complex programs can be assigned to rookies and veterans, respectively.

Many companies have modified this basic team structure and member responsibilities to suit their circumstances better.

---

bug is an error in program syntax, logic, or input/output. Ridding a program of bugs is the process of **debugging**.

SYNTAX ERRORS   Debugging a program is a repetitive process, whereby each successive attempt gets the programmer one step closer to a working program. The first step is to eliminate **syntax errors**; the programmer gets a syntax error when one of the rules for writing instructions (for example, placement of parentheses, spelling of commands, and so on) is violated. The errors on the first run are mostly typos (for example, REED instead of READ). Most compilers and interpreters display an **error message**. The error message identifies the number of the statement causing the error, and it usually provides the programmer with an idea of what the error might be (for example, "unidentified variable").

LOGIC AND I/O ERRORS   Once the syntax errors have been removed, the program can be executed. An error-free program is not necessarily a working program. The programmer now has to debug the *logic of the program* and the *input/ output formats*. To do this, **test data** and, perhaps, a **test data base** must be created so that the programmer knows what to expect as output. For example, suppose that you write a program to average three grades and assign a letter grade. If your test data are 85, 95, and 75, then you would expect the average to be 85 and the letter grade to be "B." If the output is not 85 and "B," then there is a bug in the program logic.

A program whose logic is sound might have input or output formats that need to be "cleaned up" to meet layout specifications. Suppose that your output looked like this:

THE LETTER GRADE ISB

and the layout specs called for this:

THE LETTER GRADE IS B

Then you would need to modify the output format to include a blank space between IS and the letter grade.

TEST DATA   Test data are an integral part of the test procedure. Test data are made up so that all possible circumstances or branches within the program are tested. Good test data contain both valid and erroneous data. It is always a good idea to introduce erroneous data deliberately to see if error routines are working properly. For example, in a program that averages grades, you might wish to include an error routine that questions grades greater than 100. To test this routine, you simply enter a grade of, say, 108. If the program works properly, the error routine will detect the erroneous data and display an error message. A good programmer lives by Murphy's law, which assumes that if anything can go wrong, it will! Don't assume that whoever uses your program will not make certain errors in data entry.

A program may be bug-free after **unit testing**, but eventually it will have to pass **system testing**, where all programs are tested together. Thorough system testing is essential to high-quality information systems.

You should be careful about when to go to all the trouble it takes to be different.

—— *Andy Rooney*

Step 7. Document the Program

In the business environment, a program may be used every day—for years! Over the life of the system, procedures and information requirements change. For example, because the social security tax rate is revised each year, certain payroll programs must be modified. To keep up with these changes, programs must be updated periodically, or maintained. Program maintenance can be difficult if the program documentation is not complete and up-to-date. A good program documentation package includes the following items:

- □ *Program title.* A brief descriptive title (for example, PRINT__PAY-ROLL__CHECKS)
- □ *Language.* The language in which the program is written (for example, COBOL, BASIC, FOCUS, Ideal)
- □ *Narrative description.* A word description of the functions performed
- □ *Variables list.* A list containing the name and description of each variable used in the program
- □ *Source listing.* A hard-copy listing of the source code
- □ *Detailed program design.* The structure charts, flowcharts, decision tables, and so on
- □ *Input/output layouts.* The printer and workstation display layouts, examples of hard-copy output (for example, payroll check)
- □ *Frequency of processing.* How often the program is run (for example, daily, weekly, on-line)
- □ *Detailed specifications.* The arithmetic computations, sorting and editing criteria, tables, control totals, and so on
- □ *Test data.* A test package that includes test data and expected results (The test data are used to test and debug the program after each program change.)

Some of these documentation items can be included in the actual program as *internal documentation*. Descriptive programmer remarks throughout the program make a program easier to follow and to understand. Typically, the program title, a narrative description, and the variables list would also be included as internal documentation. The example programs in Module E, "Programming Concepts and Languages," in "A Short Course in Computer Concepts" illustrate internal documentation.

CHAPTER HIGHLIGHTS

■ The systems development process is a cooperative undertaking between users who know the functional areas and MIS professionals who know the technology.

■ The two fundamental approaches to the in-house development of information systems are the systems development methodology (or prespecification) and prototyping approaches.

- The two most common ways of initiating the systems development process are to incorporate a systems project into the MIS plan and to submit a service request.

- A service request typically includes short- and long-range objectives, the fundamental operation, the scope, and the justification for the proposed system, and also the problems associated with the present system.

- One of the first duties of a project leader is to create a project schedule.

- During the system analysis and design phase of the systems development process, the following activities are accomplished: existing system review, system objectives, design constraints, requirements definition, general system design, data base design, and detailed system design.

- The work and information flow of the present system is documented by reducing the system to its basic component parts, that is, input, processing, and output.

- System design techniques include flowcharting and other more "structured" techniques, such as data flow diagrams and hierarchical plus input-processing-output.

- The project team arrives at general system objectives by engaging in interactive discussions with all end user managers who are ultimately affected by the proposed system.

- A proposed information system must be developed within the boundaries of any applicable hardware, costs, schedule, procedural, software, data base, and operating constraints.

- User feedback provides the basis for the functional specifications for system input, processing, and output requirements. These specs describe the logic of the system from the perspective of the user.

- In the systems development process, the design team begins with the desired output and works backward to determine input and processing requirements.

- The user sign-off indicates that the user has examined the work, the work and specs meet the objectives, and the user is committed to the specs.

- A well-designed computer-based system will probably require users to adjust to major procedural and input/output changes when it is implemented.

- At a minimum, the documentation for the general system design includes a graphic illustration and explanation of the fundamental operation of the proposed system and general descriptions of the outputs to be produced by the system.

- During systems development, designers describe the output requirements and determine which data are needed to produce the output.

- The detailed system design depicts the relationship between all major processing activities and the input/output associated with them.

- When adhering to structured system design, designers divide the system into independent modules for ease of understanding and design.

- Data flow diagrams enable analysts to design and document systems using the structured approach to systems development. The four symbols used in DFDs are entity, process, flow line, and data store.

- Reports, or the general presentation of information, can be either periodic or ad hoc. Based on content, reports are classified as comprehensive, summary, or exception. Based on time, reports are classified as historical, status, or predictive.

- The user interface is the mechanism by which the end user interacts with the system. User interfaces are usually designed as a hierarchy of menus.

- Structured walkthroughs, a peer-review procedure, are valuable for obtaining meaningful feedback on the proposed system design during the systems development process.

- During the programming phase of the systems development process, programs are written to create the software necessary to make the information system operational. The following activities are accomplished: system specifications review; program identification and description; and program coding, testing, and documentation.

- A typical program description would include type of programming language, a narrative description, frequency of processing, input/output, limitations and restrictions, and detailed specifications.

- For each program, the programmer describes the problem; analyzes the problem; designs the general, then the detailed logic; and codes, tests, and documents the program.

- When a programmer analyzes the problem, he or she breaks the problem into its basic components (output, input, processing, and file-interaction) for analysis.

- The structure chart permits a programming problem to be broken into a hierarchy of tasks, called modules.

- The graphic display of the program logic at the detailed level of design includes all processing activities and their relationships, calculations, data manipulations, logic operations, and all input/output.

- Programmers must debug programs to rid programs of errors in syntax, logic, or I/O.

- Programs are tested individually during unit testing. Eventually they are tested again during system testing, where all programs are tested together.

ad hoc report

bar menu

bug

comprehensive report

data dictionary

data flow diagrams (DFDs)

debugging

detailed system design

error message

exception report

flowchart (Mod. F)

flowcharting (Mod. F)

functional specifications

general system design

hierarchical plus input-
    processing-output (HIPO)
    (Mod. F)

historical report

internal (program)
    documentation

main menu

menus

menu trees

modules

periodic report

pop-up menu

predictive report

process explosion

pull-down menu

reusable code

service request

status report

structure chart

structured programming

structured systems design

structured walkthrough

summary report

syntax errors

system testing

test data

test data base

unit testing

user interface

user sign-off

window

REVIEW EXERCISES

1. Within the context of MIS, what services are usually requested in a user's service request?

2. Name three sources of information that help project team members to define data processing and information requirements for a proposed information system.

3. Differentiate between a program syntax error and a program logic error.

4. Name the four symbols used in data flow diagrams.

5. If process 3.4 in Figure 12–6 were to be exploded to three third-level processes, what would be the numerical labels of the new processes?

6. Give examples of three types of system outputs.

7. Classify the following outputs with respect to content and time: payroll register, third quarter sales forecast, and delinquent accounts report.

8. Describe the contents of a program documentation package.

9. The functional specifications describe the logic of a proposed system from whose perspective?

10. What is the function of the coordinator in a structured walk-through? The secretary?

11. What is the mechanism called that enables the end user to interact with an information system?

12. Name four types of menus.

13. What are the first and last steps in the program development process?

14. What would be included in the documentation of the general design of a proposed information system?

15. Describe the relationship between the data dictionary and the data base.

16. What is the design philosophy called that enables complex design problems to be addressed in small, manageable modules?

17. Name three system design techniques.

18. What is a structure chart, and how is it used?

DISCUSSION QUESTIONS

1. It is well known among MIS specialists that "computerizing" an existing system is a poor choice of design alternatives, yet people still do it. Why?

2. Some programmers are accused of producing "spaghetti code," so named because their indecipherable flowcharts resemble a bowl of spaghetti. What steps should their managers take to eliminate inefficient spaghetti code and improve program quality?

3. Why is the user sign-off a controversial procedure?

4. Compile a service request to upgrade a batch order entry system to an on-line order entry system. Note any assumptions that you make with regard to the existing system.

5. Why are members of an MIS project team asked to "think change" when designing an information system?

6. Discuss the similarities and differences in systems analysis and design for mainframe- and microcomputer-based information systems. Do the same for programming.

7. What are the consequences of not conducting a structured walkthrough after the completion of the detailed system design?

8. Give examples of schedule, procedural, and hardware constraints that might limit the definition and design of a proposed marketing information system for a pharmaceutical company.

9. Design a screen layout for an on-line hospital admittance system. Design only that screen with which the hospital clerk would interact to enter basic patient data. Distinguish between input and output by underlining the input.

10. What is meant by the remark "garbage in, garbage out" as applied to system specifications and programming?

11. Discuss the short- and long-term benefits of designing an information system to be user friendly.

12. Why is it important to spend time documenting and understanding the existing system if it is to be discarded after a new system is developed?

13. Would it be easier for one person or five people to do a relatively simple program? Draw a parallel to the size of a project team.

14. How does adhering to a systems development methodology help a project team to "do it right the first time"?

APPLICATION CASE STUDY 12–1

Analysis and Design of an Order Processing System

The Situation

Compu-Mail is a retailer of computer hardware, software, and supplies. Most sales are made by mail order or by telephone, although Compu-Mail does have a retail outlet. Order processing is handled currently by a computer-based batch system. The system is described in detail in Application Case Study 1–2, "Types of Decisions."

A preliminary analysis of Compu-Mail's order processing system leads to the conclusion that the system should be upgraded to an on-line system. The operation of the proposed system is discussed in Application Case Study 9–1, "Data Management for Order Processing." A project team has been organized to proceed with the development of the proposed order processing system. The team consists of a project leader, two programmer/analysts, and the assistant manager of the Order Processing Department.

The Assignment

Put yourself in the role of a programmer/analyst as you complete the following assignment.

1. Draw a first-level data flow diagram depicting the current batch order processing system. Do not explode any of the processes. Note any assumptions that you make regarding the current system.

2. Draw a first-level data flow diagram depicting the proposed on-line order processing system. Draw a second-level data flow diagram for each process. Note any assumptions that you make regarding the proposed system.

3. The systems development methodology used at Compu-Mail requires a written explanation of the differences between the existing and proposed systems. Write a narrative that identifies those current operations that will be performed differently in the proposed order processing system. Note steps that were performed manually but are now automated, duties that have changed, and timing that has changed.

4. Write a program description for the on-line program that would process a customer order. Limit the scope of the program to order processing; that is, do not include related functions such as the preparation of purchase orders. Use the outline for a program description given in the chapter.

5. Use Figure 12–10 as a format guide and draw a structure chart for the program described. Be sure to include a lower-level module that checks a customer's credit.

6. Draw a detailed system flowchart for the module that checks a customer's credit. In the flowchart, include the different actions taken for the two types of credit checks that occur. The first type of credit check is performed when a customer wants to use a charge card to pay for the order. The second type of credit check is performed when a customer submits an order in the form of a purchase order. Show what actions take place when credit is approved or rejected for each type of credit check. Do not include details on what is considered "good credit."

APPLICATION CASE STUDY 12–2

Analysis and Design of the Que-List System

The Situation

Que Software is a new company that plans to develop turnkey hardware and software packages for the real estate industry. The company's first project is Que-List, an on-line multiple listing system that will be marketed to regional realtor associations. Que-List's fundamental functions are described in Application Case Study 8–3, "A Network-Based Commercial Service Operation." Management functions of the system are described in Application Case Study 9–3, "Data Management for Real Estate Operations." In addition to these business-oriented functions, Que-List contains a client-matching expert system (see Application Case Study 3–1, "Expert Systems") and a natural language interface (see Application Case Study 3–2, "Natural Languages"). Additional operational details are given in Application Case Study 11–2, "Legal Considerations in Software Development."

A project team has been formed to develop the Que-List system. The team consists of a project leader and six programmer/analysts. In addition to these Que Software employees, consultants with specialties in expert systems, networks, and real estate have been retained and will be used as needed.

The Assignment

Put yourself in the role of a programmer/analyst as you complete the following assignment.

1. Draw a first-level data flow diagram depicting the Que-List system. Do not explode any of the processes. Note any assumptions that you make regarding the system.

2. Use Figure 12–4 as a format guide and draw a HIPO structure that breaks the Que-List system into a hierarchy of modules.

3. Construct an example Que-List system report that illustrates each of the following report classifications given (use hypothetical data):

   a. Comprehensive reports

   b. Exception reports

   c. Historical reports

APPLICATION CASE STUDY 12–3

Analysis and Design of an MRP System with Just-in-Time

The Situation

John Robson, the manager of the Computer Services Department at Gabriel Industries, has just received approval to upgrade the material requirements planning (MRP) system to include just-in-time inventory planning. Under this concept, warehousing of materials needed for production is reduced to the bare minimum or abandoned entirely. This concept was discussed in Case Study 11–1, "Economic Feasibility." John Robson plans to use EDI to facilitate the timely placing of purchase orders with vendors.

The basic MRP system is triggered by a production requirements report that shows what finished products must be produced and by what date. The report contains requirements to fulfill current customer orders and the number and types of products which must be manufactured to meet anticipated sales projections. The MRP system consists of several subsystems.

☐ The bill-of-materials subsystem uses a parts explosion to identify all items used in manufacturing a finished product. An item may be an individual part, a sub-assembly (a set of parts), or an assembly (a set of parts and subassemblies).

☐ The scheduling subsystem accesses the personnel database to determine the availability of employees having the necessary skills and training. Also, the subsystem accesses the capacity planning database to determine the availability of production equipment. The MRP software can then produce a detailed schedule of production activities. This schedule indicates what should be produced each day at each production workstation.

☐ The purchasing subsystem then uses the production schedule, the parts explosion, and the current inventory database to generate purchase orders to vendors on an as-needed basis.

The Assignment

1. The project to upgrade the MRP system was approved although no formal request was submitted. Before proceeding further, John Robson wants a formal request for the MRP system. He has asked you to prepare such a request. Use the example shown in Figure 12–1 as a format guide. Note any assumptions that you make regarding the system.

2. Draw a first-level data flow diagram depicting the proposed MRP system. Also, draw a second-level data flow diagram for the process dealing with the just-in-time ordering of raw materials. Note any assumptions that you make regarding the proposed system.

CHAPTER 13

Prototyping and Application Development Tools

CHAPTER OVERVIEW

This chapter covers prototyping as an approach to systems development and a variety of development tools, including the CASE (computer-aided software engineering) tool kit. Prototyping has its own life cycle, but it is often applied within the context of a systems development methodology; therefore, prototyping is discussed as a stand-alone procedure and as an enhancement to a traditional methodology. Prototyping and automated application development tools are presented together in this chapter because the conceptual and functional overlap between the two is substantial.

PROTOTYPING

Prototyping is one of the two fundamental approaches to systems development discussed in Chapter 11, "Systems Development and Management." The other approach involves the up-front specification of user information processing requirements and the use of a systems development methodology. This approach, which is also referred to as the prespecification approach, is covered in detail in Chapter 12, "Systems Analysis and Programming."

The Prototype System

The three objectives of prototyping are:

1. To analyze the current situation.
2. To identify information needs.
3. To develop a scaled-down model of the proposed system.

The scaled-down model, called a **prototype system**, would normally handle the main transaction-oriented procedures, produce the critical reports, and permit rudimentary inquiries. The prototype system gives users an opportunity actually to work with the functional aspect of the proposed system long before the system is implemented. Once users gain hands-on familiarity with the prototype system, they are in a position to be more precise when they relate their information processing needs to the project team.

A prototype system can be anything from a nonfunctional demonstration of the input/output of a proposed information system to a full-scale operational system. Both the prespecification and prototype approaches can result in an information system, but, in practice, most prototype systems are merely models. These models are tested and refined until the users are confident that what they see is what they want. In some cases, the software that was developed to create an initial prototype system is expanded to create a fully operational information system. However, in most cases, the prototype system provides an alternate vehicle for completing the functional specifications activity of a systems development methodology. Incomplete and/or inaccurate user specifications have been the curse of the prespecification approach to systems development. Many companies have exorcised this curse by integrating prototyping into their methodologies.

As a stand-alone technique or as an augmentation to a systems development methodology, prototyping has proven to be an effective technique for creating information systems that meet the users' information processing needs. Most users do not have enough experience in systems design to comprehend what a proposed system will eventually look like and how it will work. To overcome this lack of experience, project teams are building prototype systems to give them an early firsthand look at what the system will look like when it is implemented. The prototyping process enables users to articulate their exact information processing needs to the project team during the early phases of the project and throughout the project. The availability of this high-quality user feedback precludes having to retrofit a less than acceptable system after implementation.

The Emergence of Prototyping

Most managers have a *good idea* of what they want in an information system, but they do not know *exactly* what they want. This is a problem when it comes to developing information systems. Systems analysts and programmers must have precise specifications to create an information system. The prespecification approach forces users into committing themselves to specs long before they feel comfortable with the specs. Realistically, users cannot become comfortable with a system, nor can they recognize the potential of a system, until they have had an opportunity to work with it. In the prespecification approach, user familiarity comes after the fact and too late for quick fixes and inexpensive modifications. After implementation, even small changes to an information system can be time consuming and expensive. This point is highlighted graphically in Figure 11–3 in Chapter 11, "Systems Development and Management."

Ideally, users should experiment with and familiarize themselves with the operation of the proposed system as early in the development process as possible. Systems analysts know that any action that results in the early identification of potential misdirection or errors in design will save time and money.

Prior to the year 1982, the economic feasibility of prototyping was questionable. In fact, a prototype system would probably have cost almost as much as developing the real thing. During the past few years, the price/performance of computing capacity and software development technology have improved dramatically. It is now well within the realm of economic feasibility for a project team to use fourth-generation languages and other prototyping software to create a model of a proposed system that, to the user at a workstation, appears and acts very much like the finished product.

There is always an easy solution to every human problem—neat, plausible, and wrong.

—— *H. L. Mencken*

Approaches to Developing Prototype Systems

Throughout the twentieth century, manufacturers have built prototypes of everything from toasters to airplanes. Automobile manufacturers routinely build prototype cars according to design specifications. However, automobile prototypes have varying degrees of sophistication. Scaled-down clay models are made to evaluate aesthetics and aerodynamics. Ultimately, a full-size fully functional prototype is created that enables the driver and passengers to test all aspects of the car's functionality. If engineers see possibilities for improvement, the prototypes at the varying levels of sophistication are modified and retested until they meet or exceed all specifications. Prototyping is now becoming SOP (standard operating procedure) for software development. Like prototypes of manufactured goods, software prototypes are also created in varying degrees of sophistication:

☐ Nonfunctional prototype systems
☐ Partially functional prototype systems
☐ Fully functional prototype systems

In practice, a given prototype system may exhibit the characteristics of several levels of prototype sophistication.

Nonfunctional Prototypes

The "quick and dirty" way to give users an opportunity to experiment with the operational aspects of a proposed information system is to create a nonworking model of the system. This approach to prototyping, sometimes called **rapid prototyping**, focuses on three aspects of the design:

- The user interface
- Data entry displays
- System outputs

Prototyping tools are available that enable project team members to design demonstration menus and screens. For example, while working with the prototype system, the user is able to select the data entry option from a menu and the desired data entry screen is displayed. Then, the user can key in data, but the data are lost when the user requests another screen; that is, the data entered are superimposed on the data entry screen, but they are not transmitted to the data base. Also, the user can select menu

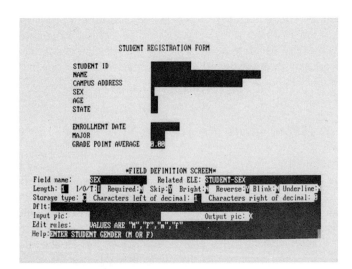

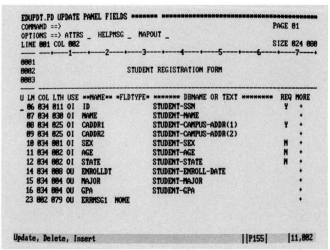

Excelerator, a product of Index Technologies, Inc., is a micro-based software package that enables the automation of many of the tasks associated with systems analysis, design, and documentation. The screen and report design facilities of Excelerator make it a handy tool for prototyping. The first photo illustrates how the software can be employed to design a student registration form. The second screen is automatically generated to indicate which data elements will be needed to insert the information on a completed form. Excelerator can be interfaced with Pansophic Corporation's TELON, an application generator, to generate the COBOL or PL/1 programs needed to produce the student registration form.

options that result in the display of a particular report. In a functional system, the information contained in a report is extracted from a data base, but in a nonfunctional prototype, the the report is based on static test data. At this point in the system development, the content and layout of the report are much more important than are the actual entries.

In nonfunctional prototype systems, the time-consuming technical intricacies of interfacing with an actual data base are avoided while permitting users to familiarize themselves with the proposed user interface and system input/output.

Partially Functional Prototypes

The next level of sophistication in the development of prototype systems is the partially functional prototype. The 80/20 rule is as applicable to information systems development as it is to inventory management (20 percent of the inventory items account for 80 percent of the inventory activity). When applied to information systems, the rule states that 80 percent of the features and functionality of an information system can be realized with 20 percent of the effort required to develop a fully functional system. In general, the more sophisticated but less frequently used features of an information system pose the greatest challenges and demand the lion's share of a project team's effort. The philosophy behind partially functional prototyping is that users, especially at the operational level, can work with most of the basic features of the proposed system during interactive practice sessions. They will even be able to make routine inquiries to the data base.

Many partially functional prototype systems are created under the premise that they will eventually be enhanced to the level of fully functional systems. Once all the kinks in the prototype system are worked out at one level of sophistication, the system can be enhanced to incorporate other user-requested features. After several iterations, the prototype system emerges as a fully functional information system. Those technologies that are used to develop the initial prototype system also can be employed to expand the scope of the system.

Fully Functional Prototypes

The most ambitious approach to prototyping is to create a fully functional prototype system. Typically, such systems are created for the sole purpose of enabling users to experiment with the system. The focus of fully functional prototype systems is functionality; therefore, performance characteristics are ignored. This means that prototype developers can ignore concerns that relate to system efficiency and volume of work. For example, the capacity of a fully functional prototype system may be limited to 10 transactions per minute where the eventual system may need to handle up to 1,000 transactions per minute.

Once familiar with the operation of the proposed system, users can provide meaningful feedback on all aspects of the proposed system. Unlike the partially functional approach, the fully functional approach is not intended to result in an operational system. The results of the fully functional approach are well-defined user specifications that can be used by the project team to create an information system that uses resources more efficiently and can handle an increased volume of work.

Prototyping: The Preferred Approach

In Chapter 11, "Systems Development and Management," the four variables in project management are identified. These variables are quality, scope, resources (people and money), and time (schedule). In the prespecification approach to systems development, project management is an ongoing concern because these variables are constantly changing. Prototyping has enabled managers to better define the scope of a proposed information system and thereby reduce the variability in the project's quality, resource requirements, and schedule. Specifications defined during prototyping are the result of careful examination and experimentation by users; therefore, users are less likely to change their minds once the development of the actual system is underway.

Prototyping enables project team members to home in on exactly what the user wants early in the development cycle. This capability has endeared prototyping to the entire MIS and user communities. In fact, over three-fourths of all new mainframe-based information systems emerge from a prototype system, and the percentage is increasing each year.

The Prototyping Process

Forming the Project Team

The composition of the project team is essentially the same for both the prototyping and the systems development methodology approaches. Both have users, programmers, systems analysts, and special function personnel (user liaison, data base manager), as required. The main difference in the team makeup for the two approaches is the size of the team. The interactive nature of prototyping demands that the size of the project team be kept as small as possible. Each member of the team must be familiar with all facets of the system and be prepared to interact with any other member at any time. In the prespecification approach, project team members can work relatively independently once the specifications have been defined.

Successful Prototype Systems

There are two keys to creating successful systems:

- *Users must be willing and committed to providing ongoing and meaningful feedback.* This feedback includes recommendations and qualitative comments that enhance the functionality of the finished system. In the prespecification approach to systems development, user feedback is more of a once-and-done activity. Prototyping is an iterative process; therefore, users must be available to examine and comment on the system design after each addition or revision to the prototype system.

- *The prototype system must be designed and created in a manner that makes it easy to modify.* The whole idea behind prototyping is to give users an opportunity to examine a menu, a report, or the overall operation of the system so that they can render their approval or recommend changes. If it is difficult to modify the prototype system, needed changes will be ignored and the finished system will fall short of user expectations.

Systems Analysis and Programming

The systems analysis, systems design, and programming maxims and techniques presented in Chapter 12, "Systems Analysis and Programming," are applicable to both the prespecification and the prototyping approaches to systems development. Project team members must analyze the existing system, interview users, create structured work and information flow diagrams (data flow diagrams and flowcharts), design the layouts for input and output, and so on.

Defining System Specifications

To appreciate the benefits of prototyping fully, you need to understand what has been done in the past. Traditionally, one of the rough spots in the prespecification approach to systems development has been the definition of system specifications. In the past, users cooperated with the project team to complete the functional specifications as early in the development cycle as possible. The specs had to be defined early because the technology (primarily third-generation languages and traditional file processing) did not provide project team members with much flexibility to modify the design of the system or the programs. In this environment, design changes were costly and, if possible, changes were avoided.

For the most part, users were unable to comprehend the scope of the proposed system during the early stages of the project, and they were often unable to convey their information requirements to the project team. The resulting functional specifications were ill defined and incomplete. Inevitably, one or more serious design oversights forced the project team to backtrack and make costly modifications. After years of backtracking, MIS professionals decided to ask users to sign-off (see Chapter 12) on the system specifications. After the sign-off, the specs were "frozen"; that is, no more changes could be made to the specs. Well, frozen specs are like ice cubes—when enough heat is applied, they melt.

With the new applications development tools, the specs do not need to be frozen. With these tools, the project team can develop a prototype system during interactive sessions with the user. To the user, the prototype version will look very much like the real thing. The system has menus, reports, various input/output screens, and a data base—all that a user needs to relate his or her desires to a project team.

Creating the Prototype System

To create a prototype system, project team members rough out the logic of the system and how the elements fit together and then work with the user to define the I/O interfaces (the system interaction with the user). During interactive sessions, project team members and users create whatever interactive display screens are required to meet the user's information processing needs. To do this, project team members use the applications development tools discussed later in this chapter to create the screen images (menus, reports, inquiries, and so on) and to generate much of the programming code. In some cases, an existing data base can be modified to service the proposed system. In other cases, a new data base must be created.

Use and Refine the Prototype System

Users can actually sit down at a workstation and evaluate portions and, eventually, all of the prototype system. Invariably, users have suggestions for improving the user interfaces and/or the format of the I/O. And, without fail, their examination reveals new needs for information. In effect, the prototype system is the beginning. From here, the system is expanded and refined to meet the users' total information needs. Prototyping software tools (discussed later in this chapter) are limited in what they can do, so the typical system may require a considerable amount of **custom coding**, probably written in third- and fourth-generation languages.

Prototyping: Advantages and Disadvantages

Just as the prespecification approach has its advantages and disadvantages, so does prototyping. The advantages of prototyping (as opposed to prespecification) are listed below.

☐ Prototyping takes less time to produce an information system than does the prespecification approach.

☐ Errors in judgment and oversights can be quickly remedied without costly redesigning or reprogramming.

☐ Users are more informed, and, therefore, the feedback to the project team is of a higher quality. This minimizes backtracking.

☐ With prototyping, user expectations for the completed system are realistic. In effect, users get exactly what they requested. In prespecification, users sometimes have unrealistic expectations of what the finished product will look like and do; consequently, they are often disappointed.

☐ Prototyping is the only way to demonstrate the product (an information system) to the users before they buy it. In most companies, information services, including systems development, are charged back to the user department.

Prototyping also has its disadvantages:

☐ Prototyping assumes full cooperation on the part of users who will ultimately be affected by the information system. The users play a big role in prototyping. They must spend many hours experimenting with the system and offering recommendations for system enhancements, and they must respond quickly after each iteration in design. If the users fail to meet their obligations, most of the advantages of prototyping are negated.

☐ For an information system that employs the software of its prototype system, the finished system may be inefficient from a hardware perspective. That is, the computing capacity required to make the system operational may be more than that required for a system developed using traditional techniques.

People whose lives are affected by a decision must be part of the process of arriving at that decision.

——— *John Naisbitt*

During the early years of prototyping (early 1980s), prototyping systems were reserved for information processing environments where decisions are unstructured (decision support systems). As the benefits of prototyping became more apparent and prototyping tools improved, prototyping became routine for all new systems development.

Integrating Prototyping into Systems Development Methodologies

In practice, information services divisions are realizing the best of both worlds by integrating prototyping into their systems development methodologies. By doing this, they can simultaneously enjoy the flexibility of prototyping and the structured framework of a systems development methodology. In this integrated environment, prototyping becomes the vehicle by which system specifications are determined. Typically, it is the nonfunctional and fully functional approaches to prototyping that are integrated into a systems development methodology. In both cases, the prototype system is discarded once the specs have been determined. From these specs, an information system is created that is capable of handling the required volume of work.

APPLICATION DEVELOPMENT TOOLS

For decades, the average MIS professional has been overworked, behind schedule, and faced with an ever-increasing backlog of work. It is not unusual for user managers to submit a service request for a new or enhanced information system, then wait two or more years for work to begin. Users are not going to stop requesting information services; in fact, requests are increasing as users strive to capture the competitive advantage and improve productivity via MIS. Until recently, MIS managers had only two solutions to addressing the backlog of service requests—hire more people or ask the existing staff to work harder. Now they have a third alternative. A plethora of computer-based **application development tools** are now available that can help MIS professionals increase their productivity by as much as 400 percent! These tools, which are enabling MIS managers to be more responsive to the information processing needs of users, include *very high-level programming languages* and a family of software packages known as *computer-aided software engineering* or *CASE* tools. Both are discussed in the following sections.

Very High-Level Programming Languages

Programming languages have evolved in generations, just as computers have. With each new generation, fewer instructions are needed to instruct the computer to perform a particular task. That is, a program written in a first-generation language that computes and prints student grade averages may require 100 or more instructions; the same program in a fourth-generation language may have fewer than 10 instructions. The first three generations of languages are discussed in Module E, "Programming Concepts and Languages," in "A Short Course in Computer Concepts."

Our Age of Anxiety is, in great part, the result of trying to do today's job with yesterday's tools—with yesterday's concepts.

——— *Marshall McLuhan*

The first two generations were known as low-level languages because their instruction sets were oriented to the most basic level of computer operation. High-level languages enabled multiple machine-level operations to be incorporated in a single instruction. Most of today's operational information systems are written in third-generation, *procedure-oriented programming languages* such as COBOL, PL/I, and RPG. However, an increasing share of the information systems developed in the 1980s have been written in even higher-level languages. These fourth-generation languages do not necessarily provide us with greater programming capabilities, but they do provide a *more sophisticated programmer/computer interaction*. In short, each new generation is easier to understand and use.

Fourth-Generation Languages

Fourth-generation languages, commonly referred to as *4GLs*, use high-level English-like instructions to retrieve and format data for inquiries and reporting. Most of the procedure portion of a 4GL program is generated automatically by the computer and the language software. That is, for the most part, the programmer specifies "what to do," *not* "how to do it." A programmer using a procedure-oriented language has to write instructions depicting "what to do" *and* "how to do it." Thus the use of 4GLs, sometimes called *query languages*, yields substantial improvements in programming productivity for certain information needs.

The features of a 4GL include English-like instructions, limited mathematical manipulation of data, automatic report formatting, sequencing (sorting), and record selection by criteria.

USING 4GLS   The 4GL example presented here gives you a feel for the difference between a procedure-oriented language, such as COBOL, and a 4GL. About 20 4GLs are commercially available, such as NOMAD2, FOCUS, Mantis, Ideal, EASYTRIEVE Plus, INTELLECT, RAMIS II, ADS/ONLINE, and DATA-TRIEVE. The example shows how a representative 4GL program can be used to generate a management report. Suppose, for example, that a personnel manager wants to make the following request for information:

> List the employee ID, sex, net pay, and gross pay for all employees in Departments 911 and 914.

To obtain the report, the manager wrote the query-language program in Figure 13–1; the report generated by this program is shown in Figure 13–2.

```
1.    FILE IS PAYROLL
2.    LIST BY DEPARTMENT NAME ID SEX NET GROSS
3.    SELECT DEPARTMENT = 911, 914
4.    SUBTOTALS BY DEPARTMENT
5.    TITLE: "PAYROLL FOR DEPARTMENTS 911, 914"
6.    COLUMN HEADINGS:   "DEPARTMENT", "EMPLOYEE, NAME";
      "EMPLOYEE, NUMBER"; "SEX"; "NET, PAY"; "GROSS, PAY"
```

FIGURE 13–1   A 4GL Program
This representative 4GL program generates the report shown in Figure 13–2. Each instruction is discussed in detail in the chapter material.

PAYROLL FOR DEPARTMENTS 911, 914

DEPARTMENT	EMPLOYEE NAME	EMPLOYEE NUMBER	SEX	NET PAY	GROSS PAY
911	ARNOLD	01963	1	356.87	445.50
911	LARSON	11357	2	215.47	283.92
911	POWELL	11710	1	167.96	243.20
911	POST	00445	1	206.60	292.00
911	KRUSE	03571	2	182.09	242.40
911	SMOTH	01730	1	202.43	315.20
911	GREEN	12829	1	238.04	365.60
911	ISAAC	12641	1	219.91	313.60
911	STRIDE	03890	1	272.53	386.40
911	REYNOLDS	05805	2	134.03	174.15
911	YOUNG	04589	1	229.69	313.60
911	HAFER	09764	2	96.64	121.95
DEPARTMENT TOTAL				2,522.26	3,497.52
914	MANHART	11602	1	250.89	344.80
914	VETTER	01895	1	189.06	279.36
914	GRECO	07231	1	685.23	1,004.00
914	CROCI	08262	1	215.95	376.00
914	RYAN	10961	1	291.70	399.20
DEPARTMENT TOTAL				1,632.83	2,403.36
FINAL TOTAL				4,155.09	5,900.88
17 RECORDS TOTALED					

FIGURE 13–2   A Payroll Report
This payroll report is the result of the execution of the 4GL program of Figure 13–1.

☐ *Instruction 1* specifies that the payroll data are stored on a FILE called PAYROLL. Although the data of only one file are needed in this example, requests requiring data from several files are no more difficult.

☐ *Instruction 2* specifies that the information in the report is to be *sorted* (Department 911 before 914) and LISTed BY DEPARTMENT. It also specifies which data elements within the file are to be included in the report of Figure 13–2. If the instruction had been "LIST BY DEPARTMENT BY NAME," then the employee names would be listed in alphabetical order for each department.

☐ *Instruction 3* specifies the criterion by which records are SELECTed. The personnel manager is interested only in those employees from DEPARTMENTs 911 and 914. Other criteria could be included for further record selections. For example, the criterion "GROSS > 400.00" could be added to select only those people (from Departments 911 and 914) whose gross pay is greater than $400.00.

☐ *Instruction 4* causes SUBTOTALS to be computed and displayed BY DEPARTMENT.

☐ *Instructions 5 and 6* allow the personnel manager to improve the appearance and readability of the report by including a title and labeling the columns. Instruction 5 produces the report title, and instruction 6 specifies descriptive column headings.

The COBOL equivalent of this request would require over 150 lines of code!

Fourth-generation languages are effective tools for generating responses to a variety of requests for information. Short programs, similar to the one in Figure 13–1, are all that is needed to respond to the following typical management requests:

☐ Which employees have accumulated over 20 sick days since May 1?
☐ Are there any deluxe single hospital rooms to be vacated by the end of the day?

☐ What is a particular student's average in all English courses taken?
☐ List departments that have exceeded their budget alphabetically by the department head's name.

Fourth-generation languages have become very sophisticated and can be used to create full-scale information systems as well as make ad hoc inquiries to data bases. Fourth-generation languages are available at two levels of sophistication. Some 4GLs are oriented primarily to users and are less likely to be used for the development of full-scale information systems. Others that are oriented primarily to MIS professionals are, as you might expect, more technical and difficult to learn; however, the more sophisticated versions of 4GLs can be used for developing comprehensive information systems. In fact, 4GLs are often the technology used to create prototype systems.

NATURAL LANGUAGE INTERFACES TO 4GLS   Some 4GLs have a **natural language interface**. With certain limitations, this interface permits users to express their queries in normal, everyday English.

List the employee ID, sex, net pay, and gross pay for all employees in Departments 911 and 914.

Instead of writing the program in Figure 13–1, the user could have entered the preceding request directly to the natural language interface. The natural language interface analyzes the request and translates it to instructions that can be interpreted by the 4GL. Natural languages are discussed in Chapter 3, "Artificial Intelligence and Expert Systems."

FOCUS, a popular 4GL/DBMS from Information Builders, Inc., provides a non-procedural alternative to traditional programming languages such as COBOL and FORTRAN. One of the add-on capabilities to PC/FOCUS, the PC version of FOCUS, is EQL (English Query Language). EQL is a natural language interface that enables users to make inquiries to the data base in simple English sentences. EQL translates the sentence into FOCUS instructions. When the sentence is not understood by EQL, the system asks for clarification. In the example, EQL did not recognize the word "units."

Information Builders, Inc.

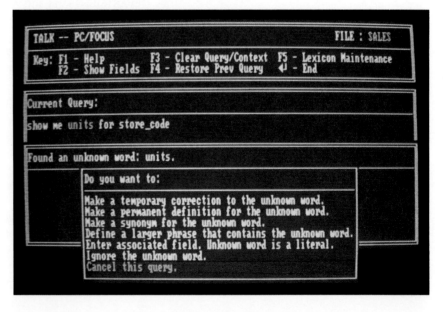

ENTREPRENEURIAL INNOVATION Procedure-oriented languages, such as FOR-TRAN and COBOL, were designed by volunteer committees and individuals, primarily for the public domain. Then, companies such as DEC, CDC, and IBM developed *compilers* and *interpreters* that could translate the FORTRAN and COBOL instructions to the type of instructions that could be executed by the computer. The 4GLs and higher-level languages are products of entrepreneurial innovation. That is, these languages (for example, NOMAD2 and EASYTRIEVE Plus) are developed to be marketed and sold. The demand for very high-level programming languages is so great that many software entrepreneurs have elected to compete in this highly competitive market.

Application Generators

Application generators are designed primarily for use by MIS professionals. The concept of an application generator is not well defined, nor will it ever be, as entrepreneurs are continually working to provide better ways to create information systems. In general, application generators are designed to assist in the development of full-scale information systems.

When using application generators, also called **code generators**, to development information systems, programmers specify what information processing tasks are to be performed by engaging in an interactive dialogue with the system. This is essentially a fill-in-the-blank process. The code generator asks a question and the programmer responds by filling in the blank. For example, the code generator might ask the user to categorize the proposed program as data entry, inquiry, report generation, or file maintenance. If the programmer responds "inquiry," then the code generator will ask the programmer to identify appropriate data bases. Code generators interpret the programmer-supplied information and actually generate the program code that enables the user to make a data base inquiry, update a data base, and so on. Most of the code generators produce code in the form of COBOL or PL/I programs. Code generators are often used for developing partially and fully functional prototype systems.

When using application generators to create an information system, systems analysts and programmers describe the data base, then specify screen layouts for file creation and maintenance, data entry, management reports, and menus. The application generator software consists of modules of **reusable code** that are pulled together and integrated automatically to complete the system.

Application generators are currently in the infant stage of development. Existing application generators do not have the flexibility of procedure-oriented languages; therefore, the generic reusable code of application generators must occasionally be supplemented with *custom code* to handle unique situations. Normally, about 10 to 15 percent of the code would be custom code. Application generators provide the framework by which to integrate custom code with generated code. When used for the purposes intended, application generators can quadruple the output of programmers and systems analysts. As application generators mature, they will play an ever-increasing role in information systems development.

Application generators, or code generators, also are considered a CASE tool and are presented later as a CASE program development tool.

The MIS manager who wants productivity improvement, but will not dedicate human resources to that challenge, is not really committed to doing what it takes. He is simply looking for a quick technology fix.

——— *Vaughan Merlyn*

Computer-Aided Software Engineering (CASE)

For years, most people were of the school of thought that the best way to improve productivity in systems development was to make it easier for programmers to create programs. Fourth-generation languages and application generators are an outgrowth of this quest for better productivity. In essence, these languages are designed to let the computer do much of the programming. In the early 1980s, people began asking the question, "Why can't the power of the computer be applied to analysis and design work as well?" Now we know that it can. Many of the time-consuming manual tasks, such as creating a data dictionary and documenting information flow, can be automated. This general family of software development productivity tools falls under the umbrella of **computer-aided software engineering** or **CASE** tools. The term **software engineering** was coined to emphasize an approach to software development that embodies the rigors of engineering discipline. Software engineering implies the use of formal procedures (for example, a systems development methodology) and an integrated set of automated design and development tools (for example, CASE tools). **Systems engineering** and **information engineering** are computerese synonyms for software engineering.

Although the concept of CASE has been around since the mid 1970s, the actual software tools that make up CASE are relatively recent innovations. The CASE tool kit consists of these tools (see Figure 13–3):

- ☐ Design tools
- ☐ Prototyping tools
- ☐ Information repository tools
- ☐ Program development tools
- ☐ Methodology tools

The foregoing complement of tools provides automated support for prototyping and the entire system's life cycle. Each of these tools is discussed in more detail in the following sections. Note that there is some overlap in functionality between the various CASE tools. Throughout this section, photographs illustrate the use and application of a variety of commercially available case tools.

CASE tools, which are also referred to as **workbench technologies**, are in their infancy. To some extent, each of the tools listed is available commercially. While no comprehensive CASE tool kit to date integrates all the various tools, some companies offer packages that integrate two or three of the tools. **Software engineers** are working overtime to develop software products that will bridge the gap between design and executable program code. It is reasonable to expect that very sophisticated integrated CASE tool kits will be commercially available in the not-too-distant future. In a two-step process, these tool kits will enable project teams to use automated software packages to help them complete the logic design (information flow, I/O), then the CASE software will translate the logical design to the physical implementation of the system (executable program code). In fact, several existing CASE products are bordering on this level of sophistication.

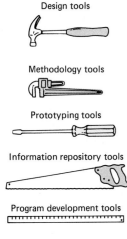

Design tools

Methodology tools

Prototyping tools

Information repository tools

Program development tools

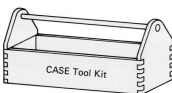

CASE Tool Kit

FIGURE 13–3 The CASE Tool Kit

Design Tools

Prior to the introduction of CASE technologies, the tool kit for the systems analyst and programmer was comprised of flowcharting and data flow diagram templates, lettering templates, rulers, scissors, glue, pencils, pens, and plenty of erasers and "white out." Once a company purchases a CASE design tool and trains MIS professionals in its use and applications, these manual tools become relics. Perhaps the *design tool* category of CASE tools offers the most apparent improvements to productivity. The introduction of these *front-end* tools in the early 1980s marked the beginning of the emergence of what we now call CASE technology. These tools help analysts and programmers to prepare the schematics that graphically depict the logic of a system or program (for example, data flow diagrams, structure charts). They do this in much the same way word processing software helps a writer prepare an article for publication. Also, they assist designers in the preparation of screen and report layouts.

All CASE design tools use structured design techniques, such as data flow diagrams, to model the work flow, information flow, and program interactions within a system. Data flow diagrams are discussed in Chapter 12, "Systems Analysis and Programming." Other design techniques are discussed in Module F, "Design Techniques Overview," in "A Short Course in Computer Concepts." Automated design tools enable an analyst or programmer to select and position symbols, such as the DFD process and entity symbols, and to connect these symbols with flow lines. Both symbols and flow lines can be labeled. For example, an analyst might label a process symbol "enter order data." Flow lines can be clarified with arrows to indicate the direction of flow and with descriptions of what is being transferred. Since all the design techniques supported by CASE products are structured design techniques, systems are ultimately depicted in several levels of generality. For example, at the highest level, the entire system might be represented in four process symbols of a data flow diagram. However, at the second level, each of these processes is broken down into finer detail and presented as a more detailed data flow diagram. The processes at the second level can be broken down into finer detail and so on. This concept is illustrated in Chapter 15, "An MIS Case Study."

Programmers and analysts can change the size of symbols to fit the diagram on the screen and/or change the color of a symbol or flow line to indicate special significance (a control procedure). They can also help to clarify the diagram by adding explanatory notations, both visible and hidden (that is, they can be called up in pop-up windows). A diagram can be exploded to the next level of generality by positioning the cursor over the appropriate symbol. The next screen would show an *explosion* (the next level of detail) of the desired process. Of course, levels of generality can be explored in both directions.

CASE design tools also aid systems analysts in the preparation of I/O specifications. While interacting with one another, analysts and users employ CASE design tools to prepare layouts for reports and screens. The layout is a detailed output and/or input specification that graphically illustrates exactly where information should be placed or entered on a workstation display screen or on a printer output. Example screen layouts are shown in the accompanying photos.

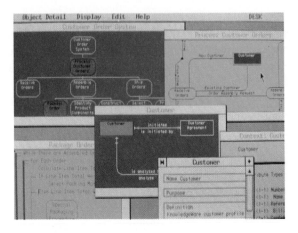

(a)

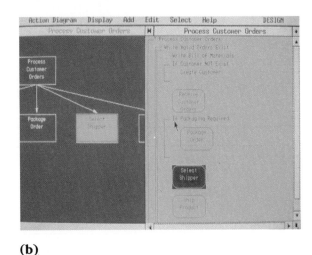

(b)

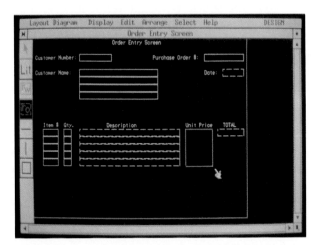

(c)

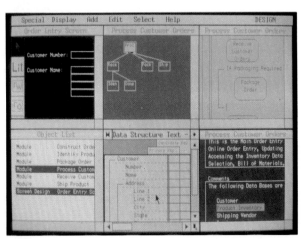

(d)

KnowledgeWare, Inc. provides an integrated CASE environment for the planning, analysis, design, and construction of information systems. The KnowledgeWare tools function as an integrated set and, independently, as stand-alone products. (a) The windows in the first screen illustrate the capabilities of the Analysis Workstation. The Analysis Workstation is an integrated set of diagrammatic tools for requirements analysis. The techniques incorporated into the software include decomposition diagrams (top left), data flow diagrams (top right), entity relationship diagrams (middle), and action diagrams (bottom left). (b) The Knowledge Coordinator component works with the Encyclopedia software to ensure that information entered in the Encyclopedia is correct and consistent, and represents systems that can be constructed. The system maintains consistency throughout the system documentation. If a change is made to an object in one diagram, other affected items of documentation are updated automatically to reflect the change. In the example, when the "choose carrier" process was renamed "select shipper" in the structure chart, it also was updated in the action diagram. (c) Knowledgeware's Design Workstation is used to capture diagrammatically knowledge about screen layouts, edit rules, program structures, procedural logic, and database and file structures. (d) Knowledgeware's Presentation Diagrammer for Screens enables project team members interactively to create screen layouts while in consultation with users.

KnowledgeWare, Inc., Atlanta, GA, USA

Some CASE design tools have the capability to validate the logic portrayed in flow diagrams. These tools highlight any inconsistencies in logic in real time; for example, the tool might point out that a newly identified process needs data that may not be available. KnowledgeWare's design tool performs a "connectivity analysis" that checks each data flow to ensure that it is connected to a valid source or destination.

Prototyping Tools

In practice, all the CASE tools have proven to be valuable assets during the creation of prototype systems. However, there is a category of CASE tools that is designated specifically for prototyping. CASE *prototyping tools* are used by project team members to create a physical representation of a proposed system at one of the three levels of sophistication discussed earlier in this chapter (that is, a nonfunctional, partially functional, or fully functional prototype system).

The basic components of prototyping tools are:

☐ *The user interface.* This capability enables the project team to design and create the user interface. Typically the user interface consists of a hierarchy of menus, which may be displayed in windows that are superimposed over the current display. In most cases, the initial screen contains the main menu. When a user selects an item from the main menu, a subordinate menu is displayed, either on a separate screen or in a window. Eventually, a user selection results in the display of an input screen, a report, or perhaps a graph. User interface concepts are presented in Chapter 12, "Systems Analysis and Programming."

☐ *Screen generators.* In the traditional programming environment, the systems analysts uses pencils, erasers, and screen layout paper to prepare a graphic rendering of a proposed display screen. From these screen specs, the programmer uses complicated formatting and data base instructions to generate the software needed to create the display. **Screen generators** offer an alternative to this time-consuming process. Screen generators, also called **screen formatters**, provide systems analysts with the capability to generate a mockup of a screen while in direct consultation with the user. Screen generation is made even easier when you consider that data specifications (field length, labels, and so on) can be recalled directly from the automated data dictionary (discussed shortly).

☐ *Report generators.* **Report generators** work similarly to screen generators, with one exception. Report generators permit summary totals by criteria and overall, and the editing of output (for example, the automatic insertion of currency notation). For example, if the report in Figure 13–2 was the product of a report generator, the summary totals by department and overall would have been generated automatically.

In summary, the prototyping tool provides the capability to model a system. The user can experiment with the model and provide precise feedback that enables system designers to fine tune the system specifications.

Information Repository Tools

When used within the context of CASE technology, the terms *information repository*, *dictionary*, and *encyclopedia* are used interchangeably in practice, even though each might have a slightly different meaning when referring to a specific vendor's CASE product. The information repository would be analogous to the data dictionary in the traditional manual approach to system design. However, the information repository contains everything the data dictionary includes and much more. As explained in Chapter 12, "Systems Analysis and Programming," the data dictionary is a listing and description of all data elements in the data base. The descriptive information includes such information as data element name, description, format, and so on. The information repository is an expansion of the data dictionary. The information repository is a central computer-based storage facility for all design information. For example, in an information repository, each data element is cross-referenced to all other components in the system. That is, the data element "customer number" would be cross-referenced to every screen, report, graph, record/file, data base, program, or any other design element in which it occurred. Cross-references are also made to processes in data flow diagrams. Once the company has had the information repository in place for a while, cross-references can be extended between information systems.

The systems development process is (or should be) systematic, leaving no stone unturned. The mechanics of looking under every stone can produce volumes of information, all of which must be readily accessible to all members of the project team. Besides the data dictionary component, the information repository permits all system documentation to be packaged electronically. That is, any part of the system—layouts, data dictionary, notes, pseudocode (nonexecutable program code), project schedules, and so on—can be recalled and displayed for review or modification. In effect, the information repository is the "data base" for the system development project. And, as does an on-line information system, the information repository reflects up-to-the-minute project status.

One of the biggest problems facing project teams is keeping documentation up-to-date so that all members are current on what has happened and what is happening in the project. Information repositories provide a long-awaited solution to this problem.

Program Development Tools

Program development tools focus on the *back-end* or the latter stages of the systems development effort. CASE program development tools are in four categories:

- □ Program structure charts
- □ Code generators
- □ Program preprocessors (error checking and documentation)
- □ Test data generators

Of course, programmers also use the CASE design tools to graphically depict the logic of their programs.

PROGRAM STRUCTURE CHARTS An information system will often be comprised of dozens, even hundreds, of programs. The program structure chart tool enables programmers to create a graphic hierarchical representation of these programs that illustrates program dependencies and interactions. The program structure chart also shows how the various programs relate to the processes depicted in the system flow diagrams.

CODE GENERATORS Code generators, which are also called application generators (see earlier discussion of high-level programming languages in this chapter), are perhaps the most valuable program development tool. Computers can write certain programs far more efficiently than can human programmers. Instead of doing the actual coding of programs, programmers use code generators to describe the structure of a data base and to create screens and report layouts in what is essentially a fill-in-the-blank process.

One hundred percent of the program code for many programming tasks can be produced entirely by code generators; however, code generators have their limitations. Most code generators cannot interpret complex system specifications; however, they can produce **skeletal code**, or a partially complete program. The skeletal code provides the foundation to which programmer-produced custom code can be added to complete the program. Code generators are becoming so sophisticated that custom code may comprise less than 10 percent of an information system. The software for some straightforward information systems is comprised entirely of programs produced by code generators.

PROGRAM PREPROCESSORS Another handy program development tool preprocesses programmer-written programs of high-level programming languages, such as COBOL and PL/I, to point out potential problems with the program logic and syntax and to generate the documentation for the program. The preprocessor simulates the execution of the program and highlights poorly structured code, hidden bugs, and possible maintenance problems. At any point in the program development process, the preprocessor can be employed to generate up-to-date program documentation automatically. This documentation software can generate many of the traditional items of program documentation, such as a list of program variable names, internal comments, and even a flowchart. Program documentation is discussed in Chapter 12.

TEST DATA GENERATORS One of the more laborious tasks associated with programming is the generation of test data. Programmers using CASE tools rely on **test data generators** to compile test data. The programmer describes the parameters of the desired data (format, ranges, distributions, and so on), and the test data generator does the rest.

Methodology Tools

The systems development methodologies described in Chapter 11, "Systems Development and Management," are usually presented in a hard-copy manual, but with increasing frequency, they are being automated and presented as on-line, interactive systems. The *methodology tool* is a computer-based version of the traditional systems development methodology manual. Both describe phased procedures and responsibilities and both provide forms and formats

The computer is no better than its program.

——— *Elting Elmore Morison*

for documenting the system. The methodology tools available in the market-place support the traditional life-cycle approach to systems development, prototyping, and a combination of the two approaches.

The primary advantage that a methodology tool has over a hard-copy manual is that much of the information relating to the project can be entered on-line. This up-to-date information is accessible to all members of the team. For example, as soon as the results of an interview with a user are recorded, all team members can view the results. The methodology tool has a check-list for each activity in each phase of the project. A checklist item can be a work activity (interview users) or an output (summary of interviews). The net effects of using a methodology tool are better control and coordination of the project team and better communication among project team members. Some methodology tools are integrated with a computer-based project management system that enables the estimation of resource requirements and the allocation and scheduling of these resources over the course of the project.

Each methodology tool reflects a different philosophy of system development. Although the systems development process is relatively standard from an overview perspective, the details of the process vary markedly between methodology tools. Some are data-driven; that is, the problem is described in terms of data elements. Some are event-driven; that is, the problem is described dynamically in terms time-phased events. Still others are function-driven; that is, the problem is conceptualized in terms of the functions that make up the process. As you might expect, those that do not fit into any of these philosophies are hybrids, perhaps embracing two or all of the philosophies outlined.

Commercially Available CASE Products

Computer-aided software engineering or CASE software products may well be the hottest area in the commercial software marketplace. About 50 companies have developed products and are vying for their share of the business; however, relatively few are realizing profits from their CASE products. Some products are mainframe-based and others are run on microcomputers. Some vendors have developed similar versions for both the mainframe and micro environments.

The following list includes some of the more commercially successful CASE tools: Excelerator and PC Prism (Index Technology Corporation), Application Factory (Cortex Corporation), Information Engineering Workbench (Knowledgeware, Inc.), Teamwork (Cadre Technologies, Inc.), CASE 2000 Designaid (Nastec Corp.), Pacbase (CGI Systems), Casepac (On-Line Software), Information Engineering Facility (Texas Instruments), and Analyst/Designer Toolkit (Yourdon/DeVry).

CASE Summary

Even though CASE is a relatively recent technology, few will argue that it will eventually be the dominant tool for systems development. Existing products are being improved and new products are being announced each month.

The advantages of using CASE technology are very convincing. In a nutshell, CASE enables information system project team members to be substantially more productive and to be better informed of what other members have done and are doing. Nevertheless, many companies are waiting to make the move to CASE until it reaches another level of sophistication or, perhaps, a clear industry leader emerges. As a result, only a small fraction, probably less than 5 percent, of potential CASE users actually use CASE.

Programmers and systems analysts who employ CASE technology are convinced that CASE tools enable them to produce higher-quality information systems. This conclusion seems only logical when you study parallels between the writer/word processing relationship and the programmer-analyst/CASE relationship. Any writer will tell you that word processing has improved the quality of their work. Frequent and substantial changes can be made to a draft of a report with relative ease. Before word processing, writers thought long and hard before making minor or major modifications to their work, because to do so might delay completion and increase the probability of error. The same can be said of CASE tools. Traditionally, programmers and analysts have been reluctant to revise their flow diagrams, most of which were hand drawn with painstaking care. Today, with CASE tools they can make needed revisions in a matter of minutes. Since many of the tasks associated with analysis, design, and programming are automated with CASE tools, the project team members can focus their efforts on the accurate definition of user requirements and the logic of the system. Word processing and CASE are both tools. However, the word processing software does not do the writing, and the CASE software does not do the analysis and design. People do these tasks.

As with any new product, be it made out of steel or bits and bytes, CASE has its problems. One of the biggest problems is lack of functionality. That is, a particular CASE product may address only one or two aspects of systems development (perhaps only logic diagrams and the data dictionary). The other major problem is integration—integration of the CASE tools and integration between a particular CASE product other commercial software. System designers would prefer that the various case tools be integrated so that information can be exchanged between the tools. Generally speaking, CASE products with multiple tools are only partially integrated. The next major step in the evolution of CASE technology will be the integration of CASE with other commercial software products. For example, system designers would like to interface the information repository tool with an actual data base product, such as DB2 and dBASE IV. In this way, the data specifications in the information repository could be used to create the design of the data base.

CASE is more than just another tool. It is a design philosophy that demands that MIS professionals and users acquire new skills and adopt new attitudes. When a company converts from traditional approaches to using CASE tools, it is making a transition to an entirely new working environment. This type of transition demands careful planning, close scrutiny by management, and a comprehensive, ongoing education program for both MIS professionals and users. With any less of an effort, expensive CASE software can quickly become shelfware (software that sits unused on the shelf).

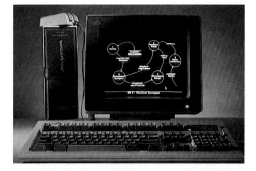

Teamwork/PCSA, a product of Cadre Technologies Inc., is a comprehensive CASE tool that, among other things, enables system designers to create and edit data flow diagrams.

Cadre Technologies Inc.

In some companies, CASE has actually been too successful. These companies are producing results so quickly that they are actually jamming the systems development process on the back end. That is, they are completing information systems so quickly that they do not have sufficient resources to convert and implement these systems. Perhaps there is something to the saying, "you can have too much of a good thing."

CHAPTER HIGHLIGHTS

■ Prototyping is one of the two fundamental approaches to systems development. The other approach involves the up-front specification of user information processing requirements and the use of a systems development methodology.

■ The three objectives of prototyping are to analyze the current situation, identify information needs, and develop a scaled-down model of the proposed system.

■ A prototype system would normally handle the main transaction-oriented procedures, produce the critical reports, and permit rudimentary inquiries.

■ Ideally, users should experiment with and familiarize themselves with the operation of a proposed system as early in the development process as possible. The prototyping process enables users to relate accurate information processing needs to the project team during the early phases of the project and throughout the project.

■ Software prototypes are created in varying degrees of sophistication: nonfunctional prototype systems (rapid prototyping), partially functional prototype systems, and fully functional prototype systems.

■ The nonfunctional prototype system focuses on three aspects of the design: the user interface, data entry displays, and system outputs.

■ Many partially functional prototype systems are created under the premise that they will eventually be enhanced to the level of fully functional systems.

■ Typically, fully functional prototype systems are created for the sole purpose of enabling users to experiment with the system.

■ Prototyping has enabled managers to define the scope of a proposed information system better and thereby reduce the variability in a project's quality, resource requirements, and schedule.

■ For prototype systems to be successful, users must be willing and committed to providing ongoing and meaningful feedback, and the system must be designed and created in a manner that makes it easy to modify.

■ Prototyping saves time, reduces errors in judgment and oversights, produces higher-quality feedback from users, encourages realistic user expectations, and provides a way to demonstrate what the system will look like and do upon implementation.

■ In practice, the MIS community is enjoying the best of both worlds by following systems development methodologies that include prototyping.

■ Application development tools are now available that can help MIS professionals increase their productivity by as much as 400 percent.

■ High-level languages enabled multiple machine-level operations to be incorporated in a single instruction.

■ The programmer/computer interaction is more sophisticated in fourth-generation languages than it is in the first three generations of programming languages.

■ Fourth-generation languages use high-level English-like instructions to retrieve and format data for inquiries and reporting. For the most part, 4GL instructions specify "what to do," not "how to do it."

■ Higher-level languages (fourth and above) are products of entrepreneurial innovation. Commercially available packages include NOMAD2, FOCUS, Mantis, and about 20 others.

■ When using application generators or code generators to develop information systems, programmers specify what information processing tasks are to be performed by engaging in an interactive dialogue with the system. Code generators interpret the programmer-supplied information and actually generate the program code.

■ Since existing application generators do not have the flexibility of procedure-oriented languages, the generic reusable code of application generators must occasionally be supplemented with custom code to handle unique situations.

■ The terms "software engineering," "systems engineering," and "information engineering" were coined to emphasize an approach to software development that embodies the rigors of the engineering discipline.

■ The CASE tool kit, also called workbench technologies, is comprised of design tools, prototyping tools, information repository tools, program development tools, and methodology tools.

■ CASE design tools help analysts and programmers prepare the schematics that graphically depict the logic of a system or program, and they assist designers in the preparation of screen and report layouts. Some CASE design tools have the capability to validate the logic portrayed in flow diagrams.

■ CASE prototyping tools are used by project team members to create a physical representation of a proposed information system.

■ The basic components of prototyping tools are the user interface, screen generators, and report generators.

■ In the information repository (also dictionary or encyclopedia), each data element is cross-referenced to all other components in the system.

■ CASE program development tools include program structure charts, code generators, program preprocessors, and test data generators.

■ The skeletal code provided by code generators provides the foundation to which programmer-produced custom code can be added to complete a program.

■ Program preprocessors analyze COBOL and PL/I programs to identify problems in the logic and syntax of a program and to document the program.

■ The methodology tool is a computer-based version of the traditional systems development methodology manual.

■ CASE enables information system project team members to be substantially more productive and to be better informed of what other members have done and are doing.

■ CASE is a design philosophy that demands that MIS professionals and users acquire new skills and adopt new attitudes. When a company converts from traditional approaches to using CASE tools, it is making a transition to an entirely new working environment.

IMPORTANT TERMS

application development tool
application generator
code generator
compiler
computer-aided software engineering (CASE)
custom coding
encyclopedia
dictionary

fourth-generation languages (4GL) (Ch. 6)
information engineering
interpreter
information repository
natural language interface
procedure-oriented programming language (Mod. E)

prototyping (Ch. 11)
prototype system (Ch. 11)
query language
rapid prototyping
report generator
reusable code
screen formatter
screen generator

skeletal code
software engineering
software engineers
systems engineering
test data generator
very high-level programming language
workbench technologies

REVIEW EXERCISES

1. Cite one of the keys to creating successful prototype systems.

2. Rapid prototyping is associated with which level of prototyping sophistication?

3. Briefly describe the make-up of a prototyping project team.

4. Which of the two approaches to systems development, pre-specification or prototyping, enables managers to define the scope of a proposed information system better?

5. Briefly describe the basic difference between a third- and a fourth-generation programming language.

6. What prompted MIS professionals to ask users to sign off on system specifications?

7. Custom code that is written to augment a prototype system is probably written in what type of programming language?

8. Name five commercially available 4GLs.

9. Procedure-oriented languages belong to which generation of languages? Name two such languages.

10. At which of the three levels of prototyping sophistication are data extracted from a data base?

11. Which CASE tool is analogous to the data dictionary in the traditional manual approach to system design?

12. Who are the users of application generators?

13. Name three commercially available CASE products.

14. What is the purpose of the CASE design tool?

15. Besides producing critical reports and permitting rudimentary inquiries, what else does a prototype system typically do?

16. What are the three basic components of prototyping tools?

17. Briefly describe the function of program preprocessors, one of the CASE program development tools.

18. Of the three levels of prototyping sophistication, which are most likely to be integrated into a systems development methodology?

19. Name the tools in the CASE tool kit.

20. What is another name for CASE tools?

21. What is the objective of prototyping?

DISCUSSION QUESTIONS

1. One application of the 80/20 rule to information systems development is that 80 percent of the features and functionality of an information system can be realized with 20 percent of the effort required to develop a fully functional system. Describe two other instances that occur in the MIS environment to which the 80/20 rule might be applied.

2. Why aren't all fully functional prototype systems installed as operational information systems?

3. Prototyping is often described as an iterative process. What does this mean?

4. One of the objectives of prototyping is to develop a scaled-down model of the proposed system. However, some prototype systems are fully functional. Describe how such a prototype system is scaled down.

5. Discuss actions that can be taken by the project team during the early stages of a project to overcome or minimize the traditional disadvantages of prototyping?

6. Describe at least three approaches that MIS managers can follow to reduce their backlogs of user service requests.

7. Discuss how a nonfunctional prototype system can improve the quality of user-defined system specifications.

8. Describe the circumstances that would prompt you to recommend the development of a nonfunctional prototype system over a fully functional one. A fully functional prototype system over a nonfunctional one.

9. In the chapter material, the author notes that most managers have a good idea of what they want in an information system, but they do not know exactly what they want. Why is it so important that they know exactly what they want?

10. Draw parallels between prototyping in the automobile industry and in software development.

11. Why is prototyping more popular in the mainframe environment than in the microcomputer environment?

12. Describe how a CASE methodology tool can complement a computer-based project management system. Describe how a computer-based project management system can complement a CASE methodology tool.

13. The potential and advantages of CASE products are well understood by the MIS community, yet most companies have not integrated CASE tools into their software development processes. Why is this so?

14. The vice president of finance would like to produce a report that lists the employees in Department 911 alphabetically by sex. He wants the name, employee number, department, net pay, and gross pay listed for each employee. How would you modify the query-language program in Figure 13–1 to generate this report?

15. Discuss the advantages of using an automated design tool versus pencils, templates, and paper to create data flow diagrams.

16. Many states prohibit people from representing themselves as consulting engineers unless they have passed a rigorous exam and become registered professional engineers. However, none of these states offers an exam in software engineering. Should they offer such an exam so that software engineers can become registered?

17. If code generators can produce functional COBOL and PL/I programs, why would anyone ever write a COBOL or PL/I program?

18. Discuss the relationship and differences between CASE and prototyping. Between CASE and 4GLs. Between CASE and application generators.

19. Some programmers say that producing certain programs from skeletal code is more trouble than it is worth. What type of programs are they talking about?

20. With CASE technology, is there a danger of producing too much system documentation? Discuss.

APPLICATION CASE STUDY 13–1

The Impact of Prototyping and Application Development Tools

The Situation

Management at Gabriel Industries has decided to make the most of information technology in an attempt to improve the company's competitive position. As a consequence of this emphasis, the Computer Services Department was inundated with service requests from all areas of the company. John Robson, manager of the Computer Services Department, has established an information center to help users fill their personal or departmental information needs (see Application Case Study 5–2, "The Information Center"). The emergence of end user computing at Gabriel has reduced the number of requests for small, independent projects, but this has not helped with the backlog of larger, more complex projects that must be developed by the programmer/analysts in the Computer Services Department.

To help alleviate the backlog, John Robson has requested permission to augment his programmer/analyst staff by three. Although his request was approved, John Robson concluded that the long-term solution to the backlog problem is to improve the productivity of his programmer/analysts. He is convinced that the judicious use of prototyping and modern application development tools will result in significant increases in productivity. He asked Mary Fiducci, the systems and programming manager, to select and acquire the necessary software and hardware. She purchased an integrated CASE software package and three workstations, all of which will be dedicated to prototyping and new system development.

The Assignment

Put yourself in the role of Mary Fiducci as you complete the following assignment.

1. Briefly describe how you would:
   a. Train the programmer/analysts in prototyping techniques and the use of the CASE package.
   b. Evaluate the effectiveness of prototyping and the CASE package at Gabriel.
2. Gabriel's existing system development methodology requires formal prespecification of the functionality, output screens, and report layouts of the proposed system. Discuss the impact of introducing prototyping into the existing methodology by answering the following questions:

a. Would users cooperate and make the time commitments necessary for successful prototyping? (See Application Case Study 6–2, "Management of End User Computing," for background information on users at Gabriel Industries.) What suggestions would you make to preempt potential problems in this regard?

b. How do you think programmer/analysts will react to the new methodology and to the need to interact more frequently with users? What suggestions would you make to preempt potential problems in this regard?

3. Different approaches to prototyping may be appropriate for projects of different sizes and complexity. The five projects listed here are currently being considered for implementation at Gabriel.

   □ Developing and implementing a new accounts receivable system (see Application Case Study 1–1, "The Decision-Making Process").

   □ Upgrading the batch personnel/payroll system to on-line (see Application Case Study 2–2, "On-line Versus Off-line").

   □ Designing and implementing a corporate communications network (see Application Case Study 8–1, "An Interstate Network").

   □ Upgrading the material requirements planning system to include just-in-time inventory planning (see Application Case Study 12–3, "Analysis and Design of an MRP System with Just-in-Time").

   □ Upgrading the batch order processing system so that Gabriel's customers can place orders using EDI.

John Robson has evaluated these projects for technological risk and business priority (see Application Case Study 10–2, "MIS Operational Planning") and for economic feasibility (see Application Case Study 11–1, "Economic Feasibility"). For each of the five projects, recommend a prototyping strategy (nonfunctional, partially functional, or fully functional) and justify your recommendation. If you feel prototyping is not applicable or not appropriate, justify your conclusion.

APPLICATION CASE STUDY 13–2
Prototyping Tools

The Situation

Compu-Mail has decided to proceed with the development of an on-line order processing system to replace the current batch system (see Application Case Study 12–1, "Analysis and Design of an Order Processing System"). The operation of the proposed system is described in Application Case Study 9–1, "Data Management for Order Processing." Additional background information on Compu-Mail's operations is given in Application Case Study 1–2, "Types of Decisions."

Arlene Wolff, manager of systems and programming at Compu-Mail, has just ordered The Generator, a comprehensive prototyping package. The Generator includes a menu generator, a screen generator, and a report generator. Ms. Wolff experimented with a prerelease version of the package at a computer exhibition and decided to use it at Compu-Mail. However, the package is back-ordered, and she does not expect to receive it for another two weeks. Nevertheless, she wants to use The Generator as the principal design aid for developing new systems. For this reason, she has instructed the project team working on the on-line order processing system to prepare manually initial versions of the menus, screens, and reports the system will include. These designs can then be entered using The Generator as soon as it is installed.

The Assignment

This assignment deals with the proposed on-line order processing system. Put yourself in the role of a programmer/analyst as you complete the assignment. In the assignment, you will be designing a user interface based on hierarchical menus. Sketch each screen on a separate sheet of paper. (Do not be concerned about exact positioning of the I/O, as this will be done automatically by the The Generator.) Label each screen so that the hierarchy of the displays is clear. That is, the main menu is 0.0. The selections on the main menu will lead to screens labeled 1.0, 2.0, and so on. Subordinate screens of the 1.0 screen will be labeled 1.1, 1.2, and so on. Subordinate screens of the 1.1 screen will be labeled 1.1.1, 1.1.2, and so on. Note any necessary assumptions.

1. Sketch the initial screen for the main menu ("Enter a Customer Order," "Enter a Return of Goods," and so on).

2. Sketch a screen for each selection in the main menu. These screens may consist of another menu, a data entry screen, or an information display screen.

3. Sketch a screen that is triggered when an customer name entry is determined to be a new customer.

CHAPTER 14

System Implementation

CHAPTER OVERVIEW

The two preceding chapters (12 and 13) discuss approaches and techniques that can be employed to create an information system. This chapter is concerned with the implementation of a newly created information system and the ongoing operation of this system. The chapter opens with discussions of the learning and reference aids that users need to learn and use the system. This is followed by a discussion on system testing procedures and an overview of the various approaches to converting to a new system. The postimplementation section addresses those activities that are initiated to ensure that the system continues to meet the information needs of the company. The chapter concludes with a presentation of those elements of system design and operation that preserve the integrity and accuracy of the system.

USER SUPPORT FOR SYSTEM IMPLEMENTATION

An information system is intended ultimately for use by its end users. Microcomputer-based systems may have one or, perhaps, several end users. A large mainframe-based system may have thousands of end users. Certainly every system designer strives to create user-friendly systems, but the effective use of such systems is still very much dependent on the quality of the user manuals, help screens, and end user training programs that accompany the information system. Preparation of these learning and reference aids is typically the responsibility of the project team.

User Manuals and Help Screens

Part of the documentation for any information system, no matter how small, is the **user manual**. The typical user manual might contain the following information.

☐ The objectives of the system.

☐ A brief description of the overall system.

☐ A glossary of terms, acronyms, and phrases that are unique to the system.

☐ Instructions on the use of the hardware.

☐ Instructions on the use and operation of the system (menus, data entry screens, system failure, and so on).

☐ Descriptions of all outputs (documents, on-line and hard-copy reports, and so on).

☐ Data collection, update, and/or distribution procedures.

☐ Flow diagrams that graphically illustrate the scope of the system and the overall operating procedures.

End users rely heavily on the user manual during the familiarization and learning period. Afterward, they use it as a reference manual and a training tool. Depending on the scope of the information system, a system may have several user manuals, one for each level of user. For example, one manual might be oriented to operational-level users and another to tactical- and strategic-level users.

With so many systems being on-line, the trend is to design systems that permit users to ask for assistance while interacting with the system. This means that users can request *context-sensitive* **help screens** at any point during the operation of the system. To get help, the user simply presses the "help" key, and a help screen appears. The help screen may include instructions or describe options and considerations that are germane to what the user is doing at the time he or she requested help. Essentially, the help screens are an on-line, interactive version of the user manual.

Training Programs

End users are usually introduced to the functionality of an information system via a one-on-one and/or group lecture training program. At a minimum, the agenda for such a program should include the following.

"COLD TURKEY" SYSTEM CONVERSIONS

Q. In four months we are scheduled to implement a homegrown material requirements planning system (MRP). I am the project leader. While drawing up the conversion plan, it became apparent that we had a real problem. The new MRP system is such a radical change from the way we have traditionally handled manufacturing systems that the conversion calls for some structural reorganization and some facilities changes.

The differences in approach and the scattering of personnel make parallel conversion impossible with current resources. We considered hiring 10 temporary people for two months, but that proposal fell through when the managers involved decided it was a waste of time and money to train temporary people on the old procedures.

Although I have recommended a direct conversion, the users say this is out of the question. They offer no alternative. Do you have one?

A. With the implementation of more and more integrated on-line information systems, direct conversion has become an increasingly appealing alternative to the traditional parallel conversion. The implementation of an MRP system is an invitation to go "cold turkey" with direct conversion. A phased conversion is not as applicable to MRP as it is to other systems.

Offset the greater risk of direct conversion with extra-thorough system testing and user training. I would suggest that you continue to press for a direct conversion effort.

In preparation for in-house user training sessions, instructors devise operational scenarios, complete with test data, to give users an opportunity to familiarize themselves with the system. During the sessions, instructors provide insight into how to make the most effective use of the system. The conversion and implementation process progresses smoothly when users feel comfortable with a system.

Photo courtesy of Hewlett-Packard Company

- ☐ Purpose and objectives of the system.
- ☐ Differences between the existing and the new system.
- ☐ Overview of system operation and procedures.
- ☐ Organization and use of the system's user manual and help screens.
- ☐ Duties and responsibilities of end users.
- ☐ Duties and responsibilities of technical support personnel.
- ☐ Demonstration of the system.
- ☐ An introductory hands-on walkthrough of the system.
- ☐ Familiarization with the system (practice using the system with test data).

Of course, the user manual and the help screens are the primary resources for the user training program. Depending on the complexity of the information system, the duration of the training program can be as short as a few hours or as long as a week.

The importance of user manuals and user training programs cannot be overemphasized. For example, to implement a sophisticated new point-of-sale (POS) system, a department store chain distributed a 200-plus-page user manual to each salesperson, told them to read it, and put the system into operation. Salespeople were given no training. As you might expect, disaster ensued. Shortly after system conversion, customers would routinely complain that salespersons would spend as much as 30 minutes recording a sale. Most of this time was spent thumbing through the user manual. The chain's business dropped off sharply before store management recognized the problem. Once the problem was identified, ongoing user training became a priority activity.

User training programs must be ongoing because employees come and go. Each new employee has to be trained in the use and operation of the system.

SYSTEM AND ACCEPTANCE TESTING

Chapter 12, "Systems Analysis and Programming," and Chapter 13, "Prototyping and Application Development Tools," present steps and approaches to creating information systems. Whether the information system is created using a traditional systems development methodology, rapid prototyping, or a combination of these, the final step before system conversion and implementation is system and acceptance testing. This testing activity encompasses everything that makes up the information system—the hardware, the software, the end users, the procedures (including user manuals), and the data. If needed, the interfaces between the system and other systems are tested as well.

Testing with Test Data

During the programming phase of systems development, programs are written according to system specifications and individually tested. Although the programs that comprise the software for the system have undergone *unit testing* (individual testing) and been debugged, there is no guarantee that the programs will work as a system. To ensure that the software can be combined into an operational information system, the project team performs integrated *systems testing*. An information system for inventory management and control may have a hundred programs and a comprehensive data base; these must be tested together to ensure harmony of operation. The purpose of the system test is to validate all software, input/output, procedures, and the data base. It is a safe bet that a few design errors, programming errors, procedural errors, or oversights will surface during system testing. Minor modifications in design and programming may be required to complete the system test to the satisfaction of the users.

To conduct the system test, the project team compiles and thoroughly tests the system with test data. In this first stage of system testing, tests are run for each subsystem (one of the functional aspects of the system) or cycle (weekly or monthly activities). The test data are judiciously compiled so that all program and system options and all error and validation routines are tested. The tests are repeated and modifications are made until all subsystems or cycles function properly. At this point the entire system is tested as a unit. Testing and modifications continue until the components of the system work as they should and all input/output is validated. For example, the numbers on a summary sales report must be what is expected.

The more ridiculous the deadline, the more it costs to try to meet it.

——— *Anonymous*

Testing with Live Data

The second stage of system testing is done with *live data*. Live data are actual data that have already been processed through the existing system. Testing with live data provides an extra level of assurance that the system will work properly when implemented. As much as programmers, systems analysts, and users try to compile test data that will test all possible options, the ultimate test is to run the system against live data.

During system testing with live data, the users get involved. A representative group of users are trained and set loose on the system. While being observed by project team members, users enter and use live data to perform routine transactions. During this stage of testing, the user manual, help screens, system procedures, and interactions between other systems are given a good test. Testing and modifications are continued until the project team and participating users are satisfied with the results of the test.

User Acceptance Testing

At this point in system testing, all the bugs should be eliminated and all system components and affected personnel should work together smoothly. The system is now presented to the scrutiny of the user managers whose departments will ultimately use the system. The purpose of this last test, called **user acceptance testing**, is to get the user's stamp of approval. User managers examine and test the operation of the system (using live data) until they are satisfied that it meets the original system objectives. Modification and testing continues until it does.

SYSTEM CONVERSION AND IMPLEMENTATION

Approaches to System Conversion

Once acceptance testing is complete, the project team can begin to integrate people, software, hardware, procedures, and data into an operational information system. This normally involves a "conversion" from the existing system to the new one. An organization's approach to system conversion depends on its *willingness to accept risk* and the *amount of time available* for the conversion. Four common approaches are parallel conversion, direct conversion, phased conversion, and pilot conversion. These approaches are illustrated graphically in Figure 14–1 and discussed in the paragraphs that follow.

Parallel Conversion

In **parallel conversion**, the existing system and the new system operate simultaneously, or in parallel, until the project team is confident that the new system is working properly. Parallel conversion has two important advan-

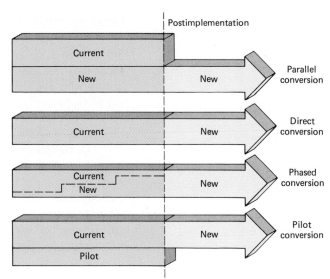

FIGURE 14–1   Common Approaches to System Conversion

tages. First, the existing system serves as backup if the new system fails to operate as expected. Second, the results of the new system can be compared to the results of the existing system.

There is less risk with this strategy because the present system provides backup, but it also doubles the work load for personnel and hardware resources during the conversion. The duration of parallel conversion is usually one month or a major system cycle. For a public utility company, this might be one complete billing cycle, which is usually a month.

Direct Conversion

As companies improve their system testing procedures, they begin to gain confidence in their ability to implement a working system. Some companies forgo parallel conversion in favor of a **direct conversion.** A greater risk is associated with direct conversion because there is no backup in case the system fails.

Companies select this "cold turkey" approach when there is no existing system or when the existing system is substantially different. For example, all on-line hotel reservations systems are implemented cold turkey.

Phased Conversion

In **phased conversion**, an information system is implemented one module at a time by either parallel or direct conversion. For example, in a point-of-sale system, the first phase might be to convert the sales accounting module. The second phase could be the inventory management module. The third might be the credit check module.

Phased conversion has the advantage of spreading out the demand for resources so that an intense demand can be avoided. The disadvantages are that the conversion takes longer, and a system interface must be developed between the existing system and the new system.

Murphy's law: Nothing is as easy as it looks; everything takes longer than you think; and if anything can go wrong, it will.

Pilot Conversion

In **pilot conversion**, the new system is implemented by parallel, direct, or phased conversion as a "pilot" system in only one of the several areas for which it is targeted. For example, suppose that a company wants to implement a manufacturing resources planning system in its eight plants. One plant would be selected as a pilot, and the new information system would be implemented there first.

The advantage of pilot conversion is that the inevitable bugs in a system can be removed before the system is implemented at the other locations. The disadvantage is that the implementation time for the total system takes longer than if the entire system were implemented at one time.

The System Becomes Operational

Once the conversion has been completed, the information system enters the production stage of the system life cycle (see Figure 11–1 in Chapter 11). During the production stage, the system becomes operational and is turned over to the users. The operations function of the information services division provides operational support for the system. This function, discussed in detail in Chapter 5, "Providers of Computer Information Services," encompasses everything associated with the running of an information system. This includes all interaction with the hardware that supports the system. The scope of operations support would typically include these major areas.

- ☐ Data entry and transaction processing, both batch and on-line.
- ☐ Interactive inquiry, both built-in and ad hoc.
- ☐ Maintenance of the data base.
- ☐ Output, including reports (summary, exception, historical, graphic, and so on) and documents (for example, utility bills, mailing labels, authorizations to build, air travel tickets).
- ☐ Transition or preprocessing (massaging data to put them in the proper format for processing, a common activity for electronic data interchange applications).

Managing Change

The development and implementation of virtually any MIS involves change; therefore, **change management** comes into play. To achieve an orderly transition from a manual system to a computer-based information system or to an enhancement of an existing information system, managers must pay particular attention to the effects of change. A good manager is proactive and does not react to the problems of change. The proactive manager keeps everyone informed, thereby silencing the "rumor mill." Inevitably, the implementation of a new information system will result in some shifts in responsibilities. The implementation of an integrated MIS may prompt a major reorganization of personnel.

Perhaps the most important managerial concern is the attitude of subordinates toward the changes brought about by automation. To combat negative attitudes, managers must demonstrate to subordinates how the proposed MIS will help them to do their jobs better and how it will provide greater career opportunities. Workers who understand the benefits of an MIS are much more willing to participate in a conversion effort.

POSTIMPLEMENTATION ACTIVITIES

If you don't know where you are, how can you know where you're going?

——— *Anonymous*

Three to six months after the hardware, software, people, procedures, and data have been integrated into an operational material requirements planning system, key members of the project team conduct a postimplementation evaluation to assess the overall effectiveness of the system.

Photo courtesy of Hewlett-Packard Company

Just as a new automobile will need some screws tightened after a few hundred miles, an information system will need some "fine-tuning" just after implementation. Thereafter, and throughout the production stage of the system life cycle, the system will be modified many times to meet the changing needs of the company.

Postimplementation Review

The **postimplementation review** is a critical examination of the system after it has been put into production. The evaluation is conducted three to six months after implementation. This waiting period allows several factors to stabilize: the resistance to change, the anxieties associated with change, and the learning curve. It also allows time for unanticipated problems to surface.

The postimplementation review focuses on the following.

☐ *A comparison of the system's actual performance versus the anticipated performance objectives.* This comparison provides management with an evaluation of the quality of the system development effort.

☐ *An assessment of each facet of the system with respect to preset criteria.* If any part of the system is judged deficient, plans are made to correct the problems.

☐ *Mistakes.* No information system has ever been developed without mistakes being made. The best way to avoid making the same mistakes again is to identify and document these mistakes.

☐ *Unexpected benefits.* Once operational, unexpected benefits will inevitably surface.

☐ *Unexpected problems.* Once operational, unexpected problems will inevitably surface. More often than not, a new information system will have an unforeseen impact on company procedures, standards, traditions, or other information systems.

System Maintenance

Once an information system is implemented and "goes on-line," the emphasis is switched from *development* to *operations*. In a payroll system, supervisors begin to enter hours worked on their workstations, and the computer center

Q. A consultant recommended that the start of a few large new development projects be delayed by at least one year. This development slowdown is designed to free up MIS resources that can be allocated to documentation, reorganization, and the development of standards and procedures.

I report to a VP who supports the recommendations in theory but is reluctant to delay the development of what he considers to be essential systems. Although everybody is in agreement with the recommendations, they are being ignored by top management. Any support?

A. During the growth of every information services department, there is a point in time at which the mess created to date must be "cleaned up." The consultant has identified that time as now.

Continued new systems development, in the absence of a development framework and standards, can only result in systems of marginal quality. Ask corporate managers if that is what they want. If management insists that the projects be continued, tell them that you will be happy to continue but cannot be responsible for the quality of the end product.

A well-ordered information services department can produce more and better services. Over the long term, these "essential systems" will be insignificant when compared to the benefits derived from the proposed development slowdown.

produces and issues payroll checks. Once operational, an information system becomes a cooperative effort between the users and the information services division.

An information system is dynamic and must be responsive to the changing needs of the company and those who use it. The process of modifying an information system to meet changing needs is known as **system maintenance**.

There are two approaches to system maintenance. The first, and least desirable, is the "reactive" approach. That is, *do nothing unless requested to do so* by the people who use it. The more effective, "proactive" approach requires the project team to *review the system* once or twice a year to see where it can be improved. Even though an information system is placed under the user's microscope each day, pertinent user feedback on system operation is not always related to persons with the authority to initiate a system change. To retrieve this feedback, a review team made up of analysts and users interviews users at all levels, from clerks to executive management, and information technology professionals assigned to the system. The focus of the interviews is system efficiency and effectiveness and/or how the system can be improved. During this review, the review team looks into such things as:

- ☐ Effectiveness of the system.
- ☐ Turnaround time, which is the elapsed time between the submission of a job and the distribution of the results.
- ☐ Response time, which is the elapsed time between when an on-line message is sent and a response is received.
- ☐ Relevance of the information generated by the system.
- ☐ Effectiveness of the user interface.
- ☐ Input/output formats and content.
- ☐ File and data base organization.
- ☐ Update, control, and backup procedures.
- ☐ Currency of system documentation.
- ☐ User suggestions for improved system performance.

The results of periodic system reviews, service requests, and occasionally, a bug in the system are what prompt system maintenance activities.

An information system cannot live forever. The accumulation of modifications and enhancements will eventually make any information system cumbersome and inefficient. Minor modifications are known as **patches**. Depending on the number of patches and enhancements, an information system will remain operational, that is, be in the production stage, from four to seven years.

Toward the end of the useful life of an information system, it is more trouble to continue patching the system than it is to redesign the system from scratch. The end of the production stage signals the "death" stage of the information system life cycle (see Figure 11–1 in Chapter 11). A new system is then "born" of need, and the system development process is repeated.

SYSTEM CONTROLS, AUDITING, SECURITY, AND BACKUP

An information system should run smoothly under normal circumstances. But as Murphy has taught us, "If anything can go wrong, it will." Users, programmers, and operators make oversights and errors in judgment. Computers sometimes fail to work as planned and sometimes they simply cease to function. System controls and information systems auditing procedures help to ensure that the system runs as planned and that errors or inappropriate procedures are detected and corrected before the system is affected.

System Controls

Because of the ever-present potential for human and hardware errors, coupled with the threat of computer crime, it is important that an organization build in controls to ensure the accuracy, reliability, integrity, and security of an information system. Without controls, an enterprising computer criminal might be able to supplement his or her checking account without making a deposit. An erroneous data entry error could result in the delivery of a red car instead of a blue one. Someone expecting a monthly pay check of $2,500 might receive $250,000. A computer operator could cause chaos by forgetting to do the daily audit run. System controls are introduced to prevent these, and any of a thousand other, undesirable events from happening.

Information system controls minimize or eliminate errors before, during, and after processing so that the data entered and the information produced are complete and accurate. Controls also minimize the possibility of computer fraud. There are four types of controls: *input validation*, *processing controls*, *output controls*, and *procedural controls* (see Figure 14–2).

Input Validation

Data are checked for accuracy when entered into the system. In on-line data entry, the data entry operator verifies the data by sight checks. Also, a variety of checking procedures are designed into the software. Two of these software control procedures are discussed next.

□ *Reasonableness check*. Suppose that a customer's maximum order to date is 250 widgets and an order is entered for 2000 widgets. Since an order of 2,000 is much greater than the maximum order to date of 250, the entry is historically unreasonable, and the probable error is brought to the attention of the data entry operator.

□ *Limits check*. A limits check assesses whether the value of an entry is out of line with that expected. For example, a company's policy guarantees 40 hours of work per week for each employee and limits overtime to 15 hours per week. A limits check on the "hours-worked" entry guarantees that a value between 40 and 55, inclusive, is entered.

Processing Controls

Systems analysts and programmers employ a variety of techniques to validate that processing is complete and accurate. Control totals and consistency checks are a few of the many techniques that can be built into the software.

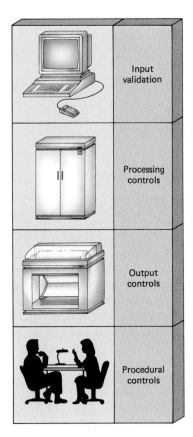

FIGURE 14–2 System Controls

□ *Control total.* A control total, or hash total, is a value that is known to be the accumulated sum of a particular data element. Control totals are used primarily to verify that processing is complete. For example, when a company's payroll checks are printed, the employee numbers are added together and compared to a known value. If the accumulated control total is not equal to the known value, the computer operator knows immediately that some checks were not processed or that some checks were processed that should not have been.

□ *Consistency check.* The consistency check compares like data items for consistency of value. For example, if a company's electricity bill for March is 300 percent higher than the bill for March of last year, the invoice would not be processed. Management would then ask the electric utility company to check the accuracy of the meter reading.

Output Controls

Some people take for granted that any computer-produced output is accurate. Such is not always the case. There are too many things that can go wrong. One of many methods of output control is *crossfoot checking*. This technique is used in reports, such as the one in Figure 14–3, that have column and row totals with some arithmetic relationship to one another. In Figure 14–3, the column totals for each beverage type should equal the total for all delivery routes.

Procedural Controls

In an information system, the work is done either by the computer system or by people. Programs tell the computer what to do. People are guided by procedures. Some procedures are built into the system for control purposes. For example, many companies subscribe to the *separation-of-duties* procedure. The theory behind this procedure is that if responsibilities for input, processing, and output are assigned to different people, most attempts to defraud the system will be foiled. It is unlikely that would-be computer criminals could solicit that much cooperation.

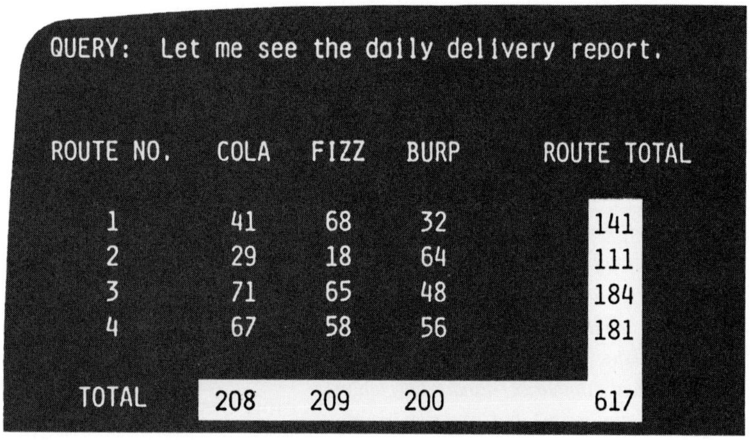

```
QUERY: Let me see the daily delivery report.


  ROUTE NO.    COLA   FIZZ   BURP     ROUTE TOTAL

      1         41     68     32        141
      2         29     18     64        111
      3         71     65     48        184
      4         67     58     56        181

    TOTAL      208    209    200        617
```

FIGURE 14–3 Crossfoot Checking
The sum of the row totals equals the sum of the column totals.

A corporation is vulnerable when one operator has sole responsibility for running a particular information system. Because of this, many companies have a mandatory vacation policy requiring programmers, operators, and others in sensitive positions to take their vacations in blocks of no less than two weeks.

Information Systems Auditing

Every corporation should have an internal information systems auditor or, perhaps, an auditing group. The information systems audit staff functions to ensure the integrity of operational information systems. There are three types of information system audits. These are *system development audits*, *operational audits*, and *application audits*.

System Development Audits

In system development audits, the information systems audit staff serves as advisors to members of the development project team. Their involvement in the project guarantees that appropriate audit controls are embedded in the original system design.

Operational Audits

Operational audits are periodically conducted on an MIS to ensure that proper system controls exist and that they are being followed. Hash totals, crossfoot checking, separation of duties, and mandatory vacations (all discussed previously) are examples of such controls and procedures. Auditors use these and a number of other techniques to minimize the possibility and opportunity for abuse of a computer-based information system.

Application Audits

The objective of periodic application audits is to validate the integrity of an information system. In an application audit, information systems auditors validate that a operational MIS is working according to design specifications. This is in contrast to a periodic system review where present and future needs as well as system effectiveness are the key considerations. To validate an MIS, auditors may trace a summary report back to the original transactions, and vice versa. They intentionally try to block or foul the system to check internal controls. Special audit software is used to aid in the information systems audit process. For example, audit programs provide the auditor with file sampling capabilities. The auditor uses these programs to check records for quality, completeness, accuracy, and efficiency.

System Security

Certainly, one of the most important considerations in the development and ongoing operation of an information system is security. As more and more systems go on-line, more people have access to the system. A company must be extremely careful not to compromise the integrity of the system. The company must be equally careful with the "engine" for the information system—the computer.

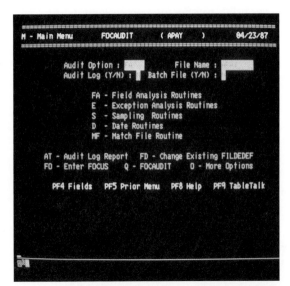

This is one of the menu screens for FOCAUDIT, a FOCUS-based computer-assisted audit package for financial auditors. FOCAUDIT includes interactive procedures for performing the full range of audit functions: analyzing fields (record counts, high-low values, and so on); sampling (attribute, interval, random, and so on) and validating data; testing and converting dates (Julian/Gregorian); and producing statistical summaries (standard deviation, quartiles, means, and so on) and exception reports (duplicate names/values, gap detection, and so on).

Information Builders, Inc.

An information system has many points of vulnerability and too much is at stake to overlook the threats to the security of an information system and a computer center. These threats take many forms: white-collar crime, natural disasters (for example, earthquakes, floods), vandalism, and carelessness.

White-collar crime is real and exists undetected in some of the most unlikely places. It is sophisticated crime with sophisticated criminals. And it is more widespread than estimates would lead us to believe. Most computer crimes are undetected; others are unreported. A bank may prefer to write off a $100,000 embezzlement rather than publicly announce to its depositors that its computer system is vulnerable.

This section is devoted to discussing the security measures needed to neutralize security threats to an information system or to a computer center.

Computer Center Security

A company's computer center has a number of points of vulnerability; these are *hardware*, *software*, *files/data bases*, *data communications*, and *personnel*. Each is discussed separately in the following sections and illustrated in Figure 14–4.

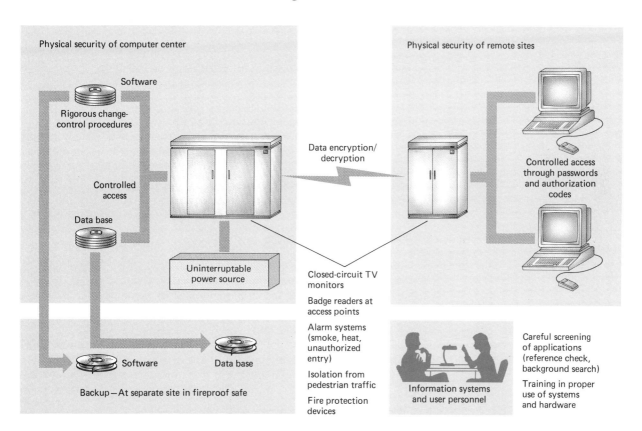

FIGURE 14–4   Security Precautions
Some, or all, of the security measures noted in the figure are implemented in most computer centers. Each precaution helps to minimize the risk of an MIS's or a computer system's vulnerability to crime, disasters, and failure.

HARDWARE   If the hardware fails, the information system fails. The threat of failure can be minimized by implementing security precautions that prevent access by unauthorized personnel and by taking steps to keep all hardware operational.

Common approaches to securing the premises from unauthorized entry include closed-circuit TV monitors, alarm systems, and computer-controlled devices that check employee badges, fingerprints, or voice prints before unlocking doors at access points. Also, computer centers should be isolated from pedestrian traffic. Machine room fires are extinguished by a special chemical that douses the fire but does not destroy the files or equipment.

Computers, especially mainframe computers, must have a "clean," continuous source of power. To minimize the effects of "dirty" power or power outages, many computer centers have installed an **uninterruptible power source (UPS)**. Dirty power, such as sags and surges in power output or brownouts (low power), causes data transmission errors and program execution errors. An UPS system serves as a control buffer between the external power source and the computer system. In an UPS system, the computer is powered by batteries (which deliver clean power), which in turn are regenerated by an external power source. If the external power source fails, the UPS system permits operation to continue for a period of time after an outage. This allows operators to either "power down" normally or switch to a backup power source, normally a diesel generator. Until recently, UPS systems were associated only with mainframe computer systems. Now, UPS systems are economically feasible for microcomputer systems.

SOFTWARE   Unless properly controlled, the software for an information system can be modified for personal gain. Thus close control over software development and the documentation of an information system is needed to minimize the opportunity for computer crime. Operational control procedures that are built into the design of an information system will constantly monitor processing accuracy. These controls are discussed earlier in this section. Unfortunately, cagey programmers have been known to get around some of these controls. Perhaps the best way to safeguard programs from unlawful tampering is to use rigorous change-control procedures. Such procedures make it difficult to modify a program for purposes of personal gain.

Bank programmers certainly have opportunities for personal gain. In one case, a couple of programmers modified a savings system to make small deposits from other accounts to their own accounts. Here's how it worked: the interest for each savings account was compounded and credited daily; the calculated interest was rounded to the nearest penny before being credited to the savings account; programs were modified to round down on all interest calculations and put the "extra" penny in one of the programmer's savings accounts. It may not seem like much, but a penny a day from thousands of accounts adds up to big bucks. The "beauty" of the system was that the books balanced and depositors did not miss the 15 cents (an average of 1/2 cent per day for 30 days) that was judiciously taken from each account each month. Even the auditors have difficulty detecting this crime because the total interest paid out for all accounts is correct. However, the culprits got greedy and were apprehended when someone noticed that they repeatedly withdrew inordinately large sums of money.

Take care of the means and the end will take care of itself.

——— *Mahatma Gandhi*

Unfortunately, other enterprising programmers in other industries have been equally imaginative.

FILES/DATA BASES   The data base contains the raw material for information. Often, the files/data bases are the lifeblood of a company. For example, how many companies can afford to lose their accounts receivable file, which documents who owes what? Having several *generations of backups* (backups to backups) to all files is not sufficient insurance against loss of files/data bases. The backup and master files should be stored in fireproof safes in separate rooms, preferably in separate buildings.

DATA COMMUNICATIONS   The mere existence of data communications capabilities, where data are transmitted via communications links from one computer to another, poses a threat to security. A knowledgeable criminal can tap into the system from a remote location and use the system for personal gain. In a well-designed system, this is not an easy task. But it can be and has been done! When one criminal broke a company's security code and tapped into the network of computers, he was able to order certain products without being billed. He filled a warehouse before eventually being caught. Another tapped into an international banking exchange system to "reroute" funds to an account of his own in a Swiss bank. In another case, an oil company was able consistently to outbid a competitor by "listening in" on the latter's data transmissions. On several occasions, overzealous young "hackers" have tapped into sensitive defense computer systems; fortunately, no harm was done.

Some companies use **cryptography** to scramble messages sent over data communications channels. Someone who unlawfully intercepts such a message would find meaningless strings of characters. Cryptography is analogous to the "code book" used by intelligence people during the cloak-and-dagger days. Instead of a code book, however, a "key" is used in conjunction with **encryption/decryption** hardware to unscramble the message. Both sender and receiver must have the key, which is actually an algorithm that rearranges the bit structure of a message. Companies that routinely transmit sensitive data over communications channels are moving to data encryption as a means by which to limit access to their information systems and their data bases.

PERSONNEL   The biggest threat to a company's security system is its own employees. Managers are paying close attention to who gets hired for positions that permit access to computer-based information systems and sensitive data. Many companies flash a message such as, "all information on this system is confidential and proprietary." It's not very user friendly, but it gets the message across to employees that they may be fired if they abuse the system. Also, someone who is grossly incompetent can cause just as much harm as someone who is inherently dishonest.

Information Systems Security

Information systems security is classified as physical or logical. **Physical security** refers to hardware, facilities, magnetic disks, and other things that could be illegally accessed, stolen, or destroyed.

This photo illustrates how cryptography works. An employee assessment is produced by a manager using word processing and is stored on disk in EBCDIC, a common 8-bit encoding system. In EBCDIC, the first word, "John," becomes a hexadecimal D1968895. However, prior to being sent to company headquarters via data communications, the EBCDIC version of the text is encrypted such that "John" becomes a hexadecimal 4A6F686E (see photo). This is a nonsensical bit configuration to anyone without the key. The encrypted version of the text (the hexadecimal numbers in the photo) is transmitted to headquarters. At headquarters, the employee assessment is decrypted to its original form for viewing.

Jones Futurex, Inc.

Personal computers are everywhere and, as such, are particularly vulnerable to unauthorized use or malicious tampering. As an alternative to passwords or as an added layer of security, many companies are opting to use a magnetic card reader as part of the user sign-on procedure. The card reader reads commonly carried credit cards, door opener cards, telephone cards, and so on. When used in conjunction with authorization codes, a PC can have the same level of security as an automatic teller machine.

Harcom Security Systems Corporation

Logical security is built into the software by permitting only authorized persons to access and use the system. Logical security for on-line systems is achieved primarily by **passwords** and **authorization codes**. Only those persons with a "need to know" are told the password and given authorization codes. On occasion, however, these security codes fall into the wrong hands. When this happens, an unauthorized person can gain access to programs and sensitive files by simply dialing up the computer and entering the codes.

Keeping passwords and authorization codes from the computer criminal is not easy. One computer criminal took advantage of the fact that a bank's automatic teller machine (ATM) did not "time out" for several minutes. That is, the authorization code could be entered without reinserting the card to initiate another transaction. Using high-powered binoculars, he watched from across the street as the numeric code was being entered. He then ran over to the ATM and was waiting when the customer left. He quickly entered the code and made withdrawals before the machine timed out. Needless to say, this design flaw has been eliminated in existing ATM systems.

Level of Risk

No amount of security measures will completely remove the vulnerability of a computer center or an information system. Security systems are implemented in degrees. That is, an information system can be made marginally secure or very secure, but never totally secure. Each company must determine the level of risk that it is willing to accept. Unfortunately, some corporations are willing to accept an enormous risk and hope that these rare instances of crime and disaster do not occur. Some corporations have found out too late that *rarely* is not the same as *never!*

System Backup

Occasionally, the worst case scenario comes to pass—total system failure. To avoid catastrophe during system failure, **backup** and **checkpoint/restart** procedures are defined during the systems development process. These procedures describe the extra processes included in the system that cope with system failures. When a system fails, backup files/data bases and/or backup transaction logs (see Chapter 9, "Data Management") are used to recreate processing from the last "checkpoint." The system is "restarted" at the last checkpoint and normal operation is resumed. Periodically during the chronology of system processing, operators establish a checkpoint such that any processing to that point in time is saved and cannot be destroyed.

All the backup files and procedures in the world are worthless if there is no hardware on which to run them. Any of a number of disasters, from fire to malicious vandalism, could render a company's computer system useless. As a backup, many company's have agreements with one another to share their computing resources in case of disaster. When this happens, both companies would operate only critical systems until a new computer system could be installed. Other companies contract with a commercial disaster recovery services. These services make a fully configured computer system available to clients in case of a disaster. Backup hardware sites are discussed in more detail in Chapter 16, "Managing Information Services."

■ A typical user manual includes system objectives, a system description, a glossary, instructions on the hardware and system operation, I/O descriptions, and flow diagrams.

■ Context-sensitive help screens, which are accessible to user during an interactive session, provide instructions or describe options and considerations that are germane to what the user is doing at the time he or she requested help.

■ End users are introduced to an information system via a training program that includes such information as the purpose and objectives of the system, differences between the existing and the new system, and the responsibilities of end users.

■ Although the programs that make up an information system have been debugged on an individual basis, they must be combined and subjected to integrated systems testing prior to implementation.

■ After system testing with live data comes user acceptance testing. During this test, user managers examine and test the operation of the system until they are satisfied that it meets the original system objectives.

■ The four common approaches to system conversion are parallel conversion, direct conversion, phased conversion, and pilot conversion. The approach that an organization selects depends on their willingness to accept risk and the amount of time available for the conversion.

■ Once the conversion has been completed, the information system enters the production stage of the system life cycle and is turned over to the users.

■ To achieve an orderly transition from a manual system to a computer-based information system or to an enhancement of

an existing information system, managers must employ the principles of change management.

■ The postimplementation review, which is a critical examination of the system after it has been put into production, is conducted three to six months after implementation.

■ An information system is dynamic and must be responsive to the changing needs of the company and those who use it. The process of modifying an information system to meet changing needs is known as system maintenance. Maintenance activities are usually initiated by periodic system reviews, service requests, and bugs in the system.

■ Companies build controls into their information systems to ensure system accuracy, reliability, integrity, and security. The four types of controls are input validation, processing controls, output controls, and procedural controls.

■ The information systems audit staff, which ensures the integrity of operational information systems, conducts system development audits, operational audits, and application audits.

■ The threats to the security of computer centers and information systems call for precautionary measures. A computer center can be vulnerable in its hardware, software, files/data bases, data communications, and personnel. Information systems security is classified as physical security or logical security. Security systems are implemented in degrees, and no system or computer center can be made totally secure.

■ To avoid catastrophe during system failure, backup and checkpoint/restart procedures are defined during the systems development process.

application audit	direct conversion	parallel conversion	reasonableness check
authorization code	encryption/decryption	password	system development audit
backup	help screen	patch	system maintenance
change management	input validation	phased conversion	systems testing (Ch. 12)
checkpoint/restart	limits check	physical security	uninterruptible power source (UPS)
consistency check	live data	pilot conversion	
control total	logical security	postimplementation review	unit testing (Ch. 12)
crossfoot checking	operational audit	procedural control	user acceptance testing
cryptography	output control	processing control	user manual

1. Which comes first during system testing, testing with live data or testing with test data?

2. List the three areas addressed during a postimplementation review.

3. Name three items of information to be included in a user manual.

4. What is the purpose of transition or preprocessing?

5. Describe what is meant when someone describes a help screen as being "context sensitive."

6. Name two types controls for validating input. Name two types of processing controls.

7. List the types of information system audits.

8. At what point during the systems development process is an information system given the user's stamp of approval?

9. What is the purpose of a "key" in cryptography?

10. What precautions can be taken to minimize the effects of hardware failure?

11. The mere fact that a system uses data communications poses a threat to security. Why so?

12. What advantage does direct conversion have over parallel conversion? Parallel over direct conversion?

13. Give two examples of uses of a control total.

DISCUSSION QUESTIONS

1. Assuming that test data are designed and compiled to test all system options, why is it recommended to continue testing with live data?

2. Develop an argument in support of the proactive approach to system maintenance as opposed to the reactive approach to system maintenance.

3. Why is change management so important when converting from a manual system to a computer-based information system?

4. In a federal agency, passwords are given to people who need access to confidential information. A new set of passwords is issued every other month. Is this extra work of issuing new passwords really necessary? Discuss.

5. Evaluate your college's (or your company's) computer center with respect to security. Identify areas where you think it is vulnerable and discuss ways to improve its security.

6. In the past, bank officers have been reluctant to report computer crimes. If you were a customer of a bank that made such a decision, how would you react?

7. Every Friday night, a company makes backup copies of all master files and programs. Why is this necessary? The company has both tape and disk drives. What storage medium would you suggest for the backup? Why?

8. As a security precaution, some MIS managers have initiated a policy that requires two programmers to be familiar with each program. Argue for *or* against this procedure.

9. A bank programmer developed an algorithm to determine the check digit for the bank's credit card numbers. The programmer sold the algorithm, one of the bank's control procedures, to an underground group that specialized in counterfeit credit cards. A year later the programmer was caught and pleaded guilty. What do you feel is a just sentence for this crime?

10. Do you feel that operator sight checks are a valid approach to data entry verification? Why or why not?

11. Discuss specific input, processing, output, and procedural controls that could be built into a payroll system.

12. During the implementation of computer applications, managers have traditionally focused on hardware and software. Now they realize that they must pay more attention to the human needs as well. What are these needs?

13. The overwhelming majority of financial institutions do not use encryption/decryption hardware, primarily because of the expense involved. The expense is trivial when compared to the potential loss. What arguments would you use to convince bank management that the cost of purchasing and installing encryption/decryption can be justified.

APPLICATION CASE STUDY 14–1

Planning for Conversion, Security, and Backup

The Situation

At Gabriel Industries the Computer Services Department has these five projects in various stages of development:

☐ Developing and implementing a new accounts receivable system (see Application Case Study 1–1, "The Decision-Making Process").

☐ Upgrading the batch personnel/payroll system to on-line (see Application Case Study 2–2, "On-line Versus Off-line").

☐ Designing and implementing a corporate communications network (see Application Case Study 8–1, "An Interstate Network").

☐ Upgrading the material requirements planning system to include just-in-time inventory planning (see Application Case Study 12–3, "Analysis and Design of an MRP System with Just-in-Time").

☐ Upgrading the batch order processing system so that Gabriel's customers can place orders using EDI.

John Robson, manager of the Computer Services Department, is concerned that planning for the critical elements of conversion, security, backup, and evaluation may be deficient or omitted entirely for some projects. He has several reasons for this concern.

☐ Many projects are being undertaken simultaneously.

☐ Several new programmer/analysts have joined the department.

☐ Rapid prototyping has been introduced into the system development methodology (see Application Case Study 13–1, "The Impact of Prototyping and Application Development Tools").

☐ Top management is pressuring John Robson to reduce the backlog of applications.

The Assignment

1. Recommend a conversion approach (parallel, direct, phased, or pilot) for each of the five projects under development. Justify your recommendations. Note any necessary assumptions.

2. Describe the security measures that you feel will need to be implemented to ensure the integrity of the upgraded order processing system. Justify your recommendations. Note any necessary assumptions.

3. Describe the backup procedures that you feel will need to be implemented to enable the upgraded personnel/payroll system to function with minimal interruption in the event of a computer system failure. Include manual or other procedures that may need to be employed on an interim basis. Justify your recommendations. Note any necessary assumptions.

4. List specific evaluation criteria that can be used to determine whether the upgraded MRP system has met its objectives once the system goes on-line.

APPLICATION CASE STUDY 14–2

User Support for System Implementation

The Situation

An on-line order processing system is currently under development at Compu-Mail. The operation of the on-line system is described in Application Case Study 9–1, "Data Management for Order Processing." Background information on Compu-Mail and the current batch order processing system is given in Application Case Study 1–2, "Types of Decisions."

Arlene Wolff, Compu-Mail's manager of systems and programming, recognizes that order processing is the lifeblood of the company. She wants the transition to the new system to be as smooth as possible, and she has assigned one of the programmer/analysts on the project team to write the user manual, design context-sensitive help screens, and develop a training plan for the users of the system.

The Assignment

Put yourself in the role of the programmer/analyst as you complete the following assignment regarding Compu-Mail's new on-line order processing system. Note any necessary assumptions.

1. Prepare a draft copy of the section of the user manual that describes the objectives of the system.

2. Prepare a draft copy of the section of the user manual that describes the procedures a clerk should follow when a customer is placing an order by telephone and wants to charge the purchase. Include the text of all appropriate "verbal scripts" that the clerk is to follow in various situations (for example, the initial greeting, the response when a customer's charge is not approved, and so on).

3. Prepare a draft copy of the section of the user manual that describes the procedures the credit manager is to follow when the system rejects a customer's purchase order.

4. On occasion, a clerk will key in a customer number or name, and the system will indicate that the customer is not in the data base. Three circumstances prompt this event. First, this may be a new customer, in which case the data entry screen for new customers is displayed and the appropriate data are entered. Second, the customer number may have been entered incorrectly by the clerk, in which case the clerk rekeys the number. Third, the customer may have provided an incorrect number, in which case the clerk searches the data base by customer name. When a match is found, the clerk confirms the match by checking the addresses.

a. Design one or more help screens that a clerk can request when the system indicates that a customer number is not in the data base. Label the screens so that the function of each screen is clear.

b. Describe how a clerk might ask for a help screen to be displayed (for example, pressing a certain key). Should the instructions for requesting help be displayed permanently on the screen? Justify your answer.

c. Describe how a clerk would leave a help screen and identify which screen would be displayed following the help screen.

5. Describe how you would approach the following aspects of the training program.

a. *A demonstration of the system.* When should this take place? Specify each step in the "program," including logging onto the system, entering orders (include the major events that may occur), and logging off the system. Who should perform the demonstration? Justify your answers.

b. *Practice sessions with test data.* When should this take place? How can you be sure that every trainee follows each step of the practice session? Who should conduct the practice sessions? How many trainees should there be in a group? Justify your answers.

c. *Describe alternatives to training replacement personnel.* Assume that new personnel arrive sporadically, one at a time (versus in a group). Which training method would you recommend? Justify your answer.

CHAPTER **15**

An MIS Case Study

KEY TOPICS

CHAPTER OVERVIEW

In this chapter, a variety of MIS and business concepts are discussed and illustrated in a case study. The case study makes it possible to demonstrate the work and information flow of an integrated MIS within the context of a business environment. The case study centers on Zimco Enterprises, a fictitious medium-sized manufacturer of handy consumer goods. Zimco's MIS has four functional components: finance and accounting, personnel, production and inventory control, and sales and marketing. Zimco is, of course, a fictional company, but it is very real in that its people, systems, methods, and planning mirror that of other successful businesses.

ZIMCO ENTERPRISES: BACKGROUND SUMMARY

This chapter presents a case study with diagrams and supporting discussions that describe an integrated management information system (MIS) for Zimco Enterprises, a fictitious light manufacturing company. The overall MIS and its four functional components are presented in this chapter.

Zimco was founded in 1876 during the post-Civil War era by Ezekiel "Zeke" F. Zimmers. During the past century, Zimco has thrived by developing and selling a variety of consumer goods that meet the market demands of the time. Zimco management adopted a simple entrepreneurial philosophy: produce a limited line of high-quality consumer products that are innovative and for which there is relatively little (or no) competition. Management figured that if it could identify a need early and produce the right product at the right price, it could corner the market. Today, Zimco produces and sells four very successful consumer products: Stibs, Teglers, Qwerts, and Farkles.

Zimco is a $150 million (annual sales) company with about 1,500 employees nationwide. Except for 100 field representatives, all employees work out of the the Dallas, Texas, headquarters office or one of the four regional plants, located at Dallas, Becker (Minnesota), Eugene (Oregon), and Reston (Virginia). Each of the four plant sites is also a *regional distribution center* and a *regional sales office* for all Zimco products (Figure 15–1).

Zimco is classically organized into four *line* divisions and one *staff* division. The four line divisions are the Accounting Division, the Sales and Marketing Division, the Personnel Division, and the Operations Division, which includes manufacturing, distribution, research and development (R&D), and purchasing. The Computer and Information Services Division, which is commonly abbreviated as CIS, provides services to all areas of corporate operation. All division heads are vice presidents and report directly to the president, Preston Smith. The corporate staff, which includes legal

FIGURE 15–1   Zimco Headquarters and Plant Sites

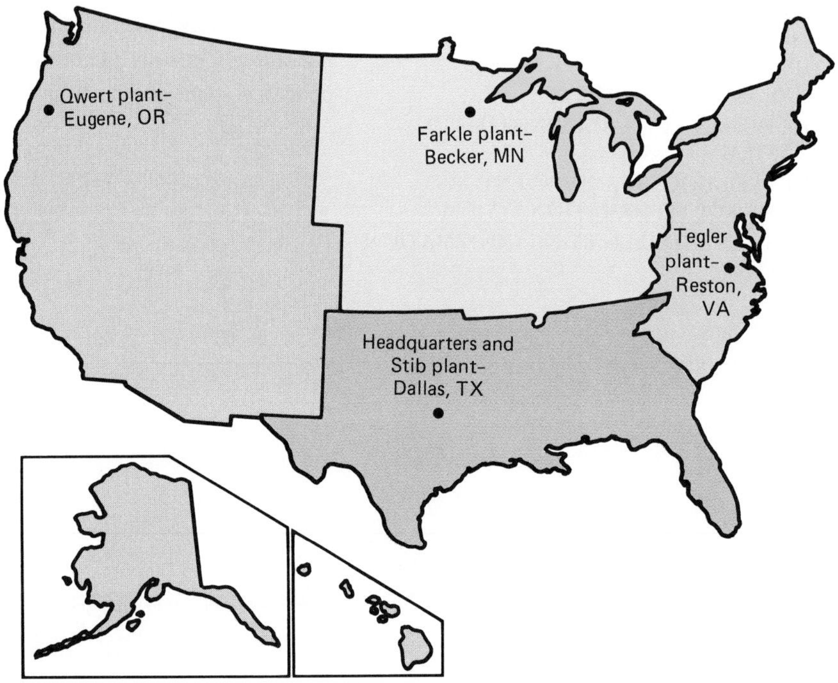

affairs, public relations, and other support groups, also reports to the president. The function and operation of CIS and the four functional divisions are described briefly:

- □ *Computer and Information Services Division (CIS).* The vice president of the Computer and Information Services (CIS) Division, Conrad Innis, is charged with the support of all Zimco Enterprises information processing requirements that are consistent with corporate objectives.

- □ *Finance and Accounting Division.* The head of the Finance and Accounting Division, Monroe Green, oversees the Finance and Accounting departments. The Accounting Department collects and manipulates monetary data to provide information that reflects Zimco's monetary activity. The Finance Department seeks to optimize Zimco's cash flow.

- □ *Sales and Marketing Division.* Sally Marcio, the vice president of the Sales and Marketing Division, is responsible for the activities of the Sales and Marketing departments. Zimco relies exclusively on field sales representatives to sell its products. The Sales Department field reps work out of the four regional sales offices (southern, northern, western, eastern) and call on thousands of retailers and wholesalers throughout the country. The Marketing Department is concerned primarily with making consumers aware of the products that Zimco has to offer.

- □ *Personnel Division.* The vice president of the Personnel Division, Peggy Peoples, has the responsibility for all personnel accounting functions. Peggy's division hires people to meet work force requirements and provides services to individuals and departments regarding personnel benefits, compensation, and other personnel matters. The department also maintains a skills inventory and does the background work for internal training sessions.

- □ *Operations Division.* Otto Manning, vice president of the Operations Division, sees that the products are made and delivered to customers. The plant managers in Dallas, Eugene, Becker, and Reston report to the manager of Manufacturing and Distribution, who, in turn, reports to Otto Manning. Associated with each plant is a regional distribution center for all Zimco products. Managers of the Research and Development Department and the Purchasing Department also report to Otto.

Details of how these divisions interact with one another via integrated computer systems (for example, information flow) are illustrated and discussed later in this chapter.

THE INTEGRATED MANAGEMENT INFORMATION SYSTEM

The four functional divisions at Zimco Enterprises (Finance and Accounting, Sales and Marketing, Operations, and Personnel) work together as a unit to accomplish the goals of the corporation. Each division is very much dependent on information derived from the others. In this section we'll take a *top-down view* of Zimco's overall management information system. To do this, we'll start at the "top" (general overview) and examine a diagram that illustrates the basic information flow between the four divisions. Later in this chapter, we'll move "down" the ladder and take a closer look (greater detail) at the information flow within each of the four divisions. The design tool used to graphically illustrate the flow of information, at both the overview and detailed levels, is the data flow diagram or DFD. The DFD technique is described in Chapter 12, "Systems Analysis and Programming."

Strategic-Level Information Flow

The CIS Division compiled the "MIS overview" of Figure 15–2 to provide top management with a strategic overview of the information flow within Zimco Enterprises. The MIS overview diagram also provides documentation of Zimco's information systems.

In the "business system" model presented in Figure 1–3 in Chapter 1, "Information Processing in Perspective," the corporate resources (money, material, people, and information), the corporate functions, and the products are shown to interact with a variety of *entities* (employees, suppliers, customers, and so on), both within and outside of a company. These interactions, as well as the basic information flow between the four functional areas, are graphically portrayed in the overview data flow diagram of Figure 15–2. These interactions are further expanded, or "exploded," in tactical- and operational-level DFDs in the the remainder of this chapter.

The function of the CIS Division is to facilitate the flow of information within Zimco Enterprises. Since all computer-based information at one time or another passes through the CIS Division (or its computers), you might say that CIS is the nucleus of information flow within Zimco. However, to simplify things, *the intermediate flow of information through CIS is omitted in the overview data flow diagram of Figure 15–2 such that information is shown to flow directly from one functional division to the next.*

The MIS overview in Figure 15–2 highlights the interdependence between the four line divisions at Zimco. For example, the Finance and Accounting Division receives purchase orders from the Operations Division, accounts receivable data from the Sales and Marketing Division, and pay and benefits data from the Personnel Division. In turn, the Finance and Accounting Division provides cost information to the Operations Division, gross sales information to the Sales and Marketing Division, and information regarding the division's work force requirements to the Personnel Division. Information flows to and from the other three divisions are illustrated in Figure 15–2.

The two entities internal to Zimco are *employees* and *managers*. The employees entity encompasses all employees, including managers. The managers entity includes managers at the operational, tactical, and strategic levels. The interaction between Zimco's integrated MIS and the employees entity generally falls into the areas of pay, benefits, and training. The interaction between the MIS and managers entity is primarily in the areas of management inquiries, reports, and directives. For example, in the Sales and Marketing Division, management routinely makes inquiries regarding the progress of sales of certain products. The system also supplies forecasts of potential sales. These forecasts eventually become input to the Operations Division.

There are many external entities from which the Zimco MIS receives input and to which it must provide output. These external entities include

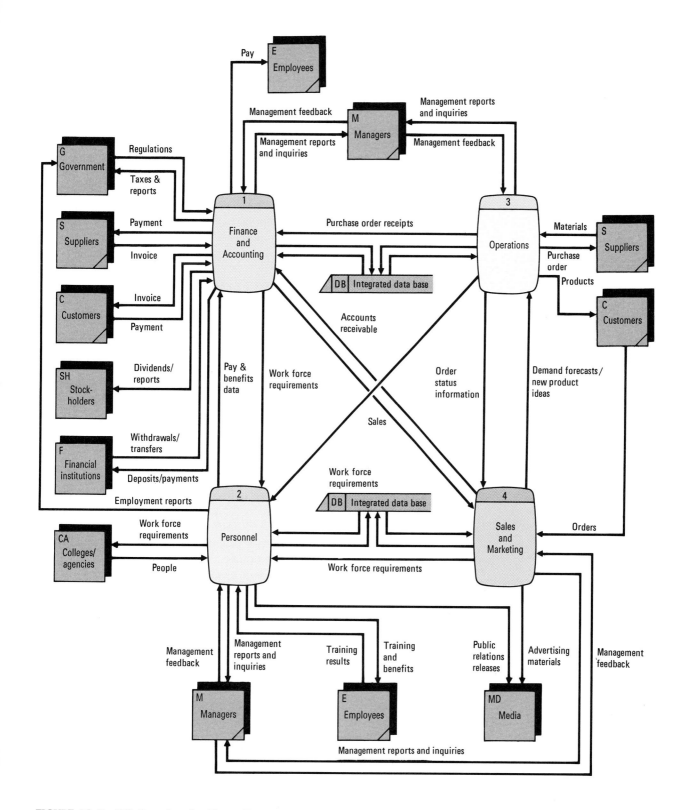

FIGURE 15–2   MIS Overview for Zimco Enterprises

the *government* (all levels), *suppliers, customers, stockholders, financial institutions, colleges/agencies,* and the *media.*

Zimco's primary interaction with the government is in the area of taxes. Payment is made to suppliers for the materials that they provide. Zimco's customers, who are primarily retailers and wholesalers, are the primary source of revenue. The stockholders own Zimco and, therefore, are interested in its ongoing well-being and its dividends. The financial institutions service Zimco in much the same way that they service individuals; that is, Zimco deposits, withdraws, transfers, and invests money as needed to meet the company's liquidity requirements. Colleges and employment agencies are the primary source of Zimco's people resources. Zimco routinely uses the media, primarily newspapers, magazines, radio, and television, to advertise its products. Also, promotions and Zimco news items are released to local newspapers.

The Integrated Corporate Data Base

The only data store (the open-ended boxes in DFD diagrams) in Figure 15–2 is Zimco's integrated data base. The data base symbol is repeated to simplify the presentation of the DFD. The diagonal line on the left end of the data store symbols indicates that the data store is repeated elsewhere in the DFD.

To explain the concept of an integrated data base, we need to back up a few years and discuss Zimco's data base as it was prior to 1980. At that time, Zimco had several dozen traditional flat files, each designed to meet a specific user group's requirements. When a file was designed and created, very little thought was given to how it would benefit Zimco as a whole. As a result, many very similar, but different, files were created. For example, basic customer data were collected and maintained in separate files for the headquarters sales office, for the Distribution Department, for the Accounting Department, and for the Customer Service Department. Imagine, when customer data changed (for example, the name of the purchasing agent), each file would have to be updated separately!

Conrad Innis, the vice president of the CIS Division, recognized that data redundancy is costly. When he first joined Zimco, he said, "data redundancy can be minimized by designing an integrated data base to serve Zimco as a whole, not a single department. To do this we'll need database management system (DBMS) software." DBMS software concepts are discussed in detail in Chapter 9, "Data Management."

Zimco first installed DBMS software in 1981 and has upgraded it several times since. The four categories of data included as part of Zimco's integrated data base are *manufacturing/inventory, customer/sales, personnel,* and *general accounting.* The Technical Support Department of CIS is responsible for maintaining the integrated data base. Zimco employees have access to all or part of the data base, depending on their need to know.

Zimco's integrated data base provides its managers with enormous flexibility in the types of reports that can be generated and the types of on-line inquires that can be made. Otto Manning, vice president of operations, said recently that "the greater access to information provided by Zimco's integrated data base enables me to make better decisions. As a result, we are able to produce a quality product at less cost than our competitors."

The Four Major Processes in Zimco's MIS

It is no coincidence that the four major information systems in Zimco's MIS correspond to the four functional divisions at Zimco (see Figure 15–2). Zimco's MIS is an on-line, interactive, menu-driven system that puts data processing and information gathering at the fingertips of end users. The functional components of Zimco's MIS are

FACS: The Finance and Accounting Control System
       (Process 1 of MIS: Finance and Accounting)

PERES: The Personnel Resources System
       (Process 2 of MIS: Personnel)

PICS: The Production and Inventory Control System
       (Process 3 of MIS: Operations)

SAMIS: The Sales and Marketing Information System
       (Process 4 of MIS: Sales and Marketing)

All the MIS component systems share a common data base, thereby eliminating much of the data redundancy that plague other nonintegrated companies.

Zimco, like just about every other company, created acronyms for its systems to make everyday conversation among workers a little more efficient. It is much easier for an end user to say "picks" (for PICS) than it is to say "Production and Inventory Control System."

THE FINANCE AND ACCOUNTING INFORMATION SYSTEM

Zeke Zimmers, Jr., then the president of Zimco Enterprises, walked into the accounting office just after a visibly tired group of accountants had completed the year-end closing for 1933. He announced bluntly: "I've hired an automation expert and I want all of you to cooperate with him. Let's bring our accounting procedures into the twentieth century. We should not have to work night and day for months just to close our books each year. Technology has provided us with machines to help us and we should be using them!"

It was apparent to Zeke that accounting was the obvious place to begin automating Zimco's administrative activities. Automation expenses were easy to justify with accounting applications. The tasks were repetitive, they involved numerous calculations, and they required the periodic storage and retrieval of data.

Zimco's administrative activities have continued to evolve with the technology. Fifty-plus years later, the Finance and Accounting Division has a sophisticated system it proudly calls the Finance and Accounting Control System, or FACS. FACS, which was developed in-house by CIS in close cooperation with the Finance and Accounting Division, is the envy of a good many businesses in the Dallas-Ft. Worth area.

During the early stages of the FACS development project, the project team spent a week mapping out the information and control flows that involve the Finance and Accounting Division. An overview result of that work is shown in Figure 15–3. The systems analysts, accountants, and financial people on the team decided to divide the system into five logical subsystems (see Figure 15–3). The subsystems are not necessarily aligned with particular

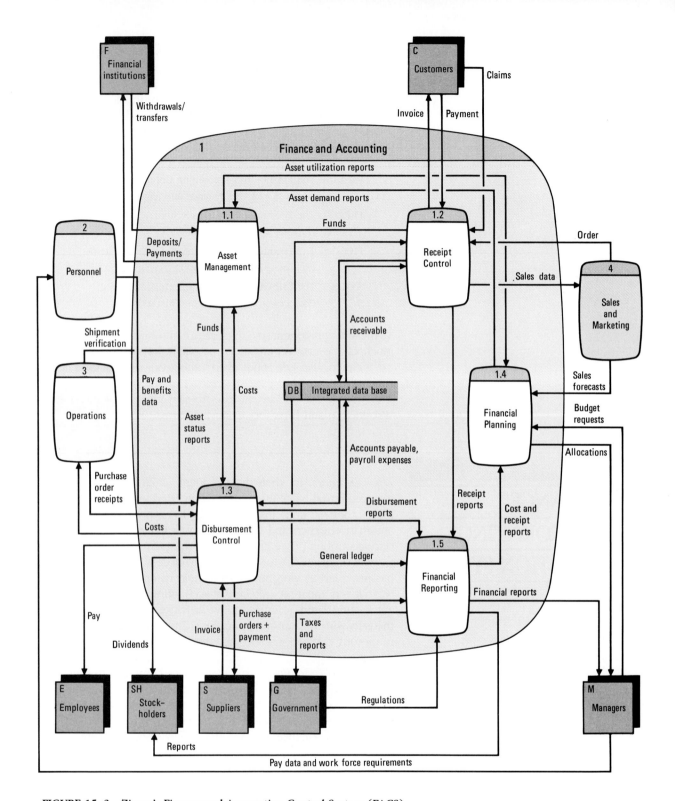

FIGURE 15-3 **Zimco's Finance and Accounting Control System (FACS)**
This data flow diagram is the explosion of the Finance and Accounting (1) process of the MIS overview data flow diagram of Figure 15-2.

departments because FACS is an integrated system that is designed to support the needs of the organization as a whole.

Notice that each of the four components of the Zimco MIS are numbered 1, 2, 3, and 4. The numbering scheme is used in data flow diagrams to identify subordinate processes. Since the Finance and Accounting process (FACS) is numbered "1," the first-level subordinate systems are identified as 1.1, 1.2, 1.3, and so on. The five subsystems are:

1.1 Asset Management

1.2 Receipt Control

1.3 Disbursement Control

1.4 Financial Planning

1.5 Financial Reporting

Perhaps the best way to explain the operation of FACS is to focus on the interaction between these five subsystems and their interaction with the external (for example, financial institutions) and internal (for example, managers) entities (see Figure 15–3). All subsystems interact frequently with the integrated data base, but some of these interactions are omitted in Figure 15–3 so that the information flow between the subsystems is more visually apparent.

Asset Management (1.1)

Just as data are input to and output from a computer systems, money is input to and output from the Asset Management Subsystem (see Figure 15–3). Money is the common denominator at Zimco and in the business world in general. The Asset Management Subsystem releases funds and takes in funds as needed. The funds, of course, are kept in various financial institutions. Zimco's accounting and financial people are responsible for ensuring that enough liquid funds are on hand to meet the ongoing operational needs of the company.

Funds received from the Receipt Control Subsystem (1.2), primarily payments from customers, are deposited with financial institutions. Funds are withdrawn and distributed to the Disbursement Control Subsystem (1.3) so that these funds can be used to meet the ongoing financial obligations of Zimco. Since the Asset Management Subsystem does most of the interaction with financial institutions, the periodic payments for bonds and loans are made through the Asset Management Subsystem rather than through the Disbursement Control Subsystem.

The Asset Management Subsystem periodically generates asset utilization reports as input to the Financial Planning Subsystem (1.4). In turn, the Financial Planning Subsystem feeds the Asset Management Subsystem with asset demand forecasts. Based on the demand forecasts, the Asset Management Subsystem does the processing required to ensure that liquid funds are made available to meet short- and long-term obligations.

Data generated by the Asset Management Subsystem become part of the integrated data base and are used by the Financial Reporting Subsystem (1.5) to produce Zimco's financial statements.

Receipt Control (1.2)

The primary function of the Receipt Control Subsystem (see Figure 15–3) is the *accounts receivable* application. Briefly, the Sales and Marketing Division is responsible for getting the order, the Operations Division is responsible for the manufacture and delivery of the order; and the Finance and Accounting Division is responsible for collecting for the order. The accounts receivable application keeps track of money owed the company on charges for products sold or services rendered (primarily the maintenance of products). When a Zimco customer purchases goods or services, the customer record in the integrated data base is updated to reflect the charge.

As soon as an order is verified within the Sales and Marketing Information Systems (SAMIS), order information is automatically recorded on the customer record and an invoice, which reflects the balance due, is sent to the customer. Upon receipt of payment, the amount due is decreased by the amount of the payment in the data base.

Management relies on the Receipt Control Subsystem (accounts receivable) to identify overdue accounts. Reports are generated that "age" accounts to identify those customers whose accounts are overdue by more than 30 days, 60 days, or 90 days. As Monroe Green puts it: "Those accounts that are 30 days overdue, we call and remind; those that are 60 days overdue, we notify that shipment of orders has been suspended; those that are 90 days overdue go on our deadbeat list and we take legal action."

Zimco's FACS system still handles traditional data processing activities, such as aging of accounts and producing invoices, but it also provides management with tremendous flexibility to retrieve the information they need. For example, Zimco can provide customers with a variety of discounts to encourage their timely payment. Management and operational-level personnel have access to the information they need to do their jobs right. Customer credit histories are on-line and the data are up to the minute. The FACS system can provide sales and marketing managers with sales analysis reports by multiple criteria. That is, they can request analysis by salesperson, territory, product, and so on. Because FACS is integrated, each accounts receivable transaction becomes an automatic entry in the general ledger portion of the integrated data base.

Disbursement Control (1.3)

The Disbursement Control Subsystem (see Figure 15–3) ensures that all external creditor entities (except financial institutions) and employees are paid promptly. The primary applications in this subsystem are *accounts payable* and *payroll*.

Accounts Payable

Zimco purchases everything from paper clips to 18-wheelers on credit. The accounts payable application is the other side of the accounts receivable application. That is, an invoice from a supplier company's accounts receivable system becomes input to Zimco's accounts payable application. When Zimco receives an invoice, the accounts payable application generates a check and adjusts the balance owed. Of course, Zimco's accounts payable application is carefully designed to take advantage of available discounts for prompt payment.

Purchase orders are generated in every department, but the Operations Division generates most of them. The purchase order is a flag to the Disbursement Control Subsystem to expect an invoice from a supplier. When the invoice is received from the supplier and receipt of the item is verified by the ordering department on the integrated data base, payment is then authorized and the supplier is sent a check.

Like accounts receivable transactions, accounts payable transactions are automatically fed to the general ledger application. The features of Zimco's accounts payable application are numerous. It has an audit program to check entries. Invoices can be selected interactively by date or vendor. For any given invoice the system computes the optimal discount strategy. The invoice aging report, purchase journal, and a variety of other timely reports help managers to control purchased inventory and overhead expenses.

Payroll

The payroll application at Zimco is a combined effort between the Personnel Division and the Finance and Accounting Division. The Personnel Division is responsible for the benefits program and for wage and salary administration. Prior to each pay period, the people in the Personnel Division verify pay and benefits data on the integrated data base. The mechanics of producing and distributing the payroll checks are handled by the Disbursement Control Subsystem in the Finance and Accounting Division. The two primary outputs of the payroll application are the payroll check and stub, which are distributed to the employees, and the payroll register, which is a summary report of payroll transactions. These transactions, of course, are logged automatically on the general ledger portion of the integrated data base.

The payroll application handles all calculations associated with gross pay, taxes, and user-defined deductions. The payroll application is capable of generating a variety of management reports, such as the federal tax summary report and the retirement contribution summary report.

Any disbursement, be it pay, dividends, or payment for goods or services, is noted in the appropriate record(s) in the integrated data base. Summary and detailed disbursement reports are input to the Financial Reporting Subsystem (1.5).

Financial Planning (1.4)

The Financial Planning Subsystem (see Figure 15–3) operates in support of the budgeting process. Each year Zimco's financial planners, in cooperation with management, must decide how the company's revenues can be allocated to over 400 accounts.

Zimco's accounting is done on a calendar year basis, so the budgeting process begins during the late summer and, if all goes well, takes effect at the beginning of the new year. During a prescribed period, managers enter their budget requests, with line-item detail, into the Financial Planning Subsystem from their workstations. Concurrent with the preparation of budget

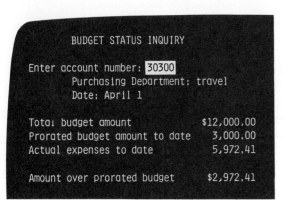

```
        BUDGET STATUS INQUIRY

Enter account number: 30300
        Purchasing Department: travel
        Date: April 1

Total budget amount              $12,000.00
Prorated budget amount to date     3,000.00
Actual expenses to date            5,972.41

Amount over prorated budget       $2,972.41
```

FIGURE 15–4 Management Budget Inquiry
The Financial Planning Subsystem of FACS enables Zimco managers to make on-line budget inquiries regarding budgets.

requests, the Sales and Marketing Division prepares a forecast of sales for the coming year. The Financial Planning Subsystem helps to translate these sales into projected revenues.

Managers often spend months preparing their departmental budgets for the coming year. To aid in this task, the *budget* application provides each manager with historical information on past line-item expenditures (for example, salaries, office equipment, office supplies, and so on). Based on this information and projected budget requirements, each manager can make budget requests for the next fiscal year.

Financial planners and top management match requests for funds against projected revenues. At Zimco, and at other companies, managers invariably ask for more than they need, knowing full well that they will never get what they request. Eventually, a workable budget is established.

Managers at Zimco frequently use the Financial Planning Subsystem to monitor expenditures in their departments. For example, Figure 15–4 illustrates the display that was generated when the manager of the Purchasing Department inquired about the status of her department's travel budget. She entered only the coded travel account number (30300) to obtain the budget status of her travel account. Other managers routinely make similar inquiries. Inordinate budget variances, such as the one shown in Figure 15–4, prompt managers to take immediate action to get certain budget items under control.

Financial Reporting (1.5)

The Financial Reporting Subsystem (see Figure 15–3) includes the *general ledger* application—the glue that integrates all the other accounting applications. In the not-too-distant past, accountants manually posted debits and credits for each account in a ledger book, thus the name "general ledger" for today's electronic system. Other "account" applications (accounts receivable, accounts payable, payroll, and so on) are sources of financial transactions and feed data to the general ledger application.

The general ledger application records every monetary transaction that occurs within Zimco. Payment of a bill, an interdepartmental transfer of funds, receipt of payment for an order, a contribution to an employee's retirement fund—all are examples of monetary transactions. The general ledger system keeps track of these transactions and provides the input necessary to produce Zimco's financial statement.

For the purposes of accounting, Zimco is divided into 14 general accounting categories, such as current assets, current liabilities, cost of goods sold, and so on. These, in turn, are subdivided into as many accounts as are needed to reflect monetary flow accurately within Zimco. Monetary transactions are recorded as a debit or a credit to a particular account. The *balance sheet*, one of two major elements of Zimco's financial statement, reflects a summary of these accounts at the end of a particular day. Zimco balance sheets for this year and the same time last year are illustrated in Figure 15–5. The balance sheet is so named because the company's assets are equated with its liabilities. Since all monetary transactions are recorded on-line as they occur via FACS, managers can request a display or hard copy of the balance sheet on any day of the year, not just at the end of each quarter.

```
========================================================================
ZIMCO BALANCE SHEET ($1000)                   This Year    Last Year
------------------------------------------------------------------------

ASSETS
------------------------------------------------------------------------

Current assets
  Cash                                           $6,750       $4,500
  Marketable securities @ cost                  $12,750       $6,900
  Accounts receivable
    Less: bad debt allowance                    $30,000      $28,500
  Inventories                                   $40,500      $45,000
                                             ------------------------
      Total current assets                      $90,000      $84,900

Fixed assets
  Land                                           $6,750       $6,750
  Building                                      $55,500      $52,500
  Machinery                                     $14,250      $12,750
  Office equipment                               $1,500       $1,425
                                             ------------------------
                                                $78,000      $73,425
      Less: accum. depreciation                 $27,000      $22,500
                                             ------------------------
      Net fixed assets                          $51,000      $50,925


Prepayments and deferred charges                 $1,500       $1,350

Intangibles (goodwill, patents)                  $1,500       $1,500

TOTAL ASSETS                                   $144,000     $138,675



------------------------------------------------------------------------

LIABILITIES
------------------------------------------------------------------------

Current liabilities
  Accounts payable                             $15,000      $14,100
  Notes payable                                $12,750      $15,000
  Accrued expenses payable                      $4,950       $4,500
  Federal income taxes payable                  $4,800       $4,350
                                             ------------------------
      Total current liabilites                 $37,500      $37,950

Long-term liabilities
  First mortgage bonds;
  9% interest, due 2000                        $40,500      $40,500

      Total liabilities                        $78,000      $78,450
------------------------------------------------------------------------
STOCKHOLDERS' EQUITY
------------------------------------------------------------------------

Common stock, $5 par;
  6,000,000 shares outstanding                 $30,000      $30,000
Capital surplus                                $10,500      $10,500
Retained earnings                              $25,500      $19,725
                                             ------------------------
      Total stockholders' equity               $66,000      $60,225
------------------------------------------------------------------------
TOTAL LIABILITIES & STOCKHOLDERS' EQUITY      $144,000     $138,675
```

FIGURE 15–5 Zimco's Balance Sheet
The balance sheet is one of the outputs from the Financial Reporting Subsystem (1.5).

The other major element of the financial statement is the *profit and loss statement*. Often called the "income statement," the profit and loss statement reflects how much Zimco makes or loses during a given period, usually a quarter or a year. Zimco income statements for this year and last year and a pro rata income statement are illustrated in Figure 7–6 in Chapter 7, "Personal Computing."

The financial planners at Zimco routinely tap into the Financial Reporting Subsystem to ask "what if" questions. For example, they use decision support software to ask: "What if gross sales are increased by 10 percent and the cost of goods sold is decreased by 5 percent, how would net earnings be affected?" Managers also find prior-year comparisons helpful.

The Securities and Exchange Commission (SEC) requires publicly held companies such as Zimco to file quarterly financial statements. Every three months Zimco and thousands of other companies transmit these reports to the SEC electronically via data communications.

Maintaining FACS

All FACS subsystems are on-line 24 hours a day. Any authorized Zimco employee can tap into the interactive, menu-driven FACS system to make inquiries or to add, delete, or revise data. The Finance and Accounting Division is responsible for maintaining that portion of the integrated data base that deals with monetary accounting, even though much of the input comes from the other divisions. On occasion, this causes some problems. Monroe Green admits that "sometimes the Personnel Division has to be prodded to get the pay and benefits data in on time. However, you can always depend on the sales reps in the field to get their expense reports in on time."

THE HUMAN RESOURCES INFORMATION SYSTEM

PERES, which is pronounced like the French city, is an acronym for Zimco's Personnel Resource System. PERES is one of the four major components of Zimco's corporatewide MIS (see Figure 15–2). PERES is essentially a personnel accounting system that maintains pertinent data on employees. Peggy Peoples, vice president of personnel, and others in the Personnel Division are the primary users of the system. Besides routine historical data, such as educational background, salary history, and so on, PERES includes data on performance reviews, skills, and professional development.

PERES is divided into three subsystems:

2.1 Recruiting
2.2 Pay and Benefits Administration
2.3 Training and Education

These subsystems are illustrated graphically in the data flow diagram of Figure 15–6. Figure 15–6 shows the explosion of the "personnel" component of the Zimco MIS. Each of these subsystems is described in the following sections.

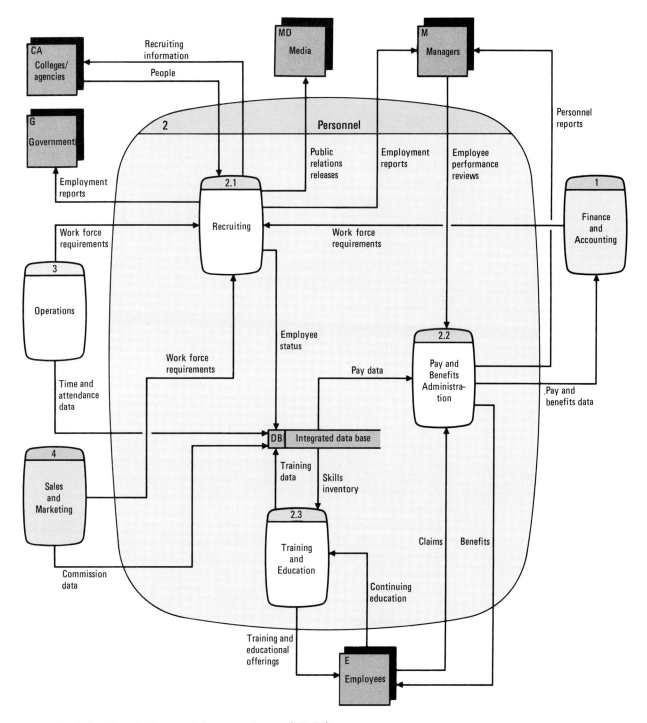

FIGURE 15–6   Zimco's Personnel Resource System (PERES)
This data flow diagram is the explosion of the personnel (2) process of the MIS overview data flow diagram of Figure 15–2.

Recruiting (2.1)

It has long been a tradition at Zimco to hire quality people and promote from within. At the beginning of each quarter, the division vice presidents enter their work force requirements into PERES. Each vice president is responsible for finding qualified candidates to fill these positions. The Recruiting Subsystem (see Figure 15–6) has proven helpful in landing the best available people.

The Recruiting Subsystem (2.1) automatically distributes predefined job descriptions to selected colleges and to several personnel search agencies. About 20 percent of these are distributed via electronic mail; the rest are generated in hard copy and sent via the postal service. The colleges and agencies suggest possible candidates, then the Recruiting Department conducts a preliminary interview. The results of the interview, which are entered into PERES, are on-line and readily accessible to management.

Managers can make on-line inquiries directly from their workstations. The following are examples of some of the on-line reports made available by the menu-driven Recruiting Subsystem:

- ☐ Work Force Summary: Current and Authorized
- ☐ Current Openings (see Figure 15–7)
- ☐ Current Candidate Summary

Peggy Peoples, vice president of personnel, says that "the first day a new hire comes to work, he or she reports to us. We give them a couple of minutes' instruction on the use of our workstations, then ask them to enter their personal data into PERES. This serves two purposes. We get the data into the system, but most important, the new hire realizes that computers are very much a part of how we conduct business at Zimco. This is the first activity of a two-day orientation that we give every new hire."

Classified ads, announcing Zimco job openings, are sent to local newspapers electronically in a format that needs no further editing by typesetters. This approach saves time and Zimco gets a discount for delivering machine-readable ad copy. The Personnel Division receives announcements of position openings each day from several departments. It responds by preparing releases to local newspapers. These releases are usually, but not always, placed in the "classified ads" section.

		Current Openings			
Division	Position	Department	Location	Salary	Requirements
Fin./Acct.	Sr. planner	Finance	Dallas	40k-55k	MBA + exp.
	End user liason	Accounting	Dallas	28k-40k	BS, BA + 1 yr.exp.
	Adm.specialist	Accounting	Dallas	15k-22k	HS + word proc.
Sales/Mkt.	Sales rep.(2)	Sales	L.A.	18k-35k	BS, BA
Operations	Robot repair	Man./Dist.	Reston	22k-32k	Assoc. degree
CIS	Programmer II	Programming	Dallas	27k-37k	Assoc. degree
	Sr. sys. anal.	Systems	Eugene	30k-45k	BS, BA (MIS pref.)
	Librarian	Operations	Dallas	20k-25k	Assoc. degree
Total number of openings: 9					

FIGURE 15–7 The Current Openings Report
This on-line current openings report is one of several that are available upon request via the Recruiting Subsystem (2.1).

In the past managers complained that both internal and public announcements of position openings were being delayed too long and that they had to operate shorthanded longer than necessary. The solution was to eliminate internal hard-copy announcements by posting all openings on the company's electronic bulletin board and by transmitting the position announcements directly to newspapers via data communications. Now, minutes after a position opening is received from a department, it is posted on the Zimco Bulletin Board System (ZBBS). The ZBBS is affectionately known to Zimco employees as "Z-Buzz."

To post an item to Z-Buzz or scan its contents, employees simply log on to the nearest workstation. Z-Buzz includes typical bulletin board items such as softball scores, "for sale" items, messages of all kinds, and of course, position announcements. Workstations, most of which are micros, are everywhere at Zimco, even in the halls, the cafeterias, and the executive washroom. Those employees that would like to transfer to another job or another office routinely scan the position announcements on Z-Buzz.

The position announcements appear immediately in the company's electronic bulletin board and they appear the same or the next day in local and regional newspapers. The Personnel Division runs want ads in 5 to 12 newspapers every day of the year. For 30 years, it mailed or called in the ads to newspapers. Now it saves time and money by using micros to transmit the ads electronically. People in the Personnel Division compose the text of the ads and insert standard electronic publishing symbols that designate size of print, centering of text, and so on. They then use one of the PERES Recruiting Subsystem's built-in features to "dial up" the computers automatically at the newspapers and transmit the ads electronically. Compositors at the various newspapers simply insert the ads in the appropriate section. No other keystrokes are required. Figure 15–8 illustrates what is sent and

```
/AT Zimco Enterprises

/CE !BREND!NDUSER LIAISON IN ACCOUNTING!RM

/T        !BRZimco!RM is seeking a !IThighly motivated!RM
individual with at least a bachelor's degree in accounting
and at least one year of experience working directly with
programmers and systems analysts.  The successful candidate
will have the interpersonal skills needed to encourage
greater automation of accounting.  Write Zimco or call Zimco
for an interview.
```

END–USER LIAISON IN ACCOUNTING
ZIMCO is seeking a *highly motivated* individual with at least a bachelor's degree in accounting and at least one year of experience working directly with programmers and systems analysts. The successful candidate will have the interpersonal skills needed to encourage greater automation of accounting. Write Zimco or call Zimco for an interview.

FIGURE 15–8   The Text of a Position Announcement
The text of a position announcement is shown prior to its electronic distribution to area newspapers and as it appears in the classified ads section.

how it appears in the "Want Ads." Because Zimco enters and formats their own ads, they pay substantially less than do other advertisers.

A variety of mandatory government reports, dealing primarily with equal opportunity employment, are generated from the Recruiting Subsystem.

Pay and Benefits Administration (2.2)

Maintenance and Preparation of Payroll Data

The *payroll application* is a joint effort between the Personnel Division and the Finance and Accounting Division. The Pay and Benefits Administration Subsystems (see Figure 15–6) is the heart of the *wage and salary administration application*. Supervisors enter hours-worked data for hourly personnel directly into their workstations. The Personnel Division makes any adjustments to pay, such as an optional purchase of Zimco stock, directly to an employee's record on the integrated data base. Then, prior to each pay period, the Personnel Division verifies pay and benefits data on the integrated data base. Once the data are prepared, the actual preparation and distribution of the checks is handled by the Disbursement Control Subsystem (1.3) of FACS.

Performance Reviews

At Zimco, every employee has a semiannual performance review—even Preston Smith, the president. Each employee is evaluated by his or her immediate manager in six areas: ability to work with others, innovativeness, contribution through achievement of goals, potential for advancement, ability to communicate, and expertise in his or her area of specialty.

Many managers record their numeric evaluations, from 1 to 10, and add a verbal support statement while interacting directly with PERES. Managers conduct performance reviews with their subordinates while both of them are seated in front of a workstation. When a subordinate comes in for an interview, the manager will have already done the rating, usually on the low side. If, by virtue of other information, a subordinate can convince the manager that he or she should be rated higher, the rating is changed on the spot. Most Zimco managers feel that there should be some give and take between manager and subordinate. The PERES system gives managers the flexibility to render a mutually agreeable performance review without unnecessarily causing hard feelings.

Management Reports

Managers at Zimco use the company's fourth generation language (4GL) to make ad hoc requests for information and reports. A manager obtains information by writing a short program that, in turn, "queries" the integrated data base. Such queries can be made to the data base for information in any functional area, not just personnel.

The 4GL used at Zimco is called FOCUS. At Zimco, 70 percent of the managers at Zimco, including top management, know, use, and like FOCUS. FOCUS is user friendly, and managers can get the information they need without having to wait in line for a programmer.

Fourth-generation languages are effective tools for generating responses to a variety of requests for information. Short user-developed programs are all that is needed to respond to the following typical Zimco management requests:

☐ Which employees have accumulated over 20 sick days since May 1?

☐ List departments that have exceeded their total budget allocation for the month of June in alphabetical order by department name.

Training and Education (2.3)

The Training and Education Subsystem (2.3) monitors and tracks the ongoing career development of Zimco employees. Any external or internal training or education received by an employee is entered into his or her "skills inventory." Included in an employee's skills inventory are any special skills or knowledge. As a matter of policy, managers first conduct an internal search to fill openings. They do this by listing desired skills, knowledge, and so on, then initiating an automatic search of the skills inventory section of the integrated data base. Frequently, there is a match and an opportunity for promotion is extended to an existing employee.

The Personnel Division administers ongoing in-house training programs and evaluates employee requests for external educational support. The Training and Education Subsystem automatically informs employees of in-house offerings by posting a notice on Z-Buzz, Zimco's electronic bulletin board.

THE PRODUCTION AND INVENTORY CONTROL INFORMATION SYSTEM

PICS, Zimco's Production and Inventory Control System, supports the Operations Division and is one of the four functional components of Zimco's integrated management information system (see Figure 15–2). Figure 15–9 graphically illustrates the scope of PICS by showing the explosion of Process 3, "Operations," of the Zimco MIS overview data flow diagram in Figure 15–2. PICS is logically divided into five subsystems:

3.1 Production

3.2 Research and Development

3.3 Schedule and Monitor Production

3.4 Acquire and Manage Materials

3.5 Shipping

The Operations Division's user liaison provides the interface between CIS people (programmers, systems analysts, and the data base administrator) and users. She made a valuable contribution to PICS during its design and implementation by facilitating and fostering verbal communication between CIS and user personnel. The user liaison explained how the project team came up with the five subsystems.

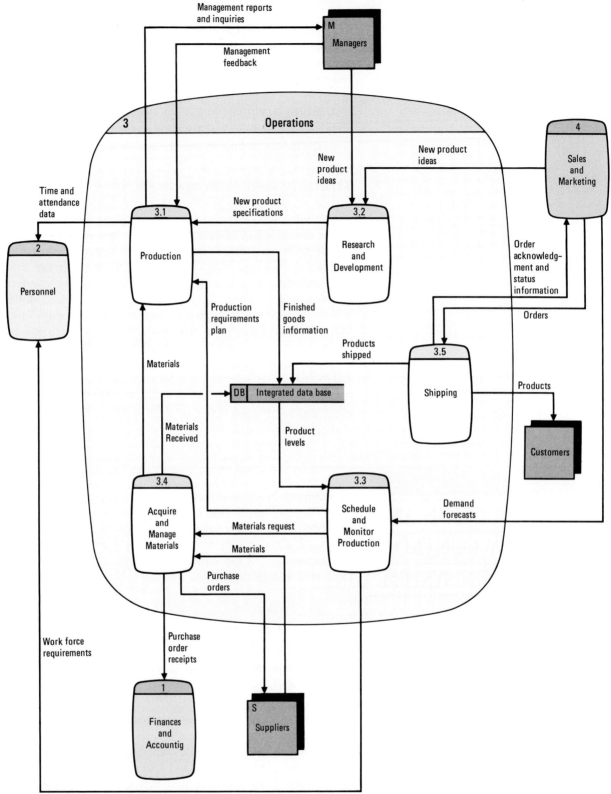

FIGURE 15–9   Zimco's Production and Inventory Control System (PICS)
This data flow diagram is the explosion of the operations (3) process of the MIS overview data flow diagram of Figure 15–2.

The project team analyzed the Operations Division from an information processing perspective, not from a departmental perspective. Because the information and processing requirements of the various departments overlapped substantially, it seemed only logical that we design PICS as an integrated system. Although there is some correlation between the subsystems and departmental lines, this was not a criterion during the design phase. Our primary concern was to design a system that would best meet the needs of the Operations Division, while complementing Zimco's overall MIS.

Otto Manning, the vice president of operations, was the real force behind the development and implementation of PICS, and he was very much a proponent of designing it around an integrated data base. He said:

The Operations Division is very dynamic and hopelessly intertwined with everything we do here at Zimco. We get input from Marketing, R&D, and Accounting. Marketing tells us what products to make, how many to make, and when to have them in stock. R&D tells us how to make them, and Accounting tells us how much we can spend. All too often Marketing wants the product before R&D is finished with the design, and Accounting doesn't allocate enough money to cover the cost of production. These and other conflicts between divisions highlight the need for people throughout the company to be better informed. To help alleviate some of our misinformation problems, we decided that the nerve center of PICS should be an integrated data base.

Production (3.1)

All activities in the Operations Division function to support the production process, and so it is with PICS. All other subsystems support the Production Subsystem (3.1). Plant managers get the specifications for new products and product enhancements from the Research and Development Subsystem (3.2). Each day, plant managers at the four plant/distribution center sites tap into the Schedule and Monitor Production Subsystem (3.3) to monitor production levels. The Acquire and Manage Materials Subsystem (3.4) ensures that raw materials needed during production are at the right place at the right time. And, of course, the Shipping Subsystem (3.5) gets the products out the door to the customer.

Plant managers rely heavily on the DSS (decision support system) software, such as linear programming and simulation models, that is embodied in the Production Subsystem to help them make the most effective use of available resources. These models help schedule the arrival of raw materials and components, the use of machine tools and assembly stations, the use of the work force, and maintenance shutdowns.

An important aspect of the production process is quality control. Zimco uses sampling techniques to maintain a high level of quality control. Each plant has inspectors on the floor who examine both work-in-process and finished goods for defects. Inspectors enter defect data directly into the Production Subsystem. The subsystem then does the necessary statistical analysis and provides inspectors with immediate feedback as to whether a lot should be given the stamp of approval, sampled further, or deemed defective.

Position	A/N	Code	Description
1	Alpha	D A	Development Application
2	Alpha	N E	New product Enhancement
3	Alpha	S T Q F X	Stib Tegler Qwert Farkle Not application
4–5	Numeric	not applicable	Unique numerical project identifier

Examples:

DES03 — Development project #03 to enhance the Stib
AET01 — Application project #01 to improve production of the Tegler
DNX08 — New product development project #08

FIGURE 15–10 Coded Data Elements
The figure illustrates the coding scheme for a five-position R&D project code. Example coded data elements are shown at the bottom.

Research and Development (3.2)

The Research and Development Subsystem (3.2) is comprised of an array of analysis, design, and project management tools that help researchers to be more productive. For example, at any given time, the Research and Development Department is working on a number of projects. Managers use the project management facility to help them manage these projects. To make an inquiry about a particular project, engineers and supervisors need only enter a five-character code. R&D projects are identified by a coded project code (see Figure 15–10). To save data entry keystrokes and storage space, PICS designers tried to code as many data elements as possible.

The project code identifies whether the project is a development or applications project, whether it deals with a new product or an enhancement to an existing product, and if it is an enhancement, the code associates the project with one of the current Zimco products (for example, Stib). The project code has a unique numerical identifier to distinguish between similar projects (for example, multiple "DES" projects). Coded data elements, such as the project code, convey a special meaning and provide information to the user. For example, the project code DES03 describes a development project (#03) to enhance the Stib (see Figure 15–10).

Schedule and Monitor Production (3.3)

The Schedule and Monitor Production Subsystem receives the demand forecast for the various Zimco products from the sales and marketing component (4) of the overall Zimco MIS. These forecasts are what drive the production process.

Mathematical models built into the Schedule and Monitor Production

Subsystem retrieve data from the integrated data base to generate a production requirements plan. This plan specifies week-by-week in-stock requirements for Zimco products. The plan tells the plant manager what the rate of production for a particular product should be over a period of time, usually six months. Plant managers take immediate action if the information they get from this subsystem suggests that production levels may fall below production requirements.

The materials request, which is a by-product of the production requirements plan, is automatically generated and routed to the Acquire and Manage Materials Subsystems (3.4).

Acquire and Manage Materials (3.4)

MATERIALS REQUIREMENTS PLANNING   Built into the overall Zimco MIS, and specifically the Acquire and Manage Materials Subsystem, is the philosophy of *material requirements planning*, often called *MRP*. MRP is essentially a set of mathematical models that accepts data for production requirements and translates these requirements into an optimal schedule for the ordering and the delivery of the components and raw materials needed to manufacture Zimco's products.

INVENTORY MANAGEMENT AND CONTROL   The Acquire and Manage Materials Subsystem gets the materials request from the Schedule and Monitor Production Subsystem (3.3). The subsystem then generates purchase orders for the raw materials and components needed to meet production schedules. These purchase orders are sent to the suppliers, some via EDI (electronic data interchange). An "electronic flag" is added to the integrated data base to notify the Finance and Accounting Division of the order.

Manufacturing companies such as Zimco must manage stock (components and raw materials) and finished goods inventories. This subsystem (3.4) monitors the quantity on hand and the location of each inventory item. Figure 15–11 illustrates the interactive, user-friendly nature of PICS with a few of the menus and input/output displays that are generated by the Acquire and Manage Materials Subsystem. The inventory inquiries in Figure 15–11 are made by a user to Zimco's integrated data base, a network data base (discussed in Chapter 9, "Data Management").

The data base subschema in Figure 15–12 illustrates that portion of the integrated data base that relates specifically to the *inventory management and control application*. The arrows indicate the one-to-many relationships between the five data base records; that is, *one* record for a Zimco product will have cross-references to the *many* records of the stock items that make up that product.

The data base subschema in Figure 15–12 is designed to minimize data redundancy. The *product* data base record contains a list of those items (for example, components and raw materials) that are combined to produce a Zimco product. The two inventory records, *finished goods* and *item*, maintain stock and order data. The *purchase order* record indicates what was ordered. The *supplier* record includes pertinent data about each supplier. The entire schema for Zimco's CODASYL-based integrated data base, which is not shown, includes relationships between these and other data base records.

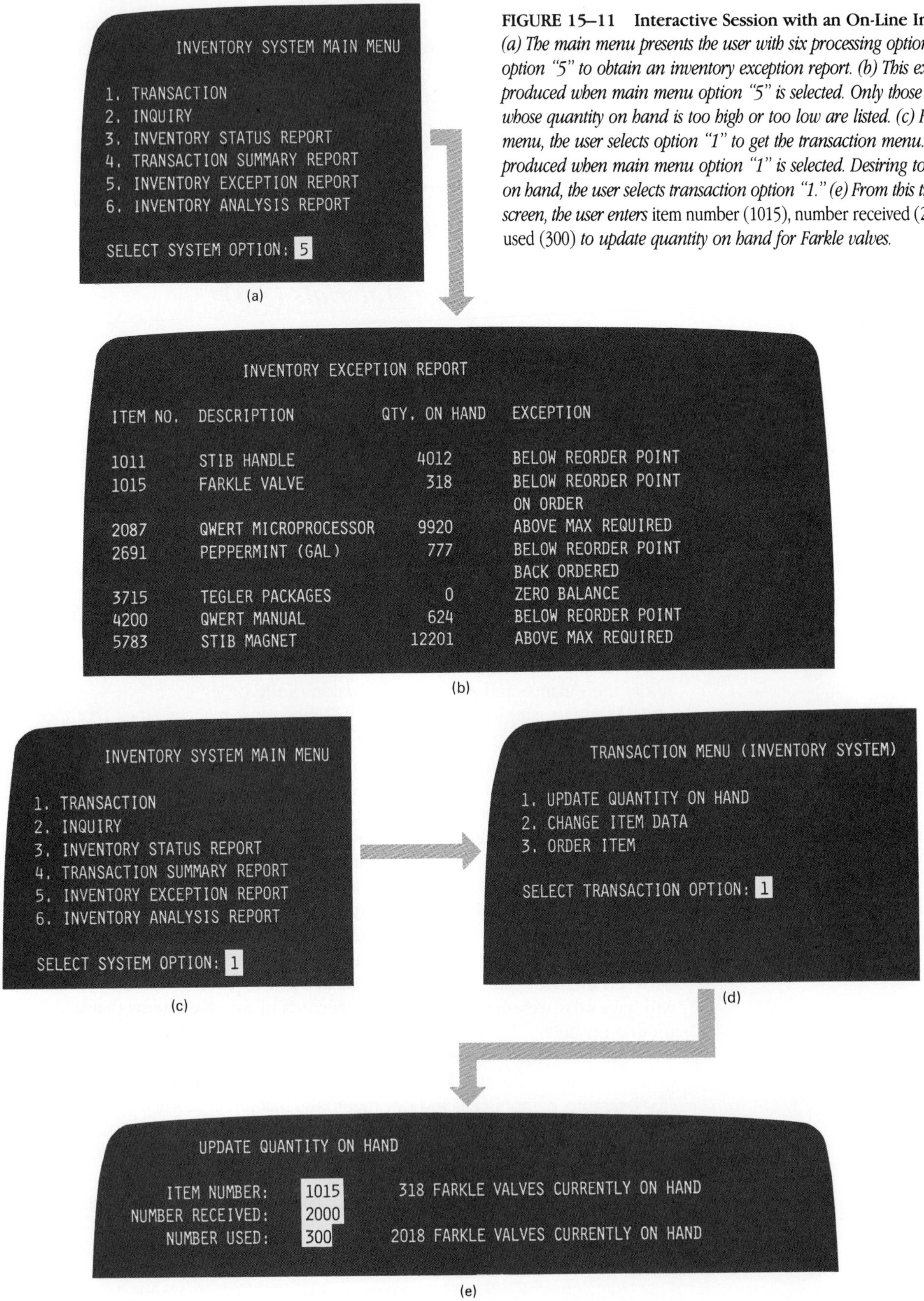

FIGURE 15–11 Interactive Session with an On-Line Inventory System
(a) The main menu presents the user with six processing options. The user enters option "5" to obtain an inventory exception report. (b) This exception report is produced when main menu option "5" is selected. Only those inventory items whose quantity on hand is too high or too low are listed. (c) From the main menu, the user selects option "1" to get the transaction menu. (d) This screen is produced when main menu option "1" is selected. Desiring to update quantity on hand, the user selects transaction option "1." (e) From this transaction display screen, the user enters item number (1015), number received (2000), and number used (300) *to update quantity on hand for Farkle valves.*

significant, Sally Marcio, vice president of sales and marketing, was less vocal about the need for SAMIS than the other vice presidents were about their systems. Second, she was relatively satisfied with the information that she and her managers were receiving from an outside time-sharing service.

Several years ago during the early summer, the vice president of sales and marketing remarked to the vice president of CIS that "The competition is getting the jump on us with better information. Also that time-sharing service has doubled their rates! We can't wait any longer, we've got to have SAMIS by the end of the year to stay competitive!"

At that time, work was not scheduled to begin on SAMIS for another 18 months. Conrad Innis, the vice president of CIS, told Sally: "We simply don't have the resources to commit to a major new in-house development project. As an alternative, would you consider buying a commercial software package?"

Zimco's Computer and Information Services (CIS) Division, like most centralized computer centers, suffers from a shortage of human resources. To help alleviate this problem, Zimco managers have occasionally opted to purchase and install commercially available software packages.

Sally Marcio did not believe that the Sales and Marketing Division could wait a couple of years for CIS to develop an in-house information system. She decided to take Conrad's advice and began looking for a packaged sales and marketing system. After evaluating seven such systems, a search team recommended a package developed by a firm in Cleveland. Sally said: "With a few minor modifications, this system will fit our needs to a tee." Since the packaged system was compatible with Zimco's database management system, the modifications were relatively minor.

Because of the immediacy of the need and the availability of a product, Zimco management decided to "buy" rather than "make" the fourth component of the Zimco MIS. SAMIS went on-line in November, five months after Sally first related her sense of desperation to Conrad.

SAMIS is that component of the integrated MIS that services the Sales and Marketing Division. The system interacts frequently with the other three MIS components: FACS, PERES, and PICS. The five subsystems of SAMIS match up perfectly with the functions of the five departments in the Sales and Marketing Division. If you will remember, this is in contrast to the subsystems of FACS, PERES, and PICS which are not aligned with the organizational structures of their respective divisions. The five subsystems of SAMIS are:

4.1 Market Research

4.2 Advertising and Promotion

4.3 Customer Services

4.4 Sales and Order Processing

4.5 Sales Forecasting and Analysis

The second-level data flow diagram of Figure 15–13 is the explosion of the "sales and marketing" component of the Zimco MIS (see Figure 15–2). Each of the five subsystems is described in the following sections.

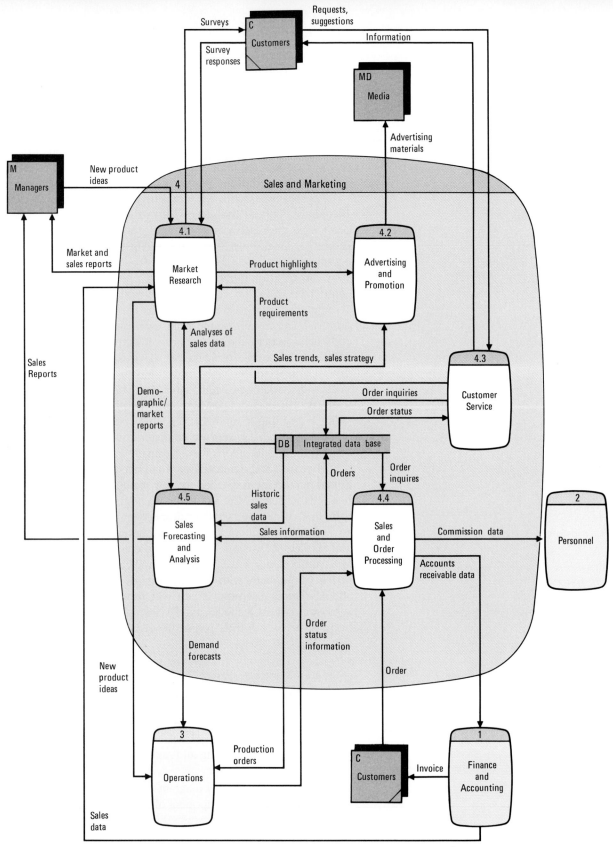

FIGURE 15–13   Zimco's Sales and Marketing Information System (SAMIS)

This data flow diagram is the explosion of the sales and marketing (4) process of the MIS overview data flow diagram of Figure 15–2.

Market Research Subsystem (4.1)

The Market Research Department systematically gathers all kinds of data that may in some way provide information that will help managers to make better decisions regarding the marketing and sale of Zimco products. Unlike accounting or personnel systems, the data gathered for input to the Market Research Subsystem are very volatile (see Figure 15–13); that is, data that are seemingly accurate today may be erroneous tomorrow. Because of the ever-changing nature of market research data, the data must be constantly updated so that the information derived from the data is representative of the current market. Inputs to the Market Research Subsystem are:

☐ Data on the marketing activities of competitors.

☐ Demographic data.

☐ Economic indicators.

☐ Data on consumer behavior.

☐ Customer responses to surveys.

Zimco subscribes to several commercially available data bases that provide much of these data. The company obtains the rest of the data by periodically distributing surveys, from Zimco's integrated data base, and from feedback from the field sales representatives.

People in the Market Research Department use SAMIS to keep an eye on demographics and customer buying trends so that they can identify untapped niches in the market. Sally Marcio says:

> Without SAMIS, certain segments of the marketplace would forever remain hidden. For example, for years we targeted our marketing campaigns for one of our products at commuters. A survey conducted by market research surfaced numerous domestic uses for this product as well. By broadening the scope of our advertising, we were able to increase sales by 18 percent during the next year.

The Market Research Subsystem automatically gathers ideas for new products and enhancements to existing products from Zimco managers and from the Customer Service Subsystem. Last year one of Zimco's distributors reported that several women complained about the "unattractive" color of one of the products. In response, the Market Research Department worked closely with the Operations Division to produce the product in pastel colors. Before releasing the product in pastel colors, Zimco test marketed them in Cincinnati and used SAMIS to monitor sales on a daily basis. The new brightly colored products test marketed very well and are now a part of the product line.

The Market Research Subsystem includes a number of models that help researchers to analyze and interpret the data. For example, each week the system determines if there is any statistically significant correlation between sales trends for the various Zimco products and other trends. For example, statistical techniques are used to correlate product sales to the consumer price index, unemployment level, furniture sales, and numerous other factors that might in some way influence the sale of a Zimco product.

If a correlation exists, market researchers can identify trends early and give management some time to react, perhaps with an unscheduled price adjustment.

Advertising and Promotion Subsystem (4.2)

Zimco promotes its products through personal selling (exclusively to retailers and wholesalers), advertising, and promotional campaigns. The latter two are supported by the Advertising and Promotion Subsystem (see Figure 15–13). The catalyst for the advertising and promotion activity is the information on sales trends and strategies provided by the Sales Forecasting and Analysis Subsystem.

Zimco routinely advertises in newspapers and magazines. The copy and graphics for these ads are generated on-line and routed directly to the print media via electronic mail. Occasionally, they advertise on television and radio. About three times a year, Zimco has promotional campaigns for each of its products. These campaigns usually involve price reductions or rebates. SAMIS has made it possible for the people at Zimco to analyze the effectiveness of their ads and promotional campaigns on a day-to-day basis. Sally Marcio is proud of SAMIS's contribution to her division's bottom line: "By identifying the most effective advertising medium, SAMIS helps Zimco managers to maximize the value of their advertising dollars."

The purchase price of SAMIS included the software and hardware for a computerized dialing system for *telemarketing*. The system, which is part of the Advertising and Promotion Subsystem, automatically dials a telephone number, then plays a prerecorded message. Sally Marcio decided to use this component of the subsystem to kick off a new promotional campaign. The telephone numbers of Zimco customers were entered into the system, then dialed automatically, one after another. Sally Marcio said:

> Telemarketing sounded like a good idea, but it wasn't. Customer feedback was all negative. They let us know immediately that they didn't appreciate these "computer" calls, so we turned the machine off the next day and haven't turned it on since. This incident reminds us that not all applications of computer technology are worthwhile.

Customer Services Subsystem (4.3)

The function of customer service representatives is to respond to any type of customer inquiry or complaint. Sally Marcio says: "Because of SAMIS, our customer service reps have on-line access to the integrated data base and just about any information that the customer would want to know."

For the more routine inquiries, many of Zimco's customers prefer the "Zimco Connection." Zimco customers are given a telephone number, a password, and an authorization code that will allow them to tap directly into SAMIS from their own workstations. Customers routinely establish an EDI link with the Customer Service Subsystem (see Figure 15–13) to track orders and shipments and to get the latest pricing information. Of course, security precautions limit what customers can access, and they can't change anything. According to Sally, "The Customer Service Subsystem has helped to build customer loyalty and has made relations with our customers much smoother. They know that if they have a question, they can ask us or they can query our data base directly."

At the end of the day, each customer service rep requests that the names and addresses of those customers with whom they have interacted be downloaded from the corporate data base to disk storage on their micro-computer workstations. Each customer service representative has a micro, with disk storage, and shares a desktop laser printer. During the last hour or so of the day, the customer service workstations become stand-alone computer systems so that representatives can use word processing and mail-merge software to write "personalized" letters to the customers that they talked with during the day. The basic form letter confirms Zimco's continuing commitment to customer service. About 50 percent of the time, the reps add a sentence or so that relates to the customer's particular situation. Sally Marcio says that this "immediate and personal follow-up to a customer's inquiry has provided immeasurable goodwill and set us apart from our competitors."

Sales and Order Processing Subsystem (4.4)

The Sales and Order Processing Subsystem (see Figure 15–13) provides the facility for Zimco's field sales reps and Zimco's customers to enter orders directly into SAMIS and the integrated data base. Every field sales rep has a portable workstation. The rep can enter an order, make an inquiry, or send a message while in a customers office. To do this, the rep simply dials the number of the Dallas mainframe on a telephone. Upon hearing the computer's high whistle "greeting," the rep inserts the telephone handset into the work-station's built-in modem. This makes the connection between the workstation and Zimco's mainframe computer.

Sally says that "the use of portables in the field has resulted in faster delivery to the customer, far less paperwork, and a better cash flow to Zimco. More often than not a sales rep can guarantee the customer that his or her order will be shipped within 24 hours. The customer appreciates that."

Just having the portable workstations gives the field reps a psychological boost. They know that they have a direct link to literally everyone in the company, even though most of them work out of their homes. All of them routinely get and receive electronic mail. Since the portable workstations double as microcomputers, the sales reps use them in stand-alone mode to do spreadsheet analysis and word processing.

The Sales and Order Processing Subsystem also provides support for electronic data interchange or EDI (see Chapter 4, "Information Systems as a Competitive Strategy," for discussions of EDI concepts and strategies). Some customers prefer to enter their orders directly from their mainframe computers into Zimco's mainframe at Dallas. Customers send the order data in a standard format, and the order is confirmed with a return message from Zimco's mainframe computer. Sally reports: "EDI benefits our customer and us. Zimco customers are able to cut their inventories since they get quicker delivery. It cuts our paperwork substantially, thereby reducing the overall cost of sales."

	Dallas	% Chg.	Eugene	% Chg.	Benton	% Chg.	Reston	% Chg.	Total	% Chg.
			6-Month Demand Schedule (Stibs)							
			Anticipated Unit Demand by Warehouse (1,000s of units)							
March	101	1.0%	210	1.5%	192	3.0%	222	0.5%	725	1.5%
April	97	-1.2%	215	4.0%	182	-2.0%	219	-1.0%	713	0.2%
May	105	5.0%	213	3.0%	183	-1.5%	225	2.0%	726	1.8%
June	109	8.0%	221	7.0%	197	6.0%	239	8.0%	766	7.2%
July	99	1.0%	206	-0.5%	184	-1.0%	230	4.0%	719	1.0%
August	110	-0.5%	205	-1.0%	187	0.5%	223	1.0%	725	0.1%

FIGURE 15–14   6-Month Demand Schedule
This report is generated each month by the Sales Forecasting and Analysis Subsystem (4.5) to help plant managers set production and finished goods inventory levels. The "% Chg." columns indicate the percentage change in the product demand estimate from the previous month's (February) "6-Month Demand Report."

Sales Forecasting and Analysis Subsystem (4.5)

The Sales Forecasting and Analysis Subsystem (see Figure 15–13) uses mathematical models to combine the historical sales data, sales forecasts, and other predictive data to extrapolate sales trends for Zimco products. The production levels at each of the plants are based on the sales forecasts. Each month, the Sales Forecasting and Analysis Subsystem generates a 6-Month Demand Schedule for each of Zimco's products. Figure 15–14 illustrates the March-August 6-Month Demand Schedule for Stibs.

The Operations Division uses these demand reports to schedule production levels at the plants and to set minimum finished goods inventory levels at each of the warehouses. Each month the "6-Month Demand Schedule" is updated to reflect current information. Notice the "% Chg." columns in Figure 15–14. These figures indicate the percentage change in the product demand estimate from the previous month's (February) "6-Month Demand Schedule." For example, the March Stibs demand for the Dallas warehouse is forecast to be 1 percent greater than it was a month ago. The bar chart in Figure 15–15 graphically highlights any major changes in the monthly total demand estimates. From the figure, it is obvious that there will be a far greater demand for Stibs in June than was earlier expected.

SAMIS Summary

The examples presented in this case study represent only a small fraction of the capabilities of SAMIS. Sales managers can request a sales summary of the top 10 accounts in their regions. Orders can be received, processed, and billed without human intervention. When sales fall below the historical norm in a particular sales territory, the appropriate regional sales manager is automatically notified via electronic mail. Sally Marcio summed up her impressions of SAMIS very succinctly. "Before SAMIS, we had too much data and not enough information. Now we use information as a competitive weapon."

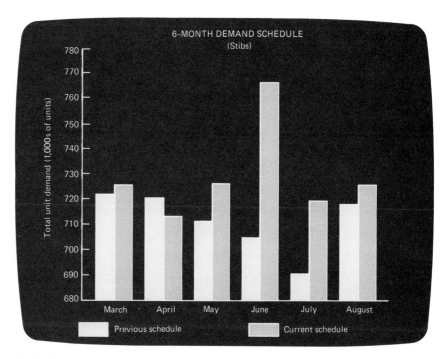

FIGURE 15–15   Bar Chart for 6-Month Demand Schedule
This bar chart graphically highlights any major changes in the total product demand forecast (for example, June) by comparing the demand estimates for the current "6-Month Demand Schedule" (see Figure 15–14) with the estimates on the previous month's schedule.

CHAPTER HIGHLIGHTS

■ Zimco's four line divisions are the Accounting Division, the Sales and Marketing Division, the Personnel Division, and the Operations Division.

■ Zimco's staff division, the Computer and Information Services Division, provides support for all Zimco Enterprises information processing requirements that are consistent with corporate objectives.

■ An overview diagram of an integrated MIS portrays the interactions between entities and the basic information flow between the functional areas.

■ At Zimco data redundancy was minimized by designing an integrated data base to serve all facets of Zimco operation.

■ At Zimco and most other companies, the first applications to be automated involve accounting.

■ The Asset Management Subsystem releases funds and takes in funds as needed.

■ The primary function of the Receipt Control Subsystem is the accounts receivable application.

■ The primary applications in the Disbursement Control Subsystem are accounts payable and payroll.

■ The Financial Planning Subsystem helps managers to decide how the company's revenues can be allocated to the various internal accounts.

■ The general ledger application records every monetary transaction.

■ The balance sheet reflects a summary of major accounting categories at the end of a particular day. The profit and loss statement reflects how much Zimco makes or loses during a given period.

■ The wage and salary administration application is the basis for the preparation, printing, and distribution of the payroll.

■ Zimco's Training and Education Subsystem monitors and tracks the ongoing career development of its employees.

■ Two of the most prominent computer-aided manufacturing applications are robotics and computer-aided design.

■ Computer-integrated manufacturing is the integration of the computer throughout the manufacturing process.

■ The Zimco Sales and Order Processing Subsystem provides electronic data interchange support that enables customers to enter their orders directly into Zimco's mainframe computer.

accounts payable application

accounts receivable application

balance sheet

budget application

computer-aided design (CAD)

computer-aided manufacturing (CAM)

computer-integrated manufacturing (CIM)

entity

general ledger application

inventory management and control application

material requirements planning (MRP)

payroll application

profit and loss statement (Ch. 7)

purchase order

robotics (Ch. 3)

telemarketing

top-down view

wage and salary administration application

Finance and Accounting Control System (FACS)

  Asset Management Subsystem

  Receipt Control Subsystem

  Disbursement Control Subsystem

  Financial Planning Subsystem

  Financial Reporting Subsystem

Personnel Resource System (PERES)

  Recruiting Subsystem

  Pay and Benefits Administration Subsystem

  Training and Education Subsystem

Production and Inventory Control System (PICS)

  Production Subsystem

  Research and Development Subsystem

  Schedule and Monitor Production Subsystem

  Acquire and Manage Materials Subsystem

  Shipping Subsystem

Sales and Marketing Information System (SAMIS)

  Market Research Subsystem

  Advertising and Promotion Subsystem

  Customer Services Subsystem

  Sales and Order Processing Subsystem

  Sales Forecasting and Analysis Subsystem

REVIEW EXERCISES

1. Employee access to Zimco's data base is dependent on what?

2. Name the four functional components of Zimco's MIS.

3. What are the two primary applications in the Disbursement Control Subsystem of FACS, one of the components of Zimco's MIS?

4. Expand the following acronyms: MRP, CIM, and CAD.

5. Name two elements of a company's financial statement.

6. Name two internal and two external entities at Zimco.

7. What symbol is used to portray the existence of a data base in a data flow diagram?

8. What application keeps track of all monetary transactions that affect cash flow?

9. Which component of Zimco's MIS embodies the philosophy of materials requirements planning?

10. Orders for Zimco products are entered into which of the four major components of the MIS?

11. List the five subsystems of SAMIS, Zimco's Sales and Marketing Information System.

1. Zimco Enterprises manufactures and sells three relatively low-tech products and one very high-tech product. Discuss the effects, if any, that the mixing of low- and high-tech products might have on the design of basic information systems such as an accounting system or an inventory control system.

2. Describe the information flow between Zimco Enterprises and all levels of government and between its suppliers, customers, and stockholders.

3. Describe the information flow between Zimco Enterprises and those financial institutions, colleges/agencies, and media organizations with whom it has business relations.

4. In Figure 15–2, Zimco's MIS is logically organized into four major processes. Discuss an alternative organization that would involve five, six, or seven major processes. Discuss the advantages of such an organization.

5. Do acronyms, such as FACS and PERES, foster cyberphobia, or do they simplify interaction between users and computer professionals? Explain.

6. Draw a data flow diagram explosion of the Receipt Control Subsystem (1.2) showing the primary information flows between appropriate processes, the customer entity, and the integrated data base. Label subordinate processes 1.2.1, 1.2.2, and so on.

7. Explain the relationship between Zimco's accounts payable application and a supplier's accounts receivables application.

8. Draw a data flow diagram explosion of the Financial Reporting Subsystem (1.5) of Figure 15–3 showing the primary information flows between appropriate processes, the managers and government entities, and the integrated data base. Label subordinate processes 1.5.1, 1.5.2, and so on.

9. Getting out the payroll at Zimco is a joint effort between the Personnel Division and the Finance and Accounting Division. Could the payroll application be made more efficient by consolidating it in one division or the other? Explain.

10. A proposal being seriously considered by Zimco's top management is to change all hourly employees to salaried employees. If adopted, what impact would this proposal have on the Pay and Benefits Administration Subsystem (2.2) of PERES?

11. Many Zimco managers conduct performance reviews with their subordinates while interacting with PERES. Discuss the pros and cons of this approach.

12. Describe three management reports that you might expect to be generated by the Training and Education Subsystem (2.3) of PERES.

13. Describe the information flow between PERES and FACS. Be specific.

14. What are the advantages of having an on-line skills inventory for all employees?

15. The Sales and Order Processing Subsystem permits field sales reps to make inquiries to the integrated data base from their portable workstations while in a customer's office. Discuss the types of inquiries that a sales rep might make.

16. Customers have limited access to the Zimco data base via EDI. Discuss the advantages and disadvantages to this customer service.

17. Of the four major systems that comprise the Zimco MIS, only SAMIS is proprietary software. Does this make any difference to the end user? How about programmers and systems analysts?

18. Describe the information flow to and from the Disbursement Control Subsystem (1.3) of FACS as illustrated in Figure 15–3.

19. Describe the information flow to and from the Recruiting Subsystem (2.1) of PERES as illustrated in Figure 15–6.

20. Describe the information flow to and from the Acquire and Manage Materials Subsystem (3.4) of PICS as illustrated in Figure 15–9.

21. Describe the information flow to and from the Market Research Subsystem (4.1) of SAMIS as illustrated in Figure 15–13.

APPLICATION CASE STUDY 15–1
Monitoring Individual Productivity

The Situation

Preston Smith, the president of Zimco Enterprises, has lunch with his five vice presidents every other Friday (see Chapter 15, "An MIS Case Study," for background information on Zimco Enterprises). The informal setting prompts discussions that have proven highly beneficial for the company. Sometimes a problem in one division can be mitigated by action in another. At other times, the discussion revolves around potential opportunities for Zimco Enterprises.

The topic of conversation at the last executive luncheon dealt with the just-completed semiannual employee performance reviews. The general consensus was that "the reviews are a necessary evil" and "thank goodness they're over!"

Peggy Peoples, vice president of the Personnel Division, said, "Maybe they're over for you, but they're not over for me. My division has to process the ratings and deal with the inevitable gripes. And wouldn't you know it, most of the complaints about ratings come from people who feel that their productivity has been rated unfairly. I wish that there was some way that we could really measure how much work a person does."

Otto Manning, vice president of the Operations Division, said, "What's the problem? We do that with our assembly people. We know how many farkles a person produces an hour, for example."

Sally Marcio, vice president of the Sales and Marketing Division, agreed, saying, "So do we. I know exactly how much each of our field reps sold."

Peggy Peoples responded, "Yes, but those are the easy ones. What about the people in marketing, or finance and accounting, or computing? Can we measure their work output? And, if so, should we do it?" She asked Conrad Innis, vice president of the Computer and Information Services Division, "Conrad, do you have any suggestions?"

Preston Smith interrupted: "Before you answer that one Conrad, I'd like to say that I'm reluctant to implement the 'Big Brother is watching you' concept in this company."

The Assignment

This assignment deals with the ethical and practical aspects of monitoring an individual's productivity in the workplace.

1. List possible productivity criteria for:
   a. A data entry operator (for example, one criterion could be the number of keystrokes per hour).
   b. A secretary.
   c. An accountant.
   d. A programmer.
   e. A vice president.
2. Information technology has been used by many companies to monitor individual productivity. For example, some companies monitor the performance of data entry operators by counting the number of keystrokes per unit time. Describe ways that information technology can be employed to measure the productivity of a secretary, an accountant, a programmer, and a vice president.
3. Discuss the desirability of monitoring individual productivity at Zimco.
4. Is it possible or advisable for the company to have one philosophy regarding the monitoring of production workers and another philosophy regarding the monitoring of nonproduction workers? Explain.

APPLICATION CASE STUDY 15–2
The Impact of a Merger

The Situation

The Board of Directors at Zimco Enterprises has made a decision that will have a major impact on every division of the company (see Chapter 15, "An MIS Case Study," for background information on Zimco Enterprises). The Board decided that, in addition to developing new products internally, Zimco should acquire other companies that produce innovative products that are consistent with Zimco's product philosophy.

Preston Smith, Zimco's president, has asked the Board of Directors to consider the Parsec Company as a candidate for acquisition. Parsec is light years ahead of its competition in the application of CAD/CAM. Consumers have reacted enthusiastically to both its products, wingers and snibeks. The company, which employs about 450 people, is located in Ann Arbor, Michigan.

The Engineering Department uses a computer-aided design system to design new products and refine current products. The manufacturing facilities are highly automated, with most processes under the control of a computer-aided manufacturing system. The design and manufacturing systems are the primary components of an integrated package. The traditional transaction processing applications (order entry, billing, and so on) have been automated, but they would not be considered sophisticated and they are not integrated. The Board of Directors has asked each vice president to assess the impact that acquiring the Parsec Company would have on his or her division.

The Assignment

Put yourself in the role of a systems analyst as you complete the following assignment. Conrad Innis, the vice president of the Computer and Information Services Division, has asked you to investigate how the merger with the Parsec Company will affect the Computer and Information Services Division.

1. Zimco's strategic plan calls for a gradual transition to a computer-integrated manufacturing environment over the next five years. Is the merger likely to help or hinder this plan? Explain.
2. Discuss the ramifications of integrating Parsec's procedures and files into Zimco's integrated management information system.
3. Discuss the pros and cons of consolidating the operations at Parsec's computer center into the operations at Zimco's centralized computer center at Dallas.

APPLICATION CASE STUDY 15–3
"Buying" Versus "Making" Software

The Situation

The Sales and Marketing Information System (SAMIS) at Zimco Enterprises is a proprietary software package that was purchased from an outside vendor (see Chapter 15, "An MIS Case Study," for background information on Zimco Enterprises). The implementation went smoothly because the package required only minor modifications to meet the needs of the Sales and Marketing Division. This positive experience with software packages encouraged Conrad Innis, the vice president of the Computer and Information Services Division, to investigate the possibility of purchasing two major packages rather than develop them in-house. When he discussed this alternative with the systems manager and the programming manager, they both said that they were opposed to the idea. Furthermore, both expressed concern that Zimco might lose some of its best programmers and analysts if these packages were purchased. The acquisition of the SAMIS package caused considerable unrest in the division. Several people were irate about the fact that they had become implementors rather than developers. These people felt that attending to the minor modifications needed to implement the SAMIS package did not constitute professional-level work. In addition, they felt that the Zimco MIS staff could have produced a better information system at a lower cost if it had been done in-house.

The Assignment

Put yourself in the role of Conrad Innis as you complete the following assignment.

1. How would you respond to the concerns of your systems and programming managers?
2. What could you say or do to create an environment within the Computer and Information Services Division that would be more conducive to the acquisition and implementation of proprietary software?

CHAPTER 16

Managing Information Services

KEY TOPICS

CHAPTER OVERVIEW

Management of the information services function is one of the major themes throughout this book. This chapter continues with this theme by focusing on high-visibility management issues and concerns. The tone of the chapter is slightly different from that of the preceding chapters because it introduces some "straight talk" to give you a feel for the gap that exists between the ideal and reality. A variety of issues and concerns are described and discussed from management's perspective: the impact of distributed processing, the automation explosion, computer crime, software piracy, user chargeback systems, contingency planning, and internal politics.

DISTRIBUTED PROCESSING'S IMPACT ON USER MANAGERS

A few years ago the management of information and computing resources was the sole domain of the director of the data processing department. Today, more and more companies are adopting the philosophy of information resource management (IRM), and the management of this resource is becoming a shared responsibility for both MIS and user management.

The organizational structure shown in Figure 16–1 is representative of companies that are retaining a centralized information services department while distributing processing capabilities into the user areas. In this type of structure, the distributed information services departments are set up as staff functions to the vice presidents and provide direct computing support for their respective functional areas. In this environment, sometimes called departmental computing (see Chapter 5, "Providers of Computer and Information Services"), the departmental computers are linked to the company's mainframe computer. To maintain control and consistency throughout the company's computer network, most companies are opting for a dotted-line relationship between the vice president of information services and the directors of the distributed information services departments. In general, the functional-area vice presidents set priorities and manage their departmental computer center, and the centralized MIS function provides standards and coordinates corporatewide MIS activities that affect these distributed facilities.

Because of the trend to IRM and distributed processing, top corporate executives and user managers in all areas are becoming intimately involved in the management of the information resource. Since the best way to manage the information resource is through judicious use of computers, they must also manage computing resources.

This trend toward distributing processing capabilities closer to the people who use them has prompted a movement of hardware, software, and computer specialists into the user departments. Forecasters are predicting

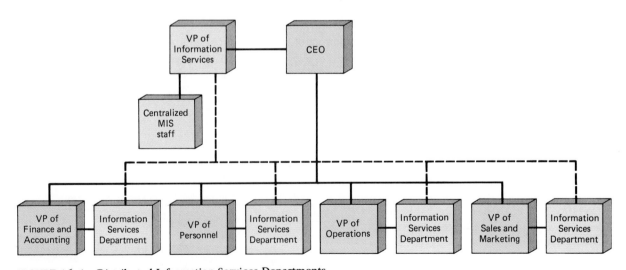

FIGURE 16–1   Distributed Information Services Departments
The organizational structure illustrates a popular alternative for the formal and informal lines of reporting for distributed information services departments.

It is a wise management that knows how to insist on and obtain detailed plans from operating personnel, and yet not use the results of such planning in a punitive manner.

—— *Anonymous*

that the majority of computer specialist positions in companies will be in the user groups by 1990 (see Figure 6–4 in Chapter 6, "End User Computing"). Even now, virtually every type of user group, from research and development to purchasing to accounting, is vigorously recruiting people with a variety of computer-related specialties. Of course, user groups need people with the traditional skills (programmers, systems analysts, operators), but they also need the new breed of computer specialists (office automation specialists, microcomputer specialists, information center specialists, and user liaisons).

Today it is not just the information services division that has computers. The information services division may have the edge in computing capacity, but the user areas have the edge in numbers of computers. The personal computer revolution has caused an explosion of computers in the user areas. With computers becoming fixtures throughout most companies, it was a foregone conclusion that computer specialists would follow. User managers who have become comfortable with their scope of responsibility and their environment are finding themselves responsible for management of certain facets of the information services function. In that regard, they are confronted with a new set of management challenges. As you can imagine, those managers with an understanding of MIS are pursuing these challenges with vigor. Those who are deficient in their understanding of MIS and computer concepts are less than enthusiastic about this irreversible trend.

The remainder of this chapter is devoted to addressing some of the more prominent issues and management considerations confronting MIS managers and user managers who have responsibilities for managing information- and computer-related resources.

Computer designers are attuned to the trend toward distributing processing capabilities closer to the user areas. Powerful minicomputers are being designed to operate in a normal office environment. Most minicomputers do not require special accommodations for temperature and humidity control. The minicomputer at this management consulting firm (on the floor next to the plant) services 32 workstations, including the 4 in the photo.

Photo courtesy of Hewlett-Packard Company

AN OVERHAUL OF CORPORATE MIS

Q. Like most companies today, increasing productivity in the area of MIS has become a major focal point of interest to us. We are an MIS staff of approximately 140 servicing a highly diversified $2 billion corporation. We are currently attempting to structure a two-year comprehensive program to improve our staff's productivity; utilize a homegrown system development methodology; incorporate increased user participation and responsibility; migrate toward user-oriented nonprocedural languages; and generally improve our product, timeliness of production and service, and credibility throughout the corporation.

Are there a few key points that you feel might help us in our endeavors?

A. You are talking about a complete overhaul of corporate MIS. To realize success in such an ambitious endeavor, attention to three areas is critical: MIS planning, system development, and user education.

1. Develop a comprehensive MIS strategic plan for corporate information services. I use the word "comprehensive" to emphasize that a plan for information services incorporates not only hardware and software, but policy, procedures, attitudes, people, education, and so on—all necessary ingredients of the information service function.

2. Relative to the system development:

   a. Integrate the user into the process. The user is as much a part of the development process as analysts and programmers.

   b. If you use a methodology, keep it simple. A lengthy, complex methodology will either fail or be more trouble than it is worth. A person's willingness to use the methodology is inversely proportional to its complexity.

   c. Do system development under the umbrella of a project management system.

   d. Take advantage of the latest technological innovations, such as CASE and fourth-generation languages. They are well worth the investment.

3. Implement an ongoing in-house user education program at all levels of the corporation. User awareness and knowledge of capabilities and potential of MIS can be the key to successful implementation of your program.

MIS ISSUES CONFRONTING USER, MIS, AND EXECUTIVE MANAGEMENT

To this point in the book, a great many management issues have been addressed, for example:

- ☐ Understanding MIS trends (Chapter 1).
- ☐ Using information systems as a strategic weapon (Chapter 4).
- ☐ Decentralizing information services (Chapter 5).
- ☐ Accommodating end user computing (Chapter 6).
- ☐ Fostering connectivity (Chapter 8).
- ☐ Integrating corporate data (Chapter 9).
- ☐ Coordinating corporate and MIS planning (Chapter 10).
- ☐ Protecting the privacy of personal information (Chapter 11).
- ☐ Identifying user and MIS roles in systems development (Chapters 12 and 13).

Other equally important issues have yet to be discussed. These issues are addressed in the following sections:

- Controlling the rapid expansion of computer-based applications.
- Thwarting the threat of computer crime.
- Dealing with software piracy.
- Creating and realizing project schedules.
- Upgrading aging software.
- Fostering corporate support for information system development.

Controlling the Rapid Expansion of Computer-Based Applications

Fifteen years ago, company executives would have been reasonably content with a data processing department that had installed a few standard applications (for example, inventory management, accounts receivable, and general ledger) and perhaps a few industry-specific applications (for example, route accounting for a beverage distributor). Today, top management is asking everyone to find ways to increase productivity and to become more competitive. In response to this request, managers and operational-level personnel are looking in every corner for a solution. More often than not, the solution revolves around automation. The net result of this constant pressure by management to achieve a higher level of productivity and greater competitiveness is a tidal wave of computer applications being suggested, approved, developed, and implemented. This emphasis on automation has caused a tremendous increase in the number of applications in a company's applications portfolio. A medium-sized company that had between 20 or 30 applications in 1970 might have hundreds of departmental- and corporate-level applications and literally thousands of PC-based applications. Coping with this rapid expansion of computer-based systems has posed a major challenge to management.

The most valuable and least used word in a manager's vocabulary is "No."

———— *Anonymous*

Companies that have been successful in coping with this explosion of systems have several things in common.

- *Coordination and cooperation.* Left unchecked, the rapid decentralization of computing capabilities via minis and micros gives rise to the potential for the proliferation of expensive autonomous and redundant information systems. Progressive companies nip this proliferation in the bud by establishing a high-level MIS steering committee (see Chapter 5, "Providers of Computer and Information Services"). Such a committee encourages coordination and cooperation in all phases of MIS endeavor. Companies with an executive mandate to cooperate tend to have less duplication and more integration.
- *Planning.* Each successful company has an MIS strategic plan that articulates strategic directions for information services. MIS strategic and operational planning is discussed in some detail in Chapter 10, "MIS Planning."

□ *Controls.* Companies making the most of information resources have a sophisticated set of controls that ensure the integrity of all operational systems. Controls are discussed in Chapter 14, "System Implementation."

Virtually all companies give lip service to coordination and cooperation. Some even have a steering committee and an MIS plan, but too often the steering committee is "paper only," and the plan simply gathers dust. In these companies, computer applications are continuing to proliferate without direction or control. To cope with the explosion of computer-based applications, corporate management should have an active MIS steering committee, follow the guidelines of carefully prepared MIS plans, and enforce system controls.

Thwarting the Threat of Computer Crime

Relatively few companies are adequately prepared to deal with the issue of computer crime. Computer crime is an issue that can be very costly, especially if the issue is ignored until after the fact. Unfortunately, a series of highly publicized and costly computer crimes may be the only thing that will convince executives that computer crime is real and should be a priority concern. It is estimated that each year, the total loss from computer crime is greater than the sum total of all robberies! In fact, no one really knows the extent of computer crime because much of it is either undetected or unreported (most often the latter). In those cases involving banks, officers may elect to

In a hierarchy, every employee tends to rise to his level of incompetence.

—— *Laurence Johnston Peter*

write off the loss rather than announce the crime and risk the loss of goodwill from their customers. Computer crime is on the rise. There are many types of computer crime, ranging from the use of an unauthorized password by a college student to a billion-dollar insurance fraud.

Computer crimes require the cooperation of experienced computer specialists. A common street thug does not have the knowledge or the opportunity to pull off a computer crime. The sophistication of the crime, however, makes it no less criminal.

Computer crime is a relatively recent phenomenon. Legislation and the criminal justice system are as ill prepared to cope with it, as is industry in general. Only a few police and FBI agents in the entire country have been trained to handle cases involving computer crime. And when a case comes to court, few judges have the background necessary to understand the testimony.

There is a growing concern that the media is glorifying the illegal entry and use of computer systems by overzealous hackers. These "electronic vandals" have tapped into everything from local credit agencies to top-secret defense systems. The evidence of unlawful entry, perhaps a revised record or access during nonoperating hours, is called a **footprint**.

A few hackers and computer professionals have chosen computer crime as a profession. But the threat of computer crime may be even greater from insiders like managers and consultants. These people are in the best position to pull off a computer crime. They know how the systems operate, and they know the passwords needed to gain access to the systems. For example, in the now-famous Equity Funding fraud (1973), officers of the company created bogus insurance policies (via computer) to make the company appear successful. Senior management perpetuated the fraud by creating fictitious policyholders and by using computer capabilities for the cover-up. The stock skyrocketed and over $2 billion disappeared before the culprits were caught.

There is no fail safe approach to avoiding computer crime. However, a business can be made considerably less vulnerable by installing a variety of security measures. System security is discussed in Chapter 14, "System Implementation."

Dealing with Software Piracy

An issue that continues to be a concern to MIS and user managers is **software piracy**. Software is protected by the Copyright Law of 1974, just as books are protected by copyright laws. This makes the duplication of copyright software illegal. This unlawful thievery of someone else's programs is sometimes called software piracy. The term **pilferage** is used to describe the situation where a company purchases a software product without a site-usage license agreement, then copies and distributes it throughout the company.

It may cost more to reproduce a book than to buy it, but a $750 commercial software product can be reproduced for $2.50 (price of storage medium) in less than a minute. Many software pirates have found the temptation too great to resist. Vendors of software for personal computers estimate that for every software product sold, two more are illegally copied. Software

SOFTWARE PIRACY

Q. I know for a fact that personal computers in my department have been used for the unauthorized duplication of proprietary software. Recently, I made it clear that I did not condone this type of activity. However, I learned through the grapevine that since that meeting, one package has been copied for home use.

Have other companies been successful in stopping software piracy? If so, what are they doing?

A. Every time I begin to think that the software pirates are losing the war, I am in some way reminded that the problem continues. Only recently, I listened as the president of a company (perhaps $30M in sales) encouraged over 100 conference attendees to save money by copying proprietary software. Software vendors are very serious about eradicating this erosion of profits.

Any company that does not have a written policy regarding the duplication of proprietary software should draft one as soon as possible. For the purposes of individual protection, any manager responsible for microcomputers should distribute a memo that articulates the company's policy on the reproduction of proprietary software.

As further protection for the company and as a warning to users, many companies are producing stick-on labels that read something like this: Unauthorized duplication of copyright software is prohibited on this machine.

piracy is a serious problem, and software vendors are acting vigorously to prosecute people and companies who violate their copyrights.

Some managers confront the issue head on and state bluntly that software piracy is a crime and offenders will be dismissed. This method has proven effective. Some, who are in reality accomplices, look the other way as subordinates copy software for office and personal use. In any company, the corporate policy can be nothing short of a public condemnation of software piracy. In fact, most companies place warning labels on company micros that remind employees of the corporate policy on software piracy.

Creating and Realizing Project Schedules

Historically, implementing information systems on schedule has been a problem. Managers at all levels recognize the need for better scheduling of projects, and many companies are beginning to take a more realistic approach to information systems planning. Several factors contribute to this ongoing management concern. The most prominent is the *I-want-it-yesterday syndrome*. That is, when user managers decide that they want a new or enhanced system, they usually want it yesterday, or at the worst, as soon as possible. To be as accommodating as possible, MIS management compiles an optimistic schedule that assumes full cooperation from affected user departments and a total commitment from MIS project team members. As so often happens after the excitement of the launch of the project, enthusiasm wanes on the part of the users and the efforts of project team members are often diverted to "hot" projects. Inevitably the implementation date begins to slip, thereby frustrating the planning efforts of both MIS and user managers.

The following corporate scenario is all too typical. A competitor company establishes a competitive advantage by announcing an electronic data interchange (EDI) system that permits customers to make inquires and enter orders directly. The vice president of sales responds by demanding that a similar system be installed as soon as possible. Top management agrees and makes the system the number-one priority and the system is scheduled to go on-line on September 1. Of course, other "high-priority" projects suffer as people resources are diverted to the new number-one project. The schedules of the other projects begin to slip indefinitely. Eventually, one or more of these neglected projects are reevaluated by top management and given a status equal to or above the EDI system. Resources are reallocated, and the EDI project schedule slips. This vacillation of priorities and the reallocation of limited resources continues indefinitely. Eventually all systems are implemented, but only after numerous "promised" completion dates have come and gone. This type of scheduling philosophy is actually more the rule than the exception and can be very frustrating to both MIS and user management.

Many MIS managers have fallen prey to the *90 percent complete syndrome*. That is, to appease anxious user managers who are desperate to get their systems installed and on-line, MIS managers sometimes tell them that the project is "90 percent complete." They do this knowing that the project may be well behind schedule and only 30 or 50 percent complete. By saying that it is 90 percent complete, the MIS manager buys some more uninterrupted time. This lack of honest communication between MIS and

> The bitterness of poor quality lingers long after the sweetness of meeting schedules is forgotten.
>
> —— *Anonymous*

user management is an ongoing issue. User management needs to be more up front about the plans for information system activity, and MIS management needs to paint a more realistic picture of project schedules. Of course, conscientious adherence to MIS strategic and operational plans can eliminate many of the problems associated with project scheduling.

Upgrading Aging Software

Practically speaking, the majority of installed information systems need serious attention. That is, they need a major upgrade or should be scrapped and replaced by a new system.

An old, and often antiquated, information system has some enticing advantages.

- □ Users are familiar with its operation and feel comfortable using it.
- □ The system works and is free of bugs.

These advantages are all that some managers need to delay the decision to initiate the inevitable hassle of converting to a new system. Not every user manager is hungry for automation. In these situations, the issue is who initiates the move to an upgrade or new system—MIS or user managers? In theory, MIS personnel are the catalysts, but ultimately it is the user who should request the upgrade. Often this is the case, but too often users are not interested in changing their information system. If MIS initiates action on a new system, then users perceive this action as an intrusion on their area of responsibility. If both MIS and user managers elect to take no action on an antiquated, inefficient, and limited information system, it can remain operational indefinitely, costing the company money and lost opportunities.

At some point in time, the utility of retaining an old information system becomes marginal. At this time the disadvantages begin to outweigh the advantages. The primary disadvantages of an old system include the following:

- □ The old system may have an autonomous data base and may not be compatible with the company's integrated data base.
- □ The old system can be a maintenance nightmare, taking more personnel resources to maintain it than it would to create a new one.
- □ The old system probably does not satisfy all the user's needs for information.
- □ The old system may not be taking advantage of the economies of the latest technology.

The determination of when to upgrade an old system requires close cooperation on the part of MIS and user management. Each year they need to evaluate each system to assess the utility of the old system and the benefits of upgrading to a new system. What to look for during periodic system evaluation is discussed in Chapter 14, "System Implementation." A system left unchecked can remain operational well after a rational evaluation would have deemed the system dated and of marginal benefit to the company.

Fostering Corporate Support for Information System Development

Most managers are staunch and open advocates of the judicious use of the company's computing and information resources. However, getting them to commit their time, the time of their subordinates, and a portion of their department's budget to MIS activities is another matter. At issue in virtually every company is the priority of MIS within the overall organization. In a consumer goods company, marketing is usually given priority status. In heavy industry, such as steel, production is the favored area. In a start-up company, research and development is the focus. In a bank, accounting is emphasized. In general, tradition has precluded MIS from becoming a priority activity. In fact, MIS has only recently become a consideration in corporate strategic planning.

Top management tends to focus on whatever comprises the backbone of corporate operations. Middle managers are concerned with their particular functional areas. Line workers are interested in making their particular job easier. Historically, MIS managers have been unsuccessful in their attempts to raise management's awareness of the potential of MIS—that is, until recently. Now that companies are beginning to use MIS as a strategic weapon, executives and managers at all levels are becoming keenly aware of MIS. Several very visible and well-publicized success stories about how companies are using computer and information technology to win the competitive advantage have done more to garner corporate support for MIS than have two decades worth of presentations by MIS managers. Also, success stories of how MIS has improved productivity have contributed to management's acceptance of MIS as a solution to a wide range of business problems. Management's awareness of MIS is a recent phenomena, and many managers have yet to get the message, but, at least this issue is well on its way to a resolution.

ALLOCATING COSTS TO END USERS

The current trend for medium and large organizations is to allocate the cost of computer and information services to the end users via **chargeback systems**. Chargeback systems are implemented to encourage the judicious use of the information/computer resource, primarily in the mainframe environment. The premise behind chargeback systems is that user managers are more deliberate when MIS funding comes directly from their budgets. Chargeback systems remain a heated issue in many companies because at some time in the past computing and information services were provided gratis to the user areas. For obvious reasons, many users would prefer to return to free services.

Many questions must be answered before a chargeback or cost allocation system can be implemented.

- Should the end user be charged for the costs of feasibility studies?
- Should charges be a fixed amount or should the charge be based on the actual time expended?

IMPROVING USER–MIS INTERACTIONS

Q. Recently I was placed in charge of developing a program to improve user interactions within our corporation. I am the assistant director of what most people would consider a large information services department. During a weekly staff meeting, our systems manager suggested that I write and see what you have to say.

Here's our situation. We have the usual problems in determining what the user wants during the design phase, and, consequently, our users are less than satisfied with the end products. What little feedback we get about the services we provide is routed through a vice president who is in charge of the Information Systems Department, as well as several other corporate services. Ultimately this feedback comes to us in the form of reprimands.

In recent years we have worked very hard to develop what we consider excellent standards and procedures within the Information Systems Department. Unfortunately, the lack of interaction with functional-area personnel precludes us from achieving the level of quality and service that we would like.

I would appreciate any ideas you might have that would help us improve our user relations and interactions.

A. First of all, the formal line of communication (user-MIS) should not be through the vice president. Designate one person, or more if necessary, to serve as a user liaison. This person is charged with the responsibility of rendering a level of satisfaction to the user. I am sorry to say that the user usually gets the runaround unless there is a formal communication link. A phone number and perhaps a sympathetic ear will do wonders for user relations.

Obviously a user liaison cannot solve all problems on the spot. When a compromise is the only solution, the user liaison can assist in arbitrating the differences. When no compromise is necessary, the liaison may work with the user to prepare a working plan.

Your confidence in your internal procedures indicates that you probably have a methodology for systems development and for other MIS functions, such as strategic planning, and so on. Is the user incorporated in your methodologies? For example, does the project team have at least one user representative? Whether it be systems development or MIS strategic planning, the user has the right to be consulted at critical milestones throughout the process. The user also has the obligation to provide feedback and ultimately an affirmative commitment at each of these milestones.

Several large corporations have provided slots within the organizational structure of the data center for user personnel from the various functional areas. These users return to their functional areas after one and a half to three years. This structure has several positive features. The user brings with him or her knowledge of the functional area and returns with a substantial knowledge of and sympathy for MIS operations. A permanent informal communication link is established when the user returns.

There are several ways to make significant improvements in user interactions that require a minimum of effort. For example, MIS managers often fall into the trap of committing themselves to an unrealistic completion date in order to relieve tension temporarily. In the long run, this does more to impede user interaction than coming up front and telling the user the bad news.

□ Should hardware utilization charges be based solely on processor utilization or should these charges be separated for each peripheral device (printer, disk storage, and so on)?

□ Should price breaks be given for volume usage?

□ Should price breaks be given for nonprime-time computer usage?

These are just a few of the questions that must be resolved when setting up a user chargeback system. As you can see, chargeback systems can be complex. In the past, the algorithms used to charge for the use of computing

MIS in practice

FLEXIBLE CHARGEBACK SYSTEMS

Q. Our company's chargeback system prorates the cost of a piece of equipment among the users of that equipment. Some analysts, therefore, are hesitant about using some new efficient devices because the charge to the user will be considerably higher than using older ones that are already heavily used. Isn't this self-defeating on a companywide basis since it would be advantageous to encourage the use of better devices? Is there a better way to prorate hardware cost?

A. The objective of a cost allocation and control system is to recover costs through efficient utilization of the corporate information services resources. New capabilities and methods are constantly changing the complexion of the resource pool. The services rate structure must be flexible enough to enable service costs to be revised to encourage an optimal use of all resources, including hardware.

---

devices was too complex to be understood easily by those paying the bill—the end users. The trend has been to simplify these algorithms. The premise behind this trend is that if the user understands the charges, he or she will strive to use computing and information resources more effectively.

There are four basic approaches to allocating costs to the end user. As one might expect, each has advantages and disadvantages. The following approaches are representative of those being used.

- ☐ Do not charge users for information services.
- ☐ Allocation of MIS funds to users upon request.
- ☐ Charging users directly for all information services.
- ☐ Charge users directly for all information services but at a reduced rate.

These approaches are discussed further in the following sections.

No Charge to User for Information Services

Until the early 1970s, most companies elected not to charge their users for their use of the company's computing and information resources. In these companies, the entire corporate information services budget was allocated to the information services division. They, in turn, were charged with providing the best possible service to the user within the constraints of the available resources. Today, relatively few medium and large companies continue using this approach, but it is still popular with small companies. This method is administratively simple and service is available to everyone at no charge. The disadvantages are that (1) the burden of priorities (without the existence of a steering committee) rest with information services management, (2) users do not appreciate the cost and do not fully analyze the benefit/cost ratio of their requests for service, and (3) invariably, the largest user gets the best service. This is, however, a viable option if and only if a strong and fair MIS steering committee exists that can allocate limited resources based on corporate need.

Allocation of MIS Funds to Users upon Request

One approach to allocating the cost of information services to the user departments is to provide each requesting department with an MIS budget. In this approach, the users are simply given whatever "funds" are needed to enable them to accomplish the desired MIS activities. There is, in fact, no internal transfer of funds. In the trade, this type of budget allocation is known as "funny money" or "wooden nickels." The advantage of this approach is that it provides a limited amount of control over the information services budget and provides the user with feedback on the MIS expenses incurred. Again, with this approach, users do not appreciate costs and do not analyze the benefit/cost ratio of their requests. Budget allocations tend not to be taken seriously since the user need only request a greater allocation when the initial allocation is exhausted. This type of chargeback system has been popular in the college environment.

In the business community, this approach is a viable option over the long term only if real dollar penalties are assessed for exceeding the initial budget allocation. In the short term, this approach is often used to help corporations make the transition from a gratis environment to a chargeback system in which actual dollars are transferred between departments. During the transition, user groups are allocated a budget and are then given "memo charges" that reflect the amount of the current charges and the amount left in their budgets. Typically, memo charges are generated for about a year. During this time, user managers gain an appreciation for what they might expect when MIS services actually are charged to the functional area budgets.

Charging Directly for All Information Services

In a direct chargeback system, user departments are charged for all hardware utilization, personnel services, and materials. The advantage of this system is that it encourages user managers to analyze the benefit/cost ratio of their request. When managers scrutinize their requests, the requests tend to reflect high-priority and cost-effective projects. The most significant disadvantage of this approach is that the cost of the service may discourage potential users from considering computer-based information systems as an alternative.

Combining Corporate Subsidy and Direct Charge

The last approach to allocating the cost of information services to the user areas involves matching user expenditures with funds from a pool of corporate information services monies. This approach enables the user to pay, through internal funds transfer, only a portion of the charges for information services. For example, the user might pay 30 percent, 50 percent, or 70 percent with the remainder being charged to the corporate information services account. The advantage of this approach is that it encourages reluctant users to invest in cost-effective computer-based systems. Although the user is charged only a portion of the total cost, there is still an awareness of cost. To a lesser extent, the disadvantages of charging users directly for services are also applicable to this approach.

CONTINGENCY PLANNING

Reorganization is a wonderful method for creating the illusion of progress while producing confusion, inefficiency, and demoralization.

——— *Anonymous*

The importance of planning has been an emphasis throughout this book. To this point, the planning discussions have centered on MIS strategic and operational planning, both of which are oriented to ongoing and long-term system considerations. There is another type of MIS plan that may never need to be implemented, but it is no less important than the MIS strategic or operational plan. Most organizations maintain a **contingency plan** for information services that details what to do if there is an environmental disaster, sabotage, gross negligence, or any other extraordinary event that drastically disrupts the operation of a computer center (personnel strike, departure of key personnel). A contingency plan describes duties and responsibilities, alternative hardware sites, and the logistics for recovering from such disasters.

Under normal circumstances, an information services division without a contingency plan can continue to provide adequate service to the company indefinitely. However, the division not prepared for other than routine operation is courting disaster. Consider the following scenario:

A small fire in the United Airlines terminal at O'Hare International Airport in Chicago damaged voice and data lines that resulted in the cancellation of 175 flights and the stranding of 10,000 travelers. Reservations personnel could not keep pace manually with processing that normally is done by computers. With a contingency plan, perhaps the impact of the disaster could have been made less severe.

Corporations have gone bankrupt because of their inability to provide information services as a result of a disaster.

Contingency planning, sometimes referred to as **disaster planning**, is serious business. A company that helps companies to recover from disasters, Sunguard Recovery Services, Inc., estimates that a large bank would be out of business in two days if its computer systems went down. It estimated that a distribution company would last three days, a manufacturing company would last five days, and an insurance company would last six days. A University of Minnesota study examined victims of disasters and concluded that the probability of long-term survival was low if they were unable to recover critical operations within 30 hours. Even with overwhelming evidence to support the need for contingency planning, it is not done in all companies. Too often top management is unaware of the consequence of not having a contingency plan until after a crisis has occurred.

Identification of Potential Disasters and Extraordinary Occurrences

The first step in the contingency planning process is to identify potential disasters or extraordinary occurrences. A company must assume some risk, in that there are marginal returns for developing contingency plans for all possible occurrences. The plan should focus on addressing those disasters that are most probable and those with the greatest potential impact on corporate operation. One of the objectives of the contingency plan is to detail what can be done to avoid or minimize the impact of certain potential disasters. For example, most computer centers have Halon fire-retarding systems. In case of fire, a fire-retarding chemical that does not damage the hardware or the magnetic storage media is automatically dumped over the equipment in the machine room.

Alternate Site Selection

If for some reason a computer center is destroyed, the first step in the recovery process is to set up operations somewhere else. One of the primary functions of contingency planning is to select a backup site. There are essentially four backup site strategies. These are illustrated in Figure 16–2 and discussed here.

1. *Reciprocal agreement with another company.* Companies with similar hardware configurations make a legally binding agreement with one another to permit short-term sharing of the unaffected computer system until the

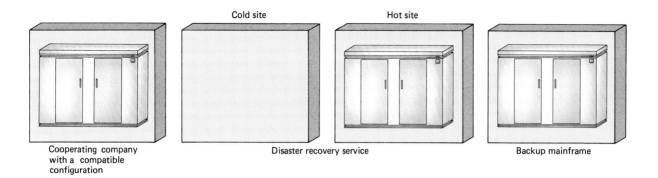

Cold site

Hot site

Cooperating company
with a compatible
configuration

Disaster recovery service

Backup mainframe

FIGURE 16–2   Backup Site Strategies

company experiencing the disaster is up and running again. When disaster occurs, both companies must cut back information services support to critical operations. The primary advantage of such an arrangement is that it is inexpensive. The disadvantages are more pronounced. The disaster could affect both companies (for example, an earthquake). Contingency planning becomes a cooperative effort between two companies. Reduced operation can continue only a few days, after which time, the operation of both companies can become tenuous.

2. *Cold site arrangement.* **Cold sites**, or **shells**, are simply facilities that are set up to accommodate a mainframe computer system (environment control, electrical service, workrooms). Companies contract with a disaster recovery service to provide a cold site in case of a disaster. It is the affected company's responsibility to provide its own hardware. The primary advantage of a cold site is its immediate availability. The primary disadvantage is that, after a disaster, a company must gather and install an entire computer system within a very short period, usually less than a day.

3. *Hot site arrangement.* **Hot sites** contain a compatible mainframe computer system that is ready to go. Companies contract with a disaster recovery service to provide a hot site in case of a disaster. The advantages are obvious. A company can take its backup tapes of data bases and programs to the hot site, load them up, and be up and running in a matter of a few hours. The big disadvantage is the expense. Because of the cost, only large, highly vulnerable companies can justify the average cost of $200,000 per year for a hot site lease. Another disadvantage is that the same disaster might affect several companies with contracts for emergency use of the same hot site.

4. *Purchase and maintain a backup computer system.* Many companies maintain a backup computer system at an alternate site. The backup system remains operational on an ongoing basis in support of noncritical applications. In case of an emergency, noncritical support is suspended, and the backup system provides support for essential applications. This option has become increasingly popular in recent years. For example, at a cost of $20,000 per minute of down time, major airlines are more than willing to invest in backup computer systems. Twenty percent of IBM's profits are derived from backup hardware.

Responsibilities and Logistics for Disaster Recovery

When a disaster occurs, time is of the essence. An army of people must act in unison in accordance with the directives in the contingency plan to get the company up and running as soon as possible. A typical contingency plan would involve personnel in the following areas.

- Management (MIS and user)
- Information services (operations, programming, systems analysis, and so on)
- Internal auditing
- Legal
- Security
- Corporate communications (public relations)
- Building maintenance
- Transportation
- Fire protection
- Insurance adjustment

The contingency plan would include detailed descriptions of duties and responsibilities for the personnel responsible for these areas. For example, the plan would even list telephone numbers of key people, directions to the backup site, and so on. The plan may also involve other companies (for example, customers and communications common carriers). The plan also addresses logistical considerations, such as the details of the physical movement of materials back and forth to the backup site.

Perhaps the most critical aspect of contingency planning is training and practice. Periodically, companies that recognize the importance of contingency planning conduct a "fire drill" to test and practice the procedures set forth in the plan. Today, top management is well attuned to the fact that good contingency planning can make the difference between continuing as a profitmaking entity and bankruptcy.

All animals are equal, but some animals are more equal than others.

—— *George Orwell*

POLITICS, INFORMATION, AND COMPUTERS

It is often said that information is power. As we all know, power and politics go hand in hand. Every organization, no matter how small, has a political infrastructure that is always highly active in attempts to influence the role and plight of information services. Whenever demand exceeds supply, which is the case for computing and information resources, politics often influences the allocation of these critical resources. To manage information services effectively, managers must factor the forces of internal politics into their decision making.

Unfortunately, information services is sometimes used as a pawn in a political game played by corporate executives desiring top priority for their special interests and information services needs. When this happens, the providers of information services become the center of corporate controversy, and decisions regarding the allocation of resources become increasingly difficult to make.

Internal politics are a fact of life, but the wise executive will harness the power and influence of the political infrastructure to effect cooperation and integration. In the long run, special interests are best served through system integration. Self-serving efforts to expedite the implementation of autonomous systems tend to maintain the status quo and impede progress.

CHAPTER HIGHLIGHTS

■ As companies adopt the philosophy of information resource management, the management of the information resource is becoming more of a shared responsibility between MIS and user management.

■ In distributed processing environments, companies are using a dotted-line relationship between the vice president of information services and the directors of the distributed information services departments. This relationship helps to maintain control and consistency throughout the company's computer network.

■ The trend toward distributing processing capabilities closer to the people who use them has prompted a movement of hardware, software, and computer specialists into the user departments.

■ The information services division may have the edge in computing capacity, but the user areas have the edge in numbers of computers.

■ Today, top management is constantly pressuring employees at all levels to achieve a higher level of productivity and greater competitiveness. This indirect emphasis on automation has caused a tremendous increase in the number of applications in a company's applications portfolio.

■ Companies that have been successful in holding the uncontrolled growth of their applications portfolio in check exhibit coordination and cooperation, participate in MIS planning, and adhere to a set of system controls.

■ It is estimated that each year, the total loss from computer crime is greater than the sum total of all robberies.

■ Insiders, like managers and consultants, are in the best position to pull off a computer crime.

■ There is no fail-safe approach to avoiding computer crime, however, a business can be made considerably less vulnerable by installing a variety of security measures.

■ The best way to address the issue of software piracy is to establish a policy condemning it, then enforce the policy.

■ To cope with the I-want-it-yesterday syndrome, MIS management sometimes compiles an overly optimistic project schedule that inevitably results in slipped implementation dates.

■ Many MIS managers have fallen prey to the 90 percent complete syndrome. That is, they appease anxious user managers by telling them that their projects are "90 percent complete," even if the projects are less than 50 percent complete.

■ If both MIS and user managers elect to take no action on an antiquated, inefficient, and limited information system, it can remain operational indefinitely, costing the company money and lost opportunities.

■ Chargeback systems are implemented to encourage the judicious use of the information/computer resource, primarily in the mainframe environment. The premise behind chargeback systems is that user managers are more deliberate when MIS funding comes directly from their budgets.

■ There are four basic approaches to allocating costs to end users: no charge for services, allocate MIS funds to users upon request, charge users directly, and charge users directly but at a reduced rate.

■ Most organizations maintain a contingency plan for information services that details what to do if there is an environmental disaster, sabotage, gross negligence, or any other extraordinary event that drastically disrupts the operation of a computer center. A contingency plan describes duties and responsibilities, alternative hardware sites, and the logistics for recovering from such disasters.

■ A study concluded that the probability of long-term survival from the loss of a company's mainframe computer system was low if the company was unable to recover critical operations within 30 hours.

■ The four basic backup site strategies are: (1) have a reciprocal agreement with another company, (2) contract with a disaster recovery service for a cold site, (3) contract with a disaster recovery service for a hot site, or (4) purchase and maintain a backup computer system.

■ Whenever demand exceeds supply, which is the case for computing and information resources, politics often influences the allocation of these critical resources. To manage information services effectively, managers must factor the forces of internal politics into their decision making.

IMPORTANT TERMS

chargeback systems	disaster planning	I-want-it-yesterday syndrome	pilferage
cold sites	footprint	90 percent complete syndrome	shells
contingency plan	hot sites		software piracy

REVIEW EXERCISES

1. What revolution is responsible for the explosion of computers in the user areas?
2. What do companies have in common that have had success in coping with the explosion in the number of installed computer-based applications?
3. Name three computer-based applications that would be considered standard in most companies.
4. Is computer crime rising or falling?
5. What term is used to describe the situation where a company purchases a software product without a site-usage license agreement, then copies and distributes it throughout the company.
6. What is to be gained from the implementation of a chargeback system?
7. What is the difference between a cold site and a hot site?
8. Within the context of computer crime, what is a footprint?
9. Name three types of MIS plans.
10. A typical contingency plan would involve personnel in a variety of areas. Name four of these areas.
11. Like an old shoe, old information systems also have their advantages. What are these advantages?

DISCUSSION QUESTIONS

1. Who is more to blame for a project not meeting a scheduled completion date: a user manager who demands an immediate response to his information needs and does not honor his personnel commitments to the project, or a director of information services who gives the user an unrealistic implementation date? Explain.
2. A computer security consultant presented two proposals to top management at a large bank. One proposal called for a $2 million computer security system. He said that he was 95 percent sure that such a system would prevent computer crime at the bank. The other proposal was for a $4 million system. He was 99 percent sure that the more expensive system would prevent computer crime at the bank. Which proposal would you select and why?
3. Explain how a medium-sized company that had between 20 and 30 computer-based applications in 1970 might have hundreds or even thousands of applications today.
4. In Figure 16–1 there is a dotted-line relationship between the directors of the distributed information services departments and the vice president of information services. Would there be any merit to having the dotted line relationship between the distributed information services departments and the functional-area vice presidents and the solid line to the vice president of information services? Explain.
5. A number of management issues have been addressed in this book, such as using information systems as a strategic weapon (discussed in Chapter 4), accommodating end user computing (discussed in Chapter 6), and integrating corporate data (discussed in Chapter 9). Which of the preceding three issues do you consider to be the most pressing and why?
6. What considerations should be built into a contractual agreement between two companies that plan to provide backup protection for one another in the case that disaster strikes one of their computer centers?
7. A major insurance company has 10,000 employees, 2,000 agents, and millions of policyholders. Describe the scenario during the first two hours following the devastation of the insurance company's primary computer facility.
8. Would you recommend a chargeback system that is subsidized by the corporation or one that charges 100 percent of the services back to the user? Defend your choice.
9. Describe seven events that could render a company's mainframe computer system inoperable.

10. Today, distributed processing is a well-defined trend, yet some user managers are continuing to ignore it. If these managers ask you for advice on how to improve their prospects for career advancement, what would you tell them?

11. A surprisingly high percentage of existing home security systems were installed in response to a burglary. Do you think that the instance of a computer crime may be the only thing that will convince management to act on thwarting computer crime? Explain.

12. Explain how the continued operation of an antiquated, inefficient, and limited information system results in unnecessary cost to the company.

13. Certain questions must be resolved before a cost allocation system can be implemented. Respond to the following questions as if you were creating a chargeback system for your company (or college). Should charges be a fixed amount or should the charge be based on the actual time expended? Should price breaks be given for volume usage? Should price breaks be given for nonprime-time computer usage?

14. A company policy requires that a warning label be affixed to the front of every one of the company's microcomputers. The label reads, "This computer is not to be used for the unlawful duplication of copyright software." What do you suppose prompted top management to implement such a policy?

APPLICATION CASE STUDY 16–1
Allocating Costs to End Users

The Situation

When John Robson became manager of the Computer Services Department at Gabriel Industries, all computer-based information systems were operating in batch mode. Users were not charged for systems development or computer processing. All such costs were absorbed by the Computer Services Department, and the department was funded from corporate overhead. John Robson was dissatisfied with this system because there was no incentive for users to make efficient use of computing resources. Also, users were submitting service requests for the development of information systems that could not be justified on a cost-benefit basis.

John Robson succeeded in convincing top management that a chargeback system was necessary and that it would benefit the company. He was given approval to implement a partial chargeback system that required users to pay the cost of system operation after implementation; that is, development costs would still be absorbed by the Computer Services Department. John Robson was not completely happy with the decision, but he accepted it as a step in the right direction. He implemented a system that charged users for each unit of computing resources they consumed. Charges aligned with the following categories:

1. Processor time used.
2. Number of disk accesses (reads or writes).
3. Disk storage space used, per day.
4. Number of tape accesses (reads or writes).
5. Magnetic tape reels stored, per day.
6. Number of lines printed.
7. Number of data entry keystrokes.
8. Off-line services (for example, separating multiple copy reports).

In addition to these cost categories, users were charged for supplies used by their applications (for example, preprinted forms).

The Computer Services Department is currently developing several on-line information systems. John Robson wants to modify the chargeback system such that it will be able to reflect more accurately the operational costs of on-line systems. He views this reassessment of the chargeback system as an opportune time to change it so that users pay for all or at least a portion of the development costs for new or enhanced systems. John Robson has an additional concern: How will the proliferation of end user computing affect his department's budget?

The Assignment

Put yourself in the role of John Robson as you complete the following assignment.

1. Describe the computing resources for which users of on-line systems would be charged.

   a. List each resource category given in this case study for batch systems and state whether the charges incurred for each resource are likely to increase, stay about the same, or decrease when the conversion is made to an on-line system. Justify your answers.

   b. What new resource categories will need to be added to the existing categories to accommodate on-line systems?

2. What arguments would you use to convince users and top management that charging for system development activities is a good idea.

3. Assume that your proposal for modifying the chargeback system to include development costs is approved. Identify the source(s) of funding for each of the following items. Justify your answers.

   a. An upgrade to the mainframe hardware or its software.

   b. Modifications to information systems software necessitated by upgrades to the mainframe hardware or its software.

   c. Additional personnel for the Computer Services Department.

   d. The information center staff and facilities.

4. How will the proliferation of end user computing affect the Computer Services Department budget? For example, will a smaller mainframe suffice? Justify your answers.

APPLICATION CASE STUDY 16–2

Contingency Planning for End User Computing

The Situation

Users at Gabriel Industries have three fundamental sources of computing available to them: personal computing (microcomputers), departmental computing (minicomputers and micro networks), and the mainframe computer operated by the Computer Services Department. An information center provides technical support and advisory services for personal and departmental computing. The manager of the Computer Services Department, John Robson, has developed a contingency plan for the corporate computer center. His plan incorporates a reciprocal arrangement with a nearby company that has a mainframe hardware and software configuration similar to that at Gabriel Industries. Both companies store backups of software and data files in safes at each other's sites.

Although John Robson feels confident about the contingency plan for the mainframe environment, he is very concerned about the lack of planning among users who have personal computers and microcomputers.

The Assignment

Put yourself in the role of John Robson as you complete the following assignment.

1. What should the role of the Computer Services Department be regarding contingency planning among end users? Justify your answer.

2. What role (if any) should the information center play in helping end users with contingency planning?

3. Prepare guidelines for the preparation of end user contingency plans. At minimum, address personnel duties and responsibilities, alternative hardware sites, and the logistics of recovery procedures for:

   a. A personal computer.

   b. A departmental local area network made up of microcomputers.

   c. A departmental minicomputer.

CHAPTER **17**

Evaluation, Selection, and Acquisition of Hardware and Software

KEY TOPICS

CHAPTER OVERVIEW

Most MIS books and courses emphasize the use and application of computer and information technologies, but relatively little is said about obtaining these technologies. Too often, not knowing how to obtain hardware, software, and information services results in their use being deferred indefinitely or, worse, the selection and purchase of the wrong system. As in Chapter 16, the material in this chapter demands more "straight talk." This chapter is devoted to discussing the topics associated with the evaluation, selection, and acquisition of hardware, software, and information services. The chapter concludes with the presentation of an acquisition methodology.

ACQUISITION PHILOSOPHIES

Individuals and companies, whether conscientiously or unconscientiously, eventually develop a philosophy regarding the acquisition of hardware, software, and information services. In practice, three distinct philosophies have emerged. These acquisition philosophies include being a vendor loyalist, being a leading edge technocrat, and being a conservative.

The Vendor Loyalist

For whatever reason, some individuals and companies are very loyal to one, or perhaps, a few vendors. For example, one large midwestern company buys all of its minicomputers and mainframe computers and most of its peripheral devices from one company (it buys its disk drives from another company). The decision makers at this company have been pleased with the service of the primary vendor and do not want to risk the possibility of having to settle for a reduced level of service, so they stay with the same vendor. A small eastern company made the decision to wait for the next release of a popular microcomputer database package, never even considering the possibility that other currently available software might be less expensive, provide better features, and be easier to use. Managers and operational people at this company are familiar with the product and, to the person, have no interest in learning another database package.

The reasons that companies and individuals habitually return to the same vendor vary dramatically. Some seek the security of doing business with a well-established company. Others like the products or, perhaps, even the salesperson. Compatibility concerns are often cited as reasons for remaining loyal to a particular vendor. Some loyalists are very outspoken about their commitment to a particular vendor and even discourage other vendors from calling. Although others may encourage competitive bidding, in the end, they remain loyal to a particular vendor. Even given the possibility that these companies may pay a premium price for their products, decision makers are convinced that, in the long run, the costs are less than they would be if they switched vendors. And, often this is the case.

Certainly many hardware and software vendors have established a loyal following, but without question, the International Business Machines Corporation has the largest base of vendor loyalists. IBM is often referred to as "Big Blue" because of its predominately blue hardware. It follows then that IBM loyalists are "true blue," a nickname that IBM loyalists accept with pride.

The Leading-Edge Technocrats

A relatively small group of companies want to be perpetually on the leading edge of the technology. They are always on the lookout for innovative new products that may have the potential to benefit their companies. These adventuresome companies are willing to work directly with vendors to iron out the bugs in the hardware or a software package in return for the privilege of being among the first to install the product. These companies often agree to be a **beta test** site for a vendor, that is, they agree to test a product in a live environment. Before being released for beta testing, products will have

We are becoming the servants in thought, as in action, of the machines we have created to serve us.

―――― *John Kenneth Galbraith*

At IBM's Software Usability Laboratory, software engineers monitor subjects while they learn and use software packages that may some day be released as commercial software products. The objective of this phase of alpha testing is to gather feedback that enables system designers to fine tune the user interface before the software is released for beta testing.

Courtesy of International Business Machines

passed an **alpha test** (an in-house vendor test). By agreeing to be a beta test site, a company has an opportunity to get in on the ground floor of the emergence of a potentially exciting product. The vendor provides prerelease versions of the product gratis to the beta test sites in return for their comments on the accuracy, effectiveness, and overall quality of the product.

Being first has its drawbacks. Implementing a new product can be time consuming and costly. Most off-the-shelf products are bug-free. This is not the case with prerelease versions and even products that have just reached the market. Prerelease versions of software products and some newly released products invariably have bugs and sometimes major design flaws. Companies using these products must be willing to cope with setbacks and delays for the right to be first. Even being first is a small consolation when a product does not live up to its prerelease hype.

The Conservatives

In contrast to the leading-edge technocrats, the conservative buyers have no interest in being on the leading edge, or as they call it, the "bleeding edge." They are perfectly content to let other companies experience the pain and expense of working through the learning curve. The conservatives want to buy a proven product. They feel that delaying implementation by six months or a year is a small price to pay for the satisfaction of knowing that a product works. Before buying, the conservatives ask vendors to point to examples of success stories; then they confirm these reports by talking directly with representatives of the companies using the product.

COMPATIBILITY AND CONNECTIVITY CONCERNS

Now, after almost four decades into the availability of commercial computers, most companies have sizable investments in hardware and software. Only a very unusual set of circumstances would cause a company to upgrade to a computer system that was not compatible with the majority of their existing software, and vice versa. Applications software is not as portable as we would like. An information system is designed and coded to be run in a specific *computing environment*, defined by the programming language, computer, and operating system. This is true for both micros and mainframes. When software written for one environment can be run on another, the environments are said to be compatible. On the other hand, environments are not compatible when the programs can be run under one environment or the other, but not both.

The expense of upgrading to hardware or software that is not compatible with the existing environment is an expense that managers try to avoid if at all possible. When systems are not compatible, programs may require substantial and expensive modification before they can be run. When evaluating hardware and software, managers may limit their search to alternatives that are compatible and can offer **upward compatibility**. Systems that permit upward compatibility enable a company to purchase proprietary software at one level of sophistication and, then, at a later date, upgrade the existing system to one with greater capabilities without the need for redesigning and reprogramming.

MIS in practice

HARDWARE AND SOFTWARE OBSOLESCENCE

Q. Both our mainframe computer systems are circa 1978. We purchased three packaged systems in the late 1970s and all are in use today. Users are vocal about their dissatisfaction of our service, yet my requests to upgrade our hardware and software are denied.

Our current resources are inadequate to service the company's computing needs sufficiently. How can I convince management to loosen the purse strings?

A. I am assuming that during the last five years you have surely espoused the obvious and probably the not-so-obvious benefits of using state-of-the-art computing resources. I would suggest that you try making an analogy between your department's end product (that is, information) and the end product of your company.

Management personnel in the manufacturing industry understand the consequences of using outdated equipment and inefficient procedures in the manufacturing processes. Inevitably, a low-quality product is produced at an inordinately high cost. When this happens, management must confront the alternatives— shut down or upgrade.

With an information services department, the alternatives are slightly different. Realistically speaking, management must rule out a shutdown. The options usually boil down to continuing the status quo or to allocating funds to upgrade the department. State-of-the-art hardware and software offer greater potential to provide "quality" information. In general, companies that continue to use dated computing resources end up paying a premium price for "low-quality" information.

I would suggest that you give management concrete examples of "quality" information. Paint a vivid verbal scenario of what kind of service they can expect in a couple of years if they continue to neglect their computing resources. Sometimes management has to be reminded of the benefits of progress and the consequences of inactivity.

In recent years, with the trend toward networking and electronic data interchange (EDI), managers are as concerned about connectivity as they are about compatibility. Typically, their strategy is to minimize the expense of linking and integrating hardware and software (especially database software) into a network. Connectivity concepts are addressed in Chapter 8, "Connectivity and Data Communications."

INDUSTRY STANDARDS

Official and de facto (commonly accepted) industry standard hardware and software have had a tremendous impact on the buying habits of the computer community. People do not want to make a large investment in hardware or software and find out later that the rest of the industry in moving in a different direction. In the microcomputer market, the IBM PC became the de facto industry standard within a year after it was announced in 1981. Through the 1980s, dozens of companies have manufactured and sold fully compatible clones of the IBM PC. IBM's new PS/2 series of microcomputers may well follow suit and become the industry standard. Because it is made up primarily of IBM components, cloning the PS/2 will pose a much greater challenge (the IBM PC is a product of off-the-shelf components). Several companies have cloned the de facto industry standard electronic spreadsheet, Lotus 1-2-3. When a hardware or software product achieves "standard" status, other vendors begin to create software and/or hardware that is compatible with the standard. For example, a number of companies have created applications software to be run on the de facto industry standards for micro database software, dBASE III PLUS and dBASE IV. An entire industry is being created in response to the need for add-on products to support IBM's DB2 database management system.

Managers migrate to industry standard hardware and software for a number of reasons. First and foremost, the pool of people who have expertise with a particular standard product is much larger. This makes the recruiting of qualified personnel to fill open positions a doable task. Also, training expenses are reduced because people learn about the product in college or during their previous employment. Finally, managers can feel secure that the hardware and software they have selected will be improved and supported for the foreseeable future. On the down side, the exclusive use of industry standard products may be expensive and preclude the company from using a superior product. For example, the company that has the industry standard electronic spreadsheet charges two or three times as much for its product as some competitors who have comparable or, according to some published reviews, even superior products.

The following are examples of commonly accepted industry standards:

- *Operating systems.* For mainframes—IBM's MVS and VM, DEC's VMS, AT&T's UNIX; for micros—Microsoft's MS-DOS, IBM/Microsoft's OS/2.
- *Data access.* SQL, now an official standard (see Chapter 9, "Data Management").
- *Electronic spreadsheet.* Lotus Development Corporation's Lotus 1-2-3.
- *Database.* For mainframes—IBM's IMS and DB2 (see Chapter 9); for micros—Ashton Tate's dBASE III PLUS and dBASE IV.

□ *Microcomputer communications protocols*. For data communications—XON/XOFF; for file transfer activities—XMODEM.

Although WordPerfect Corporation's WordPerfect word processing software is the market leader, the market is diluted by numerous successful packages. In this and other similar cases (4GLs, DSS software), a clear de facto industry standard does not exist. In the computer industry, standards are very volatile. An overwhelmingly superior product can displace a vulnerable standard.

VENDOR RELATIONS

The Role of Vendors

Vendors of hardware, software, and information services play a significant role in whether a company is successful or not in their application of computer technology. This is especially true of the mainframe environment. In the mainframe environment, hardware and software marketing representatives meet with management at the company's site and provide on-site servicing and training. Typically, marketing representatives sell the products and the more technically oriented systems engineers support them once they have been installed. Marketing representatives hold a technical sales position that requires a broad knowledge of the company's products and their capabilities. The systems engineer is the technical "expert" and is often called on by customers for advice on technical matters. Together, the marketing representatives and systems engineers do a good job of keeping customers and potential customers abreast of the latest technological innovations. In this respect, they can be a valuable resource for information.

Generally speaking, vendors provide adequate to excellent service before and after the sale. However, miscues between sales and production are perhaps more frequent than in other less volatile industries. Sometimes, it behooves us to recognize the youth of the industry. After all, the average age of hardware and software vendors is less than 10 years. Apple Computer, Inc., a major player in the computer industry, just completed its first decade. Companies with comparable influence in other industries may have already celebrated their centennial year. In many cases, hardware and software vendors are expanding so rapidly that their growth sometimes undermines service to the customer.

Dealing with Vendors

The relationship between vendors and customers can be a warm and healthy friendship, but customers should be ever cognizant that the vendor's ultimate objective is to sell something. When decision makers keep this relationship in its proper perspective, both sides benefit. Fifteen or 20 years ago, customer companies enjoyed some independence from hardware and software manufacturers. This is not the case today as the selection of a major product is usually the beginning of a 10-year-plus commitment. This is especially true

A tight budget brings out the best creative instincts in man.

—————— *Robert Townsend*

of large mainframe computers, database management systems, and comprehensive integrated financial and accounting systems. This implied no-divorce clause demands that the vendor/customer relationship be stable and amicable. When management makes a decision to go with a product, the company actually becomes locked in, that is, management will be extremely reluctant to scrap their substantial investment and begin another expensive start-up activity.

In dealing with hardware and software vendors, decision makers should heed the following warnings.

☐ Vendor claims can be misleading, even untrue, and must be tempered with the realization that the zeal of the marketing staff may sometimes obscure reality.

☐ Vendors will oversell if they are permitted to do so.

☐ Vendors preannounce new products, often as much as a year in advance of the scheduled release date. Unfortunately, it has become common practice for vendors to equate their most optimistic date of completion with the projected release date of the product. Vendors do this to entice potential customers into waiting for their product rather than purchasing one from a competitor. Seldom do vendors actually meet their projected release dates for new products.

☐ Be wary of vendors who tout their products as "revolutionary" or the "next generation." Only a handful of vendors have earned the right to make such claims. For others, such claims are merely marketing hype.

Multivendor Environments

An integrated computer-based information system is a complex collection of hardware and software. Most small companies and virtually all medium and large companies support environments that are invariably made up of hardware and software from several vendors. *Multivendor environments* can function indefinitely without incident. However, when a problem arises, vendors have been known to point fingers at one another rather than cooperate to solve the problem. For example, at one company a communications specialist was having difficulty downloading and uploading data from a distributed minicomputer. The two computers and their respective communications software packages were manufactured and supported by two competing companies. Not surprisingly, each company identified the other company's hardware and software as the source of the problem. To complicate the situation further, both said that if the problem could not be isolated to the other company's computer, then the data communications common carrier was surely the culprit. Of course, the common carrier pleaded innocent and asked management to double-check the affected hardware and software before calling them again. Eventually, the source of the error was determined and corrected, but only after management had begged each of the three vendors to examine its part of the system.

Similar scenarios are played out many times each year in multivendor environments. Practically speaking, multivendor environments are a fact of life in modern-day computing. They are hard to avoid. Nevertheless, forward-thinking managers can minimize the adverse impact of such an environment by paying careful attention to the wording in maintenance contracts.

BUYING MICROCOMPUTERS AND THEIR PERIPHERAL DEVICES

More than a million people a year go through the process of buying a microcomputer, micro peripheral devices, and related software. This section contains information that will help those planning to purchase a microcomputer to spend their money wisely.

Retail Sales

Where to Buy

Microcomputers and related hardware and software can be purchased at thousands of convenient locations. Retail chains, such as ComputerLand, ENTRE Computer Center, 20/20, and MicroAge, market and service a variety of small computer systems. Radio Shack stores carry and sell their own line of computers. Micros are also sold in the computer department of most department stores. The demand for micros has encouraged major computer system manufacturers to open retail stores.

There is an alternative to buying a computer at a retail store. If you know what you want, you can call any of several mail order services, give them a credit card number, and your PC will be delivered to your doorstep.

The Perks of Employment

You might be able to acquire a micro through your employer. Many companies offer their employees a "computer perk." In cooperation with vendors, companies make volume purchases of PCs at discount rates and then offer them to employees at substantial savings. Many colleges sponsor similar programs to benefit students and professors.

Micro Manufacturers

Visions of tremendous profit opportunities have lured scores of companies into developing products to meet the growing demand for personal computers. The number of personal computer manufacturers may have peaked in 1983, with over 150 companies manufacturing about 700 PCs. Recent failures of both small and large companies have caused potential entrepreneurs to think twice before going head to head with dozens of established, well-financed companies. Industry analysts are predicting that at least half the existing micro vendors will not survive the decade.

Commodore Business Machines, Apple, Tandy, Compaq, Eagle, Leading Edge, Epson, Zenith, Panasonic, Toshiba, and Kaypro are just a few of many manufacturers of microcomputers. Computer giants such as IBM and DEC did not enter the microcomputer market until 1981. The giants may have

BENCHMARK TESTS

Q. Our company first bought a computer in 1959. Since that time our information services function has experienced a rapid growth in people (from 3 to 400) and equipment. The entire operation is centralized.

I was appointed to serve as a representative of the Accounting Division on a committee to select the hardware for decentralizing our MIS operations. I am the only user on the committee.

The committee was formed two months ago. Since then, the emphasis has been on developing specifications for benchmark tests. Although reasonably computerwise, I have been unable to help in the development of these highly technical specs. The committee is going around in circles trying to identify circumstances that can be used to evaluate equitably the various alternatives.

Having no previous experience in hardware selection, I would be interested in knowing if other companies devote so much time to preparing benchmarks and how much emphasis is placed on benchmarks in the evaluation process.

A. Fifteen years ago the benchmark test was very popular because one vendor's computer system could be configured like another's. Therefore, qualitative evaluations could be made relative to performance. Not so any more.

A computer system, especially in the MIS environment, is much more complex today. With so many variables, the results will probably require an asterisk or two that negate the possibility of any real comparison. As an alternative to benchmarks, consider using performance data compiled by current users to validate the vendor's claims.

Under most circumstances, benchmark results are difficult to interpret and may have little to contribute to the selection process. In the final analysis, other factors play a more vital role in the hardware evaluation and selection process. Cost, vendor reputation, service, compatibility, and availability of support software are much more critical to success.

had a late start, but they have been making up for lost time by taking substantial shares of the micro market. Almost immediately after it was announced, the IBM PC became an industry phenomenon. During most of the 1980s it has been the industry standard. At one time, over 30 companies manufactured IBM PC-compatible micros. These supposedly would run the same software and accomplish the same functions as the IBM PC. A few IBM PC-compatible micros are indeed completely compatible, but others are only partially compatible. If history repeats itself, the new IBM Personal System/2 (PS/2), which is compatible with the IBM PC series, may well be the standard bearer in the 1990s.

Steps to Buying a Microcomputer

Buying a microcomputer can be a harrowing experience, or it can be a thrilling and fulfilling one. If you approach the purchase of a micro haphazardly, expect the former. If you go about the acquisition methodically and with purpose, expect the latter. This section contains a seven-step procedure that will help you in the evaluation and selection of a microcomputer (see Figure 17–1).

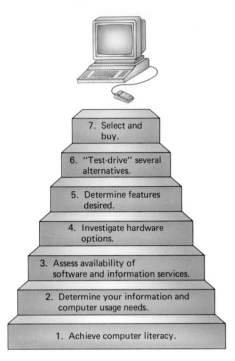

FIGURE 17–1   Seven-Step Process for Buying a Microcomputer System

1. *Achieve computer literacy.* You do not buy an automobile before you learn how to drive, and you should not buy a microcomputer without a good understanding of its capabilities and how you intend to use it.

2. *Determine your information and computer usage needs.* There is an old adage, "If you don't know where you are going, any road will get you there." The statement is certainly true of choosing a PC. Knowing where you are going can be translated to mean "How do you plan to use the PC?"

Do you wish to develop your own software or purchase commercially available software packages? Or perhaps do both? If you want to write your own programs, you must select the programming language that is best suited to your application needs. The only programming language that is supported by all microcomputers is BASIC. If you plan on purchasing the software, determine which general application areas you wish to have supported on the proposed PC (spreadsheet, accounting, word processing, home banking, or others).

3. *Assess availability of software and information services.* Determine what software and information services are available to meet your prescribed needs. Good sources of this type of information include a wide variety of periodicals (*PC*, *Byte*, *Software*, *Computerworld*, and *Personal Computing*, to name a few), salespersons at computer stores, and acquaintances who have knowledge in the area.

Several hundred micro productivity software packages are available commercially. Commercially available software packages vary greatly in capabilities and price. Software with essentially the same capabilities may be priced with differences of as much as several hundred dollars. Some graphics software creates displays of graphs in seconds, while others take minutes. Some software packages are easy to learn and are accompanied by good documentation, while others are not. Considering the amount of time that you might spend using micro software, any extra time you spend evaluating the software will be time well spent.

4. *Investigate hardware options.* If you select a specific software product or an information service, your selection may dictate the general computer system configuration requirements and, in some cases, a specific microcomputer system. In all likelihood, you will have several, if not a dozen, hardware alternatives available to you. Become familiar with the features and options of each system.

5. *Determine features desired.* You can go with a minimum system configuration, or you can add a few "bells and whistles." Expect to pay for each feature in convenience, quality, and speed that you add to the minimum configuration. For example, people are usually willing to pay a little extra for the added convenience of a two-disk system, even though one disk will suffice. On the other hand, a color monitor may be an unnecessary luxury for some applications. The peripherals that you select depend on your specific needs and volume of usage. For example, the type of printer that you choose will depend on the volume of hard-copy output that you anticipate, whether or not you need graphics output, whether or not you need letter-quality print, and so on.

6. *"Test drive" several alternatives.* Once you have selected several software

When searching for a personal computer, this industrial engineer identified portability as her primary criteria. She purchased a lap PC because it gave her the flexibility to carry her files and the power of a computer into the field.

All change is not growth, as all movement is not forward.

—— Ellen Glasgow

and hardware alternatives, spend enough time to gain some familiarity with them. Do you prefer one keyboard over another? Does a word processing system fully use the features of the hardware? Is one system easier to understand and use than another? Use these sessions to answer any questions that you might have about the hardware or software. Salespersons at most retail stores are happy to give you a test drive—just ask.

7. *Select and buy*. Apply your criteria, select, and then buy your hardware and software.

Factors to Consider When Buying a Micro

1. *Future computing needs*. What will your computer and information processing needs be in the future? Make sure the system you select can grow with your needs.

2. *Who will use the system?* Plan not only for yourself but for others in your home or office who will also use the system. Get their input and consider their needs along with yours.

3. *Availability of software*. Software is developed for one or several microcomputers, but not for all microcomputers. As you might expect, a more extensive array of software is available for the more popular micros. However, do not overlook some of the less visible vendors if their products, in your mind, are superior to the other alternatives.

4. *Service*. Computing hardware is very reliable. Even so, the possibility exists that one or several of the components will eventually malfunction and have to be repaired. Before purchasing a micro, identify a reliable source of hardware maintenance. Most retailers service what they sell. If a retailer says that the hardware must be returned to the manufacturer for repair, choose another retailer or another system.

Most retailers or vendors will offer a variety of maintenance contracts. Maintenance contract options range from on-site repair that covers all parts and service to carry-in service that does not include parts. Most domestic users elect to treat their micros like their televisions and autos: when the warranty runs out, they pay for repairs as they are needed. Under normal circumstances, this strategy will prove the least expensive.

Service extends beyond hardware maintenance. Service is also an organization's willingness to respond to your inquiries, before *and* after the sale. Some retailers and vendors offer classes in programming and in the use of the hardware and software that they sell.

5. *Hardware obsolescence*. "I'm going to buy one as soon as the price goes down a little more." If you adopt this strategy, you may never purchase a computer. If you wait another six months, you will probably be able to get a more powerful micro for less money. But what about the lost opportunity?

There is, however, a danger in purchasing a micro that is near or at the end of its life cycle. Focus your search on micros with state-of-the-art technology. Even though you may get a substantial discount on the older micro, you will normally get more for your money with the newer one.

6. *Software obsolescence*. Software can become obsolete as well. Software vendors are continually improving their software packages. Each package

is assigned a **version number**, the first *release* being 1.0 (referred to as one point zero). Subsequent updates to version 1.0 become version 1.1, version 1.2, and so on. The next major revision to the package is released as version number 2.0. Make sure that you are buying the most recent release of a particular software package.

7. *Other costs*. The cost of the actual microcomputer system is the major expense, but there are numerous incidental expenses that can mount up that may influence your selection of a micro. If you have a spending limit, consider these costs when purchasing the hardware (the cost ranges listed are for a first-time user): software ($100-1,500), maintenance ($0-500 a year), diskettes and tape cassettes ($50-200), furniture ($0-350), insurance ($0-40), and printer ribbons or cartridges, paper, and other supplies ($40-400).

CAPACITY PLANNING

End users make microcomputer and micro software purchasing decisions as a matter of routine. However, end users are less involved with the evaluation and selection of mini and mainframe computer systems. These decisions often demand a level of technical expertise that relatively few users have (or need). Typically MIS professionals evaluate alternatives and make a recommendation to top management for approval. The primary input to the evaluation and selection process for mainframe computers comes from capacity planning.

The process by which planners determine how much hardware resources are needed to meet anticipated demands is known as **capacity planning**. Capacity planning is traditionally treated as a separate planning activity in MIS planning (see Chapter 10, "MIS Planning"). This type of planning is important because the lead time for installing additional mainframe and mini hardware can be as much as a year. The primary inputs to capacity planning are:

☐ *Existing hardware performance and utilization data*. To plan for the future, capacity planners must monitor the ongoing performance of hardware, software, networks, and so on to determine if current service levels are adequate.

☐ *The MIS operational plan*. The operational plan (see Chapter 10) highlights when new information systems and enhancements to existing systems will be installed.

From the instant a company installs its first computer, the need for hardware capability or capacity continues to increase. It is the job of the capacity planner to make sure that demand for capacity never exceeds supply. If the hardware is not in place when it is needed many things can happen, all of which are bad. A publisher put off ordering new hardware and simply ran out of computing capacity. As a stopgap measure, users had to work weekends, on overtime, because during the workweek the system did not have the capacity to meet routine processing demands. At a mailorder house, the volume of orders became so heavy that it had to increase salespersons;

THE CONFLICT BETWEEN POLICY AND NEED

Q. Last year we purchased three microcomputers and electronic spreadsheet software for the accounting office staff. All three micros were idle for about six months until someone decided to figure out how to use them. Since then, a half dozen people in accounting, and at least as many in other offices, keep the systems tied up continuously. To alleviate this bottleneck, we decided to order three more.

Our company's policy on hardware acquisition has been recently revised. Now, all micro purchases must be approved by the hardware committee in the MIS department. As their first official decision, the committee denied our request. The reason given was that we had just purchased several accounting systems that would provide us with similar or better capabilities.

These systems will not be implemented for at least a year. We look forward to that, but what about now? We have three overloaded micros that have paid for themselves many times over.

The purchase of these micros is a matter of continuous debate. The committee wants to hold down the proliferation of micros within the company (we now have 13). Money has never been a question.

Do you think we should give up the idea of purchasing the micros or keep the issue alive?

A. I, too, am against the uncontrolled proliferation of micros. However, you have an established need and an immediate opportunity to increase productivity. It sounds a little like the hardware committee is overemphasizing the proliferation issue. In so doing, they may have lost sight of the fact that for a few thousand dollars, life can be made a whole lot easier for people throughout the company.

Keep the issue alive!

---

however, in so doing it overloaded the system's ability to accept and process orders. The company lost business because it neglected capacity planning.

The ultimate objective of capacity planning is to optimize the computer system's configuration while meeting the organization's information processing needs. Capacity planning ensures that capacity requirements are met while avoiding costly excess capacity. If 10 *gigabytes* (10 billion characters of secondary storage) of DASD (direct-access storage device) is sufficient, there is no reason to have 20 gigabytes.

Besides examining the performance of an entire computer system, the capacity planner must also examine each component of a computer system's configuration separately to ensure that each will meet anticipated capacity requirements. Planners consider capacity requirements for the processor (65 percent utilization is considered optimal), DASD, workstations, front-end processors, down-line processors, printers, and so on. Based on historical performance data and the MIS operational plan, the capacity planner uses simulation and modeling techniques to forecast and plan system enhancements and upgrades. Hardware is evaluated and selected and then ordered so that it can be installed in time to meet forecasted capacity requirements.

One of the peripheral objectives of capacity planning is to investigate ways to increase the performance of existing hardware. There are a number of hardware and software products that can enhance a system's performance. For example, one software product speeds up the process of sorting records, another hardware/software product reduces the response time for end users at a workstation.

EVALUATION, SELECTION, AND ACQUISITION METHODOLOGY

Hardware and software costs can consume as much as 50 percent of an MIS division's budget and as much as .5 to 3 percent of the total corporate budget. However, a rule of thumb places hardware and software costs at 20 to 35 percent of the MIS budget. These figures highlight the significance of having a hardware/software evaluation and selection methodology in place that consistently results in the acquisition of products that optimize the computing environment. A company that purchases or signs a lease for the wrong hardware may be locked into an unfavorable situation for as much as five years. A company that purchases the wrong software may run the risk of alienating employees toward MIS, or, if the software is not used, it becomes expensive **shelfware**. Shelfware is software that is purchased with great enthusiasm and for whatever reason is never used or implemented. This section presents a proven method for the evaluation and selection of major pieces of hardware and proprietary software packages.

The Selection Committee

The evaluation and selection process for major hardware and software acquisitions is best done by a group of knowledgeable persons. There are too many variables that require subjective evaluations to place such a responsibility on the shoulders of an individual. Collective evaluations tend to yield a more acceptable set of alternatives. The most effective selection committees are made up of MIS personnel and, in some cases, interested and technically informed users.

Communication with the Vendor

If done correctly, a vendor should receive at most three documents requesting input into the evaluation and selection process:

1. The request for information (an optional document)
2. The request for proposal
3. The decision statement

These documents should be the only formal communications with the vendor. The RFI is optional.

The Request for Information

The **request for information** or **RFI** is helpful when the corporation is not well informed of the scope and availability of applicable hardware and software. The receipt of helpful information is the primary benefit of an RFI, however, it has a valuable side benefit that may not be apparent when it is sent to the vendors. The RFI can be used to identify interested vendors. Those who do not respond or respond in a lukewarm manner can be immediately scratched as potential vendors. The RFI is not meant to be a request for proposal, and this should be stated in the RFI. The RFI is simply a letter sent to appropriate vendors for the purpose of canvassing the marketplace and determining which suppliers have viable alternatives and/or are willing to compete for the business. The RFI should include:

- □ A general description of the existing MIS environment.
- □ The changes in operations and/or technology that prompted the RFI.
- □ Some historical perspective.
- □ The computer system configuration of the system (if any) that will be replaced or a brief description of the existing software (if any) that will be replaced.
- □ A brief statement of any problems, constraints, or limitations.

The Request for Proposal

The **request for proposal** (**RFP**) is comprised of information and directions for the vendor, standardized forms, and requests for specific data and information. The RFP is a formal request to a vendor for a proposal. It is recommended that the RFPs be distributed at a joint meeting of the selection committee and competing vendors. During the meeting, the RFP can be explained in detail and vendors are invited to ask questions about the RFP. The joint meeting eliminates the possibility of unknowingly giving an unfair advantage to a vendor.

　　Unless standardized forms are used for responses to the RFPs, the evaluation and selection committee will find it difficult to compare various alternatives proposed by vendors. It is to the vendor's advantage to put the requesting company in a situation where they are comparing apples to oranges. In hardware and software evaluation and selection, cost is seldom the ultimate bottom line. The use of standardized forms, such as those illustrated in Figures 17–2 through 17–5, provides a common denominator for the evaluation of the RFPs.

　　Whether for the acquisition of hardware or software, the text of the RFP should include:

- □ A general description of the past and present computing and MIS environment.
- □ A time-phased definition of the objectives for the proposed acquisition (objectives for the first year, second year, and so on).
- □ A description of alternative approaches being considered.
- □ Guidelines for the RFP responses (scope, format, and deadline).
- □ Details of cost presentation (purchase only, lease, lease-purchase, discount rate, depreciation schedules, tax rate, horizon, and so on).
- □ References (companies who can support vendor claims).
- □ Award procedure.
- □ Award criteria.
- □ Proposed implementation schedule.
- □ New systems requirements (a listing of the basic requirements that are expected to be met by any proposal).

□ Contact person within the corporation (vendors should be restricted as to whom they can contact).

Included in the RFP after the foregoing introductory material are applicable standardized forms and instructions for completing the forms. The following would be considered representative of forms that might be included in an RFP.

□ *Hardware/software vendor questionnaire.* The questionnaire poses specific questions to the vendor for which the company expects a response. A vendor desiring the business will be more than happy to answer these questions. The questions could be extensive, depending on the hardware or software being investigated. For example, for the acquisition of a mainframe, a company would want information on available systems software, communications capabilities, environmental and power specifications, access controls, reliability statistics, and so on.

□ *System characteristics.* The system characteristics form, Figure 17–2, allows the company an opportunity to list features that are of particular interest to it. It is not a specifications sheet. It is intended to display cost, availability, and any comments regarding these specifically listed features. The vendor's responses can be more easily compared when each vendor addresses specific customer-defined characteristics for the proposed system.

□ *Cost summary.* The cost summary form in Figure 17–3 provides a vehicle by which cost can be presented in a standard format for ease of comparison among vendors. The cost can be presented over time if future system upgrades are proposed.

□ *Benchmark results.* The benchmark results form, Figure 17–4, ensures a standardized presentation of the results of a **benchmark test**. Bench-

Form: SYSTEM CHARACTERISTICS	Vendor: HAL, INC.		
Feature	Included in bid	Available — Week of / Cost	Comments
User training	No	3/10/90 4/20/90 / $500/ person	
MIS training	Yes	N/A / N/A	Delivered in house on two consecutive weeks at convenience of company
Operating system	Yes	3/1/90 / N/A	
16M memory	Yes	N/A / $13,000	Standard configuration is 8M
Completed by Company ←	→ Completed by Vendor		

FIGURE 17–2 System Characteristics Form
This System Characteristics Form is used in conjunction with the example hardware/software acquisitions methodology discussed in the chapter. The company distributing the RFP enters the features and the vendor fills in the remainder of the form.

Form: COST SUMMARY	Vendor: HAL, INC.											
Item	**Init. Purc./Rent**		**Year 2**		**Year 3**		**Year 4**		**Year 5**		**Total**	
	Desc.	Cost	Desc.	Cost	Desc.	Cost	Desc.	Cost	Desc.	Cost	Desc.	Cost
Processor	408 MOD-X	30K	—	30K	680 MOD-Y	40K	—	40K				
Disk subsystem	x2 MOD-E	14K	Add 800 M	12K	—	12K	—	12K				
Printer	ABC MOD-1	10K	—	—	Trade in MOD-1 for MOD-2	10K	—	—				
Maintenance – continual (A)		5K		6K		7K		7K				
Maintenance – by job (B)		2K (est.)		8K (est.)		9K (est.)		10K (est.)				
Total Net Cost, with: Maintenance plan A Maintenance plan B		59K 56K		48K 50K		69K 71K		59K 62K				＊235K 239K

Completed by Company ◄—   —► Completed by Vendor   Total costs are not discounted or adjusted for inflation.

FIGURE 17–3   Cost Summary Form

This Cost Summary Form is used in conjunction with the example hardware/software acquisitions methodology discussed in the chapter. The company distributing the RFP enters the items to be detailed and the vendor fills in the remainder of the form.

Form: BENCHMARK RESULTS	Vendor: HAL, INC.				
Job name	**Circumstances**	**CPU time (seconds)**	**Elapsed time (minutes)**	**Response time (seconds)**	**Comments**
XXX32Q	50K partition	400	14.5		
XXX14R	1 disk 100M			1.4 sec. (avg.)	
XXX14R	2 disks 100M each			1.1 sec. (avg.)	
ZZZ81P	Standard configuration	80	28		files supplied had no standard labels

Completed by Company ◄—   —► Completed by Vendor

FIGURE 17–4   Benchmark Results Form

This Benchmark Results Form is used in conjunction with the example hardware/software acquisitions methodology discussed in the chapter. The company distributing the RFP enters the job name and appropriate circumstances for that job and the vendor fills in the remainder of the form.

UPWARD COMPATIBILITY

Q. We have outgrown our present computer system and are in the market for another. The vice president to whom I report has asked me to review alternative systems and to submit proposals from at least two vendors for final review by the executive committee. All expenditures in excess of $100,000 must be approved by the executive committee.

I solicited proposals from six vendors. Five responded, but only two met the specifications. These two were submitted for final review. Since my job description (manager of information services) called for the "selection of computing hardware," I submitted a written recommendation that encouraged the committee to select the more expensive alternative. I reiterated my feelings during a presentation.

The committee authorized the purchase of my second choice. It has several distinct advantages: the operating system is more versatile, has greater processing capacity, is more state of the art, and, perhaps most important, it costs $80,000 less. However, the installation of the system will require that modifications be made to all existing programs. The system that I recommended is compatible with our current system.

The entire MIS staff consists of myself and four others. If we order a noncompatible system, we will spend most of the next year modifying programs. To date, I have refused to order a new computer system because our current staff is not adequate to meet ongoing operational, development, and maintenance demands, much less a major system conversion. Our current system is operating at capacity, but the situation will get worse if we order the approved system. Where do I go from here?

A. Present your case in dollars and cents. If tradition holds, user requests for service will hold steady or increase, with or without a new computer. Calculate the cost of the work force augmentation needed to maintain the current level of service while modifying systems and programs to run on the new computer system. That cost may well exceed the difference in the cost of the two systems. This bottom-line approach may encourage the committee to reexamine your recommendation from a different perspective.

---

mark tests are used to compare the performance of several computer systems while they run the same software or to compare the performance of several programs that are run on the same computer. The increasing complexity of computer systems has made it difficult for evaluators to create a benchmark problem that does not have an embedded bias toward one of the products being tested. For this reason, benchmark testing is not as popular as it was during the past. A form of the type shown in Figure 17–4 is intended for only the most basic types of information; however, it does allow the selection committee a method of easy comparison of benchmark results between vendors.

Evaluation of Vendor Responses

The evaluation is accomplished by the evaluation and selection committee. The proposal evaluation worksheet shown in Figure 17–5 is used to display graphically both individual and cumulative evaluations for each proposal.

Alternatives / Criteria %/100	BIG	HAL #1	HAL #2	ACME	XYZ			
Total system cost 25	20 / 3	10 / 4	22 / 1	10 / 4	22 / 1			
Availability of software 20	20 / 1	15 / 4	10 / 5	20 / 1	18 / 3			
System flexibility 15	10 / 3	15 / 1	10 / 3	15 / 1	10 / 3			
System reliability 10	2 / 5	8 / 3	10 / 1	9 / 2	6 / 4			
Compatibility 10	2 / 5	5 / 4	8 / 3	10 / 1	9 / 2			
Backup 10	2 / 5	5 / 4	7 / 3	10 / 1	8 / 2			
Overall evaluation 10	8 / 2	9 / 1	5 / 5	7 / 3	7 / 3			
Total points / Overall rank	64 / 5	67 / 4	72 / 3	81 / 1	80 / 2			

Form: PROPOSAL EVALUATION WORKSHEET

FIGURE 17–5 Proposal Evaluation Worksheet
This Proposal Evaluation Worksheet is used in conjunction with the example hardware/software acquisitions methodology discussed in the chapter. The form can be used to report individual and collective evaluations.

Cheerful obedience to the computer leads to worse performance by society. It makes it easier for dictators to accomplish their ends. It brings a lessening of freedom. Being loyal to the computer means selling out . . . The computer is there only to serve man—not to be served by him.

—— *H. Matusow*

In this matrix form, each company-defined criterion (total system cost, availability of software) is given a relative point value (25/100, 20/100, and so on) for evaluating each proposal (100 total points possible). The vendors and/or vendor alternatives are listed on the top of each column (BIG, HAL #1, HAL #2, and so on). Each criterion with its associated relative point value is placed in the respective boxes for each row.

Each evaluator rates each proposal against each criterion. In addition to the vendors' RFPs, certain information may be assembled to help evaluators rate the criteria. For example, the results of the benefit/cost analyses (see Chapter 11, "System Development and Management") would be helpful in rating the "total system cost" criterion and the "overall evaluation" criterion (see Figure 17–5). The completed individual worksheets are gathered from the committee members, and the results are tabulated and displayed on a cumulative worksheet as illustrated in Figure 17–5. Each proposal can be ranked relative to each criterion and overall. The rankings and relative point values provide valuable insight to the selection process. Sometimes one alternative emerges as the clear choice, but often the rankings serve only to highlight the top two or three alternatives, as is the case in the example in Figure 17–5. In these instances, the committee must factor other subjective considerations into the process before reaching a collective decision.

CHAPTER HIGHLIGHTS

■ Individuals and companies tend to adopt a philosophy regarding the acquisition of hardware, software, and information services. The three most distinct philosophies found in practice are being a vendor loyalist, being a leading edge technocrat, and being a conservative.

■ Once a proposed commercial software product passes alpha testing at the vendor's site, the product is distributed to beta test sites for further testing.

■ An information system is designed and coded to be run in a specific computing environment. The computing environment is defined by the programming language, computer, and operating system.

■ When evaluating hardware and software, managers are often concerned with upward compatibility. Systems that permit upward compatibility enable a company to purchase proprietary software at one level of sophistication, and then, at a later date, upgrade the existing system to one with greater capabilities without the need for redesigning and reprogramming.

■ Today, the selection of a major hardware or software product is usually the beginning of a 10-year-plus commitment to that product.

■ Managers can minimize the problems associated with multivendor environments by paying careful attention to the wording in maintenance contracts.

■ Micros and PCs can be purchased at computer and traditional retail stores everywhere. There are a number of computer vendors of microcomputers, but in recent years the vendors of mainframe computers, such as DEC and IBM, have made micros a major segment of their product lines.

■ Buying a microcomputer, whether for home or business, should be approached methodically and with purpose. Factors to consider when buying a micro include future computing needs, those who will use the system, availability of software, service, obsolescence, and other costs.

■ The process by which planners determine how much hardware resources are needed to meet anticipated demands is known as capacity planning.

■ The primary inputs to capacity planning are existing hardware performance and utilization data, and the MIS operational plan. The ultimate objective of capacity planning is to optimize the computer system's configuration while meeting the organization's information processing needs.

■ Hardware and software costs can consume as much as 50 percent of an MIS division's budget and as much as .5 to 3 percent of the total corporate budget. However, a rule of thumb places hardware and software costs at 20 to 35 percent of the MIS budget.

■ Because of the many variables that require subjective evaluations, the evaluation and selection process for major hardware and software acquisitions is best done by a group of knowledgeable persons.

■ If done correctly, a vendor should receive at most three documents requesting input into the evaluation and selection process. These are the request for information, the request for proposal, and the decision statement.

■ The request for information is helpful when an organization is not well informed of the scope and availability of applicable hardware and software.

■ The request for proposal is comprised of information and directions for the vendor, standardized forms, and requests for specific data and information.

■ Benchmark tests are used to compare the performance of several computer systems while running the same software or to compare the performance of several programs that are run on the same computer. However, it is difficult to remove biases from benchmark tests.

IMPORTANT TERMS

alpha test	capacity planning	gigabyte	request for proposal (RFP)
benchmark test	computing environment	multivendor environments	shelfware
beta test	de facto industry standard	request for information (RFI)	upward compatibility

1. Which comes first, the alpha test or the beta test?

2. What defines a computing environment?

3. What would be the version number for the first upgrade to version 2.0 of an electronic spreadsheet package?

4. Name three retail chains that specialize in the sale of small computer systems.

5. List three hardware or software products that have attained the status of industry standard.

6. What is considered optimal for processor utilization, 50 percent, 65 percent, or 80 percent?

7. What is the test called that is used to compare the performance of several computer systems while they are running the same software?

8. Describe what is meant by upward compatibility.

9. What are the three hardware and software philosophies that are commonly found in practice?

10. Expand the following acronyms: RFI and RFP.

11. What type of planning involves determining how much hardware resources are needed to meet anticipated demands?

12. List four items that should be included in a request for proposal.

13. What are the primary inputs to capacity planning?

1. Someone with a philosophy that parallels that of a leading-edge technocrat is hired as the new director of MIS into a company that has traditionally been conservative in its approach to hardware and software acquisitions. Do you see this conflict of philosophies as positive or negative? Explain.

2. In their rush to be first, companies have been known to release software products before receiving the results from beta test sites. Is this business practice unethical?

3. In the chapter material the author made the statement that vendors will oversell if they are permitted to do so. Do you agree or disagree? Explain.

4. Compare the influence of official industry standards on the computer community to that of de facto industry standards.

5. A small consumer goods company decided to standardize on the HAL PC and a HAL PC compatible, the Zap-100. Since the compatible costs 30 percent less than the actual HAL PC, why didn't the company just standardize on the compatible?

6. Identify the general categories of recurring costs of an on-line sales information system.

7. What would you look for when taking a word processing package for a "test drive"?

8. Identify the types of expenses that a product manager for a durable goods company can expect to incur during the first year if he or she purchases and uses a microcomputer system, primarily for word processing and as a workstation.

9. "I'm going to wait a few more months for the price to go down." How would you respond to a manager who, year after year, uses this excuse for not buying a micro?

10. A search team, made up of people from both the MIS and marketing divisions, was formed to evaluate commercially available sales and marketing software packages. Suggest criteria the team might use to evaluate available packages.

11. Most of the companies that make up the hardware and software industry are relatively youthful. Does this mean that they may be less mature in their dealings with customers than would well-established companies in other industry types?

12. Some companies avoid the expense of compiling a capacity plan for computing. These companies respond to slow response times, overloaded disk capacity, and other such circumstances by ordering more hardware. Are they really saving money? Explain.

13. Some very successful MIS divisions devote as much as 75 percent of their budgets to hardware and software. How can this be the case if the median budget amount allotted to these items in MIS divisions is well below 35 percent?

14. Word processing software, one of the popular and useful micro productivity packages, is often relegated to shelfware status. Speculate on what the circumstances might be that would cause a fully functioning word processing package to become shelfware.

15. In the chapter, the author's acquisition methodology recommends a formal relationship between the purchasing company and competing vendors. Do you think that the proposal and bidding process can be just as fair with less formality? Explain.

APPLICATION CASE STUDY 17–1
The Request for Proposal

The Situation

Que Realty is a successful independent real estate company with about 140 real estate agents who work out of 16 offices. Joan Magee, Que's owner, is an avid proponent of using information technology as a competitive strategy. Under her leadership, industry-specific information systems have been implemented (see Application Case Studies 3–1, "Expert Systems," and 3–2, "Natural Languages"). Que Realty is also committed to using office automation and personal computing where appropriate (see Application Case Studies 6–1, "Office Automation" and 7–1, "Personal Computing").

A consultant conducted a study of Que's operations and developed a list of state-of-the-art hardware and software that have the potential to enhance the productivity of Que's personnel (see Application Case Study 4–2, "Leveraging Information Systems"). The top item on the consultant's list was providing a lap personal computer for each real estate agent. Joan Magee has asked the consultant to proceed with the acquisition of the lap PCs.

The consultant compiled the following list of tasks that agents should be able to perform with their lap PCs, whether at the office, at home, in a client's office or home, or anywhere there is a telephone.

- ☐ Calculate monthly payments for a mortgage.
- ☐ Calculate commissions, points, and other fees.
- ☐ Make inquiries into the listing data base.
- ☐ Enter a new listing into the data base.
- ☐ Prepare memos and other documents and submit them to Que's office automation system.
- ☐ Send and receive electronic mail.

The Assignment

Put yourself in the role of the consultant as you complete the following assignment.

1. Prepare the requirements portion of a Request for Proposal for the lap PCs from a capabilities viewpoint (that is, list the performance objectives that the lap PCs must satisfy). The vendor will then configure the equipment to meet the specified objectives. For example, the lap PC must be able to communicate with Que's minicomputer at 1,200 baud from any telephone.

2. Prepare the requirements portion of an RFP for a specific configuration for the lap PCs (that is, list the technical specifications for the lap PCs). For example, the lap PC must have a 1,200- baud internal modem. Information on technical specifications is available in Chapter 8, "Connectivity and Data Communications," and "A Short Course in Computer Concepts" that follows Chapter 17.

3. Write the section of the RFP that specifies the vendor's liabilities in the event the lap PCs are not delivered by a mutually agreed-upon date.

4. Included in the RFP will be a request for references who can support vendor claims. Prepare a list of questions for the references and describe the rating structure; for example: "How is the vendor's technical support?" Responses could range from "excellent" to "poor." Be sure to include categories for "never used" or "don't know."

APPLICATION CASE STUDY 17–2

Replacement Considerations and Strategies

The Situation

Monica Roberts, the director of Academic Computing at Peterson College, has recently completed a strategic plan for academic computing at the college (see Application Case Study 8–2, "A Local Area Network"). The plan includes the following desired capabilities and facilities:

☐ Replace the minicomputer with a newer model.

☐ Provide the capability for all microcomputers in the existing laboratory to route output to a dot-matrix printer, a daisy-wheel printer, a laser printer, and a plotter.

☐ Provide the capability for all microcomputers at Peterson College to download files from the minicomputer and to upload files to it.

☐ Provide a cluster of three or four microcomputers and a printer in each of the three dormitories and in the main classroom building, called the Learning Center.

☐ Provide each faculty member with a microcomputer in his or her office.

☐ Provide access to the library's proposed on-line catalog from any workstation (micro or terminal, on or off campus).

☐ Provide access to computing facilities at other cooperating colleges from any workstation. (Certain restrictions would accompany this capability because there will be a charge for the use of another college's facilities.)

☐ Provide access to Peterson College's computing facilities for students and faculty at other cooperating institutions.

☐ Provide access to the minicomputer from the current and proposed satellite campuses.

☐ Provide access to the minicomputer from off-campus workstations; that is, provide access for individuals who have a workstation at home or at their place of employment. This is essential for the master's degree students and desirable for faculty and undergraduate students.

The key item in the preceding list is the replacement of the minicomputer. This is an eight-year-old machine with 16 terminals and no communication facilities.

The Assignment

Put yourself in the role of Monica Roberts as you complete the following assignment.

1. Prepare a list of hardware and software requirements for the replacement computer system.

2. How important is it that the new hardware and software be compatible with that of the current system?

3. Peterson College is deciding which arrangement to use to acquire the new minicomputer. Discuss the advantages and disadvantages of each of the following alternatives:

   a. Purchase the mini from the vendor.

   b. Lease/purchase the mini from the vendor (under this arrangement, a portion of the lease payments accrue toward the purchase of the equipment).

   c. Lease the mini from a third party.

A SHORT COURSE IN COMPUTER CONCEPTS

MODULE A

Computer Systems

Uncovering the "Mystery" of Computers

What Is a Computer?

The word "computer" is an integral part of just about everyone's daily-use vocabulary, but to many people, it is some kind of miraculous "black box." Technically speaking, a **computer** is any counting device. But in the context of modern technology, we define the computer as *an electronic device capable of interpreting and executing programmed commands for input, output, computation, and logic operations*. The computer, also called a **processor**, is the "intelligence" of a *computer system*.

      Computers may be technically complex, but they are conceptually simple. A computer system—any computer system, small or large—has only four fundamental components: **input**, *processing*, **output**, and *storage*. Note that a *computer system*, not a computer, has four components. The actual computer is the processing component and is combined with the other three to form a **computer system** (see Figure A–1). Generally, computer systems are classified as **microcomputers**, **minicomputers**, and **mainframe computers**.

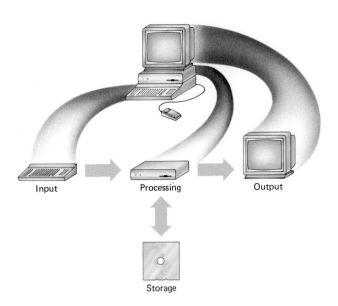

FIGURE A–1 The Four Fundamental Components of a Microcomputer System

In a microcomputer system, the storage and processing components are often contained in the same physical unit. In the illustration, the diskette storage medium is inserted into the unit that contains the processor.

How a Computer System Works

A computer system can be likened to the biological system of the human body. Your brain, which is the processing component, is linked to the other components of the body by the central nervous system. Your eyes and ears are input components that send signals to the brain. If you see someone approaching, your brain matches the visual image of this person with others in your memory (storage component). If the visual image is matched in memory with that of a friend, your brain sends signals to your vocal chords and right arm (output components) to greet your friend with a "Hello" and a handshake. Computer system components interact in a similar way.

      The payroll system in Figure A–2 illustrates how data are entered and how the four computer system components interact to produce information (such as a "year-to-date overtime report") and the payroll checks. The hours-worked data are *input* to the system and are *stored* on the personnel master file. Note that the storage component of a computer system stores data, not information!

      The payroll checks are produced when the *processing* component, or the computer, executes a program. In this example, the employee record is recalled from storage, and the pay amount is calculated. The *output* is the printed payroll checks. Other programs extract data from the personnel master file to produce a year-to-date overtime report and any other information that might help in the decision-making process.

The Hardware

In the microcomputer-based payroll example, data are entered (input) on a typewriterlike **keyboard** and displayed (output) on a televisionlike (video) screen, called a **monitor**. The payroll checks are then output on a device called a **printer.** Data are stored for later recall on **magnetic disk**. The wide variety of **input/output (I/O)** and storage devices are discussed in Module C, "I/O and Data Storage Devices."

      The principles just discussed apply equally to microcomputers, minicomputers, and mainframe computers. Each has the four components, and each uses data to produce information in a similar manner. The difference is that microcomputers are more limited in their capabilities and are designed primarily for use by *one person* at a time. Minicomputers and mainframe computers can service *many users*, perhaps even thousands, all at once.

What Can a Computer Do?

The last section discussed how the input/output and data storage hardware components are configured with the processing compo-

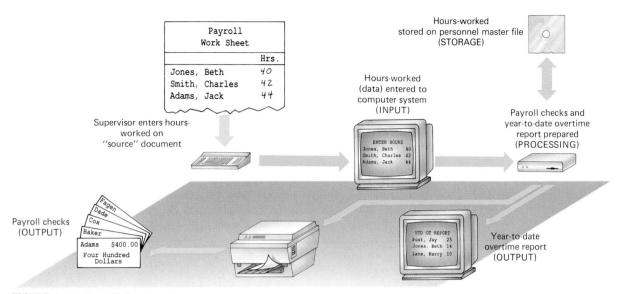

FIGURE A–2 Payroll System

This microcomputer-based payroll system illustrates input, storage, processing, and output.

nent (the computer) to make up a computer system (see Figure A–1). The focus of this section is on the the operational capabilities of a computer system.

INPUT/OUTPUT OPERATIONS The computer *reads* from input and storage devices. The computer *writes* to output and storage devices. Before data can be processed, they must be "read" from an input device or data storage device. Input data are usually entered by a user via a keyboard or some other input device or retrieved from a data storage device, such as a magnetic disk drive. Once data have been processed, they are "written" to an output device, such as a printer, or to a data storage device.

Input/output (I/O) operations are illustrated in the payroll system example in Figure A–2. Hours-worked data are entered and read into the computer system. These data are written to magnetic disk storage for recall at a later date.

PROCESSING OPERATIONS The computer is totally objective. That is, any two computers instructed to perform the same operation will arrive at the same result. This is because the computer can perform only *computation* and *logic operations*.

The computational capabilities of the computer include adding, subtracting, multiplying, and dividing. Logic capability permits the computer to make comparisons between numbers and between words and, based on the result of the comparison, perform appropriate functions. In the payroll system example of Figure A–2, the computer calculates the gross pay in a computation operation (40 hours at $10 per hour = $400). In a logic operation, the computer compares the number of hours worked to 40 to determine the number of overtime hours that an employee worked during a given week.

Computer System Capabilities

In a nutshell, computers are fast, accurate, and reliable; they do not forget anything; and they do not complain.

SPEED The smallest unit of time in the human experience is, realistically, the second. With the second as the only means of comparison, it is difficult for us to comprehend the time scale of computers. The operations (the execution of instructions) for microcomputers are measured in **milliseconds** and **microseconds** (one-thousandth and one-millionth of a second, respectively). Larger processors are measured in **nanoseconds** and **picoseconds** (one-billionth and one-trillionth of a second, respectively). To give you a feeling for the speed of computers, a beam of light travels down the length of this page in about 1 nanosecond!

ACCURACY You may work for years before experiencing a system error, such as an updating of the wrong record or an incorrect addition. Errors do occur, but precious few can be directly attributed to the computer system. The vast majority of these errors can be traced to a program logic error, a procedural error, or erroneous data. These are human errors.

RELIABILITY Computer systems are particularly adept at repetitive tasks. They don't take sick days and coffee breaks, and they seldom complain. Anything below 99.9 percent *uptime* is usually unacceptable. Unfortunately, *downtime* sometimes occurs at the most inconvenient times. Fortunately for microcomputer users, a *backup* micro is usually no farther away than the next room. Some companies have backup mainframe computers that take over if the primary computer fails.

MEMORY CAPABILITY   Computer systems have total and instant recall of data and an almost unlimited capacity to store these data. A typical microcomputer will have the capacity to store and recall from 1 to 100 million characters and, perhaps, some graphic images. Storage on mainframe computer systems is measured in the billions and trillions of characters. To give you a benchmark for comparison, this book contains approximately 1,500,000 characters.

Microcomputers

Microprocessors

Microprocessors play a very important role in our lives. You probably have a dozen or more of them at home and may not know it. They are used in telephones, ovens, televisions, greeting cards, cars, and, of course, microcomputers.

The microprocessor is a product of the microminiaturization of electronic circuitry; it is literally a "computer on a chip." The first fully operational microprocessor was demonstrated in March 1971. Since that time, these relatively inexpensive microprocessors have been integrated into thousands of mechanical and electronic devices, even elevators and ski boot bindings. In a few years, virtually everything that is mechanical or electronic will incorporate microprocessor technology into the design.

Microcomputer Electronics

The microprocessor is sometimes confused with its famous offspring, the microcomputer. A keyboard, video monitor, and memory were attached to the microprocessor and—the microcomputer was born!

In a microcomputer, the microprocessor, electronic circuitry for handling input/output signals from the peripheral devices, and "memory chips" are mounted to a single circuit board, called a **motherboard**. Before being attached to the circuit board, the microprocessor and other chips are mounted on a *carrier*. Carriers have standard-sized pin connectors that permit the chips to be attached to the motherboard.

The motherboard, the "guts" of a microcomputer, is what distinguishes one microcomputer from another. The motherboard is simply "plugged" into one of several slots designed for circuit boards. The processing components of most micros have several empty **expansion slots** so that you can purchase and plug in optional capabilities in the form of **add-on boards**. For example, you can purchase more memory, a board that permits graphics output, or a modem (a device that permits data communications between computers).

Microcomputer Defined

During the last decade, people have described microcomputers in terms of cost, physical dimensions, size of primary storage, and amount of data processed at a time, but all definitions proved confusing. A **micro** is just a small computer. Perhaps the best definition of a micro is *any computer that you can pick up and carry*. But don't be misled by the "micro" prefix. You can "pick up and carry" some very powerful computers!

A microcomputer is also called a **personal computer** or **PC**. The label "personal computer" was associated with microcomputers because they were designed for use by one person at a time. For the most part, this one-to-one relationship still holds. However, some micros or PCs can handle several users simultaneously.

Pocket, Lap, and Desktop PCs

Personal computers come in three different physical sizes: *pocket PCs*, *lap PCs*, and *desktop PCs*. The pocket and lap PCs are light (a few ounces to 8 pounds) and compact and can operate without an external power source—so they earn the "portable" label as well. There are also a number of "transportable" desktop PCs on the market, but they are more cumbersome to move. They fold up to about the size of a small suitcase, weigh about 25 pounds, and usually require an external power source. Most desktop PCs are not designed for frequent movement and are, therefore, not considered portable.

The power of a PC is not necessarily in proportion to its size. A few lap PCs can run circles around some of the desktop PCs. Some user conveniences, however, must be sacrificed to achieve portability. For example, the miniature keyboards on pocket PCs make data entry and interaction with the computer difficult and slow. On lap PCs, the display screen is small and does not hold as much text as a display on a desktop PC.

Configuring a Microcomputer System

Normally, computer professionals are called upon to select, configure, and install the hardware associated with minicomputers and mainframe computers. But individuals, often users, select, configure, and install their own micros, so it is important to know what makes up a microcomputer system.

The microcomputer is the smallest computer system. Even so, it has the same components as mainframe computer systems: input, output, storage, and processing. As you might expect, the input/output components are much slower, and the storage component has a smaller capacity than do the larger systems.

The computer and its peripheral devices are called the computer system **configuration**. The configuration of a microcomputer can vary. The most typical micro configuration consists of:

1. A computer.
2. A keyboard for input.
3. A televisionlike display called a monitor for **soft-copy** (temporary) output.
4. A printer for **hard-copy** (printed) output.
5. One or two disk drives for permanent storage of data and programs.

Some of the more powerful desktop microcomputers actually sit under or to the side of a desk. This provides more space for the keyboard, monitor, printer, and other peripheral devices.

Courtesy of International Business Machines

In some microcomputer systems these components are purchased as separate physical units and then are linked together. In others, two, three, and even all of the components can be contained in a single unit. With a few rare exceptions, the printer is usually a separate unit.

Micros that give users the flexibility to configure the system with a variety of peripheral devices (input/output and storage) are said to have an **open architecture**. A component stereo system provides a good analogy to illustrate the concept of open architecture. In a stereo system, the tuner is the central component to which record turntables, equalizers, tape decks, compact disk players, speakers, and so on can be attached. A microcomputer system with an open architecture is configured by linking any of the many peripheral devices discussed in Module C to the processor component. As a rule of thumb, if there is a need for a special type of input/output or storage device, then someone markets it. In a **closed architecture**, the system is fully configured when it is sold.

The storage medium of most microcomputers is normally a **diskette** or a **microdisk**. The diskette can be compared to a phonograph record, but it is thinner and more flexible and is permanently enclosed within a 5¼-inch square jacket. Because the diskette is flexible, like a page in this book, it is also called a **flexible disk** or a **floppy disk**. Some microcomputers use rigid microdisks (3¼ or 3½ inches in diameter) for storage. The more powerful microcomputers use hard disks. These and other storage media are discussed in detail in Module C.

Multiuser Micros

In the early 1960s, mainframe computer systems were able to service only one user at a time. By the mid-1960s, technological improvements made it possible for computers to service several users simultaneously. A quarter of a century later, some mainframes service thousands of users, all at the same time!

We can draw a parallel between what happened to the mainframe in the 1960s and what is happening to microcomputers today. Until recently, micros were "personal" computers—for individual use only. But technological improvements have been so rapid that it has become difficult for a single user to tap the full potential of state-of-the-art micros. To tap this unused potential, hardware and software vendors are marketing products that permit several users on the system at once.

These multiuser micros are configured with up to 12 keyboard/monitor pairs, called **workstations**. These workstations, often located in the same office, share the microcomputer's resources and its peripheral devices. With a multiuser micro, a secretary can be transcribing dictation at one workstation, a manager can be doing financial analysis at another workstation, and a clerk can be entering data to a data base at another workstation. All of this takes place at the same time on the same multiuser micro.

Micros as Workstations

A workstation is the hardware that allows you to interact with a computer system, be it a mainframe or a multiuser micro. A *video display terminal* (*VDT*) is a workstation. A microcomputer can also be a workstation. With the installation of an optional data communications adapter, a micro has the flexibility to serve as a *stand-alone* computer system or as an "intelligent" workstation to a multiuser micro, a minicomputer, or a mainframe computer.

The term "intelligent" is applied to workstations that can also operate as stand-alone computer systems, independent of any other computer system. For example, you can dial up any one of a number of information services on travel, securities, and consumer goods; link your micro to the telephone line and remote computer; and then use your micro as a workstation to obtain information. Both the micro and the VDT can transmit and receive data from a remote computer, but only the micro workstation can process and store the data independently.

Minicomputers

Until the late 1960s, all computers were mainframe computers, and they were expensive—too expensive for all but the largest companies. About that time vendors introduced smaller, but slightly "watered-down," computers that were more affordable to smaller companies. The industry dubbed these small computers minicomputers, or simply **minis**. The name has stuck, even though some of today's so-called minis are many times as powerful as the largest mainframes of the early 1970s.

There is no clear-cut or generally accepted definition for a minicomputer. The passing of time and a rapidly changing technol-

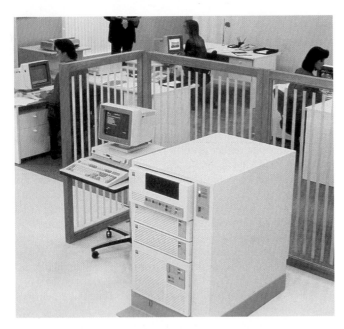

The minicomputer system at this East Coast automotive parts distributor helps administrative personnel keep track of orders and shipping information.

Courtesy of International Business Machines

ogy have blurred the distinction between categories of computers. The more powerful multiuser micros look very much like small minis, but minis are now accomplishing processing tasks that have traditionally been associated with mainframes. Minis bridge the gap between micros and mainframes, but the manner in which they are used makes them more characteristic of mainframes than of micros. Creating a rigorous definition of a minicomputer is like trying to grab a speeding bullet. Since technology has created a moving target, we will describe the minicomputer simply as a small mainframe computer.

Minicomputers usually serve as stand-alone computer systems for small businesses (10 to 400 employees) and as remote computer systems linked to a large centralized mainframe computer. Minis are also common in research groups, engineering firms, and colleges.

As the definition of a minicomputer becomes more obscure, the term "minicomputer" will take its place beside "electronic brain." But for now, it remains a commonly used term, even though it lacks a commonly accepted definition.

Mainframe Computers

Besides the obvious difference in the speeds at which they process data, the major difference between minicomputers and other mainframe computers is in the number of remote workstations that they can service. As a rule of thumb, any computer that services more than 100 remote workstations can no longer be called a minicomputer. Some **supercomputers**, the fastest and most powerful of mainframes, provide service to over 10,000 remote workstations.

The speed at which medium and large mainframe computers can perform operations allows more input, output, and storage devices with greater capabilities to be configured in the computer system. The computer system in Figure A–3 is used by the municipal government of a city of about 1 million people. This example should give you an appreciation of the relative size and potential of a medium-sized mainframe computer system. The hardware devices illustrated are discussed in Module C. The components are described briefly as follows.

☐ *Processing.* Mainframe computer systems, including some minis, will normally be configured with the mainframe or **host processor** and several other processors. The host processor has direct control over all the other processors, storage devices, and input/output devices. The other processors relieve the host of certain routine processing requirements. For example, the **back-end processor** performs the task of locating a particular record on a data storage device. The **front-end processor** relieves the host processor of communications-related processing duties—that is, the transmission of data to and from remote workstations and other computers. In this way, the host can concentrate on overall system control and the execution of applications software.

A typical configuration would have a host processor, a front-end processor, and perhaps a back-end processor. The host is the main computer and is substantially larger and more powerful than the other *subordinate* processors. The front-end and back-end processors control the data flow in and out of the host processor. Although the host could handle the entire system without the assistance of the subordinate processors, overall system efficiency would be drastically reduced without them.

☐ *Storage.* All mainframe computer systems use similar direct and sequential storage media. The larger ones simply have more of them, and they usually work faster. In Figure A–3 there are 4 magnetic tape drives and 10 magnetic disk drives. The total on-line data storage capacity in the example is 800 megabytes of sequential storage (tape) and 16,000 megabytes of direct-access storage (disk).

☐ *Input.* The primary means of entering data to the system is the same, no matter what the size of the computer system. The only difference between a large and a small system is in the number and location of the workstations. In the example of Figure A–3, 150 workstations are dedicated to service and administrative functions, 30 are used for programming, and 16 **ports** are available for those who might wish to use their PCs to dial up and log on to the mainframe computer. A port is an access point in a computer system that permits data to be transmitted between the computer and

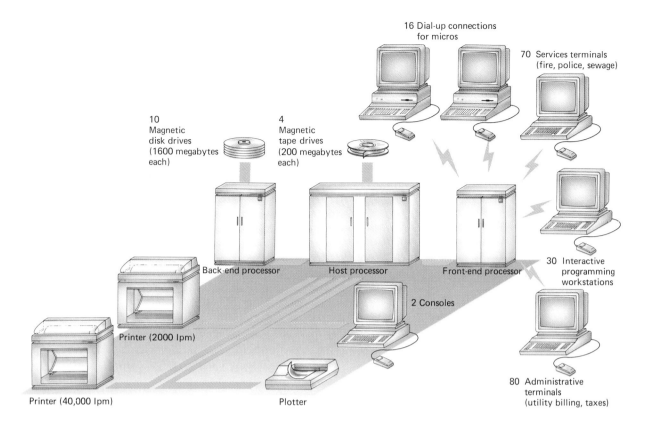

16 Dial-up connections for micros

70 Services terminals (fire, police, sewage)

10 Magnetic disk drives (1600 megabytes each)

4 Magnetic tape drives (200 megabytes each)

Back-end processor

Host processor

Front-end processor

30 Interactive programming workstations

2 Consoles

Printer (2000 lpm)

Printer (40,000 lpm)

Plotter

80 Administrative terminals (utility billing, taxes)

FIGURE A–3   A Mainframe Computer System
This mid-sized mainframe computer system supports the administrative processing needs for the municipal government of a city with a population of about 1 million.

a peripheral device. Two **operator consoles** in the machine room are used by operators to communicate instructions to the system.

□ *Output*.   The hard copy is produced on high-speed printers and the soft copy on workstations. In the example, there are two printers: a line printer with a speed of 2,000 lines per minute and a page printer that uses laser printing technology to achieve printing speeds of over 40,000 lines per minute. The *plotter*, also pictured in the configuration, is used by city engineers to produce hard copies of graphs, charts, and drawings.

Computer Systems Summary

There has never been a common definition for terms such as microcomputer, minicomputer, and supercomputer. Consequently, their meanings become even more obscure with each leap in technological innovation. Nevertheless, people still use these terms to refer to general classes of computers. Just remember that one person's (or vendor's) microcomputer may be another's minicomputer.

Perhaps the most important point to be made in this module is this: a personal computer, a mainframe, a mini, or any other

The clean lines of this mainframe computer system hide the thousands of integrated circuits, and even gold, that make up the inner workings of a computer system. This data center provides information processing support for hundreds of end users.

Photo courtesy of Hewlett-Packard Company

kind of computer system differ only in size and how they are applied.

Important Terms

add-on board	microcomputer, micro
backup	microdisk
back-end processor	microprocessor
closed architecture	microsecond
computation operation	millisecond
computer	minicomputer, mini
computer system	monitor
configuration	motherboard
desktop PC	nanosecond
diskette	open architecture
downtime	operator console
expansion slot	personal computer (PC)
flexible disk	picosecond
floppy disk	plotter
front-end processor	pocket PC
hard copy	port
host processor	printer
input	processor
input/output (I/O)	soft copy
keyboard	supercomputer
lap PC	uptime
logic operation	video display terminal (VDT)
magnetic disk	workstation
mainframe computer	

Review Exercises

1. What are the four fundamental components of a computer system?
2. Which component of a computer system executes the program?
3. Light travels at 186,000 miles per second. How many milliseconds does it take for a beam of light to travel across the United States, a distance of about 3,000 miles?
4. In computerese, what is meant by "read" and "write"?
5. What is a motherboard?
6. In terms of physical size, how are PCs categorized?
7. What is the name given to printed output? Output on a monitor?
8. Give two examples each of both input hardware and output hardware.
9. What is the difference between a diskette and a microdisk?
10. Briefly describe a typical configuration for a microcomputer system.

Self-Test

1. A printer is an example of which of the four computer system components?
2. The two types of processing operations performed by computers are _____ and _____ .
3. A microsecond is 1,000 times longer than a nanosecond. (T/F)
4. The computer and its peripheral devices are called the computer system _____.
5. A microcomputer cannot be linked to a mainframe computer. (T/F)
6. The microdisk is also known as a floppy disk. (T/F)
7. Another name for a microcomputer is personal computer. (T/F)
8. Minicomputers are now accomplishing processing tasks that have traditionally been associated with mainframe computers. (T/F)
9. Each peripheral device is connected to a mainframe computer through a port. (T/F)
10. The _____ relieves the host processor of communications-related processing duties.

SELF-TEST ANSWERS   1. output; 2. computation, logic; 3. T; 4. configuration; 5. F; 6. F; 7. T; 8. T; 9. T; 10. front-end processor

MODULE B

Inside the Computer

Bits and Bytes

The computer's seemingly endless potential is, in fact, based on only two electrical states, *on* and *off*. The physical characteristics of the computer make it possible to combine these two electronic states to represent letters and numbers. An "on" or "off" electronic state is represented by a **bit**. The term "bit" is short for *binary digit*. The presence or absence of a bit is referred to as *on-bit* or *off-bit*, respectively. In the **binary numbering system** (base 2) and in written text, the on-bit is a 1 and the off-bit is a 0.

Physically, these states are achieved in a variety of ways. In the computer's solid-state memory (memory chips), the two electronic states are represented by the direction of current flow. Another approach is to turn the circuit on or off. In rotating memory (disks), the two states are made possible by the magnetic arrangement of the iron oxide coating on magnetic disks.

Bits may be fine for computers, but human beings are more comfortable with letters and decimal numbers (the base 10 numerals 0 through 9). Therefore, the letters and decimal numbers that we input to a computer system must be translated to 1's and 0's for processing and storage. The computer translates the bits back to letters and decimal numbers on output. This translation is performed so that we can recognize and understand the output, and it is made possible by *encoding systems*.

Encoding Systems: Combining Bits to Form Bytes

Computers do not talk to each other in English, Spanish, or French. They have their own languages that are better suited to electronic communication. In these languages, bits are combined according to an **encoding system** to represent letters (**alpha characters**), numbers (**numeric characters**), and special characters (such as *, $, +, and &). One such encoding system is the seven-bit **ASCII** (American Standard Code for Information Interchange, pronounced *AS-key*), which is used primarily in micros and for data communications. In ASCII a B and a 3 are represented by 1000010 and 0110011, respectively. In the eight-bit **EBCDIC** encoding system (Extended Binary-Coded Decimal Interchange Code, pronounced *EBB-see-dik*), which is used primarily in mainframe computers, a B and a 3 are represented by 11000010 and 11110011, respectively.

Letters, numbers, and special characters are collectively referred to as **alphanumeric characters**. Alphanumeric characters are *encoded* to a bit configuration on input so that the computer can interpret them. The characters are *decoded* on output so that we can interpret them. This coding, which is based on a particular encoding system, equates a unique series of bits and no-bits with a specific character. Just as the words *mother* and *father* are arbitrary English-language character strings that refer to our parents, 1000010 is an arbitrary ASCII code that refers to the letter B. The combination of bits used to represent a character is called a **byte** (pronounced *bite*).

The seven-bit ASCII code can represent up to 128 characters (2^7). An eight-bit version of ASCII can represent up to 256 characters (2^8). The binary (and decimal) value for the codes of the first 128 characters of the eight-bit ASCII code are the same as those represented by the seven-bit code. You might ask why an eight-bit code is needed when the English language has considerably fewer than 256 alphanumeric characters. The extra bit configurations are needed to communicate a variety of activities to the processor. For example, several codes cause special symbols to be displayed (such as a "happy face"), another code causes a beep sound, and another causes the blinking cursor to move one character position to the right. Many of the extra codes can be used to display graphic symbols that can be combined to display meaningful graphic images. Figure B–1 shows the binary value (the actual bit configuration) and the decimal equivalent of commonly used ASCII characters.

The Processor and RAM

We have discussed how data are represented inside a computer system in electronic states called bits. We are now ready to expose the inner workings of the nucleus of the computer system—the processor.

The internal operation of a computer, or processor, is interesting, but there really is no mystery about it. There are literally hundreds of different types of computers, both large and small, marketed by scores of manufacturers. The complexity of each type may vary considerably, but in the end, each processor, also called the **central processing unit** or **CPU**, has only two fundamental sections: the *control unit* and the *arithmetic and logic unit*. **Random access memory**, or **RAM** (pronounced *ram*), also plays an integral part in the internal operation of a processor. These three (RAM, the control unit, and the arithmetic and logic unit) work together. Their functions and the relationships between them are described in the following discussions and illustrated in Figure B–2. Figure B–2 uses a microcomputer as the basis for illustration. These principles are equally applicable to minicomputers and mainframe computers.

Character	ASCII Code Binary Value	Decimal Value
A	100 0001	65
B	100 0010	66
C	100 0011	67
D	100 0100	68
E	100 0101	69
F	100 0110	70
G	100 0111	71
H	100 1000	72
I	100 1001	73
J	100 1010	74
K	100 1011	75
L	100 1100	76
M	100 1101	77
N	100 1110	78
O	100 1111	79
P	101 0000	80
Q	101 0001	81
R	101 0010	82
S	101 0011	83
T	101 0100	84
U	101 0101	85
V	101 0110	86
W	101 0111	87
X	101 1000	88
Y	101 1001	89
Z	101 1010	90
a	110 0001	97
b	110 0010	98
c	110 0011	99
d	110 0100	100
e	110 0101	101
f	110 0110	102
g	110 0111	103
h	110 1000	104
i	110 1001	105
j	110 1010	106
k	110 1011	107
l	110 1100	108
m	110 1101	109
n	110 1110	110
o	110 1111	111
p	111 0000	112
q	111 0001	113
r	111 0010	114
s	111 0011	115
t	111 0100	116
u	111 0101	117
v	111 0110	118
w	111 0111	119
x	111 1000	120
y	111 1001	121
z	111 1010	122

Character	ASCII Code Binary Value	Decimal Value
0	011 0000	48
1	011 0001	49
2	011 0010	50
3	011 0011	51
4	011 0100	52
5	011 0101	53
6	011 0110	54
7	011 0111	55
8	011 1000	56
9	011 1001	57
Space	010 0000	32
.	010 1110	46
<	011 1100	60
(	010 1000	40
+	010 1011	43
&	010 0110	38
!	010 0001	33
$	010 0100	36
*	010 1010	42
)	010 1001	41
;	011 1011	59
,	010 1100	44
%	010 0101	37
—	101 1111	95
>	011 1110	62
?	011 1111	63
:	011 1010	58
#	010 0011	35
@	100 0000	64
'	010 0111	39
=	011 1101	61
''	010 0010	34
½	1010 1011	171
¼	1010 1100	172
▒	1011 0010	178
■	1101 1011	219
▬	1101 1100	220
I	1101 1101	221
▪	1101 1110	222
	1101 1111	223
√	1111 1011	251
n	1111 1100	252
2	1111 1101	253
■	1111 1110	254
(blank)	1111 1111	255

FIGURE B–1   ASCII Codes
This figure contains the binary and decimal values for commonly used ASCII characters.

Random Access Memory (RAM)

Unlike **secondary storage** devices such as magnetic disk and tape, RAM, or **primary storage**, is solid state and has no moving parts. With no mechanical movement, data can be accessed from RAM at electronic speeds, close to the speed of light. RAM, also called **main memory**, provides the processor with *temporary* storage for programs and data.

All programs and data must be transferred to RAM from an input device (such as a keyboard) or from magnetic storage (such as a disk) before programs can be executed or data can be processed. RAM space is always at a premium; therefore, after a program has been executed, the storage space occupied by it is reallocated to another program that is awaiting execution.

A program instruction or a piece of data is stored in a specific primary storage location called an **address**. Addresses permit program instructions and data to be found, accessed, and processed. The content of each address is constantly changing as different programs are executed and new data are processed.

A special type of RAM called **read-only memory** (**ROM**) cannot be altered by the programmer. The contents of the ROM are hard-wired (designed into the logic of a memory chip) by the manufacturer and can be "read only." For example, when you turn on a microcomputer system, a program in ROM automatically performs diagnostic functions such as checking RAM and readies the computer system for use. Then, a ROM program loads the operating system into RAM. Some microcomputers can be purchased with word processing software and other applications software that can be loaded from ROM rather than disk.

A variation of ROM is programmable read-only memory or **PROM**. PROM is ROM into which you, the user, can load "read-only" programs and data. Some microcomputer software packages, such as electronic spreadsheets, are available as PROM units as well as on diskette. Once a program is loaded to PROM, it is seldom, if ever, changed. However, if you need to be able to revise the contents of PROM, there is **EPROM**, erasable PROM.

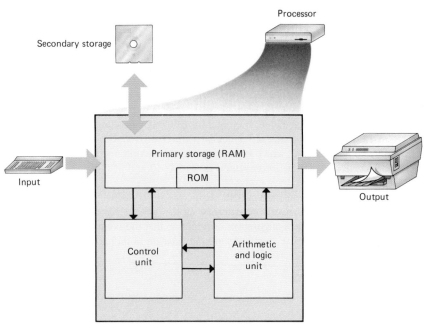

FIGURE B–2   Interaction Between Primary Storage and Computer System Components
All programs and data must be transferred from an input device or from secondary storage before programs can be executed and data can be processed. Output is transferred to the printer from primary storage.

The Control Unit

Just as the processor is the nucleus of a computer system, the **control unit** is the nucleus of the processor. The control unit has three primary functions:

1. To read and interpret program instructions.
2. To direct the operation of internal processor components.
3. To control the flow of programs and data in and out of RAM.

Any program (word processing or database, for example) must first be loaded to RAM before it can be executed. During execution, the first in a sequence of program instructions is moved from RAM to the control unit where it is **decoded** and interpreted. The control unit then directs other processor components to carry out the operations necessary to execute the instruction. Productivity software programs, such as electronic spreadsheets, are made up of thousands of instructions.

Arithmetic and Logic Unit

The **arithmetic and logic unit** performs all computations (addition, subtraction, multiplication, and division) and all logic operations (comparisons). An example of a computation operation is the summing of the numbers in a column of an electronic spreadsheet. In a logic operation, two pieces of data are compared. For instance, when employee records in a data base are alphabetized, the letters in the names are compared in a logic operation (for example, "Smith" is placed before "Smyth").

Describing the Processor

The processing component of a computer is described in terms of *processor speed*, *RAM capacity*, and *word length*.

PROCESSOR SPEED On microcomputers, a *crystal oscillator* paces the execution of instructions within the processor. A micro's processor speed is rated by its frequency of oscillation or the number of clock cycles per second. Most personal computers are rated between 5 and 25 **megahertz** or **MHz** (clock cycles). The elapsed time for one clock cycle is 1/frequency (one divided by the frequency). For example, the elapsed time to complete one cycle on a 20-MHz processor is 1/20,000,000 or .00000005 seconds or 50 nanoseconds. Normally, several clock cycles are required to *retrieve, interpret,* and *execute* a single program instruction. The shorter the clock cycle, the faster the processor.

On mainframe computers, processor speed is usually measured in **MIPS**, or millions of instructions per second. The processing speed of today's mainframe computers is in the range 20 to 1,000 MIPS.

RAM CAPACITY The capacity of RAM is stated in terms of the number of bytes that can be stored. A byte is roughly equivalent to a character, like A, 1, or &.

This mainframe computer, which is one of the world's fastest computers, is sometimes called a supercomputer. It has a word size of 64 bits and offers up to 1,024 megabytes of primary storage.

The memory capacity of microcomputers is usually stated in terms of **K** (kilo) bytes and **M** (mega) bytes, convenient designations for 1,024 (2^{10}) bytes of storage and 1,048,576 (2^{20}) of bytes of storage, respectively. RAM capacities in micros range from 256K bytes (or simply 256KB) in small micros to 8M bytes (or simply 8MB) in the more powerful multiuser micros. Memory capacities for mainframe computers range from 4M bytes to 8 billion bytes.

WORD LENGTH A **word** is the number of bits that are handled as a unit for a particular computer system. The word size of modern microcomputers is normally 16 or 32 bits. The newer 16- and 32-bit micros are as much as 10 times faster than are the early 8-bit PCs. Supercomputers have 64-bit words.

Important Terms

address	decoded
alpha character	EBCDIC
alphanumeric character	encode
arithmetic and logic unit	encoding system
ASCII	EPROM
binary numbering system	K (kilobyte)
bit (binary digit)	M (megabyte)
byte	main memory
central processing unit (CPU)	megahertz (MHz)
	MIPS
control unit	numeric character

off-bit

on-bit

primary storage

PROM

random access memory
  (RAM)

read-only memory (ROM)

secondary storage

word

Review Exercises

1. Which two functions are performed by the arithmetic and logic unit?

2. Write your first name as an ASCII-bit configuration.

3. What are the functions of the control unit?

4. Distinguish between RAM, ROM, PROM, and EPROM.

5. How many EBCDIC bytes can be stored in a 32-bit word?

6. List examples of alpha, numeric, and alphanumeric characters.

7. Computers are described in terms of what three characteristics?

Self-Test

1. Bit is the singular of byte. (T/F)

2. The ASCII bit configuration for the uppercase letter "X" is _____ .

3. The _____ is that part of the processor that reads and interprets program instructions.

4. The arithmetic and logic unit controls the flow of programs and data in and out of main memory. (T/F)

5. Data are retrieved from temporary secondary storage and stored permanently in main memory. (T/F)

6. The word length of a mainframe computer can be as much as 64 bits. (T/F)

7. MIPS is an acronym for "millions of instructions per second." (T/F)

SELF-TEST ANSWERS   1. F; 2. 1011000; 3. control unit; 4. F; 5. F; 6. T; 7. T

MODULE C
I/O and Data Storage Devices

Input/Output Devices

Data are created in many places and in many ways. Before data can be processed and stored, they must be translated to a form that the computer can interpret. For this, *input* devices are needed. Once the data have been processed, they must be translated back to a form that we can understand. For this, *output* devices are needed. These **peripheral** input/output (I/O) devices enable communication between us and the computer.

Relatively few people have an opportunity to visit a machine room that houses a mainframe computer and its associated peripheral devices. Even fewer people are involved in the acquisition and operation of mainframe-based I/O and data storage devices. On the other hand, millions of people are frequently involved in the acquisition and operation of all facets of microcomputer systems. Since the microcomputer is more accessible to the vast majority of people, microcomputer I/O and data storage devices are emphasized in this module. For the most part, any device that can be linked to a microcomputer also can be adapted to the mainframe environment. Peripheral I/O and data storage devices that are designed specifically for the mainframe environment are similar in function and operation to microcomputer peripheral devices, but they are faster and have greater capacities.

Input Devices

THE KEYBOARD   All micros come equipped with a keyboard for input. The typical key-driven data entry device has a standard *alphanumeric keyboard* with an optional numeric keyboard, called a *10-key pad*. Some keyboards also have *special-function keys* that can be used to instruct the computer to perform a specific operation that may otherwise require several keystrokes.

The standard QWERTY alphanumeric keyboard comes with micros unless you specifically request the alternative, the Dvorak keyboard. The layout of Dvorak keyboard places the most frequently used characters in the center of the keyboard.

RANDOM CURSOR CONTROL   For some applications the keyboard is too cumbersome. For example, you might need to "draw" a line to connect two points on the micro's display screen. Such applications call for devices that go beyond the capabilities of keyboards.

This microcomputer is configured for desktop publishing applications. It has three input devices and a desktop laser printer (right). Besides the keyboard and the mouse, the configuration also includes a digital scanner (left) that permits images of photos and charts to be digitized and stored on disk. Once on disk, the images can be recalled for inclusion in an output document.

MicroAge Computer Stores, Inc.

These devices permit random movement of the **cursor** to create the image. A cursor, or blinking character (usually an underscore or a rectangle), indicates the location on the screen of the next input. The joystick, digitizing tablet (or pad) and pen, and mouse are among the most popular cursor movement and input mechanisms.

The **joystick** is a single vertical stick that moves the cursor in the direction in which the stick is pushed. The **digitizing tablet and pen** is a pressure-sensitive tablet with the same *X-Y* coordinates as the screen and a pen. The outline of an image drawn on a tablet is reproduced on the display screen. The **mouse**, sometimes called the "pet peripheral," is now standard equipment on some micros. The mouse, attached to the computer by a cable, is a small device that, when moved across a desktop, causes comparable movement of the cursor.

VOICE DATA ENTRY **Voice data entry**, or **voice recognition**, devices can be used to enter limited kinds and quantities of data. Despite being limited to the ability to interpret relatively few words, voice data entry has a number of applications. The use of voice data entry is valuable for those who require "hands-free" operation such as quality control inspectors. A computer-based audio response unit or a speech synthesizer (both covered later in this module) make the conversation two-way.

OPTICAL SCANNERS **Optical scanners** bounce a beam of light off an image and then measure the reflected light to determine the value of the image. Optical scanners can recognize printed characters and various types of codes. These scanners can "learn" to read almost any typeface, including this book! The "learning" takes place when the structure of the character set is described to the optical scanning device. One primary application for optical scanners on microcomputers is to read printed material into a word processing document file.

Output Devices

MONITORS Alphanumeric and graphic output are displayed on the micro's video **monitor**. Because display on the monitor's screen is temporary, it is sometimes referred to as **soft copy**. The three primary attributes of monitors are the *size* of the display screen, whether the display is *color* or *monochrome* (usually white, green, or amber), and the *resolution* or detail of the display. The size of the screen varies from 5 to 25 inches (diagonal dimension).

In *RGB monitors*, the colors red, green, and blue are combined to produce up to 64 colors. If you are willing to compromise on the quality of the display and amount of information that can be displayed, you can use an *RF modulator* to adapt a color television for use with microcomputers.

Some PC monitors have a much higher **resolution**, or quality of output. Resolution refers to the number of **pixels**, or addressable points on the screen, that is, the number of points to which light can be directed under program control. A strictly alphanumeric monitor has about 65,000 such points. A PC monitor used primarily for computer graphics may have over 250,000 points. The high-resolution monitors project extremely clear images that look almost like photographs.

This engineer is using a CAD (computer-aided design) system to design a part. The three-dimensional solid model display of the part demonstrates the clarity that can be achieved with a high-resolution color monitor.

Photo courtesy of Hewlett-Packard Company

Most PCs that are equipped with *flat panel monitors* use *liquid crystal* technology. Since liquid crystal monitors display the image by reflecting light, you must have some light to read the display. Those flat panel monitors that use *gas plasma* technology are easier to read in situations with poor lighting.

PRINTERS AND PLOTTERS The most common "output-only" devices are printers and plotters.

Printers. Printers produce **hard-copy** output, such as management reports, payroll checks, and program listings. Microcomputer printers are generally classified as **character printers** or **page printers**. Printers are rated by their print speed. Print speeds for character printers are measured in *characters per second* (*cps*), and for page printers, they are measured in *pages per minute* (*ppm*). The print-speed ranges for the two types of printers are 40 to 450 cps and 8 to 20 ppm, respectively.

Character printers are the primary hard-copy output unit for microcomputers. *Impact* character printers rely on **dot-matrix** and **daisy-wheel** technology. *Nonimpact* character printers employ **ink-jet** and **thermal** technology. Regardless of the technology, the images are formed *one character at a time* as the print head moves across the paper.

FIGURE C–1   Dot-Matrix Printer Character Formation
Each character is formed in a 7 × 5 matrix as the nine-hammer print head moves across the paper. The two bottom hammers are used for lowercase letters that extend below the line (for example, g and p).

FIGURE C–2   Letter-Quality Dot-Matrix Character Formation
The 18-hammer print head permits dots to be overlapped to increase the density and, therefore, the quality of the image.

This ink-jet color graphics printer combines vivid color graphics with near-letter-quality text.

Photo courtesy of Hewlett-Packard Company

The *dot-matrix printer* configures printed dots to form characters and all kinds of images in much the same way as lights display time and temperature on bank signs. One or several vertical columns of small print hammers are contained in a rectangular print head. The hammers are activated independently to form a dot character image as the print head moves horizontally across the paper (see Figures C–1 and C–2). Dot-matrix printers can produce graphic output as well as text output.

The *daisy-wheel printer* produces high-quality output for word processing applications. An interchangeable daisy wheel containing a set of fully formed characters is spun to the desired character. A print hammer strikes the embossed character on the print wheel to form the image.

Ink-jet printers squirt "dots" of ink on the paper to form images in a manner similar to that of the dot-matrix printer. The heat elements of *thermal printers* are activated to produce dot-matrix images on heat-sensitive paper. The big advantage that these two nonimpact character printers have over the impact printers is that they can produce *multicolor* output.

Microcomputer page printers, often called **desktop laser printers**, use laser technology to achieve high-speed hard-copy output by printing *a page at a time*. The nonimpact laser printers have many inviting characteristics: they are quiet, they can print near-typeset-quality text and graphics, they can mix type styles and sizes on the same page, and they are much faster than character printers.

Figure C–3 contrasts the output from a dot-matrix printer, in both normal and *near-letter-quality* (*NLQ*) modes, a daisy-wheel printer, and a laser printer.

```
This sentence was printed on a 9-pin dot-matrix printer.
This sentence was printed in NLQ mode on a dot-matrix printer.
This sentence was printed on a daisy-wheel printer.
This sentence was printed on a desktop laser printer.
```

FIGURE C–3   Printer Output Comparison

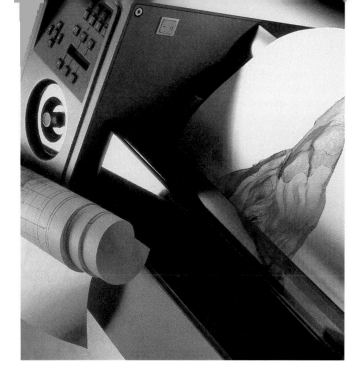

Cartographers use pen plotters to portray terrains in three dimensions.

Photo courtesy of Hewlett-Packard Company

Plotters. A **pen plotter** is a device that converts computer-generated graphs, charts, and line drawings to high-precision hard-copy output. The plotter that is commonly used with micros has one or more pens that move concurrently with the paper to produce the image. Several pens are required to vary the width and color of the lines. Pens are selected and manipulated under computer control.

SOUND AND SPEECH   One of the standard capabilities of most micros is the ability to output sounds of varying duration and frequency. This micro output feature is used for everything from warning users of a keying error to playing melodies of popular songs.

Speech synthesizers convert raw data to electronically produced speech. The existing technology produces synthesized speech with only limited vocal inflections and phrasing. Still, the number of microcomputer applications for speech synthesizers is growing.

Mainframe Input /Output Devices

Although certain I/O devices are not necessarily unique to the mainframe environment, they are more often associated with mainframes than micros. These devices include workstations, magnetic ink character recognition, magnetic stripes and smart cards, portable data entry, line printers, and high-speed laser printers. Each of these hardware devices is described briefly in the following sections.

WORKSTATIONS   A **workstation** is a device that allows us to interact with a computer from just about anywhere. A microcomputer can serve as a stand-alone computer or as a workstation linked to a mainframe. A workstation's primary input mechanism is usually a keyboard, and the output is usually a monitor. Workstations, sometimes called **video display terminals** (**VDTs**) or simply **terminals**, come in all shapes and sizes and have a variety of input/output capabilities. Also, the VDT is affectionately known as the "tube," short for **cathode-ray tube**.

The trend in workstations is to provide processing as well as I/O capability. This, in effect, means that by the next edition of this book, virtually all workstations will be microcomputers with stand-alone processing capability.

MAGNETIC INK CHARACTER RECOGNITION   **Magnetic ink character recognition** (**MICR**) is similar to optical scanning and is used exclusively by the banking industry. MICR readers are used to read and sort checks and deposits. You have probably noticed the *account number* and *bank number* encoded on all your checks and personalized deposit slips. The *date* of the transaction is automatically recorded for all checks processed that day; therefore, only the *amount* must be keyed in.

MAGNETIC STRIPES AND SMART CARDS   The **magnetic stripes** on the backs of charge cards and badges offer another means of data entry. The magnetic stripes are encoded with data appropriate for the application. For example, the account number and privacy code are encoded on cards for automatic teller machines.

The **smart card**, which is similar in appearance to charge cards, contains a microprocessor that retains certain security and personal data in its memory at all times. The smart card is really a portable computer that fits in a billfold. Since it will be almost impossible to duplicate, it may be the charge and/or identification card of the future.

PORTABLE DATA ENTRY   **Portable data entry** devices are hand-held and usually off-line. The typical portable data entry device would have a limited keyboard and a magnetic cassette tape on which to "capture" the data. After the data have been entered, they are batched to the host computer for processing.

One portable data entry device combines a hand-held optical wand with a keyboard. Stock clerks in department stores routinely use such devices to collect and enter reorder data. As clerks check the inventory level visually, they identify the items to be restocked. First, the price tag is scanned by the wand, then the number to be ordered is entered on the keyboard.

LINE PRINTERS   Line printers are found primarily in the mainframe environment. These printers are impact printers that print *a line at a time*. The three most popular types of line printers are the band printer, the chain printer, and the matrix line printer. Band and chain printers have a print hammer for each print position in the line of print (usually 132). On a band printer, several similar character sets of fully formed characters are embossed on a horizon-

This hand-held industrial computer is designed for remote data collection in manufacturing environments. The stock clerk is using a keyboard and optical wand scanner to enter data to the device. At the end of the day, he transmits the data to the company's host computer via a telephone hookup.

Photo courtesy of Hewlett-Packard Company

tal band that is continuously moving in front of the print hammers. On a chain printer, the characters are embossed on each link of the print chain. On both types, the paper is momentarily stopped, and as the desired character passes over a given column, the hammer is activated and the image is formed on the paper.

Matrix line printers print a line of *dots* at a time. Needlelike hammers are lined up across the width of the paper. Like matrix printers that print one character at a time, characters are formed in rectangular dot configurations, and they are capable of producing graphic output. The print speed of line printers can reach up to 3,600 lines per minute.

HIGH-SPEED PAGE PRINTERS   Very high-speed page printers, which are unique to the mainframe environment, use laser printing technology to achieve hard-copy output by printing *a page at a time*. Print speed for these high-speed devices can reach 40,000 lines per minute.

Data Storage Devices and Media

Secondary Storage: Permanent Data Storage

Within a computer system, programs and data are stored in *RAM* (also called *primary storage* or *main memory*) and in *secondary storage*. Programs and data are stored *permanently* for periodic retrieval in **secondary storage**. Programs and data are retrieved from secondary storage and are stored *temporarily* in high-speed RAM for processing.

The various types of **magnetic disk drives** and their respective storage media are the overwhelming choice of micro users for secondary storage. In the microcomputer environment, **magnetic tape drives** are used exclusively to back up and store disk files.

Magnetic tape is for **sequential access** only. Magnetic disks have **random** or **direct access** capabilities as well as sequential-access capabilities. You are quite familiar with these concepts, but you may not realize it. Magnetic tape is operationally the same as the one in home and car tape decks. The magnetic disk can be compared loosely to the phonograph record. When playing music on a cassette tape, you have to wind the tape forward to search for the song you want. With a phonograph record, all you would have to do is move the needle "directly" to the track containing the desired song. This simple analogy demonstrates the two fundamental methods of storing and accessing data, *sequential* and *random*, respectively.

MAGNETIC DISKS   Magnetic disk drives are secondary storage devices that provide a computer system with **random** *and* **sequential processing** capabilities. In random processing, the desired programs and data are accessed *directly* from the storage medium.

A variety of magnetic disk drives (the hardware device) and magnetic disks (the media) are manufactured for different user requirements. The two most popular types of *interchangeable* magnetic disks are the **diskette** and the **microdisk**.

☐ *Diskette.* The diskette is a thin, flexible disk that is permanently enclosed within a 5¼-inch square jacket. Because the diskette is flexible, like a page in this book, it is also called a **flexible disk** or a **floppy disk**.

☐ *Microdisk.* The microdisk is a rigid disk that is either 3¼ or 3½ inches in diameter.

Once inserted in a disk drive, the programs and data on the diskette or microdisk are said to be on-line. This means that the programs and data on the disk are accessible to and under the control of a computer system. Once the programs and data are no longer needed for processing, the disks can be removed for off-line storage. The storage capacity of diskettes and microdisks ranges from about 320K to 1.2M bytes.

Not all disk storage media are interchangeable. In fact, the trend is to permanently installed **hard** or **fixed disks**; a microcomputer hard disk is called a **Winchester disk**. Most of the newer personal computers are configured with at least one diskette drive and one hard disk. The storage capacity of hard disks ranges from about 10M to 80M bytes, which is as much as 250 times the capacity of a diskette.

A hard disk, which may have several disk platters, spins continuously at a high speed. The floppy, however, is set in motion only when a command is issued to read from or write to disk. An indicator light near the disk drive is illuminated only when the disk is spinning. The rotational movement of the disk passes all data under or over a **read/write head**, thereby making all data available for access on each revolution of the disk.

The manner in which data and programs are stored and accessed is very similar for both hard and floppy disks. The disk storage medium has a thin film coating of cobalt or iron oxide. The thin film coating on the disk can be electronically magnetized by the read/write head to represent the absence or presence of a bit (0 or 1). Data are recorded *serially* in concentric circles called **tracks** by magnetizing the surface to represent bit configurations (see Figure C–4).

Personal computers and some mainframe computers use **sector organization** to store and retrieve data. In sector organization, the recording surface is divided into pie-shaped sectors, from 8 to 15 (see Figure C–4). Each sector is assigned a unique number; therefore, the *sector number* and *track number* are all that is needed to comprise a **disk address** (the physical location of data or a program). To read from or write to a disk, an **access arm** containing the read/write head is moved under program control to the appropriate *track*. When the appropriate sector passes under or over the read/write head, the data are read or written.

The **access time** is the interval of time between the instant when a computer makes a request for a transfer of data from a secondary storage device and the instant when this operation is completed. The access time for hard disks is significantly less than that for floppy disks because the hard disk is in continuous motion.

Disks come in a wide variety of shapes and storage capacities. The type used depends on the volume of data that you have and

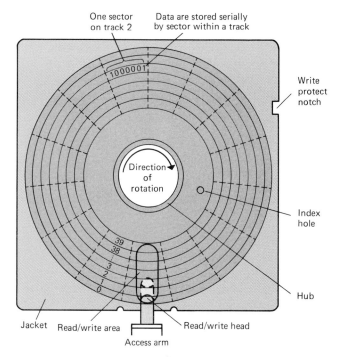

FIGURE C–4   Cutaway of a 5¼-Inch Diskette
Photoelectric cells sense light as it passes through the index hole. This feedback enables the computer to monitor which sector is over the read/write head at any given time. Data are read or written serially in tracks, within a given sector.

These 3½-inch Winchester disk drives have capacities of 42 (left) and 84 (right) megabytes. The 42-megabyte drive has two disks and three read/write heads, and the 84-megabyte drive has three disks and six read/write heads.

the frequency with which those data are accessed. All types of disks are available for both micros and mainframes; however, most micros use microdisks, floppies, or Winchester disks (small fixed disks).

Magnetic disks range in storage capacity from low-capacity floppy disks that can store about 320K characters to very high-density mainframe-based rigid disks that can store over 30M characters on 1 square inch of recording surface. That is the equivalent of the text of this and 20 other books on a space the size of a postage stamp!

MAGNETIC TAPE   The primary use of magnetic tape storage for micros and mainframes is as a backup medium for the hard disk. For backup, a **tape cassette** is taken from off-line storage and mounted into a tape drive, and the contents of a disk file are "dumped" from the disk to the tape. The tape is removed and placed in off-line storage as a backup to the operational disk. Details of backup procedures are discussed and illustrated in Chapter 9, "Data Management."

The mechanical operation of a magnetic tape drive is similar to that of a reel-to-reel or cassette audio tape deck. A thin Mylar tape passes under a read/write head, and the data are either (1) read and transmitted to primary storage or (2) transmitted from primary storage and written to the tape.

Modern technology has taken away some of the romance associated with the computer mystique. Today's computers don't have hundreds of multicolored blinking lights and swirling tapes. In the photo, eight traditional tape drives are compared to eight modern tape drives. The much smaller high-density tape cartridges used in modern tape processing can store 200 million characters each, about 20 percent more than a 10½-inch tape reel.

Courtesy of International Business Machines Corporation

A tape drive is rated by the **density** at which the data can be stored on a magnetic tape as well as by the speed of the tape as it passes under the read/write head. Combined, these determine the **transfer rate**, or the number of characters per second that can be transmitted to primary storage. Tape density is measured in **bytes per inch** (**bpi**) or the number of bytes (characters) that can be stored per linear inch of tape. Tape density varies from 800 to 20,000 bpi. A 6,250-bpi tape traveling under the read/write head at 300 inches per second is capable of a transfer rate of 1,875,000 characters per second.

Like magnetic disks, tapes come in a wide variety of shapes and storage capacities. All micros and a growing number of mainframe computers use some type of tape cassette. A single tape cassette can store from 20M to 60M bytes. **Magnetic tape reels** with capacities of up to 180M bytes continue to be popular in the mainframe environment, but reels are being phased out in favor of the more convenient tape cassettes.

OPTICAL LASER DISKS Some industry analysts have predicted that **optical laser disk** technology, now in its infancy stage of development, may eventually make magnetic disk and tape storage obsolete. With this technology, the read/write head of magnetic storage is replaced with two lasers, one for read and one for write operations. Optical laser disks for micros are *write once/read only*. That is, once the data have been written to the medium, they can only be read, not updated or changed. Nevertheless, because the storage capacity of optical laser disks is many times that of a hard disk, there are many applications for this technology.

We may be approaching the technological limits of magnetic data storage. When this happens, sophisticated optics and lasers (light amplification by stimulated emission of radiation) may help to take up the slack. A single CD ROM disk can hold the equivalent of 13,000 images, 250,000 pages of text, or 1,500 floppy disks. CD ROM disks can be used with personal computers, minis, or mainframes because the manufacturing standard ensures that all CD ROM readers will be compatible with all CD ROM disks.

Philips and DuPont Optical Company

The actual optical laser disks storage media comes in three formats, 5-inch **CD ROM disk** (compact disk read-only memory) and the 8- and 12-inch **video disk**. *CD ROM readers* and *video disk readers* permit random access to the data or images stored on CD ROM and video disks, respectively. One vendor markets a CD ROM disk that contains the entire text of a 20-volume set of encyclopedias. The disk contains an index that enables users to access the text by key word. Another vendor markets a video disk that contains images of the great works of art over the last four centuries. Video disk readers are usually used in conjunction with very high resolution monitors that can display images with a clarity that approaches that of a color photo in a magazine.

Important Terms

access arm	magnetic tape reel
access time	microdisk
alphanumeric keyboard	monitor
bytes per inch (bpi)	mouse
CD ROM disk	near-letter-quality (NLQ)
CD ROM reader	optical laser disk
cathode-ray tube	optical scanners
character printer	page printer
characters per second (cps)	pages per minute (ppm)
cursor	pen plotter
daisy-wheel printer	peripheral devices
density	pixel
desktop laser printer	RAM portable data entry
digitizing tablet and pen	random access
direct access	random processing
disk address	read/write head
diskette	resolution
dot-matrix printer	RF modulator
fixed disk	RGB monitors
flat panel monitor	secondary storage
flexible disk	sector organization
floppy disk	sequential access
hard copy	sequential processing
hard disk	smart card
ink-jet printer	soft copy
joystick	special-function key
magnetic disk drive	speech synthesizers
magnetic ink character recognition (MICR)	tape cassette
	10-key pad
magnetic stripe	terminal
magnetic tape drive	thermal printer
track	voice data entry
transfer rate	voice recognition
video disk	Winchester disk
video disk reader	workstation
video display terminal (VDT)	

Review Exercises

1. List devices, other than key-driven, that are used to input source data to a computer system.

2. Name two types of impact printers and two types of non-impact printers.

3. A program issues a "read" command for data to be retrieved from a magnetic tape. Describe the resulting movement of the data.

4. Give at least one alternative name for each of the following: a personal computer, direct processing, a hard disk, and a diskette.

5. What component of a disk drive is positioned over a disk track for the purpose of reading or writing data to the disk?

6. Which monitor has the higher resolution, one with 65,000 pixels or one with 250,000 pixels?

7. What output device converts raw data to electronically produced speech?

Self-Test

1. Input devices translate data to a form that can be interpreted by a computer. (T/F)

2. The primary function of I/O peripherals is to facilitate computer-to-computer data transmission. (T/F)

3. The input device that is rolled over a desktop to move the cursor is called a joystick. (T/F)

4. The quality of output on a workstation's monitor is determined by its _____.

5. The _____ card contains a tiny microprocessor.

6. Ink-jet printers are classified as impact printers. (T/F)

7. All magnetic disks have both _____ and _____ access capabilities.

8. In a disk drive, the read/write head is mounted on an access arm. (T/F)

SELF-TEST ANSWERS 1. T; 2. F; 3. F; 4. resolution; 5. smart; 6. F; 7. random, sequential; 8. T

MODULE D

Software Concepts

Programming and Software

In Modules A, B, and C, discussions centered on computer hardware. But computer hardware is useless without **software**, and software is useless without hardware. This module and Module E, "Programming Concepts and Languages," address the topic of software.

A computer system does nothing until directed to do so. A **program**, which consists of instructions to the computer, is the means by which we tell a computer to perform certain operations. These instructions are logically sequenced and assembled through the act of **programming**. **Programmers** use a variety of **programming languages**, such as COBOL and BASIC, to communicate instructions to the computer.

We use the term "software" to refer to the programs that direct the activities of the computer system. Software falls into two general categories: applications and systems. **Applications software** is designed and written to perform specific personal, business, or scientific processing tasks, such as payroll processing, order entry, or financial analysis. **Systems software** is more general than is applications software and is usually independent of any specific application area. The *operating system* is classified as systems software.

The Operating System

Just as the processor is the nucleus of the computer system, the **operating system** is the nucleus of all software activity. The operating system is a family of systems software programs that are usually, though not always, supplied by the computer system vendor. Although microcomputer and mainframe operating systems ultimately perform similar functions, they are conceptually quite different. The micro user has frequent interaction with the operating system. In the mainframe environment, the operating system is used almost exclusively by MIS professionals and is transparent to the end user. Because of these differences, micro and mainframe operating systems are discussed separately.

Microcomputer Operating Systems

Some of the more popular micro operating systems are **MS-DOS**, **Operating System/2 (OS/2)**, and **UNIX**. Microsoft Corporation's MS-DOS is the base operating system for the IBM PC series of computers, the IBM Personal System/2 (PS/2) series of computers, and IBM PC-compatibles. The high end of the IBM PS/2 series also uses OS/2, a more user-friendly operating system. Unix is popular with micros running in a multiuser environment. You

may encounter spin-offs of these operating systems. Unfortunately, the logic, structure, and nomenclature of the different operating systems vary considerably. This makes it difficult for an end user to maintain competence in more than one operating system.

All hardware, software, and input/output are controlled by the operating system. One of the family of operating system programs is always *resident* in RAM during processing. For example, an MS-DOS program, called COMMAND.COM, loads other operating system and applications programs into RAM as they are needed or as directed by you, the user.

Besides controlling the ongoing operation of the microcomputer systems, the operating system has two other important functions.

- □ *Input/output control.* The operating system facilitates the movement of data between peripheral devices, the processor, RAM, and programs.
- □ *File and disk management.* The operating system and its file and disk management utility programs enable users to perform such tasks as making backup copies of work disks, erasing disk files that are no longer needed, making inquiries about the number and type of files on a particular diskette, and preparing new diskettes for use. The operating system also handles many file- and disk-oriented tasks that are transparent to the end user. For example, the operating system keeps track of the physical location of disk files so that we, as users, need only to refer to them by name (such as myfile) when loading them from disk to memory.

Before you can use a microcomputer, you must load the operating system, or **boot** the system. The procedure for booting the system on most micros is simply to load the operating system from disk storage into random access memory. In most micros, this is no more difficult than inserting the operating system disk in a disk drive, closing the disk drive door, and flipping the switch on. On micros with hard disks, all you have to do is turn on the system, and the operating system is automatically loaded from the hard disk to RAM.

Mainframe Operating Systems

Mainframe operating systems are vastly more complex than micro operating systems in that they must be capable of controlling many devices with substantially greater capabilities, and they must be able to accommodate from 10 to thousands of end users simultaneously.

DESIGN OBJECTIVES Like micro operating systems, mainframe operating systems vary considerably in design; however, each is designed with the same three objectives in mind:

1. Minimize turnaround time (elapsed time between submittal of a job, for example, print payroll checks, and receipt of output).

2. Maximize **throughput** (amount of processing per unit time).

3. Optimize the use of the computer system resources (processor, primary storage, and peripheral devices).

THE SUPERVISOR The operating system program that is always resident in primary storage (see Figure D–1) is called the **supervisor**. The supervisor loads other operating system and applications programs to primary storage as they are needed. For example, when you request the execution of a particular applications program, the supervisor loads the program from disk storage to primary storage for processing.

ALLOCATING COMPUTER RESOURCES In a typical mainframe computer system, several jobs will be executing at the same time. The operating system determines which computer system resources are allo-

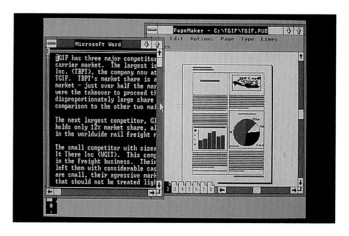

For occasional users, operating system commands can be difficult to learn and use. There are, however, programs that provide users with a user-friendly interface between the operating system, applications software, and user files. The term "operating environment" is sometimes used to describe the use of such an interface. Microsoft's Windows, shown here, permits an operating environment.

Microsoft Corporation

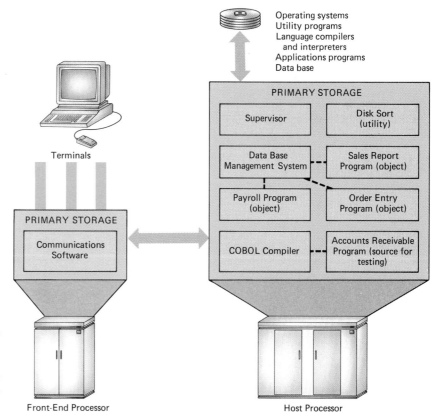

FIGURE D–1 Software, Storage, and Execution
The supervisor program is always resident in primary storage and calls other programs, as needed, from secondary storage. For example, applications programs rely on data base management system software to assist in the retrieval of data from secondary storage. Software in the front-end processor handles data communications-related tasks.

cated to which programs. As an example, suppose that a computer system with only one printer has three jobs whose output is ready to be printed. Obviously, two must wait. The operating system continuously resolves this type of resource conflict to optimize the allocation of computer resources.

OPERATOR INTERACTION The operating system is in continuous interaction with computer operators. The incredible speed of a mainframe computer system dictates that resource allocation decisions be made at computer speeds. Most of these decisions are made automatically by the operating system. For decisions requiring human input, the operating system interrogates the operators through the operator console. The operating system also sends messages to the operator. A common message is "Printer no. 1 is out of paper."

COMPATIBILITY CONSIDERATIONS Applications programs are not as portable between operating systems as we would like. This is true for both micros and mainframes. Therefore, programs that work well under one operating system may not be compatible with a different operating system.

Multiprogramming

All computers, except small micros, have **multiprogramming** capability. Multiprogramming is the *seemingly simultaneous execution* of more than one program at a time. A computer can execute only one program at a time. But the internal processing speed of a computer is so fast that several programs can be allocated a "slice" of computer time in rotation; this makes it appear to us that several programs are being executed at once.

The great difference between processor speed and the speeds of the peripheral devices makes multiprogramming possible. A 40,000-line-per-minute printer cannot even challenge the speed of an average mainframe processor. The processor is continually waiting for the peripheral devices to complete such tasks as retrieving a record from disk storage, printing a report, or copying a backup file onto magnetic tape. During these "wait" periods, the processor just continues processing other programs. In this way, computer system resources are used efficiently.

In a multiprogramming environment, it is not unusual for several programs to require the same I/O device. For example, two or more programs may be competing for the printer. Rather than hold up the processing of a program by waiting for the printer to become available, both programs are executed, and the printer output for one is temporarily loaded to magnetic disk. As the printer becomes available, the output is called from magnetic disk and printed. This process is called **spooling**.

Virtual Memory

In Module B, "Inside the Computer," the point is made that all data and programs must be resident in primary storage to be processed. Therefore, primary storage is a critical factor in determining the throughput, or how much work can be done by a computer system per unit of time. Once primary storage becomes full, no more programs can be executed until a portion of primary storage is made available.

Virtual memory is a systems software addition to the operating system that effectively expands the capacity of primary storage through the use of software and secondary storage. This allows more data and programs to be resident in primary storage at any given time.

The principle behind virtual memory is quite simple. Remember, a program is executed sequentially—one instruction after another. Programs are segmented into **pages**, so only that a portion of the program being executed (one or more pages) is resident in primary storage. The rest of the program is on disk storage. Appropriate pages are *rolled* (moved) into primary storage from disk storage as they are needed to continue execution of the program. The paging process and use of virtual memory is illustrated graphically in Figure D–2.

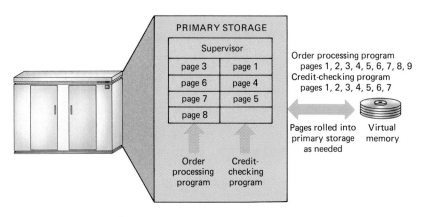

FIGURE D–2   Virtual Memory
Pages of the order processing and credit-checking programs are rolled from virtual memory on disk into "real" memory (primary storage) as they are needed.

The advantage of virtual memory is that primary storage is effectively enlarged, giving programmers greater flexibility in what they can do. For example, some applications require several large programs to be resident in primary storage at the same time (such as the order processing and credit-checking programs illustrated in Figure D–2). If the size of these programs exceeds the capacity of "real" primary storage, then virtual memory can be used as a supplement to complete the processing.

Important Terms

applications software	programming
boot	programming language
MS-DOS	software
multiprogramming	spooling
operating system	supervisor
Operating System/2 (OS/2)	systems software
pages	throughput
program	UNIX
programmer	virtual memory

Review Exercises

1. What are the two general categories of software? Give an example of each.

2. Which MS-DOS program is always resident in RAM during processing?

3. List the three design objectives for mainframe computer-based operating systems.

4. Why is it necessary to spool output in a multiprogramming environment?

Self-Test

1. Software that is designed and written to perform specific personal, business, or scientific processing tasks is called _____ .

2. One of the functions of a microcomputer operating system is input/output control. (T/F)

3. The _____ is the nucleus for all software activity.

4. The operating system program that is always resident in the primary storage of a mainframe computer is called the supervisor. (T/F)

5. Programs are segmented into pages before they are spooled. (T/F)

SELF-TEST ANSWERS 1. applications software; 2. T; 3. operating system; 4. T; 5. F

MODULE E
Programming Concepts and Languages

Concepts and Principles of Programming

A computer program is made up of a sequence of instructions that are executed one after another. These instructions, also called **statements**, are executed in sequence unless the order of execution is altered by a "test-on-condition" instruction or a "branch" instruction. The purpose of this section is to familiarize you with the general types of programming instructions that would be found in any procedure-oriented programming language. Each language has an instruction set with at least one instruction in each of the following *instruction classifications:* input/output, computation, control, data transfer and assignment, and format.

INPUT/OUTPUT Input/output instructions direct the computer to "read from" or "write to" a peripheral device (for example, printer, disk drive). For example, a READ EMPLOYEE instruction in a payroll program might request that an employee record, including pay data, be read from the data base. The instruction WRITE EMPLOYEE might cause an updated record to be written to disk storage.

COMPUTATION Computation instructions perform arithmetic operations (add, subtract, multiply, divide, and raise a number to a power). For example, the instruction PAY = HOURS * RATE computes gross earnings for hourly employees.

CONTROL (DECISION AND/OR BRANCH) Control instructions can alter the sequence of the program's execution. *Unconditional* and *conditional instructions* prompt a decision and, perhaps, a branch to another part of the program or to a subroutine. For example, in a payroll program, a conditional instruction such as IF SALARY-CODE = HOURLY THEN PERFORM HOURLY-PROCEDURE would cause processing to branch to that part of the program that computes wages for hourly employees. An unconditional branch instruction might be GOTO FINISH.

DATA TRANSFER AND ASSIGNMENT Data can be transferred internally from one primary storage location to another. In procedure-oriented languages, data are transferred or "moved" by *assignment instructions*. These instructions permit a *string constant*, also called a *literal value*, such as "The net pay is", or a *numeric value*, such as 234, to be assigned to a named primary storage location.

In a program, a primary storage location is represented by a **variable name** (for example, PAY, HOURS, NET). A variable name in a program statement refers to the contents of a particular primary storage location. For example, a programmer may use the variable name HOURS in a computation statement to refer to the numeric value of the *hours worked* by a particular employee.

FORMAT Format instructions are used in conjunction with input and output instructions; they describe how the data are to be entered or output from primary storage. On output, format instructions position headings on reports, line up columns of data, edit output (for example, 23456 becomes $23,456.00), and, generally, present data in a readable format.

With these few types of instructions, you can model almost any business or scientific procedure, be it sales forecasting or guiding rockets to the moon.

Generations of Programming Languages

We "talk" to computers within the framework of a particular programming language. There are many different programming languages, most of which have highly structured sets of rules. The selection of a programming language depends on who is involved and the nature of "conversation." The president of a company may prefer a different type of language than that preferred by a professional programmer; languages used for payroll processing may not be appropriate for ad hoc (one-time) inquiries.

Like computers, programming languages have evolved in generations. With each new generation, fewer instructions are needed to instruct the computer to perform a particular task. That is, a program written in a first-generation language that computes the total sales for each sales representative and then lists those over quota, may require 100 or more instructions; the same program in a fourth-generation language may have fewer than 10 instructions.

The hierarchy of programming languages, shown in Figure E–1, illustrates the relationships between the various generations of programming languages. The later **high-level languages** (third and later generations) do not necessarily provide us with greater programming capabilities, but they do provide a *more sophisticated programmer/computer interaction*. In short, each new generation is easier to understand and use. For example, in the fourth generation languages, we need only instruct the computer system *what*

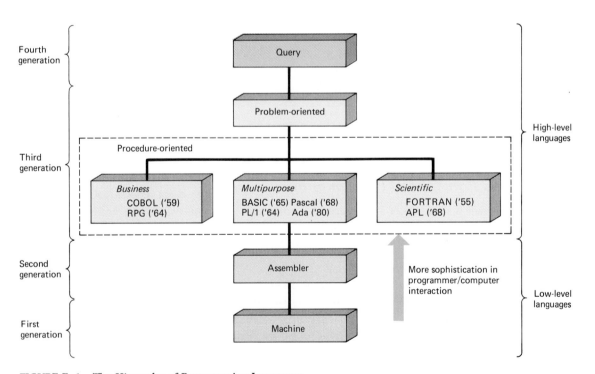

FIGURE E–1 The Hierarchy of Programming Languages
As you progress from one generation of programming languages to the next, fewer instructions are required to perform a particular programming task.

to do, not necessarily *how to do it*. When programming in one of the first three generations of languages, you have to tell the computer what to do *and* how to do it.

The ease with which the later generations can be used is certainly appealing, but the earlier languages also have their advantages. All generations of languages are in use today. According to a recent survey of companies that use IBM mainframe computers, approximately three-fourths of their applications programs are developed with third-generation languages. Fourth-generation languages account for 14 percent of the development effort and first- and second-generation languages account for 6 percent. The remaining 4 percent falls in the "other" category. The trend, however, is to greater use of fourth-generation languages, also called **4GLs**, and other very high-level languages.

First-, second-, and third-generation languages are discussed and illustrated in this module. Very high-level languages, such as 4GLs, are introduced in Chapter 6, "End User Computing," and illustrated in Chapter 13, "Prototyping and Applications Development Tools."

First- And Second-Generation Languages

Machine Language

Each computer has only one programming language that can be executed—the **machine language**. We talk of programming in COBOL, Pascal, and BASIC, but all these languages must be translated to the machine language of the computer on which the program is to be executed. These and other high-level languages are simply a convenience for the programmer.

Machine-language programs, the *first generation*, are written at the most basic level of computer operation. Because their instructions are directed at this basic level of operation, machine language and assembler language (discussed next) are collectively called **low-level languages**. In machine language, instructions are coded as a series of 1's and 0's. As you might expect, machine-language programs are cumbersome and difficult to write. Early programmers had no alternative. Fortunately, we do.

Assembler Language

A set of instructions for an **assembler language** is essentially one to one with those of a machine language. Like machine languages, assembler languages are unique to a particular computer. The big difference between the two types is the way the instructions are represented by the programmer. Rather than a cumbersome series of 1's and 0's, assembler languages use easily recognized symbols, called **mnemonics**, to represent instructions (see Figure E–2). For example, most assembler languages use the mnemonic "MUL" to represent a "Multiply" instruction. The assembler languages ushered in the *second generation* of programming languages.

Compilers and Interpreters

No matter which high-level language a program is written in, it must be translated to machine language before it can be executed. This conversion of high-level instructions to machine-level instructions is done by systems software programs called *compilers* and *interpreters*.

Compilers

The **compiler** program translates the instructions of a high-level language, such as COBOL, to machine-language instructions that the computer can interpret and execute. A separate compiler (or an interpreter, discussed in the next section) is required for each programming language intended for use on a particular computer system. That is, to execute a COBOL and a Pascal program, you must have a COBOL compiler and a Pascal compiler. High-level programming languages are simply a programmer convenience; they cannot be executed in their source, or original, form.

The actual high-level programming-language instructions, called the **source program**, are translated or **compiled** to machine-language instructions, called an **object program**, by a compiler. It is the compiled object program that is executed by the computer.

```
COMP$PAY        PROC PUBLIC
;
;       COMP$PAY - procedure to compute gross pay (PAY = HOURS * RATE)
;
        MOV     AX,HOURS              ;multiplicand
        MUL     RATE+2                ;  times second word of multiplier
        MOV     PAY+2,AX              ;store the product in PAY
;
        MOV     AX,HOURS              ;multiplicand
        MUL     RATE                  ;  times first word of multiplier
        ADD     PAY+2,AX              ;add the product to PAY
        ADC     PAY,DX                ;add the carry, if any
        RET                           ;end procedure
COMP$PAY        ENDP
```

FIGURE E–2   An Assembler Program Procedure
These assembler instructions compute PAY by multiplying the number of HOURS times the RATE.

Interpreters

An **interpreter** is a systems software program that ultimately performs the same function as a compiler—but in a different manner. Instead of translating the entire source program in a single pass, an interpreter translates and executes each source program instruction before translating and executing the next.

Third-Generation Languages

A quantum leap in programmer convenience accompanied the introduction of the *third generation* of programming languages. A third-generation language is placed in one of two categories: **procedure-oriented languages** or **problem-oriented languages** (review Figure E–1).

Procedure-Oriented Languages

The flexibility of procedure-oriented languages permits programmers to model almost any scientific or business procedure. Instructions are **coded**, or written, sequentially and processed according to program specifications.

Unless triggered by program logic to do otherwise, the processor selects and executes instructions in the sequence in which they are written. In a production payroll system, for example, a particular sequence of program instructions is executed for each salaried employee; another sequence is executed for each hourly employee.

Procedure-oriented languages are classified as *business, scientific,* or *multipurpose*. These are illustrated in Figure E–1 and are discussed in the paragraphs that follow.

BUSINESS LANGUAGES Business programming languages are designed to be effective tools for developing business information systems. The strength of business-oriented languages lies in their ability to store, retrieve, and manipulate alphanumeric data.

The arithmetic requirements of most business systems are minimal. Although sophisticated mathematical manipulation is possible, it is cumbersome to achieve, so it is best left to scientific languages.

COBOL. **COBOL**, the first business programming language, was introduced in 1959. It remains the most popular. The original intent of the developers of COBOL (*Common Business Oriented Language*) was to make its instructions approximate the English language. Here is a typical COBOL *sentence*: "IF SALARY-CODE IS EQUAL TO H' MULTIPLY SALARY BY HOURLY-RATE GIVING GROSS-PAY ELSE PERFORM SALARIED-EMPLOYEE-ROUTINE." Note that the sentence contains several instructions and even a period.

The American National Standards Institute (ANSI) has established standards for COBOL and other languages. The purpose of these standards is to make COBOL programs *portable*. A program is said to be portable if it can be run on a variety of computers. Unfortunately, the ANSI standards are followed only casually; consequently, it is unlikely that a COBOL program written for a DEC computer, for example, can be executed on a Data General computer without some modification.

Figure E–3 illustrates a COBOL program that computes gross pay for hourly wage earners. Notice that the program is divided into four divisions: identification, environment, data, and procedure. The procedure division contains the logic of the program;

```
0100 IDENTIFICATION DIVISION.
0200 PROGRAM-ID.            PAYPROG.
0300 REMARKS.              PROGRAM TO COMPUTE GROSS PAY.
0400 ENVIRONMENT DIVISION.
0500 DATA DIVISION.
0600 WORKING-STORAGE SECTION.
0700 01 PAY-DATA.
0800      05 HOURS        PIC 99V99.
0900      05 RATE         PIC 99V99.
1000      05 PAY          PIC 9999V99.
1100 01 LINE-1.
1200      03 FILLER       PIC X(5)      VALUE SPACES.
1300      03 FILLER       PIC X(12)     VALUE "GROSS PAY IS ".
1400      03 GROSS-PAY    PIC $$$9.99.
1500 01 PRINT-LINE.        PIC X(27).
1600 PROCEDURE DIVISION.
1700 MAINLINE-PROCEDURE.
1800      PERFORM ENTER-PAY.
1900      PERFORM COMPUTE-PAY.
2000      PERFORM PRINT-PAY.
2100      STOP RUN.
2200 ENTER-PAY.
2300      DISPLAY "ENTER HOURS AND RATE OF PAY".
2400      ACCEPT HOURS, RATE.
2500 COMPUTE-PAY.
2600      MULTIPLY HOURS BY RATE GIVING PAY ROUNDED.
2700 PRINT-PAY.
2800      MOVE PAY TO GROSS-PAY.
2900      MOVE LINE-1 TO PRINT-LINE.
3000      DISPLAY PRINT-LINE.
```

FIGURE E–3   A COBOL Program
This COBOL program accepts the number of hours worked and the pay rate for an hourly wage earner, then computes and displays the gross pay amount. The resultant input/output is shown in an interactive session.

```
Enter hours and rate of pay
43, 8.25
    Gross pay is $354.75
```

that is, the sequence of instructions that instructs the computer to accept, process, and display data.

For the purpose of comparison, the COBOL program in Figure E–3 and all other examples of third-generation programs (Figures E–4 through E–7) are written to perform the same input, processing, and output activities: compute gross pay for hourly wage earners. The interactive session (see Figure E–3) is the same for all these programs.

RPG. **RPG** (*Report Program Generator*) was originally developed in 1964 for IBM's entry-level punched-card business computers and for the express purpose of generating reports. As punched cards went the way of vacuum tubes, RPG remained—evolving from a special-purpose problem-oriented language to a general-purpose procedure-oriented language. Its name has made RPG the most misunderstood of the programming languages. People who do not know RPG still associate it with report generation when, in fact, it has become a powerful programming language that matured with the demands of RPG users.

RPG has always differed somewhat from other procedure-oriented languages in that the programmer specifies certain processing requirements by selecting the desired programming options. That is, during a programming session, the programmer is presented with *prompting formats* at the bottom of the workstation screen. The programmer requests the prompts for a particular type of instruction and then responds with the desired programming specifications.

SCIENTIFIC LANGUAGES   Scientific languages are algebraic/formula-type languages. These are specifically designed to meet typical scientific processing requirements, such as matrix manipulation, precision calculations, iterative processing, the expression and resolution of mathematical equations, and so on. For example, engineers and actuaries turn to scientific languages when writing programs for statistical analysis.

FORTRAN. **FORTRAN** (*For*mula *Trans*lator), the first procedure-oriented language, was developed in 1955. It was, and it remains, the most popular scientific language. The FORTRAN program in Figure E–4 performs the same processing functions as the COBOL program in Figure E–3.

APL. **APL** (*A Programming Language*), introduced in 1968, is a symbolic interactive programming language that is popular with engineers, mathematicians, and scientists. A special keyboard with "shorthand" symbols helps to speed the coding process.

MULTIPURPOSE LANGUAGES   Multipurpose languages are equally effective for both business and scientific applications. These languages are an outgrowth of the need to simplify the programming environment by providing programmers with one language that is capable of addressing all of a company's programming needs.

BASIC. **BASIC**, developed in 1964, is the primary language supported by millions of personal computers. BASIC is also used extensively on mainframe computer systems, primarily for one-time "quick and dirty" programs.

BASIC is perhaps the easiest third-generation language to learn and use (see Figure E–5). It is commonly used for both scientific and business applications—and even for developing video games. The widespread use of BASIC attests to the versatility of its features. In fact, BASIC is the only programming language that is supported on virtually every computer.

```
         program payprog
c
c        payprog        - Program to compute the pay for an employee,
c                         given hours worked and the employee's pay rate.
c
         real hours, rate, pay               !define the variables
c
         write(6,1)                          !input prompt
1        format(1H,'Enter hours and rate of pay')
         read(5,*) hours, rate               !accept hours & pay rate
         pay = hours * rate                  !compute pay
         write(6,2) pay                      !display gross pay
2        format(1H,5X,'Gross pay is $',F7.2)
         end
```

FIGURE E–4   A FORTRAN Program
This FORTRAN program accepts the number of hours worked and the pay rate for an hourly wage earner, then computes and displays the gross pay amount. The resultant interactive session is the same as that of Figure E–3.

FIGURE E–5   A BASIC Program
This BASIC program accepts the number of hours worked and the pay rate for an hourly wage earner, then computes and displays the gross pay amount. The resultant interactive session is the same as that of Figure E–3.

```
100 REM payprog              Program to compute the pay for an employee,
110 REM                      given hours worked and the employee's pay rate.
120 REM
130 PRINT "Enter hours and rate of pay"      'input prompt
140 INPUT HOURS, RATE                        'accept hours & pay rate
150 LET PAY = HOURS * RATE                    'compute pay
160 PRINT TAB(5);"Gross pay is $";PAY         'display gross pay
170 END
```

Pascal. During the last decade, **Pascal**, named after the seventeenth-century French mathematician Blaise Pascal, has experienced tremendous growth. Introduced in 1968, Pascal is considered the state of the art among widely used procedure-oriented languages (see Figure E–6).

Pascal's power, flexibility, and self-documenting structure have made it the language of choice in many computer science curriculums and for many developers of systems software. Currently, only 1 to 2 percent of the business system programs are written in Pascal, but it is enjoying a growing acceptance in the business community.

C. The results of a recent employment survey showed **C** programmers to be in the greatest demand. Developers of proprietary packaged software are very interested in C because it is considered more transportable than other languages. That is, it is relatively machine independent: a C program written for one type of computer (see Figure E–7) can be run on another type with little or no modification.

PL/I. **PL/I** (*Programming Language/I*), introduced in 1964, was hailed as the answer to many of the shortcomings of existing programming languages, such as COBOL and FORTRAN. It has not, however, won the acceptance that was originally anticipated, but it is widely used.

Ada. **Ada** is the most recent and perhaps the most sophisticated procedure-oriented language. Ada is a multipurpose language developed for the U.S. Department of Defense. The language was named to honor the nineteenth-century pioneer, Lady Augusta Ada Lovelace, considered by some to be the first programmer. Ada developers are optimistic that as more people begin to study it, Ada will gain widespread acceptance not only in the military but in the private sector as well.

Problem-Oriented Languages

A problem-oriented language is designed to address a particular application area or to solve a particular set of problems. Problem-oriented languages do not require the programming detail of procedure-oriented ones. The emphasis of problem-oriented languages is more on *input and the desired output* than on the *procedures or mathematics involved.*

Problem-oriented languages have been designed for scores of applications: simulation (for example, GPSS, SLAM), programming machine tools (for example, APT), and analysis of stress points in buildings and bridges (for example, COGO).

```
program payprog(input,output);
{       Program to compute the pay for an employee,
        given hours worked and the employee's pay rate. }

var     hours, rate, pay : real;                (define the variables)

begin
  writeln(output,'Enter hours and rate of pay');   (input prompt)
  readln(input,hours,rate);                    (accept hours & pay rate)
  pay := hours * rate;                         (compute pay)
  writeln(output,'     Gross pay is $',pay:0:2) (display gross pay)
end.
```

FIGURE E–6   A Pascal Program
This Pascal program accepts the number of hours worked and the pay rate for an hourly wage earner, then computes and displays the gross pay amount. The resultant interactive session is the same as that of Figure E–3.

```
/*      payprog.c     - Program to compute the pay for an employee,
                        given hours worked and the employee's pay rate. */

main()
{
        float hours, rate, pay;                 /* define the
                                                   variables used */
        printf("Enter hours and rate of pay\n"); /* input prompt */
        scanf("%f %f", &hours, &rate);          /* accept hours
                                                   and pay rate */
        pay = hours * rate;                     /* compute pay */
        printf("\tGross pay is $%.2f\n",pay);   /* print gross pay */
}
```

FIGURE E–7   A C-Language Program
This C program accepts the number of hours worked and the pay rate for an hourly wage earner, then computes and displays the gross pay amount. The resultant interactive session is the same as that of Figure E–3.

Important Terms

Ada	low-level languages
APL	machine language
assembler language	mnemonics
BASIC	numeric value
C	object program
COBOL	PL/I
coded	Pascal
compiled	problem-oriented languages
compiler	procedure-oriented
FORTRAN	languages
4GLs (fourth-generation	RPG
languages)	source program
high-level languages	statements
interpreter	string constant
literal value	variable name

Review Exercises

1. Associate each of the following with a particular generation of languages: 4GLs, mnemonics, and Ada.

2. Name a procedure-oriented programming language in each of the three classification areas: business, scientific, and multipurpose.

3. What are the programs called that translate source programs to machine language? Which one does the translation on a single pass? Which one does it one statement at a time?

4. What are the four divisions of a COBOL program?

5. Which third-generation scientific language uses a special keyboard with "shorthand" symbols?

6. Which multipurpose language was developed for the U.S. Department of Defense?

Self-Test

1. A source program in a third-generation language is compiled to create an _____ program.

2. Assembler-level languages use mnemonics to represent instructions. (T/F)

3. A fourth-generation program will normally have fewer instructions than will the same program written in a third-generation language. (T/F)

4. The type of programming instruction that permits data to be transferred internally from one primary storage location to another is the _____ instruction.

5. Only the first two generations of programming languages would be classified as procedure-oriented languages. (T/F)

6. Each computer has only one programming language that can be executed. (T/F)

SELF-TEST ANSWERS   1. object; 2. T; 3. T; 4. assignment; 5. F; 6. T

MODULE F
Design Techniques Overview

Systems analysts, programmers, and users employ a variety of techniques to assist them in the design and documentation of an information system. This module introduces you to a representative sample of commonly used techniques. Included in the overview are *data flow diagrams, flowcharting, HIPO, SADT, Warnier-Orr, pseudocode,* and *decision tables.*

Data Flow Diagrams

Data flow diagrams, or **DFDs**, encourage analysts and programmers to examine the system from the top down (that is, from the general to the specific). The result is a more structured design. DFDs use the four symbols illustrated in Figure F–1 (entity, process, flow line, and data store) to document the system at several levels

of generality. DFD concepts are discussed in Chapter 12, "Systems Analysis and Programming," and the application of DFDs is illustrated in Chapter 15, "An MIS Case Study."

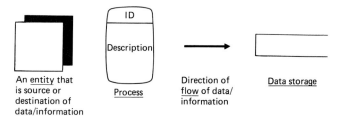

An **entity** that is source or destination of data/information

Process

Direction of **flow** of data/information

Data storage

FIGURE F–1   Data Flow Diagram Symbols

Flowcharting

In **flowcharting**, **flowcharts** are used to illustrate data, information, and work flow through the interconnection of *specialized symbols* with *flow lines*. The combination of symbols and flow lines portrays the logic of the program or system.

Flowcharting Symbols

Each symbol indicates the *type of operation to be performed*, and the flowchart graphically illustrates the *sequence in which the operations are to be performed*. The more commonly used flowchart symbols are shown in Figure F–2 and discussed here.

□ *Computer process* symbols (rectangles) signify some type of process. The process could be as specific as "compute net pay" (in a program flowchart) or as general as "produce payroll checks and register" (in a system flowchart).

□ *Predefined process* symbols (rectangles with extra vertical lines) are a special case of the process symbol. The predefined process refers to a group of operations that may be detailed in a separate flowchart.

□ *Input/output* symbols (parallelograms) refer generally to any type of input to, or output from, the program or system.

□ *Decision* symbols (diamond shaped) mark the points at which decisions are to be made. In a program flowchart, a

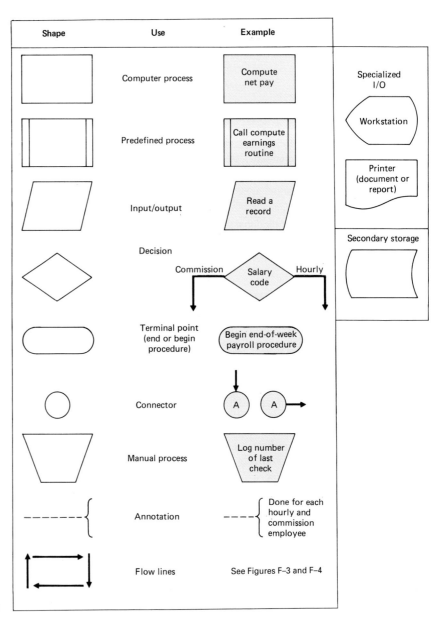

FIGURE F–2 Flowchart Symbols

particular set of instructions is executed based on the outcome of a decision. For example, in a payroll program, gross pay is computed differently for hourly and commission employees; therefore, for each employee processed, a decision is made as to which set of instructions is to be executed.

☐ *Terminal point* symbols (ovals) are used to indicate the beginning and the end of flowcharts.

☐ *Connector* symbols (small circles) are used to break and then link flow lines. The connector symbol is often used to avoid having to cross lines.

☐ *Manual process* symbols (trapezoids) indicate that a manual process is to be performed. Contrast this with a computer process represented by a rectangle.

☐ *Bracket* symbols permit descriptive notations to be added to flowcharts.

☐ *Workstation* symbols are used to indicate output to or input from a video display terminal.

☐ *Printer* symbols denote hard-copy output.

☐ *On-line data storage* symbols are used to represent files or data bases on disk storage.

☐ *Flow lines* depict the sequential flow of the program or system logic.

These symbols are equally applicable to system and program flowcharting and can be used to develop and represent the logic for each.

System and Program Flowcharts

A **system flowchart** for a payroll system is illustrated in Figure F–3. The example system flowchart illustrates the weekly payroll

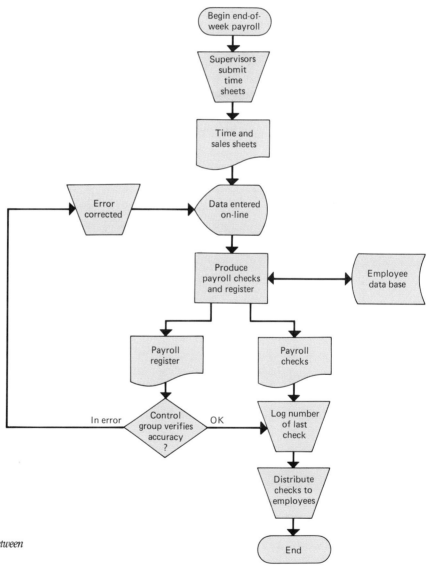

FIGURE F–3   General Systems Flowchart
This systems flowchart graphically illustrates the relationship between I/O and major processing activities in a payroll system.

process for hourly and commission employees (salary employee checks are processed monthly). Gross earnings for hourly employees are computed by multiplying hours-worked times the rate of pay. For salespeople on commission, gross earnings are computed as a percentage of sales.

Contrast the system flowchart in Figure F–3 with the **program flowchart** of Figure F–4. The example program flowchart portrays the general logic of a program to compute and print payroll checks for commission and hourly employees. In structured programming, each program has a **driver module** that causes other program modules to be executed as they are needed. The driver module for the example payroll program in Figure F–4 is a *loop* that "calls" each of the subordinate modules, or **subroutines**, as they are needed for the processing of each employee.

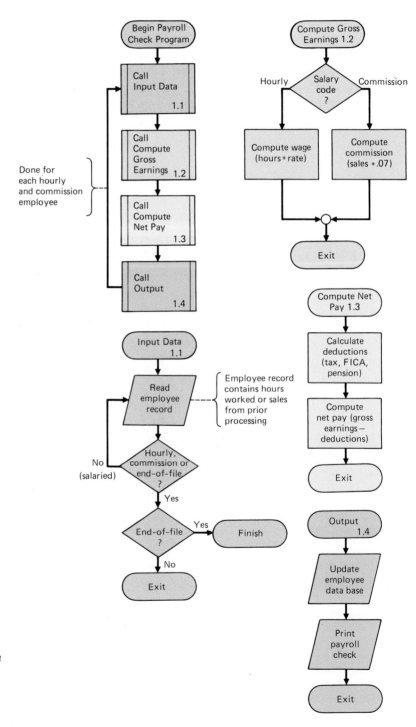

FIGURE F–4 Program Flowchart
This structured program flowchart portrays the logic of a program to compute and print payroll checks for commission and hourly employees. The logic is designed so that a driver module calls subroutines as they are needed to process each employee.

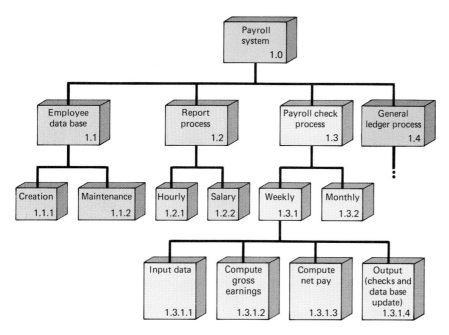

FIGURE F–5 HIPO Structure Chart
This structure chart breaks a payroll system down into a hierarchy of modules.

The program is designed such that when the payroll program is initiated, the "input data" module (1.1) is executed, or "performed" first. After execution, control is then returned to the driver module, unless there are no more employees to be processed, in which case execution is terminated (the "Finish" terminal point). For each hourly or commission employee, modules 1.2, 1.3, and 1.4 are performed, and at the completion of each subroutine, control is passed back to the driver module.

Hierarchy Plus Input-Processing-Output

Hierarchy plus input-processing-output, or **HIPO** (pronounced *HI-poe*), is a top-down design technique that permits the project team to divide the system into independent modules for ease of understanding and design. HIPO follows the "divide and conquer" line of reasoning.

HIPO has several standard forms. A *structure chart* breaks a system down into a hierarchy of modules. For example, a structure chart for a payroll system is shown in Figure F–5. In the structure chart, the system is decomposed into modules at finer levels of detail until a particular module can best be portrayed in terms of procedural logic. Eventually, the logic for each of the lowest-level modules is represented in detailed in step-by-step *overview diagrams* that illustrate the interactions between input, processing, output, and storage activities for a particular module. Figure F–6 shows an overview diagram for module 1.3.1 (weekly payroll processing) of Figure F–5.

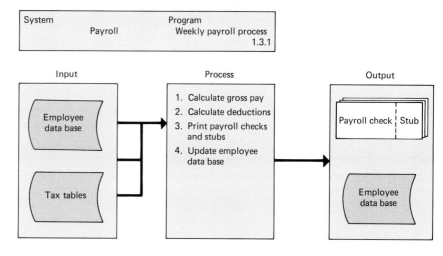

FIGURE F–6 HIPO Overview Diagram
The example overview diagram illustrates the input, processing, and output components of module 1.3.1 of Figure F–5.

Like DFDs, HIPO encourages top-down design. This advantage is, to some extent, offset by the cumbersome volume of paperwork required to document the system.

Structured Analysis and Design Technique

Structured Analysis and Design Technique, or **SADT**, is also a top-down design technique. Under SADT, a system is conceptualized as being composed of things and activities and the relationships between them. This conceptual view is described graphically using *actigrams* (activity diagrams) and *datagrams* (data diagrams).

Actigrams, which are models of the activities carried out by the system, are made up of *activity boxes* (Figure F–7). Each activity box may have input and output data, constraints that are placed upon the activity, and sources of support for the activity. The activity within a system is described by creating an SADT activity box for each procedural function in the system and combining them into an actigram (Figure F–8).

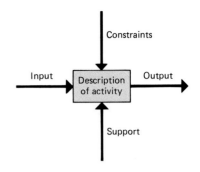

FIGURE F–7   SADT Activity Box

Datagrams are models of the data relationships within the system. The *data box* (Figure F–9) is the foundation element in the datagram. The data box contains a description of the data and indicates which activity generates the data, which activity utilizes

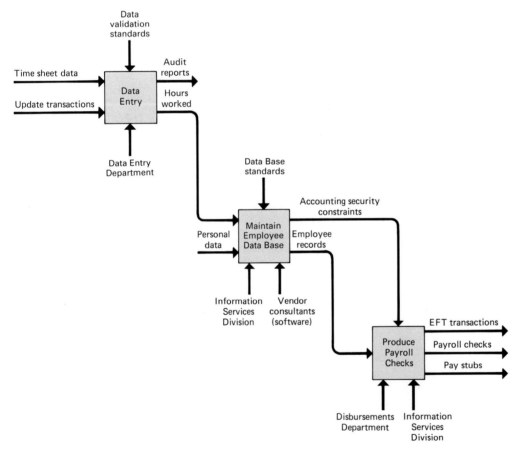

FIGURE F–8   SADT Actigram for a Payroll System
SADT actigrams are compiled by linking the activity boxes that depict the procedural functions of a payroll system.

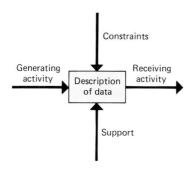

FIGURE F–9   SADT Data Box

or receives the data, and what constraints are placed on the data. The data box may also show support activities or data storage areas. Data boxes for a system are combined into a datagram in a manner similar to the way that activity boxes are combined to create an actigram.

Warnier-Orr

Warnier-Orr diagrams, which were developed in the late 1960s, can be used to design an overall system, data structure, report contents, data elements, and procedures. The premise behind the Warnier-Orr diagram is that the system should be designed around the data structures. The greatest advantage of Warnier-Orr diagrams is their applicability to a variety of circumstances. Warnier-Orr diagrams are constructed using *universals* or braces. The braces serve to illustrate the hierarchy of the data or procedure being modeled.

Warnier-Orr diagrams can illustrate several control structures. A sequence of procedures is represented by simply listing the procedures below each other. An example of this can be found in Figure F–10. In the second universal, the procedures "Produce payroll register" and "Verify accuracy of register" are performed in sequence. A *repetition* (loop) *control structure* is represented by placing the number of times to execute a procedure in parentheses under the procedure name. In the example, "Register accurate" occurs zero times or one time (0,1). A (0,n) notation indicates that the procedure may be executed 250 times if the value of n is 250. The *selection control structure*, also shown in Figure F–10, is represented by listing two conditions and an exclusive OR symbol (a circled plus sign). Note that placing a bar or line over a condition negates that condition. When expressed verbally, the selection structure in Figure F–10 becomes: "If the [payroll] register is accurate, print the payroll checks. Otherwise, if the register is not accurate, make the corrections and reverify the register."

Pseudocode

Another design technique that is used almost exclusively for program design is called **pseudocode**. While the other techniques represent the logic of the program graphically, pseudocode represents the logic in programlike statements written in plain English. Since pseudocode does not have any syntax guidelines (that is, rules for formulating instructions), you can concentrate on developing the logic of your program. Once you feel that the logic is sound, the pseudocode is easily translated to a procedure-oriented language that can be executed. In Figure F–11, the logic of a simple program is represented in pseudocode and with a flowchart.

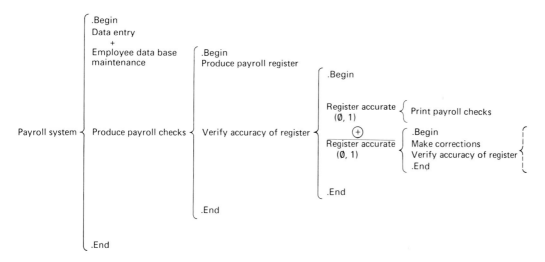

FIGURE F–10   Warnier-Orr Diagram of a Payroll System
Warnier-Orr diagrams are constructed using universals to illustrate the hierarchy of the data or procedure being modeled.

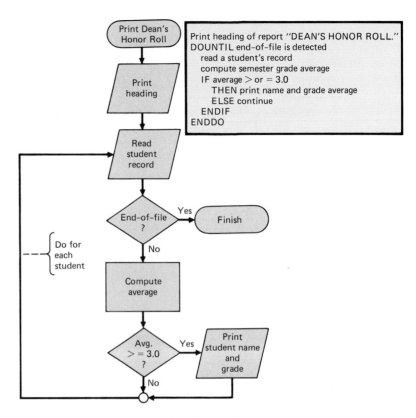

```
Print heading of report "DEAN'S HONOR ROLL."
DOUNTIL end–of–file is detected
    read a student's record
    compute semester grade average
    IF average > or = 3.0
        THEN print name and grade average
        ELSE continue
    ENDIF
ENDDO
```

FIGURE F–11   Pseudocode with Flowchart
This pseudocode program depicts the logic of a program to compile a list of students who have qualified for the dean's honor roll. The same logic is shown in a flowchart.

Decision Tables

The **decision table** is a handy tool that analysts and programmers use to depict graphically what happens in a system or program for occurrences of various circumstances. The decision table is based on "IF . . . THEN" logic. *IF* this set of conditions is met, *THEN* take this action. Decision tables are divided into quadrants (see Figure F–12). Conditions that may occur are listed in the *condition stub* (the upper left quadrant). The possible occurrences

for each condition type are noted in the *condition entries* (the upper right quadrant). Each possible set of conditions, called a *rule*, is numbered at the top of each column. Actions that can result from various combinations of conditions, or rules, are listed in the *action stub* (the lower left quadrant). For each rule, an action-to-be-taken entry is made in the *action entries* (the lower right quadrant).

The decision table in Figure F–13 illustrates what action is taken for each of several sets of conditions. For example, *IF* the employees to be processed are salaried and it is the end of the month (rule 1), *THEN* both paychecks and a payroll register are printed. *IF* the employees to be processed are on a commission and it is the end of the week (rule 4), *THEN* paychecks only are printed.

The decision table is not a good technique for illustrating work flow. It is, however, very helpful when used in conjunction with the other techniques discussed in this module. The major advantage of decision tables is that a programmer or analyst must consider *all* alternatives, options, conditions, variables, and so on. With decision tables, the level of detail is dictated by the circumstances. With flowcharts and other design techniques, the level of detail is more a matter of personal preference.

FIGURE F–12   Decision Table Format
Decision tables are divided into four quadrants: condition stub, condition entries, action stub, and action entries.

Payroll type/output chart	Rules				
	1	2	3	4	5
Salaried employee	Y	N	N	N	N
Hourly employee	N	Y	Y	N	N
Commission employee	N	N	N	Y	Y
End of week	N	Y	N	Y	N
End of month	Y	N	Y	N	Y
Print paychecks	X	X		X	X
Print payroll register	X	X	X		X

FIGURE F–13   Decision Table
This decision table depicts what payroll outputs would be generated for various payroll types and conditions.

Important Terms

actigram

action entry

action stub

condition entry

condition stub

data flow diagram (DFD)

datagram

decision table

driver module

flowchart

flowcharting

hierarchy plus input-
    processing-output (HIPO)

overview diagram

program flowchart

pseudocode

structure chart

structured analysis and
    design technique (SADT)

subroutine

system flowchart

universals

Warnier-Orr diagram

Review Questions

1. Draw the flowcharting symbols for manual process, terminal point, workstation, and decision.

2. Write a pseudocode program that represents the logic of module 1.1 (Input Data) in Figure F–4.

3. In structured programming, what is the module called that causes other program modules to be executed as they are needed?

4. Name the three control structures that can be illustrated graphically with Warnier-Orr diagrams.

5. Name four design techniques other than flowcharting.

6. What is the shape of an SADT data box? A Warnier-Orr exclusive OR? A DFD entity symbol?

Self-Test

1. Flowcharting is used primarily for program design and rarely for systems design. (T/F)

2. Warnier-Orr diagrams are constructed using braces, or _____ .

3. Actigrams and datagrams are integral to the preparation of data flow diagrams. (T/F)

4. SADT, HIPO, and DFD are all top-down design techniques. (T/F)

5. The HIPO overview diagram illustrates the interactions between the input, _____ , output, and storage activities for a particular module.

6. In a decision table, each possible set of conditions is called a _____ .

SELF-TEST ANSWERS   1. F; 2. universals; 3. F; 4. T; 5. processing;
6. rule

HANDS-ON EXERCISES
Electronic Spreadsheet, Graphics, and Database

Microcomputer-based electronic spreadsheet, graphics, and database software have become popular productivity tools at all levels of business endeavor. Chapter 7, "Personal Computing," contains a conceptual overview of the capabilities, applications, and use of these tools. This appendix contains a variety of hands-on exercises that are designed to help students develop skills in the application and use of these tools.

Although the exercises are, for the most part, generic and applicable to any electronic spreadsheet, graphics, and database package, parts of the more advanced exercises may ask you to accomplish certain software-specific tasks. When this occurs, the exercises are oriented to Lotus 1-2-3, dBASE III PLUS, and the MS-DOS operating system.

Most commercial electronic spreadsheet packages are actually integrated packages that combine the capabilities of spreadsheet, graphics, and database into a single software product. To accommodate these commercial products better, the hands-on exercises for integrated electronic spreadsheet software are divided into three categories (see the listing that follows), and the hands-on exercises designed specifically for database software follow.

□ Electronic Spreadsheet Hands-on Exercises (Spreadsheet Capabilities)

□ Electronic Spreadsheet Hands-on Exercises (Graphics Capabilities)

□ Electronic Spreadsheet Hands-on Exercises (Database Capabilities)

□ Database Hands-on Exercises

Electronic Spreadsheet Hands-on Exercises (Spreadsheet Capabilities)

1. a. The following data represent the unit sales data for the past year for Diolab, Inc., a manufacturer of a diagnostic laboratory instrument that is sold primarily to hospitals and clinics.

DIOLAB INC. SALES (UNITS)

REGION	QTR1	QTR2	QTR3	QTR4
NE REGION	214	300	320	170
SE REGION	120	150	165	201
SW REGION	64	80	60	52
NW REGION	116	141	147	180

Enter the title, headings, and data in an electronic spreadsheet. Place the title in the range B1, the column headings in the range A2..E2, the row headings in the range A3..A6, and the sales data in the range B3..E6.

In the remaining portion of this exercise, each part builds on the results of the previous part. If the exercise is to be handed in, print out the initial spreadsheets and then print them out again for each revision.

b. Add another column heading called SALES/YR in F2 of the Diolab spreadsheet. Enter a formula in F3 that sums the sales for each quarter for the NE Region. Copy the formula to the range F4..F6. SALES/YR should be 1004 for the NE Region and 636 for the SE Region.

c. Add average sales per quarter, AVG/QTR, in column G. AVG/QTR should be 251 for the NE Region and 159 for the SE Region.

d. Add two more columns that reflect sales per salesperson. In column H, add number of salespersons per region, PERSONS: 5, 3, 2, and 4, respectively. In column I, add formulas that compute sales per person, SALES/PER (from the data in SALES/YR and PERSONS columns). SALES/PER should be 200.8 for the NE Region and 212 for the SE Region.

e. In the range B8..F8, use functions to total sales for each quarter and for the year. The total sales for all regions should be 2480.

f. Copy the range A2..A6 to A12..A16 and B2..E2 to B12..E12. Diolab, Inc., sales are estimated to be 120 percent of last year's sales. Complete the newly created spreadsheet by multiplying last year's quarterly sales data by 1.2 and placing the result in the spreadsheet. Title this set of data ESTIMATED DIOLAB INC. SALES—NEXT YEAR. The NE Region first quarter sales should be 257 (rounded), and the SE Region second quarter sales should be 180.

g. Each of the lab analysis units sells for $2,000. Add formulas in column F to compute estimated GROSS sales ($2,000 times the total of the estimated quarterly sales) for each region. Also format the GROSS sales values as currency with no decimal places so that the NE Region amount appears as $2,409,600 and the SE Region as $1,526,400. You may need to expand the width of column F to 11 positions.

2. a. Create a spreadsheet that summarizes an individual's monthly budget in two general categories: expenditures and income. Use formulas to compute the totals for the two categories, the percentage of the total, and the ratio of total expenditures to total income. Format your spreadsheet like the following:

	A	B	C
		Amount	Percent of Total
1	EXPENDITURES		
2	Category	Amount	Percent of Total
3	Housing	495.00	33.01%
4	Utilities	125.45	8.37%
5	Food	369.29	24.63%
6	Clothing	85.00	5.67%
7	Transportation	265.17	17.68%
8	Entertainment	100.00	6.67%
9	Other	59.50	3.97%
10		- - - - - - - -	
11	TOTAL	$1,499.41	
12	= =		

	A	B	C
13	INCOME		
14	Category	Amount	Percent of Total
15	Wages	2,400.00	96.00%
16	Tips	0.00	0.00%
17	Gifts	100.00	4.00%
18	Other	0.00	0.00%
19		- - - - - - - -	
20	TOTAL	$2,500.00	
21	= =
22	Ratio of expenditures to income:		.60

b. Print the spreadsheet.

c. Enter new amounts for various categories of expenditures and income, and print out the spreadsheet.

3. a. Create a spreadsheet that will allow you to compare this year's monthly electric utility bills with last year's bills. Use the sample data shown here or use your own data. Format your spreadsheet like the following:

	A	B	C	D
1	Month	This Year	Last Year	Difference
2				
3	January	140.23	154.24	−14.01
4	February	160.54	168.30	−7.76
5	March	90.77	87.22	3.55
6	April	65.12	56.61	8.51
7	May	30.98	50.15	−19.17
8	June	50.00	48.08	1.92
9	July	69.33	74.04	−4.71
10	August	45.20	48.59	−3.39
11	September	35.61	22.62	12.99
12	October	70.02	69.11	0.91
13	November	98.87	106.04	−7.17
14	December	128.09	140.01	−11.92
15		- -	
16	TOTAL	$984.76	$1,025.01	

b. Print the spreadsheet.

4. The following data represent sales by division for each month of the first quarter for Begonia's Clothing Store for Women.

DIVISION	JANUARY	FEBRUARY	MARCH
Coats	$6,780	$14,780	$12,700
Dresses	$12,600	$13,580	$15,794
New Ideas	$14,670	$16,871	$17,400
Swimwear	$1,260	$1,150	$2,140
Casual	$8,600	$9,890	$11,502
Designer's	$15,890	$18,274	$21,252
Junior's	$13,680	$15,732	$18,296
Handbags	$6,400	$7,360	$9,580
Accessories	$9,580	$11,017	$12,813
Shoes	$7,650	$8,798	$11,400
Fragrances	$4,200	$6,700	$7,792
Spec Sizes	$12,400	$14,260	$16,584

a. Enter the data into an electronic spreadsheet. Reset the width of column A to 12 and the width of columns B through G to 10. Place a separator line in row 3, columns A through G. Enter the column heading DIVISION in A4. Right align the headings JANUARY, FEBRUARY, and MARCH in B4..D4.

Place a second separator line in A5..G5. Enter each division's name in A6..A17. Format B6..D17 as currency with 0 decimals and enter the sales data. Save the spreadsheet as BEGONIA1 on your data disk.

b. Add a column of formulas in column E. Right align the heading TOTAL in E4. Use the SUM function to total the amounts in each row for rows 6 through 17 (create the formula for row 6 and copy the formula to rows 7 through 17). Format E6..E17 as currency with 0 decimals. Save the spreadsheet as BEGONIA2.

c. Add another column of data in column F. Right align the heading LAST YEAR (total sales for the past year) in F4. Enter the following sales data in column F.

	LAST YEAR
6 (Coats)	$32,670
7 (Dresses)	$39,750
8 (New Ideas)	$38,600
9 (Swimwear)	$4,260
10 (Casual)	$26,000
11 (Designer's)	$49,123
12 (Junior's)	$40,234
13 (Handbags)	$18,500
14 (Accessories)	$27,400
15 (Shoes)	$23,690
16 (Fragrances)	$19,900
17 (Spec Sizes)	$42,800

Format F6..F17 as currency with 0 decimals. Save the spreadsheet as BEGONIA3.

d. Add two more separator lines in row 18 and row 20 (copy A3..G3). Enter the row heading TOTALS in A19 and use the SUM function to total each of the columns B through F (create the formula for column B and copy the formula to C through F). Format B19..F19 as currency with 0 decimals. Save the spreadsheet as BEGONIA4.

e. Right align the final column heading %CHG in G4. Create a formula to calculate the percentage change in sales from last year to this year (subtract last year's sales from this year's sales and divide the result by last year's sales). Enter the formula in G6 and copy the formula to G7..G17 and G19. Format G6..G17 and G19 as a percentage with two decimal places.

Enter the heading BEGONIA'S CLOTHING STORE FOR WOMEN with six leading spaces in B1. Enter the heading RETAIL SALES—FIRST QUARTER in C2. Save the spreadsheet as BEGONIA5.

f. Print the spreadsheet.

g. Exit your spreadsheet program and return to DOS. At the DOS prompt, enter a command that displays the file names BEGONIA1 through BEGONIA5. [Hint: Use the DIR command and the ? wildcard character.] Use the print-screen command (for MS-DOS, SHIFT-PRTSC) to print the list of files.

5. This exercise is a follow-up to Hands-on Exercise 4. Use absolute cell referencing to calculate the percentage of total sales for each division.

a. Load the electronic spreadsheet program and retrieve the file BEGONIA5.

b. Insert a new column at column F.

c. If necessary, enter connecting separator lines in F3, F5, F18, and F20. Reset the width of column F to 18.

d. Right align the column heading % TOTAL SALES in F4.

e. Enter a formula in F6 that calculates the sales for Coats Division as a percentage of total sales for the store (divide the division's sales total in E6 by the store's sales total in E19).

f. Edit the formula that you entered in F6 so that the reference to total sales (E19) is an absolute cell address.

g. Copy the revised formula in F6 to F7..F17. Format F6..F17 as a percentage with two decimal places.

h. Save the spreadsheet as BEGONIA6. Print the range A1..F20.

6. Use an IF function to create a spreadsheet that will determine a bank's service charge for a checking account.

a. Set the width of column A to 20 and enter text data and separator lines as shown here (remember that labels can spill over into empty adjacent cells):

	A	B	C
1		Bank Service Charges	
2			
3			
4	Account balance:		
5			
6	------------------------------		
7	$6.00 charge if less than $500		
8	$3.00 charge if $500–$999.99		
9	No charge if $1,000 or greater		

```
             A          B          C
10  - - - - - - - - - - - - - - - - - - - - - - - - - - -
11
12  Service charge:
13
```

b. Enter a formula in B12 that determines the service charge of an account for which the balance is entered in B4. [Hint: The formula includes two IF functions, one nested inside the other.]

c. Format B4 and B12 as currency with two decimal places.

d. Enter 499 into B4, position the pointer in B12, and use the print-screen command to print the spreadsheet.

e. Repeat (d) but use 500.

f. Repeat (d) again but use 1000.

g. Save the spreadsheet as CHARGE on your data disk.

7. Use the financial function PMT (principal, fixed interest rate, and term), and create a spreadsheet that will permit the calculation of monthly mortgage payments.

a. Set the width of column A to 25 and column B to 18. Enter text data and separator lines as shown:

```
                         A                        B
 1
 2  Mortgage Payment Calculation
 3
 4
 5  - - - - - - - - - - - - - - - - - - - - - - - - - - - - - -
 6  Amount of loan
 7  Annual rate of interest
 8  Term (in years)
 9  - - - - - - - - - - - - - - - - - - - - - - - - - - - - - -
10
11  Monthly payment
12
```

b. Format B6 as currency with zero decimal places, B7 as a percentage with one decimal place, B8 as fixed with zero decimal places, and B11 as currency with two decimal places.

c. Enter the formula that calculates the monthly payment in B11 (the word ERR will appear in B11). Use the PMT function. The PMT function calculates the loan payment, given the amount of the loan (principal), the rate of interest, and the term of the loan. To arrive at PMT arguments needed to calculate the monthly payment amount, divide the annual interest rate by 12 and multiply the term (in years) by 12.

d. Save the spreadsheet as MORTGAGE on your data disk.

e. When you enter 65000 in B6, .115 in B7, and 25 in B8, the display in B11 should be $660.70.

f. Enter 92500 in B6, position the pointer in B11, and use the print-screen command to print the spreadsheet.

Electronic Spreadsheet Hands-on Exercises
(Graphics Capabilities)

8. a. Use the following Diolab, Inc., sales data (from Hands-on Exercise 1). Produce a bar graph showing the total unit sales by region for Diolab, Inc. Title the graph "Total Sales by Region" with a subtitle "Diolab, Inc.", label the *y* axis "Unit Sales," and label the bars "NE Region," "SE Region," "SW Region," and "NW Region."

DIOLAB INC. SALES (UNITS)				
REGION	QTR1	QTR2	QTR3	QTR4
NE REGION	214	300	320	170
SE REGION	120	150	165	201
SW REGION	64	80	60	52
NW REGION	116	141	147	180

Each of the remaining parts of this hands-on exercise deal with the Diolab, Inc., data or graphs produced from these data.

b. Produce a pie graph showing the total unit sales by region for Diolab, Inc. Title the graph "Total Sales by Region" with a subtitle "Diolab, Inc." and label the pieces "NE Region," "SE Region," "SW Region," and "NW Region."

c. Compare the information portrayed in the bar and pie graphs.

d. Produce a clustered-bar graph showing quarterly unit sales by region for Diolab, Inc. Title the graph "Quarterly Sales by Region" with a subtitle "Diolab, Inc.", label the *y* axis "Unit Sales," label the clusters of bars "Qtr1," "Qtr2," "Qtr3," "Qtr4," and include a legend as a cross-reference to the four regions (NE, SE, SW, NW).

e. Produce a line graph showing quarterly unit sales by region for Diolab, Inc. Title the graph "Quarterly Sales by Region" with a subtitle "Diolab, Inc.", label the *y* axis "Unit Sales," label points on the lines "Qtr1," "Qtr2," "Qtr3," "Qtr4," and include a legend as a cross-reference to the regional lines (NE, SE, SW, NW).

f. Compare the information shown in the clustered-bar and line graphs.

9. Use an integrated software package to produce a line graph for the spreadsheet data in Hands-on Exercise 3. Label the *y* axis "Payment" and the *x* axis "Month." Set the origin at $20 and plot the data for "This Year" and "Last Year." Display the graph and then print it.

10. This is a follow-up exercise to Hands-on Exercise 4. Use the file BEGONIA5 as the basis for creating two bar graphs and a pie graph.

a. Load the electronic spreadsheet program and retrieve the file BEGONIA5.

b. Create a bar graph that displays the total sales for each division (E6..E17). Make the first line of the graph's title BEGONIA'S CLOTHING STORE FOR WOMEN and the second line RETAIL SALES (QTR 1).

c. Place the name of each division at the top of the bar representing the sales for that division.

d. Save the graph settings as BAR–SALES.

e. Revise the current settings to create a second bar graph that displays the percentage change in sales for each division (G6..G17). Revise the second line of the heading to read %CHG FROM LAST YEAR'S SALES (QTR 1).

f. Save the graph settings as BAR–%CHG.

g. Recall the settings for the initial graph BAR–SALES. Revise the graph-type selection to create a pie graph that displays each division's quarterly sales.

h. Revise the graph settings to explode the pie segments for the Coats and New Ideas divisions.

i. Save the settings as PIE–SALES.

j. Print the BAR–%CHG graph.

Electronic Spreadsheet Hands-on Exercises (Database Capabilities)

11. a. Set up a spreadsheet data base to accept the following sales data for Diolab, Inc., a manufacturer of a diagnostic laboratory instrument that is sold primarily to hospitals and clinics.

DIOLAB INC. SALES (UNITS)				
REGION	QTR1	QTR2	QTR3	QTR4
= = = = = = = = = = = = = = = = = =				
NE REGION	241	300	320	170
SE REGION	120	150	165	201
SW REGION	64	80	60	52

Each of the remaining parts of this hands-on exercise is a follow-up to the previous part.

b. Enter the Diolab data into the data base.

c. Revise the NE Region first quarter sales to be 214.

d. Add the following NW Region record to the data base.

REGION	QTR1	QTR2	QTR3	QTR4
= = = = = = = = = = = = = = = = = =				
NW REGION	116	141	147	180

e. Obtain a printout of the data base and store the data on a disk file named DIOLAB.

f. Select and list all Diolab regions (records) that sold more than 150 units in the fourth quarter (all but the SW Region).

g. Select and list all Diolab regions (records) that sold more than 150 units in the fourth quarter *and* for which fourth quarter sales are greater than third quarter sales (SE and NW regions).

h. Sort the Diolab data base in ascending order by QTR1 sales.

i. Sort the Diolab data base in descending order by QTR4 sales.

12. Create a name and address data base. Sort the data base, and extract various records from the data base.

a. Start with a blank spreadsheet. Set the width of columns A and B to 12, columns C and D to 17, and column E to 4.

b. Enter the following text data:

	A	B	C	D	E	F
1	First Name	Last Name	Address	City	ST	ZIP
2	Phil	Cline	1915 N.W. 25th	Oklahoma City	OK	73107
3	Sherry	Howard	3587 Lee Dr.	Jackson	MS	39208
4	Bill	Allred	630 W. Call	Tallahassee	FL	32308
5	Warren	Sherman	3745 Rogers	Ft. Worth	TX	76109
6	Malcolm	Haney	642 Tulane Av.	Little Rock	AR	72204
7	Sharon	Bias	125 Lake View	Gainesville	GA	30501
8	Janet	Roche	432 Oak St.	Nashville	TN	37203
9	Joyce	Phinney	345 Pratt Dr.	New Orleans	LA	70122
10	Michael	Howard	3587 Lee Dr.	Jackson	MS	39208
11	Alison	Haney	933 Hilltop	Little Rock	AR	72204
12	Kristine	Haney	3216 West End	Nashville	TN	37203
13	- -
14						
15						
16	- -
17						

c. Prepare the spreadsheet for data query (for example, for Lotus 1-2-3, copy A1..F1 to both A14..F14 and A17..F17).

d. Define the data query ranges [for example, for Lotus 1-2-3, define input (A1..F12), criterion (A14..F15), and output (A17..F20) ranges].

e. List the records of those people who live in Arkansas. Use the print-screen command (for MS-DOS, SHIFT-PRTSC) to print the current display.

f. List the records of those people who have the last name "Haney". Use the print-screen command to print the current display.

g. Sort the data base alphabetically in ascending sequence by last name. Use the print-screen command to print the current display.

h. Sort the data base alphabetically in ascending sequence by state. Use the print-screen command to print the current display.

i. Sort the data base alphabetically in ascending sequence using LASTNAME as the primary field and FIRSTNAME as the secondary field. Use the print-screen command to print the current display.

Database Hands-on Exercises

13. a. Design a data entry screen to accept the following sales data for Diolab, Inc., a manufacturer of a diagnostic laboratory instrument that is sold primarily to hospitals and clinics.

REGION	QTR1	QTR2	QTR3	QTR4
DIOLAB INC. SALES (UNITS)				
= =				
NE REGION	241	300	320	170
SE REGION	120	150	165	201
SW REGION	64	80	60	52

Each of the remaining parts of this hands-on exercise is a follow-up to the previous part.

b. Enter the Diolab data into a data base.

c. Revise the NE Region first quarter sales to be 214.

d. Add the following NW Region record to the data base.

REGION	QTR1	QTR2	QTR3	QTR4
=== === === === === === === === === === === ===				
NW REGION	116	141	147	180

e. Obtain a printout of the data base and store the data on a disk file named DIOLAB.

f. Select and list all Diolab regions (records) that sold more than 150 units in the fourth quarter (all but the SW Region).

g. Select and list all Diolab regions (records) that sold more than 150 units in the fourth quarter *and* for which fourth quarter sales are greater than third quarter sales (SE and NW regions).

h. Select and list only the REGION and QTR4 fields of those Diolab regions for which the average sales for the first three quarters is less than the sales for the fourth quarter (SE and NW regions).

i. Make an inquiry to the Diolab data base that results in a display of the average unit sales for each quarter (QTR1=128).

j. Make an inquiry to the Diolab data base that results in a display of the total unit sales for each quarter (QTR1=514).

k. Sort the Diolab data base in ascending order by QTR1 sales. Print out the sorted data base.

l. Sort the Diolab data base in descending order by QTR4 sales. Print out the sorted data base.

m. Generate and print a formatted report from the sorted DIOLAB data base that is entitled DIOLAB INC. SALES (UNITS) and has the following column headings: Sales Region, 1st Qtr, 2nd Qtr, 3rd Qtr, and 4th Qtr. The report should include the total sales for each quarter.

14. a. Create a database to keep track of an individual's library of recordings: compact discs (CDs), long-playing (LP) records, and audio tapes. The database should have the following fields defined:
   (1) FORMAT (CD, LP record, or tape)
   (2) ARTIST
   (3) TITLE
   (4) [Playing] TIME
   (5) [Number of] SONGS

b. Enter the following data into the audio database.

FORMAT	ARTIST	TITLE	TIME	SONGS
CD	Depeche Mode	Some Great Reward	38.59	13
CD	The Cure	The Cure?	32.32	10
RECORD	London Symphony	Mozart: Requiem	61.25	1
TAPE	Pet Shop Boys	Please	32.15	10
CD	Depeche Mode	Black Celebration	41.19	12
RECORD	Depeche Mode	People Are People	32.37	11
TAPE	O.M.D.	The Pacific Age	43.00	12
CD	The Cure	Standing on the Beach	52.18	15
RECORD	The Ramones	End of the Century	36.28	16

c. Use the audio data base and appropriate criteria to generate and print reports that contain
   (1) The entire data base sorted alphabetically by title.
   (2) All LP records and tapes sorted by playing time.
   (3) All CDs that were recorded by Depeche Mode.
   (4) All LP records and tapes with playing times in excess of 40 minutes.

d. Make the following inquiries to the audio data base.
   (1) The total number of songs on CD.
   (2) The average playing time for all recordings.

e. Produce and print a formatted report that contains all entries in the data base, is sorted alphabetically by artist, and has subtotals for playing time for each artist. The report should look something like this:

ARTIST	TITLE	PLAYING TIME	TOTAL FOR ARTIST
Depeche Mode	Some Great Reward	38.59	
Depeche Mode	Black Celebration	41.19	
Depeche Mode	People Are People	32.37	
			112.15
London Symphony	Mozart: Requiem	61.25	
			61.25
O.M.D.	The Pacific Age	43.00	
			43.00
Pet Shop Boys	Please	32.15	
			32.15
The Cure	The Cure?	32.32	
The Cure	Standing on the Beach	52.18	
			84.50
The Ramones	End of the Century	36.28	
			36.28

15. a. Write an interactive database program that permits a manager to request a quarterly sales summary for any of the four regions of Diolab, Inc. (use the Diolab data base from Hands-on Exercise 13). A sample interactive session is illustrated below.

   Enter sales region to be summarized: **NW REGION**

   NW REGION SALES SUMMARY
   = = = = = = = = = = = =

   First quarter: 116
   Second quarter: 141
   Third quarter: 147
   Fourth quarter: 180
   -
   Total for year: 584

b. Activate the DOS printer echo (for MS-DOS, CTRL-PRTSC) feature and execute the program. Request a sales summary for the SE Region. Deactivate the printer echo.

c. Document the database program with internal comments. Print out the program.

16. Create a name and address data base. Sort and list the data base in various ways.

    a. Create a data base that includes the following fields: FIRSTNAME, LASTNAME, ADDRESS, CITY, ST, ZIP. If your data base program requests field type and field width, enter the following:

Field Name	Type	Width
FIRSTNAME	Character	12
LASTNAME	Character	15
ADDRESS	Character	15
CITY	Character	15
ST	Character	2
ZIP	Character	5

    Call the data base NAMES.

    b. Enter the following data into the data base.

FIRSTNAME	LASTNAME	ADDRESS	CITY	ST	ZIP
Phil	Cline	1915 N.W. 25th	Oklahoma City	OK	73107
Sherry	Howard	3587 Lee Dr.	Jackson	MS	39208
Bill	Allred	630 W. Call	Tallahassee	FL	32308
Warren	Sherman	3745 Rogers	Ft. Worth	TX	76109
Malcolm	Haney	642 Tulane Av.	Little Rock	AR	72204
Sharon	Bias	125 Lake View	Gainesville	GA	30501
Janet	Roche	432 Oak St.	Nashville	TN	37203
Joyce	Phinney	345 Pratt Dr.	New Orleans	LA	70122
Michael	Howard	3587 Lee Dr.	Jackson	MS	39208
Alison	Haney	933 Hilltop	Little Rock	AR	72204
Kristine	Haney	3216 West End	Nashville	TN	37203

    c. List the data base. Use the print-screen command (for MS-DOS, SHIFT-PRTSC) to print the current display.

    d. If your data base program displays record numbers, list the data base again, but this time without record numbers. Use the print-screen command to print the current display.

    e. List the records of those people who live in Arkansas. Use the print-screen command to print the current display.

    f. List the records of those people who live in Arkansas or Mississippi. Use the print-screen command to print the current display.

    g. Sort the data base alphabetically in ascending sequence by last name. List only the LASTNAME field. Use the print-screen command to print the current display.

    h. Sort the data base alphabetically in ascending sequence by STATE. List only the LASTNAME and STATE fields. Use the print-screen command to print the current display.

i. Sort the data base alphabetically in ascending sequence using LASTNAME as the primary field and FIRSTNAME as the secondary field. List only the LASTNAME and FIRSTNAME fields. Use the print-screen command to print the current display.

j. List the records of those people whose ZIP code begins with 7. Use the print-screen command to print the current display.

GLOSSARY

Abacus Traced back at least 5,000 years, probably the original mechanical counting device. Beads are moved along parallel wires to count and perform arithmetic computations.

Absolute cell address A cell address in an electronic spreadsheet that always refers to the same cell.

Access arm The disk drive mechanism used to position the read/write heads over the appropriate track.

Access time The time interval between the instant a computer makes a request for a transfer of data from a secondary storage device and the instant this operation is completed.

Accumulator The computer register in which the result of an arithmetic or logic operation is formed.

Acoustical coupler A device in which a telephone handset is mounted for the purpose of transmitting data over telephone lines. Used with a modem.

Ada A multipurpose, procedure-oriented language.

Add-on boards Circuit boards that contain the electronic circuitry for a wide variety of computer-related functions (also called *add-on cards*).

Add-on cards See *add-on boards*.

Address (1) A name, numeral, or label that designates a particular location in primary or secondary storage. (2) A location identifier for terminals in a computer network.

ALGOL [ALGOrithmic Language] A high-level programming language designed primarily for scientific applications.

Algorithm A procedure that can be used to solve a particular problem.

Alpha A reference to the letters of the alphabet.

Alpha test The in-house testing of a software product by the vendor prior to its release for beta testing (contrast with *beta test*).

Alphanumeric Pertaining to a character set that contains letters, digits, punctuation, and special symbols (related to *alpha* and *numeric*).

Analog computer A computer that operates on data that are expressed as a continuously changing representation of a physical variable, such as voltage (contrast with *digital computer*).

Analog-to-digital (A-D) converter A device which translates an analog signal to a digital signal (contrast with *digital-to-analog converter*).

ANSI [American National Standards Institute] An organization that coordinates the setting of standards in the United States.

APL [A Programming Language] An interactive symbolic programming language used primarily for mathematical applications.

Application A problem or task to which the computer can be applied.

Application generators A very high-level programming language in which programmers specify, through an interactive dialog with the system, which processing tasks are to be performed (also called *code generator*).

Applications portfolio The current mix of existing and proposed information systems in an organization.

Applications software Software that is designed and written to address a specific personal, business, or processing task.

APT [Automatically Programmed Tools] A special-purpose programming language used to program machine tools.

Architecture The design of a computer system.

Arithmetic and logic unit That portion of the computer that performs arithmetic and logic operations (related to *accumulator*).

Arithmetic operators Mathematical operators [add ($+$), subtract ($-$), multiply ($*$), divide ($/$), and exponentiation ($\char94$)] used in electronic spreadsheet and database software for computations.

Array A programming concept that permits access to a list or table of values by the use of a single variable name.

Array processor A processor that is composed of several processors, all under the control of a single control unit.

Artificial intelligence (AI) The ability of a computer to reason, to learn, to strive for self-improvement, and to simulate human sensory capabilities.

ASCII [American Standard Code for Information Interchange] An encoding system.

ASCII file A generic text file that is stripped of program-specific control characters.

Assembler language A low-level symbolic language with an instruction set that is essentially one-to-one with machine language.

Assistant system A type of knowledge-based system that helps users make relatively straightforward decisions (contrast with *expert system*).

Asynchronous transmission Data transmission at irregular intervals that is synchronized with start/stop bits (contrast with *synchronous transmission*).

Attribute A data element in a relational data base.

Auto-answer A modem function that permits the automatic answering of a call from a remote computer.

Auto-dial A modem function that permits the automatic dialing of the number of a remote computer.

Automatic teller machine (ATM) An automated deposit/withdrawal device used in banking.

Automation The automatic control and operation of machines, processes, and procedures.

Auxiliary storage See *secondary storage*.

Back-end processor A host-subordinate processor that handles administrative tasks associated with retrieval and manipulation of data (same as *data base machine*).

Backup Pertaining to equipment, procedures, or data bases that can be used to restart the system in the event of system failure.

Backup file Duplicate of an existing production file.

Badge reader An input device that reads data on badges and cards (related to *magnetic stripe*).

Bar code A graphic encoding technique in which vertical bars of varying widths are used to represent data.

Bar graph A graph that contains vertical bars that represent specified numeric values.

Bar menu A menu in which the options are displayed across the screen.

BASIC A popular multipurpose programming language.

Batch file A disk file that contains a list of commands and/or programs that are to be executed immediately following the loading of the operating system to main memory.

Batch processing A technique in which transactions and/or jobs are collected into groups (batched) and processed together.

Baud (1) A measure of the maximum number of electronic signals that can be transmitted via a communications channel. (2) Bits per second (common-use definition).

Benchmark test A test for comparing the performance of several computer systems while running the same software or comparing the performance of several programs that are run on the same computer.

Beta test The testing of a software product in a live environment prior to its release to the public (contrast with *alpha test*).

Binary notation Using the binary (base-2) numbering system (0, 1) for internal representation of alphanumeric data.

Bit A *bi*nary digi*t* (0 or 1).

Bits per second (bps) The number of bits that can be transmitted per second over a communications channel.

Block A group of data that is either read from or written to an I/O device in one operation.

Blocking Combining two or more records into one block.

Boilerplate Existing text in a word processing file that can in some way be customized so that it is applicable to a variety of word processing applications.

Boot The procedure for loading the operating system to primary storage and readying a computer system for use.

BPI [Bytes Per Inch] A measure of data-recording density on secondary storage.

Bridge A protocol-independent hardware device that permits communication between devices on separate local area networks.

Buffer Intermediate memory that temporarily holds data that are en route from main memory to another computer or an input/output device.

Bug A logic or syntax error in a program, a logic error in the design of a computer system, or a hardware fault.

Bulletin board system (BBS) The electronic counterpart of a wall-mounted bulletin board that enables end users in a computer network to exchange ideas and information via a centralized data base.

Bus An electrical pathway through which the processor sends data and commands to RAM and all peripheral devices.

Bus architecture See *open architecture*.

Bus topology A computer network that permits the connection of terminals, peripheral devices, and microcomputers along an open-ended central cable.

Business Systems Planning (BSP) A structured process for MIS planning that is based on the premise that data are a corporate resource that must be carefully evaluated with respect to organizational needs.

Byte A group of adjacent bits configured to represent a character.

C A transportable programming language that can be used to develop both systems and applications software.

CAD See *computer-aided design*.

CAI See *computer-assisted instruction*.

Callback procedure A security procedure that results in a remote user being called back by the host computer system after the user password and authorization code have been verified.

CAM See *computer-aided manufacturing*.

Capacity planning The process by which MIS planners determine how much hardware resources are needed to meet anticipated demands.

Carrier Standard-sized pin connectors that permit chips to be attached to a circuit board.

Carrier, common [in data communications] A company that furnishes data communications services to the general public.

CASE [Computer-Aided Software Engineering] A collective reference to the family of software development productivity tools (also called *workbench technologies*).

Cathode ray tube See *CRT*.

CBT See *computer-based training*.

CD ROM disk [Compact Disk Read-Only Memory disk] A form of optical laser storage media.

Cell The intersection of a particular row and column in an electronic spreadsheet.

Cell address The location, column and row, of a cell in an electronic spreadsheet.

Central processing unit (CPU) See *processor*.

Channel The facility by which data are transmitted between locations in a computer network (e.g., workstation to host, host to printer).

Channel capacity The number of bits that can be transmitted over a communications channel per second.

Character A unit of alphanumeric datum.

Chargeback system A system that is designed to allocate the cost of computer and information services to the end users.

Checkpoint/restart When a system fails, backup files/data bases and/or backup transaction logs are used to re-create processing from the last "checkpoint." The system is "restarted" at the last checkpoint and normal operation is resumed.

Chief information officer (CIO) The individual responsible for all information services activity in a company.

CIM [Computer-Integrated Manufacturing] Using the computer at every stage of the manufacturing process, from the time a part is conceived until it is shipped.

Clone A hardware device or a software package that emulates a product with an established reputation and market acceptance.

Closed architecture Refers to micros with a fixed, unalterable configuration (contrast with *open architecture*).

Cluster controller See *down-line processor*.

Clustered-bar graph A modified bar graph that can be used to represent a two-dimensional set of numeric data (for example, multiple product sales by region).

Coaxial cable A shielded wire that is used as a medium to transmit data between computers and between computers and peripheral devices.

COBOL [COmmon Business Oriented Language] A programming language used primarily for administrative information systems.

CODASYL [COnference on DAta SYstems Languages] An organization chartered to oversee and approve software tools and procedures, such as programming languages and database management systems.

Code (1) The rules used to translate a bit configuration to alphanumeric characters. (2) The process of compiling computer instructions in the form of a computer program. (3) The actual computer program.

Code generator See *application generator*.

Cold site A backup site that is equipped for housing a computer system (contrast with *hot site*).

Collate To combine two or more files for processing.

Column A vertical block of cells that runs the length of a spreadsheet and is labeled by a letter.

COM [Computer Output Microfilm/Microfiche] A device that produces a microform image of a computer output on microfilm or microfiche.

Command An instruction to a computer that invokes the execution of a preprogrammed sequence of instructions.

Command driven Pertaining to software packages that respond to user directives that are entered as commands.

Common carrier [in data communications] See *carrier, common*.

Communications See *data communications*.

Communications channel The facility by which data are trans-

mitted between locations in a computer network (same as *line* and *data link*).

Communications protocols Rules established to govern the way that data are transmitted in a computer network.

Communications software Software that enables a microcomputer to emulate a terminal and to transfer files between a micro and another computer.

Compatibility (1) Pertaining to the ability of one computer to execute programs of, access the data base of, and communicate with another computer. (2) Pertaining to the ability of a particular hardware device to interface with a particular computer.

Competitive advantage A term used to describe a company's leveraging of computer and information technologies to realize an advantage over its competitors.

Compile To translate a high-level programming language, such as COBOL, to machine language in preparation for execution (compare with *interpreter*).

Compiler Systems software that performs the compilation process.

Computer See *processor*.

Computer console That unit of a computer system that allows operator and computer to communicate.

Computer network An integration of computer systems, workstations, and communications links.

Computer system A collective reference to all interconnected computing hardware, including processors, storage devices, input/output devices, and communications equipment.

Computer-aided design (CAD) Use of computer graphics capabilities to aid in design, drafting, and documentation in product and manufacturing engineering.

Computer-aided manufacturing (CAM) A term coined to highlight the use of computers in the manufacturing process.

Computer-assisted instruction (CAI) Use of the computer as an aid in the educational process (contrast with *computer-based training*).

Computer-based training (CBT) Using computer technologies for training and education (contrast with *computer-assisted instruction*).

Computerese A slang term that refers to the terms and phrases associated with computers and information processing.

Concatenation The joining together of labels or fields and other character strings into a single character string in electronic spreadsheet or database software.

Concentrator See *down-line processor*.

Configuration The computer and its peripheral devices.

Connectivity Pertains to the degree to which hardware devices, software, and data bases can be functionally linked to one another.

Contention A line-control procedure in which each workstation "contends" with other workstations for service by sending requests for service to the host processor.

Contingency planning A plan that details what to do in case an event drastically disrupts the operation of a computer center.

Control clerk A person who accounts for all input to and output from a computer center.

Control field See *key data element*.

Control total An accumulated number that is checked against a known value for the purpose of output control.

Control unit That portion of the processor that interprets program instructions, directs internal operations, and directs the flow of input/output to/from main memory.

Conversion The transition process from one system (manual or computer-based) to a computer-based information system.

Cooperative computing An environment in which businesses cooperate internally and externally to take full advantage of available information to obtain meaningful, accurate, and timely information.

Coprocessor An extra processor under the control of the main processor that helps relieve the main processor of certain tasks.

Core memory A main memory technology that was popular in the 1950s and 1960s.

Cottage industry People using computer technology to do work-for-profit from their homes.

Counter One or several programming instructions used to tally processing events.

Critical Path Method (CPM) A network modeling technique that enables managers to show the relationships among the various activities involved in a project and to select the approach that optimizes the use of resources while meeting project deadlines (similar to *Project Evaluation and Review Technique or PERT*).

Critical success factors (CSF) A procedure by which a manager identifies areas of business activity that are "critical" to the successful operation of the functions within his or her scope of responsibility.

CRT [Cathode Ray Tube] The video monitor component of a workstation.

Cryptography A communications crime-prevention technology that uses methods of data encryption and decryption to scramble codes sent over communications channels.

Cursor A blinking character that indicates the location of the next input on the display screen.

Cyberphobia The irrational fear of, and aversion to, computers.

Cylinder A disk storage concept. A cylinder is that portion of the disk that can be read in any given position of the access arm (contrast with *sector*).

Daisy-wheel printer A letter-quality serial printer, with its interchangeable character set located on a spoked print wheel.

DASD [Direct-Access Storage Device] A random-access secondary storage device.

Data A representation of fact. Raw material for information.

Data base (1) An organization's data resource for all computer-based information processing in which the data are integrated and related so that data redundancy is minimized. (2) Same as a file in the context of microcomputer usage.

Data base administrator (DBA) The individual responsible for the physical and logical maintenance of the data base.

Data base machine See *back-end processor*.

Data base management system (DBMS) A systems software package for the creation, manipulation, and maintenance of the data base.

Data base record Related data that are read from, or written to, the data base as a unit.

Data bits A data communications parameter that refers to the number of bits in a message.

Data communications The collection and/or distribution of data from and/or to a remote facility.

Data communications specialist A person who designs and implements computer networks.

Data dictionary A listing and description of all data elements in the data base.

Data diddling The unauthorized revision of data on entry to a system or in storage.

Data element The smallest logical unit of data. Examples are employee number, first name, and price (same as *field*; compare with *data item*).

Data entry The transcription of source data into machine-readable format.

Data entry operator A person who uses key entry devices to transcribe data into a machine-readable format.

Data flow diagram (DFD) A design technique that permits documentation of a system or program at several levels of generality.

Data item The value of a data element (compare with *data element*).

Data link See *communications channel*.

Data management software See *database software*.

Data PBX A computer that electronically connects computers and workstations for the purpose of data communication.

Data processing (DP) Using the computer to perform operations on data.

Database An alternative terminology for microcomputer-based data management software (contrast to *data base*).

Database software Software that permits users to create and maintain a data base and to extract information from the data base (also called *data management software*).

DB2 IBM's mainframe-based relational DBMS.

Debug To eliminate bugs in a program or system (related to *bug*).

Decimal The base-10 numbering system.

Decision support system (DSS) An interactive information system that relies on an integrated set of user-friendly hardware and software tools to produce and present information that is targeted to support management decision making that involves semistructured and unstructured problems.

Decision table A graphic technique used to illustrate possible occurrences and appropriate actions within a system.

Decode The reverse of the encoding process (contrast with *encode*).

Default options Preset software options that are assumed valid unless specified otherwise by the user.

Density The number of bytes per linear length of track of a recording medium. Usually measured in bytes per inch (bpi) and applied to magnetic tapes and disks.

Departmental computing Any type of computing done at the departmental level.

Desktop computer Any computer that can be placed conveniently on the top of a desk (same as *microcomputer*, *personal computer*).

Desktop publishing Refers to the hardware and software capability of producing near typeset-quality copy from the confines of a desktop.

Diagnostic The isolation and/or explanation of a program error.

Dial-up line See *switched line*.

Digital computer A computer that operates on data that are expressed in a discrete format (e.g., an on-bit or off-bit). (Contrast with *analog computer*.)

Digital-to-analog (D-A) converter A device that translates a digital to an analog signal. (Contrast with *analog-to-digital converter*.)

Digitize To translate data or an image into a discrete format that can be interpreted by computers.

Digitizing tablet A pressure-sensitive tablet with the same *x-y* coordinates as a computer-generated screen. The outline of an image drawn on a tablet with a stylus or puck is reproduced on the display.

DIP [Dual Inline Package] A toggle switch that is typically used to designate certain computer system configuration specifications (e.g., amount of RAM).

Direct access See *random access*.

Direct conversion An approach to system conversion whereby operational support by the new system is begun when the existing system is terminated.

Direct-access file See *random file access*.

Direct-access processing See *random processing*.

Direct-access storage device See *DASD*.

Director of information services The person who has responsibility for computer and information systems activity in an organization.

Directory A list of the names of the files that are stored on a particular diskette or in a named area on a hard disk.

Disaster plan See *contingency planning*.

Disk, magnetic A secondary storage medium for random-access data storage. Available as microdisk, diskette, disk cartridge, or disk pack.

Disk drive, magnetic A magnetic storage device that records data on flat rotating disks (compare with *tape drive*).

Diskette A thin flexible disk for secondary random-access data storage (same as *floppy disk* and *flexible disk*).

Distributed data processing Both a technological and an organizational concept based on the premise that information systems can be made more responsive to users by moving computer hardware and personnel physically closer to the people who use them.

Distributed DBMS Software that permits the interfacing of data bases located in various places throughout a computer network.

Distributed processor The nucleus of a small computer system that is linked to the host computer and physically located in the functional area departments.

Documentation Permanent and continuously updated written and graphic descriptions of information systems and programs.

Domain expert An expert in a particular field who provides the factual knowledge and the heuristic rules of thumb for input to a knowledge base.

DOS [Disk Operating System] A generic reference to a disk-based operating system.

Down-line processor A computer that collects data from a number of low-speed devices, then transmits "concentrated" data over a single communications channel (also called a *concentrator* and *cluster controller*).

Download The transmission of data from a mainframe computer to a workstation.

Downtime The time during which a computer system is not operational.

DP Abbreviation for data processing.

Driver module The program module that calls other subordinate program modules to be executed as they are needed.

Dump The duplication of the contents of a storage device to another storage device or to a printer.

Earth station An earth-based communications station that can transmit and receive data from communications satellites.

EBCDIC [Extended Binary Coded Decimal Interchange Code] An encoding system.

EDP Abbreviation for electronic data processing.

Education coordinator The person who coordinates all computer-related educational activities within an organization.

EFT [Electronic Funds Transfer] A computer-based system allowing electronic transfer of money from one account to another.

EGA [Enhanced Graphics Adapter] A circuit board that enables the interfacing of high resolution monitors to microcomputers.

Electronic bulletin board A computer-based "bulletin board" that permits external users access to the system via data communication for the purpose of reading and sending messages.

Electronic Data Interchange (EDI) The use of computers and data communications to transmit data electronically between companies.

Electronic dictionary A disk-based dictionary that is used in conjunction with a spelling checker program to verify the spelling of words in a word processing document.

Electronic funds transfer See *EFT*.

Electronic mail A computer application whereby messages are transmitted via data communications to "electronic mailboxes." Also called E-mail.

Electronic spreadsheet See *spreadsheet, electronic*.

Encode To apply the rules of a code (contrast with *decode*).

Encoding system A system that permits alphanumeric characters to be coded in terms of bits.

End user The individual providing input to the computer or using computer output (same as *user*).

End user computing A computing environment in which the end users handle both the technical and functional ends of the information systems projects.

End-of-file (EOF) marker A marker placed at the end of a sequential file.

EPROM Erasable PROM [programmable read-only memory] (related to *PROM*).

Exception report A report that has been filtered to highlight critical information.

Executive support system (ESS) A system that is designed specifically to support decision making at the strategic level (contrast with *decision support system* and *management information system*).

Expansion slots Slots within the processing component of a microcomputer into which optional add-on circuit boards can be inserted.

Expert system An interactive knowledge-based system that responds to questions, asks for clarification, makes recommendations, and generally helps users make complex decisions (contrast with *assistant system*).

Expert system shell The software that enables the development of expert systems.

Facsimile Equipment that transfers images of hard-copy documents via telephone lines to another office.

Fault-tolerant system Pertaining to a computer system that can operate under adverse environmental conditions.

Feasibility study A study performed to determine the economic and procedural feasibility of a proposed information system.

Fetch instruction That part of the instruction cycle in which the control unit retrieves a program instruction from main memory and loads it to the processor.

Feedback loop In a process control environment, the output of the process being controlled is input to the system.

Field See *data element*.

File (1) A collection of related records. (2) A named area on a secondary storage device that contains a program, data, or textual material.

Filtering The process of selecting and presenting only that information which is appropriate to support a particular decision.

Firmware Logic for performing certain computer functions that is built into a particular computer by the manufacturer, often in the form of ROM or PROM.

Fixed disk See *hard disk*.

Flat files A traditional file structure in which records are related to no other files.

Flexible disk See *diskette*.

Floppy disk See *diskette*.

Flops Floating point operations per second.

Flowchart A diagram that illustrates data, information, and work flow via specialized symbols which, when connected by flow lines, portray the logic of a system or program.

Footprint The evidence of unlawful entry or use of a computer system.

FORTH A programming language particularly suited for microcomputers that enables users to tailor the language's set of commands to any application.

FORTRAN [FORmula TRANslator] A high-level programming language designed primarily for scientific applications.

Fourth-generation language (4GL) A programming language that uses high-level English-like instructions to retrieve and format data for inquiries and reporting (also called a *query language*).

Frequency division multiplexing A method of simultaneously transmitting several communications signals over a transmission media by dividing its bandwidth into narrower bands, each carrying a communications signal.

Front-end processor A processor used to offload certain data communications tasks from the host processor.

Frozen specifications System specifications that have been approved and are not to be changed during the system development process.

Full-duplex line A communications channel that transmits data in both directions at the same time.

Full-screen editing This word processing feature permits the user to move the cursor to any position in the document to insert or replace text.

Function A predefined operation that performs mathematical, logical, statistical, financial, and character-string operations on data in an electronic spreadsheet or a data base.

Function key A special-function key on the keyboard that can be used to instruct the computer to perform a specific operation (also called *soft key*).

Function-based information system An information system designed for the exclusive support of a specific application area, such as inventory management or accounting.

Functional specifications Specifications that describe the logic of an information system from the perspective of the user.

Functionally adjacent systems Information systems that feed each other, have functional overlap, and/or share all or part of a data base.

Gateway Software that permits computers of different design architectures to communicate with one another.

Gateway computer A subordinate computer that translates communications protocols of remote computers to a protocol that is compatible with the host computer, thereby enabling the transmission for data from external sources.

General-purpose computer Those computer systems that are designed with the flexibility to do a variety of tasks, such as CAI, payroll processing, climate control, and so on (contrast with *special-purpose computer*).

Geosynchronous orbit An orbit that permits a communications satellite to maintain a fixed position relative to the surface of the earth (also known as geostationary orbit).

Gigabyte (G) Referring to 1 billion bytes of storage.

GIGO [Garbage In, Garbage Out] A euphemism implying that information is only as good as the data from which it is derived.

Global memory Pertaining to the random access memory that is shared by several processors.

Grammar checker An add-on program to word processing software that highlights grammatical concerns and deviations from conventions in a word processing document.

Grandfather-father-son method A secondary storage backup procedure that results in the master file having two generations of backup.

Hacker A computer enthusiast who uses the computer as a source of enjoyment.

Half-duplex line A communications channel that transmits data in both directions, but not at the same time.

Handshaking The process by which both sending and receiving devices in a computer network maintain and coordinate data communications.

Hard carriage return In word processing, a special character that is inserted in the document when the carriage return is pressed. Typically the character denotes the end of a paragraph or a string of contiguous text.

Hard copy A readable printed copy of computer output.

Hard disk Permanently installed, continuously spinning magnetic storage medium that is made up of one or more rigid disk platters (same as *fixed disk*; see also *Winchester disk*).

Hard-wired Logic that is designed into chips.

Hardware The physical devices that comprise a computer system (contrast with *software*).

Hashing A method of random access in which the address is arithmetically calculated from the key data element.

Head crash A disk drive malfunction that causes the read/write head to touch the surface of the disk, thereby resulting in the loss of the disk head, the disk, and the data stored on the disk.

Help command A software feature that provides on-line explanation or instruction on how to proceed.

Help screen The display that results from initiating the help command.

Hertz One cycle per second.

Heuristic knowledge Rules of thumb that evolve from experience.

Hexadecimal A base-16 numbering system that is used in information processing as a programmer convenience to condense binary output and make it more easily readable.

Hierarchical data base A data base whose organization employs the tree data structure (contrast with *relational data base* and *network data base*).

High-level programming language A language with instructions that combine several machine-level instructions into one (compare with *machine language* or *low-level programming language*).

HIPO [Hierarchical Plus Input-Processing-Output] A design technique that encourages the top-down approach, dividing the system into easily manageable modules.

Historical reports Reports generated from data that were gathered in the past and do not reflect the current status. Reports based solely on historical data are rare in practice.

Host computer See *host processor*.

Host processor The processor responsible for the overall control of a computer system. The host processor is the focal point of a communications-based system (also called *host computer*).

Hot site A backup site that is equipped with a functioning computer system (contrast with *cold site*).

I/O [Input/Output] Input or output, or both.

Icons Pictographs that are used in place of words or phrases on screen displays.

Idea processor A software productivity tool that allows the user to organize and document thoughts and ideas (also called *outliner*).

Identifier A name used in computer programs to recall a value, an array, a program, or a function from storage.

Image processor A device that uses a camera to scan and digitize an image that can be stored on a disk and manipulated by a computer.

Index file Within the context of database software, a file that contains logical pointers to records in a data base.

Index sequential-access method (ISAM) A direct-access data storage scheme that uses an index to locate and access data stored on magnetic disk.

Inference engine The logic embodied in the software of an expert system.

Information Data that have been collected and processed into a meaningful form.

Information center A facility in which computing resources are made available to various user groups.

Information center specialist Someone who works with users in an information center.

Information engineering A term coined to emphasize the handling of the information resource using the rigors of engineering discipline.

Information management system (IMS) IBM's mainframe-based hierarchical DBMS.

Information network See *information service*.

Information overload The circumstance that occurs when the volume of available information is so great that the decision maker cannot distinguish relevant information from that which is not.

Information repository A central computer-based storage facility for all system design information (also called *dictionary* and *encyclopedia*).

Information resource management (IRM) A concept advocating that information be treated as a corporate resource.

Information service An on-line commercial network that provides remote users with access to a variety of information services.

Information services auditor Someone who is responsible for ensuring the integrity of operational information systems.

Information services department The organizational entity or entities that develop and maintain computer-based information systems.

Information society A society in which the generation and dissemination of information becomes the central focus of commerce.

Information system A computer-based system that provides both data processing capability and information for managerial decision making.

Information-based decisions See *nonprogrammed decisions*.

Input Data to be processed by a computer system.

Inquiry An on-line request for information.

Insert mode A data entry mode in which the character entered is inserted at the cursor position.

Instruction A programming language statement that specifies a particular computer operation to be performed.

Instruction cycle The cycle of operations performed by the processor to process a single program instruction: fetch, decode, execute, and prepare for the next instruction.

Integer Any positive or negative whole number and zero.

Integrated circuit (IC) Thousands of electronic components that are etched into a tiny silicon chip in the form of a special-function electronic circuit.

Integrated information system An information system that services two or more functional areas, all of which share a common data base.

Integrated software Two or more of the major microcomputer productivity tools integrated into a single commercial software package.

Intelligent Pertaining to computer aided.

Intelligent terminal A terminal with a built-in microprocessor.

Interactive Pertaining to on-line and immediate communication between the end user and computer.

Interblock gap (IBG) A physical space between record blocks on magnetic tapes.

Intercompany networking See *electronic data interchange*.

Interpreter Systems software that translates and executes each program instruction before translating and executing the next (compare with *compiler*).

Interrupt A signal that causes a program or a device to stop or pause temporarily.

Intracompany networking The use of computers and data communications to transmit data electronically within a company (see also *cooperative computing*).

ISAM See *index sequential-access method*.

ISO [International Standards Organization] An organization that coordinates the setting of international standards.

Job A unit of work for the computer system.

Joystick A single vertical stick that moves the cursor on a screen in the direction in which the stick is pushed.

K (1) An abbreviation for kilo, meaning 1,000. (2) A computerese abbreviation for 2 to the 10th power or 1,024.

Kernel An independent software module that is part of a larger program.

Key data element The data element in a record that is used as an identifier for accessing, sorting, and collating records (same as *control field*).

Keyboard A device used to key data entry.

Keyboard template Typically a plastic keyboard overlay that indicates which commands are assigned to particular function keys.

Keyword See *reserved word*.

Knowledge acquisition facility That component of the expert system shell that permits the construction of the knowledge base.

Knowledge base The foundation of a knowledge-based system that contains facts, rules, inferences, and procedures.

Knowledge engineer Someone who is trained in the use of expert system shells and in the interview techniques needed to extract information from a domain expert.

Knowledge worker Someone whose job function revolves around the use, manipulation, and dissemination of information.

Knowledge-based system A computer-based system that helps users to make decisions by enabling them to interact with a knowledge base.

Large-scale integration (LSI) An integrated circuit with a densely packed concentration of electronic components (contrast with *very-large-scale integration* or *VLSI*).

Layout A detailed output and/or input specification that graphically illustrates exactly where information should be placed/entered on a VDT display screen or placed on a printed output.

Layout line A line on a word processing screen that graphically illustrates appropriate user settings (margins, tabs). Also called a format line.

Leased line A permanent or semipermanent communications channel leased through a common carrier.

Lexicon The dictionary of words that can be interpreted by a particular natural language.

Librarian A person who functions to catalog, monitor, and control the distribution of disks, tapes, system documentation, and computer-related literature.

Light-emitting diode (LED) A device that responds to electrical current by emitting light.

Limits check A system check that assesses whether the value of an entry is out of line with that expected.

Line See *communications channel*.

Line graph A graph in which conceptually similar points are plotted and connected so that they are represented by one or several lines.

Linkage editor An operating system program that assigns a primary storage address to each byte of an object program.

Liquid crystal display (LCD) An output device that displays characters and other images as composites of actuated liquid crystal.

LISP [LISt Processing] A programming language that is particularly suited for the manipulation of words and phrases and is often used in applications of artificial intelligence.

Live data Test data that have already been processed through an existing system.

Load To transfer programs or data from secondary to primary storage.

Local area network (LAN or local net) A system of hardware, software, and communications channels that connects devices on the local premises.

Local memory Pertaining to the random access memory associated with a particular processor or peripheral device.

Logic bomb A program, planted in a computer system by a malicious programmer, that is designed to destroy or alter programs or files when triggered by a particular sequence of events or the passage of a certain point in time.

Logic operations Computer operations that make comparisons between numbers and between words, then, based on the result of the comparison, perform appropriate functions.

Logical operators Used to combine relational expressions logically in electronic spreadsheet and database software (such as AND, OR).

Logical record See *record*.

LOGO A programming language that is often used to teach children concepts in mathematics, geometry, and computer programming.

Logon procedure The procedure by which a user establishes a communications link with a remote computer.

Loop A sequence of program instructions that are executed repeatedly until a particular condition is met.

Low-level programming language A language comprising the fundamental instruction set of a particular computer (compare with *high-level programming language*).

M See *megabyte*.

Machine cycle The time it takes to retrieve, interpret, and execute a program instruction.

Machine independent Pertaining to programs that can be executed on computers of different designs.

Machine language The programming language that is interpreted and executed directly by the computer.

Macro A sequence of frequently used operations or keystrokes that can be recalled and invoked to help speed user interaction with microcomputer productivity software.

Magnetic disk See *disk, magnetic*.

Magnetic disk drive See *disk drive, magnetic*.

Magnetic ink character recognition (MICR) A data entry technique used primarily in banking. Magnetic characters are imprinted on checks and deposits, then "scanned" to retrieve the data.

Magnetic stripe A magnetic storage medium for low-volume storage of data on badges and cards (related to *badge reader*).

Magnetic tape See *tape, magnetic*.

Magnetic tape drive See *tape drive, magnetic*.

Mail merge A computer application in which text generated by word processing is merged with with data from a data base (e.g., a form letter with an address).

Main memory See *primary storage*.

Main menu The highest-level menu in a menu tree.

Mainframe computer A large computer that can service many users simultaneously.

Maintenance The ongoing process by which information systems (and software) are updated and enhanced to keep up with changing requirements.

Management information system (MIS) An integrated structure of data bases and information flow over all levels and components of an organization, whereby the collection, transfer, and presentation of information is optimized to meet the needs of the organization.

Manipulator arm The movable part of an industrial robot to which special-function tools are attached.

MAP [Manufacturing Automation Protocol] A communications protocol, developed by General Motors, that enables the linking of robots, machine tools, automated carts, and other automated elements of manufacturing into an integrated network.

Master file The permanent source of data for a particular computer application area.

Megabyte (M) Referring to 1 million bytes of primary or secondary storage capacity.

Memory See *primary storage*.

Memory-resident program A program, other than the operating system, that remains operational while another applications program is running.

Menu A workstation display with a list of processing choices from which an end user may select.

Menu driven Pertaining to software packages that respond to user directives that are entered via a hierarchy of menus.

Message A series of bits sent from a workstation to a computer or vice versa.

Metal-oxide semiconductor (MOS) A technology for creating tiny integrated circuits in layers of conducting metal that are separated by silicon dioxide insulators.

Methodology A set of standardized procedures, including technical methods, management techniques, and documentation, that provides the framework to accomplish a particular function (e.g., system development methodology).

MHz [megahertz] One million hertz.

Micro/mainframe link Linking microcomputers and mainframes for the purpose of data communication.

Microchip An integrated circuit on a chip.

Microcomputer (micro) A small computer.

Microcomputer specialist A specialist in the use and application of microcomputer hardware and software.

Microdisk A rigid $3\frac{1}{4}$- or $3\frac{1}{2}$-inch disk used for data storage.

Microframe A high-end microcomputer.

Microprocessor A computer on a single chip. The processing component of a microcomputer.

Microsecond One millionth of a second.

Milestone A significant point in the development of a system or program.

Millisecond One-thousandth of a second.

Minicomputer A midsize computer (also called a *mini*).

MIPS Millions of instructions per second.

MIS See *management information system*.

MIS steering committee A committee of top executives who are charged with providing long-range guidance and direction for computer and MIS activities.

Mnemonics Symbols that represent instructions in assembler languages.

Modem [Modulator-Demodulator] A device used to convert computer-compatible signals to signals suitable for data transmission facilities, and vice versa.

Modula-2 A multipurpose procedure-oriented programming language.

Monitor A televisionlike display for soft-copy output in a computer system.

Motherboard A microcomputer circuit board that contains the microprocessor, electronic circuitry for handling such tasks as input/output signals from peripheral devices, and memory chips.

Mouse A small device that when moved across a desktop a particular distance and direction causes the same movement of the cursor on a screen.

MS-DOS [MicroSoft Disk Operating System] A microcomputer operating system.

Multicomputer A complex of interconnected computers that operate in concert while sharing memory or the individual computers can operate independently.

Multidrop The connection of more than one terminal to a single communications channel.

Multifunction add-on board An add-on circuit board that performs more than one function.

Multiplexing The simultaneous transmission of multiple transmissions of data over a single communications channel.

Multiprocessing Using two or more processors in the same computer system in the simultaneous execution of two or more programs.

Multiprogramming Pertaining to the concurrent execution of two or more programs by a single computer.

Multiuser microcomputer A microcomputer that can serve more than one user at any given time.

Nanosecond One-billionth of a second.

Natural language A programming language in which the programmer writes specifications without regard to instruction format or syntax. Essentially, using common, human language to program.

Nested loop A programming situation where at least one loop is entirely within another loop.

Network, computer See *computer network*.

Network data base A data base organization that permits children in a tree data structure to have more than one parent (contrast with *relational data base* and *hierarchical data base*).

Node An end point in a computer network.

Nonprocedural language A programming language that can automatically generate the instructions needed to create a programmer-described end result.

Nonprogrammed decision A decision that involves an ill-defined and unstructured problem (also called *information-based decision*).

Numeric A reference to any of the digits 0–9 (compare with *alpha* and *alphanumeric*).

Object program A machine-level program that results from the compilation of a source program.

Object-oriented language A programming language that is structured to enable the interaction between objects, that is, user defined concepts (e.g., a computer screen, a list of items) that contain data and operations to be performed on the data.

Octal A base-8 numbering system used in information processing as a programmer convenience to condense binary output and make it easier to read.

Off-line Pertaining to data that are not accessible by, or hardware devices that are not connected to, a computer system (contrast with *on-line*).

Office automation (OA) Pertaining collectively to those computer-based applications associated with general office work.

Office automation specialist A person who specializes in the use and application of office automation hardware and software (see *office automation*).

On-line Pertaining to data and/or hardware devices that are accessible to and under the control of a computer system (contrast with *off-line*).

On-line thesaurus Software that enables a user to request synonyms interactively during a word processing session.

Opcode Pertaining to that portion of a computer machine language instruction that designates the operation to be performed. Short for operation code.

Open architecture Refers to micros that give users the flexibility to configure the system with a variety of peripheral devices (contrast with *closed architecture*; also called *bus architecture*).

Open systems interconnect (OSI) A standard for data communications within a computer network established by International Standards Organization (ISO).

Operand Pertaining to that portion of a computer machine language instruction that designates the address of the data to be operated on.

Operating environment (1) A user-friendly DOS interface. (2) The conditions in which a computer system functions.

Operating system The software that controls the execution of all applications and systems software programs.

Operator The person who performs those hardware-based activities necessary to keep information systems operational.

Operator console The machine room operator's workstation.

Optical character recognition (OCR) A data entry technique that permits original-source data entry. Coded symbols or characters are "scanned" to retrieve the data.

Optical fiber A data transmission medium that carries data in the form of light in very thin transparent fibers.

Optical laser disk A read-only secondary storage medium that uses laser technology.

Optical scanners Devices that provide input to computer systems by using a beam of light to interpret printed characters and various types of codes.

Orphan The first line of paragraph that is printed as the last line on a page in a word processing document.

Outliner See *idea processor*.

Output Data transferred from primary storage to an output device.

Packaged software Software that is generalized and "packaged" to be used, with little or no modification, in a variety of environments (compare with *proprietary software*).

Packet switching A data communications process in which communications messages are divided into packets (subsets of the whole message), transmitted independent of one another in a communications network, then reassembled at the source.

Page A program segment that is loaded to primary storage only if it is needed for execution (related to *virtual storage*).

Page break In word processing, an on-line command or special character that causes the text that follows to be printed on a new page.

Page offset The distance between the left edge of the paper and the left margin in a word processing document.

Page-composition software The software component of desktop publishing software that enables users to design and make up pages.

Pagination The word processing feature that provides automatic numbering of the pages of a document.

Parallel Pertaining to processing of data in groups of bits versus one bit at a time (contrast with *serial*).

Parallel conversion An approach to system conversion whereby the existing system and the new system operate simultaneously until the project team is confident that the new system is working properly.

Parallel host processor A redundant host processor used for backup and supplemental processing.

Parallel port A direct link with the microcomputer's bus that facilitates the parallel transmission of data, usually one byte at a time.

Parallel processor A processor in which many, even millions, of processing elements simultaneously address parts of a processing problem.

Parity bit A bit appended to a bit configuration (byte) that is used to check the accuracy of data transmission from one hardware device to another (related to *parity checking* and *parity error*).

Parity checking A built-in checking procedure in a computer system to help ensure that the transmission of data is complete and accurate (related to *parity bit* and *parity error*).

Parity error Occurs when a bit is dropped in the transmission of data from one hardware device to another (related to *parity bit* and *parity checking*).

Parsing A process whereby user-written natural language commands are analyzed and translated to commands that can be interpreted by the computer.

Pascal A multipurpose procedure-oriented programming language.

Password A word or phrase known only to the end user. When entered, it permits the end user to gain access to the system.

Patch A modification to a program or information system.

Path The logical route that an operating system would follow when searching through a series of directories and subdirectories to locate a specific file on disk storage.

PC [Personal Computer] See *microcomputer*.

PC-DOS [PC Disk Operating System] A microcomputer operating system.

Peripheral equipment Any hardware device other than the processor.

Personal computer (PC) See *microcomputer*.

Personal computing A computing environment in which individuals use microcomputers for both domestic and business applications.

Personal identification number (PIN) A unique number that is assigned to and identifies a user of a computer network.

Phased conversion An approach to system conversion whereby an information system is implemented one module at a time by either parallel or direct conversion.

Pick-and-place robot An industrial robot that physically transfers material from one place to another.

Picosecond One trillionth of a second.

Pie graph A circular graph that illustrates each "piece" of data in its proper relationship to the whole "pie."

Pilferage A special case of software piracy where a company purchases a software product without a site-usage license agreement, then copies and distributes it throughout the company.

Pilot conversion An approach to system conversion whereby the new system is implemented by parallel, direct, or phased conversion as a "pilot" system in only one of the several areas for which it is targeted.

Pipe Under the Unix operating system, the "connection" of two programs such that the output of one becomes the input of the other.

Pitch Horizontal spacing (characters per inch) in printed output.

Pixel An addressable point on a display screen to which light can be directed under program control.

PL/I A multipurpose procedure-oriented programming language.

Plotter A device that produces hard copy graphic output.

Point-of-sale (POS) terminal A cash-register-like terminal designed for key and/or scanner data entry.

Point-to-point connection A single communications channel linking a workstation or a microcomputer to a computer.

Pointer The highlighted area in an electronic spreadsheet display that indicates the current cell.

Polling A line-control procedure in which each workstation is "polled" in rotation to determine whether a message is ready to be sent.

Pop-up menu A menu that is superimposed in a window over whatever is currently being displayed on the monitor.

Port An access point in a computer system that permits communication between the computer and a peripheral device.

Postimplementation evaluation A critical examination of a computer-based system after it has been put into production.

Prespecification An approach to information systems development where users determine their information processing needs during the early stages of the project, then commit to these specifications through system implementation.

Primary storage The memory area in which all programs and data must reside before programs can be executed or data manipulated (same as *main memory*, *memory*, and *RAM*; compare with *secondary storage*).

Printer A device used to prepare hard copy output.

Printer spooler A circuit board that enables data to be printed while a microcomputer user continues with other processing activities.

Private line A dedicated communications channel between any two points in a computer network.

Problem-oriented language A high-level language whose instruction set is designed to address a specific problem (e.g., process control of machine tools, simulation).

Procedure-oriented language A high-level language whose general-purpose instruction set can be used to produce a sequence of instructions to model scientific and business procedures.

Process control Using the computer to control an ongoing process in a continuous feedback loop.

Processor The logical component of a computer system that interprets and executes program instructions (same as *computer*, *central processing unit*, *CPU*).

Program (1) Computer instructions structured and ordered in a manner that, when executed, cause a computer to perform a particular function. (2) The act of producing computer software (related to *software*).

Programmed decisions Decisions that address well-defined problems with easily identifiable solutions.

Programmer One who writes computer programs.

Programmer/analyst A position title of one who performs both the programming and systems analysis function.

Programming The act of writing a computer program.

Programming language A language in which programmers communicate instructions to a computer.

Project Evaluation and Review Technique (PERT) A network modeling technique that enables managers to show the relationships among the various activities involved in the project and to select the approach that optimizes the use of resources while meeting project deadlines (similar to *Critical Path Method* or *CPM*).

Project leader The person in charge of organizing the efforts of a project team.

Prolog A descriptive programming language that is often used in applications of artificial intelligence.

PROM [Programmable Read-Only Memory] ROM in which the user can load read-only programs and data.

Prompt A program-generated message describing what should be entered by the end user operator at a workstation.

Proportional spacing A spacing option for word processing documents for which the spacing between characters remains relatively constant for any given line of output.

Proprietary software Vendor-developed software that is marketed to the public (related to *packaged software*).

Protocols Rules established to govern the way that data are transmitted in a computer network.

Prototype system A model of a full-scale system.

Pseudocode Nonexecutable program code used as an aid to develop and document structured programs.

Puck A flat hand-held device with cross hairs that is used in conjunction with a digitizing tablet to translate an image into machine-readable format.

Pull-down menu A menu that is "pulled down" and superimposed in a window over whatever is currently being displayed on a monitor.

Purging The act of erasing unwanted data, files, or programs from RAM or magnetic memory.

Quality assurance An area of specialty that is concerned with monitoring the quality of every aspect of the design and operation of information systems, including system efficiency and documentation.

Query language See *fourth-generation language*.

RAM [Random Access Memory] See *primary storage*.

Random access Direct access to records, regardless of their physical location on the storage medium (contrast with *sequential access*).

Random file A collection of records that can be processed randomly.

Random processing Processing of data and records randomly (same as *direct-access processing*; contrast with *sequential processing*).

Range A cell or a rectangular group of adjacent cells in an electronic spreadsheet.

Raster scan monitor An electron beam forms the image by scanning the screen from left to right and from top to bottom (contrast with *vector scan monitor*).

Read The process by which a record or a portion of a record is accessed from the magnetic storage medium (tape or disk) of a secondary storage device and transferred to primary storage for processing (contrast with *write*).

Read/write head That component of a disk drive or tape drive that reads from and writes to its respective magnetic storage medium.

Real-time computing   The processing of events as they occur, usually in a continuous feedback loop.

Reasonableness check   A system checking procedure that determines whether entered or generated data is reasonable when compared to historical data.

Record   A collection of related data elements (e.g., an employee record).

Recursion   Pertaining to the capability of a program to reference itself as a subroutine.

Register   A small, high-speed storage area in which data pertaining to the execution of a particular instruction are stored. Data stored in a specific register have a special meaning to the logic of the computer.

Relational data base   A data base in which data are accessed by content rather than by address (contrast with *hierarchical data base* and *network data base*).

Relational operators   Used in electronic spreadsheet and database formulas to show the equality relationship between two expressions [= (equal to), < (less than), > (greater than), <= (less than or equal to), >= (greater than or equal to), <> (not equal to)]. See also *logical operators*.

Relative cell address   Refers to a cell's position in an electronic spreadsheet relative to the cell containing the formula in which the address is used.

Replace mode   A data entry mode in which the character entered overstrikes the character at the cursor position.

Report generator   Software that produces reports automatically based on user specifications.

Request for information (RFI)   See *RFI*.

Request for proposal (RFP)   See *RFP*.

Reserved word   A word that has a special meaning to a software package (also called *keyword*).

Resolution   Referring to the number of addressable points on a monitor's screen. The greater the number of points, the higher the resolution.

Response time   The elapsed time between when a data communications message is sent and a response is received (compare with *turnaround time*).

Responsibility matrix   A matrix that graphically illustrates when and to what extent individuals and groups are involved in each activity of a systems development process.

Reusable code   Modules of programming code that can be called and used as needed.

Reverse video   Characters on a video display terminal presented as black on a light background; used for highlighting.

RFI   [Request For Information] A request to a prospective vendor requesting information about a particular type of product.

RFP   [Request For Proposal] A formal request to a vendor for a proposal.

Ring topology   A computer network that involves computer systems that are connected in a closed loop, and no one computer system is the focal point of the network.

Robot   A computer-controlled manipulator capable of locomotion and/or moving items through a variety of spatial motions.

Robotics   The integration of computers and industrial robots.

ROM   [Read-Only Memory] RAM that can only be read, not written to.

Root directory   The directory at the highest level of a hierarchy of directories.

Row   A horizontal block of cells that runs the width of a spreadsheet and is labeled by a number.

RPG   A programming language in which the programmer communicates instructions interactively by entering appropriate specifications in prompting formats.

RS-232-C   A "recommended standard" 25-pin plug that is used for the electronic interconnection of computers, modems, and other peripheral devices.

Run   The continuous execution of one or more logically related programs (e.g., print payroll checks).

Scheduler   Someone who schedules the use of hardware resources to optimize system efficiency.

Schema   A graphical representation of the logical structure of a CODASYL data base.

Screen formatter   See *screen generator*.

Screen generator   A system design tool that enables a systems analyst to produce a mockup of a display while in direct consultation with the user (also called a *screen formatter*).

Scrolling   Using the cursor keys to view parts of a word processing document or an electronic spreadsheet that extends past the bottom or top or sides of the screen.

Secondary storage   Permanent data storage on magnetic disk and tape (same as *auxiliary storage*; compare with *primary storage*).

Sector   A disk storage concept. A pie-shaped portion of a disk or diskette in which records are stored and subsequently retrieved (contrast with *cylinder*).

Self-booting diskette   A diskette that contains both the operating system and an applications software package.

Semiconductor   A crystalline substance whose properties of electrical conductivity permit the manufacture of integrated circuits.

Sequential access   Accessing records in the order in which they are stored (contrast with *random access*).

Sequential files   Files that contain records that are ordered according to a key data element.

Sequential processing   Processing of files that are ordered numerically or alphabetically by a key data element (contrast with *direct-access processing* or *random processing*).

Serial   Pertaining to processing of data one bit at a time (contrast with *parallel*).

Serial port   A direct link with the microcomputer's bus that facilitates the serial transmission of data, one bit at a time.

Service request   A formal request from a user for some kind of computer- or MIS-related service.

Set   A CODASYL data base concept that serves to define the relationship between two records.

Shelfware Software that was purchased but never used or implemented.

Simplex line A communications channel that transmits data in only one direction.

Situation assessment An MIS planning activity that results in a definition of where the information services division and the functional areas stand with respect to their use of computer and information technologies.

Skeletal code A partially complete program that is produced by a code generator.

Smalltalk An object-oriented language.

Smart card A card or badge with an embedded microprocessor.

Smart modems Modems that have embedded microprocessors.

SNA [Systems Network Architecture] IBM's scheme for networking its computers.

Soft carriage return In word processing, an invisible special character that is automatically inserted after the last full word within the right margin of entered text.

Soft copy Temporary output that can be interpreted visually as on a workstation monitor (contrast with *hard copy*).

Soft key See *function key*.

Software The programs used to direct the functions of a computer system (contrast with *hardware*).

Software engineering A term coined to emphasize an approach to software development that embodies the rigors of engineering discipline.

Software package One or more programs that are designed to perform a particular processing task.

Software piracy The unlawful duplication of proprietary software (related to *pilfering*).

Sort The rearrangement of data elements or records in an ordered sequence by a key data element.

Source document The original hard copy from which data are entered.

Source program The code of the original program (compare with *object program*). Also called source code.

Special-purpose computer Computers that are designed for a specific application, such as CAD, video games, robots (contrast with *general-purpose computer*).

Speech synthesizers Devices that convert raw data to electronically produced speech.

Spelling checker An add-on program to word processing that checks the spelling of every word in a word processing document against an electronic dictionary.

Spooling The process by which output (or input) is loaded temporarily to secondary storage. It is then output (or input) as appropriate devices become available.

Spreadsheet, electronic Refers to software that permits users to work with rows and columns of data.

Stacked-bar graph A modified bar graph in which the bars are divided to highlight visually the relative contribution of the components that make up the bar.

Star topology A computer network that involves a centralized host computer that is connected to a number of smaller computer systems.

Statement See *instruction* (for a computer program).

Status report A report that reflects the current status (contrast with *historical report*).

Structured programming A design technique by which the logic of a program is addressed hierarchically in logical modules.

Structured Query Language (SQL) The ANSI and ISO standard data access query language for relational data bases.

Structured walkthrough A peer evaluation procedure for programs and systems under development. It is used to minimize the possibility of something being overlooked or done incorrectly.

Style checker An add-on program to word processing software that identifies deviations from effective writing style in a word processing document (for example, long and complex sentences).

Stylus A penlike device that is used in conjunction with a digitizing tablet to translate an image into computer format.

Subdirectory A directory that is subordinate to a higher-level directory.

Subroutine A sequence of program instructions that are called and executed as needed.

Subscripts Characters that are positioned slightly below the line of type.

Summary report A report that presents a summary of information about a particular subject.

Supercomputer The category of computers that includes the largest and most powerful computers.

Superscripts Characters that are positioned slightly above the line of type.

Supervisor The operating system program that loads programs to primary storage as they are needed.

Switched line A telephone line used as a regular data communications channel. Also called dial-up line.

Synchronous transmission Transmission of data at timed intervals between terminals and/or computers (contrast with *asynchronous transmission*).

Syntax The rules that govern the formulation of the instructions in a computer program.

Syntax error An invalid format for a program instruction.

Sysop [system operator] Sponsor of an electronic bulletin board system.

System Any group of components (functions, people, activities, events, and so on) that interface with and complement one another to achieve one or more predefined goals.

System development methodology Written standardized procedures that depict the activities in the systems development process and define individual and group responsibilities.

System life cycle A reference to the four stages of a computer-based information system—birth, development, production, and death.

System maintenance The process of modifying an information system to meet changing needs.

Systems analysis   The analysis, design, development, and implementation of computer-based information systems.

Systems analyst   A person who does systems analysis.

Systems engineering   See *software engineering*.

Systems software   Software that is independent of any specific applications area.

Systems testing   A phase of testing where all programs in a system are tested together.

Tape cassette   Magnetic tape storage in cassette format.

Tape drive, magnetic   The hardware device that contains the read/write mechanism for the magnetic tape storage medium.

Tape, magnetic   A secondary storage medium for sequential data storage. Available as a reel or a cassette.

Task   The basic unit of work for a processor.

Technology transfer   The application of existing technology to a current problem or situation.

Telecommunications   Communication between remote devices.

Telecommuting   "Commuting" via a communications link between home and office.

Teleconferencing   A meeting in which people in different locations use electronic means to see and talk to each other and to share charts and other meeting materials.

Teleprocessing   A term coined to represent the merging of telecommunications and data processing.

Template   A model for a particular microcomputer software application.

Terminal   Any device capable of sending and receiving data over a communications channel.

Terminal emulation mode   The software transformation of a microcomputer so that its keyboard, monitor, and data interface emulate that of a terminal.

Test data   Data that are created to test all facets of an information system's operational capabilities.

Thesaurus, on-line   See *on-line thesaurus*.

Three-tier network   A computer network with three layers—a host mainframe at the top which is linked to multiple minicomputers which are linked to multiple microcomputers.

Throughput   A measure of computer system efficiency; the rate at which work can be performed by a computer system.

Throwaway system   An information system that is developed to support information for a one-time decision, then discarded.

Time-division multiplexing   A method of concurrently transmitting several communications signals over a transmission media.

Timesharing   Multiple end users sharing time on a single computer system in an on-line environment.

Toggle   The action of pressing a single key on a keyboard to switch between two or more modes of operation such as insert and replace.

Top-down design   An approach to system and program design that begins at the highest level of generalization; design strategies are then developed at successive levels of decreasing generalization, until the detailed specifications are achieved.

Trace   A procedure used to debug programs whereby all processing events are recorded and related to the steps in the program. The objective of a trace is to isolate program logic errors.

Track, disk   That portion of a magnetic disk face surface that can be accessed in any given setting of a single read/write head. Tracks are configured in concentric circles.

Track, tape   That portion of a magnetic tape that can be accessed by any one of the nine read/write heads. A track runs the length of the tape.

Trackball   A ball mounted in a box that when moved results in a similar movement of the cursor on a display screen.

Transaction   A procedural event in a system that prompts manual or computer-based activity.

Transaction file   A file containing records of data activity (transactions); used to update the master file.

Transaction-oriented processing   Transactions are recorded and entered as they occur.

Transcribe   To convert source data to machine-readable format.

Transistor   An electronic switching device that can be used to vary voltage or alter the flow of current.

Transmission rate   The number of characters per second that can be transmitted between primary storage and a peripheral device.

Transparent   A reference to a procedure or activity that occurs automatically and does not have to be considered in the use or design of a program or an information system.

Trojan horse   A public domain program with inviting functional capabilities that, when downloaded from a bulletin board system and executed, does irreparable damage to the disk files of an unknowing victim.

Tuple   A group of related fields (a row) in a relational data base.

Turbo Pascal   A microcomputer version of the Pascal programming language.

Turnaround document   A computer-produced output that is ultimately returned to a computer system as a machine-readable input.

Turnaround time   Elapsed time between the submission of a job and the distribution of the results.

Twisted-pair wire   Two twisted copper wires. The foundation of telephone services through the 1970s.

Two-tier network   A computer network with two layers—a host mainframe at the top that is linked directly to multiple minicomputers and/or microcomputers.

Uninterruptible power source (UPS)   A buffer between an external power source and a computer system that supplies clean and continuous power.

Unit testing   That phase of testing in which the programs that make up an information system are tested individually.

Universal product code (UPC) A 10-digit machine-readable bar code placed on consumer products.

Upload The transmission of data from a workstation to the main-frame computer.

Uptime That time when the computer system is in operation.

Upward compatibility A computing environment that can be upgraded without the need for redesign and reprogramming.

User See *end user*.

User acceptance testing That stage of system testing where the system is presented to the scrutiny of the user managers whose departments will ultimately use the system.

User friendly Pertaining to an on-line system that permits a person with relatively little experience to interact successfully with the system.

User interface A reference to the software, method, or displays that enable interaction between the user and the application or system software being used.

User liaison A person who serves as the technical interface between the information services department and the user group.

User sign-off A procedure whereby the user manager is asked to "sign off" or commit to the specifications defined by the systems development project team.

Utility program An often-used service routine such as a program to sort records.

Value added network (VAN) A specialized common carrier that "adds value" over and above the standard services of common carriers.

Variable A primary storage location that can assume different numeric or alphanumeric values.

Variable name An identifier in a program that represents the actual value of a storage location.

VDT [Video Display Terminal] A terminal on which printed and graphic information is displayed on a televisionlike monitor and data are entered on a typewriterlike keyboard.

Vector scan monitor An electron beam forms the image by scanning the screen from point to point (contrast with *raster scan monitor*).

Version number A number that identifies the release version of a software package.

Very-large-scale integration (VLSI) An integrated circuit with a very densely packed concentration of electronic components (contrast with *large-scale integration* or *LSI*).

Video disk A secondary storage medium that permits storage and random access to video or pictorial information.

Video display terminal See *VDT*.

Videotext The merging of text and graphics in an interactive communications-based information network.

Virtual machine The processing capabilities of one computer system created through software (and sometimes hardware) in a different computer system.

Virtual memory The use of secondary storage devices and primary storage to expand effectively a computer system's primary storage.

Virus A program that is written with malicious intent and loaded to the computer system of an unsuspecting victim. Ultimately the program destroys or introduces errors in programs and data bases.

Vision input systems A device that enables limited visual input to a computer system.

Voice data entry device A device that permits voice input to a computer system (also called a *voice recognition device*).

Voice message switching Using computers, the telephone system, and other electronic means to store and forward voice messages (contrast with *electronic mail*).

Voice recognition device See *voice data entry device*.

Voice response unit A device that enables output from a computer system in the form of user-recorded words, phrases, music, alarms, or anything that might be recorded on tape.

Walkthrough, structured See *structured walkthrough*.

Widow The last line of a paragraph that is printed as the first line on a page in a word processing document.

Wildcard (character) Usually a ? or an * that is used in micro-computer software commands as a generic reference to any character or any combination of characters, respectively.

Winchester disk Permanently installed, continuously spinning magnetic storage medium that is made up of one or more rigid disk platters (see also *hard disk* and *fixed disk*).

Window (1) A rectangular section of a display screen that is dedicated to a specific activity or application. (2) In integrated software, a "view" of a designated area of a worksheet, such as a spreadsheet or word processing text.

Window panes Simultaneous display of subareas of a particular window.

Word For a given computer, an established number of bits that are handled as a unit.

Word processing Using the computer to enter, store, manipu-late, and print text.

Word wrap A word processing feature that automatically moves or wraps text to the next line when text that is added to the line exceeds the right margin limit.

Workbench technologies See *CASE*.

Workstation The hardware that permits interaction with a computer system, be it a mainframe or a multiuser micro. A VDT and a microcomputer can be workstations.

Worm A program that erases data and/or programs from a computer system's memory, usually with malicious intent.

WORM (write-once, read many) disk An optical laser disk that can be read many times after the data are written to it, but the data cannot be changed or erased.

Write To record data on the output medium of a particular I/O device (tape, hard copy, workstation display; contrast to *read*).

WYSIWYG [What You See Is What You Get] A word processing package in which what is displayed on the screen is very similar in appearance to what you get when the document is printed.

XMODEM A standard data communications protocol for file transfers.

XON/XOFF A standard data communications protocol.

X.12 An ANSI communications protocol that has been adopted for electronic data interchange transactions.

X.25 A standard communications protocol for networks that involve packet switching.

X.75 A standard communications protocol for networks that involve international interconnections.

Zoom An integrated software command that expands a window to fill the entire screen.

INDEX

Multiuser micros, 493
MVS, 469

Nanosecond, 491
Natural language interface, 370
Natural languages, 67–68, 79–82, 91–92, 170, 370
Negligence, 318
Network DBMS, 258, 260–62
Network modeling techniques, 51
Network topologies, 232–33
Networks (see Data communications, networks or Computer network)
Node, 232
Nominal group technique, 296
Nonprogrammed decisions, 16–17
Numeric, 497
Numeric entry (electronic spreadsheet), 197–99
Numeric value, 512

Object program, 513
Occurrence (in a data base), 259, 262
Office automation (OA) applications, 59, 164–67, 180
Office information systems, 59
Off-line processing, 37–38
On-line processing, 10, 17, 37–38, 40, 99
On-line thesaurus, 143, 191
Open architecture, 141, 493
Open Systems Interconnection (see OSI)
Operating system, 186, 469, 508–10
Operational planning, 274–75, 278, 291–96, 476
Operational-level information, 21–22
Operations group, 135–36
Operator, 135, 139
Operator console, 495
Optical fiber, 229
Optical laser disk, 266, 506
Optical scanners, 501
OS/2 (Operating System/2), 469
OSI (Open Systems Interconnection), 224
Output, 35, 187, 490–91, 495
Output controls, 395
Output devices, 490, 501–4

Page, 510
Page printers, 502, 504
Parallel conversion, 389
Parse tree, 80–81
Parsing, 80–81
Pascal, 516
Pascal, Blaise, 516
Passwords, 400
Patch, 393
Payroll systems (see Applications of computers, general)
PBX (see Data PBX)
PC DOS, 186
Pen plotter, 503
Peripheral devices, 500 (see also Input devices, Output devices, and Storage, secondary)

Personal computer (PC), 186–87, 492, 501–2 (see also Microcomputer)
Personal computing, 183–213, 216
Personal System/2 (PS/2), 185, 469
Phased conversion, 390
Picosecond, 491
Pie graph, 56, 200, 203
Pilferage, 174, 449–50
Pilot conversion, 391
Pixel, 501
PL/I, 516
Planner, 136
Planning, 52, 162, 273–96, 300–301
Plotters, 142–43, 503
Pocket personal computer, 186–87, 492
Pointer, 255
Point-of-sale (POS) terminal, 100–101
Point-to-point connection, 235–36
Polling, 235–36
Pop-up menu, 344
Port, 494
Portable computer, 12, 186–87, 248, 475
Portable data entry, 503
Postimplementation evaluation, 313–14, 392–93
Power user, 176–77
Presentation graphics, 56, 143, 200–204
Prespecification, 311, 330, 335
Primary storage (see Storage, primary)
Printers, 143, 490, 502
Private line, 231–32
Problem-oriented languages, 516
Procedural controls, 395–96
Procedure-oriented languages, 514–16
Process control, 33
Processing, 34–35, 187, 490–91, 494, 497–99
  controls, 394–95
Processors, 187, 226–28, 490
  internal components, 499
  speed and capacity of, 497
  types, 494–95
Productivity, 163, 346
Productivity software, 163–64, 169
  communications, 144, 209–11
  data management (database), 48–50, 143, 162, 204–9
  desktop publishing, 143, 193–94, 501
  electronic spreadsheet, 143, 194–200
  graphics, 56, 142, 162, 200–204
  idea processor, 143
  word processing, 143, 166, 188–93
Program, 508 (see also Programming)
Program development tools, 376–77
Program flowchart, 520
Program processors, 376–77
Programmable read-only memory (see PROM)
Programmed decisions, 16
Programmer, 134–35, 138, 508
Programmer/analyst, 135
Programming, 313, 345–52, 508
  concepts, 511–12
  instruction classifications, 511–12
Programming languages, 367–71, 508, 512–16
Project leader, 319
Project management (see Applications of computers, general)
Project team, 138–39, 314, 344, 364
PROM (programmable read-only memory), 498